*igel Regiment:
story of the Twenty-Sixth Wisconsin Volunteer Infantry 1862-1865*
nes S. Pula

8 7 6 5 4 3 2 1
Hardcover Edition

1-882810-20-1

ded bibliographic references and index

Publishing Company
S. Bascom Avenue, Suite 204,
bell, California 95008
732-3669

ographic credits: Unless otherwise specified, the photographs appearing in this
were taken from *Germania und Abend Post (Germania).*

book is printed on 50-lb. Glatfelter acid-free paper.

paper in this book meets or exceeds the guidelines for permanence and durabili-
the Committee on Production Guidelines for Book Longevity of the Council
brary Resources.

The Sigel Regime

A History of the Twenty-Sixth Wis Volunteer Infantry, 1862-186

by

James S. Pula

For My Mother
Whose Patience, Support, and Compassion
Merit a "Medal of Honor."

❦

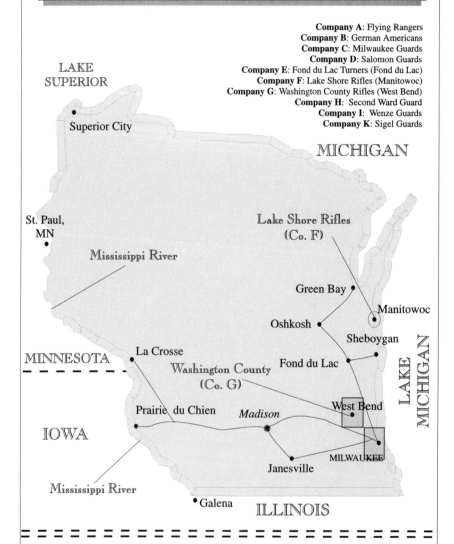

Wisconsin was organized as a territory on July 4, 1836, and originally included much of what would eventually become Iowa, Minnesota, and the Dakotas. The first German settlers, together with Irish immigrants, arrived in Milwaukee in 1839. By 1846 the city's population had surged to 7,600, and within four years topped 21,000. Fully 40% were German. Wisconsin was particularly appealing to Germans. Its weather, religious tolerance, work ethic, and geography were pleasantly familiar to these Europeans.

By the time Southern guns fired on Fort Sumter in April 1861, most Germans were solidly behind the Lincoln administration and the Union. In August 1862, Lincoln called for another 300,000 soldiers, and the president authorized Maj. Gen. Franz Sigel to raise a dozen regiments of German troops. One of the regiments would be raised in the Milwaukee area. It was designated the 26th Wisconsin, although it was known locally as "The Sigel Regiment," or *Unser Deutsches Regiment* (our German regiment). As the Battle of Antietam roared in Maryland on September 17, 1862, its 38 officers and 959 enlisted men were quietly mustered into service in Milwaukee.

Theodore P. Savas

Table of Contents

continued. . .

PHOTOS AND ILLUSTRATIONS

(continued)

(continued from previous page)

(continued from previous page)

CARTOGRAPHY

PUBLISHER'S PREFACE

*W*hile thousands of young men were being killed and maimed along a once-tranquil creek in western Maryland on September 17, 1862, Col. William H. Jacobs' 26th Wisconsin Volunteer Infantry was quietly mustered into service in Milwaukee. The regiment was made up primarily of German immigrants and Americans of German descent. By the war's second autumn few in its newly-formed ranks harbored illusions that the conflict would end quickly. Indeed, the result was still being hotly debated with rifles and artillery across grassy fields and through broken wood lots across the divided nation.

The 26th Wisconsin's service began rather fortuitously. It was initially absorbed into the Army of the Potomac and attached to the 2nd Brigade, 3rd Division, 11th Army Corps. Colonel Jacobs was new to the craft of war, having earned his living previously in banking and insurance. The brigade, however, was headed by Col. Wtodzimierz Krzyżanowski, a competent officer and Polish refugee with European military experience. Divisional leadership was similarly situated with the bespectacled Carl Schurz in command, a capable Prussian immigrant and former journalist and European revolutionary. As part of the army's Reserve Division, the Wisconsinites missed the opportunity of firing their muskets in anger at the Battle of Fredericksburg in December 1862. Thereafter the 26th's fortunes angled off in a new direction.

The afternoon of May 2, 1863, found the regiment in Oliver O. Howard's 11th Corps on the army's far right wing in the thickets near a small crossing named Chancellorsville. The neophyte "Sigel Regiment," named after German General Franz Sigel, was about to experience the receiving end of one of the most successful surprise attacks in military history. The value of well-drilled stock and solid regimental leadership rose to the fore. Outnumbered, outflanked and caught in a crossfire, the battling Colonel Jacobs refused to fall back before the onslaught until twice ordered to do so by his brigade commander. The cost to the 26th Wisconsin for its lonely and conspicuous stand was 204 men. Similar ill luck two months later ensconced the regiment north of Gettysburg, where the Badger State troops, this time under Lt. Col. Hans Boebel, left another 250 men on the field. By the time the 26th Wisconsin shipped out that fall for service in the Western Theater, hardened combat veterans who had seen the worst war has to offer populated its ranks.

Service in Tennessee with the Army of the Cumberland lessened the regiments' exposure to hard combat only temporarily. With Krzyżanowski and Schurz still leading the brigade and division, respectively, Maj. Frederick C. Winkler assumed the reins of regimental leadership and took his Wisconsin troops through the Chattanooga and Knoxville campaigns. The spring of 1864 heralded both a new season of campaigning and a change in organization when the 26th Wisconsin was transferred into the 3rd Brigade, 3rd Division, 20th Corps, with which it served for the balance of the war. Over the following months the Germans distinguished themselves on a number of fields, including Resaca, New Hope Church, Kennesaw Mountain, and Peach Tree Creek. Winkler's thinning regiment achieved special distinction during the latter action when it managed to capture the flag of the 33rd Mississippi Infantry. The March to the Sea and Carolinas Campaign followed, with the 26th seeing action at both Averasboro and Bentonville. By the end of its service some 1,089 men had served in the 26th's ranks; more than 17% were killed or mortally wounded.

Throughout their remarkable odyssey the men of the 26th Wisconsin remained faithful to both their ethnic roots and their new country. Indeed, their sacrifices for their adopted homeland are inextricably linked forever to the scarred lands stretching from near our nation's capital to beyond the Appalachian Mountains—a pantheon to the fallen. That their story is not better known today is a mystery, for during the Civil War the men of the 26th stood apart and were recognized by their contemporaries as a regiment of distinction.

The colonel of the 2nd Massachusetts Infantry, when referencing the 26th's achievements in the Eastern Theater, hailed it as "one of the finest military organizations in the service." Readers of James S. Pula's gracefully written and superbly researched *The Sigel Regiment: A History of the Twenty Sixth Wisconsin Volunteer Infantry, 1862-1865,* will likewise claim he has penned one of the finest regimental histories published to date.

Theodore P. Savas
Publisher
February 16, 1998

ACKNOWLEDGEMENTS

or any success this work might enjoy, I am indebted to many individuals and institutions who offered their assistance and resources in its preparation. Fred Turk provided extensive copies of his valuable collection of articles from several Wisconsin newspapers, put me in contact with descendants and other researchers, shared his own research, and provided continual encouragement. Russell Scott, developer of an excellent Web Page on the 26th Wisconsin, likewise shared unselfishly his own research and sources, as well as seeking out others to contribute to the effort at recording the experience of the Sigel Regiment.

Particular thanks go to Carmen Gonzalez for her enthusiastic and reliable research assistance, and to Barbara Lunati who translated several German newspaper articles. Others who generously contributed personal papers, photographs, or other information on their ancestors who served with the 26th Wisconsin included Conrad Baetz, Emerson P. Baetz, Thomas Baetz, Patrick Brennan, W. L. Damkoehler, Robert T. Ewens, Donnabelle Gerhardt, Richard H. Haviland, Eliot Held, George H. Kenny, John J. Kuhn, Thomas A. Kuhn, William M. Lamers, John C. Leitzmann, Robert D. Medley, Steven Miske, Dennis R. Moore, John

G. Peisen, Florence M. Petterson, James H. Roth, D. JoAnn Schiefelbein, Erv Seeger, Lucy Storch, Michael Telzrow, and Alfred Wickesberg.

Among the many archivists, historians, and librarians who aided my research were Dr. Richard Sommers of the U.S. Army Military History Research Institute; Judith A. Simonsen, Curator of Research Collections, and Steve Daily, Assistant at the Milwaukee County Historical Society; Dawn F. Schumann, Executive Director, and Rosemarie Barber of The Milwaukee Turner's Foundation, Inc.; Tim Erickson of the Urban Archives at the University of Wisconsin-Milwaukee; Lynette M. Wolfe, Richard W. Harrison, Mark van Ells of the Wisconsin Veterans Museum; Cheryl A. Pula, reference librarian at the Dunham Public Library in Whitesboro, New York; Robert P. Fay, Executive Director, and Edward Ehlert, Secretary, of the Manitowoc County Historical Society; Robert B. Roesler, Curator, Greenfield Historical Society; John Ebert and Thomas Kuechenberg of the Fond du Lac County Historical Society; Troy Harman of the Gettysburg National Military Park; Evelyn Zarling of the Washington County Historical Museum and Howard Michael Madaus, an expert on Civil War flags. My appreciation also goes to the staffs of the following institutions that were both accommodating and supportive of my research: the State Historical Society of Wisconsin, the Milwaukee Public Library, The Wisconsin State Military Museum, The Mullen Library at The Catholic University of America, The National Archives, and The Library of Congress.

To these, and everyone else who offered assistance and encouragement, I am deeply indebted.

Chapter 1

OFF TO WAR
Unser Deutsches Regiment

apid stacatto drumbeats pierced the deep bass tones of martial brass as long lines of marching men moved steadily down the street amid shouts and applause from the throngs that lined the pathways. Here and there men saluted or removed their caps as the colors swung past. Necks turned and twisted to catch a glimpse of father or husband, brother or son, while several young ladies rushed forward to drape floral bouquets about the muzzles of their sweethearts' muskets. Shouts of recognition and friendly waves came from well-wishers as the marchers passed. Ludwig! Hans! Friedrich! Franz! It was not Berlin; it was not 1914 or 1939. It was the United States of America, it was 1862, and the 26th Wisconsin Volunteer Infantry was marching off to war.

When Milwaukee's German population turned out to cheer its own as they left for as yet unknown battlefields that second autumn of the Civil War, Wisconsin had not yet entered its second decade of statehood. First organized as a territory on July 4, 1836, it originally included much of what would later become Iowa, Minnesota, and the Dakotas. Its most inhabited location, Milwaukee, boasted a population of only 1,200, but a serious economic depression reduced that number to a mere 700 citizens within two years. Despite the decline, the town incorporated on March 11, 1839, and its population soon began to rise with the arrival that summer of Irish settlers from Fall River, Massachusetts, and the first small groups of German immigrants. The new arrivals quickly increased the population to over 1,700 by the end of the year.[1]

German immigrants found Wisconsin attractive for many reasons. The climate and the gently rolling, wooded hills of the central and eastern portions of the territory were pleasantly familiar to people from southern and central Germany, while the comparatively inexpensive price of land and the availability of public financing made property ownership a realistic goal for most early immigrants. In the decade beginning in 1845 over 90% of German immigrants to Wisconsin came from the geographically similar areas of Nassau, Hesse, Pfalz, Baden, Württemberg, Bavaria, and the Rhineland in southwestern Germany, areas plagued by blights, crop failures, and generally inefficient farming caused by the breakup of estates into individual plots frequently too small to support an average family. Given these circumstances, the earnestly optimistic letters of early immigrants were often enough to encourage families, or large portions of entire villages, to migrate to this wondrous new land.[2]

The initial effect of this increasing stream of immigrants was seen by many in Wisconsin as an economic stimulus. "The effect of the arrival of these hardy sons of toil," wrote businessman J. S. Buck, "with their gold and silver wherewith to purchase homes for themselves and their children upon the country was electric."[3] So positive was their arrival viewed that citizens groups printed pamphlets in German describing the advantages of Wisconsin and distributed them widely in Europe to encourage immigration to the western territory. In 1852 the legislature established a Commission of Immigration with Herman Haertel, a German land agent from Milwaukee, as Immigration Commissioner. Haertel used the New York and European press to good effect in advertising the benefits of relocating in Wisconsin. A resident agent in New York distributed information in Europe encouraging immigrants to move to Wisconsin, and Haertel succeeded in recruiting Dr. Hildebrandt, U. S. Consul General in Bremen, Germany, and a former resident of Mineral Point, Wisconsin, to publicize the Badger State among German emigrants.[4]

Religious motivations were also important for many Germans. As early as 1840 Wisconsin boasted Catholic, Lutheran, and Methodist churches, as well as several smaller groups who generally met in private homes. By the end of the decade the German Congregationalists, Evangelicals, and Evangelical Zionists also built places of worship. In 1850 the Lutheran Wisconsin Synod came into existence. Roman

Catholics also arrived early and in large numbers. In 1843 a group of Rheinlanders founded a German Catholic church in Greenfield. In July of the following year Bishop John Martin Henni delivered part of his first sermon in Milwaukee in German, and parishioners laid the cornerstone for St. Mary's Church, the city's first Catholic parish, in 1846. An outspoken advocate of immigration, Bishop Henni actively promoted the recruitment of Germans and others to increase Wisconsin's Catholic population.[5]

The political disturbances that beset Germany leading to the unsuccessful democratic revolutions of the "Springtime of Nations" in 1848 provided further impetus to migration. Motivated by the French Revolution's ideals of liberty and equality, the "Forty-Eighters" were deeply idealistic, educated, and determined to succeed in building a better society in America than they left behind in Germany. "What I am looking for in America is not only personal freedom, but the chance to gain full legal citizenship," Carl Schurz explained. "If I cannot be the citizen of a free Germany, then I would at least be a citizen of a free America." [6]

Though intensely democratic in thought, many were equally intense in their distrust of organized religion, both Catholic and Protestant, which they regarded as anti-democratic, state-supported churches in their homelands. As a result, a high percentage of Forty-Eighters were not only educated journalists, teachers, scientists, and physicians, but anti-clerical freethinkers as well.[7]

As the pace of immigration quickened, Milwaukee's population rose dramatically from 1,700 in 1840 to over 9,600 in 1846 and more than 21,000 in 1850. Fully 40% of the city's population was by this time German, and as their numbers grew so did their cultural and community life. The *Schuetzen Verein* [Hunting Society] was popular among sportsmen, while intellectuals and those with political inclinations supported *Die Freie Gemeinde* [The Free Commune], an organization for discussing and propagating the rationalist and humanitarian principles of Thomas Paine. The *Deutscher Unterstützungs Verein* [German Charity Society] provided aid to impoverished new immigrants, while musical societies proved very popular within the new German community. The *Beethoven Gesellschaft* [Beethoven Society], founded in 1843, was the first musical society. Under the leadership of Forty-Eighter Hans Balatka, the Milwaukee *Musikverein* [Music

Society] supported a male chorus, a string quartet, and a full concert orchestra. It produced fourteen operas in a seven-year period, while the *Liederkranz* singing society and several amateur theatrical organizations proved influential in keeping German language and culture alive and relevant in the American setting. The *Garten-Verein* [Horticultural Society] was popular during the 1850s, as was the *Soziale Männer Gesang Verein* [the Men's Social Choral Society], the *Gesangverein Deutscher Arbeiter* [The German Worker's Choral Society], the *Theater Verein* [Theater Society], and *Der Bund Freier Männer* [The Free Men's Organization]. Laws prohibiting commercial and recreational activities on Sunday were largely ignored as the German community enjoyed a weekly day of *gemütlichkeit* [good-natured sociability] including sports, music, and liquid refreshment at places like Bielfeld's Garten, Melms Biergarten, Mozart Hall, Milwaukee Garten, and Schlitz Bier Garten.[8]

The first labor union in Milwaukee was *Der Arbeiterbund* [The Workingman's Organization] founded in 1852, followed by *Der Schreinerbund* [The Carpenter's Organization]. There was a printer's union, a building society, and a fire insurance company which later became Mechanics Mutual Insurance Company.[9] The many advertisements in local newspapers testified to the rapid growth of a diversified middle class of shopkeepers, merchants, and manufacturers.

Nor was education neglected. In 1850 Dr. Aigner began a *Schulverein* [School Society] with Peter Englemann as the first teacher. Under the teacher's leadership, this rapidly evolved into the prestigious German-English Academy. Englemann also founded the *Naturalhistorische Verein* [Natural History Society] which later became the Milwaukee Museum. In another form of education, publications grew to facilitate communication and support many of the growing variety of societies and political viewpoints. The liberal *Wiskonsin Banner* [Wisconsin Banner], the first daily German newspaper in Wisconsin, was soon challenged by the *Volksfreund* [People's Friend], founded by the owners of the *Milwaukee Sentinel* to support Whig political positions within the German community. Freethinkers supported the *Humanist*, those subscribing to rationalism and natural philosophy read the *Anthropologist*, while women's suffrage advocates eagerly read each issue of *Die Deutsche Frauenzeitung* [The German Women's' News]. *Atlantis* was a literary and scientific monthly, while Utopian socialists published *Der Arbeiter* [The Worker].[10]

Preeminent among German organizations was the *Turnverein* [Gymnastic Society]. Originally an organization devoted to physical development and social improvement, the *Turnverein* became involved in the liberal political movements leading to the "Springtime of Nations." In Milwaukee, Edward Schulz and Fritz Anneke established a Turner school for boys at Becker's Cafe Français on Market Square in March, 1850. In June, 1852, a group of adults met at Kossuth Hall to establish the *Teutonia Turnverein*, with its *Turnplatz* at Melms Biergarten on the banks of the Menomonee River. In the following year August Willich led a group that founded *Der Soziale Turnverein* [The Social Gymnastic Society] at Bielfeld's Garten on the east side of the Milwaukee River. Both anti-clerical and anti-capitalist, the society's constitution adopted the "Red Flag of Socialism" and proclaimed itself opposed to Jesuits and Papal reactionaries. Because of these beliefs a fractious war of words developed with the liberal *Wiskonsin Banner,* and later the Whig-supported *Volksfreund*—which combined into the *Banner und Volksfreund* in 1852—trading venomous editorials with the more conservative *Seebote* [The Lake Messenger], founded in 1852 as a quasi-official voice for the Catholic Church.[11]

As time passed, tempers and politics moderated. *Der Soziale Turnverein* eventually changed its name to the *Milwaukee Turnverein*, became more inclusive, and developed into arguably the largest and most influential German organization in the city. Taking as their motto the German expression "Frisch, Frei, Stark und Treu" [Vigorous, Free, Strong and True], the Milwaukee Turners developed a comprehensive gymnastics and physical education program, but were also active in promoting social and economic development and supporting the fine arts and literary expression. In 1855 they joined the National Turner Bund, with Hans Boebel traveling to Buffalo, New York, to attend the national convention in September. Blonde, blue-eyed, and handsome, Boebel, a tailor by trade, was a freethinker and founding member of both the *Turnverein* and the *Bund Freier Menschen* [The Free Men's Organization]. A prominent member of Milwaukee's liberal political community, as well as its social and cultural societies, he possessed no formal higher education but was nevertheless described as "thoroughly versed" in history, science, classical poetry, read Shakespeare and Longfellow both in English and in German translation, and could quote from Schiller and Goethe. His prestige rose further two years later when, under his leadership, Milwaukee hosted a national month-long *Turnfest,* a Turner gymnastic festival.[12]

As the number of German settlers increased, they developed a community characterized by vitality, culture, and a passion for social and political involvement that impressed Frederika Bremer during her visit to the city in 1850. "Here one sees German houses, German inscriptions over the doors or signs, German physiognomies," she wrote. "Here are published German newspapers; and many Germans live here who never learn English, and seldom go beyond the German town. Their music and dances, and other popular pleasures, distinguish them from the Anglo-American people, who, particularly in the West, have no other pleasure than 'business.'"[13] By 1850, the variety and quality of cultural, intellectual, recreational, and charitable institutions within Milwaukee's German community won for it the widely recognized sobriquet *"Deutsche Athen"* — the German Athens.[14]

Political Schisms

With the vast increase in newly arrived immigrants came a growing resentment on the part of some of the earlier residents. Although citizens could vote after residing in the territory for only six months, when a proposal emerged to extend this same privilege to immigrants if they declared their intention to become citizens, the Whigs, sensing an opportunity for political advantage, rose in opposition. Their ally, the *Milwaukee Sentinel,* complained: "This is going too far. If one really wanted to confer equal rights on these foreigners, who are by birth, education, language, and customs entirely different people than the Americans, then one would seriously imperil local institutions. It is an injustice to tear such uncultured, monarchically inclined barbers out of their legitimate sphere, to flatter them, and to fill their heads with high thoughts which they are unable to understand...They may admire us but they can never be our equals."[15]

The issue of immigrant voting rights defined a crucial division between the Whigs and the Democrats in Wisconsin politics. While the Whigs wanted to deny immigrants the suffrage because of their tendency to support the Democrats, the latter favored the voting provision for precisely the same reason. To support the measure, the Ger-

Dr. Franz Huebschmann, a physician and political leader from Milwaukee.

Courtesy of the Milwaukee County Historical Society

man community elected Franz Huebschmann co-chair, along with Irishman John White, of a joint German-Irish committee to support the voting measure. Born in 1817 in Reithnordhausen, Grand Duchy of Weimar, Hueb- schmann completed his early edu- cation in Erfurt and Weimar before pursuing professional stud- ies at the University of Jena where he received his medical degree in 1841. Migrating to the United States a few months after graduation, he lived with relatives in Boston for a brief time before moving to Mil- waukee during the winter of 1841-42. According to Carl Knoche, "Huebschmann was an ambitious man and probably felt that the fairly small but rapidly expanding village of Milwaukee offered him a better chance of success than the large cities in the East." Once in Milwaukee he opened a practice in a small office and took an immediate interest in civil and political activities. He became involved in a successful peti- tion to Congress to designate Milwaukee a port city, proved instru- mental in obtaining federal funds for the construction of piers and other commercial improvements, and was conspicuous in promoting unity among the German population. In 1844 he served as a member of the committee to draft the first city charter, proving to be a strong advocate for immigrant rights.[16]

While the Irish could reach their own community and the general English-speaking population throughout their newspaper, the *Courier*, the Germans lacked such a voice. To remedy this, Huebschmann approached Moritz Schoeffler, editor and publisher of the German-lan- guage *West Chronik* in Jefferson City, Missouri. With his support and $170 collected from the German populace, Huebschmann began the *Wiskonsin Banner* to rally German support for the Democrats. Later that year he formed the German Democratic Association, serving as its first president. Despite constant criticism from the *Sentinel*, including ridicule of the new *Wiskonsin Banner* as "a feast for those that are fond of munching Dutch jawbreakers," the efforts of Huebschmann and his associates brought success. In 1844 the territorial legislature voted to allow anyone who was a resident for at least six months to vote in the election for members of the constitutional convention, and anyone who was a resident for at least three months to vote on the proposed constitution.[17] In the resulting elections, his fellow-citizens elected him a delegate to the constitutional convention where he served actively on several committees including the important Committee on Suffrage and Franchise.[18]

Wisconsin entered the Union on May 29, 1848. The Democratic Party dominated political life in the new state, with opposition from the Whigs and a small Liberal Party. In the voting for the first governor, the Democrats polled 19,875 votes to 14,621 for the Whigs and only 1,134 for the Liberals. The Whigs, smarting from their defeat at the polls, blamed the loss directly on the immigrant vote they previously sought to exclude. Portraying themselves as "defenders of American institutions" against foreign assault in order to appeal to American-born voters, most agreed with a Whig publication called the *Grant County Herald* when it complained: "The party professing to be democratic, has taken foreign pauperism into its alliance and has beaten us with the votes of aliens. Our Sovereigns are the ragged rabble of Europe."[19]

In the first decade of statehood, however, old political alliances would be sorely tested, with few issues causing more division and political realignment than the question of slavery. Wisconsin had a strong anti-slavery faction long before statehood. As early as 1842, C. C. Sholes, publisher of the *Milwaukee Democrat*, frustrated by the Democrat's national policy on slavery, changed the name of his newspaper to the *American Freeman* and adopted an anti-slavery platform. Within the state, Milwaukee was home to a strong pro-slavery group, but only the state's Quaker population was known to be more heavily anti-slavery than the Germans. This difference in outlook frequently placed German Milwaukee at political odds with the rest of the city. As early as 1844 Germans were subject to verbal attack for their anti-slavery sentiments, and by 1848 the slavery issue began to create divisions within the Democratic Party. In that year, bouyed by the appeals of the *Volksfreund*, the new Free Soil Party made serious inroads into the Democrat's previous German support.[20]

Despite these inroads, when the Republican party came into being in 1854 the three German language newspapers in Milwaukee remained steadfastly Democratic, probably because many Whigs joined the Republicans, tainting the new party, in the eyes of the immigrants, with the loathsome burden of nativism. Understanding the need for a press to propagate their views, German radicals in Milwaukee began publishing *Korsär* [Corsair], a Republican political organ supported by Rufus King of the *Milwaukee Sentinel,* as a means of spreading Republican ideals within the German community. As editor they selected Bernhard Domschcke. A native of Freiberg, Germany, who studied theology and philosophy, he established himself as a revolutionary editor in Saxony before moving to the United States in 1851. An ardent defender of liberalism and the anti-slavery crusade, he worked in New York before moving to Boston where he became a close associate of radical editor Karl Heinzen while employed by the *Neu-England Zeitung*. Moving to Louisville, Kentucky, the two published an uncompromising anti-slavery journal. In 1854 the pair authored the radical Louisville Platform which denounced all racial and class privileges, attacked slavery and the Fugitive Slave Law of 1850, and advocated free lands for settlers, easier and quicker naturalization procedures, and equal political and social rights for blacks and women. Burned out by a Louisville mob, Domschcke was penniless and destitute when he arrived in Milwaukee, conditions that did not in the least mellow his beliefs or his methods.[21] In Milwaukee, according to historian Richard N. Current, the "youthful Forty-Eighter…immediately distinguished himself by the virulence of his attacks on both the Roman Catholic Church and what he called the 'Democratic Church.'"[22] "Slavery and religion is the platform of the Democrats," Domschcke wrote. "How well the two harmonize; a slavery both mental and physical." [23]

During the election campaign in 1856 the Republicans, who selected western explorer John C. Frémont as their first presidential candidate, made a serious effort to win over German voters. Prominent German speakers traveled from one community to another, while campaign literature was distributed in German. The Democrats, promoting the candidacy of James Buchanan, attacked Republicans over the slavery issue and the anti-clericalism of many radical supporters of

Bernhard Domschcke, a radical newspaper editor from Milwaukee

Courtesy of the Milwaukee County Historical Society

Republicanism. The *News* wrote that any "Adopted Citizen" who voted for the Republican candidate "votes to rob himself of his religion and political rights, and to put in power a party that seeks to elevate the native negro at the expense of the foreign-born white man."[24]

In Milwaukee, the German Republican Club held meetings, raised funds, and sent speakers throughout the community to rally support for Frémont. An important speaker was editor Domschcke who delivered many orations on the issues of slavery and the nativist plague of Know-Nothingism. On one such occasion the *Sentinel* commented that he "exhibited great ability. His speech is said to have been truly eloquent and closely reasoned."[25] Regardless of Domschcke's efforts, Germans stayed away from the polls in large numbers in 1856, seemingly equally repelled by the taint of nativism hovering about the Republicans and the pro-slavery stance of the Democrats.[26]

In the aftermath of the Democratic victory in 1856, Franz Huebschmann determined to run for governor in the 1857 state election. Aside from his prominence in the controversy over immigrant voting rights, which gained him widespread recognition among the Irish community and other English-speaking groups throughout the state, the doctor had been active in politics in the intervening years. Elected to the Milwaukee Board of School Commissioners in 1849, he served in that capacity until 1853. He also served as a presidential elector in 1848, was elected city alderman in 1850 and again in 1852, became a member of the City Council and County Supervisor from 1848 to 1867, won a term in the state legislature in 1850, and served as Superintendent of Indian Affairs of the Northern Superintendency under President Franklin Pierce from 1853 through 1857. Despite his prominence, however, the Democrats chose as their standard-bearer James B. Cross, mayor of Milwaukee, because, as they explained to a disappointed Huebschmann and his followers, the doctor "lacked a political following outside Milwaukee."[27] In the ensuing campaign, the Democratic *Banner und Volksfreund,* in an effort to retain German voters for that party, renewed its charges that the Republicans were only anti-foreign Know-Nothings in disguise, intent upon giving the vote to blacks at the expense of immigrants. Despite these Democratic efforts, Huebschmann's rejection as a suitable candidate, coupled with growing concern over the slavery issue, caused many Milwaukee Germans to abandon the Democrats and vote Republican in the fall elections.[28]

The economic panic that began in 1857 led to further defections from the Democratic ranks, as did the Republican strategy of nominating Carl Schurz as lieutenant governor. A prominent German revolutionary who led an assault on the Seigsburg arsenal during the "Springtime of Nations" in 1848, Schurz later rescued revolutionary political leader Gottfried Kinkel from a Berlin prison, gaining for himself hero status among German liberals. Arriving in Wisconsin in 1853, he joined the infant Republican Party in the following year. Schurz proved an effective campaigner, winning over not only Germans, but non-Germans as well with what Current described as his "eloquence and the charm and power of his masterly oratory." Once again, however, the Germans were disappointed. Although Republican Alexander W. Randall narrowly won the governorship, Schurz lost the race for lieutenant governor by a mere 107 votes.[29]

In the following months, emotionalism grew as the gulf between Democrats and Republicans fractured both the state and its German community. In the political battle for the hearts and minds of Wisconsinites, Milwaukee's German-language newspapers generally supported the Democrats. The *Banner und Volksfreund* continued to rail against Republican anti-slavery policies and perceived anti-foreignism, while the Catholic *Seebote*, generally a staunch enemy of the anti-Catholic *Banner und Volksfreund*, strongly denounced the Republicans as "Temperance men, abolitionists, haters of foreigners, sacrilegious despoilers of churches..., killers of Catholics—these are the infernal ingredients of which this loathsome Republican monstrosity is composed."[30]

By the time of the 1860 election, emotions ran high throughout the country, so much so that the dominant Democratic Party could not agree on a presidential candidate. Instead, the northern wing of the party nominated Stephen A. Douglas of Illinois, while the southern wing chose John C. Breckinridge of Kentucky. Arrayed against the two Democratic candidates were Republican standard-bearer Abraham Lincoln and Constitutional Union Party candidate John Bell. In Wisconsin, Carl Schurz, a member of the Republican national executive committee, chaired the state delegation to the Republican national convention in Chicago where he initially seconded the nomination of William H. Seward, but later seconded the motion for a unanimous nomination of Lincoln once the Illinoisan's nomination gained a majority. A member of the committee sent to notify Lincoln of his nomination, Schurz became a close friend of the nominee and was appointed Minister to Spain following the inauguration of the Republican administration in 1861.[31]

In Milwaukee the election was even more spirited than the 1856 contest. Douglas visited the city on October 13, speaking before an enthusiastic crowd of 8,000 in Market Square. That evening a torchlight parade escorted him to a reception at the Newhall House. Five days later Republicans held a similar city-wide parade, while neighborhood speeches and processions occurred almost daily as the campaign neared a conclusion. Franz Huebschmann, Bernhard Domschcke, and a host of other German speakers promoted the cause of Republicanism with the result that serious inroads were made in the city's Democratic majority. Whereas all nine of the city's wards returned Democratic majorities in 1856, three went for Lincoln in the 1860 contest, with Huebschmann gaining election to the city's Common Council.[32]

Lincoln's election set the wheels of secession in motion. South Carolina voted to leave the Union in December, 1860, with most of the Deep South states following its lead in the first month of 1861. As the crisis increased, Wisconsin prepared for the worst. When Confederate shells fell on Ft. Sumter, the Wisconsin legislature voted to give the governor authority to "provide for the defense of the state and to aid in enforcing the laws and maintaining the authority of the Federal government."[33] To meet the crisis, President Lincoln called on April 15 for 75,000 volunteers. The following day, Governor Randall issued a proclamation urging prompt fulfillment of the state's quota of volunteers. Support ran high. In those emotional times, differences were generally discarded and support for the Union became the popular, overriding concern. The *Banner und Volksfreund*, heretofore virulently anti-Lincoln, reflected this new spirit of unity on April 16 when it announced its position as "The Union above all! We must help the president as long as he does not act against the Constitution, even though he was elected by a party we don't approve of. The Capital is in danger!" A month later the 1st Wisconsin Volunteer Infantry, made up of existing militia units and new recruits from Madison, Beloit, Fond du Lac, Horicon, and Kenosha, took the oath of federal service in Milwaukee.[34]

Rally Boys! Rally!

With the beginning of the war, most of the German factions rallied to support the Union. Radical socialists, liberal Forty-Eighters, Catholics, Protestants, Turners, and freethinkers, veterans of the struggles for social reform in Europe, came together to form a benevolent society to support those effected by the war. Members of the rival *Liederkranz* and *Liedertafel* musical societies joined the same German regiment. On April 18, 108 Turners enlisted together as a sharp-shooter company—Company C, "Turner Rifles"—in the 5th Wisconsin Volunteer Infantry. The 9th Wisconsin Volunteer Infantry, known as the "German Regiment," recruited almost wholly from that ethnic group. Those who could not serve provided support in various ways. Social and cultural organizations furnished money, supplies, and other support.[35]

Despite early enthusiasm, the war did not go well for the North. Defeat followed defeat during the first months of the conflict—Bull Run and Ball's Bluff in 1861; the Peninsula Campaign, Jackson's Valley Campaign, and Second Bull Run in 1862. Even the Union victory at Shiloh appeared hollow once the appalling casualty lists became public. By mid-1862, the Union was in desperate condition. Popular support waned in many states, while anti-war fever increased. To make matters worse, Secretary of War Edwin Stanton terminated Northern recruiting efforts in the mistaken belief that enough troops were on hand to quell the rebellion. Losses in the spring and early summer of 1862 proved him wrong. In this darkest of hours, President Lincoln called on July 2 for 300,000 more troops to serve for three years, following this, as losses continued to mount, with a request in August for yet another 300,000 men. Wisconsin's quota in these two calls was 42,557 men.

By the summer of 1862 war had become a reality. The long lists of killed, wounded, maimed, and missing from the first twelve months of the fratricidal conflict brought with them a more realistic understanding of the human costs of war than the heady days of early 1861. War was no longer a glorious crusade, but long, terrible suffering and sacrifice. With initial enthusiasm for the war long since gone, the state Adjutant General's office issued General Order No. 17 on August 12 calling for the recruitment of infantry regiments number 26 through 37 by August 22 with the proviso that any "deficiency...then existing will be drafted." In preparation, county sheriffs began to register all able-bodied men between the ages of 18 and 45 for a draft initially scheduled to be held on September 3, but later postponed for logistical reasons to November 10.[36]

That same August, Lincoln authorized General Franz Sigel, the preeminent German leader in America, to recruit twelve regiments from among the German communities nationwide. One of these was to be raised in Wisconsin. On August 13 the *Milwaukee Sentinel* car-

Rekruten Verlangt

für das

26. Regiment

Wisc. Volunteers!!

Ver. Staaten Bounty: $402 für ehrenhaft aus dem Dienst entlassene Veteranen!

$302 für Neue Rekruten!

27 Dollars und eine Monats-Löhnung im Voraus werden bezahlt, wenn die Mannschaft in den Dienst gemustert wird. Löhnung und Beköstigung beginnt vom Tage der Anwerbung.

Jeder Deutscher sollte sich diesem Regimente anschließen.

Rekrutirungs-Office: Vier Thüren oberhalb der Stadt-Halle, an Ostwasserstraße, 7. Ward, Milwaukee.

Recruiting Poster for the 26th Wisconsin Volunteer Infantry

Courtesy of the State Historical Society of Wisconsin

ried a story titled "German Americans for Gen. Sigel's Command" that invited all men, regardless of nationality, to enlist for service under "that gallant commander" in Virginia.[37] To lead the new regiment, which would be designated the 26th Wisconsin Volunteer Infantry, and popularly known as the "Sigel Regiment," or simply "*Unser Deutsches Regiment*" [Our German Regiment], Governor Salomon appointed William H. Jacobs. A native of Braunschweig, Germany, who migrated to the United States in 1850, the thirty-year-old Jacobs was a successful banker and a fine tenor in the Milwaukee *Sängerbund*. After working in the bank of Marshall & Haley, in 1855 he organized the Second Ward Savings Bank and was elected its first cashier [president].[38] The *Sentinel* informed its readers "He is a well-known citizen and an old resident, a German, perfectly acquainted with the English language, a banker and businessman, long and favorably known to our mercantile community, a democrat in the days of party, and now a loyal man, heart and soul for the Government, and for the vigorous prosecution and early close of the war. He holds now the office of Clerk of the Circuit and County Courts, to which he was elected over a very popular man, and has discharged the duties of that post in a manner, to which it is compliment enough to say that he well fills Mr. Keenan's place. Colonel Jacobs is an educated gentleman, of unusual ability and industry, and although not a soldier by profession, is capable of becoming one as soon as any person we know of. There is no doubt of his re-election to the lucrative office he now holds, and his acceptance of the military rank will be no small evidence of patriotism...Success to the Sigel Regiment! May they only be equal to their illustrious name!"[39]

Among the regiment's officers were some of the most prominent men in Milwaukee's German community. The lieutenant colonelcy went to Charles Lehmann. Claiming twenty years experience as a cavalry officer, Capt. Lehmann led the Benton Hussars, a Milwaukee cavalry company serving in Von Deutsch's Milwaukee Dragoons, off to save St. Louis for the Union in 1861. The *Sentinel*, noting the company's excellence in drill, proclaimed it "the pride of the Regiment," and its captain an accomplished soldier worthy of his commission in the new Sigel Regiment.[40]

Philip Horwitz became major. A veteran of the Mexican War who marched to Mexico City with General Winfield Scott, and an early vol-

Colonel Wilhelm H. Jacobs, a banker from Milwaukee.

Courtesy of the Milwaukee County Historical Society

Franz Lackner, a law student from Milwau kee.

Capt. Frederick C. Winkler, a lawyer from Milwaukee

Courtesy of the U.S. Army Military History Institute

Courtesy of the Milwaukee County Historical Society

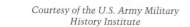

unteer in the 1st Wisconsin, Horwitz established a headquarters at Schroges' Hotel in Menasha from which he was instrumental in establishing recruiting stations for the 9th Wisconsin, a German regiment under Colonel Salomon. This completed, he turned his attention to recruiting for the 26th, winning in the process his commission.[41] As surgeon, the regiment was fortunate to enlist one of the most prominent Germans in the state, Dr. Franz Huebschmann.

Typical of Milwaukee's support for the 26th Wisconsin was the organization of Company B, the German Americans. On August 13 the *Sentinel* announced that a committee headed by Federick C. Winkler, Franz Lackner, Karl Doerflinger, and Louis C. Heide had been formed to raise a "first rate" company. Born in Bremen, Germany, in 1838, Winkler remained in Germany when his father migrated to America in 1842, making the voyage himself when the elder Winkler sent for his wife and child two years later. As a youth, Winkler attended the Milwaukee public schools and graduated from the German-English Academy of the noted educator Peter Engelmann. In 1856 he began reading law in the offices of Henry L. Palmer, an attorney and insurance company executive. He then joined the prestigious law office of Abbott, Gregory, and Pinney in Madison where he gained admittance to the bar in April, 1859, and argued his first case before the State Supreme Court in 1860. In this national crisis, he closed his law office to go off to war.[42]

Franz Lackner was a young man studying for a career in law in 1862. When the call came to raise the 26th, Lackner was commissioned a recruiting agent along with Louis C. Heide, William Steinmeyer, and Henry Sonntag. While their work progressed, first one and then another of his friends enlisted. As their urgings increased, Lackner decided to follow their lead, yet he still harbored misgivings. "I felt 'mean'," he confided to his diary, "had not yet spoken to father about it & had not yet made up my mind really to go—if at that moment I could have honorably withdrawn from the field I would have done it—but pride & duty forbade."[43]

Karl Doerflinger was born on February 17, 1843, in Ettenheim, Baden, Germany. His father was a German official who supported the revolution in 1848, escaping with the failure of the movement and migrating to the United Stated in 1851. Educated in Milwaukee in the German-English Academy, he gained from the experience "an enthusiasm for liberty, for republican principles, a patriotic sentiment toward his adopted country and had awakened within him that interest in progress and in scientific advancement which have marked his career."[44] Keenly interested in education, nature, science, and promoting scientific endeavors, financial difficulties forced him to leave school at the age of fourteen to become a newsboy, a printer's apprentice, and then an architect's apprentice. Between 1860 and 1862 he was engaged in mining and farming when he answered the call to his adopted country's service along with many of his former schoolmates.[45]

By August 14, the *Milwaukee Sentinel* reported, "Nearly three hundred men have been obtained for the German regiment."[46] That evening "a large and enthusiastic" crowd met at Reinel's Hall in the Ninth Ward to recruit for Milwaukee's new regiment. Patriotic speeches were delivered by Winkler, editor Bernhard Domschcke, Charles Schroeder, and others. The audience responded with some $500 in contributions to the Ninth Ward war fund. Joseph Ammann, "having no money, gave his best cow, worth $40." The committee planned to auction the cow the next day.[47]

Milwaukee's German community responded quickly to Lincoln's call for volunteers. On August 16 the Milwaukee *Turnverein* passed a resolution that every member who was able should volunteer for service. Any who did not would be expelled from the society. In addition to those who had already left, some 90 members enlisted in the coming weeks. Altogether, more than half of the entire membership of the society served in the war. To care for those left behind, the *Turnverein* added a 25-cent per month surcharge to each member's dues. Profits from the 1862 Thomas Paine celebration were contributed to the fund, which provided money, food, and other support for the dependents of those in the service.[48]

On August 20 some 400 recruits paraded through the city's streets behind a lively brass band, and the same day the Chamber of Commerce voted to present the new regiment with a flag. The following day Bernhard Domschcke closed the offices of his daily newspaper and, together with his foreman, compositors, carriers, and clerk, enlisted as a private. The *Milwaukee Sentinel* commented that "Mr. Domschcke has long been a prominent man among the Germans of this community and is known throughout the country as one of the ablest of our German writers. He sets a good example."[49] Domschcke was soon elected lieutenant and presented with a "handsome" new sword by his friends. "Sword presentations have got to be every day occurrences," the *Sentinel* commented, "but we know of none so worthy to receive a testimonial of this kind than Mr. Domschcke[c]ke. He will use it as he has always used his pen, vigorously and fearlessly for freedom, and in support of law."[50]

Enthusiasm also ran high in Washington County. "Rally Boys! Rally!" blared the West Bend *Post* announcing an upcoming "grand war meeting" to be held on August 13. "Let every man that has a spark of patriotism in his soul, be present, and bring his neighbor with him. The very foundation of our government is being undermined. The constitution and flag for which our fore-fathers so nobly fought and bled, is being trampled into the dust. The fate of our existence as a Nation, is at stake."[51] The meeting, held in the West Bend Court House, resolved "to raise men and money to put down the rebellion." A collection raised $395 to support the "Washington County Rifles," and twelve recruits stepped forward to declare their intention to enlist in the company. The first to volunteer included: Jacob Dexheimer, Charles Hafemann, Jacob Heip, John Horn, Julius Jewlson, Conrad Mack, John Remmel, Killian Schnepf, John Schultz, Peter Stoffel, Robert H. Templeton, and Jacob Wagner. They were soon joined by Karl Karsten, a farmer also from West Bend. Not to be outdone, the citizens of Barton raised some $1,200 for the cause, and frenzied recruiting continued for the next two weeks.[52]

"Adieu, Patrons! farewell," advised Jacob E. Mann, editor of the *Post,* in an editorial on August 30. "My country calls me and I am going."[53] Mann enlisted, leaving his wife Carrie to run the newspaper in his absence. The county's residents treated the recruits, 97 in all, to supper and a ball held in their honor in Vieths' Hall. On September 4 Captain Jacob Mann led the men off to war. They made it as far as Schleisingerville where they planned to board the LaCrosse and Milwaukee Railroad for the journey to Milwaukee, but no cars were available to carry them. The company had to wait more than two days, which provoked a great outcry of disgust in the *Post.*[54]

In Manitowoc County, Henry Baetz worked ceaselessly from his headquarters in Klingholz Hall to recruit men for the Lake Shore Rifles. Born in the Grand Duchy of Hesse in 1830, he received his education in the German common schools and emigrated to the United States in 1853. Settling eventually in Manitowoc, he became a land agent, a notary public, and served as town clerk, treasurer, and president of the village of Manitowoc. He resigned his position as the county register of deeds to accept the captaincy of Company F.[55]

Among those who followed him off to war were several fellow-members of the *Manitowoc Freier Sängerbund* [Free Singing Society]. Including in its membership a large number of idealistic "Forty-Eighters," the *Freier Sängerbund* was a hotbed of pro-Union, anti-slavery sentiment. When war came, several quickly joined Company A of the 5th Wisconsin and Company B of the 9th Wisconsin. By the end of the war, more than half of the singers had enlisted, with two-thirds rising to become officers. Joining Baetz in Company F, 26th Wisconsin, were Charles Pizzala, formerly a member of the 5th Wisconsin and a *Sängerbund* officer, editor Otto Troemel, a former director of the society, Paul Leubner, Nikolaus Roeder, Henry Greve, William H. Hemschemeyer, and Nicholas Wollmer.[56]

Over 2,000 citizens gathered to bid farewell to the Lake Shore Rifles and, reported the *Manitowoc Tribune,* to "bid them God Speed."

"To War Patriots!" reads this recruiting poster used by Charles Pizzala and Henry Baeetz for the Lake Shore Rifles, Company F, 26th Wisconsin.

Courtesy of Emerson P. Baetz and Thomas Baetz

Packed aboard the steamer *Sunbeam*, "the soldiers received a farewell greeting from a thousand throats, and the cheers were exchanged back and forth across the water as long as they could be heard by the parties to whom they were intended." The *Tribune* expressed the sentiments of those left behind toward the company when it wished "Good luck to it, for there will be gallant hearts beating under the folds of its banner."[57]

In the truest sense of its founding principles, the Fond du Lac *Turnverein* met to select officers for the "German Turner Company." Anton Kettlar was unanimously selected captain, Charles W. Neukirch became first lieutenant, John Hagen second lieutenant, and Anton Vogt orderly sergeant. When a rumor spread that the governor would disregard the election and appoint a 2nd lieutenant of his own choosing, Neukirch wrote to an influential friend to assure him that "Mr. Hagen is an experienced soldier, having served in the Mexican War, as

Some of the Greenfielders in Company C

Adam Muenzenberger (right)

Courtesy of William Lamers

(Below) Left to Right, Jacob Michel, Nicholas Friedrich, and Lewis Manz.

Courtesy of William Lamers

also in the present, as 3 months service, and to ask your influence in his favor." Whether the letter was influential or not cannot be determined, but Hagen was confirmed in his rank and he, Neukirch, and their fellow Turners marched off to become Company E, 26th Wisconsin.[58]

In the small town of Greenfield, out near the Janesville Plank Road, Adam Muenzenberger weighed an important decision. At thirty-two years of age, the father of four children was described as "round faced, with kindly blue eyes, brown hair, and a light complexion."[59] A cobbler who made boots and shoes in his home, secretary of the Greenfield *Burger-Verein* [Citizen's Society], he was also a deeply devout Catholic worried about his debt-plagued Blessed Sacrament Church.

Without help the parish might soon be bankrupt. The bounty for enlisting was a huge sum to the cobbler and his wife Barbara. According to the Milwaukee *Sentinel,* a volunteer could expect bounties from the federal government totalling $125, government bonuses of $8.00 to anyone (himself in this case) presenting a recruit, a bounty of $35 from the local Central War Committee, one month's advance pay of $13 from the federal government, a bonus of $25 raised by private citizens, and $117.00 for nine months pay if the war was over by spring of 1863. Altogether, a recruit could receive $323, a small fortune that might save their church. The couple talked it over, thought, prayed for guidance, then Adam joined his sixteen-year-old brother-in-law Adam Wuest and his Greenfield friends Leopold Drewes, Nicholas Friedrich, Asmus Holz, Lewis Manz, Jacob Michel, and Julius Stirn as a new member of Company C, the Milwaukee Guards, under the command of Capt. John P. Seemann, a prominent businessman from Milwaukee's Second Ward.[60]

Up the coast from Milwaukee, near the tiny community of Sturgeon Bay, Ernst Damkoehler also made a difficult decision. A veteran of both the Prussian army and the French Foreign Legion, Damkoehler settled in East Troy, Wisconsin, in the 1840s before moving by oxcart with his wife Mathilde to Sturgeon Bay. There the couple built a log cabin and earned a living as farmers. That momentous August of 1862, Mathilde was pregnant with their sixth child.[61] When he decided to enlist, he did not have the heart to look at his wife as the ship pulled off into Lake Michigan. "I went on the other side of the boat to save my strength," he later confided to her in a letter. "I did not have the heart to look at you again and to keep quiet."[62]

From Sturgeon Bay, Damkoehler, accompanied by his friends Georg Boyer, Phillip Feldman, and George Heilmann, journeyed to Menominee where the group stayed overnight before continuing on to Green Bay. There a recruiting officer approached them with an offer to join "the Green Bay Company," but Damkoehler did not trust the agent. "The Green Bay Company was put together from all kinds of trash from the city, and spoiled advocates were candidates for officer's positions." He and the other Germans present declined to join, deciding instead to continue on to Milwaukee. But the Green Bay men were not to be dissuaded and the Sturgeon Bay men finally agreed to sign on with them the next day to avoid a confrontation. They arose early the next morning, ate breakfast, then drove in a horse and wagon to Two Rivers where they once again took ship for Milwaukee to enlist in Company I of the Sigel Regiment. "I had recommendations to the Colonel," Damkoehler explained to Mathilde, "and we received the warmest welcome." Sworn in the next day, they were assigned "comfortable quarters at Landa Restaurant, along with our Captain, an old gray-bearded soldier" named Franz Landa.[63]

On the 25th the soldiers, "headed by their excellent band," paraded down Water Street, while meetings and torchlight rallies continued to recruit men and raise funds for the support of the soldiers and those left behind.[64] "Passing by the Turner's Hall on Friday," a reporter for the *Milwaukee Sentinel* wrote, "we were attracted by the noise of marching in the building, and looked in. We found Major Horwitz there, engaged in drilling the non-commissioned officers of the 26th Regiment. They were being put through all the maneuvers of marching, so that they may be able to drill their men promptly. We understand that they drill thus in a body every day, and that the commissioned officers are also drilled in a similar manner, at a different hour. This is as it should be, though we have not noticed the practice with other of our regiments."[65]

The 26th Wisconsin rendezvoused at Camp Sigel, Milwaukee, on September 6, 1862.[66] The occasion prompted Franz Lackner to begin a diary. The first thing he did was ruminate on his uncertain decision to enlist:

> The fate of man is molded by circumstances....Four weeks ago, if any one should have predicted, that I would at this day be a soldier, wear the blouse, the flannel shirt & blue cap, I should have laughed at him, & yet it is so—A mixture of pride & patriotism accompanied by a "train of circumstances" have changed the quiet law-student, who touched a sharp weapon with as much pleasure as he would a red hot iron, into a "bould sojer boy"; the hopes of future juridical eminence cherished for four happy years, during which time I have been laboring hard to substantiate them, have been suddenly laid aside, dismissed for the present; a new life, with new plans, new hopes, new disappointments is begun—& why? By a free exercise of the will, certainly, but what guided & directed the will? Was it patriotism? A goodly portion of it & it would have been purely so, were I convinced, that this war is real-

ly for the good of the "patria"; but considering the spirit manifested by the south I have serious doubts of the practicality—or benefit of a re-union. A fair proportion of pride had also its influence;
with head & heart a northern man, I cannot bear to see the north
"whipped" & it shall not be, if I can prevent it. Take patriotism &
pride & the "circumstances" in the shape of drumming & fifing,
singing of patriotic airs, meetings, speeches, flings & sneers by
those who had already enlisted, prospect of lieutenancy, bright
shoulder straps, fine uniform, & c & c & my firm purpose not to
become a soldier (for the purpose to remain a law-student
amounts to the same thing) was changed where I am—second
lieutenant in Compy "B." 26 Regt. Wis. Vol. Infantry. Now to a soldiers life.[67]

With more men arriving in camp daily, drilling and tactical studies intensified. "Camp life is very monotonous," Ernst Rietz wrote to
the *Pionier*, "the routine is every day the same, nearly every day there
is drill and officers and men exert themselves in trying to learn the
drill as soon as possible. It is a veritable joy to see these men drill, all
have a longing and a love for the life of a soldier; also the discipline
must be called good, since nearly all the under officers are soldiers
who have seen service, who know how to instill respect. Permission
to go to the city is often received, many who cannot obtain the desired
permission take the shorter route and steal out of the camp; the same
is surrounded with posts yet many succeed to crawl through the posts
and to roam around the city until accompanied by a patrol they find
their way back to the camp. On beautiful days our camp is a place of
pastime for the dwellers of the city. Many are led out by curiosity but
by far the greatest number come to meet acquaintances, friends and
relatives."[68]

The hectic pace made it impossible for Lackner to fulfill his
intent to keep a daily diary, because "writing utensils are scarce, hands
stiff & eyes sleepy & here my excuses." He spent most of his time
drilling. "I am beginning to understand the tactics & find them quite
interesting, am on good terms with our Company so far & hope to
command their confidence soon." Though not yet ready for the front,
he received an unexpected dose of wartime reality: he received a letter
from his close friend William F. Bode, only to learn a few days later that
Bode had been killed at Antietam the day after penning the letter.[69]

September 17, 1862, was the bloodiest single day in American military history. On that day, Northern and Southern armies met on the rolling fields along Antietam Creek, pounding each other until more than 26,000 casualties lay strewn about the ground. In Milwaukee, rain fell most of the day, dampening the muster-in ceremony of the 26th Wisconsin. Despite the weather, Capt. J. M. Trowbridge, U. S. Mustering Officer, administered the oath transforming the citizens into soldiers. The inspection and mustering in process for 38 officers and 959 enlisted men took some three hours, after which, Karl Karsten reported, the men received their bounties. "The boys had rather a hard time of it," the *Sentinel* reported, "very few were rejected, and the regiment numbers probably 1,050 men. The boys are in good health and spirits. The heavy rains trouble them a little in their leaky barracks."[70] Of the 997 who presented themselves for inspection, six were discharged for disability, two were discharged as minors on the request of their parents, and one recruit died two days later. The remaining 988 mustered in as the 26th Wisconsin Volunteer Infantry.[71]

For Lackner, the occasion presented another opportunity to question his decision to enlist. As he waited for the physician to examine him, he "was in hopes the old fellow would reject me," but instead he "was accepted & sworn in on [the] same day & felt better, a great deal better—even cheerful." From that time he determined to spend his time "drilling, recruiting & trying to get a lieutenancy."[72]

Others also questioned the wisdom of their decision. "We have had here all kinds of expenses," Ernst Damkoehler wrote to his wife Mathilde. "We had to buy our caps and duty utensils, and there are plenty of opportunities to spend money in other ways. . .After each drill we march into a beer hall where we are treated by the officers with money we were cheated out of. It is still better than in an American Regiment, where the officers keep everything." Yet, Damkoehler had more to worry about than the usual complaints of camp-bound soldiers. Rumors of impending Indian hostilities were circulating and his home in the north of the state might be in danger. "My dear Mathilde, there came alarming rumors from Sheboygan that the Indians were getting restless. As soon as you anticipate the smallest danger move away. When I know you are in danger I could desert in order to protect you, but I hope it is only a rumor. I will write to Gustav and if there should be danger, you move to him. When I think about it I believe I would have been just as smart to stay with you and would have risked it to be drafted like all the other neighbors, but now it is too late."[73]

While some debated their decisions, and others, like Damkoehler, had more pressing concerns, some in the regiment spent their off-duty hours in town. Not all went well. On September 22 members of the 26th were involved in a fight with hackmen on East Water Street, and on the 28th a fight broke out at a dance in Birchard's Hall. When police arrived to arrest one of the participants, the others met the constables with their muskets and one policeman was wounded by a rock thrown by a member of the 26th. Later, when a fire broke out on West Water Street, the *Sentinel* reported "a Lieutenant from the Twenty-sixth Regiment was very conspicuous there, rushing about with a drawn sword, ordering people indiscriminately and brandishing his weapon in a dangerous and ludicrous manner."[74]

More serious was an organized transgression of civil law by none other than the regiment's lieutenant colonel. Enraged by a critical article that appeared in the *Milwaukee Sentinel*, Lehmann ordered two companies of the regiment to assemble on Market Square at 2:00 p.m., September 8. When the men assembled, Lehmann led them to the newspaper's offices "to demand redress or satisfaction." With the troops, armed with clubs, drawn up in front of the building to prevent its occupant's escape, the lieutenant colonel entered, followed by several other officers, to confront A. O. Wheeler, the lone editor on duty. Demanding an explanation, Lehmann did not wait for the man to complete his reply before striking him a flurry of blows. According to the *Sentinel*, Lehmann "announced his entrance with an oath and enforced his physical authority with blasphemous vituperation, foaming at the mouth, gesticulating wildly, and threatening destruction to the office." As he assaulted the editor, Lt. Henry J. Berninger and "several of those who were with him" cried "Kill him" and "hit him." The assailants "would listen to no explanation, and would hear no reply to their bullying threats." His retribution complete, Lehmann marched his men away, ordering them to give three cheers as they retired.[75]

When the editor preferred charges, the matter came before a civil court. Found guilty of assault, the court fined Lehmann five dollars and costs. Now it was the *Sentinel's* turn to be outraged. Commenting that according to the judge "a military commander" can "take the law into his own hands upon the slightest provocation, assault and beat an editor, violate the very sanctity of private citizen's places of abode or business. . .provided he pays to the city and County of Milwaukee five dollars and costs." Ominously, the newspaper concluded that since it "cannot depend upon the court for protection" it would be forced to take the law into its own hands.[76]

Despite its venom, the newspaper did note that "the large body of men" in the regiment and its "gentlemanly" colonel "denounce the outrage." Most of the men in camp "expressed their surprise and indignation in unequivocal terms. We have been waited upon by officers and privates in great number, all of whom desired us to place the blame and odium where they properly belonged."[77]

But the case did not end there. Soon Governor Salomon intervened, causing Lehmann to stand trial, placing the other officers under arrest, and ordering the non-commissioned officers and privates to perform extra guard duty as punishment for their participation in a conflict between military and civil authority.[78] Outraged newspapers throughout Wisconsin and the surrounding states weighed in with their condemnation of the lieutenant colonel, but the most serious effect was a lingering rift between Lehmann and his supporters on one side and Colonel Jacobs and his supporters on the other. This division would cause recurring difficulties for months to come.

"Our Citizens, Our Neighbors, and Our Friends"

By the end of September, the regiment's training and organization were as complete as they could be before taking the field. On the last day of the month, Capt. Trowbridge informed General John Pope, commander of the Department of the Northwest, that the 26th Wisconsin Volunteer Infantry had completed organization with a "strength of line" of 985. All were armed and "partially clothed but [with] no camp equipage or accoutrements except cartridge boxes and belts."[79] The officers and men were a representative cross-section of Wisconsin's German population, with some non-Germans filling out its ranks. Like most Union regiments, farmers predominated forming 38.5% of those enrolled. Laborers were the next most numerous at 10.6%, follower by carpenters with 7.0%, shoemakers 4.8%, coopers at 3.5%, blacksmiths 3.0%, butchers 2.4%, clerks 2.1%, and tailors 2.0%.

Combining the various categories under general rubrics, 5.8% could be classified as professionals and 38.9% as artisans or skilled workers. More than two-thirds were from Milwaukee, with some being veterans of Wisconsin's earlier regiments which had already seen service during the conflict.[80]

Democrats predominated in the regiment, but there was also a strong component of Republicans, especially among the officers. Its rolls were dotted with scores of prominent, widely-traveled, well-read men making it one of the most literate organizations in the service. It contained a rich mixture of mature men who learned their discipline in the Old Country, with younger men, often sons of the early immigrants, who were new to the demands of war, adding youthful zest and energy to the steadied discipline of their elders.[81] A correspondent for the *State Journal* who viewed the regiment informed his readers "It is certainly one of the finest Regiments organized in the Badger State...most of the men being very stout and high statured, so that some of the companies could at once be mustered into the 'Prussian Guards.' Among the officers are 13 who have seen service, 11 of whom have been in war, either in this country or in Europe. One-half, if not more, of the non-commissioned officers, and one-fifth of the privates have been in military service before. Though the regiment has been but a few weeks in camp, it really excels in drill a great many others. Col. Jacobs, though lacking military experience, develops such zeal and energy that officers and men are getting more and more confident that he will soon become a first rate Colonel. Among the officers are very educated men, and the whole corps of officers show a military address which is very seldom seen in new regiments....Whoever has an opportunity to see this regiment and to observe its character, will be satisfied that in the fight for Union and Liberty it will do full credit to the American as well as to the German name, and be worthy to fight under a hero like Gen. Sigel." [82]

On September 30, 1862, the Sigel Regiment received marching orders. That same day Adam Muenzenberger wrote to inform his wife the regiment would receive its flag. "If you would like to come it would give me the greatest pleasure to have you with me here, as I see you only as a guardian angel."[83]

In preparation for their departure, on Saturday, October 4, the men assembled at Camp Sigel, prepared for a full dress parade. At 2:00

p.m. Colonel Jacobs led his troops forward, marching steadily through town amidst the cheers and applause of the populace. The *Daily Milwaukee News* reported the soldiers were "well uniformed, all were praised by every one who saw them for their soldierly appearance and proficiency in discipline. Composed of hardy men, inured to toil and being already respectably drilled, they go from the state as well able to do it honor on the field of battle as any that have preceded it." At the Newhall House, George W. Allen, acting on behalf of the Milwaukee Chamber of Commerce, presented a new set of colors to the regiment.[84] Taking the rostrum, Allen began a brief but emotional speech:

> Col. Jacobs and Officers and Soldiers of the Sigel Twenty-sixth Regiment:
>
> That patriotic body, the Chamber of Commerce of this city, has deputed me to present to you, on this occasion, your State colors. More interest pertains to this occasion than ordinarily attends those of a kindred character.
>
> Yes, go forth to unite with the thousands and the hundreds of thousands of other men, in common efforts to preserve the government of our common country. You are to unite your efforts with theirs in solving the great problem whether a representative government can be preserved when attacked by powerful force—whether a government founded by the people and existing by the people, has vitality enough and force enough to withstand the shock of those arrayed against it—whether there be vitality enough in a people, thus possessing and being the government, to rise up and protect that government, assailed by a foreign or a domestic foe.
>
> Your own position as a regiment is interesting and peculiar. You were born in another and distant land. You bid adieu to the groves and the green fields and beautiful hills of your native land, and came here by choice to cast in your fortunes with the first of those who were to this manor born.
>
> With effections thus divided—lingering memories of a distant nativity—of its green groves—of its living and loved kindred—then struggle in your hearts while you behold the present and future of your adopted land. How much greater the homage that should be paid to your loyalty than to those who go forth to the battle who were to the manor born! Before leaving your native hills and fields, you had heard of the great trans-Atlantic Republic. The civil and religious freedom there enjoyed. You had heard of its

free and powerful government—among the greatest in the family of nations. You choose to cast in your lot with the nation and its people. You came here and found a great nation—great in all the elements of national greatness—you found it a united, a happy, and a prosperous nation. How changed—in an evil hour red ambition resolved upon its destruction. True to the instincts of your hearts—true to the instincts of yourselves and the great body of humanity, you have come forward in this dark hour and offered the sacrifice of your time, your labors, and if need be, your lives, to the course of protecting and defending our common heritage.

You go forth to fight under the banners of the gallant Sigel. Of all the names that have arisen on the field since the commencement of this war, none shines out with a brighter luster than that of General Franz Sigel. It is not reported that he has yet met with a failure or with disaster. Skillful in all his combinations and all his movements, success has ever perched upon his banners. Overborne by numbers he may have been but always saved his command in a manner that commanded the admiration of his country and the world. No adverse criticism has yet been passed upon any of his actions in the field, a fact that renders complaints by words powerless.

At the battle of Pea Ridge, it is stated that the enemy determined to take the life of Sigel—that they selected twelve sharpshooters for that purpose—and though he was surrounded and compelled to cut his way through, yet came out untouched. The favored and protected of Heaven, he was reserved for other and greater services to hes adopted country.

You requested of the Chamber of Commerce that it should inscribe upon the folds of this flag, that it was presented by the Chamber of Commerce of the city of Milwaukee. The Chamber has departed from your request. It has placed an engraved plate upon its staff, thus rescinding your request. But it has left its ample folds free, to be inscribed with the names of the victories that your heroic deeds shall render immortal!

Go forth, then, to this holy war, under this banner. You go from us—for you are of us. Most of you are our citizens, our neighbors, and our friends. A city's eyes will follow you—a city's prayers will ascend unto Him with whom are the issues of life, that in the day of battle, when bracing up bravely amidst the tempest of fire and the storm of leaden hail, His shield may be around you, and that you may return, crowned with the victor's wreath, to those homes and firesides you have known and loved so well.[85]

Deafening applause and shouts followed Allen's speech. When they began to subside, S. T. Hooker, president of the Chamber of Commerce, handed the colorful new flag to the regiment, saying: "Officers and Men of the Twenty-sixth (Sigel) Regiment, Wisconsin Volunteers. In behalf of the Chamber of Commerce, I present you with this banner. May the Almighty God preserve and protect you, and all who fight under its folds and lead you on to victory, granting that we may be here to welcome you on your return, with your Banner filled with the records of your victories."[86]

Once again cheers and applause filled the air as Colonel Jacobs rose to accept the gift. "Gentlemen," he began:

in accepting at your hands this beautiful emblem, in behalf of the regiment I have the honor to command, allow me to express to you my heart-felt gratitude which I know to be shared by every soldier here, for your appropriate gift. Coming from the Chamber of Commerce, it speaks to us the patriotism and sincere solicitation for our welfare, of the community. For it is through the Chamber of Commerce that the patriotic sentiment of the people finds utterance, in deeds of kindest benevolence for the soldier in the field. We thank the good people of Milwaukee for the universal kindness shown us. We heartily thank you, gentlemen of the Chamber of Commerce, for this the latest and I may say to us the dearest manifestation of that kindness. For what is there dearer to the soldier's heart than the flag under which he fights? And where among the nations of the earth is there another flag that represents principles so dear to man; so intimately interwoven with the problem of constitutional liberty, as the standard under which we rally? My friends, words are as nothing—verbal professions of little value—We hope and trust that the opportunity will be offered us when we may show by deeds that we are worthy of the mark of esteem with which you honor us to-day. When amid the flash of musketry and the roar of cannon, it shall be our proud duty to carry this noble emblem of liberty with strong arms, and unquailing hearts, high above the din of battle, "onward and upward and true to the line." Gentlemen, the best wishes of the regiment are yours.[87]

The speeches concluded, three cheers were given for the Milwaukee Chamber of Commerce, followed by three more for Franz Sigel, whereupon the regiment formed into line and marched back to its camp. "The appearance of the men elicited considerable surprise," commented the *Sentinel*. "Their efficiency in drill, their discipline, and their uniformity of appearance being remarkable, and all were lauded loudly. Major Horwitz, and Dr. Huebschmann, both thorough officers, were conspicuous, with the Colonel, and were noticeable for their soldierly bearing and promptness. Altogether the regiment created a decidedly favorable impression, and it was generally remarked that it was the best drilled and best appearing body of men that has yet left the State."[88]

The following day, Sunday, October 5, some 5,000 relatives and friends crowded into Camp Sigel to wish their soldiers well, enjoy what Adam Muenzenberger described as "a genuine Sunday dinner," and observe a full dress parade.[89] Lackner found it "almost impossible to wind ones way through the dense crowd. Everybody bids farewell; everybody has a kind word, a hope for our welfare to express—may

1862 Issue National Flag of the 26th Wisconsin Volunteer Infantry.

Courtesy of the Wisconsin Veterans Museum

their hopes be realized. Poor father! He came in on Sunday to see me once more, for I had been to take leave of him at home."[90] Ernst Rietz described one compelling scene to the readers of the *Pionier am Wisconsin:* "Here one sees a young woman taking leave from her husband with tearfilled eyes, a blooming boy whom she leads by the hand whispers to his father a fond farewell. Casting another affectionate look upon his loved one this strong man returns to his quarters; he has preferred to be of service to his fatherland and sacrificed his domestic happiness and all. Such touching scenes occur frequently. It is left to the future historian to record these scenes."[91]

On Tuesday, October 7, the regiment bid adieu to Camp Sigel for the final time. The day began with driving rain squalls, but around 10:00 a.m., as the men began forming ranks, the clouds broke, bathing the long blue lines in bright sunlight. About 10:30 a.m. Colonel Jacobs led his men once more through the streets of Milwaukee on their way to a waiting train at the Lake Shore Depot. Down Prospect Street to Division the long column marched, then along Division to East Water Street. The streets had been crowded since early in the morning with well-wishers. As the regiment appeared they greeted it with cheers and applause accompanied by the waving of flags, handkerchiefs, and hats. According to the *Sentinel*, the regiment marched "in fine order, made a splendid appearance, and well deserved the applause and enthusiasm which it met everywhere along the march."[92] The *Daily Milwaukee News* marveled that "not fifty of the whole number of these men who start South for the maintenance of the American Constitution and American liberty, were born on American soil," yet "the regiment moved through our streets already a model in soldierly discipline."[93]

At Market Square the regiment halted briefly in front of the St. Charles Hotel where friends furnished refreshments to the departing soldiers. Then it marched on toward the depot, its soldiers struggling to maintain their ranks amid the constant coming and going of people wanting to bid one last farewell to friends and loved ones. Frederick Winkler marveled that "All along the road down to the depot people crowed upon us, rushed upon us, pulling the boys out of the ranks, shaking hands and kissing them and bidding them a final farewell."[94]

Franz Lackner's father kept pace with the marchers. "He bid me a last farewell four different times with tears in his eyes," Lackner confided to his diary. "That march I can never forget. The streets were lined with people; everywhere waving of handkerchiefs; my sword was continually in my left hand, for I had to use the right to shake hands." On one corner his three sisters stood "weeping piteously. A hasty farewell & they were lost to my sight—perhaps forever."[95] Karl Doerflinger was struck by "a noble woman who kept pace on the sidewalk with her only son marching in the street: she was leading two little girls who were smiling and wafting farewells to their big brother; the mother suppressed by an extreme effort her anguish and her tears, in order not to depress the spirit of her boy, who was her and the little girls only reliance."[96]

"The scene at the depot," Winkler wrote, "was one of the most affecting I have ever witnessed. A tearful crowd waved a last farewell and tearfully our soldiers answered it. The most happy and light hearted wept."[97] The *Sentinel* reported "There was scarcely a dry eye in the immense throng. Wives, mothers and sisters pressed forward to give their last blessing and receive the last fond farewell from those they cherished in their hearts. We noticed one lady whose grief was touching. She had lost two sons in the war, and the third and last son was now going. May God spare her only son to cherish and protect her in her declining years."[98] Every minute was taken up with sad goodbyes. Those whose loved ones were present spent as much time with them as they could. Those whose loved ones were in West Bend or Sheboygan, Greenfield or Kenosha, thought longingly of home while exchanging farewells with strangers only too happy to accommodate.

"Few regiments of such strong, stalwart and brave men have left this state," the *Sentinel* told its readers. "The hopes and prayers of every earnest man will go with them."[99]

Chapter 2

"WE ARE COMING, FATHER ABRAHAM"
Soldiering

lowly the heavily laden train pulled out of the Lake Shore Depot. Christian Crusius, a private in Company I, reflected in a letter to the *Pionier* that "the departure from this city was very touching, even I, accustomed to such scenes, was deeply moved although I took leave from only a few friends and countrymen."[1] "How strange I felt when the cars began first to move," Lackner confided to his diary, "the first tug of the cars & one feels as though he was torn, root & all, from the mother soil. It pains & then all is lost in insensibility. Trees, houses, men & women fly past & they are but dry objects of no interest; the unconscious eye glides over the most beautiful scenery & knows not its presence for the mind is at home—with the dear ones there."[2] According to Winkler, emotions ran high and tears were commonplace among civilians and soldiers alike, "but it was only for the moment of parting. Once gone all were in good spirits and a more cheerful, happy and sprightly party has never been known."[3]

Rumbling south from Milwaukee along the shores of Lake Michigan, the train took seven hours to reach Chicago. There the men detrained, formed in line, and marched to the Union Depot where they received food and coffee from the Southern Michigan Railroad. The officers retired to a "splendid supper" in the prestigious Tremont House. The contrast was not lost on Lackner who noted the officers "had a superb supper—the men had almost nothing."[4] Another opinion was relayed to Milwaukee by a correspondent of the *Sentinel*. "Satiated as Chicago is with military displays," he boasted, "the passage of the Twenty-Sixth through the streets attracted considerable attention, and the precision of its marching was commented on favorably."[5] The stay, however, was short. Arriving in the city at 8:00 p.m., the regiment was already leaving on the next leg of its trip in less than two hours.[6]

From Chicago it traveled slowly across northern Indiana and Ohio to Toledo and Cleveland, then on along Lake Erie into New York State. It arrived at Dunkirk fifteen minutes after midnight the following evening. There the officers received "supper and other necessary refreshments in the depot dining saloon" while the men "were regaled with coffee outside." By 3:00 a.m. they were back aboard, heading once again eastward toward Elmira "in the best of spirits."[7] "They left Dunkirk," the *Milwaukee Sentinel* informed its readers, "in the best of spirits, with a renewed determination to 'fight mit Sigel.'"[8] Winkler found the trip a delight, "good cars, good fare, and above all the most delightful weather, a bright sun by day and fair moon by night." As they neared Elmira he found himself passing "through some really fine scenery this morning, smiling valleys—surrounded by hills higher than any I have ever seen before—crossed by shining streamlets."[9]

From Elmira they turned south through the mountains to Harrisburg, Pennsylvania, and then on to Baltimore, arriving there about noon on October 9 to be received with a sumptuous lunch including fresh seafood delicacies. "At all places which we passed through on our trip to Washington our regiment made a good impression and were well received by the Germans in a number of cities," Christian Crusius informed the *Pionier*.[10] "Our trip was enjoyable from the beginning to the end," Adam Muenzenberger told his wife. "At every station we were received with the greatest enthusiasm."[11] Not everyone shared his opinion. "A railroad trip of three days and nights in uncomfortable freight cars brought us to Baltimore and Washington," wrote Karl Doerflinger, "a large percentage of the boys arrived there with their legs swollen enormously; some of them had to be left behind in a temporary hospital at Baltimore," but most, Doerflinger included, "insisted on continuing with the regiment [despite] their elephantic limbs, the delicious and plentiful steamed oysters of Baltimore notwithstanding."[12]

After waiting all day in vain for transportation to Washington, the regiment stacked arms and knapsacks between the tracks and bedded down on the grounds of the railroad yard to sleep under the open sky. Not until late afternoon on the following day did they continue their journey. Back aboard train, what Winkler describes as a "slow and tedious" ride brought them to Washington about 8:00 p.m. amid a heavy rainfall. They were taken to a "Soldier's Rest" near the depot where they enjoyed a dry dinner and a few hours of sleep. Winkler and some of the other officers walked to Willard's Hotel where they found the accommodations more to their liking, but Lackner stayed with the men. He recalled "a poor supper & worse bed in a large but crowded barrack, on the floor."[13]

The next morning Winkler and his fellow officers enjoyed a warm breakfast at Willard's. By afternoon the weather worsened, a drizzling rain turning the already muddy streets into a slippery slime. In the midst of this uncomfortable scene the regiment marched through Washington, across the long bridge over the Potomac, and on to where it camped in the open near Ft. Cochrane.[14] Karsten reported using his bayonet "to make sparks to create a fire."[15] Their tents did not arrive, forcing them to camp beneath the stars, but this did not appear to bother them. "Tents we had none," Crusius explained, "but wood was brought from the woods and soon every company had a sky high fire around which wrapped the mantels we camped and enjoyed sweet rest."[16] Lackner felt "wearied & tired," but "slept in the open air, thoroughly moistured with dew."[17] That night Muenzenberger was no doubt one of many to write home to inform family and friends he was "well and happy...Remember me to all who inquire for me," the Greenfield cobbler told his wife, and "kiss the children for me."[18]

The next day their tents and waterproof blankets arrived and once again drilling commenced in earnest. Everything was done to prepare them, according to Doerflinger, "to protect 'our national capital and our national bureaucrats,' as some of the boys put it in good natured jest."[19] Yet, some of what they met in this, their first camp "in the field," was not so good natured. Here Doerflinger experienced "the first results of 'army grub' and indigestion had to be overcome, by frequent and strong doses of some remedies that may originally have been invented for horses, and where, emancipated from the fostering care of women, we were put through a full course of the coarsest domestic science before our regiment was considered fit" for further service.[20]

With the tents came Major Horwitz bearing orders for the regiment to join General Sigel's command. Nothing could have pleased the men of the Sigel Regiment more than to be assigned to their namesake, the most famous and cherished German American leader in the field.

Assigned to the 2nd Brigade of Gen. Carl Schurz's 3rd Division, the men felt at home in Sigel's Eleventh Corps, which contained a large percentage of German regiments, as well as in Schurz's division which was almost exclusively German. The troops knew Schurz well from his tenure in Wisconsin politics, as well as from his ardent campaigning on behalf of Abraham Lincoln in 1860. To them, the combination of Sigel and Schurz as corps and division commanders could not have been better. Even the Democrats, who despised Schurz's Republican affiliations, admired him as a champion of the German revolutionary movement. They also found him a kind, humane, compassionate commanding officer.[21]

The Wisconsin troops were not familiar with their brigade commander, Col. Wlodzimierz Krzyżanowski of the 58th New York Infantry. They soon learned that he came to the United States as a political exile from the ill-fated 1846 Mieroslawski Insurrection in Poland. A liberal Republican and a philosophical democrat, he loudly denounced slavery while speaking on behalf of Abraham Lincoln's candidacy in 1860. They soon found he, like Schurz, was a humane officer who cared much for the welfare of his men.[22]

Krzyżanowski's brigade consisted of four regiments of what were then referred to as "foreign" troops. In addition to the Sigel Regiment, there was the 75th Pennsylvania under Col. Franz Mahler, the 58th New York under Lt. Col. Frederick Gellman, and the 119th New York under Col. Elias Peissner. The latter, like the 26th, was a new regiment, while the other two were veterans of the fighting against Stonewall Jackson in the Shenandoah Valley and the Second Bull Run campaign. Of the four, aside from the Sigel Regiment's Company G, only the 119th New York enrolled significant numbers of so-called "native American" troops.

On Tuesday, October 15, Company G was detached for guard duty while the rest of the regiment began the fifteen mile march to Fairfax Court House where Crusius expected to "contact the brave Franz."[23] It was the regiment's first real march in the field with full packs, weapons, and accoutrements—about 45 pounds of equipment per man— and it was soon evident the men were not yet in prime condition. "After the boys had marched about 2 miles with their knapsacks," Lackner reported, "it was found that they could not carry them & they were drawn on wagons." Despite easily wearied legs, their enthusiasm

Brig. Gen. Carl Schurz, commanding the Third Division, Eleventh Corps.

*Courtesy of the U .S. Army Military
History Institute*

ran high, with "considerable anxiety & beating of hearts."[24] But the journey proved uneventful, the column arriving at its destination about 5:00 p.m. with no enemy in sight.

The regiment was assigned to "a pleasant meadow surrounded by forests, about a mile from Fairfax Court House," where they were welcomed by a fellow immigrant Badger, Gen. Carl Schurz. Winkler found Schurz's welcome warm, but could not help reflecting on the incongruity of Schurz's invitation to make themselves comfortable. "This was certainly one of the most striking and original ideas that the famous orator ever uttered. Make ourselves comfortable! If you have Webster at hand, see what comfort means; see whether it means after a long, wearisome, toilsome march over rough roads, up hill and down again, all worn out and hungry, to lie down without bedding, without blanket, upon the bare earth and thus pass the night. If that is comfort, then indeed the General's invitation was generous."[25]

Since the wagon train lagged behind, and the new soldiers proved unable to carry their knapsacks and accoutrements, they paid the price by spending their first night in Fairfax Court House with neither tents nor blankets. "The first night was a miserable one for us," Lackner complained, because of "an exceedingly heavy dew, not to speak of the cold."[26] Although Ernst Damkoehler felt "happy to be able to rest up a little after all this activity," he found, after only one march, the "hardships of hunger and campaign under the open skies with a terrible rain and other inconveniences were without limit." He estimated a quarter of the regiment was sick with "diarrhea, fever and colds."[27]

Life in camp at Fairfax Court House may have seemed grim to those accustomed to the accommodations at Milwaukee's Camp Sigel, or even the relative ease of their first camp at Arlington Heights, but the men of the Sigel Regiment generally appear to have enjoyed their new surroundings. "We are getting better accustomed to camp life day by day," Winkler felt, "and every day brings some little improvement adding to comfort and convenience ingeniously contrived." For his part, Winkler fashioned a chair for himself made of "a round stick of wood branching off in three branches—these are the legs—a board nailed on the other side offers a seat."[30] Others chose intellectual diversions rather than physical improvement, with one captain spending his off-duty hours reading Shakespeare. Still others found enjoyment in reading the news from home. The *Pionier* arrived regularly, Christian Crusius reported, "about a week after it is printed."[31]

Appointed corporal by Colonel Jacobs and assigned as one of his secretaries, Adam Muenzenberger had access to time and writing materials that allowed him to carry on a frequent correspondence with his wife Barbara. "Dear wife," he wrote, "as happy as I would be to be in your midst, I am not sorry to be here. The soldier's life suits me well enough and I therefore urge you not to worry about me."[32] Later in the month he informed her "We are all well and happy and wish very much to be remembered. The drinking water here is wonderfully pure—all spring water. There is a great plenty of wood, and as far as we have gone

Colonel Wlodzimierz Krzyzanowski,
commander of the Second Brigade, Third Division, Eleventh Corps.

Courtesy of the Library of Congress

the district is not nearly as thickly settled as Wisconsin. The whole country hereabouts is covered with shrubbery and woods and no one can imagine how it looks."[33]

Lackner found his tent large and comfortable and marveled it was "astonishing what a good appetite I continue to have. Our whole thoughts are concentrated on the cooking of our meals. Just now Paul [a cook] is getting ready to make potatoe pancakes; that with beefsteak, bread & molasses constitutes our dinner for to-day. We buy what we want at the quartermasters—chocolate, pickles, sardines & c & can live well. I know not what to write as our days, at present pass away monotonously, one as the other."[34] Winkler, too, felt increasingly comfortable, commenting on the "variety of eatables" and noting the "weather here is perfectly delightful; the days are sunshiny and warm, the nights exceedingly cool and moist, but we are amply provided with blankets and manage to keep comfortable on our beds of hay."[35]

Others, including Ernst Damkoehler, anticipated orders that would bring them in harm's way. "Now, dear Mathilde, I desire only of you that if you perhaps receive no letter from me for some time, not to be disturbed. There are times here when it is almost impossible to write, but that should not in the least keep you from writing to me. In case that anything should happen to me, I have it arranged with our officers and with Adam and Philip to inform you of any accident that should happen to me."[36]

Complaints continued to be minor, involving typical concerns of camp life. "Liquors are contraband and very difficult to receive," Damkoehler explained. "Bad liquor was sold, but was forbidden by the Command because it caused diarrhea. But I was invited by our 2nd Lt. Berninger to drink a glass with him and he procured an excellent glass of bitters, which I can assure you did not taste bad at all to me."[37] Karl Wickesberg, a carpenter from Herman in Sheboygan County, enlisted because of a broken love affair.[38] "We live here happy and healthy all day long," he wrote. "The worst is, we do not have any girls here. But we get along without girls too."[39] To Adam Muenzenberger, the worst problem was a lack of stamps. "Please send me for 25 or 30 cents nine three cent post stamps in order that I can send you more letters. We cannot get them here. Here the price for them is already ten cents."[40]

To Lt. Lackner, the worst part was picket duty. His first picket included a sergeant, three corporals, and thirty men stationed about a mile from the camp. It began one Sunday at noon and continued until noon the next day, "and such a picket. Rain all day, rain for 24 hours,...We built two large fires, but had no shelter from the rain. So we sat or stood all night around the fire, our backs toward the rain, our feet cold and wet, our faces so near the fire, that we had to cover them with our handkerchiefs. It was a dreary and endless night. Monday noon we were at last relieved, just as it stopped raining. Such a life must break the strongest constitution. I got over this time, however, with a slight cold."[41] He was lucky to escape with a "slight cold." With a bright fire illuminating their position, faces to the fire and "backs toward the rain," it must have been a rather lackadaisical picket. If Confederates had put in an appearance the entire group may have found themselves marching off into captivity, or worse.

Even without an immediate threat from the enemy, life on the picket line could be dangerous. Before the end of the month Lackner noted in his diary that "A man of another regiment was shot by our picket accidentally to-day, while they were discharging their guns. Poor fellow—perhaps a valuable life is thus uselessly lost. But what is one life when so many are daily lost. It creates no excitement whatever."[42]

Winkler and several other officers took the time to visit Fairfax Court House and some of the neighboring campsites. The impression was sobering. "When you come here and meet the scattered remnants of regiments that, but a year ago, marched forth as full in numbers and as buoyant in spirit as we do now, and listen to the story of their existence, it would seem as if the angels of Heaven, moved by pity, would come down and bid us cease this bloody strife."[43]

While at Fairfax Court House the regiment also received several visitors from Milwaukee, including city and county politicians courting votes for the upcoming election. Generals Sigel and Schurz visited camp frequently, giving the regiment an opportunity to develop opinions on their new commanders. Winkler believed Sigel looked "very much like his pictures." He found the famous general "slight and unassuming in manner. His cheeks are thin and show hard toil. He is very animated in speaking. The sentiments he uttered were noble and manly."[44] Muenzenberger felt encouraged by their new division commander: "It is said that as far as the soldiers are concerned Carl Schurz is the best division commander as he takes the best care of them."[45]

On Wednesday, October 15, Brigadier General Adolf von Steinwehr arrived in camp to inspect the regiment before it was reviewed by General Sigel. "Early in the morning," Winkler explained, "the regiment was at work brushing clothes, blackening shoes, burnishing plates, guns, etc., and at the appointed time we formed in line of battle, ready for review."[46] Damhoehler was proud that von Steinwehr "praised the regiment a lot because of our Prussian drills with the weapons."[47]

The preliminaries concluded, the regiment was drawn up in line for review by their idol. Standing stiffly at attention, their eyes fixed on the general officer about to review the new addition to his corps. Shoulders back, chests out, each soldier stood rigid with pride as their corps commander strode before them. "At last brave Sigel came," Muenzenberger told his wife. "He paraded up and down and inspected us from head to foot. He admired the Germans from Wisconsin and said that it was only through the Germans that anything would be accomplished. He told the officers that only in the soldier's life was there a unity in two parts, namely, one that commands and one that obeys. 'I demand from you officers that you expect no more from the soldiers than you know they can do and that you care for them and teach them. You soldiers, obey your superiors in order that brotherly love shall always prevail.'"[48] Damkoehler called it "an enthusiastic address."[49] "He spoke to us earnestly as behooves a soldier," Lackner wrote. Sigel said "that Justice would be dealt out to soldiers & officers alike; that we should not expect a comfortable life, but trying times, days of hardship; he flattered us not, but entreated us to uphold the national honor as hitherto it had been upheld. And so we will!"[50] The review ended "amid thundering hurrahs" with everyone very pleased with Sigel, his speech, and themselves.[51]

The review concluded, the regiment settled down for a few days of drill. "We have drills seven hours a day and the other time of the day is filled up in cleaning our things and other tiring things....We are situated in a lovely place, on a slope so that rain or water doesn't bother us in the least," Damkoeher reported. But to Muenzenberger, "The land here looks desolate. All the houses that are not in ruins are unoccupied...Everything is trodden down, all the fences are burned, even fruit trees have been chopped down and burned. There is no beef to be found here, other than that which belongs to the army for slaughter. We have fresh beef twice a week."[52] Despite the constant drilling, Damkoehler, a veteran of two previous armies, did not feel much progress was being made. "On the whole, we learn only very little; even the officers learn nothing."[53] An opportunity soon arose to demonstrate this before distinguished observers.

Early on the morning of October 20 word passed for everyone to be "in marching trim" by 8:00 a.m.[54] Excitement prevailed as the men quickly prepared breakfast and made ready to march. At the appointed hour they formed ranks and marched two or three miles to a large field where they joined six other infantry regiments and two artillery batteries for review by General Sigel. Formed into close columns, they stood waiting for what Winkler considered "a long, long time" before the general and his staff arrived to conduct the review. The formalities at an end, the regiments and batteries marched three to four miles further to another large field "covered with brushes and briars" where they were moved from place to place in mock combat maneuvers.[55]

As the maneuvers progressed, Sigel ordered the 26th placed in line of battle to cover Schirmer's Battery, a common battlefield maneuver when artillery was posted in the front lines in close proximity to the enemy. Under the command of Major Horwitz, the regiment was ordered to "advance, fire kneeling & then charge bayonet."[56] For some inexplicable reason, the order to advance "was forgotten—so we kneeled down & fired on our own battery (no cartridge, of course) to their immense delight."[57] Winkler described the scene with biting sarcasm that betrayed his great frustration and humiliation at the regiment's performance: "Under the magnificent direction of an efficient Major, we were made to pour a most murderous fire into Sigel's best battery, which we were to defend. Our 'splendid' regiment, I dare say, reaped nothing but ridicule there. It vexed me.[58]

Compounding the initial error, the bayonet charge Horwitz ordered turned into a fiasco with the officers losing all control of their men. "Charging bayonets through a wood at double quick in two ranks" was, Winkler confessed, something "we never practiced, never thought of, and were entirely unequal to."[59] The effort, Lackner acknowledged, "scattered our men in all directions." Sigel was visibly "displeased."[60]

The poor showing of the regiment caused much soul-searching and finger-pointing, particularly among the officers and would-be-officers. Most agreed with Corporal Muenzenberger that "Colonel Jacobs is the best man that could be found for his soldiers. We have him to thank for everything good that happens here."[61] The primary recipients of cen-

Major Gen. Franz Sigel, commanding the Eleventh Army Corps.

Courtesy of the U. S. Army Military History Institute

sure were Lt. Col. Lehmann and Major Horwitz. Muenzenberger characterized both as "haughty" officers who did not care for the men.[62] "Our
major acts like a fool," asserted Lackner, "swearing & scolding & doing
nothing. We must get him off the regiment."[63]

Meanwhile, others assessed their chances for promotion.
Damkoehler calculated that if rumors about the impending resignations of Lehmann and Captain Franz Landa were correct, his friend
First Lieutenant Berninger would become captain and he would be in
line for a position as orderly. This would place him "first in line for
advancement to Lieutenant."[64] When Landa resigned, however, he was
replaced by William Smith from Company G and Berninger was
instead transferred out of Company I to fill a vacancy left by the resignation of Lt. Jacob Heip in Company K. Berninger's departure was,
according to Crusius, "very much to our regret." He is an "efficient officer who had been schooled in Baden under Sigel and who later had an
opportunity to continue his training in Algiers," but "was arbitrarily
taken away from his men who loved and respected him. Many joined
the Company only on account of him. A petition to the chief which
had the purpose of retaining Berninger was not at all considered."[65]

As the days passed, however, there was little time for intrigue.
Seemingly endless drills continued for six hours each day, broken only
by unpopular picket duty or
occasional reviews. On
October 22 the Sigel Regiment
received forty rounds of
ammunition per man. The following day, Karsten reported
"We learned to shoot, to load,
and to lie down," target practice with live ammunition following for the first time on the
24th.[66] "We have marched
around quite a bit in this
vicinity," Dr. Huebschmann

Julius Froehlich, Company B,
a clerk from Milwaukee.

complained to his wife, "without having done any good thereby, nor has it meant anything. Many pranks happen in the regiment and there are many rascals there."[67]

The dreary routine prompted many to long for more exciting activities. "I for my own part am calm," Damkoehler reported to his wife, "and to tell the truth I wish that we would have a battle tomorrow and stay at the battle and bring the war to an end."[68] Winkler chose a different battlefield, making a checker board and using buttons from his sewing kit for pieces until he discovered that one of the lieutenants had a set of chess pieces, after which chess became the evening routine for several of the officers.[69]

At the end of the month Secretary of the Treasury Salmon P. Chase and his daughter visited prompting in his honor a full dress review of two entire divisions of Sigel's corps.[70] About the same time, orders arrived to prepare to march. "It is difficult for us to depart from this camp located so high from which we enjoy the most beautiful views, above all since we found the tents so well equipped and felt ourselves bedded in down," wrote Pvt. Crusius. "Only the thought that soon we shall meet the rebel hordes and inflict upon them a defeat can reconcile us with this order to march."[71]

Chapter 3

"EVERYONE HOPES FOR THE BEST"
On The March

ollowing the bloody Battle of Antietam on September 17, 1862, Robert E. Lee's rebel army retreated south from Maryland into Virginia, followed at a distance by McClellan's Army of the Potomac. Although Lincoln prodded McClellan to attack swiftly before Lee's forces escaped, the Northern general went into camp complaining of fatigued horses and the need for reinforcements and resupply. In an effort to concentrate the entire army for a strike at the Confederates, the Eleventh Corps received orders to move to Centreville, and thence west to Thoroughfare Gap to rendezvous with McClellan's army and participate in the anticipated campaign against the Army of Northern Virginia.

The First Campaign

With the arrival of marching orders, the camp came to life in preparation to move out the next day. "As I write these lines by the meagre light of a lamp in my tent," wrote Crusius, "there is life and activity both in our regiment and in the surrounding regiments. Virile war songs resound, the men grouped together picturesquely, many crowd around the fires who can hardly wait until the meat is cooked. The cook has his hands full for salt meat must be cooked for three days. Also the orderlies and the sergeants are not idle; from a large barrel the crackers are distributed: another packs the things which cannot be taken in the knapsacks for only the most necessary things can be carried in the knapsacks. From this we must assume that difficult marches and bivouacs will be our portion for some time."[1]

Orders arrived for the regiment to be ready to march at 7:00 a.m. on November 2. "We are all to go in the lightest trim," Winkler reported. "The men are allowed to carry nothing but a change of underclothes, a pair of shoes and their blankets in their knapsacks. The officers are also reduced to the minutest limits. The small valise is all that is expected to be carried under any circumstances, and even that will probably not keep up with the progress of the march. No mess chest, no cooking utensils of any kind will be carried along, each officer will have a tin cup and that will answer all our requirements....We have as yet seen little, nay nothing, of the hardships of war, but the time is coming."[2]

The objective of the movement, to drive Confederate troops from Thoroughfare Gap and occupy the surrounding area, brought a thrill of anticipation. "We all expected a brush & hence some excitement," noted Lackner.[3] For many, it was a time not only of excitement and anticipation, but self reflection. "I see clearly what awaits us," Winkler confided in a letter home, "and with firm step and unquailing heart I hope to do my duty, not do I feel as if the trials I am to undergo were hard, unreasonably hard; no, I am cheerful while I am determined. I know that the cause we fight is just. This, and a firm reliance on the providence of God, lends me the strength I possess."[4]

The men were awakened at 4:00 a.m. the next morning so they could cook the two day's rations they would carry in their knapsacks. After breakfast they received fresh ammunition, sixty rounds per man. Anticipation was everywhere, "the boys jokingly bidding one another farewell." To Winkler, the scene was emotionally overwhelming: "To me, as I looked upon the array of trusty men—a company of men as true, as noble as ever enlisted in the cause of war, and every one of whom I had learned dearly to love and knew to be devoted to me, it was no subject for joking; and while I could not but smile at their witticisms, I had to turn my face from them to disguise the tears that rushed to my eyes."[5]

The column swung into motion at 8:00 a.m., moving steadily through Fairfax to Centerville, which they reached about noon, before stopping an hour for a rest. To Lackner, "The sight of a whole Corps, or at least half a one marching was quite a novelty to me. The whole road was literally covered with soldiers, batteries, wagons &c."[6] Winkler found "the face of the country is very hilly and our march was continually up hill and down."[7]

At Centerville the regiment relaxed for about an hour. A few of the soldiers took advantage of the respite to consume some of their rations and brew coffee, while others became acquainted with men from Gen. Julius Stahel's brigade stopped nearby. Stahel's troops assured the Wisconsin men they would meet the rebels before nightfall.[8] The lighthearted humor of early morning turned quiet in anticipation of the work ahead.

The men fell in and moved out again about 1:00 p.m., but covered only four miles before stopping for the night some two hours later. Nevertheless, Winkler found the march "fatigued me very much." He felt "perfectly worn out" by the time they stopped for the evening. Colonel Jacobs invited Winkler to share his tent that night, providing the captain with "a sound sleep" after which he "felt like a new man."[9] Lackner spent "a cold, windy night pretty comfortably" in a tent with Major Horwitz and a lieutenant.[10]

The following morning the troops were once again up early, marching over the Bull Run bridge into countryside so recently the scene of furious combat. "The desolation which stares one in the face, between here & the Gap is really pitiable," Lackner observed. "No fences—fields trodden hard—houses demolished—here and there the carcass of a dead horse, all can tell the story of war."[11] To Pvt. Crusius the sight of the battlefield of Second Bull Run, fought only two months before, brought a realization of "the horrors of the war in its entirety. Fragments of human skeletons and the carcasses of horses lie around everywhere and those who in life hated each other are here united in death with their bones."[12] Lackner continued: "Graves can be seen in the middle & on the sides of the roads, with heads and limbs protruding & in all conditions—a horrible sight. Sometimes a rail fence, or a tombstone, in the shape of a board with a lead pencil inscription, shows that friendship lives even in the field."[13]

Somber from the experience, the troops marched steadily, feeling always that the enemy was near. About a mile from Gainesville the column halted, formed into divisions, and advanced cautiously as if expecting a confrontation at any moment. Soon it stood at the junction of the Warrenton Turnpike and the Manassas Gap Railroad, about eleven miles from Thoroughfare Gap. Anxiously, Lackner thought of the regiment's empty weapons and "wondered why we did not load."[14] Just before entering the town the column turned down a road to the right, marching through the little hamlet of Haymarket whose inhabitants peered from windows and stood warily along the streets. "They looked at us insolently," Muenzenberger recalled, "but our men sang in a loud voice, 'In the south, in the south, where the German guns explode and the rebels fall.'"[15] The "rebels" thus chastised, the column pushed on to Thoroughfare Gap, arriving about 4:00 p.m.[16]

The two-day march covered twenty-six miles. At Thoroughfare Gap, Muenzenberger reported, "We were given immediate orders to set up our tents. We had barely finished with this when the younger soldiers of the regiment went out foraging and brought in pigs, chickens, ducks, turkeys and geese in large numbers. We roasted and cooked them."[17] With an opportunity for fresh food, the regiment apparently acquitted itself better at foraging than it did during the maneuvers before leaving Fairfax Court House. "Here," Crusius wrote, "it was possible for us to recuperate somewhat after the strenuous march and we hunted sheep, chickens, pigs and various other two and four legged creatures to which we made the most pleasant grimaces[,] the farmers on the other hand the most terrible[.] [E]ven if we were not as mischievous as the Wallensteiner to whom the Capuchian preached[,] nevertheless we made use of everything that we saw."[18] Karl Karsten reported resting and taking "horses, sheep, pigs, chickens, ducks, geese, honey, [and] apples from the countryside. We cooked and fixed the meat all day and had a good time."[19] "We are now completely in secession country," Karl Wickesberg reported, "and around here have taken away everything that they had from the secessionists."[20]

Winkler found the forager's conduct deplorable and attempted to portray his regiment in the best possible light with the people at home. "The country around seems to be as richly supplied with all the wealth that farmers have, as if no army has ever been here before, but the troops robbed and pillaged yards, barns and houses in a most disgraceful manner yesterday; our regiment, I am happy to say, was the most moderate of all and kept within some bounds of decency. Company B brought in nothing but a few sheep and a pig."[21]

Lackner found the new campsite "pleasant," but had little time to enjoy it. Before he could settle in, his company was detailed to the picket line under the overall command of Captain Boebel. Retracing their steps back toward Haymarket, they established their picket line along the roadway a suitable distance from camp. "Stragglers came through all night laden with [booty] &c which they had taken from Haymarket, claiming it to be infected by secesh." When he returned to the main camp the following day, Winkler's attempt to minimize his company's foraging notwithstanding, Lackner found "sheep, geese, pigs & c. were plenty. I had for dinner a fried chicken & some honey—a great luxury."[22]

In the camp at Thoroughfare Gap the regiment had an opportunity to participate in the fall elections. Emotions ran high. After the long series of federal disasters on the battlefield, followed by McClellan's failure to destroy Lee's army in the sanguinary Battle of Antietam, anti-war sentiment in the North was on the rise. Republicans and their pro-war Democratic allies feared losing control of Congress and various state legislatures to anti-war Democrats. "On the 4th of Nov. we voted," Lackner wrote.[23] But all, apparently, did not go well, the political strife in the civilian community apparently being mirrored in the regiment. "We expected tickets for the election on the 4th," Crusius complained, "but have not yet received them."[24] Adam Muenzenberger was more pointed: "Today is election day. All companies have voted except ours. Our officers are all Republicans and our soldiers are all Democrats, and so they've cheated us—or rather the candidates."[25]

Back in Wisconsin, the Madison *Patriot*, a Democratic publication, implied some irregularities. "Our company in the Twenty-sixth regiment gave 90 democratic and 9 republican votes. Did the other companies vote? If not, why?"[26] The *Milwaukee Sentinel* answered in an equally accusatory tone: "Yes, other companies did vote; one at least giving a unanimous vote for Brown, and the regiment giving a majority the same way. Is it not possible for the *Patriot* and other democratic sheets to exhibit common honesty with reference to the soldier's vote? If not, why."[27]

Although the election resulted in disappointment for the Republican candidates in many state and national races, in Milwaukee voters elected a War Democrat, James S. Brown, to the House of Representatives.[28] Though not a Republican, men of that political persuasion in the 26th were generally satisfied that the anti-war faction was not victorious.

Before the results of the election were known, tragedy struck. On the night of November 5, men from Companies B and I went on picket duty. With them were 2nd Lt. Lackner from Company B and 2nd Lt. John Orth of Company I.[29] Orth, accompanied by Pvt. Crusius, was assigned to take the new password to the picket outposts. Arriving at the furthest outpost from the camp, manned by a corporal and six privates, "Orth passed the guard in an open place in the woods" while Crusius "and the corporal proceeded to the fire in order to give him the pass word." Crusius transmitted the password, but had barely done so when a shot rang out, followed by Orth's voice crying for help. "In the greatest excitement all ran to the place where we beheld a terrible scene," Crusius recalled. "The poor Lieut. lay in his blood[,] fifteen

Left to Right: Jacob Stauff, George P. Träumer, John Koege, John Orth, Philip Waldorf.

paces away stood the guard who had inflicted the wound which he alone could give. The sentry (by no means a recruit but a soldier in the service of the Prussian army) stated that the Lieut. had not answered according to order; but if one considers that the night was bright and the distance was only fifteen paces away[,] that the surrounding territory is clear[,] then must one draw the conclusion that the sentry either from malice or out of revenge acted thus because he claimed to be sick and was placed by the Lieut. to this extreme outpost. Orth who would never do harm to a child possibly questioned him concerning this affair. Be that as it may if Orth had answered according to instructions probably everything would have been OK."[30]

The bullet entered Orth's abdomen. The unfortunate lieutenant was carried to the hospital tent where Damkoehler remembered that "by probing of the urethra blood showed up and the doctors called the

Left to Right: Adolph Weidner, L. Meier, George Schuele, Henry Erdmann. Heinrich Ulrich, Charles Weidner, J. Steil (probably John Style).

wound very critical. I was with him all night and cooled his wound."
Orth was removed to Washington for treatment at the earliest opportunity. For Damkoehler, it "was a hard blow." "Lieutenant Berninger was
transferred through some plotting of our Company and some good-for-
nothing by the name of Smith was put in his place," he lamented, "and
now Orth is lost to us. Both were my friends and they had the best in
mind for me. This last sad accident was only due to the inexperience of
the Lieutenant and of the soldier. With some instructions it could have
been prevented."[31]

Following the shooting, the nights continued terribly cold with
winds making the "tents quake." On the 7th, orders arrived for the regiment to march through Thoroughfare Gap the next day. The column
moved out of camp about 7:00 a.m. on November 8. Soon it began
snowing as the men "defiled through the gap and then marched over a
stony, hilly road about five miles to a collection of three houses, with
barnes, stables, etc., which constitutes the village of New Baltimore."[32]
Lackner felt the Gap "can boast of a magnificent scenery," but the "cold
& snowy day" dampened some of the spirits.[33] "We marched in the
mountains," Damkoehler recalled. "On the way it started to snow and
after our arrival here we had to clear the place from snow first before we
could pitch our tent. Today, while I am sitting in my little tent, everything is white outside and my fingers are pretty cold."[34]

The next morning the men were up early again, moving out at
8:00 a.m. on the road to Gainesville where they arrived after a rapid
three-hour march.[35] Pickets were thrown out to secure the new campsite, while the men set about constructing their tents and making the
accommodations as hospitable as they could under the circumstances.
"We now have small tents like we had in Africa," Damkoehler wrote,
comparing the new camp to those he recalled from his experience in
the French Foreign Legion. "These are only about 4 feet high and
arranged for 3 men, and each one has to carry his part with him." In
camp, three men secured their portions together to form a single tent
to cover all.[36]

Sergt. William Steinmeyer, Sergt. Karl Doerflinger, and Lt. Franz
Lackner constructed a small log hut to protect themselves from the
weather. Hungry for fresh food, Capt. Winkler and Lt. Lackner gave
Pvt. Ferdinand Huebner ten cents and sent him to buy some things
from the local farmers. "He came home with a canteen full of milk, a

chicken, potatoes & honey &—his ten cents. On the whole we lived pretty comfortably there."[37] Soon, however, "the Captain was appointed Judge Advocate of the Corps, took leave of the Company, who gave him three rousing cheers & were very much moved—the command devolved on H[uttmann], whom the boys began to dislike very much."[38] Surprised by the unanticipated appointment, Winkler marvelled that he would now "have a commodious tent at headquarters and a horse to ride." While vowing "faithfully and religiously to balance the scales of justice," he was "sorry to leave the regiment—to leave my company. My company is the best—the standard company of the regiment—the material it is made of necessarily makes it such," he wrote with obvious pride. "I love those boys."[39]

Winkler was very concerned about what would happen to his "boys." He held no confidence in 1st Lt. William Huttmann, the next ranking company officer. Huttmann, he felt, "is a youth without distinction or the least weight of character, in point of education inferior to one-half the men in the ranks; this circumstance greatly adds to my regret at leaving the company." His only solace was that 2nd Lt. Lackner was "a good and reliable man." After roll call the next morning Winkler gathered the men around him, announced his new appointment, thanked them for their faithful service, and asked them "to be true to their duty in the future." Silence followed the announcement, until Lackner "called for three cheers for the Captain, that were given with a unanimity and heartiness that deeply moved" Winkler. "Tears came into my eyes and I could only falter in reply, 'I thank you, boys!' Then they came around me individually and you could see in their faces that they were really sorry." Winkler left that afternoon, but was so affected by the parting he "could not sleep all night."[40]

Once in camp, newspapers arrived trumpeting the great victory of Schurz's division at Thoroughfare Gap. "I see by a Baltimore paper that General Schurz' Division 'drove the enemy through Thoroughfare Gap' at the time of our march," Winkler wrote sarcastically. "I was there. I saw the 'drive.' Oh, it was terrible! Not a gun was fired, not a foe was seen! Great Victory!"[41]

General Sigel's headquarters was at Gainesville, which gave officers in the 26th an opportunity to renew acquaintances with some of his staff whom they had known before the war. On the 10th, the entire brigade, complete with artillery, "marched out in parade style and formed a brilliant line along the road near by to receive with due honors George B. McClellan." The men stood in line "a few hours," but the commanding general never arrived. Eventually, disappointed, they "marched home again without having seen anything of the little General." Rumors abounded until word arrived that McClellan had been relieved the previous day, replaced as commander of the Army of the Potomac by Ambrose P. Burnside.[42]

Many took advantage of the opportunity afforded by camp life to write home. Pvt. Crusius wrote that he expected to begin digging trenches the next day. "With my comrade I have already erected a stronghold against the inclemency of the weather. Today once more the sun shines after heaven had opened for four days its floodgate and we in our thin tents had no reason to complain of a shortage of water."[43]

Ernst Damkoehler was depressed about the transfer of Lt. Berninger, the shooting of Lt. Orth, and the lack of opportunity for advancement. Now he received a letter from his wife bearing the troubling news she was having financial difficulties. Damkoehler collected two dollars owed him by the captain and another from his friend Georg Bayer and sent the money to her. "I was thinking of buying a pair of gloves for myself since the weather is so rough," he wrote, "but I think I will get along."[44] Rumors circulated that the paymaster would soon arrive, so he promised to send her more as soon as he was able. Depressed, he confided his frustration to his wife in a letter dated November 10: "As I wrote to you in my last letter, it is almost impossible to get ahead. Had I been a saloon or barkeeper in Milwaukee I would have a fine future, but knowledge and merits don't count."[45] The following day he continued the theme in another missive: "My dear Mathilde, the whole war is only a humbug and had I known as much three months ago as I do now I would not have enlisted under my own free will....[T]o write to you of prospects of advancement would be nonsense. Our Regiment gives no consideration to knowledge and learnings. To the contrary, it seems to me the most stupid ones are chosen."[46]

"We are still held in reserve," Adam Muenzenberger told his wife Barbara. "We have seen no rebels but here and there the wives and children who have been left behind stare at us, sometimes sadly, sometimes hatefully....No horse or cow is safe from the old regiment. The soldiers take everything along on the plea that they wish to pay the rebels for the treatment at the last battle of Bull Run." But he too was worried about his wife's financial circumstances. "We hear that our wives have received no assistance from the government, and a lot of other idle talk. Please write and tell me how everything is at home....We haven't received any pay as yet, and haven't heard when we will be paid. If you haven't sent me any post stamps as yet, send me some—but all new ones, and I will write you one or even two letters every week. Stamps cannot be obtained here."[47]

Adam's concern grew when another Greenfielder, Fritz Awe, received a letter from his parents informing him that Barbara Muenzenberger was ill. But soon a welcome letter arrived from Barbara to comfort him. "Your letters arrived as we lay in our tents, and you can't imagine how happy their arrival made me. I had been very much depressed because I had heard that you were seriously ill....Now as I hear your sweet voice again in your letter I find peace again, but this only through prayer....I am very happy to hear that our children are so diligent in study and especially in penmanship, which as you know was always my greatest pleasure....My clothing is still in good shape. I wash my blue shirts and my underwear every week....Only the soles of my boots are worn through. My shoes and the new grey shirts which I received from the government are like new. We have received no money as yet, nor do I know when we will receive any, but as soon as we are paid I will write and send you some....I was just invited to a sausage lunch by Jacob Michel, Louis Manz, and Nikolaus Friedrich. We live as well here as we can. The food is good and the crackers taste—or rather must taste—good to us. We have fresh meat almost every day. Don't give up hope, old lady, trust in the Lord. In the wish that these lines find you in the best of health as they leave me I salute you all heartily....You can't imagine the pleasure I get from looking at your picture."[48]

While many wrote home, others spent their time maneuvering for advantage within the regiment as the old cleavages from the earlier "Lehmann Affair" in Milwaukee appear to have resurfaced. "Intriguing also commenced," Lackner noted, "as is usual in German regiments." Colonel Jacobs "issued an order giving us 6 hours drill every day & at this the Lt. Col. [Lehmann] endeavored to excite dissatisfaction in the Camp. The Col. made a speech to the regiment, telling them that he would not allow intrigues. Lt. [Christian] Sarnow was put under arrest & lt. [Jacob] Heip & Capt. [Franz] Landa handed in their resignations."[49]

On November 18 the regiment broke camp and marched east to Centreville, once again moving over the recent battlefields near Bull Run where it "passed one grave from which two parched black hands protruded." Arriving in the midst of a heavy rain, the Sigel Regiment encamped within the fortifications of that sprawling supply base.[50] Muenzenberger found it "a charming little village with fine mills and a fairly large church, but now it is an abandoned nest. The mill has been destroyed by fire and the church has been converted into a hospital and quartermaster's station. The people have moved out of the place and the houses are occupied by officers, soldiers and negroes. We are expected to camp here for an indefinite period. Where we go then we don't know. Our army is falling back—why, no one knows."[51]

For the most part the men were discouraged by their first "campaign." They expected to be in the front lines when they marched to Gainesville, but instead they watched as portions of the Army of the Potomac marched by on their way in pursuit of the Confederates. As disappointed as they were about the lack of activity in Gainesville, they felt worse about the movement back to Centreville where they "expected to take up winter quarters and stay there all winter." Damkoehler explained: "The soldiers were angry at the thought of lying around all winter."[52] They preferred to get into action and end the war as soon as possible.

To make matters worse, the *New York Times* published a story about panic in "a Wisconsin regiment" in General Sigel's command during the withdrawal from Thoroughfare Gap. As bad as the story was for morale, it's ill effects were magnified many times when the November 26 edition of the *Milwaukee Sentinel*, picking up the story, printed the following headline: "The retreat from Gainsville to Fairfax Court House—A Panic amongst the New Regiments—The Twenty-Sixth Wisconsin abandon their Tents—are sent back for Them." In the accompanying story, readers were informed that "the falling back was not the most orderly....The Twenty-sixth Wisconsin abandoned a large number of tents and muskets. Gen. Sigel, when he heard of this, ordered the regiment, accompanied by a sufficient force, to return, and, if possible, obtain the abandoned property. Some property was also necessarily left at Thoroughfare Gap, owing to the order to move being so sudden, that there was not time to order forward sufficient means for transporting everything. The property was subsequently sent for. There seems, also, to have been a slight panic at this place."[53]

Stung by this blatant falsehood, officers and men could only wonder what their friends and relatives at home would think. Reaction among the officers brought a swift denunciation by General Sigel himself. On December 4 the *Sentinel* printed under the heading "The Twenty-Sixth Wisconsin Vindicated" a letter from Sigel, "correcting a foul slander upon the Twenty-sixth Wisconsin, which appeared in the New York papers."[54] The letter read as follows:

Headquarters Eleventh Corps,
Army of the Potomac,
Fairfax C.H., Va, Nov. 27, 1862.

To His Excellency, Gov. Salomon, Madison, Wis:

DEAR SIR:-Probably you will have read in one of our papers, that "a Wisconsin regiment" did not behave well on the withdrawal of our forces from Thoroughfare Gap, by throwing away their arms and burning their tents. Although I am sure that you have more confidence in the valor and discipline of the noble Twenty-sixth (the only regiment of Wisconsin soldiers attached to this corps), than to believe such a scandalous report, I think it nevertheless my duty to say, that the Twenty-sixth Wisconsin was not at Thoroughfare Gap, when we marched from there to Centerville, and that the whole story about throwing away arms and burning tents is a most malicious and infamous misrepresentation and lie, brought up by some treacherous scoundrel, who should be regarded and held up before the public as an official rebel agent and sensationist.

It affords me pleasure to say, that the Twenty-sixth Wisconsin is in the best spirits, and, by constant exercise and drill, in excellent health.

With the greatest respect, yours truly,

F. Sigel, Maj. Gen.

The letter notwithstanding, the damage was done. Feelings of outrage, pain, and frustration circulated through camp. Among those who wrote to correct the impression at home was Adam

Muenzenberger:

You do not know how surprised I was to learn from your letter
that the 26th Wisconsin and the 119th New York ran away at
Gainesville, and left their blankets and guns behind them. It is
laughable and at the same time annoying to have anything of that
kind said or written about a regiment such as ours.

It is laughable to this extent. Up to this time our regiment has
not had the honor even to meet a southern soldier with the excep-
tion of those whom our pickets took prisoner....

It is annoying because we hear that these rumors are given
out in part by the *Milwaukee Sentinel* and in part by the
Milwaukee Seebothe. Of course you can't blame the *Sentinel* in
this matter. It hasn't forgotten the slur our Lieutenant [Colonel]
Lehman[n], gave it. It certainly would be aggravating to get a
good dig from a Dutchman and not to be able to return it. You
know, we are no Yankees.

One can forgive the *Seebothe* because the editor simply doesn't
understand the affair and I know the old man. He screams when
the other one shouts and he is angry besides because his
Napolean, McClellan, was relieved of duty.

Beloved, believe me—and I wouldn't lie—we marched back in
the same order and with the same packs that we had when we left
here. In the same way that you saw us march from Camp Sigel we
marched from Gainesville to Centerville with our stomachs
empty. The whole company grumbled because our equipment
wasn't hauled there, in spite of the fact that we knew two days
ahead of time that we were going to Centerville. I firmly believe,
though, that our regiment would let itself be shot to pieces before
it would retreat. Let me repeat once more, then, that as yet we
haven't seen the enemy, and that the whole tale is an ugly slander
against us.[55]

Centreville

Once in camp, Muenzenberger was assigned to picket duty. "We
did picket duty before a house where we get a quart of milk every
morning and evening. I was the corporal of the watch. We didn't know
what to do to pass the time without getting into mischief. We are in

good health, and have plenty to eat, and an over-abundance of good, healthy appetite. But Babbette, you can't imagine the poverty among the people here, especially among the farmers. At every retreat the Rebels make they plunder everything that isn't fastened down. If the Northern Army retreats they do the same. They [the natives] think the North has some very tough soldiers, but they always have a word of praise for the 26ers, they are always sent back for guard."[56] Doerflinger also recalled opportunities to acquire food while on picket duty. "[W]e paid a good U.S. dollar for each 'Johnny cake' baked by the Virginia beauties whose husbands or brothers were or seemed absent, possibly lying in ambush for us somewhere in the wilderness."[57]

Despite the occasional opportunities for food, picket duty was always an onerous task, particularly in bad weather. Just as Muenzenberger and his group received their assignment for outpost duty, "it began to snow and snow fell until eight o'clock in the evening. During all this time we stood in the snow around a fire. The officers and the non-commissioned officers don't have to undergo as much hardship as the privates do who are on picket duty. Every two hours pickets are changed. At nine P.M. the weather cleared and the wind whistled so coldly that we thought we would freeze....[T]hese duties are very hard—twenty-four hours without shelter. It is terribly cold here now. There are traces of snow and the wind is biting. We built little fireplaces in our tents, and they feel good as long as we can remain by them. But what can we do? Duties must be performed."[58]

While Muenzenberger was on picket duty Adam Wuest received a "heartbreaking" letter from his girlfriend, Christina Schmidt. When the cobbler returned from picket, he also found a letter waiting for him. Hastening to reply to his wife's communication, he wished her "congratulations on your namesday, and to wish you many more happy returns of the day with your children. But my greatest wish is that I could be united with you and the children soon again." He lamented the fact they had not been paid and thus he could not send her any money, also expressing the universal wish of all soldiers away from home that she write to him more often. "There is nothing more consoling to a father far away from home than to hear good news and often from his folks."[59] In another letter he thanked Barbara for her comments on the draft situation which caused some hard feelings between those who volunteered and those who did not. "I was encouraged by the fact that you comforted me about the draft. I'm perfectly satisfied that things are as they are; and, if God wills, the war will soon be over and we will have the opportunity, volunteers as well as drafted men, to talk to one another."[60]

Soon his wish for more mail was fulfilled. "My wholehearted thanks for your loving congratulations on my namesday," Barbara wrote. "My greatest wish is to have you return to me. Beloved, you write that I write so little. Hereafter I will send you a letter every Sunday. You don't know how much work I have—especially with the wood, because since your absence I have cut every piece myself. God be praised though, it goes better now....Money is scarce....Farewell, may the good Lord be your protector."[61] Though troubled by Barbara's toil and the shortage of money, Adam was at least comforted to read her handwriting and know that she and the children were in good health.

The drudgery of camp life, the increasingly inclement weather, frustrations at their seeming retreat without contacting the enemy, and the unflattering newspaper stories took their toll on the men's morale. Two men deserted at Centreville, raising to six the number of desertions since their muster-in. Captain Franz Landa of Company I, Lieutenant Christian Sarnow of Company A, and Lieutenant Jacob Heip of Company K resigned on November 19 and left for home. Several other officers returned home to recuperate from illness, or perhaps ponder their own resignations.[62] "Lt. H[uttmann] is sick of soldiering," Lackner confided to his diary. "He feigned sickness & asked me the other day to write his resignation, which I did. It will probably return accepted to-morrow & then he will start for home; he talks of nothing else." If Huttmann's resignation was accepted, Lackner reasoned, he stood to be promoted and Doerflinger made 2nd lieutenant. "Just now I feel very ambitious of promotion & have a belief," he wrote, "that I shall yet do so."[63] Huttmann resigned on December 8. When he heard the news, Winkler felt pleased Lackner and Doerflinger would no doubt be promoted, but could not resist a sarcastic comment on Huttmann: "He has the ear-ache so bad! He cannot stand it! Now...Company B will flourish again."[64]

The same day Huttmann resigned, the fiery West Bend editor, Captain Jacob E. Mann, resigned from Company G to return to his civilian profession. Back home in Wisconsin Mann's fighting spirit apparently returned as he sought to justify his action. "Six months ago," he explained to readers of the West Bend *Post*, "being inspired with patriotism and love of country, we raised a company of brave and sturdy young men, and joined the 26th Reg., bound to fight, bleed and die in defense of that glorious constitution bequeathed us, by our forefathers. But Alas! how soon was our youthful ardor dampened under the influence of a Southern clime, hard crackers, and mother earth for a pillow. All our ambition and eagerness for the bloody strife; all our anticipations of a glorious death on the battle-field, soon vanished, and after a protracted illness, we turned our face homeward, and now having once more resumed the pen, which, in the hands of the righteous is more powerful than the sword, we shall still battle for our country and the constitution. To our friends we once more extend our hand for their friendly grip. To our enemies we say come on, we are prepared to meet you."[65]

Back in Virginia, weakened from lack of rest, Colonel Jacobs fell ill with "chills and fever," causing great concern among those loyal to him. Corporal Muenzenberger commanded the watch in front of his quarters, recalling that, despite the colonel's illness, "In the morning he treated us with a bottle of brandy. He is in all respects the best officer in the regiment."[66] One of those who visited the ill officer was Lt. Lackner, who found him greatly concerned over the course of the war. "I was at the Colonels this afternoon. He claims that the democracy is adverse to a peace policy & that no peace could be made because southern leaders would not accept of any, except the basis of recognition. At the same time he fears, that a second draft would be resorted to, which might lead northern people to anti-war demonstrations & compell a hasty peace." Lackner was not quite as pessimistic, preferring to believe that cooler heads would eventually prevail. "It seems to me," he wrote, "that if an honorable peace be proposed in Congress, making no recognition, it would be accepted by the southern *people* although not by Jeff. Davis & his Cabinet. If the northern people can compell its administration to propose a peace, the southern people can compell Davis to accept one, I think. And in fact the prospects of peace are not so very distant, to Judge from the presidents message; besides it seems to me, that the republican Congress would in this, its last session, try to secure a fair & honorable peace, to regain the good-will of the people which it has lost by this war & the manners in which it has been carried on—whether it so lost it Justly or unjustly, need not be here spoken of. It cannot be denied, that at the present moment, there is a large proportion of the northern people in favor of peace on almost any Condition; the same state of things probably exists at the south; we also have men of immense influence elected to important offices in the north (I need only mention Seymour's name) who represent that party & will endeavor to execute its designs. I, for my part, am not so very anxious for peace, although I should like to see home. In fact I have an idea, that I can yet partly gratify my ambition in this war, if my youth is not in the way, & hence I want a little more time."[67]

Colonel Jacobs's illness gave the regiment a brief respite from battalion drills as, according to Lackner, a Jacobs partisan, Lt. Col. Lehmann "cannot drill a regiment."[68] Confirmation of his observation came when Col. Krzyżanowski, the brigade commander, arrived to observe battalion drill. Left with no alternative, Lt. Col. Lehmann attempted to conduct the exercise but succeeded only in making himself appear "perfectly ridiculous." "I wonder what the consequences of this will be," mused Lackner.[69] Another of Lehmann's detractors was Corporal Muenzenberger. To him, Lehmann's haughtiness and cruelty marked him as one of the worst officers in the regiment, if not the entire service. To the corporal, the lt. colonel was "a beast and is drunk most of the time" and "doesn't know how to treat the men decently."[70] Apparently others shared this opinion because an anonymous letter from a soldier in the 26th that appeared in the *Milwaukee Sentinel* described the lt. colonel as a "leading miscreant" fit only as "a good corporal."[71] Such attitudes contributed greatly to the general discontent in the regiment that fall.

In this depressing atmosphere, rumors proliferated. "Rumors of all kinds concerning peace and a return to Milwaukee are floating around," Muenzenberger told his wife. "I don't think you can find a single soldier in the entire army who wouldn't rather go home today than tomorrow. Everyone sees this big humbug with wide-open eyes. The man who stays well here is fortunate. Our doctors are absolutely worthless."[72]

The general consensus of camp gossip had the regiment spending the winter in Centreville. Several groups used their spare time to make their tents more comfortable. Lackner and his "tentmates" constructed beds out of boards for their old wall tent, outfitted it with a writing table and oilcloth cover, and purchased a small stove. The smoke, however, made the tent more uncomfortable with the stove than without, and several different chimney designs failed to solve the problem. Finally they induced Pvt. Heinrich Lingsch to build them a fireplace which brought warmth to the cold evenings without the aggravation of suffocating smoke.[73]

Tents erected, the men gradually settled into a daily routine that to some brought welcome stability after weeks of movement and uncertainty. Lackner spent time studying tactics and reading Milton. When he finished the latter, he borrowed Hesekiel's *Rome and Berlin* from 2nd Lt. Hermann Fuerstenberg in Company D and finished it in two days.[74] Many followed with interest and concern newspaper reports of the new draft in Wisconsin. Drafting began everywhere except Milwaukee on November 10, the selection in that city being delayed by errors in the draft list. Throughout the state emotions ran high. In Ozaukee County rioters burned the draft commissioner's home. A riot in Port Washington proved serious enough to require eight companies of the 28th Wisconsin Infantry to restore order. In Milwaukee, a protest march took place in the Ninth Ward in which a loud brass band led 150 men down Grand Avenue behind a banner reading "NO DRAFT! NO! NO!" Crowds lined the street, but only a few joined in the protest.[75] The *Sentinel* reported a group of women assaulted a draft commissioner, while state authorities were worried enough to order the 1st Wisconsin Volunteers into the city to maintain order. Although some blamed the disturbances in Milwaukee on the city's Germans, they offered no proof for the accusation.[76]

The Sigel Regiment's *freiwilligen*, who took great pride in their status as volunteers, were very much concerned with this turn of events on the home front. "Report has it that there has been drafting in Wisconsin and great resultant scandal," Muenzenberger informed his wife. "We have had a great laugh at the simpletons who laughed at us because we volunteered. Please let me know who was drafted, if you can find out, so that I can laugh at their lot the way they laughed at mine."[77] Capt. Winkler felt outraged at the conduct of his fellow citizens in Wisconsin. "I hope that every man who participated in those riotous proceedings will be ferreted out and severely punished."[78]

Each day men went out to take target practice in small groups of twenty, a duty not devoid of danger. On December 2 Karsten reported that Lewis Grosshaus accidentally shot himself in the leg with his own weapon while at target practice. Companies and squads rotated on picket duty, with "several" presumed rebels being captured daily on charges of spying. Captain John P. Seemann, serving as provost marshal, dutifully sent each batch of captives on to Washington.[79]

Despite the cold, the boredom, and the recurring illnesses, the men gradually became accustomed to life in camp. "Troubled with loneliness and with my thoughts forever with the loved ones at home," Muenzenberger told his wife, "I take my pen in hand to write you a short letter. We are, God be praised, in the best of health, and hope that this letter finds you the same. We enjoy happy times here in the camp at Centerville. We take long walks, and pass our time in the easiest fashion....Every two days we get good wheat bread; the other days we have crackers. We likewise have fresh beef every two days. On the other days we have salt pork and bean soup. We have received no money as yet, and I don't know when we will receive any, but as soon as I do get some I will write to you. The weather here is about the same as it is in October at home. It freezes just a little at night and there is a light frost. We are camped here in our cotton tents, quite well satisfied and filled with the hope that the war will be over in spring."[80]

Snow began falling on December 8, covering the ground with a gentle white blanket by the following day. Despite the attractiveness of the scenery, Lackner found it "cold & stormy & about impossible to keep a comfortable heat in our tent."[81]

On the 9th, Muenzenberger took advantage of a few minutes of inactivity to again write his wife. Lackner returned from picket duty about noon, anxious for some rest, but soon orders arrived for the regiment to move to Falmouth, a small Virginia town located along the Rappahannock River opposite Fredericksburg.[82] There the new commander of the Army of the Potomac, General Ambrose P. Burnside, planned to concentrate his army before crossing the river to attack Lee's Army of Northern Virginia. That evening, as the regiment prepared to move out in the morning, Lt. Huttmann gave Lackner a bottle of rum as a gesture of thanks for his help preparing his resignation, then left for Washington on the first leg of his homeward journey.[83]

Fredericksburg

The next morning the men struck their tents and were on the move with the arrival of daylight. "We had established ourselves very comfortably and left this place unwillingly," Crusius asserted. When they left camp the ground was frozen, but the morning sun brought pleasantly warm weather, "an old women's summer" according to Crusius, that began melting the ground by 9:00 a.m., converting it into a soft, muddy mess.[84] The men marched steadily at a regular pace, but as the day wore on the combination of warming weather and marching feet caused the dirt roads to deteriorate rapidly. By early afternoon "the clay roads of Virginia had been converted into a mass of mud" that Crusius found "most difficult....If one considers the ravines, the steep hills and forests then a person can form an idea of the difficulties that confront us."[85] Marching on despite the difficulty, the regiment reached Fairfax Station, a distance of only some seven miles for the day's march, about 3:30 p.m. and pitched their tents for the evening.[86] Lackner "had a cup of chocolate in the evening" with Major Horwitz and Lt. Domschcke. The major "commenced to be sick," so Lackner shared a tent with Corp. Frederick Ehlert, Pvt. Carl Friedrich, Pvt. William Penner, and Sgt. Karl Doerflinger, enjoying a "first rate" sleep.[87]

The next day they were again up early to continue the march. "All that day we struggled through the mud," Muenzenberger recalled, arriving at Wolf's Run Shoals where they camped for the night after a fourteen mile march.[88] The roads continued to be "awful" and Lackner found the campsite at the edge of a woods to be "cold & wet with melted snow & we felt very uncomfortable." Karsten had the unenviable job of guarding the wagons which he had to constantly push and pry from the mud. By evening, Sergt. William Steinmeyer was very sick, while others suffered to a greater or lesser degree from colds and respiratory problems because of the dampness and fluctuating temperatures.[89]

The third day of the march the men were once again awakened before daybreak, hastily heating some morning coffee before taking to the roads. The weather continued "warm and clear" during the day according to Muenzenberger, "about the way it is at home in October."[90] Around noon, while the regiment halted for a rest, Gen. Sigel and his staff rode by, stopping to converse with Lt. Col. Lehmann, in command during Col. Jacobs's continuing absence in the hospital. Lackner watched as the general spoke to Lehmann in "friendly" terms, offering him a cigar. "If he only knew what an incompetent officer he is," Lackner thought.[91] Resuming the march, the regiment continued on until it arrived within a mile of the small village of Dumfries, some twenty-two miles from Fredericksburg, about 4:00 p.m. Lackner's Company B and Company D were assigned to picket duty near where a federal wagon had been ambushed by rebel guerrillas only two hours before, but the evening proved quiet and they were relieved by Ohio troops about 11:00 p.m.[92]

On the 13th the regiment rested before moving on, but Muenzenberger and his friends had little opportunity to enjoy the beautiful weather as the "rest" brought only picket duty. By now, the three days rations the men carried were exhausted, leaving many as hungry as they were weary. Once the wagon trains caught up with the troops at Dumfries, each soldier received five hardtack crackers and one tablespoon of coffee to last two days.[93]

Nor was Lackner happy. After waiting hours for the regimental wagons to catch up, he found to his dismay that a crackerbox he was using for a mess chest had been inexplicably burned by the teamsters and "some valises were also missing & we scared the quartermaster almost out of his wits till the valises were at last found in a wagon."[94]

One of those who caught up with the regiment on the 13th was Ernst Damkoehler. Shortly before the 26th received orders to move out, Damkoehler was transferred to the ambulance corps. "I took it thinking to get a better place," he explained, "but was disappointed that my job turned out to be a carrier. Usually the crew consists of fellows unable to fight in the Regiment and rough people on top of it....My job was to empty five gallon jugs and refill them with fresh water." Soon, however, Brigade Commissary Wendt appointed him "second issue clerk" which brought more interesting work and the added incentive of a pay increase. "There is plenty of work and at times hard work. We...work through whole nights and up to now haven't had time to wash my clothes...and this is the reason dear Mathilde that I had to keep you waiting" for a letter.[95] When the regiment left Centreville, Damkoehler remained behind until enough wagons could be found to supply the need. By the time he left, all the other troops had already departed. "We left five o'clock in the afternoon and two o'clock at night until five in the morning we rested. There were thousands of wagons and they moved along slowly. In the evening we usually slept on top or underneath the wagons or I should say shivered in the cold weather."[96]

Despite their assorted complaints, however, more ominous thoughts no doubt filled their minds. Throughout the day the men "heard the terrible cannonading of the battle which raged at Fredericksburg during that day & thought it gunboats shelling the rebel batteries."[97] While they listened, Burnside threw his legions against Robert E. Lee's entrenchments on the slopes of Marye's Heights above Fredericksburg. Fourteen times he sent piecemeal attacks across a wide plain into the teeth of a very strong natural position manned by Confederate veterans supported by artillery on the heights above. When the day's slaughter finally ended, absolutely nothing had been gained for the loss of 12,700 Union casualties, more than twice the loss sustained by the defending Confederates in one of the most lopsided Union defeats of the war.

Unaware of the tragedy that transpired while they were at Dumfries, the 26th once again struck its tents early on the morning of the 14th, marching until 8:30 p.m. when it camped about two miles from Stafford Court House.[98] "This march was one of the hardest the Regt. ever made," Winker later wrote. "Rain & melting snow had made the roads almost impassable; arriving at our camping grounds generally late in the evening the tents had to be pitched in the snow & mud; rations, too, were very much reduced a part of the time."[99] Others agreed. "I never was more tired in my life," confessed Lackner. "I slept with my former comrades who took good care of me—our rations had given out & we all were very hungry."[100]

On the 15th they marched through the village of Stafford which Muenzenberger pronounced "about the most beautiful I have seen on our whole march."[101] From there it was on to the railroad station at Brooks Station, about eight miles from Fredericksburg, where they were finally reprovisioned, each soldier receiving twenty hardtack crackers and six tablespoons of coffee. Christian Crusius and his friends "strengthened ourselves with a strong mocca,"[102] and Muenzenberger agreed that "Now we are in good condition as far as eating is concerned."[103]

After marching all day, the Sigel Regiment arrived at Falmouth, one and one-half miles from Fredericksburg, at 4:00 p.m. on Tuesday, December 16. "We rested," Lackner noted, "not having any idea yet of what bloody scenes had transpired in our neighborhood a short time before." Soon they were ordered to fall in, and rumor passed that "we were going to fight, as our Cartridge boxes had Just been replenished."[104] After standing in line for some time, however, the order came to stand down and they encamped for the night. "We have pitched camp a mile and a half from Fredericksburg," Muenzenberger wrote that evening. "The rebels in their forts are only four miles away. For five days now a battle has been going on, and no one knows yet if it is over. We have heard that ten thousand of our men have been killed or captured. With much enthusiasm our people smashed everything in the town. We are hourly awaiting a renewal of the battle, inasmuch as the rebels don't want to withdraw. This evening we received orders to retreat—where to, no one knows but the generals. Hourly new troops are arriving on our side."[105]

Gradually, the full magnitude of the disaster at Fredericksburg filtered through the ranks. "We were too late to take part in the battle," Karl Wickesberg told his parents. "And we were satisfied with that, because the people were slaughtered for nothing."[106]

The battle over, the stay near Fredericksburg was brief. The next morning the regiment fell in and marched back along eight miles of muddy roads to Stafford Court House in the midst of a snow storm.[107] "We pitched our tents immediately," Muenzenberger recalled. "By the time they were up the snow had stopped falling. How happy I was when our quartermaster brought our mail and I received a letter from my precious wife. I immediately thought, I must finish this letter which I started at Fredericksburg. God be praised, I still am in the best of health as are Adam [Wuest], Leopold [Drewes], John Kraemer, [Andreas] Stubanus the basketmaker. I hope that this letter finds you the same. We have plenty to eat again, but we don't know what's going to happen to us and where we will be sent next."[108]

Although staples were much more available than they had been, it remained difficult to obtain some items. "Sutler stores are very scarce," Lackner reported, "as the rebels trouble the poor fellows very much." Because of the uncertain supply, a loaf of bread rose to fifty cents, butter increased to sixty cents, and tobacco was exceptionally scarce.[109]

One item in abundant supply was rumor, a commodity often as widespread as it was wild. Patrols went our regularly, but could detect no major Confederate activities save the usual guerrilla attacks on isolated wagons or picket posts. "It seems there is no thought of establishing winter quarters for the troops," Crusius wrote to the *Pionier am Wisconsin*, while Muenzenberger passed along his view of the prevailing camp wisdom: "They say that Sigel's corps is to go to Richmond by water with the fleet. General Banks is before Richmond, and Sigel is to support him. Tonight it is rumored that General Banks took Richmond, but whether the report is true we don't know. We hope that it is."[110]

Rumors aside, the regiment began settling in, not yet knowing if

Stafford Court House was destined to be its winter quarters. Crusius reflected this ambiguity in a letter to the *Pionier:*

> Everything is now at the point of establishing itself comfortably. Material of every kind is brought together and is laid and fastened by artistic hands. In a few days perhaps we shall march again and all the glory must be left behind. Thus it is with us homeless, we rove through the forests of Virginia, now erecting our habitat here and then there and then to tear it down just as quickly. And how exquisite tastes the coffee prepared under so many difficulties over smoking fire, how comfortably one quaffs this precious drink with a few crackers and then lie together so closely in the narrow tents. One dreams of attacks, the clash of swords, the thunder of cannons until the reveille awakes us and then we bound up and make fire. After the coffee has been consumed the tent is loosened each one takes his part on his knapsack, the cover is placed under the flap of the knapsack and the call to fall in rank is awaited. When the weather is favorable bivouacking is tolerable but if a torrent of rain falls suddenly while one enjoys a rest under the canvas tent then the affair becomes very cold. The thin material lets the water through, one is constrained to get up and to sit near the fire longing for the day to dawn. The day breaks one has no time to dry the covering and the tent; they are packed up while damp thereby adding to the weight of the knapsack considerably which in itself is heavy enough. The regiment stands the marching and fatigues well; all the sick were sent away from Centerville. The nights are very cold, during the day the sun often shines agreeably. Just now the cook called, "the rye soup is done" hence I must close since the stomach demands its rights.[111]

Stafford Court House

Once in camp, mail arrived with more frequency. Among the Greenfielders in Company C, Adam Muenzenberger received a letter from his wife Barbara. His brother-in-law, Adam Wuest, was disappointed at not receiving a letter from his girlfriend Christina Schmidt, but did receive a note from Mary Wuest Wiskirchen, a relative in La Crosse. Muenzenberger quickly set about replying to his letter.

"Dearest, I pity you because you have to cut the wood and do all the hard work. But be satisfied, true soul. This hard lot is merely a test for us. If God wills I can return and we will have wonderful—in fact the most wonderful days of our life together. Now don't give up. God still lives and I trust that he will let me return in the best of health and will reunite us."[112]

Promotions also arrived for many. Adam Muenzenberger's efforts were rewarded with promotion from fifth corporal to third, while his friend Jacob Michel received sergeant's stripes. Among the officers, Lt. Charles Pizzala rose to captain of Company G to replace the departed Jacob Mann. Lackner's wish for promotion was also fulfilled as he was appointed first lieutenant to replace the departed William Huttmann. William Smith rose to captain of Company I, and Karl Doerflinger received his coveted second lieutenancy in Company B.[113]

Settling into camp life, the regiment returned to daily drills. Company drill took place between 9:00 and 11:00 a.m., giving newly promoted officers a chance to adapt to their new roles. Battalion drill lasted from 2:00 to 4:00 p.m., but despite the daily practice criticism of Lt. Col. Lehmann continued unabated. "The Lt. Col. takes half of the regiment to drill every day & makes the sorest blunders under the eyes of Genl. Schurz," reported Lackner. "I wonder what will become of it. He certainly can not lead us in battle."[114] Muenzenberger agreed, adding that Lehmann "becomes more bestial day by day. No soldier has any respect for him. They sneer at his commands. Sometimes he hasn't nerve enough to come into camp until after midnight. The regiment likes our commander [Colonel Jacobs] more every day. They say that he is a very good man and a very successful officer. Everyone has the greatest respect for him."[115]

As the year neared an end, the regiment had been in the service three months with nothing to show for its exertions but miles of muddy marching, hours of freezing picket duty, personal intrigues, and false newspaper accusations. And then there were the debilitating illnesses that already claimed the lives of six: Joseph Kowall of Company I on September 19, Philip Stamp of Company H on October 26, Gottlieb Sommer of Company H on November 17, Heinrich Jaeger of Company A on November 30, Conrad Mack of Company G two days before Christmas, and William Sprangenberg of Company A on New Year's Eve.[116] Even the smallest illness could develop into life-threatening proportions in a matter of hours. There were no great battles to write home about, no heroism, no glory. Yet, while many harbored animosity for those profiting from the war, most cherished news from loved ones at home while determining to see the war through to a conclusion.

"You can't imagine how pleased I am every time I receive a letter from you," Muenzenberger told his wife. "I get added pleasure from the knowledge that you are all well and happy. A letter from you always brings healing medicine to my heart, which beats only for you, my loved ones. I am highly pleased to hear that Ernest and Mary like to study. Tell them to keep on so that when I return I may be very proud of them. They can please me better in no other way. Should I return I will surely bring them a beautiful gift, if they study hard. How are Henry and little Adam?...I am not sorry I enlisted, but I do wish that those who talked war constantly would have to perform an American soldier's duties for eight days. Then there would be peace in a short time. The newspapers say that the army is well satisfied with the conduct of the war. That is nothing but a lie. There isn't a regiment that isn't looking for peace, saying that war is nothing but moneymaking and humbug. This war doesn't concern the Union but the almighty purses of the officers and contractors, speculators and dealers. For these the war hasn't lasted nearly long enough. As long as Uncle Sam pays, the war will last. The weather is now pretty cold. We have only wood to use for fire to warm ourselves. Nothing would warm me more, though, than a letter from you and a greeting from your faithful heart."[117]

As their first Christmas away from home approached, many took the opportunity to write home. "I send you best wishes from my whole heart and I wish you a merry Christmas and a very happy New Year in the best of health," Muenzenberger wrote.[118]

"I am sitting in my cold tent drinking coffee with sugar so that I can write to you," explained Ernst Damkoehler. "My dear Wife and children, in two days it is Christmas and I wish you your health and my best good wishes for a happy new year. May our Dear God grant that this war may end and in favor of the Union so that we who are married may be united to the circle of our families...what I would give only to see you again. My dear wife as long as I am in our [commissary] business, I most likely won't see much of the enemy, and this way my dear, so far your wish has come true. Now don't you worry, you will not be the only widow to mourn over a husband. Be sure I will do my duty."[119]

"Dear Parents," Karl Wickesberg wrote, "I hope you can celebrate Christmas better than I. As I and another four men from our company have to leave today and work on the telegraph. I do not know how long that is going to take. The others have to do outpost duty. That is how we celebrate Christmas. I hope I will be in your midst next year."[120]

In Company C the Greenfielders did its best to prepare for Christmas. Muenzenberger teamed with Adam Wuest, Leopold Drewes, Asmus Holz, and Andreas Springling from Milwaukee as tent-mates. Although Wuest was suffering from the effects of a cold, he spurned the hospital and accompanied Holz on a "hunting" expedition, returning with a dismembered cow. "We have plenty of fresh beef now," Muenzenberger wrote, "but there isn't enough hardtack."[121]

On Christmas Eve Capt. Winkler, Lt. Charles Neukirch, and Sergt. William Steinmeyer spent the evening with Lt. Lackner enjoying rum punch and trying "to forget the homesickness which took hold of us." Lackner spent most of Christmas Day reading. Karsten received a box of crackers from home, purchased some cookies for fifty cents, then sat down to write his parents.[122]

The following week additional changes took place. Major Horwitz fell ill and left for Washington on a twenty-day sick leave; or, if one believes Lackner, the major "pretends to be sick." Few expected him to return.[123] Lieutenant Colonel Lehmann was called before a Board of Examiners to determine his competency, and rumor spread that he would tender his resignation. He was "the worst person in the whole army," Muenzenberger commented.[124] Lackner speculated that Captains John Seemann, Hans Boebel and Frederick Winkler were the leading candidates to fill the vacancies left by Lehmann and Horwitz. "I rather think that Boebel will be Lt. Col. & Winkler Major," he wrote. "We shall see."[125]

Dr. Huebschmann was called before a court martial, accused of stealing government wine furnished for the sick soldiers. Although Muenzenberger thought the doctor would "land back in Milwaukee before long," Huebschmann was found innocent of the charges. "By and by our regiment will be cleared of all rascals," Muenzenberger wrote, while at the same time lauding the colonel. "Our colonel behaves himself very well. He is liked by everyone. Every morning he visits the hospital."[126]

As the year wound down, one last spurt of excitement occurred.

On Sunday afternoon, December 28, as the regiment prepared for a ceremonial dress parade, orders arrived to march immediately to Dumfries where Confederates were attacking Gen. Alexander Schimmelfennig's brigade. "We were ready in about 5 minutes," Lackner explained, and "marched till we came to the Little Potomac, about 4 miles." There they halted for about an hour after receiving word the enemy cavalry attack had been repulsed. Retracing their steps, they arrived back in camp "very tired" about 7:30 p.m.[127]

On New Year's Eve the regiment formed for the formal review held every two months. "Our regiment was acclaimed the best and the neatest," Muenzenberger reported with pride. "Our colonel received merited praise for this." That evening its brigade commander, Col. Krzyżanowsk,i provided each regiment in his command with a barrel of whiskey to celebrate the appearance of the new year. Muenzenberger received a drink "as big as an inch."[128] Lackner found the night "not very pleasant. The Company had whiskey punch, of which we partook a little."[129] Karl Wickesberg felt differently: "We had a pretty amusing evening yesterday because our Brigade General Crisanowski [*sic*] had given our regiment a barrel of whisky and many a soldier was a little tipsy. Especially the officers." Captain Boebel came around about 1:00 a.m. to wish his men a happy new year, at the same time warning them to keep themselves "prepared because the Southern Cavalry was going to launch a surprise attack."[130]

On New Year's Day the officers visited Col. Krzyżanowski and were "well received." Later in the afternoon they picked a location for a new camp, while Lackner and Doerflinger made plans to build "a neat blockhaus" in the new location.[131] Captain Winkler wrote: "The common wish of a Happy New Year, I have heard from a hundred lips today. If we were to regard the weather as an omen, it would promise good to Virginia, war-beaten Virginia. This morning is clear and bright and genial, as if angels ruled the skies, and the day has been a lovely Indian summer day."[132]

Adam Muenzenberger took time to write an ebullient letter to his wife. "As healthy as ever, I take my pen in hand this 1st day of January, 1863, to tell you, beloved, about our activities here in Virginia. We are, God be praised, still in good health; and I hope, dearest, that this letter finds you the same. We think that we will have our money in a few days, as I hear that the entire regiment will be paid here. Should this happen I will send it to my dear ones as soon as possible, since it is my greatest pleasure to bring happiness to my beloved family at home. With this letter I am sending you a little New Year's present. It is a ring which I whittled out of wood here. It is the same wood out of which they make pipe bowls. It got too small for me. I had made it larger but through steaming it is shrunk. I will be very sorry if it is too small for you. I am going to whittle a prettier and larger one for you and for Mary. We have made many pipes, many of which are fully as nice as those you get in Milwaukee. Everyone is whittling pipes and rings, and tries to outdo everyone else. I am going to begin another one today. It is sure to be elaborate."[133]

Some of the men celebrated with culinary delicacies. "Dear Parents," wrote Wickesberg, "this morning we received flour and molasses. And because I, the sergeant, and the corporal are in the same tent, I always get a little bit more than the others. So we baked some pancakes. That was the first time I had any as long as I am a soldier. It is true the eggs were missing, but they still tasted very good." He too began making plans to build permanent winter quarters on the morrow. "So, this winter everything is just about over. And I think they won't start again [until] next spring. However, a person never knows how everything will go. Everyone just hopes for the best."[134]

"ALL THIS HUMBUG"
Marking Time

*I*n Wisconsin, friends and family of the men in the Sigel Regiment spent an apprehensive holiday season awaiting news that their loved ones were not involved in the Fredericksburg debâcle. Always concerned with their soldiers at the front, the Ladie's Soldiers Aid Society of Milwaukee knitted mittens for the men during the fall, solicited money to send them food and clothing, held benefit concerts, and provided support for widows and orphans. During 1862 the women raised $3,195.92 in cash and sent thousands of articles to soldiers in the field. The German Soldiers Aid Society canvassed the community for donations, while the Milwaukee *Turnverein* "donated a series of their beautiful tableaux" to a supper and dance sponsored by the Soldiers' Aid Society, and provided food and money for needy soldiers' families at home. The *Turnverein* voted to donate the proceeds of its annual Thomas Paine dinner of 1862 to providing for the welfare of the families of Turner soldiers. In 1863 it mailed local newspapers to the men at the front, and in 1863, 1864 and 1865 proceeds of the dinner were used to support soldiers' widows and also the orphaned.[1]

When letters arrived from Virginia, the welcome word that the regiment missed that terrible battle at Fredericksburg spread from one community to another. On January 6 the *Milwaukee Sentinel* noted the promotion of several men in the 26th: Sergeant Major Peter Fernekes to 2nd Lieutenant, Co. I; 2nd Lieutenant Bernhard Domschcke to 1st Lieutenant, Co. G; 1st Sergeant Robert Muller to 2nd Lieutenant,

Co. C; 1st Lieutenant Charles Pizzala to Captain, Co. G.[2]

On the motion of the Hon. W. K. Wilson, the Milwaukee Common Council honored the regiment's corps commander, Gen. Franz Sigel, with a resolution complementing him on his conduct and contributions to the war effort. In response, the flattered general sent a letter of acknowledgement that was printed in the *Sentinel* on January 27:

HEADQUARTERS GRAND RESERVE DIVISION
ARMY OF THE POTOMAC,
Stafford C.H., Va., January 16, 1863.
Hon. Horace Chase, Mayor of the City of Milwaukee, Wis:

DEAR SIR:-The resolutions of the Common Council of Milwaukee, expressing the generous confidence of that body in my behalf, were duly received, but the multiplicity of my duties has prevented an earlier acknowledgment.

Allow me at this late day to say, that such an expression from your honorable body is more honor than I can appropriate to myself. I have endeavored to do my duty as a citizen and a soldier, but have accomplished less than my heart has desired. The brave men who have served under me deserve the highest incomiums for their devotion and courage, and since they necessarily share all the credit that may be attributed to me, cannot shrink from the responsibilities which those generous expressions of confidence involve.

Accept, therefore, and please present to the Common Council, my hearty thanks for the expressions of regard and confidence contained in those resolutions, and believe me to be

Gratefully and truly,

F. SIGEL, Maj. Gen. U.S. Vols.[3]

While those in Milwaukee honored their commanding general, those in his namesake regiment tried to make themselves comfortable. The holidays made Adam Wuest feel homesick, longing for letters from home. Ernst Damkoehler spent the last days of 1862 and the first of 1863 trying to recuperate from "a terrible rheumatic tooth and headache and a bad catarrh."[4] One who did not escape was John Crowley who died on the morning of January 5. His comrades in Company G buried him that same afternoon, right after battalion drill.

As they lowered him into his shallow grave and filled in the dirt over him, Sergt. John Horn commanded a squad to fire three rounds over his last resting place.[5]

Christian Crusius informed the *Pionier* that as soon as they arrived at Stafford Court House they were advised "to make ourselves comfortable which in view of the impending winter quarters, was immediately carried out. In a few days our settlement, to which the proud name of New Milwaukee was given, was completed. Over several huts pompous names such as New Hall House [and] American Hotel were attached, every company gave a name to its street and kept it clean. It is not exaggeration to say that we had the best and the most tasteful shanties in the entire division, something that was admitted even by Gen. Schurz."[6]

Lt. Lackner and his tentmates completed their "blockhaus" in which they felt "very comfortable," their only fear being "that we may be driven off soon." The structure was "10 x 11 & walls 5 feet high, covered with a fly—a fine bed & fireplace we have also & enough to eat." Soon the good weather that blessed the New Year turned ominous. "It looks decidedly like rain at present," Lackner commented, "I should not wonder if the rainy season should set in at last." Yet, he was confident "Our boys are all comfortably quartered & we can defy the weather." To pass the time he studied military tactics, read Milton and *Catherine of Brunswick*, and studied every newspaper he could find."[7] He also began riding a horse, and planning a trip to Falmouth with Charles Neukirch to visit a friend from Wisconsin. "It went off tolerably, but I find that it hurts me to[o] much to undertake a ride to Falmouth."[8]

Adam Muenzenberger and his friends in Company C built themselves "some fine bunk houses, about the size of our pig-pen, 12 x 8 feet. Each one accommodates five men. We then built two bed bunks, one above the other. Three sleep in the lower and two in the upper bed, and that gives us a little room in the shanty." As their accommodations changed, so did Adam's appearance. "I am still one of the healthiest in the whole regiment, but I have lost some weight, and so before long I will be back to the weight of my youth. But that is nothing. I am now an entirely different fellow, with a mustache and a pair of whiskers, as I have not shaved since I left Milwaukee. If you met me I doubt if you would know me."[9]

The chief complaint during the first days of the new year was the lack of pay. "The regiment is becoming more and more dissatisfied," Muenzenberger wrote. "At first they told us that we would receive our pay by January 10th, 1863. Now the rumor is floating around that we won't be paid until March. What will happen we don't know."[10] Damkoehler heard rumors the regiment would be paid soon, but such rumors passed about frequently and he did not believe them. "It makes my heart bleed as I wrote you in my last letter to sell the sled or see if you could get an advance from Harris," he wrote to his wife Mathilde. "I am so much the more sorry because I am well off, at least well fed and well clothed."[11] Karl Wickesberg relayed the rumor about being paid in a letter home, but was soon acknowledging the rumor "is all humbug. Everyone hoped for it longingly. I wish our regiment could go to Washington once and could act there as it pleased. It would hang Lincoln and the whole cabinet."[12]

To make matters worse, the money promised to the families of those who enlisted had still not been paid after all these months. "I am satisfied with what I have," wrote Muenzenberger to his wife, "but—if you don't receive any money this month, I am afraid we will have a rebellion right here in the regiment."[13]

Adam Wuest received a letter with some money from his mother, and Muenzenberger received help from his financially strapped wife. "I can't thank you enough for the two dollars which you sent because, although everything to help us pass time is very scarce, I never would have taken the liberty to write you for money if only we would have known when we would receive ours. But I will pay you back very soon, as they say that the paymaster is here. Our colonel promised us that our regiment would be paid out on the 13th or 14th. As he says, the money that we signed for in Milwaukee should be paid out to you. That pleases us very much here because you can't trust anyone."[14]

Despite the promises, the paymaster did not arrive in camp until January 29, and when he did the news was still disappointing. Instead of being paid through January 1 as the men expected, they received pay only through November 1. Lt. Lackner received "about $153, of which $75 was allotted & about $75 paid to me. By paying debts &c I have reduced that sum to about $20."[15] Still, rank did have its advantages. By contrast, Adam Muenzenberger received $36.90, less a $20 allotment for his family, which left him with only $16.90 for his two and one-half months service. From this he paid $1 to the sutler, kept 90¢, and sent the remaining $15 to his "beloved ones....We were much dissatisfied with our pay, as we expected money for four months at least."[16]

Ernst Damkoehler received $18.20. After he paid his accumulated debts, he had only $13.00 to send home to his pregnant wife and five children. "My dear Mathilde," he wrote, "you can imagine how my heart bled, that I could not send you any more under your present circumstances...don't lose your courage. From many soldiers in the Regiment I heard that their wives had received assistance from the state: if your conditions permit you will have to call on Harris once more. I don't think it is right for the State Treasurer to give out assistance to women who already get assistance of 5 to 8 dollars a month from their towns or wards and our women, who, due to the poverty of the county can't get assistance, still don't get any help from the State. You have to explain things to Harris as I write it to you and refer to the local support, that you get none and women in other towns both. After it is once in order with our pay I hope that you shall not suffer any more."[17]

Another pressing concern was health. "Many are sick in bed," Muenzenberger explained. "Others are lying around. I do not think that our regiment has more than eight hundred serviceable men. If this humbug doesn't stop soon there will be many who will die as soon as the weather warms up after the January rains."[18] One day, while he was helping pass out rations, the corporal watched as Colonel Jacobs questioned one of the soldiers:

"What's the matter with you, son?"

"Oh Colonel," he answered, "I have such a cough that I can hardly keep up any longer."

As Muenzenberger watched, "The colonel told the boy to go to the doctor and to get something for the cough, and to keep himself warm. He has the warmest sympathy for the sick. His first duty every morning is to go to the hospital. He is the best officer who came from Milwaukee with us, and even superior officers are surprised at the progress he has made. Every morning he examines the captains in command of the regiment and in this way he sees what is going on."

Wickesberg was less generous: "There lies the poor soldier and is a little sick. If he had his money he would buy something for it and he would feel better soon. But now if there is something wrong with him he has to go to the doctor. And then he is really bad off. Because these are no doctors, they are human torturers."[19]

Capt. Winkler recalled passing through the camp of the 26th one day and being particularly struck by the appearance of four graves. "A very neat picket fence encloses them; two of them have stone slabs with the name of the sleeper, his description, age and time of death painted upon them. The two latest are completely surrounded by wreaths of the Virginia holly; the outline of a heart is also traced on each of the latter with a soft and tender light green moss ornamented with the holly berries. These two graves are indeed beautiful and testify that his dead comrade is not an object of indifference to the soldier."[20]

For some, thoughts of health were also cause for concern with family at home. When Adam Wuest received a letter from his family it brought the unwelcome news that Muenzenberger's young son Adam was seriously ill. "I am very sorry that you should have this trial with him," the corporal wrote to his wife, "and to show you my sympathy I am writing immediately. I am wishing the little fellow a speedy recovery, and you and yours the best of health. I am writing this letter with tears in my eyes, so deeply sympathetic I am with you poor, forsaken ones. But who can alter it? Therefore, be comforted, beloved; there is One above us who will correct all this."[21] A few days later he wrote once again: "I am sending this little present to Ernest because he studies so hard. I will whittle and send a ring to Mary. Tell her to be good and industrious. I will send a present later on to Henry and Adam."[22]

News from home could effect the soldier's mental health as well. Doerflinger later wrote that during the winter the regiment was subjected to anti-war sentiments, "infected to a slight degree by that general epidemic thru letters and a certain class of newspapers." Regardless, he felt the men "maintained a good spirit, performing their hard duties in a loyal humor; confidence and good feelings toward officers were the rule, as was also that *stern sense of duty* on the part of the officers not only in strictly military matters, but in the ever watchful control of the Commissary Department by the Colonel and his staff."[23]

The lieutenant's optimism notwithstanding, morale fell and many blamed the officers for not doing more to secure their back pay and otherwise make their lives more comfortable. "Then there are, these gentlemen, our officers," Wickesberg complained. "They do not deny themselves anything. Our aide-de-camp is donating 150 bottles of wine to the generals and staff officers this afternoon. But we poor souls do not even get one whiskey."[24] But some of the officers were very concerned about the men. Aside from his frequent visits to the hospital, Col. Jacobs made every effort to secure adequate food for the men and even bought small items for them out of his own resources. At the bimonthly muster in February, for example, the colonel gave each company four dozen packages of tobacco sent by his wife.[25] Muenzenberger, who was in a position to view many of the regiment's officers at close hand, felt Colonel Jacobs was an excellent officer, and was favorably disposed toward Capt. Hans Boebel, Capt. William George, and Lt. John Fuchs. Nevertheless, he complained that: "We are very short of things here. We receive our rations very irregularly, and every day the incompetence of the officers becomes more apparent. We must drill for hours every day, not so much to teach the soldiers as to teach the officers. And they *can command*—but they can't understand the commands. In this fashion we have to play poodle dog for the officers. No other regiment drills the way we do. The others watch us."[26]

Morale was also damaged by incessant camp rumors and a lack of discipline in many of the regiments. "Since the battle of Fredericksburg," Muenzenberger reported, "some of the soldiers of the old regiments have been wandering around not knowing where their companies are. Some of them don't want to find their regiments. They curse the Union and all the administration to the depths of hell. Only the thought of their families keeps them from suicide. That's the patriotism that reigns in the army. It disappears more and more every day. But enough of all this humbug."[27] On another occasion he emphasized the depression commonplace in the ranks: "Regarding an armistice, we down here have heard nothing but rumors, but everyone would be glad if this humbug were at an end. I only wish that all the folks from Wisconsin were here once— just once—to get a glimpse of soldier life. The whole thing is a swindle from beginning to end. The officers know nothing except making money—and that is all the war is concerned with."[28]

Capt. Winkler was repulsed not only by the deserters, but by the reaction of many in the North who supported their actions. "Oh, what a mean spirit has come over the North; it is almost disgusting. Multitudes of deserters from drafted regiments, instead of being hooted and scorned as they deserve, are treated as heroes—yea, as martyrs who have suffered for people's rights. It is a shame, I am glad I am not at home to see it."[29]

Lt. Lackner summarized the general feeling well when he wrote:

"In regard to the future I am decidedly of the opinion, that the present spirit of opposition to the government will increase & become bolder, as the number of those who are sufferers in this war becomes greater & that it will in a short time break out at mass meetings in the shape of anti-war resolutions. The government will be entreated & threatened into a shameful peace & the south will obtain all it wants. Nothing but a great & decisive victory in Virginia can save us, & as there is no prospect of that, considering the incapacity of our generals & the demoralization & fright of our troops, there is scarcely a ray of hope left. Although I am as anxious as every other soldier to see home again & rest in the security of civil life, yet I do not wish shamefully to abandon this war at the present moment. I like the present life—it has its pleasures, at least in camp, where one can read as comfortably as at home—it opens too, a wide, wide field for the ambitions & then last, but not least, the honor & perhaps the freedom of the Country of my birth is at stake."[30]

Rumors, complaining, and prophesying were abruptly interrupted when "all at once and entirely unexpectedly came the order to march on January 14." Crusius reported they "had to pack up our tents and everything had to be in readiness even in the middle of the night; then we were ordered to remain but always to be ready to march."[31]

The Mud March

Orders finally arrived on January 20. That same day the Eleventh Corps left to participate in Gen. Burnside's plan to move the Army of the Potomac upstream, crossing the Rappahannock above Fredericksburg at Banks's Ford and outflanking Lee's Confederates. After days of waiting, Crusius reported, "the colony finally set out, the 119th New York started the parade, the 75th Penna. followed, and the 58th New York marched an hour later."[32] No sooner did the troops take to the road than it began raining heavily, a condition that lasted for several days before turning into heavy snow. "It is bad luck for us that this weather should set in just as we are starting out on a campaign," Winkler felt.[33] But the 26th did not follow the corps immediately. Instead, it was sent beyond Stafford where it was assigned to guard the ammunition train and man the former Eleventh Corps picket lines until relieved by Gen. Slocum's Twelfth Corps.[34]

Lt. Doerflinger, disgusted with the drills, the weather, and the constant false alarms, disliked being "selected for the honor of bringing up the rear,...neither our old country veterans nor we of the younger generation relished the onerous, tedious and dreary task."[35] Crusius told the *Pionier* "We were by no means idle, rather [we] had to do the strictest picket duty; every other day we had the pleasure of doing picket duty and at the same time it rained and stormed to your heart's content."[36] Lackner experienced "many days of suffering & of hardships." Many fell ill from the severe weather. The regiment settled in the former camp of the 153rd New York which it found not nearly as nice as the one it left. Companies A and F were detached on a "bye-road" as pickets, while Companies C and E also left to man another portion of the picket line.[37] "It was a dark night," Muenzenberger explained, "we still had two and a half miles to march, and we didn't know the direction. Then we paraded along in the night like a blind man in the rain. We couldn't find the place where we were to camp, and we had to post our sentries to prevent an attack."[38] The company soon arrived at "a house made of corn stalks" where it camped for the night. On the picket line, Leopold Drewes approached a house apparently sheltering several rebels. When a man left the house, Drewes challenged him three times. Receiving no answer, he fired his musket, but he "only made a hole in old mother nature." The instant the shot rang out, both companies took arms and rushed forward. Lt. John Fuchs, Corporal Ferdinand Krueger, and Muenzenberger were the first to arrive at Drewes side, but by then whatever or whoever prompted Drewes to shoot had vanished. "Up to the time of writing this letter," Muenzenberger wrote, "we do not know just what he was shooting at."[39]

About half the regiment would be on picket at any given time. "The weather was miserable," according to Lackner. "One cold rainstorm chased the other & the night which I was on picket was most disagreeable." After two days in camp the men moved to the quarters formerly occupied by the 8th New York, which they found "*very* neatly built."[40] Damkoehler told his wife that "a terrible unfavorable weather started. It started to rain, the next day an awful snowstorm. All the pontoons to build bridge[s] and artillery were stuck in the mud and the Secesh pickets amused themselves by putting big signs on long sticks which they held up high [saying] 'Burnside is stuck in the mud.'"[41]

The horrible weather turned the roads into nearly impassable mire, ruining any chance of success for what became known as Burnside's "Mud March." He finally canceled the operation on January 23. Once again, the Sigel Regiment experienced only rain, snow, mud, cold, and frustration. "Like the whole people of the North," Doerflinger explained, "we were tired of camping, marching and countermarching in the bottomless clay, the 'three days and night's system of picket service in the mixed rain, sleet and snow of a Virginia winter, with 'nothing doing' that could bring to light the 'baton of command' which each of us knew—like Napoleon's grenadiers—fate had snugly tucked away somewhere in his knapsack. We were weary of sham midnight calls to arms to see how quickly we could appear in our company boulevards with all our tin-cups and other accoutrements safely strapped on; we were surfeited with the sham tactics of daily drill and sham strategy or tragedies of our knee-deep marches. We knew all about them. We yearned for the real things....But this was only the reflection of the impatience which pervaded the whole north and brought Abraham Lincoln and his palladins still greater worry, more sleepless nights and—it seems like a miracle—a still firmer determination to surmount all difficulties and maintain the Union."[42]

Winter Quarters

With the failure of Burnside's flanking movement, large-scale campaigns ended for the winter. Once relieved by Gen. Slocum's Twelfth Corps, the Sigel Regiment hurried off to catch up with its own brigade. It waded through the mud some nine miles to Maria Church, a small village about twelve miles from Stafford Court House. "When we arrived there," Christian Crusius wrote, "we found nothing more than a slimey wet place in the woods which was assigned to us as a camp. The first night was a sleepless one, rain and snow fell unmercifully on us poor worms of the earth[,] even the camp fire could not keep us warm. The next day was not much better[,] the snow whirled in thick flakes throughout the air and Virginia was denounced and damned by some from the bottom of their hearts. Surely it demands a hardened nature and a nature of steel to endure these hardships."[43]

But Lackner reported that despite the weather they went to work and "with an old fly & some shelter tents & logs fixed up a tolerable comfortable place."[44] Within a short time the new campsite was dotted with "snug huts of log, with their chimneys of clay." These were only just completed when the regiment received orders to return to Stafford Court House.[45]

The first day "it rained and was miserable weather throughout." They marched only four miles before camping for the evening. By the next day the roads were "awful"; slippery in some places, covered in lakes of oozing mud in others.[46] Damkoehler left Maria Church a day later with the commissary trains. "It was terrible weather. The first day it snowed continuously, and the second day it rained and we had to suffer a lot with the bad weather and messy roads."[47]

When they arrived back at their old camp near Stafford they found the huts they had so painstakingly constructed occupied by Slocum's corps. Instead of rest, the weary troops were put to work constructing new shelters.[48] As they began, they "had a terrible storm here for a couple of days and today the snow is one and one-half feet deep. You can imagine," Damkoehler complained, "how miserable it is to work the whole day in this weather, but our shift can't stand still. I can assure you, dear Mathilde, that the blood ran out of my fingers from the strenuous work of rolling the heavy kegs in the terrible mud, besides sometimes carrying one under my arm. Every evening I was so tired that I could not sleep due to exhaustion and pain."[49]

Adam Muenzenberger also felt frustrated and depressed. "Our soldier's life is a very hard one now. In the first place we were cheated in our pay. Then the weather here is so bad that we can hardly stand it. It has been raining continuously and during these last few days the rain has turned into snow. We marched in the rain, arrived in the rain, and pitched our tents in the rain. The mud is so terrible that no wagon can get through. But why complain? We simply must be satisfied. I derive my only consolation from my good and loving wife and children at home, who pity their husband and father in this cursed war; and I keep my courage up with the thought that if it is God's will I will see you all again....The picture that I have is my only consolation in all this misery."[50]

Not everyone felt so dejected. "We have once more built log huts," George Jones wrote to the *West Bend Post*, "and with not much to do, and plenty of hard crackers and fat pork with which to supply the inner man, we live quite comfortably. If it rains all night at the rate it is com-

ing down now, Uncle Sam will probably allow us to enjoy the fruits of
our labor for some time to come for the roads will be impassable....
Since being in this camp we have received two or three rations of soft
bread, with a promise of having it once or twice a week. I assure you it
was highly prized as we had not had any before in two months, some of
the boys sold their loaves as high as 25 cents."[51]

Despite the occasional soft bread, time passed slowly and monotonously in camp. One day it would snow, the next day rain. "Yesterday
it snowed & to-day it rains furiously," Lackner wrote, "causing the
water to trickle into our Cabin everywhere. The ground is wet, the
chimney smokes & altogether it is not so comfortable as it might
be."[52] Damkoehler felt all the "marching and then lying around again
effects the discipline of the soldiers."[53]

Aside from continuing drills, for the most part time was taken up
making their new quarters comfortable and finding diversions to help
pass the monotonous days. "During the winter the military High
School added new courses to its curriculum," Doerflinger reported, "as
for instance the construction of log cabins, bunks, mattresses, sweet-
brier pipes and chess figures; and for the esthetic daubing of log-chim-
neys with that stickiest of all substances, Virginia red clay which was
discovered in many varieties and exploited in every possible experi-
ment by Burnside's artillery and our boys who were kept busy all day at
one place or another pulling it out of holes 'knee deep.' And still we
had not seen a genuine 'rebel' yet, except an occasional guerrilla posing
as a peaceful citizen at his fireside and watching with eager eyes his
wife's Johnny-cake gold mine."[54]

Some of the soldiers found diversion, and perhaps comfort, by
frequenting a fortune teller in the 74th Pennsylvania who, "for twenty five cents will let everyone who desires to do so look into the
future. The tent of this fortune teller is a veritable place of pilgrim-
age," Crusius explained sarcastically, "to which many who are credulous go and then return with transfigured faces for this wonder
worker, this modern prophet has clearly proved to them from the
constellation of the cards that within two months at most the war
will come to an end. That such prophecies electrify the mind and
heart of many credulous it is hardly necessary to mention. It is
indeed a surprise that no keen mind has had the idea of selling
amulets which will make the bearer immune to blows and bullets; in

this way it would be possible in the second half of the 19th century to earn something."[55]

Washington's birthday provided one occasion for diversion in camp. Muenzenberger explained: "In honor of Washington's birthday we erected a triumphal arch between the rows of tents in the streets, and draped it with garlands. I helped make a garland forty feet long, which we draped into four loops. In the center of it we had a cross with our Company initial 'C' on it. Our quarters here appear very friendly and homelike."[56]

Adam Wuest borrowed five dollars from his brother-in-law and invested it in card games. Each day he "rushes from his duties, has barely time to cram down his meals," and then rushes off to play poker with Corporal Heinrich Urich and Pvt. Christopher Burkhardt. For his efforts he won nine dollars, but used it to buy food at inflated prices from the sutler to supplement his normal rations. Lackner spent his free time reading *The Pickwick Club*.[57]

Adam Muenzenberger passed the time by reestablishing himself as a cobbler. When his shoes gave out he "had to go around with the dirt and mud over my ankles" until he could get materials to mend the footwear. "I received the tea, awls, and zinc nails which you sent so lovingly," he wrote Barbara. "[S]end me more nails, pegs, and some stronger sewed soles and thread. Send me soles and thread every week, as I can earn quite a little money—at least enough to give me something for my own use, and now and then I might be able to send a few shillings home as there is plenty of work here."[58] Julius Schoenleber helped Muenzenberger with his new shoe repairing business which quickly had "very much work." Cobbling and his duties as Colonel Jacobs's clerk consumed most of his time. "I do all of the correspondence for the whole company, as none of the other sergeants can write. The colonel helps me whenever he can. I can do this correspondence in front of the fireplace sitting on my bed, as the time at which it must be done is not specified."[59] He also thought promotion might be in store for him. I am very well liked, and I think that in the future you will see a change in my pay. Our lieutenant [John W. Fuchs] asked me if I was still repairing shoes. I asked him why, and he told me that I was to make out the big clothing book, and, besides, that if one wanted to become an officer as I do, one has to give up shoe repairing."[60]

Illness also sapped the men's strength, increasing their depression and magnifying their complaints. Among the Greenfielders in Company C, Leopold Drewes was sick, and worried about both his own health and the welfare of his family in Wisconsin. Fritz Awe and Asmus Holz were both ill. Lewis Manz and Nicolaus Friedrich were in the hospital. Corporal Muenzenberger "caught a heavy cold" while serving on picket duty. By the end of February he had lost twenty-five pounds since enlisting. "If I were to call on my loved ones unexpectedly I doubt whether they would know me," he wrote. "We don't undress more than once a week, and then only when we change our shirts and underwear. That more than anything else keeps us thin. Then imagine the comfortable camps we have on the march. They are either in snow or mud. This keeps us thin too."[61]

In the midst of this depressing scenario, resignations began to increase among the officers. Lt. Col. Lehmann resigned in January, just before Burnside's Mud March. An anonymous letter from a member of the Sigel Regiment to the *Milwaukee Sentinel* commented: "The leading one of those miscreants was allowed to remain in the regiment, only because he was considered superior military talent, and indeed, when we came into the field, we found that he would make a most excellent Corporal, whose squad would always have the most polished buttons, clean coats, and neatly trimmed whiskers; but alas! when it came to drilling a regiment he was found to be sorely deficient. His superiors were cruel enough to 'resign' him on account of so unimportant a matter. So with the other officers of the same stripe."[62]

February brought new defections. Major Horwitz resigned on the 5th, Lieutenants August Mueller and Julius Meisswinkel on the 6th, Lt. John F. Hagen on the 12th, and Lt. Joseph Wedig on the 26th. To fill the vacant field officer positions, Colonel Jacobs looked to Captains Winkler and Boebel, but the former, after some reflection, declined promotion. Since he had been away from the regiment for some time serving at corps headquarters, and he respected Boebel's ability, Winkler did not feel right being considered for the position of lieutenant colonel. On the other hand, he could see no advantage to leaving his post as judge advocate for promotion to major, a position he felt had little responsibility. Winkler's decision frustrated Lackner because Colonel Jacobs told the lieutenant he wanted to promote him to captain, but did not want to transfer him out of his company to do so.[63]

So, Lackner concluded, "I am destined to remain *acting* Capt. yet I suppose."[64] When Jacobs asked for further recommendations for major, both Winkler and Lackner suggested Capt. Henry Baetz, a popular officer well liked by many. A register of deeds from Manitowoc whom Winkler considered "a worthy officer and a refined gentleman," Baetz was confirmed in his new position on March 15.[65]

Occasionally the foul weather broke, only to return with a vengeance. "Yesterday we had a July sun," Crusius explained, "this morning a foot of snow has fallen. In fact a peculiar change. Yesterday a person could have worn the lightest summer clothes, today one freezes in double clothes." One of the bright spots in the otherwise dull days was the arrival of mail. "The Pionier reaches us regularly," Crusius wrote to the editors of that paper. "The mail always brings new life into the camp; how eagerly everyone listens whether his name is called off and how he rejoices when he hears something from home, be it a letter from a dear friend or only a paper that he has received."[66] George Jones expressed similar sentiments in a letter to the *West Bend Post*: "To a soldier, separated from all the ties of home and friends, a newspaper is always welcome, and a letter doubly welcome."[67]

Yet, for many the news was not always encouraging. As much as he enjoyed hearing from his wife, Ernst Damkoehler agonized that he was not at home with her and the children during her pregnancy. "My dear Mathilde, you probably know how depressing it is for me to know that the time comes nearer when our family circle will increase, and the time of pain is in the future, and I can't stay at your side. Perhaps I am not even sure of a homecoming. Dear Mathilde, always have good courage, and then with the good courage you can bear a lot. I hope to receive shortly some enjoyable news from you....I can't plead with you often enough to write more often. It would give the greatest pleasure to me to write you every week, if I could only spare the time."[68]

Nor was the news from home encouraging for Adam Wuest. Rumors circulating in Greenfield that he had met and married a girl in Virginia created considerable difficulty between him and Christina Schmidt. Muenzenberger wrote reassuringly to his wife: "The story about your brother Adam is a mass of lies. People at home must be out of their minds to circulate something like that....There are no women to be seen here, and the only letters your brother has written are to you and Christina. He can't get away from camp without a furlough and he can't get a furlough. Up to now he has not been away—and he has not been married."[69] But it seems Wuest's girlfriend was herself flirting about. "I've known a long while what kind of bird little Christina is," Muenzenberger told his wife. "I've told Adam hundreds of times that he should quit writing letters to her, and that it would be much more sensible for him to write a letter to his mother....He and Leopold [Drewes] went away together and sneakingly wrote the letter to Christina. She sent him stamps frequently—sometimes as many as six and seven at a time—and such endearing letters with a lot of hugs and kisses in them, as you saw by the letter of Adam's I copied and sent you. 'Dear Adam,' in the beginning; 'Dear Adam,' in the middle; 'Dear Adam,' at the end—that is about the entire contents of the letters."[70]

But Muenzenberger had more to worry about than his brother-in-law's romance. First he received news that the son of his godfather, Adam Muehl, had died. Then came news that his own son Henry was gravely ill. Adam sent him a shovel as a present. "In your last letter you wrote me that dear Henry was ill," he told Barbara, "and that makes the longing for a letter from you, dear heart, so much keener....You have no idea with what longing I look forward to your letters, and with what happiness I receive and read them. A letter from you is always balsam for my heart, bleeding for my loved ones. On that account, write as often as you can. You can never write too often or too much."[71] Yet, when another letter came it brought still worse news. The next day John Beres, a private from Granville, came to Muenzenberger's tent to tell him he had received bad news from home. Henry was dead, a victim of diphtheria. Beres's mother heard the news when she visited the Blessed Sacrament Church. Confirmation of the dreaded news soon came from Muenzenberger's wife. Tearfully, he sat down to try and find words of comfort to his family so far away: "Be so kind, dearly beloved Barbara, as to comfort yourself, and although I cannot be with you to console you in word and deed I will do so as much as I am physically able in my letters. Cheer up, dear, the Ruler of everything disposes everything for our best. Think with Job: 'The Lord giveth, the Lord shall taketh. Blessed be the name of the Lord.' And let us pray a few 'Our Father's daily, in the hope that Henry has gone to the Father of all, where misery has an end where we all sooner or later must go. Don't give up, dear. You have a husband who has the greatest sympathy for you, and should I have the good fortune to return shortly I will surely remember your many trials and tribulations which you endured in my absence. And I will never forget how steadfast and loving you were to the children and to me. Therefore take my deepest and most heartfelt sympathy and trust in the Lord who directs all things for our benefit. Do not grieve for my absence and for our loss, because these cannot be helped and your worry won't assist matters any. Look up, then, and trust in the Lord."[72]

Another who was deeply saddened was Henry Thiele, a merchant from Milwaukee serving in Company B. Frustrated, tired, discouraged, he was further saddened by deteriorating family relations. One day he received a letter from home informing him he had been disinherited. Greatly depressed, he returned to his tent where he penned a brief note to his tentmate Theodor Prengel explaining the great pain he felt over the state of his family affairs. Then, picking up his musket, he carefully placed the muzzle to his forehead, grasped his bayonet in his other hand, extended his arm, pushed the trigger with the tip of his extended bayonet, and blew his brains out. Thiele's death was announced while the company officers were eating dinner. The next day his remains were laid to rest without the normal honors.[73]

Hooker Takes Command

On January 26, as the ill-fated "Mud March" came to an end, Burnside's tenure as commander of the Army of the Potomac also concluded. He was replaced by Gen. Joseph Hooker. Many agreed with Winkler that although Burnside "gained no glory" during his tenure in command, he had behaved in "the truest spirit of manliness" by accepting blame for the debâcles of December and January and asking to be relieved of command.[74] "Tho we did not hold Burnside responsible for the Fredericksburg disaster," Lt. Doerflinger concluded, "the necessity of 'something new,' of 'something doing,' of 'a change' was in the air, and when the news came that Gen. Burnside was superseded by Gen. Hooker, whose familiar title 'Fighting Joe' carried inspiration, a wave of relief, of new hope, passed thru our long lines of blue traversing the hills, the valleys and plains of Northern Virginia....Every one of us green soldiers now became a strategian; euchre, whist, 'ramsh,' and chess lost some of their charm; in every dog-tent, and log-hut forced marches, grand evolutions, night attacks and other surprises were planned and executed, and great victories marked out and won on the pounded clay floors."[75] In the ranks, Damkoehler also thought the change was for the best, although he, like many, longed for the return of a former commander. "I think it was a wise move. The armies had no trust in him and I heard many say they would not fight under Burnside. McClellan is in good standing with them and I believe myself that if McClellan would have stayed at the rudder, brilliant results would have been obtained."[76]

The Sigel Regiment met its new commanding general for the first time on February 16. That morning it drilled under the direct observation of Gen. Schurz, returning to its camp about 11:00 a.m. The men had "hardly undressed" when the "order came that a dress parade would be staged" at noon. Pvt. Crusius described the scene thusly: "With an empty stomach and many curses things were somewhat put in order and we marched onto the prairie and find there the other regiments of the brigade at attention. Adjutants ride hither and yon, through the woods one can see the dark contours of the other regiments with fluttering banners through the wood. Therefore something must be back of this. After a long wait the guns are placed together and all rest on the prairie grass. He lets us wait a long time they say, we could have taken our midday meal first, for whom are we waiting anyway? naively asks a young fellow who had his mind on the meat and the soup. Finally we hear a command, the roll of drums and the sound of horses hoofs. The division Steinwehr is set up yonder and is now inspected by the new General Hooker. After all the regiments have marched by our turn also comes, an orderly comes running, the commander knows what he brings, his command is given to 'fall in.' The plain on which we are stationed is oval shaped[,] in front rise wooded hills, the rest is enclosed by woods. On the right at the edge of the woods the Major General with his numerous staff is stationed. In the company of Sigel, Schurz and others he rides past the regiment set up in columns, meanwhile arms are presented and at the same time the drummers beat three rolls. To this mark of honor he responds by doffing his hat and bows his head. As far as Hooker is concerned he is a man of medium height with white hair and a weathered tanned face that is scarred. Sigel still looks very worn. All regiments march by the Generals and then home. Neither hurrah shouts nor a national melody was heard at this review, the only band of the division played German melodies, among also 'schleswig-Holstein meerumschlungen.' Several of us who had taken up arms for our adopted fatherland merely because they were soldiers asked themselves the question, will Hooker be able to reorganize the Potomac army which was animated with such high hopes once upon a time? Will he be able to reestablish the confidence of the troops shattered by so many defeats? Will he be able to dispel the dissatisfaction caused by the failure to pay the salaries? Is he the man who will be able to remove all these evils and to lead the army to glory and victory? Who knows? The future will tell."[77] Winkler felt the review "passed off very creditably."[78]

Hooker immediately tried to restore the flagging morale of his battered army. He arranged for new uniforms to be distributed, more attention given to the quantity and quality of food, and attempts made to see that back pay was forthcoming. Morale quickly improved. "We now have as much to eat here as we can swallow," wrote Wickesberg, who pronounced himself in "the best of health."[79] Muenzenberger also noted that "We receive our supplies very promptly now—bread, potatoes, white beans, meat, molasses, etc."[80] Gradually, better rations and improving conditions brought a return to better physical health. Among the Greenfielders, for example, Muenzenberger, Wuest, Drewes and Holz were all well by mid-March. Only Fritz Awe remained ill, confined to Douglas Hospital in Washington for more than a month.[81]

Another of Hooker's moves was to try and weed out unfit officers and non-commissioned officers to provide a more professionally competent leadership at the regimental and company levels. In the 26th, Captains William George, Anton Kettlar, and Louis Pelosi all resigned and headed home. Captain Hans Boebel became lieutenant colonel to replace Lehmann, Captain Henry Baetz was confirmed as major, Lackner was promoted to captain of Company F, Lt. John Fuchs became captain of Company A, 2nd Lt. Doerflinger became first lieutenant in Company K, and 2nd Lt. Edward Carl became first lieutenant in Company D. Major Baetz, Capt. Charles Pizzala, Capt. Fuchs, and Lt. Hermann Fuerstenberg were appointed as a board to examine the sergeants for promotion. In three days they examined 29 sergeants, with the result that William Steinmeyer became second lieutenant in Company B and Henry Rauth was promoted to second lieutenant in Company C. In the ranks, Karl Wickesberg became corporal.[82]

Under Hooker, a new assertiveness spread through the army, animating it with determination. Company drills continued every morning except Sunday, followed by battalion drill in the afternoon. In addition to the normal picket duty, fatigue parties "which consist in work on the roads and cutting down trees" increased as an effort was made to make the campsites and roadways more suitable. Crusius admitted the effect of the changes was startling. "Under Lieut. Col. Boebel the regiment has made considerable progress, the discipline has considerably improved, also the spirit and confidence of the troops. The old spirit of carelessness has ceased; Hooker unlike his predecessors is energetic, he is a go-getter, deserters are shot and other transgressions punished according to their offense." Yet, at the same time the private was angry about some of the resignations and promotions: "As gratifying as these conditions are, just as deplorable is the manner in which our commander appoints officers. Arbitrarily without ascertaining the opinion of the officers he appoints any spit licker a Lieutenant whether he is fit for the position or not. The resignations continue and so yesterday three Captains have left us and other officers wish to follow since they have the misfortune of having been born as men not as suckers. No one is concerned about seniority, men who a short time ago were orderlies now act as first Lieutenants....[T]he Sergeants were examined recently, but if a person knows these conditions you draw the conclusion that it is only proforma."[83]

Corporal Muenzenberger also felt progress was being made, but lamented the fact that so many of their officers were new to command. "[B]ecause all our officers are young and newly commissioned, we must drill long and hard.....If the colonel [Jacobs] or lieutenant colonel [Boebel] isn't commanding, the regiment goes the same old way and doesn't listen to the officers. If they did, they would be led astray and our newly commissioned officers would have to march along. I only wish you could see that confusion."[84] An anonymous letter from the 26th to the *Milwaukee Sentinel* was more positive: "Dissatisfaction and despair, however, give way to new hope and confidence, when we behold the changes that have been wrought by a few months in the army so far as its efficiency and spirit is concerned. While then everything was against us, so is now everything in our favor; yes, even the Administration seems to be inspired with new vigor. The more the army sees of Hooker, the greater is its confidence in him, the more

Hooker sees of his 'demoralized' army, the greater must be his pride to lead it triumphantly against the foe. He knows only one way and that is the straight way to victory. No 'digging,' no 'strategy,' no 'anaconda'—But battle and victory."[85]

Among the changes in command was one that affected every soldier in the Eleventh Corps. Concerned with the shortcomings in supply, pay, and reinforcement that plagued the Eleventh Corps, Gen. Sigel lobbied long and hard in Washington for better treatment of his troops, only to meet with continual rebuffs from the War Department. When Hooker took command he reorganized the army, eliminating the system of "Grand Divisions" and reassigning the officers who commanded them. One of those effected was Franz Sigel who reverted from commander of the Reserve Grand Division to command of the Eleventh Corps. Angered by the perceived neglect of his troops, his self-esteem now ruffled by the seeming demotion, Sigel sought assurances that his small corps would be increased to a size more befitting his rank. When no such assurances were forthcoming, the popular general tendered his resignation.

The *Milwaukee Sentinel* reprinted a story from the *Chicago Tribune* characterizing Sigel's resignation as "unwise and uncalled for," even if he had suffered some slight.[86] In the Sigel Regiment, feelings and disappointment ran high. Winkler believed Sigel's action in tendering his resignation to be "the most ill-advised step he could have taken."[87] Doerflinger felt Sigel had never really been given a chance to prove himself. "We, who had enlisted under his banner, regretted and were displeased that he resigned the command of our Eleventh Corps. We had unlimited confidence in him. We knew from our strenuous drilling, picket and other service that he kept the reins well in hand, that he was conscientiously alert to his duty, watchful of all approaches; and we loved him because he had always been among the pioneer fighters for and defenders of human liberty in the old fatherland as well as in Missouri. The spirit of our corps was excellent, and it was a mistake that no special effort was made to induce Sigel to stay, rather than change the command at a time when people were peremptorily demanding a decisive 'advance upon Richmond,' foreshadowing events in the near future that would make confidence and good spirit generally in the various Corps particularly desirable. This was a case of 'swapping the horse while crossing the river.'"[88]

With Sigel's resignation, most of the troops in the Eleventh Corps expected Carl Schurz, the ranking division commander, to be elevated to corps command. Instead, the assignment went to an officer outside the corps, Oliver Otis Howard. At the age of thirty-four, the Maine general possessed a spotless military record including instances of courage and daring under fire that cost him an arm at the Battle of Fair Oaks during McClellan's Peninsula Campaign, a fight for which he received the Medal of Honor. Howard took command on March 2. Although he knew a few words of German and attempted to build a rapport with the men, his personal prejudices and intolerances remained only thinly veiled and his demeanor offended many in his new command. A deeply religious man, the "native Americans" in the Eleventh Corps came to dislike his excessively pious attitudes and pronouncements, while the German "freethinkers" were repelled by a religiosity they found much too reminiscent of the clericalism they despised. Then too, many unjustly blamed him for Sigel's departure. Whatever the reason, the corps never warmed to Howard and it was no small task to raise a cheer in the ranks when the general rode past.[89]

While the change in command provided food for gossip and speculation, as the spring dragged on the men longed all the more for news from home. Damkoehler was concerned at not having a letter from his pregnant wife in some time. "With anxiety I have been waiting for two weeks already for a letter from you, but always in vain. You can't imagine in what unrest I find myself and not a moment passes by that my thoughts are not with you. What is the reason for the long silence? This uncertainty could drive me crazy because I know what situation you are in."[90]

Adam Muenzenberger expressed the same sentiments to his wife Barbara. "How are you? How are the dear little ones? Are they still well and how does it happen that I haven't received a letter this week? As I yearn terribly for a letter from you, and wait evening after evening and fail to receive one, I become uneasy. I don't know whether or not something has happened which prevents you from writing. I beg of you dear heart, be so kind as to write me a letter every week so that I can know how the family is getting along, whether they are in good health or not, and how everything is getting along at home, and if there is any news. What do the folks at home think of the draft? How are all our friends? What does your teacup say? Is peace at hand or not? And how is business of all kinds in Milwaukee and vicinity?"[91] When news arrived from home it put his mind at ease. He received a letter containing Barbara's "beloved portrait." Everyone at home was in good health. "You and the little ones look very well, and I am greatly pleased that you sent it. I still feel fine, and I send you my love and my portrait. It was taken March 4th, and from it you can see what I look like here in the wilds of Virginia."[92]

That spring, one of the most persistent topics of conversation was politics. With local elections rapidly approaching, many sought news from home on the political situation in Wisconsin. The spread of the anti-war "Copperhead" movement was of particular concern to many. Capt. Lackner thought about applying for a furlough to visit home, but decided against it. "I don't feel like going at all, especially as I would not meet anything but Secessionists at home anyhow."[93] Corporal Muenzenberger thought there was favoritism in the way the mail was delivered. "If you send anything else, send it [wrapped] in a 'Know-Nothing' paper, as then I will surely get it. It seems as if they are trying to hold back all the Democratic papers."[94] He was also concerned that corrupt politicians and profiteers would prolong the war. "They talk quite a bit about peace here, and about us leaving this place. Almost every hour some news arrives, and before long we're so filled with rumors that you might well say that we believe nothing that we hear. When we left Milwaukee they said, 'Just let November pass. The Democrats will be elected and immediately things will change.' In November they said that if there hadn't been a decisive battle in favor of the North by New Years it would all be over with. When the first of the year came the rumor spread: 'The 4th of March—that is the day of salvation for those in the chains of the once great republic.' Look at the prospects now. November, 1862, January 1863, and the saving March 4 have come and gone, and conditions are just as bad—if not worse in fact—than at the beginning of the war. And the reason—the big pockets of the swindlers and contractors haven't been sufficiently filled yet."[95]

"A political party can only be judged by the few prominent leading individuals," a soldier in the 26th wrote to the *Milwaukee Sentinel*, "their opinion is also the opinion of their followers, the wishes of these the others perform. Should we judge of the peace party accordingly, the question arises at once: 'Is it possible that these men ever intend to do good?' While every one, that knows somewhat of the past of the leading stars of these 'Peace Democrat's answers this question in the negative, the faction howls into our ears the word 'peace.' Obtained by means of our arms, peace is the glorious aim the patriot strives for, the much wished for end of bloody combats the wearied soldier longs for the regeneration of the Union, the beginning of her everlasting happy continuance. That peace however the peace party can and will procure for us is the beginning of everlasting reproach, disgraceful oppression, and as a necessary consequence, an eternal dissension."[96]

When the election finally came and votes were tallied, the 26th Wisconsin gave 341 votes to the Democratic candidate for Supreme Court, and only 101 to the Republican. But the heavily Democratic vote did not mean the majority of the soldiers favored peace at any price. Rather, they distinguished between "Peace" and "War" Democrats, rejecting the former as they voted for the latter.[97]

When the Illinois legislature passed a resolution in favor of ending the war, Ernst Damkoehler conveyed his feelings to his wife in no uncertain terms: "You probably read about the decision of the Illinois Legislature, but I hope you don't believe in it. I hope that you have enough patriotism to bear our longer parting instead of seeing me coming home to such an eerie peace. I am still as good a patriot as I was the first day of my enlistment."[98] He was not the only one concerned that the growth of the Northern peace movement would force an end to the war at the price of Southern secession. Led by Colonel Jacobs, the Sigel Regiment's officers signed a resolution expressing their views and sent it to the *Milwaukee Sentinel*. Quartermaster Frederick W. Hundhausen, visiting Milwaukee on leave, verified the sentiments to be true. He "assures us," the newspaper informed its readers, "that the resolutions signed by Col. Jacobs and other officers, which gave the Milwaukee Copperheads so much distress, a short time ago, were most heartily endorsed by the entire Regiment, which hates traitors aboveboard whether found North or South." Hundhausen "says he is, and always has been, a staunch Democrat, but he is not of the Copperhead variety by any means."[99]

Another expression of the regiment's feelings appeared in an anonymous letter from the 26th to the editor of the *Sentinel*, possibly written by Lackner: "[I]n an impending crisis like the present, where the fate of the country depends upon the events of the next few days, it is improper and unjust to speak of matters of less importance, and which are not in some degree calculated to support the cause of freedom. I do not possess vanity enough to think that this correspondence will in any way influence the opinion of any individual, but I claim that every work from the army giving a positive assurance that its sympathies are not with the 'Copperheads,' that it is not 'demoralized,' but willing and anxious to fight, is a blow to northern treachery and a stroke for freedom. Hence these lines. The soldier's heart must be filled with shame and mortification when he contrasts the opinion in which he was held at the time of his enlisting with that which is expressed of him now. Six months of constant hardship and of perpetual danger have changed the 'patriot,' the 'grave defender of our liberty,' into a 'base hireling, an outlaw who ought not to be allowed to vote,' a 'culprit,' who supports the administration at all hazards, and threatens destruction to slavery and its supporters north and south. We are ashamed, not of Copperheads, for of that class of people we never were proud, but of the loyal part of our northern friends, who allow those vipers to dart their poisonous tongues at us. We insist that if the soil had not been very fertile, if the opposition had not been very weak and undecided, they would never have dared to show themselves so openly.[100]

Still another letter to the *Sentinel* placed the soldier's feelings in very practical, human terms: "When a soldier, in a stormy night, lies cowering near his picket fire, wrapped up in his torn and tattered cloak, trying in vain to warm his cold limbs, or to dry his wet feet, an infinite bitterness must fill his heart when he reflects that those of whom he expected aid and comfort, are mocking him and calling him by the name of hireling; that he, when misfortune has made him a cripple, shall, on returning home, be derided and insulted, instead of being gratefully received with open arms, and relieved from his sad fate!...I am decided in my opinion that nothing has more contributed towards awakening the true spirit, the enthusiasm in the army than the outbreaking treason at the North. Every one involuntary calls to his mind such from the circle of his acquaintances at home, who might be denominated by the name of 'Copperhead's and what does he find? Oh! I do not like to go into personalities, but it is certain that every man not yet entirely fallen and hardened turns with wrath and disgust from such men, and their bad cause."[101]

By the end of March came pleasant weather the men associated more with May or June in Wisconsin. And with the change in weather came a change in the men's dispositions. "We have May weather now,"

Private Carl Staib, Company B,
a clerk from Milwaukee.

Private Frederick Upmann,
Company A,
a shoemaker from Milwaukee.

Winkler wrote before the end of March, "birds—robbins and meadow larks—are very plentiful and make the air resound with their songs."[102] A soldier informed the *Sentinel* that since his "last correspondence, none but pleasant occurrences came to pass. Everything goes on improving, the weather and the roads, the dispositions of the army; even the administration seems to be endowed with a better spirit, and with a new enthusiasm, I may almost say, a certainty of victory, we long for the approaching Spring campaign. Hooker is full of energy, and gaining the general confidence."[103]

Adam Muenzenberger also felt the change, but tempered it with reality. "Here in our camp things look just like springtime. Robins sing, other birds whistle, grass is growing—and yet in spite of all this loveliness and these messengers of spring the thunder of the cannon, the roll of the drums, and the flash of the bayonets hasn't stopped yet—and neither has the war. In such weather the imagination at times wanders to the distant home, and to the dear wife and children. But that doesn't help one. One must be a man, resigned to whatever happens to him. Hope is the only prop for our spirits in these difficult times. We hope that the worst of things is over now, and I pray that a star of peace will arise from the distant ocean and take all war and strife from this unhappy land."[104]

On Good Friday the regiment staged a review for Gen. Howard, the corps commander. "After the review he visited our camp," wrote Muenzenberger. "When he found that the woolen blankets were hanging in the sun he asked us whether we aired them every day. We told him we did. He laughed and said, 'That's right.' Then accompanied by General Schurz and his whole staff he rode away to Schurz's headquarters. Up to now all is quiet here. What will happen is in the hands of Him to Whom I trust my destiny."[105]

Easter Sunday was issue day for the brigade, a time for the men to obtain new supplies. A heavy snowstorm blanketed the camp, making the day "uncomfortable," but the arrival of mail made it a joyous occasion for many.[106] Muenzenberger received a welcome letter, but otherwise the day passed like any other. "We have poor holidays here," he wrote. "Nobody paid any attention to the fact that it was Easter. In fact no one went to church. Much less did one see children with Easter eggs. But you can stand all this when you know that in your distant home four kindly hearts beat lovingly for the husband and father, and share every pain with him."[107]

That week they received a special visitor when President Lincoln arrived to review the Eleventh Corps. The weather was beautiful, warm, and clear, if somewhat windy.[108] "Father Abraham is notoriously not a handsome man," Winkler observed, "but there is that in his looks which says that he is not a common man."[109] The chief executive impressed Karsten as "a long, thin, and haggard man."[110] Muenzenberger described the scene thusly: "Our regiment was the second last. It is the largest in the whole 11th Corps. Also the cleanest and the neatest. Our coats are still as good as new, and each man now has his second pair of trousers. On that account our regiment looks as though it had just come to the field. Our colonel said, 'Look at the bums. In spite of the fact that our regiment has performed all its winter duties it is still the trimmest and the best looking.' 'Boys,' he said, 'when you march past act as though I were in front holding review so that we get praise again the way we always do.' You know our regiment is always praised by everybody. As we marched past the President one of Carl Schurz's daughters asked him: 'General, what regiment is that?' Schurz answered, 'That is the 26th Wisconsin.' Then she said, 'That is the finest looking regiment in the army.' The place where the other regiments paraded was too small for us, and so the drums had to be placed back. We marched in divisions [two companies] in flanks past the President. Our colonel is very proud of his regiment because it is praised by everyone."[111] To Noah Brooks, occupying the reviewing stand with the other dignitaries, the Sigel Regiment "impressed us as the best drilled and most soldierly of all who passed before us during our stay."[112]

As April wore on, the signs of an impending campaign were unmistakable. Drills took on a new urgency. The sick and anyone else unable to take to the field were sent to the rear along with excess baggage and all the accumulated property that could not be easily carried on the march. Pack mules arrived to carry ammunition and necessities, the ammunition train distributed sixty rounds of fresh ammunition, and orders arrived to prepare eight day's provisions.[113] The camps came alive with excitement and anticipation as everyone looked forward to their first real confrontation with the rebel army. Finally, orders arrived on April 14 for the regiment to be ready to march at any time.[114] Damkoehler described it as "a day of work and unrest for us. We are not sure yet if we will march tomorrow or not, but we have to be prepared every moment. . . . Now we are at the eve of big events and how many a good friend will in a short time be among those who offered their lives for our righteous affair."[115]

When he received news of the orders, Muenzenberger's first thought was to write his family. "As we received orders to move this morning I will have to write to you immediately, as my feelings as husband and father bid me to do. Where we go we do not know, but this much is sure, we are advancing. . . .Perhaps a battle will have been fought by the time you receive this letter. We surely hope to be victors and in Richmond soon, but don't worry unnecessarily about us. Be comforted and trust in the Lord as I do, and He will make everything all right. It will please me immensely if I can be back in your circle again. But if we rest here quietly and do nothing the war will never end, as both sides are too stiffnecked for either to give in and make peace. Therefore be satisfied. We trust that the campaign won't be very difficult. . . .Farewell, beloved wife. Kissing the pictures of you and the children, in memory of our mutual promise until death, your loving husband, Adam Muenzenberger."[116]

Preparations complete, the men waited throughout the day without further orders arriving. On alert to move out at any time, they spent the next few days biding their time, hoping the alert was not just another false alarm. While they waited, they were assigned another three-day shift on the picket line in weather that seemed to turn "very bad" as soon as they arrived at their stations. Luckily, however, the regiment was one of the largest in the corps, which meant that each man had to serve only half as long on the picket line as did soldiers in other regiments. "The first four companies served a day and a half," Muenzenberger explained, "and then the next four companies served a day and a half. It rained terribly hard 2 days and a half of the time they served on picket duty. It rained quite hard one day we were on duty, and we didn't know how to get dry, as the rain put out the fire."[117]

During the time they waited, Corp. Muenzenberger was appointed acting sergeant. In recognition of the occasion, 1st Lt. Robert Mueller called the company into line and presented him with a sword as a token of his authority. "The company cheered and shouted: 'That's right. Muenzenberger deserved this long ago. He has to do all the writing anyway, and so he might as well have the job."[118]

Wisconsin Governor Edward S. Salomon arrived to visit on the 19th. In anticipation of his arrival the men "decorated the camp with green boughs and festoons."[119] When he arrived, the regiment fell into line for a brief inspection, after which the governor addressed the troops, assuring them "that he would never forget the honor which the Twenty-sixth yielded him. Then he said that the State of Wisconsin was proud of the Twenty-sixth." That evening the *"Milwaukee Sänger Bund,"* a regimental singing society organized by Milwaukeeans in the Sigel Regiment, serenaded Colonel Jacobs, Governor Salomon, and General Schurz with a variety of German melodies including two that were particular favorites in the regiment, "In der Heimat ist es Schoen" [It Is Beautiful in Our Homeland] and "Das treue deutsche Herz" [The True German Heart]. "In my whole life," the governor said, "I have never before been so proud of my German descent as I am now in the camp of the Twenty-sixth Regiment." The serenade and speeches con-

cluded, the men "were supposed to give three cheers for the Union, but they didn't go so well. And when the colonel asked for three cheers for the Governor they didn't go so well either. But when he called for three cheers for General Schurz, they went! Schurz merely smiled. You know he was just a guest of the Governor and the Colonel."[120]

By the last week in April the entire camp was anxious for excitement. They were tired of drills, reviews, and picket duty. "Nothing has

Governor Edward S. Salomon. He told the Sigel Regiment he was never as proud of his German heritage as when he was in their camp. *Courtesy of the State Historical Society of Wisconsin* changed with us and we are still at the same place," Damkoehler wrote. "Since a few days ago, we have had beautiful weather. The streets are getting dry and we will surely have to march in a very short time and soon we will encounter the Rebels and may God permit that the battle turns out in our favor. . .our Army is in tip top condition. Almost all had new uniforms and also all looked well nourished and I think, there is no army [in the] world provided for better than ours."[121] Lackner was tiring of chess, and he had read every book on tactics and the art of war that he could find. He was ready to put his training to the test, to "see the elephant" as old soldiers said. Winkler, too, was tired of chess and a daily routine he found "too tedious." Everyone wanted to break camp, to get on with ending the war. The wait finally ended on April 27 when the entire corps struck its tents and took to the roads. Winkler spoke for everyone when he wrote: "I am glad we are going. . . .We have been here so long, it has almost come to seem as if we lived here."[122]

Chapter 5

SEEING THE ELEPHANT
Chancellorsville

As the long winter months gradually came to an end, replaced by the warmer days of April, so too did the months of tedious drill, picket duty, and review. At the head of the largest, best equipped Union army yet to take the field, "Fighting Joe" Hooker felt it was time to implement his carefully laid plans to capture the Confederate capital at Richmond. Across the Rappahannock River from the Federal camps, Robert E. Lee must have wondered how he could turn back such a large, well-equipped force. Although the Northern army received continuous reinforcements during the winter months, his own Army of Northern Virginia mustered fewer troops to begin the third year of campaigning than it had the previous spring. With the meager forces at his disposal Lee would be hardpressed to hold his positions against Hooker's plan to put half his army across the upper Rappahannock, in position to cut off Lee's supply lines and threaten the rear of the Confederate army based at Fredericksburg, while at the same time leaving enough troops at Fredericksburg to hold Lee's forces in position there and prevent him from consolidating against one portion of the Northern army.

Hooker's campaign began ominously on the rainsoaked morning of Monday, April 27, 1863. The Sigel Regiment rose early, cooked its coffee and breakfast, then packed its belongings and made ready to march. The men were in line by 5:30 a. m., each carrying eight day's rations and 60 rounds of ammunition. Marching orders called for the Eleventh Corps to move, in company with the Twelfth Corps, west along the Rappahannock some twenty-seven miles to Kelly's Ford. Excited at long last to be leaving their camps for a movement against the enemy, the men marched off "in high glee." To Lackner, "Every body felt well & the army was in excellent condition."[1]

That first day they marched over the muddy roads to a location near Berea Church where they camped for the night. Winkler thought the march was "not so very hard" on the officers on horseback, "but for the troops, with the very heavy loads for them to carry, it was hard indeed."[2] By 4:00 a.m. the next morning they were on the road again. "We had fine clear weather until about nine o'clock when it clouded up with a thunderstorm," Muenzenberger wrote. "It rained that afternoon."[3] Despite the weather, they soon passed through "a little village called Grove Church," covering the eighteen remaining miles to Kelly's Ford by 3:00 p.m. While they waited their turn to cross, the men brewed coffee, ate a dinner of hardtack and salt pork, and slept.[4] "There we rested & saw the Pontoons & batteries pass by & be placed in position," Lackner wrote. Their brigade commander, Col. Krzyżanowski, called the officers of the regiment together, "telling them that they would probably be in a fight that night & encouraging them to do their best."[5]

About 10:00 p.m. their turn came. Col. Jacobs, forming the regiment into column of four, led it to the heights above the Rappahannock where it had to wait another two hours before being ordered down to the river's edge. Winkler was taken by "what a beautiful night it was, the moon shone out through a thin haze and it was so calm, so quiet, it seemed as if the heavens were smiling upon us."[6]

Finally, about midnight, they moved down to the pontoon bridge spanning the river. To Lackner, "It was a solemn, awe inspiring march & we expected to be attacked on the other side. Nothing was heard but the low tramp of infantry on the bridge. When we reached the other shore we formed in double column & advanced."[7] Lt. Doerflinger recalled the regiment continued "the march all night, in a drizzling rain much of the time," while Winkler noted that it had become "very foggy" making it difficult to find the way in the dark. The "soft swamp ground" made the marching very difficult, leaving the troops "worn and tired out."[8] Lackner remembered marching "for about 5-6 miles when we reached the first brigade & half dead with fatigue lay down to sleep."[9]

Shortly after they awoke the next morning, April 29, as Lackner washed himself, the camp was suddenly "fired into by a few pieces of rebel artillery," but they were "soon driven away" without loss. Taking to the road once again, the regiment reached Germanna Ford on the Rapidan River at 4:00 p.m.[10] There they "Pitched tents in [a] crowded area and slept until 11 p.m." when they were "aroused & crossed the Rapidan."[11] The scene greatly impressed Winkler. "The banks of the river were over one hundred feet high; there were the foundations of the bridge that once stretched from bank to bank, but now destroyed; there was also new timber lying about; the rebels were in the act of rebuilding the bridge." Crossing the river made no less an impression on Lackner. "Never in my life did I see a more romantic scene....The river is here very rapid & runs through rocks which served as a support for planks & c on which we crossed. Three immense fires gave us light on our perilous way. Having reached the other shore we marched about a mile & there [*sic*] lay down to rest, while a drizzling rain was falling."[12] Doerflinger called it "a short sleep in the mud or water between the corn hills of a level field."[13]

Not everyone went directly to sleep. According to Lackner, "The boys went out foraging" and to see "the burning mill" [Germanna Mills] which had been set afire because an officer in another regiment "had been shot by the owner." At 2:00 a.m. the "regiment started again, marching on a plank road through a splendid Country to the place of our destination," Locust Grove near the Chancellor House. They arrived about noon, once again covering the miles amid a continuing rain. There, "We pitched tents on a splendid field" in a small clearing surrounded by a desolate wilderness of second-growth pine and scrub oak.[14]

Since leaving their camps, the men had covered some forty-five miles over muddy, rainswept roads, while crossing two major rivers. The movement placed them, along with their comrades-in-arms in the Eleventh, Twelfth, and Fifth Corps, on the exposed left flank of the Confederate position at Fredericksburg. Morale soared with the knowledge they succeeded in catching the rebels off guard. "[A]ll were happy, cheerful and confident of victory," Winkler reported.[15] From his headquarters, Hooker issued General Order No. 47, read to the regiment on the morning of May 1:

It is with heartfelt satisfaction the commanding general announces to the army that the operations of the last three days have determined that our enemy must either ingloriously fly or come out from behind his entrenchments and give us battle on our own ground where certain destruction awaits him.

The operations of the 5th, 11th, and 12th Corps have been a succession of splendid achievements.[16]

Dawn on the first of May impressed Lackner as "splendid." While he accompanied Captains Charles Neukirch and August Schueler "to the creek to wash, the boys cleaned their guns & were anxious for a chance to use them."[17] Winkler took advantage of the lazy morning to write home, comparing the day to the May Day festivals celebrated in Germany. The sun was shining for the first time in days and "so it is to us almost a festive day....You have no idea how cheerful, how happy, we feel."[18]

Excitement swept through the camp when Col. Jacobs read a dispatch from Hooker ordering a general advance to press his advantage on Lee's flank. This was the moment they waited for so long. The anticipation of combat shown in the tenseness of their faces. Before they moved, Col. Krzyżanowski arrived to address the men. He spoke calmly, impressing upon them the importance of the task before them. The Eleventh Corps, he said, would hold the position of honor on the right wing of the army. Theirs would be the position the enemy would no doubt choose to attack. The speech concluded, Col. Jacobs ordered his men into columns and led them off down the Plank Road to begin their work.[19]

About the time the Sigel Regiment moved out, the leading Northern infantry ran into Confederate skirmishers at Tabernacle Church. A sharp fight developed. Rather than press the issue, as the commanders on the scene urged, Hooker ordered a withdrawal. "The major general commanding," he explained, "trusts that a suspension in the attack today will embolden the enemy to attack him."[20]

By halting his advance at Tabernacle Church, Hooker relinquished the initiative. General Darius Couch, watching the disappointed infantrymen marching back to their original positions, commented that "the observer required no wizard to tell him...that the high expectations which had animated them only a few hours ago had given place to disappointment."[21] Yet, not everyone was discouraged. Completing the letter he had begun that morning, Winkler noted that "Our troops are in excellent spirits, and this morning the weather was so fair, all felt so happy and enthusiastic that it may well be said that we had our May Day." It was 11:00 p.m., and the captain was ready to retire for a few hours sleep before what he was sure would be a coming day of battle. "I shall write you more after the battle," he wrote. "I have full faith that I will live through it, but if I should fall, it will be for the cause of our country."[22]

Chancellorsville

According to Muenzenberger, the men "passed a good night."[23] Dawn on May 2 found the Eleventh Corps strung out for roughly one and one-half miles along the turnpike leading through the Wilderness area west of Chancellorsville. Gen. Charles Devens's division held the extreme right, followed by those of Carl Schurz and Adolf von Steinwehr. The men dug rifle pits and erected some light works facing south, but the far right flank appeared completely neglected. Indeed, the exposed flank lay protected by only two small regiments from Leopold von Gilsa's brigade of Devens's division.

Throughout the day reports arrived at the various Eleventh Corps divisional headquarters indicating Confederate infantry on the move. Dust raised by their columns became visible at many places along the Union line. Officers observed, through clearings in the forest, Southern infantry heading off toward the southwest. General Daniel E. Sickles, commanding the Third Corps, now in line on the Eleventh Corp's left flank, sent a warning to General Howard as early as 9:00 a. m. Soon thereafter, at 9:30 a. m., a similar note arrived from General Hooker. The reports multiplied during the afternoon, but Howard paid them no heed.[24]

Hooker, besieged by a multitude of such reports, became convinced his plan was succeeding. He interpreted the sightings as evidence Lee knew his defeat was imminent. Obviously, Hooker reasoned, this was an attempt by the Southern general to escape toward his supply base at Gordonsville. It all fit so well with his preconceived notion of the campaign that he dismissed any other possibilities from his mind. He ordered Sickles out to intercept Lee with the Third Corps, and required Howard to detach Barlow's brigade to support the move. Sickles rushed forward, only to find the quarry already beyond his reach. He contented himself with a brief rearguard action in which he made prisoners of a number of Southern stragglers.[25]

Hooker viewed Lee's move as a precipitate withdrawal. In reality, what his men saw were 28,000 infantry commanded by Stonewall Jackson. Supported by 1,450 cavalrymen, 2,240 artillerymen, and 112 guns, Jackson planned to move southwest until he could turn north undetected to fall upon the unprotected flank of the Union Army, the position held by the Eleventh Corps.[26] Hooker's belated half-measures only served to make Jackson's task that much simpler. Sickle's movement successfully isolated the Eleventh Corps from its nearest support by more than a mile of dense wilderness undergrowth. The committing of Barlow's brigade to support Sickles deprived the Eleventh Corps of its only tactical reserve. As the afternoon wore on, Howard's men thus became isolated, without support, in a dangerous and potentially disastrous position.

Behind the lines of the Eleventh Corps General Schurz discussed the continuous stream of sightings with his brigade commanders. At 2:30 p.m. opposing skirmishers ran into each other out beyond the right flank. Shots rang out. Neither Hooker nor Howard appeared concerned. Carl Schurz was. He requested permission to place his entire division facing west toward the exposed flank. Howard refused. Instead of investigating, the commander of the Eleventh Corps retired for a nap.[27] Despite Howard's rebuff, Schurz determined to make at least some provision to resist an attack should one come from the unprotected right flank. Without orders, he moved the 58th New York and 26th Wisconsin of Krzyżanowski's Brigade north of the turnpike to the vicinity of the Hawkins Farm, placing them under the personal command of the Polish colonel. This placed the two small regiments perpendicular to the rest of the Union line. To support them, Schurz moved the 82nd Ohio and 157th New York to a position near the Dowdall Tavern to the east of Krzyżanowski's command, and later moved the 82nd Illinois north to cover the gap between Krzyżanowski and the main line along the turnpike. To reach its new position the 26th, which had just finished digging rifle pits along the turnpike south of the Wilderness Church, marched first north and then west, its columns splitting at the church so the regiment passed along both sides of the building to reform at the far end. Once in its new position, it passed the afternoon awaiting further orders.[28]

By 5:00 p.m. Jackson completed his movement. Out beyond the exposed Union flank he formed nearly 32,000 men into three parallel lines that stretched for a mile on either side of the turnpike. Seventeen

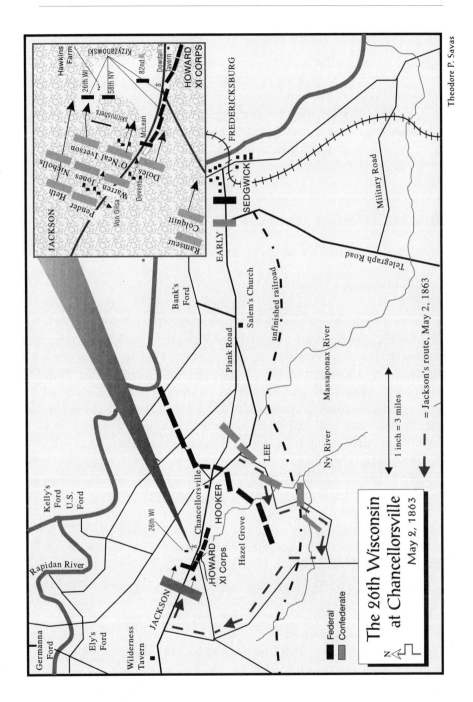

Theodore P. Savas

The 26th Wisconsin
at Chancellorsville
May 2, 1863

regiments stood in the first line, supported by nineteen in the second: a total of over 17,000 men about to strike 9,000 isolated troops in the Eleventh Corps. Behind these two lines, in reserve, stood 12,000 men of A. P. Hill's division. Two hours of daylight remained as seventy-four Southern regiments moved slowly into position for their attack on twenty-three ill-prepared blue units.[29]

The Sigel Regiment found itself posted "on a ridge in an open field, about a quarter of a mile from the road" with the 58th New York protecting the left flank of the Wisconsin regiment. The Badger's right flank was "wholly uncovered," the regiment being the farthest north of its brigade and the Eleventh Corps. Although orders from corps headquarters allowed the troops to stand down for the night, no attack being expected, Schurz and Krzyżanowski made provisions for the safety of their commands. As part of these precautions, Capt. Charles Pizzala led the Sigel Regiment's Sharpshooter Company, the ten best marksmen from each of the ten companies, into the woods to the west of the open field where the regiment lay. Pizzala's mission was to form a skirmish line to protect the regiment, and the brigade, from surprise attack. With him went Lts. Karl Doerflinger and Albert Wallber. Moving into the dense wood, Pizzala stationed himself on the exposed right flank, placing Wallber in command of the left and Doerflinger the center. At the same time, Col. Jacobs posted companies B and K as a reserve near the edge of the woods to the east of the open field as a further precaution should an emergency arise.[30]

The balance of the regiment settled down to cook its evening meal. Karl Wickesberg saw some of his comrades "boiling coffee" while others were already "sleeping."[31] Along the turnpike, men of the Eleventh Corps lay about with stacked arms. Here and there they played cards, slept, or cooked their evening meals. Horses and beeves grazed lazily behind the lines. The sound of laughter rose from around the campfires. "The regiments had stacked its arms and the men were cooking their coffee," Winkler wrote. "Bands played national airs and nothing indicated that an enemy was near or foreboded the terrible storm that was approaching."[32]

Suddenly, the skirmish line was "startled by the boom of a cannon" and Doerflinger's ears picked up "the new experience of the rattle of musketry in a Southwesterly direction. Not knowing whether it came from our own or the Confederate forces, our excitement and suspense were intense. Being stationed on somewhat level and low ground, I first detected bodies skipping from tree to tree far back in the dusky forest; a few minutes later I could recognize human figures, still later the gray uniforms; and I sent word to the Captain who warned us not to fire, fearing the gray might be an illusion. Soon, however, the enemy's dense skirmish line, advancing upon us rapidly, left no doubt, and we began firing, our boys taking cover, as well as possible, behind trees; there was no time to send for orders to the Captain, who was on higher ground where he could not yet see the enemy."[33]

Before the Badger skirmishers could reload an explosion of flame and smoke jumped from the woods ahead as the full weight of a Confederate battle line poured a volley into the Wisconsin Germans. One ball smashed through Pizzala's skull, silencing forever the vibrant tenor of the Manitowoc *Sängerbund*. With thousands of high-pitched yells, the rebels charged toward Doerflinger, Wallber, and the badly outnumbered handful of men in the path of the onrushing Confederates. Doerflinger and Wallber yelled to be heard over the sudden commotion, urging their men to return fire with all haste. Yet on the rebels came, advancing to within fifty yards of Doerflinger's position before the order arrived for the sharpshooters to fall back and rally on the regiment.[34] As he ran through the woods toward the clearing where the Sigel Regiment rushed to form its battle line, bullets cut whining paths through the trees, splintering branches and bones alike. One missile struck the lieutenant's sword sheath, bending it from the impact. Another sliced the straps on the haversack slung about his hip, severing it without injuring him.[35]

Emerging from the woods, Doerflinger found himself opposite the color guard of the 58th New York, the regiment to the left of the 26th. Without hesitation the *Turnverein* gymnast ran for the relative safety of the friendly line, praying his comrades in arms would recognize the skirmishers as friends and not open fire. "I started on my 'homerun' in doublequick across the intervening space of about 75 yards," he explained. "[B]efore I was halfway, the boys of the 58th, seeing the enemy appearing in great numbers at the edge of the timber, began to shout to us to *hurry* so as to clear the space for their fire; and we did hurry; we then and there annihilated all our previous records for 75 yard runs. At about the same time I felt that some part of my accoutrement on the left side had given way; instinctively grasping for what-

ever it might be, I caught the straps of a leather pouch and of a haversack in my left hand, they had both been severed by a bullet; without
halting, I continued in the tallest running-match of my life, seemingly
swinging my booty, i.e. my own provisions, in triumph, while the
sword in my right in its gyrations seemed thirsting for blood and the
metal scabbard on my left was indented and bent by another bullet.
Fortunately or unfortunately, no kodaks and kodak-fiends existed in
those days to perpetuate such interesting and often ludicrous events
for the edification of posterity. The humor of the occasion certainly
was at once completely obliterated by the tragic fate of a large number of
comrades of our company of sharpshooters who did not live to see the
light of the next morning or their cherished regimental colors."[36]

On the other side of the small clearing the Sigel Regiment waited
in line of battle. At the first echo of fire from the right, Col.
Krzyżanowski ordered the 58th New York and 26th Wisconsin into
close column with deploying distance between them, the New Yorkers
to the left and the Badgers to the right. As soon as the men formed
ranks, the colonel ordered them to deploy in line of battle. Reacting
quickly, Col. Jacobs issued the necessary orders and his men responded
as if on parade, moving swiftly into line. With his right "in the air,"
Jacobs was particularly concerned he might be flanked through the
dense woods on the right. To guard against a surprise from that direction he ordered the reserve, Companies B and K, to assume a position
in the woods to the right with its flank refused to prevent the main battle line from being taken in flank and rear.

In Company C, Adam Muenzenberger peered fearfully across the
field to catch a glimpse of his brother-in-law, a member of the Sharpshooter Company deployed under Pizzala's command. Suddenly his
brother-in-law's unmistakable silhouette emerged from the woods and
began the dash to safety. Rebels followed closely, their minie balls searing the air and kicking up earth about the running men. Muenzenberger expected to see him fall at any moment, but luck was with Adam
Wuest this day. He came out of the woods and across the field without
a scratch, surviving the day to laughingly tell his friends how "The
rebels didn't get me, but I stretched out my share."[37]

Many were not as lucky as Wuest. Outflanked and attacked end-
on by more than three times their number of rebels, the Northern
units had no chance of making a meaningful defense. Only two small

Capt. Charles Pizzala, Company G. A soldier from Manitowoc. Killed in action while commanding the skirmish line at Chancellorsville.

Lt. Philip J. Schlosser, Adjutant., a merchant from Milwaukee.

regiments faced the point of attack and they were swept away by overwhelming force within moments. Against a hurriedly prepared front of one or two regiments at a time, 30,000 Confederates overlapped the beleaguered Federals of Devens's division so far they threatened imminent encirclement to any who attempted a stand. All along the line the Union regiments found themselves stacked up like so many dominoes. On the attackers came, flanking, circling, and smashing everything in their path. To the north of the road, where their lines greatly overlapped the federals, the Confederates advanced unfettered until they ran into Pizzala's sharpshooters. Now all that stood between the advancing rebel waves and the rear of the Union position was the thin blue line near the Hawkins Farm.

The clearings about the Hawkins Farm formed an important position. Aside from being General Schurz's headquarters, it marked the only place along the axis of the Confederate advance where troops were deployed north of the turnpike to meet the assault. Schurz ordered Col. Krzyżanowski to command the position in person, signifying its importance. If it fell quickly, Confederate infantry could swing in behind the embattled Federals along the turnpike, cutting off their avenue of retreat and capturing all the artillery and

Lt. Karl Doerflinger, Company K, an architect from Milwaukee. Wounded at Chancellorsville and had his left leg amputated.

Courtesy of the Milwaukee County Historical Society

baggage wagons. The line had to be held until this vital equipment could safely withdraw and the other units rally upon the reinforcements that were sure to double-quick to their support. At the far northern flank of that line stood some five hundred Wisconsin *freiwilligen* grimly awaiting their fate.

Gasping for breath, his adrenaline pumping his heart faster than ever before, Doerflinger reached the line of the 58th New York just as the regiment opened with a volley on the Confederates emerging from the woods. Panting for breath, he ran past the New York colorguard, turned left, and headed for his own regiment. As he ran, the reserve companies came forward on Col. Jacobs order, allowing the regiment to shift to the right to extend its line toward the woods. In a few moments Doerflinger found Company K, but not his captain, August Schueler, who had been badly wounded in the leg and carried to the rear. As the senior company officer, Doerflinger "immediately took command of the company." While Confederate sharpshooters peppered the 26th with missles of death, Doerflinger examined his line, noting that on the right flank "there was a space of perhaps ten yards between it and the next company to the right [Co. E]; there had evidently been no time after the shift to the right to close up by a 'right dres's; the other company was partly hidden from the enemy; but its left wing was exposed particularly to the deadly fire of the enemy's sharpshooters." One of the victims was Company E's captain, Charles Neukirch, "a young man of noble and amiable traits, belonging to one of the Milwaukee Old Settler's families." Shot through the fleshy part of his left arm, Neukirch turned down Col. Jacob's offer of his horse to carry the captain to the rear, preferring to walk back to the hospital under his own power.[38]

While Doerflinger realigned his troops to cover the gap, Confederates burst from the opposite woods in force. Up and down the line the command to "Fire!" rose above the din as the Sigel Regiment sent a sheet of flame, smoke, and lead toward the onrushing rebels. Volley followed volley back and forth across the small clearing stinging both sides with the shock of sudden loss. In Company H, Captain Domschcke's sword was as active this day as his pen had been in the service of radical liberalism. In the ranks, Karl Wickesberg was surprised at how quickly "the bullets come flying right in our midst. But like lightening we were in battle formation. And stood there coldbloodedly and shot at the Rebs."[39] The volleys that slashed across the field cut into the ranks with every passing moment, ending the lives of Wenzel Gott-fried, Jacob Hartmann, Friedrich Werner, and John Zinke. Others fell wounded at an alarming rate.[40]

Particularly hard hit was Company C, located near the right of the battle line. All of its officers fell wounded—Capt. John P. Seemann, 1st Lt. Robert Mueller, and 2nd Lt. Henry Rauth. Col. Jacobs sent Capt. Lackner to the right to steady the men while another dozen in the hard-hit company fell. Amid the turmoil Adam Muenzenberger rammed charge after charge into his musket, firing as fast as he could load. All about him his friends, relatives, and Greenfield neighbors in Company C fought furiously for their very lives. Shot once in the thigh, his friend and tentmate Andreas Springling was hit again as he lay wounded upon the ground. Sergeant Jacob Michel fell grievously wounded in the head and shoulder. A minie ball struck Lewis Manz a painful blow to the hand. Julius Stirn also felt the shocking sting of a rebel minie ball. Still Adam Muenzenberger, Adam Wuest, Asmus Holz, Leopold Drewes, and the other survivors fought on.[41]

The tremendous numerical superiority of the Confederates made resistance a costly affair. A continuous stream of stretcher bearers car-ried the wounded to the Hawkins farmhouse. There they placed the injured on the bare floor, packed so tightly the two available surgeons could scarcely move between them.[42] One determined rush by the rebel infantry could not possibly have failed to annihilate the small regiment. But the unexpected resistance of these fighting *freiwilligen* momentarily halted the advanced elements, causing the impetus of the assault to wane.[43] The Confederate rush faltered, then receded back into the woods from whence it came. It was the first repulse the Con-federate attack received, and it gained valuable time for the escape of the corp's artillery, baggage wagons, cattle, and other property. Their left protected somewhat by the gallant stand of the 119th New York, also of Krzyżanowski's brigade, the 82nd Illinois, the 82nd Ohio, and the 157th New York, the Sigel Regiment held on doggedly at the extreme right of this makeshift line. It was an unequal battle of hun-dreds against thousands, a fight the vastly outnumbered Northern infantry could not hope to win. All they could do was buy time for the rest of the corps to rally and assistance to arrive from other commands.

Recovering from their unexpected rebuff, the Confederates opened a steady fire on the Wisconsin regiment, which fell back slight-

Lt. Henry Greve, Company K, a carpenter from Manitowoc, Wounded twice at Chancellorsville.

Heinrich Bremser, Company K, a trunkmaker from Milwaukee. Wounded at Chancellorsville.

ly to take advantage of the partial cover of a small rise. Overlapping the Federal line by more than a quarter mile, rebel infantry had no difficulty moving under cover of the dense woods around the right flank of the 26th, catching the regiment in a deadly crossfire. To meet the flanking move, Col. Jacobs refused the right flank companies, prolonging the fragile Union line still further northward and bending it back to the east to cover the exposed flank. All of Jacobs's men were now on the firing line. He had no other reserves left to meet the ever-widening flanking move. Deadly enfilading volleys raked the lines from the right, while a constant fire from the woods in front steadily thinned the ranks.[44]

In Company I Capt. William Smith and Lt. Albert Wallber held an exposed position that cost the Wenze Guard dearly. Although Ernst Damkoehler was behind the lines with the commissary department, his Sturgeon Bay friends fought amid growing carnage. Sergt. Georg Wachter was killed, along with W. Joseph Stellenwerk, Henry Behnke, John Lau, and Friedrich Nero. A sudden, searing pain traced the path of a musket ball through the neck and upper arm of nineteen-year-old

Capt. Henry Rauth, Company C, a printer from Milwaukee. Wounded and captured at Chancellorsville.

Wenzel Lastofka. Fifteen in the company were wounded, including the *Pionier* correspondent Christian Crusius.[45]

In Company G, the men Jacob Mann recruited for the Washington County Rifles, their leader long since departed, suffered heavily. With the loss of Capt. Pizzala, Lt. Hermann Fuerstenberg assumed command, cheering his men under a severe fire that killed eleven others and wounded fifteen, more than a quarter of those present.[46]

The silence of death mingled everywhere with the cries of the wounded as the Confederates regrouped to press home their attack. Colonels Krzyżanowski and Jacobs rushed about amid the debris of battle issuing orders, cheering their men, and looking nervously over their shoulders for the help that never came.[47]

Losses mounted to staggering proportions. Capt. Neukirch's Company E, now led by 1st Lt. Peter Fernekes, lost five killed and eleven wounded. A minie ball shot Winkler's horse from under him, while another unhorsed Col. Jacobs. A spent ball struck the colonel a glancing but painful blow, while another pierced Major Baetz's coat without injuring its wearer. A minie ball passed through the neck of Adjutant Schlosser's horse. Another missile snuffed out the life of Sergt. Major Hugo Carstangen. Losses rose with every minute, yet still they fought on against an enemy pressing their front and flank with overpowering numbers. On they fought—five minutes, ten, fifteen, twenty. Desperately seeking to hold the position, Col. Krzyżanowski sent an aide, Lt. Louis H. Orlemann, to General Schurz with an urgent appeal for reinforcements. There were none. The remainder of the army still lay a mile away wondering what all the commotion was. Mercifully, Schurz ordered the battered remnant of the 26th to retire.[48]

When the order arrived, Krzyżanowski told Jacobs to face his men about. Filled with emotion, the colonel could not bring himself to order his men to abandon the field they paid for with their blood. It was a brave gesture, but Confederate skirmishers had already infiltrated their rear, the deadly crossfire was costing lives every moment, and the Confederate infantry to their front was clearly forming for a new assault. Any further delay, perhaps even a minute or two, might spell doom for the entire regiment. With a large proportion of the company officers incapacitated, the men fired, reloaded, and fired again in rapid, mechanically repetitive motions, the long days of drill paying dividends in their cool conduct in this, their first combat. Six volleys, eight volleys, ten volleys—the toll mounted on both sides. More then one-third of the men who awoke so full of hope that morning were casualties. With time of the essence, Krzyżanowski spurred his horse in among the embattled infantrymen to lead them to safety. In Company K, Lt. Doerflinger ran about steadying and encouraging the men until a minie ball shattered his left leg, throwing him painfully to the ground. As he lay there in agony, he looked out over the scene of destruction where his company lost more than thirty men. His eyes focused on Krzyżanowski "galloping along leaning forward on his steed under the hail of lead in the fashion of his Polish countrymen."[49]

"For God's sake, men," the colonel pleaded with the stubborn Badgers, "fall back."[50] Still Jacobs, overcome by his men's sacrifices, would not abandon the casualties. Lt. Col. Boebel stepped forward, "grabbed him by the arm and urged him to leave the field." Reluctantly, the distraught colonel gave the order to retire, knowing it would mean abandonment of the many wounded who could not escape.[51] It was a very difficult order to give, but it was necessary if the survivors were to be saved.

Once the order was given, the battered regiment withdrew rapidly, Company B coming off the field last, but not before a ball smashed Henry Fink's forearm. "We ran towards the woods behind us loosing men all the way," Lackner recalled. The regiment faced about twice to fire at its pursuers, then halted at the woods to fire again before continuing eastward. In the woods, the dense trees and underbrush broke any alignment the regiment may have had, scattering men from the flank companies in small groups as they made their way to the rear. Lackner found himself in a group with 2nd Lt. William Steinmeyer of Company B, 1st Lt. Hermann Fuerstenberg of Company G, Adjutant Philip Schlosser, and about thirteen men from his company. "My throat was parched & I had a violent pain in my side so that I could only get along with difficulty." They moved to the left in hopes of meeting the rest of the regiment, and soon they found Col. Jacobs rallying men about one of the regimental colors with Col. Krzyżanowski and one of his aides. "We joined him & soon had about 50 men of the regt. together." The small group, gathering others as they advanced, marched back toward the enemy, falling into line with Col. Buschbeck's brigade as the rebels once more attacked. Shells burst all along the line, but the remnant of the Eleventh Corps held for another twenty minutes before once again being outflanked on both left and right, necessitating a withdrawal to avoid capture.[52]

From the Buschbeck line the small band of survivors retired in orderly fashion. Corporal George Jones of Company G walked "up the slope of the hill east of Hunter's Creek (also named Gold Run on account of its carrying gold) leisurely" with Col. Jacobs who "bewailed disconsolately the great losses and misfortune of his regiment in its first great battle."[53] *Mein schönes Regiment!* the colonel moaned over and over in grief and disbelief, "My beautiful regiment!"[54]

The 26th formed in an open field not far from General Hooker's headquarters at the Chancellor House. Soon it was again called upon to joint the reinforcement that finally arrived to help halt the rebel pursuit. Accompanied by several Eleventh Corps units—82nd Ohio, 82nd Illinois, 157th New York—it served in this last defensive line until the Confederate threat ended for the night around 9:00 p.m. Then the men retired under orders to the open field near Gen. Hooker's headquarters where they slept for two hours. Still overcome with shock and weariness, they were awakened and "marched back to a place near U. S. Ford" where the survivors of the Eleventh Corps took position behind entrenchments. The remnants of Companies B, G and C of the 26th were sent out on picket, about a quarter mile outside the earthworks. "To our left," Lackner recalled, "was the remnant of a fort & to our right a house. We were very tired & sleepy."[55]

Back near the Hawkins Farm, unable to rise because of his shattered leg, Lt. Doerflinger lay on the field as his comrades-in-arms disappeared into the woods to the east. "The bullets passed me from all sides. Then the rebels approached us like an avalanche in four short sequences, approximately 40,000 men. How could our division of 4,000 men resist them, one to ten?"[56] As his thoughts wandered, he felt himself "rapidly weakening on account of a great loss of blood, I calmly awaited death; however I counted 6 ranks of the victors passing over me, then lost consciousness, regaining this during the cool night and suffering from thirst, I found that my tin canteen had been taken from under my neck. I had been left for dead." He would not be taken from the field for seventeen hours.[57] About noon the next day, his wound still untreated, he summoned his remaining strength and "slid a little bit toward the road to draw attention, and could finally get some rebels to carry me to a farm."[58] But Doerflinger was lucky. Some of his fellow soldiers were already beyond hope, while others died from shock, loss of blood, or mere neglect during the long night they lay unattended on the field. Still others, mostly those seriously wounded and seeking shelter, crawled off into the nearby woods only to be "incinerated when the grove was accidentally set on fire by a shell."[59] More than four dozen of his comrades-in-arms would never see the light of another day.

Sharpshooters and Skirmshers

The Battle of Chancellorsville did not end on May 2. Following Jackson's surprise attack, Hooker ordered the Eleventh Corps to the left flank of the army near the Rapidan River where, for the next three days the Sigel Regiment duelled with sharpshooters while the now outnumbered but relentlessly aggressive Confederates succeeded in pushing Hooker's remaining troops from one position after another, gradually driving them back closer and closer to the river.[60]

Officers awoke the men early on May 3. By 6:10 a.m., they took up a position to the left of United States Ford near the junction of the Mineral Spring road and the road from Chancellorsville to Ely's Ford. About 1:00 p.m. the enemy began gathering opposite the position of the 26th and soon rebel skirmishers appeared. The German skirmishers opened fire and the rebels disappeared back into the woods. Some of the 26th's sharpshooters "went into the second story of the house where they had a good opportunity to fire," Lackner recalled. "The skirmishing was very brisk till about 10 o'clock p.m. during which time we burnt down the house & killed 2 or three secesh. 'Nobody hurt' on our side." The 119th New York relieved the skirmishers that night and they returned to the regiment. They had been asleep for only an hour, however, when they were again roused and marched "a mile forward to the entrenchments where we lay in double column ready for a bayonet charge should the entrenchments be taken. Every time when we had layn down for a 1/4 of an hour the firing commenced in front & we jumped up again. The situation was most miserable."[61]

The morning of May 4 was relatively quiet. Lackner received an unexpected treat when Ehlert Tiedemann "came & gave me a cigar & some bread & ham to my intense satisfaction." About noon the rebels assaulted the far right wing of the army, the sounds of heavy fighting drifting back to the position of the 26th on the other end of the line. The men listened as the sounds alternately grew in intensity, then receded. Except for the occasional skirmishing, however, their section of the line remained uninvolved.[62]

Adam Muenzenberger remembered May 5 only as a quiet, rainy day. "We heard a little gunfire to our left again. It was always quieted, however. In the afternoon we had a thunderstorm. The rain came pouring down and we were soaked through and through. The thunderstorm turned into a slow rain."[63] Lackner had much the same opinion. "We lay there in feverish excitement till about 11 o'clock p.m. Tuesday when we relieved [an]other regt. in the entrenchments, while a continual rain rendered our miserable condition more miserable."[64]

Mathias Weber, Company C, a black-smith from Milwaukee. Wounded at Chancellorsville.

John Grundke, Company B, a carpenter from Wauwatosa. Wounded at Chancellorsville.

Another person who was miserable that evening was Joseph Hooker. The massive campaign, begun with such hope and anticipation of success only a week before, was now in shambles. Battered by attacks from Confederate forces half his number for three consecutive days, Hooker found himself unable to use his large numerical advantage to any good effect. Rather, battered and bruised by the relentless rebel assaults, he gave ground until his forces were contained within a small semicircle whose flanks rested along the banks of a river suddenly beginning to rise with the new rainfall. Outmaneuvered and outfought by Lee, his confidence shattered, faced now with the possibility of a rising river to his rear, "Fighting Joe" gave up the fight. That evening he ordered a general retreat back across the Rappahannock River.

The retreat began in great haste, under a drenching rain, on the morning of May 6. Alerted to the imminent move, the Sigel Regiment awoke at 1:20 a. m. The order to prepare for retreat arrived about 3:00 a.m., causing the regiment to form ranks for the march. Then it waited, wet to the skin, as minutes turned into hours without the arrival of its orders. Finally, at 6:00 a. m. the movement began, "amid a cold chilly rain storm" with Gen. Schurz, fearing a Confederate attack while his troops were most vulnerable, arriving in person to lead them.[65] "We ran more than we walked & found an immense number of troops at the pontoons eager to cross," Lackner wrote. "After one half hour of suspense we crossed & notwithstanding the rain & mud marched to our old camp."[66] Muenzenberger recalled they "were sent across the Rappahannock in great haste and were lucky enough to get across when we heard that we were to return to our old camp."[67]

Ahead of them lay the long, muddy, rainswept roads to Brooke's Station, roads they and their departed comrades so cheerfully traversed only a few days earlier.[68] "We proceeded," Muenzenberger wrote, "and arrived there at seven in the evening. We had marched 28 miles that day."[69] By the time they arrived at their destinations, most agreed with Lackner who felt "half-dead."[70] The next day, Muenzenberger took the earliest opportunity to reassure his wife he was safe. "God be praised, I am in the best of health and so is your brother, but for many these last ten days were difficult and for some they were last hours. God deserves much gratitude for getting us out of this butchery." Speaking of their return to their old camp grounds, he told Barbara "We felt very much at home there, only our muscles were rather sore from the hardships of the battle. I forget all my hardships, though, when I think that I can write to you, beloved, that no bullet touched either Adam or me. I hope that you and ours are happy and that this swindle will end pretty soon. This affair is nothing more or less than the greatest fraud ever concocted."[71]

Winkler was struck with the attitude of the troops. "The army, at least our corps, is demoralized; officers talk of resigning and a spirit of depression and lack of confidence manifests itself everywhere; this may be, and I hope is, transitory. It may be better tomorrow after a good night's rest."[72] Lackner, too, felt discouraged. "The feeling in the regt. was miserable," he wrote, "next day nearly all officers tendered their resignations (Steinmeyer, myself, Doms[ch]cke, Fuchs & staff excepted) which were however not accepted." During the day Colonel Jacobs spoke with his officers individually and in small groups about the gloomy situation. Opinions were varied, but Lackner reported that "we came to the conclusion that nothing was left to be done, but to redouble our energy & brave all misfortunes."[73]

From the ranks, emotions were just as strong. "No one can have any idea of what we had to endure," Muenzenberger told his wife, "eight days and nights without sleep, with packed knapsacks on our backs, bread bags at our sides filled with rations for eight days, bullet pouches with sixty cartridges, and guns on our shoulders and bayonets at our sides. Then march ahead! Anyone can imagine how it feels to make twelve or twenty miles a day. But that is nothing compared to what we had to undergo here. When we reached our camp again, and pitched our tents, we saw only misery. One-third of the tents in camp were empty. And why? Because those who had occupied them were no more. Where are they?

Charles Baje, Company C, a blacksmith from Milwaukee. Wounded at Chancellorsville.

Courtesy of U.S. Army Military History Institute

Dead! In the hospitals. Captured by the rebels. That is the worst thing that could happen to a regiment that once was so excellent. We have only three hundred men in active service. We crossed the Rappahannock with six hundred. Another affair like this and there will be no regiment."[74] Why had this happened? To Muenzenberger there was but one answer: "The fault of it is this, Sigel isn't with us anymore, and the others are merely humbug generals."[75]

On May 10 General Schurz reviewed his division. The 26th Wisconsin, nearly a thousand strong when it left Milwaukee seven months earlier, mustered only 260 men fit for duty.[76]

The Result

At Chancellorsville the Sigel Regiment "saw the elephant." Those who survived the battle, and the war, would never forget the experience. The regiment had 471 men engaged at Chancellorsville, suffering 53 killed in action, more than 11% of its total, and one of the highest fatality rates of any regiment in the battle. Its aggregate loss of 204 was the fifth highest of any Union regiment in the battle.[77]

Although forced to retreat by overwhelming odds, the regiment performed very well in its inaugural action. With very little advanced warning, the men rushed into ranks in an open field, shielded only by some brush and the undulations of the ground, to meet Stonewall Jackson's surprise assault. Greatly outnumbered, outflanked, and caught in a crossfire, the inexperienced Germans held their ground for twenty minutes until ordered twice by their brigade commander to withdraw from the field. Rallying to the rear, they rejoined the fight first at the Buschbeck line, and later in the final repulse of the last Confederate assault that evening.

They fought well. "[O]ur boys never flinched and showed the pluck of old veterans." Doerflinger wrote in the "Personal War Sketches" volume of E. B. Walcott Post No. 1, Grand Army of the Republic. "I am firmly convinced that the stand made by our brigade after the extreme right-wing had been crushed and was in full flight—that by our firm stand, the impetuous Stonewall Jackson's avalanche was checked and probably prevented the destruction of the entire Army."[78] Other observers agreed.

Adin Underwood, an officer participating in the battle with the 33rd Massachusetts, commented that the "26th Wisc. stood in line 20 minutes." Attacked by "a largely superior number, who had the advantage of a screening forest, [they] stood and fought unflinchingly until the enemy had largely doubled around their flanks, both right and left" and retired "in good order."[79]

According to its brigade commander, the 26th "stood its ground until it became untenable." In his report on the battle, Col. Krzyżanowski singled out "Col. W. H. Jacobs, Lieutenant-Colonel Boebel, Major Baetz, and Adjutant Schlosser, all of the Twenty-sixth Wisconsin Volunteers, who led their men to the best of their abilities and with coolness."[80]

The division commander, Gen. Schurz, was even more laudatory.

"The Twenty-sixth Wisconsin," he wrote in his official report, "flanked on both sides and exposed to a terrible fire in front, maintained the unequal contest for a considerable time. This young regiment, alone and unsupported, firmly held the ground where I had placed it for about twenty minutes; nor did it fall back until I ordered it to do so. There is hardly an officer in the Twenty-sixth Wisconsin who has not at least received a bullet through his clothes. Had it not been for the praiseworthy firmness of these men, the enemy would have obtained possession of the woods opposite without resistance, taken the north and south rifle-pits from the rear, and appeared on the Plank road between Dowdall Tavern and Chancellorsville before the artillery could have been withdrawn."[81]

Commenting on the regiment's role in the battle, the noted Civil War historian and veteran William F. Fox concluded that although the 26th Wisconsin was placed in "an extremely disadvantageous position," it made a "creditable fight," and "held its ground there until nearly surrounded, gallantly, but vainly, trying to stem the victorious onslaught of Jackson's charge."[82]

The stand of Krzyżanowski's small force, anchored steadfastly on the right flank by the 26th Wisconsin, bought the time necessary for the Federal artillery to escape and the remainder of the troops to rally into a makeshift defensive line. Their stubborn resistance took the impetus out of the Confederate offensive, while denying to Jackson's men the objectives they sought to achieve before dark and providing time for the rest of the army to prepare for the onslaught.

The Aftermath

The day after the battle near the Hawkins Farm, Confederate soldiers found Lt. Doerflinger lying beside the road where he crawled to attract attention. They took his sword, belt, revolver, haversack, and even the shoes from his feet. Somehow he managed to conceal his money and watch. Their pillaging done, the rebels took him to the Hawkins house where he met Capt. Schueler and many other wounded from his regiment. In and about the house hundreds of wounded were being treated by two Northern physicians. The most serious cases, mostly from the 26th, lay tightly about the floor of the house. The others "were housed in little shelter tents, commonly called dog tents, exposed to all kinds of weather, unavoidable want and neglect."[83]

For the next eight days they "barely got anything to eat until we received food and brandy from Uncle Sam under a flag of truce." His wound largely untended, Doerflinger experienced "little pain" and recalled an occasional cigarette tasted "great." Eventually, rumors spread of a prisoner exchange. The injured lieutenant spent much of the passing days "longing for the moment when the ambulance would take us back under the Star Spangled Banner. They finally came yesterday and you should have seen the excitement." But the suffering was not over. Ahead lay a torturous twenty-mile ride in uncomfortable, jostling wooden wagons. Many "were in terrible pain...having their shattered bones shaken in ambulances, that had to make their way over debris, roots and stones, partly where nearly four hundred pieces of artillery had made a hell out of the beautiful forest, and left a scene of destruction now still plainly to be recognized in the crippling of many large trees." Painful though it was, most made it through this ordeal to reach friendly Union lines.[84]

Back in Wisconsin the newspapers brought the first word of a great battle in Virginia within twenty-four hours. News was incomplete, and sometimes contradictory, but it was obvious hard fighting was taking place. Casualties would certainly be high. With great apprehension, family and friends of those in the service sought news of their loved ones, hoping their names would not be among the lists of casualties that soon began to appear. Reports were agonizingly slow arriving. On May 7 the *Milwaukee Sentinel* published casualty lists including several wounded from the 26th, but reports continued to be fragmentary, and sometimes contradictory, for weeks. Often the confusion was heightened by the mangled spelling of names or the misidentification of units. Then too, some sources of information were no longer available. After the battle Christian Crusius's letters to the *Pionier* ominously stopped. As late as May 23 the *Herold* complained: "We still have not received a reliable report from 26. Regiment. However, it has been confirmed that Lieutenants Doerflinger, Cordier, and Rauth are not dead, but lightly wounded and in good spirits. However, the brave Schueler, the well-known Neukirch of Fond du Lac, and Pizzala are dead."[85] Shortly after his death, Pizzala's new bride gave birth to a son. The body of the baby's father was never identified.[86]

For many, the horrible truth became reality when the *Sentinel* published a letter to the governor of Wisconsin from the acting adjutant of the 26th, Lt. Albert Wallber, forwarding the casualty list of the regiment. "To His Excellency, the Governor of Wisconsin: I have the honor to hand you enclosed, a report of the casualties in this regiment after the late battle at Chancellorsville, Va., on the 2d day of May last. Those reported as missing have been mostly taken prisoners by the rebels. From private sources I learn that many of our men taken prisoners have been paroled, and are now at the camp parole near Annapolis, Md. The larger portion of our wounded are in the division hospital, near Brook's Station, Va."[87] There followed a list all too lengthy detailing those killed and wounded.

While the newspapers were slow to bring to Wisconsin accurate news of casualties, they were quick to launch an assault as deadly to the reputation of the Badgers and their Eleventh Corps brethren as the Confederate minie balls had been in the wilderness around Chancellorsville. This new trial began on May 7 when, for the first time in quite a while, recent newspapers circulated through the camps. Eagerly the men scanned the pages for some account of their desperate stand, some accolade for their heroism. Instead, their eyes fell upon shocking, incomprehensible stories informing readers they had abandoned their positions behind prepared breastworks to rush in panic toward the rear. The *New York Times* told its readers the Germans ran too fast to suffer many casualties and credited General Hooker's superb generalship with saving the bulk of the army. All over the North from New York and Pittsburgh to Indianapolis and Milwaukee, newspapers echoed the same sentiments, always casting aspersions on Gen. Schurz and the German troops without reference to the so-called "American" regiments that formed the bulk of the Eleventh Corps.[88]

Stunned at first, reactions quickly turned to pain followed by anger as newspapers passed from campfire to campfire. It was not the first time journalists blamed the "foreigners" for some indiscretion—as, for example, at Thoroughfare Gap where they were not even present—but this was different, a blatant attack on men who suffered so much in blood for their loyalty to the Union. Placed in a terrible position through the ineptitude of their commanding generals—Hooker and Howard—the men fought desperately. They purchased crucial time with the blood of more than one-third of their number. Now, instead of praise, the newspapers castigated them more severely than ever.

Papers in hand, men appeared at the tents of their officers seeking some explanation. They received none, of course, for the officers felt as startled and appalled as their men. Gen. Schimmelfennig wrote a scathing letter of protest in which he attributed the stories to "the prurient imaginations of those who live by dipping their pens in the blood of the slain." Schurz complained to Hooker, maintaining that in fact the only fighting done on May 2 was by the "foreign" brigades of Krzyżanowski, Schimmelfennig, and Buschbeck. When his protest bore no fruit he published a letter in the *New York Times* calling for a Congressional investigation.[89]

While few came to their aid, the German language *Milwaukee Herold,* relying on information from its correspondent in the field, sought to reassure those at home about the conduct of their troops. "The five day battle near Chancellorsville and Fredericksburg is still the subject of discussion and critique. The 11th Army Corps, mainly consisting of German regiments, is the one that is mainly being blamed. The American regiments, of which there are many in the 11th Corps, are not mentioned at all. Only the 'cowardly dutchmen,' led by General C. Schurz, who are supposed to have fled, are mentioned. I talked to many experienced and impartial military men about the fight of the 11th Corps and the result was: The main person to blame is the commander of the 11th Corps, General Howard."[90]

The *Milwaukee Sentinel* also came to the defense of the regiment, carrying a description of its stubborn fight headed by the following introduction: "The reckless statements of an irresponsible correspondent branded all the regiments in the Eleventh Army Corps with cowardice at the battle of Chancellorsville. We now know that at least one of those regiments, in whose honor we feel a peculiar interest, fought as bravely as any troops in the field. We allude to our Twenty-sixth, Col. Jacobs, of whose gallantry we have already spoken, but take pleasure in presenting the following detailed account of their conduct...."[91]

"I deem it my duty as a husband and father," wrote Adam Muezenberger, "to write to you again and more particularly because the newspapers have published so much trash about the 11th Corps which no doubt disturbed you as well as others....Our regiment suffered heavily during the strenuous campaign and battle of Chancellorsville, and of companies which were not wounded, half fell sick from wet and cold. During these last days our company alone had seventeen men in the camp hospital, eighteen wounded and missing, and eleven in different United States hospitals."[92]

Ernst Damkoehler expressed similar thoughts to his wife Mathilde. "Our Regiment stood up well after it was ordered back twice, and only after it was partly surrounded and was in a terrible crossfire it fell back, only to collect itself again behind a hill, to give the enemy a couple more rounds, from where it had to retreat then....The number of dead and wounded are sure evidence how the Regiment stood up and even though the whole Corps which had covered the retreat last summer at Bull Run under Sigel and saved the whole Army from being imprisoned, has lost its good name through the stupidity of a General, Howard, still our regiment is well respected."[93]

"The stories which are said to circulate in northern papers, charging the whole affair to the cowardice of the 3rd Division," Winkler wrote, "are utterly false; the attack was made on our right flank, which was held by the 1st Division....Our division did more than any other to check the enemy as they came on, and the 26th Wisconsin, in particular, distinguished itself."[94]

"No troops in the world would have withstood better such a sudden, unexpected onslaught as was made upon our 'right flank in the air' by a force three times as numerous," wrote Karl Doerflinger. Years later, after the mellowing effect of time, he drew a distinction between the conduct of Hooker and Howard and that of the press. "Erring is human. The patriotic, loyal and courageous commanding officers, whose errors in judgment alone were responsible for the disaster of the Army of the Potomac at Chancellorsville, deserve our compassion, because their conscience was weighted with a terrible burden; but no term of reproach is too severe for those contemptible criminals who conspired in the fabrication of the lies and calumnies heaped upon the Eleventh Corps as a whole and especially its contingent of men and officers of German birth and descent, whom the narrow-minded representatives of prejudiced chauvinism designated as the 'flying Dutchmen,' altho their loyalty, their patriotism, their love of liberty, their military spirit and discipline, their culture, their proportion of enlistment and their fighting quality compared favorably with any other element of our American people."[95]

Karl Wickesberg was less charitable. Incensed by an article that appeared in the Milwaukee *Christliche Beobachter*, he wrote home to defend his comrades. "We stood firm," he insisted. "And they say we ran away out of our trenches. I would like to see some trenches. We were standing in front of a bush....All the papers write lies. There are a few of those (either drunken or runaway) scoundrels who have those things put into the paper. In time the truth will come out....It was all General Howard's fault. He is a Yankee, and that is why he wanted to have us slaughtered, because most of us are Germans. He better not come into the thick of battle a second time, then he won't escape."[96]

Chapter 6

"TEDIOUS MARCHES"
North to Pennsylvania

he hasty retreat concluded, the Sigel Regiment lingered in its camp until May 16 when it moved to healthier ground near its old campsite at Brooks Station. Gradually the temperatures moderated and the April rains subsided. It is "delightful May weather," Winkler reported by mid-month. "[W]e have our headquarters on a beautiful green hill close by a farm house surrounded by young fruit and shade trees. We came here yesterday, only half a mile from our old camp. We were in a wood of large pine trees before; that is pleasant enough in winter, but in spring, when everything else that has been in repose leaps into life again, the unchanging somber hue of these evergreens seems very gloomy, almost dismal."[1] Muenzenberger thought it "a good campsite with clear water" where "we can get good bread almost every day."[2] Damkoehler was even more effusive. "Our new camp is wonderful! It's in the middle of the forest with a famous view towards Falmouth and the surrounding country. Naturally, we left some trees standing to have some nice shady places and we fixed everything so that we might live as nicely as possible."[3]

Quickly they settled into the familiar camp routine. Every day they arose early to cook breakfast and boil coffee. Company drill consumed the hours between 7:00 a.m. and 9:00 a.m., while battalion drill lasted from 4:00 p.m. to 6:00 p.m. Picket duty broke the routine for some; for others there were various diversions. To fill his idle hours, Adam Wuest joined some of the younger men in continuous card games that consumed nearly all of their off-duty time. Lackner began reading a treatise on military history and resumed playing chess.[4] "Here we gather—drink lemonade, smoke cigars & enjoy ourselves," the captain wrote. "Upon the whole however the matter is tedious & I long for more activity, especially as it brings peace nearer."[5]

Most took advantage of the relative leisure to write home. "Perhaps in the fall, if I am still alive I can get a furlough," Damkoehler hoped. "Oh, dear Mathilde, what I would give to see you all for a short time!"[6] Muenzenberger wrote home almost every day, revealing his thoughts and activities while longing for word of his loved ones at home. "This evening, on the ninth anniversary of our happy marriage, I received your dear letter of May 17th, and I was additionally pleased that the letter from my dearly beloved wife surprised me by appearing on that never to be forgotten day. It makes me the more unhappy, though, that I must live in this confusion of war while you live in our quiet home, forsaken by your husband. At the same time I feel comforted that the Good Father in heaven has protected me and my little ones. The ninth anniversary of our marriage was certainly a sad one, but I hope that the tenth will be the happier for it. I am well, and I hope that this letter finds you the same....am greatly pleased that Ernest and Mary are so busy studying. I take the greatest pleasure from it. Tell them they should be busy little children and pray for me....I was happy to learn that you ordered a Mass and received the sacraments on our wedding day. I wish that I could have done the same, but here one sees no church or religion—nothing but woods and soldiers."[7]

Picket duty provided some activity, but was on the whole just a tedious routine. Winkler managed to get assigned to a patrol that "went to a number of farms near the picket line, where we arrested some gentlemen with southern proclivities suspected of being spies, and took a good deal of contraband property."[8] Occasional scouting patrols also provided some relief from the routine, but on the whole there was little to do but wait. "Every day," Damkoehler complained, is "the same monotony."[9]

On May 12 a sudden stir of excitement caused a brief diversion from the daily routine. Capt. Winkler explained: "Just now a dispatch from General Hooker tells us that the Richmond papers announce the death of General Stonewall Jackson, from wounds received in his last engagement; he has been very successful as a general, and dies in the noonday of his glory. I believe that he possessed to some extent the elements of greatness. I believe that he was a sincere man and believed in the cause he had so often and so victoriously fought. His earthly career is past, may he be forgiven the sins of his treason."[10]

Another distraction occurred four days later when many of the wounded returned from Confederate captivity. They "came to the hospital from the other side of the river," Winkler explained. "I saw a great many of them—many of them who had been supposed to be dead. It is a sad sight, almost a sickening sight, to see such a collection of mutilated human beings. I feel now that it is my duty to go again; it is a duty that ought to be cheerfully done, but it is a constitutional infirmity of man to hardly bear to look on human suffering. We are glad to meet those whom we deemed dead alive and comparatively slightly wounded. On the other hand, it is terrible to see others felicitating themselves on the slightness of their injuries when the surgeon's probe has ascertained the fact that life is impossible, death inevitable." Despite the terrible sights, Winkler resolved to return to the hospital "to bring to the sufferers what little pleasure and comfort I can."[11]

Lackner visited the nearby division hospital at Brooks Station several times and found "our wounded are doing tolerably well."[12] Adam Muenzenberger and Leopold Drewes also visited the division hospital. "I wish you could see one of these hospitals," Muenzenberger wrote, "the cleanliness and orderliness with which they are run." Muenzenberger found General Schurz visiting the hospital. "He visits the wounded, tent after tent, and in this way he found out that the division doctors had been neglecting their duties, and he had them put under arrest. He said he couldn't have things like that happen. The soldiers had done their duty, and he certainly expected the doctors to do theirs; and if they didn't, he certainly would show them that they were treating human beings and not animals. He cares for the soldiers like a father for his children."[13]

Visits or not, the pain and suffering of the wounded continued for many weeks, months, or even years. Wenzel Lastofka, wounded through the neck and arm, had his right arm amputated on May 15. He remained in the hospital until August 13 when he received a discharge for disability. Henry Fink, shot in the right forearm, saw his wound turn gangrenous before a surgeon from the 20th Massachusetts removed the damaged bones on May 16. Transferred to the Veteran Reserve Corps on March 10, 1864, he could not close his fingers correctly and eventually received a disability pension. Karl Doerflinger, his shattered ankle amputated at Washington on June 27, suffered severely from a botched operation that left the end of the bone protruding from the muscle tissue. Particulary sensitive to the slightest change in weather or temperature, the exposed nerve endings in the stump caused constant pain that made it almost impossible to sleep.[14]

Capt. Charles Neukirch of Milwaukee, his wound considered slight, had walked to the field hospital to have it treated. From there he was sent to Seminary Hospital in Georgetown on the outskirts of Washington, D.C. From there he wrote his sister that the wound was slight and he expected to return to duty in a few days. But soon his conditioned worsened. A correspondent from the *Herold* visited the hospital where he found Neukirch and Lieutenant Henry Greve of Manitowoc. "I visited last Monday and stayed with these brave men for over two hours," the correspondent reported. "I witnessed Neukirch's terrible suffering. I learned from the hospital's doctors, and Dr. Wolcott of Milwaukee, that Neukirch would not be able to survive. The poor brave man felt his destiny and asked me to help him. He had just made it through a dangerous operation in which the bullet in his upper arm had been removed. Greve suffered a grazing shot in his right foot, and a shot in his left thigh. So far, the physicians have not been able to locate the bullet. Otherwise, Greve is without pain, and well off, hoping for a quick recovery. Therefore, his family and friends may not worry." Neukirch died on May 12. The *Daily Milwaukee News* informed its readers the captain was "remarkable for his sterling good sense, pleasing manners and sound integrity."[15]

Despite the warmer weather, a better diet, and less strenuous conditions, the men were slow to recover from the rigors of Hooker's brief campaign. In Muenzenberger's small company alone, less than half of the men on the rolls were present and fit for duty. Among the Greenfielders, Andreas Springling was recovering from his wounds in the hospital in Alexandria. Jacob Michel, released from Confederate captivity, recuperated in the parole camp at Annapolis, Maryland. Lewis Manz rested in a hospital in Annapolis recovering from the loss of the index finger on his right hand. During his stay there he sent Muenzenberger a letter scribbled with his left hand. Most of the ill, or the more lightly wounded who escaped capture, lay nearby in the division hospital at Brooks Station. Among Muenzenberger's other acquaintances, Fritz Awe "complained continually about pains in his chest, and he could scarcely breathe." He obtained a furlough to recuperate, but back home in Wisconsin was judged "dangerously ill." Nicolaus Friedrich recovered after a month in a Philadelphia hospital, but was detailed as an orderly there and did not know if he would return to the regiment or not. By May 21, the regiment, which numbered 825 on paper, reported 548 present, of whom only 471 were fit for duty.[16]

As the days slowly passed, everyone wondered what would happen next. "How long shall we remain in inactivity?" Winkler asked rhetorically. "When will we be ready to advance again? These are puzzling questions."[17] Everyone had an opinion. "According to rumor," Muenzenberger informed his wife, "we will be stationed here for a while yet, as our army corps is to be recruited to full strength. Every week some of the old German troops return home when their time is up."[18] Lackner reported that Schurz was trying to get his division transferred to Tennessee to join Gen. Rosecrans army. Domschcke reported three possibilities as the prevailing opinions: "Some thought our army would withdraw to defend Washington, to protect the capital from the enemy's thrusts. Others imagined a third clash on Bull Run's charnel fields. Another group expected an engagement along the Shenandoah."[19] Winkler, however, felt they would stay in Virginia in a reorganized command. "It is said that General Sigel is coming back to the Army of the Potomac to have an enlarged command, his old corps included," he explained. "I hope it is so. He is the man to command this corps, all have confidence in him, while very little confidence is felt in General Howard. Troops without confidence in their leaders are worth nothing."[20]

The first change to occur was an addition to Krzyżanowski's brigade. To replace the losses sustained at Chancellorsville and bring the brigade back up to its previous strength, the authorities assigned to it the 82nd Ohio Volunteer Infantry. The buckeye regiment enlisted 931 men at Kenton, Ohio, on the last day of December, 1861. Veterans of many a battlefield, the 82nd Ohio lost its colonel, James Cantwell, at Groveton. After fighting at Second Bull Run and as an unattached regiment assigned to Schurz's division at Chancellorsville, the unit now mustered only 350 men under Colonel James S. Robinson. Its addition lifted the active strength of the brigade to 1,555.[21]

Other changes also occurred in the Sigel Regiment because of the recent losses. Among the field staff, Alexander Metzel, a sergeant in

Frederick "Fritz" Reuss, Company B. Regimental Quartermaster Sergeant. A clerk from Milwaukee.

Photo Courtesy of Michael E. Telzrow.

Company B, replaced deceased Sergeant Major Hugo Carstanjen. In the various companies, it was necessary to replace the captains who would not be returning: in Company E, Peter Fernekes replaced Charles Neukirch; in Company G, Hermann Fuerstenberg replaced Charles Pizzala; and in Company K, Edward Carl replaced August Schueler.[22]

Many positions remained vacant while the wounded recovered, or until promotions could be confirmed. Exhausted and sensing no immediate action, Col. Jacobs left for Milwaukee on a furlough. Rumor had it the colonel had tendered his resignation, a thought, according to Winkler, that "met with little encouragement." If Jacobs did resign, Winkler reasoned, he would be in line for promotion to major. "I should like to be Colonel of the 26th," he confessed. "I must take my promotion now, because I can do more good in the regiment than I can do here, even if I am not the commander. The interests of the regiment demand it. I must say that I do not like this staff very much."[23]

Although Muenzenberger was not yet confirmed as sergeant, he did receive a change in duties. Lt. Martin Young appointed him company orderly, which meant he no longer had to stand picket duty but remained in camp to perform his new duties. "I am content with my fortune," he wrote. "I hope and pray that luck will turn her face toward us once more and we can be together again....I lean upon God, and I hope that with His help and with the help of the Blessed Virgin we will be happily reunited."[24]

One thing that did not change was the monotony. Although ordered "to have three day's rations in readiness for instant march," little else changed in the daily routine.[25] "The only thing that reminds us that we are awaiting a march order," Damkoehler explained, "is that we always have to have on hand eight rations. Our troops are in good spirits and I am sure the biggest part of them are looking forward to getting together against Lee another time. They all seem to be sure of winning."[26] Rumors continued to circulate, with most now feeling confident of victory in their next confrontation with the rebels. Winkler reported "There is a good deal said about General Lee's coming to the north of the Rappahannock shortly for our especial entertainment; if he does, we will have a fight, and if we don't whip him soundly, I think the Army of the Potomac had better be discharged for disability."[27]

By June 11 preparatory activities convinced Winkler they would not have much longer to wait. "We shall enter upon a new campaign very soon. All the preparations are made and a portion of the army has already left; in two or three days we will probably take our departure.... I have full faith that I shall go through another campaign unharmed."[28] Muenzenberger also noted increased activity. "Our wounded are all recovering, and some of them are back with their companies again, and the rest will be back within a few days. The severely wounded will be sent to Washington just as soon as they can stand the trip. From there they will be sent home on a furlough until they are entirely cured." As to himself, he felt, "thank God, hale and hearty," but wondered what the future would bring. "What does the teacup say?" he asked Barbara. "Does the end come soon?"[29]

The Movement North

Following his defeat at Chancellorsville, Hooker moved his huge army into a defensive position to meet an anticipated follow-up assault by the Army of Northern Virginia. Realizing the folly of attacking Hooker's men in their prepared positions, Lee decided upon a bold movement north. The Southern commander reasoned a successful invasion of the North would allow him to gather recruits in Maryland and much needed supplies in the rich farmlands of Pennsylvania, it would certainly draw Hooker out into the open where he might be attacked with greater opportunity for success, and a victory on Northern soil might convince Northerners the war was hopeless, thus leading to a peace based on Southern independence. Leaving a token force at Fredericksburg, Lee struck northwest toward the Shenandoah Valley, then north for the Potomac.

When Lee's strategy became apparent, Hooker proposed moving his army South to attack Richmond. Horrified at the thought of Lee's army marching unopposed through Maryland and Pennsylvania, fearing also for the safety of the capitol, Lincoln refused permission for the movement south and ordered Hooker north to do battle with Lee's invading army. Slowly, and with some aggravation, Hooker began moving west to follow Lee. At last realizing that Lee's objective was not the Shenandoah Valley but an invasion of the North, Hooker belatedly turned his columns in that direction. The race for Pennsylvania had begun.[30]

Marching orders arrived suddenly in the camp of the Sigel Regiment at 9:00 a.m. on June 12. "[A]ll is bustle around us," Winkler reported. "Some people have a way of making an immense fuss when a move takes place."[31] Within an hour the regiment was on the road to Hartwood Church under the command of Lt. Col. Hans Boebel. Bivouacking that night in the woods alongside Catlett's Station on the Alexandria and Culpepper Railroad, the next day the men arose at 3:00 a.m.[32] "We rose from our beds where we had rested well," wrote Muenzenberger, "and after we had our black coffee and crackers we marched on. We passed through very beautiful—very beautiful—country. Here and there we saw fields planted with wheat and Welsh corn."[33]

Clear skies magnified the June heat, turning Virginia's roads into dust bowls that all but asphyxiated men marching at the rear of the columns. During their brief rest stops men broke ranks to assault near-by cherry orchards, ripping whole trees to the ground in the process. Plentiful strawberry and blackberry patches were left naked as the troops indulged themselves in these juicy treats to quench thirsts made all the more urgent by the clouds of dust. "Whole trees were ripped apart" Muenzenberger recalled. Lackner commented only that they were "tedious marches."[34]

The troops reached Centreville on the evening of June 14 after marching 24 miles that day. There they rested two days, moving into position on the Gainesville Road near Bull Run as the advanced guard. "After three days hard marching, we have come to a halt at Centreville," Winkler wrote. "It is reported that Lee is in the Shenandoah Valley, threatening an invasion of Pennsylvania; we will probably follow him closely if it is true....The weather is very warm and dry, and our marches have been and will be pretty hard....We crossed the famous Bull Run last night very near the battlefield, and our present camping ground is near that historic field." The march from Catlett's Station "was over fields that had more than once been trod by hostile armies and have seen many scenes of blood. We passed over farms where rich clover was growing, but deserted ruins only mark the spots where the Virginia husbandman and his family once were happy."[35]

Centreville was a welcome sight to Muenzenberger. "[H]ow glad we were when we saw the old nest before our eyes again. Here we camped on the very earthworks the Rebels had made. During the day the weather is very hot but at night is very cold. The other morning we had to march through Centreville again and toward the Bull Run Road, where we pitched our camp in an open place under the scorching sun."[36]

After a two-day rest, the men broke camp at 3:00 a.m. on June 17 and began "a very long and fatiguing march" through "the most trying heat and dust."[37] The suffocating heat engulfed the sweating men in an unrelenting cloud of dust. They marched until 5:00 p.m., covering 27 miles in what Damkoehler referred to only as "a terrible heat." Domschcke thought it "a long and tiring march in heat and dust." Karsten reported that some fell out with sunstroke in "terrible heat," but Muenzenberger was more descriptive: "The weather is so hot that we think we scarcely can stand it and yet we have to march with our entire equipment, loaded like pack mules. You'd think this is a race—and it is, for the southern general, Lee, is marching in the same direction through the Blue Ridge, and we have to march rapidly to block his way, which we have been lucky enough to do."[38]

When they reached Goose Creek, about half way between Gum Spring and Leesburg, some five miles from Edward's Ferry on the Potomac River, the men made the best of the opportunity afforded by the shallow creek bed to cool off and cleanse their bodies of irritating coats of sticky paste.[39] They had covered 214 oppressively hot, dusty miles since the movement began. The next day the skies finally relented. "Rain at length—refreshing rain—is delighting this parched country," Winkler wrote, "it is the first rain since our recrossing the Rappahannock on the 6th of May."[40]

The column halted at Goose Creek while Hooker decided on a course of action. The men found the uncertainty and lack of information unsettling. "We know very little and don't get any papers," Damkoehler complained. To Albert Wallber, acting regimental adjutant, "An uncertainty seemed to prevail, whether we were to meet the enemy in Virginia or across the Potomac." Winkler was more emphatic: "We have had no mail and no newspaper, and are wholly ignorant except of these two facts, that Grant has not taken Vicksburg and Lee has not taken Harrisburg. I get a little homesick, when we are here so idle and uncomfortable, in every way disagreeably situated, deprived of everything. I rather wish that we march continually; this idleness is unendurable, but I must not complain." "Our camp is quite comfortable," Muenzenberger wrote, "but how long we will be here only God Himself knows."[41]

The respite at Goose Creek finally enabled the regiment's mail to catch up with it, cheering, at least temporarily, the mood of the troops. For Ernst Damkoehler the mail brought the welcome news of a new baby boy. "That you will call the little boy Henry or Harry I like very well, but I would like it much better if I could see the youngster once. Who knows if the little one is allowed to get to know his father."[42]

For Adam Muenzenberger, the mail was not so good, bringing news of illness at home. Concerned, he hastened to pen a reply to his wife Barbara: "I received your long-wished for letter today. My happiness was great when I heard that we were to receive letters, but our happiness, or rather mine, did not last long because on opening your letter I saw to my very great grief that our Ernest is ill. I hope that it will be nothing serious and until I receive the next letter I will live in the hope that he is recovering. Let God's will be done though. The fate of man is in His hands. Tell Ernest to be resigned and he will get better."[43]

Feeling helpless, filled with concern, Muenzenberger awaited news of his son. He did not have to wait long. Two days later another letter arrived informing him of young Ernst's death. Twice within the space of a year tragedy struck the family. While his friends prepared to resume the march, he once again took up his pen in an effort to comfort his wife:[44]

> I think of the trouble you are in, and the way your heart must be torn by this trial. But what can that help? You know how I love our children with heart and soul, but I must counsel you to be consoled, dearest. The Lord tries us in these days of tribulation. We too can say, "Whom the Lord loveth he chastiseth." Therefore be comforted. After the long night the sun must shine again. Of course it is hard. It is hard for me, too, as a father, because I am so far away from you. But I give myself patiently and with resignation to my fate. And I pray the good God that He preserve us and our little ones, and if it is His will that He will have us meet again.
>
> Of course for you, sweetheart, it has been considerably harder because it was your lot all alone to watch the suffering and pain of the children without my being of the least help to you. But be consoled, dear, if we have good luck, and if after this foolishness is ended, we should come together again, rest assured I will never forget what you have done for our little ones. I owe you many thanks, and I hope that the Lord will repay you a hundred-fold.

...I am still well, and although this news staggers me for the minute, I am quite consoled in thinking, "Lord, Thy will be done." I hope that you, too, beloved may raise your self above these sorrows, and think, "The Lord has given, the Lord shall take. Blessed be the name of the Lord."

I know, dear, that you are strong in adversity. Do me the favor, be comforted. Don't worry because we can't help matters in any way.

...Be comforted, dear. After the rain comes the sunshine.[45]

There was little time to mourn. The men arose early on June 25, washed down some hardtack with coffee, and fell into line. By 4:00 a.m. they were on the road to Edward's Ferry on the Potomac. Amid great rejoicing, musicians struck up lively tunes while the regimental color guard unfurled their battle-torn flags. Cheerfully the men broke into song as they followed their colors across the undulating pontoons. Delighted to leave Virginia's bloody soil behind them, they were among the first elements of the Army of the Potomac to cross back into Northern territory. "[A]fter so many crusades and pilgrimages hither and yon in decrepit Virginia," Domschcke wrote, "we gained the Maryland shore, God's country." Drawing upon the skills of his earlier profession, he committed his impressions to paper. "Everywhere in northern Virginia we met not progress but stagnation, not renovation but decay, and not freedom's blessing but slavery's curse. How antiquated everything seemed! A sad place, a locus of damnation, or perdition, as still as the grave, everywhere." Solemnly he recalled "The bodies of our comrades in arms lay mouldering in the red soil of that stygian land: the thousands who had forsaken home, prosperity, and happiness to secure the Republic against its foe."[46]

While Domschcke's thoughts were of the land they were leaving, others focused on the contrast between the countryside north and south of the river. "[W]e have left the deserted fields of Virginia and come to a smiling, happy, thrifty land, to Maryland," Winkler exulted. "We crossed the river on a pontoon bridge and marched through a land of exquisite rural beauty, such farms, such fields of heavy grain—some gathered—some ripening—at one place already bending under the reaper's cradle; the meandering river, the ranges of hills or mountains, it did the eye good to look upon them and made our very hearts happy. Of course, we suffered no want. We had an excellent dinner at a large farm house. We camped outside the pleasant little village of Jefferson about dark, and took our headquarters at a farm house....We had a good supper and breakfast."[47] Wallber was equally excited: "Having tramped around Northern Virginia with its corduroy roads, its red soil, and viewed nothing but those melancholy pine forests, barren, impoverished fields, old and dilapidated homes, a country where everything was so monotonous, where a deathlike stillness prevailed, interrupted at night only by the lamentation of the whippoorwill, our feelings may be imagined when we stepped on Maryland's shore and beheld the fertile fields, rich pastures, well-kept gardens, white farm houses with green shutters, all showing the prosperity of the inhabitants. The contrast between the two shores was so conspicuous that we really feasted on the beauty of the landscape. With a light heart and swinging step we marched on to Jefferson."[48]

The next morning they were again on the road early, marching most of the day until they reached Middletown, nestled in a valley between South Mountain and the Catoctin Mountains, about 6:00 p.m. Marching through northern territory, the troops acquired a new determination to rid the North of its Southern invaders.[49] "It is a small town of decidedly Union sentiments," Winkler noted. "[A]s we came through, flags were displayed, ladies appeared at the windows [and] waved handkerchiefs, and everywhere we see manifestations of pleasure at our appearance....I think, if we have an engagement here or anywhere north, our soldiers will fight with great courage; it cannot be otherwise. The entire population, who treat them so kindly, will anxiously look on to shower upon them benedictions for victory, but scorn and indignation for defeat; the soft beams of sympathy which have smiled upon them has already brought a new spirit into the army. You should see them as they come from the village or a neighborhood farm house, laden with bread and milk and pies. The whole female population is baking, and they sell to the soldiers with pleasure at very moderate prices. A number of neighbors have come in and tendered their services as guides and scouts; it is evident that we will have one great advantage, that of reliable information in fighting in our own country."[50]

On the 28th a major change took place in the army. Piqued by his disagreements with the War Department, Hooker asked to be relieved of command. Secretary of War Stanton, with Lincoln's endorsement, accepted the resignation. Command of the army passed to George G. Meade. With some misgivings, Meade applied himself to the enormous task of assuming command of an army on the eve of battle.[51]

The same day the Sigel Regiment took to the roads again, moving over the Catoctin Mountains some twelve miles to Frederick, Maryland, a town Karsten described as about "half the size of Milwaukee." "[I]t was pretty late when we started and we were much delayed by other troops and trains on the road," Winkler explained, "so that we did not arrive at our camping ground until near nine o'clock.... [F]rom the heights that valley presented the most beautiful scene I have ever witnessed." The regiment stopped for the night at "a palatial mansion about a mile from Frederick. There were two young ladies there whose conversation seemed to delight two musical members of our staff; a very fine piano was played by the skillful hands of some of our officers for an hour, and then we composed ourselves to sleep on a large covered stoop in front of the house, to get up again at three a.m. At that hour reveille was sounded and we jumped up."[52]

Lt. Col. Hans Boebel, a printer from Milwaukee, seen here in a faded amd worn postwar image.

On the 29th they marched over twenty-four miles, much of it in a pouring rain, passing through Utica and Craegerstown before arriving in Emmitsburg at 6:00 p.m.[53] "We arrived here this morning worn out with strenuous marches," Muenzenberger wrote. "I still feel pretty good, although I can hardly push one foot ahead of the other these days. We must march like dogs, and now that the rainy weather has started, the road is pretty bad."[54]

They camped about "a mile from the village" under orders to march again in the morning. "It is 9 p.m.," Winkler wrote. "Have only had one meal to-day and am very hungry and must try and get something to eat before I lie down." Before reveille sounded the next morning, orders arrived countermanding the march. According to Winkler, "We were not sorry to be allowed to sleep a couple of hours longer."[55]

The bimonthly muster fell on June 30. The Sigel Regiment reported 16 officers and 293 men present for duty. It rained most of the day, the air heavy with moisture between the showers. In the afternoon the regiment marched about two miles closer to the mountains, where Lt. Col. Boebel detached Lt. George Traeumer with a detail of men for picket duty that night. The balance of the regiment camped for the evening on the grounds of the Saint Joseph's Academy staffed by the Sisters of Charity. Domschcke thought it "an imposing edifice of many windows and numerous little doors on all sides; a handsome place, with outbuildings, enclosed by splendid gardens."[56] The Sisters gave Winkler and some of the officers a tour of the grounds and buildings. "This institution is magnificent, and yet everything is quite simple," he wrote. "The Sisters gave us a very good dinner to-day, which all enjoyed heartily."[57]

That evening Gen. Schurz ordered the German band of the 45th New York to play for the priest and nuns at the academy. In the dwindling evening light, the small group played patriotic songs, marches, and polkas for the assembled crowd. Once the day's activities were concluded, the men gathered about their campfires and speculated on the battle they were sure was about to be joined. The growing darkness provided a background of eerie calm for "Morgenrot," always a favorite song among the German soldiers. On this occasion it proved prophetic:

Morgenrot,	Morning glow,
Leuchtest mir zum frühen Tod?	Are you calling me to an early death

Bald wird die Trompete blasen,	Soon the trumpets will blow
Dann muss ich mein Leben lassen,	then I must give up my life
Ich und mancher Kamerad!	Mine and many comrades!
Kaum gedacht,	Suddenly,
War der Lust ein End' gemacht.	All joy came to an end.
Gestern noch auf stolzen Rossen,	Yesterday, still proudly on horseback,
Heute durch die Brust geschossen,	Today, shot through my breast,
Morgen is das kühle Grab!	Tomorrow in a cold grave.
Ach, wie bald	Oh, too soon,
Schwindet Schönheit und Gestalt!	The beauty and vision of clouds,
Tust du stolz mit deinen Wangen,	Proudly displayed
Die wie Milch und Purpur prangen?	like milk and blood, fade away,
Ach, die Rosen welken all!	Alas, even a rose wilts.
Darum still	Therefore,
Füg' ich mich, wie Gott es will.	Humbly I obey God's will.
Nun, so will ich wacker streiten,	And if death should come to me
Und sollt' ich den Tod erleiden,	I will have died
Stirbt ein braver Reitersmann.	A brave Cavalryman.

By candlelight, some of the men took the opportunity to write home. "We have our camp close beside the convent," Muenzenberger told his wife. "Should we stay here for a while—which I doubt—I will receive Communion. Be consoled my dear. I didn't think much of home until we landed in a civilized country again. Put the sad thoughts out of your mind and ask God to protect us and to give us a speedy return. I was quite exhausted by the campaign recently, but I hope it will soon be ended. They say that we are headed for Harrisburg, Pennsylvania."[58]

Winkler proved more prophetic: "It is said that the rebels are marching upon Gettysburg, Pennsylvania, that is the place that we intended to go to to-day. If they do march upon it, they are coming directly towards us."[59]

Chapter 7

"BULLETS THICK AS HAIL"
Gettysburg

y daylight on July 1, the drowsy campsite was a hub of activity. Soon a courier brought news that rebel infantry was on the outskirts of a small Pennsylvania crossroads known as Gettysburg, some thirteen miles distant. Orders came for the regiment to be prepared to move at 7:00 a.m. After waiting for the First Division to move out, the 26th was on the road at 8:00 a.m. Lt. Col. Boebel found the road clogged with baggage trains from the First Corps, so he followed the rest of the division along the route leading via the Taneytown Road. Although two miles longer than the direct road, the longer route was unimpeded by other troops or wagons, promising a faster march. They moved "Up and down miles of improved and unimproved roads," Domschcke remembered, "over fields and fences, across creeks and swamps filled by long rains the day before."[1]

The column marched at common time of ninety steps per minute, covering about seventy yards in that time, but without the normal ten minute rest each hour. Shortly after it crossed the Mason-Dixon line into the Keystone State the muffled thud of artillery fire could be heard in the distance. Another orderly soon arrived, bringing news of skirmishing. General Reynolds was about to go into action, he said, and the Eleventh Corps should move forward to support the First as quickly as possible.[2] The "march was hastened with all possible speed."[3] In Company E the pace was particularly hard on Sergt. Joseph Arnold. Suffering from illness, he was ordered to ride in the ambulance because of his condition, but found them all full. Instead, he plodded on, trying to keep "as close to the Regiment as possible."[4]

As they marched, a driving rainstorm turned the earthen roads into a quagmire. Many of the men marched barefoot, their shoes having worn out on the tedious trek from Brooke's Station. Those with footwear slogged along, water filling their shoes while the mud sucked at their feet in an effort to tear the coverings from them.[5] "Now commenced a most toilsome and fatiguing march," Wallber recalled. "We reached the hilly country and, running, climbed rocky hills. The rain fell in torrents; the atmosphere was extremely sultry, so that the soldiers, burdened with their accoutrements, heavily-packed knapsacks, blankets, haversacks and arms could proceed onward only with the greatest exertion. But Orderlies, one after another, came galloping up, spurring us on in haste. We heard the roaring of cannon at a distance."[6]

At 10:30 a.m. they reached Horner's Mill. There the rain ceased, revealing a bright, humid July day. Just past the mill, another messenger brought the brigade orders to hurry up. Boebel pushed his men forward at the quick-step, the pace increasing to 110 steps per minute that moved the column forward at 86 yards every sixty seconds. Struggling forward, the troops fought to maintain their footing in the slippery mud. From above, a now unshielded sun beat down upon them without mercy. Domschcke considered it one of "our hardest and most tiring treks."[7] Few would have disagreed.

As they neared the soon to be famous crossroads town, the column crested Cemetery Ridge from which the men could see Gettysburg, "and beyond it the smoke of battle."[8] It was about 12:30 when they came within sight of Gettysburg, having covered the thirteen miles from Emmitsburg, an average day's march in that era, in only four and one-half hours, the last ten miles with not a single rest stop. Huffing and puffing, their feet already heavy with the weight of many miles, their ears picked up the rattle of musketry beyond and to the left of the village. Rushing toward the sound of the firing, Lt. Col. Boebel raced his men the last mile into town at the double-quick, 140 steps per minute covering 109 yards each time the second hand completed a revolution.[9] "Exerting what remained of our strength," Domschcke recalled, "we finally reached the town and hurried through its streets at double-quick."[10] Sergt. Arnold was not with them. Having fallen behind because of his weakened condition, he caught up as the regiment crested Cemetery Ridge, but again fell behind when Boebel ordered the double-quick. As he struggled to follow his comrades the roaring of the guns foretold "the terrible storm that was approaching."[11]

Panting for breath, their faces streaming with sweat, the men entered the southern edge of town. As they trotted through the hamlet citizens waved and cheered from their windows and porches. Some obliging samaritans rushed forward offering buckets of water for the men to quench their thirsts. Here and there people held out loaves of bread or rolls to the famished soldiers.[12] Exhausted, the men moved mostly by habit rather than through conscious effort. "We were wet as cats, hungry as wolves," commented Sergt. Wickesberg, "our thirst was satisfied by the good citizens when we ran in full gallop through their town."[13]

While the Eleventh Corps regiments poured into the crossroads, the First Corps was heavily engaged west of the town and in danger of being outflanked on its right. Gen. Reynolds was dead, killed by a Confederate sharpshooter, leaving Gen. Howard in command of the field. Howard, yielding command of the Eleventh Corps to Schurz, ordered him to take his division, now under Gen. Alexander Schimmelfennig, and Barlow's division to support the endangered right flank of the First Corps north of Gettysburg. Von Steinwehr's division, together with the reserve artillery, went into line on Cemetery Hill, a position Howard determined to hold as a likely spot upon which to form the primary defensive works. Howard hoped to hold the lines north and west of town as long as possible, then retreat to Cemetery Hill where the Twelfth and Third Corps would form. The former, under Henry Slocum, lay at Two Taverns, some five miles from Gettysburg. The latter, led by Daniel Sickles, was at Emmitsburg.[14]

Moving rapidly through the streets, the regiment emerged from the north end of town. "Everyone's blood flows quicker," Domschcke wrote, "every pulse beats louder, every nerve is more sensitive, and every one feels that he is living faster than he was half an hour since."[15] They were no longer novices to war. They knew what the firing meant, what horrors lay ahead of them, but they pushed on.

Beyond the town, Lt. Col. Boebel rested his weary men briefly in the shade of an apple orchard while the sergeants called the roll. Despite the grueling pace of the march and the imminent threat of battle, there were remarkably few stragglers. Before the roll call ended, Sergt. Arnold arrived, leaving only three men missing. The sergeants recorded them as deserters.[16]

Capt. Winkler, still assigned to a staff position with corps head-quarters, was waiting near the orchard as the regiment arrived. "Our men were very tired when they got there," he observed, "they had marched a great distance at a very rapid rate through deep mud."[17] To their left, the contest already raged with unremitting fury. With the sounds of battle growing closer by the moment, the infantrymen knelt in silent prayer or meditation. They were an exhausted but resolute group of men. Only too well aware of the abuses heaped upon them after the Chancellorsville debâcle, and the crucial significance of this invasion of the North, they were determined to do their duty.[18]

While the regiment made ready for battle, the musicians, who functioned as stretcher bearers during times of battle, were sent to the rear to await developments. In the commissary department, Ernst Damkoehler and his comrades also went the rear for the protection of their wagons and supplies. On the following day Quartermaster Freder-ick W. Hundhausen and Commissary Sergeant Samuel Meyer led them to a place of safety in Westminster where they stayed until they returned to the regiment in Gettysburg on July 4.[19]

Soon the order came to move forward. Held in a reserve position, they were placed in the middle of a wheat field "in double column closed in mass" so as to be able to move to the support of the first line when necessary.[20] While they awaited the call, the rebel artillery on Oak Hill to their left found the range, sending shells arching through the humid summer sky toward their position. Other Confederate guns soon opened from the right, beyond Rock Creek, catching them in a crossfire of bursting metal that Karsten labeled "a strong artillery fire."[21] We "were assigned to a position in an open field to the north of the town," Wallber recalled, "with orders to lie down to escape the shot and shell which came flying over our heads."[22]

Two federal batteries clamored forward to bring their ten guns into play against the Confederates. Their fire brought some relief as they forced the Confederates to change position, thus reducing their rate of fire. Schurz had less than 6,000 men north of Gettysburg, not enough to ade-quately fill the gap between the First Corps and Rock Creek. About 2:30 p.m. Barlow, without authorization from Schurz, moved his division for-ward to take possession of a small knoll that would henceforth bear his name. This forced Schurz to advance his line, making it impossible to close a gap of nearly a quarter of a mile between the First and Eleventh Corps.[23]

Schurz ordered Krzyżanowski's brigade forward to strengthen the front line, now overextended by Barlow's ill-advised advance. Before the order arrived, however, Confederate troops moved to the attack. Marching toward the sound of distant guns, Jubal A. Early's division of rebel infantry arrived on the battlefield across Rock Creek, beyond the right flank of the Eleventh Corps.[24] Jones's artillery battalion, from Early's division, placed twenty-four guns across Rock Creek from Barlow's exposed flank, many of which were actually behind the Union lines. Together with Carter's battalion on Oak Hill, these forty-eight guns caught the entire length of the Eleventh Corps lines in a terrific crossfire of exploding shells and deadly shrapnel.[25]

Shot and shell tore into the thin blue ranks as Early sent Gordon's brigade of six Georgia regiments into action against Barlow. To Gordon's rear, the brigades of Hays and Hoke stood ready to exploit their success. To their right, George Doles's Georgia brigade of Robert Rode's division joined Gordon's assault, catching Barlow's line in a devastating crossfire.

Taken at the same instant in flank and rear, nearly encircled, Barlow's embattled infantrymen, the same division that bore the initial brunt of the Confederate attack at Chancellorsville, held briefly before crumbling under the onslaught.[26] As they began to fall back, Krzyżanowski's brigade moved to their assistance, deployed with the 82nd Ohio on the left, the 119th New York, and the 26th Wisconsin on the right. The 75th Pennsylvania was held in reserve slightly behind the left with the color guard of the 58th New York behind the Sigel Regiment. Before the Badgers could fully deploy, the fugitives from Barlow's shattered line began falling back through their ranks as they changed formation under increasing fire from columns "into line of battle about one hundred yards from the rapidly advancing enemy."[27] To their right, as at Chancellorsville, their flank was unprotected save by the scattered fugitives from Barlow's 1st Division.[28]

Quavering rebel yells pierced the roar of bursting shells as Gordon's and Doles's Georgians, joined by some of O'Neal's Alabamians closed on the blue defenders. In the Sigel Regiment Lt. Col. Boebel hastened his men into line as Confederate minie balls added new dangers to the fragments of bursting artillery shells. A minie ball struck him in the right leg, but he gallantly refused to leave the field. Soon a shell fragment caught Boebel in the same leg, slashing the flesh and crushing the bone.[29] Rushing the men into ranks, the field staff lost heavily. Major Baetz fell painfully wounded. Command of the regiment devolved on the senior captain, John Fuchs of Company A.[30] First Lieutenant Martin Young took command of the company, but was soon killed. A ball slashed through the fleshy part of 2nd Lt. Conrad Grode's right leg. Grode stayed at his post, despite the pain, but in a few moments two more balls struck him simultaneously in the right shoulder, one cutting throughout the upper part of his lung and passing through his body while the other lodged near his spine between the sixth and seventh vertebrae. 1st Sgt. Frank Feiss took command. Seven men fell wounded and two were killed, but Feiss kept the company in line.[31]

In Company B, 2nd Lt. Steinmeyer fell wounded as Confederate fire decimated the company led by 1st Lt. Adolf Hensel. In minutes shells and musket balls killed nine men. A minie ball shattered Corp. Henry Klinker's left ankle, while a dozen other wounded littered the ground.[32] Amid the nightmare of whistling minie balls punctuated by exploding shells, the men loosed a volley, then fired at will as fast as they could reload. Men fell by the scores. In the color guard Corp. John Ritger fell severely wounded early in the fight, followed quickly by Corp. Carl Krueger. Down went both regimental colors, but other hands grabbed the staffs and hoisted the banners aloft again. Within minutes Confederate fire killed or wounded every member of the color guard, but others came forward to take their places as soon as they fell.[33]

In Company C, Muenzenberger and his friends found themselves again fighting for their lives in an open field. Corporals Philip Berlandi and Joseph Koch were killed, along with Privates Johann Dallman, Henry Leken, Joseph Neumann, and Peter Rook. A musket ball smashed into Morris Wingler's head, breaking the frontal bone and exposing the membrane beneath. Nearby in Company D a pistol shot smashed the skull of 1st Sergt. Peter Guttmann, while a musket ball entered Ludwig Kuhn's right scapula and lodged in his thoracic cavity causing a very painful and bloody wound. George Chalaupka, an aging Bohemian carpenter from Caledonia, loaded and fired as quickly as his skilled hands would move. Suddenly the movement stopped, his arms went limp, and he topped into the ditch fronting the battle line. A rifle ball had crushed his skull killing the father of five instantly. His body was never recovered and probably lies today beneath one of the all-too-many gravestones in the Gettysburg

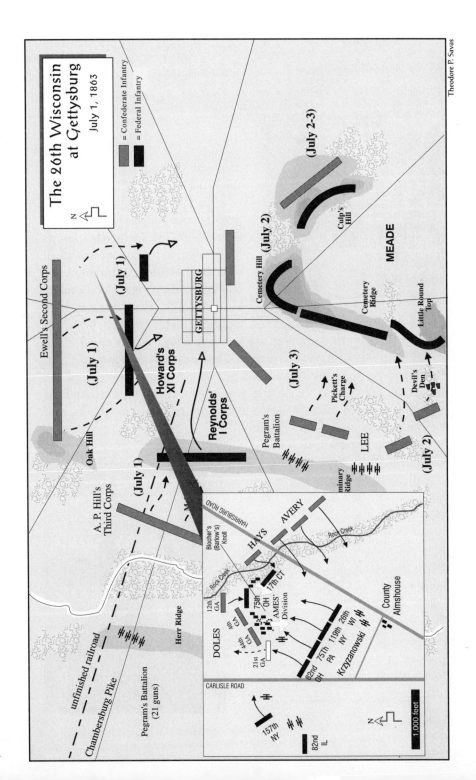

The 26th Wisconsin
at Gettysburg
July 1, 1863

= Confederate Infantry
= Federal Infantry

N

Theodore P. Savas

Ewell's Second Corps

(July 1)

(July 1)

Oak Hill

Howard's
XI Corps

(July 1)

A. P. Hill's
Third Corps

GETTYSBURG

Reynolds'
I Corps

Cemetery Hill **(July 2)**

Culp's
Hill

(July 2-3)

MEADE

Cemetery
Ridge

Little Round
Top

Devil's
Den

(July 2)

(July 3)

Pegram's
Battalion

Pickett's
Charge

LEE

Seminary
Ridge

Herr Ridge

unfinished railroad

Chambersburg Pike

Pegram's Battalion
(21 guns)

CARLISLE ROAD

HARRISBURG ROAD

Blocher's
(Barlow's)
Knoll

Rock Creek

12th
GA

DOLES

4th
GA

44th
GA

21st
GA

75th
OH

17th CT

AMES'
Division

82nd
OH

75th
PA

119th
NY

26th
WI

Krzyzanowski

HAYS

AVERY

Rock Creek

County
Almshouse

157th
NY

82nd
IL

N

1,000 feet

George Chalaupka, Company D, a carpenter, Racine. Killed in action at Gettysburg, July 1, 1863

Courtesy of the U.S. Army Military History Institute

National Cemetery engraved with the haunting legend "Unknown."[34]

To Carl Wickesberg in Company H, the "bullets came as thick as hail."[35] First Lieutenant Joseph Maschauer was wounded and a ball tore into William Ehrmann's leg leaving in its path a bloody mess. In the ranks, twelve more were wounded and four killed, but Capt. Domschcke kept the survivors in line, firing as fast as they could. Harder hit still was Company G where Confederate fire wounded Capt. Fuerstenberg, the only officer present. Of 32 men who entered the field, only seven survived unhurt. Among the wounded were Andreas Stubanus, one of Adam Muenzenberger's Greenfield neighbors, and Charles Hafemann who had followed editor Mann off to war from West Bend.[36]

Riddled by enemy fire in their exposed positions, the men stuck to their work grimly, animated as much by their constant training as by their determination. Sweating from the day's travail, the men appeared to their brigade commander to be possessed by some ani-

Jan Simonek, Company F, a laborer from Manitowoc. Wounded at Gettysburg.

Courtesy of JoAnn Schiefelbein.

Lt. Frank M. Fiess, a carpenter from Milwaukee. As a sergeant, he led Company A when all of the officers became casualties on July 1, 1863.

Lt. Albert Wallber, Acting Adjutant, a clerk from Milwaukee. Was knocked unconscious and then captured at Gettysburg.

Philip Kuhn, Company H, a saloonkeeper from Milwaukee. Wounded at Gettysburg.

Courtesy of John J. Kuhn

Major Henry Baetz, a register of deeds from Manitowoc. He was wounded at Gettysburg.

mal-like thirst for blood. Blackened by the gunpowder from their cartridges and the billowing smoke, their bloodshot eyes painted a horribly grotesque picture Krzyżanowski likened to "a portrait of hell."[37]

In this exposed position the whole brigade suffered grievous losses. In the 82nd Ohio, more than 150 of its 258 men were casualties.
The 75th Pennsylvania, moving up to support the hard-pressed left
flank, lost more than 100 of the 194 it took into action, and the 119th
New York, exposed to partial flanking fire on its left as the 26th was on
the right, lost over 100 casualties in fifteen minutes. Every one of the
regimental commanders were killed or wounded and the brigade commander was injured when his horse was shot from under him. Still the
onslaught of shot and shell continued.[38]

Protected somewhat on the left by the gallant stand of the 119th
New York, the 26th was assailed from the front and, as at Chancellorsville, from its exposed right flank, all the while rebel shells burst to
its rear. Pummeled by both infantry and artillery fire, casualties
mounted. In Company E a ball cut a path through Carl Behling's left
lung, while in Company F another missile smashed Franz Benda's hip
and femur. Capt. Fuchs fell rallying his men along the line in the vicinity of the almshouse where the fierce Union resistance impressed some
Confederates as truly heroic. "[T]he Yankees stopped and made a desperate stand," recalled G. W. Nichols of the 61st Georgia in Gordon's
Brigade. "Their officers were cheering their men and behaving like
heroes and commanders of the 'first water'."[39]

With more Confederates arriving by the minute, the situation
deteriorated from hopeless to suicidal. To the left, Confederate pressure doubled the 119th New York back onto the flank companies of
the 26th as both regiments fought desperately to hold their positions.
To the right, regiments from Early's Confederate division moved
around the Union flank, threatening to encircle the battle line and
cut the regiments off from Gettysburg and Howard's position on
Cemetery Hill. Schurz sent a desperate plea to Howard for a brigade
to halt Early's envelopment. A similar request arrived at Howard's
headquarters from General Abner Doubleday whose First Corps
became flanked on the left by Pender's rebel brigade. Howard had
only two brigades in reserve. He did not want to risk losing Cemetery
Hill so he sent word to the two beleaguered commanders to retreat,
rallying upon his position. Howard then ordered a reserve brigade for-

Anton Czoernig, Company A. A Laborer from Milwaukee.

Henry H. Mueller, Company G, a blacksmith from Addison. Wounded at Gettysburg.

Courtesy of Lucy Storch

Courtesy of Lucy Storch
Print provided by Troy Harman of the
Gettysburg National Military Park

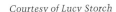

ward to cover the withdrawals.[40]

When the order to retreat into town and on to Cemetery Hill finally arrived, Confederates were in some places within twenty yards of the Sigel Regiment's position. All of its field officers were already casualties, and the firing line was becoming "confused" as both of its flanks came under severe pressure. A shell fragment struck down Sergt. Major Metzel, who fell against Sergt. Arnold knocking him to the ground. Before he could extricate himself, another man fell wounded across him. "[B]y the time I had gotten out from under the wounded man," Arnold explained, "I was told to surrender by one of the Rebs or they would blow my brains out. Being that there was no use to resist I submitted." Arnold asked his captors what troops they were and was told he had been taken by the 21st Georgia of Doles's Brigade and the 8th Louisiana of Hays's Brigade.[41]

The Sigel Regiment had to retreat across an open field raked by

Joseph Scholz, Company A, a butcher from Milwaukee. He was captured at Gettysburg. Note the Eleventh Corps cresent on his hat.

deadly fire from front and flank that added greatly to the casualty list. Retiring toward Gettysburg, bullets slashed through Sergeant Wickesberg's right arm and wrist. Another shot Lackner through the right calf. A fragment from an exploding shell threw Adjutant Wallber to the ground, stunned and unconscious. By the time the remnants formed on the outskirts of town, only four officers in the entire regiment—Captains Edward Carl and Peter Fernekes and Lts. Charles Schmidt and Henry Rauth—remained uninjured. Since the commissions of both captains ranked from the same date, it is not known who assumed command, if, indeed, any one person did. Under the circumstances, Winkler explained, "[i]t is not strange therefore that the regiment became considerably scattered in the retreat."[42]

Desperately seeking help to hold the Confederates back long enough to save the artillery and conduct an orderly retreat, Schurz sent Winkler with orders to hurry reinforcements to the right flank. Winkler rode through Gettysburg to Cemetery Hill where he found Coster's brigade of Howard's reserve ready to move forward. Leading the troops back through Gettysburg, Winkler passed the

Henry W. Rintelmann, Company A, a farmer from Cedarburg. Captured at Gettysburg.

remnants of the First Division crowding the streets in its retreat. Emerging north of town, he ran into Schurz who ordered the reinforcements to fall in on the right of the Carlisle Road. To the left the general placed the survivors of Krzyżanowski's brigade.[43]

As they rallied the troops, Schurz and Winkler came upon "thirty-two men with the colors of the 26th Wisconsin, but without any officer." When they rode past, the men called to Winkler who, with Schurz's permission, dismounted "and took command of this gallant squad." Winkler formed the men into two ranks "and had them sit down in the road." He knew further resistance could not possibly stop the Confederate assault, but he hoped to buy time for the rest of the troops from the First and Eleventh Corps to retreat into position on Cemetery Hill. To his right, the rebel assault fell on Coster's Brigade which he had just led into position. Caught in a maelstrom of fire, Coster's men melted away, leaving Winkler and his small command crouching in the road as the rebels regrouped for another attack. Just in time, one of Krzyżanowski's aides rode by and ordered Winkler to fall back.[44]

The little band retired to "a little white cottage" on the outskirts of town where the remnant of the brigade formed in the yard and opened fire on the approaching Confederates. Outflanked once again and in danger of being surrounded by the rebels moving past its right flank into the town, the command again received an order to retire. Winkler felt "enraged" and "furious" at the retreat, but there was little that could be done at that point to halt the Confederate advance. "I had ridden up and down its streets from one end to the other three times that day," he lamented, "and everywhere there were manifestations of joy; handkerchiefs were waving everywhere, and ladies stood in the streets offering refreshments to the soldiers as they passed. It seemed so awful to march back through those same streets whipped and beaten. It was the most humiliating step I ever took."[45]

Covering the rear of the retreating divisions, the 119th New York moved south along Washington Street, fighting as it went, while the greater part of the Sigel regiment covered the retreat along the town's "main thoroughfare." As the survivors retreated, Lackner "limped to the hospital" located in a church in town. Wickesberg made his way back through town where "a woman saw my bloody hand, she called me into the house, washed my wound and bandaged it. And then I had to stay for dinner yet, which did me a world of good. In the meantime, the cannonballs were flying into the town."[46] Capt. Fuchs also made his way through the crowded streets to the hospital, as did many others. There, Dr. Franz Huebschmann worked as quickly as he could, one surgeon among hundreds of wounded, to care for those in need. When the order arrived to evacuate, the doctor, knowing capture might mean months, or even years of confinement in Confederate prisons, elected to remain behind to treat the wounded. Nine men from the 26th volunteered to remain with him as hospital stewards, hoping the humanitarian nature of their work would spare them from imprisonment.[47]

Closely pressed by the surging grey infantry, the Eleventh Corps moved into Gettysburg. Once it reached town disorder set in when the two retreating corps came together in the middle of town. Several dead-end streets heightened the confusion. Few officers knew which roads led where, and several groups went astray while trying to find a way through the crowded streets or while looking for a passage free from Confederate fire. A group from the Sigel Regiment led by Capt. Domschcke of Company H took an unfortunate turn into one of these dead end street where they were trapped by the advancing Confederates. Among the unfortunate captives were luckless Adam Muenzenberger and his friend Asmus Holz.[48]

In the hospital, Lackner found himself being cared for along with Sgt. Major Metzel and several others from the regiment.[49] Amid the fury that reigned outside, Dr. Huebschmann and his nine volunteers worked feverishly to tend the ever-lengthening line of wounded awaiting their care. Eventually, some 500 patients crowded the hospital and its environs. While they worked, shells fell in the fields nearby and Southern skirmishers sent their deadly missiles whining through the streets outside the hospital's windows. Annoyed by the dangerous conditions outside, the doctor's concern grew until he could restrain himself no longer. Setting aside his instruments, he walked out the door into the nearby field where his large frame, conspicuously clad in a blood-spattered white coat, made an excellent target. Ignoring the danger, Huebschmann lifted his arms above his head as if to signal a halt, and in the same "booming voice" he used so often in Wisconsin's antebellum political wars, "implored the troops to stop firing on the wounded and pick on healthy soldiers who could defend themselves." The firing ceased. "Few could forget the courageous 'Dutch' doctor," a witness recalled, "who,

Charles John Trapschuh, Company A, a carpenter from Milwaukee. Captured at Gettysburg.

with his energetic interference, saved many lives."[50]

On the field north of town, Adjutant Wallber awoke to find himself "inside the rebel lines. A soldier shouted several times, 'where is an officer?' Upon seeing me lying on the ground, he levelled his gun and was about to pull the trigger, when an officer of his company stepped in front of me and beckoning to his men said: 'Come on, my brave boys, come on.' It was a sorrowful sight passing over the battle field. Many a friend lay there lifeless; others, more or less seriously wounded, begged for water, but my captors

refused to allow me to render assistance and after relieving me of my sword and revolver, told me to walk back. In doing so, I went across the battle field of the rebels, where the dead outnumbered the wounded, mostly shot in the head or through the breast, which proved that the aim of our soldiers was good." Moving to the rear, Wallber was taken to "a field near a farm" where he found "several thousand other prisoners," among them Capt. Domschcke and other men from the Sigel Regiment.[51]

Domschcke, captured amid the town's confusing streets, had been disarmed and sent to the rear

Charles Grochowsky, Company K, a shoemaker from Milwaukee. Wounded at Gettysburg as a member of the color guard.

Courtesy of the U.S. Army Military History Institute.

The road is the Baltimore Pike looking from Cemetery Hill toward the south end of Gettysburg where Union troops retreated along Baltimore Street. The 26th Wisconsin defended the stone wall, with its skirmishers occupying the buildings to its front. *NA*

over the roads and fields where his regiment only minutes before fought for its collective life. The rebel officer in charge of the prisoners allowed him to "take one last look" at that bloody field. "I found many a dear friend dead or wounded. Compared to the wounded how fortunate the dead! The wounded usually suffer ghastly agony, pitiful to behold. Here many cried out to me, but I could not help. Some called my name, but blood covered their faces and I could not tell who they were."[52]

The remnants of Krzyżanowski's battered brigade, bringing up the rear of the retreating corps, began arriving at Cemetery Hill about dusk. The Sigel Regiment's survivors formed behind a low stone wall near the base of the hill with their flank resting on the Baltimore Pike. There they took defensive positions to contest any attempt by the rebels to move beyond the town they now occupied. As they waited, Sergt. Karsten counted six separate bullet holes through the rubber blanket he carried slung over his shoulder, a miraculous escape for one who emerged unscathed from the maelstrom north of Gettysburg. His wound having been dressed at the hospital, Capt. Fuchs soon returned to resume command of the regiment while it worked to fortify its new position. Lt. Traeumer also arrived from Emmetsburg with the detail assigned to picket duty south of that town the night before. Fuchs sent Traeumer's group over the wall to take possession of the nearest buildings in Gettysburg for use as picket posts and sniper positions. Pressed spiritedly by rebel skirmishers, they lost two killed and two wounded but carried out their assignment. Darkness rapidly approached and the Confederate brigades needed time to reorganize and redeploy. The time the First and Eleventh Corps purchased with their blood precluded any Southern attempt on Cemetery Hill that evening.[53] The position Howard selected for the battle was secure for the moment.

That night a profound silence hung about the battlefield, broken only by the beating of horses hoofs and the dull tramp of new troops moving into position. Losses had been severe. Over one-half of those present on the brigade's firing line that afternoon did not answer when their names were called that evening. Some were being tended to in the hospitals, some were in captivity, some lay wounded upon the field, and some would never answer.

The Repulse

Dawn found the men kneeling uncomfortably behind the stone wall. The position held vital importance because artillery posted on the hill above could command the Federal line which spread out to the left along Cemetery Ridge. Throughout the morning and early afternoon of July 2 they listened to the sounds of battle echoing down the line from the Round Tops where Confederate infantry launched a desperate attempt to flank the Union line. From the outlying buildings of Gettysburg, including a church steeple, Southern sharpshooters trained their weapons on Federal officers moving about Cemetery Hill. Twelve volunteers from Schurz's division, their rifles fitted with Swiss made telescopic scopes, silenced the troublesome rebel snipers, but firing continued sporadically all day along the front held by the Sigel Regiment.[54]

Shortly after 3:30 p.m., fifty-five guns from A. P. Hill's corps began shelling Cemetery Hill. Although firing at extreme ranges, the gunners proved quite accurate. Shells began bursting all over the hill. Some caused considerable damage to horses positioned on the reverse slopes, while others exploded with enough force to crack the headstones in the cemetery. The men crouched nervously behind the stone walls, seeking what little protection they offered, but the barrage was aimed behind them and few shells fell close to their position. Amid the sounds of bursting shells and ricocheting fragments, incongruously out of place, the unmistakable sounds of familiar waltzes and polkas drifted their way across the plain from some unseen Confederate band. Intended, no doubt, to relieve the tension of the sweating rebel artillerymen, the ironically appropriate tunes calmed the frayed nerves of the German infantrymen holding Cemetery Hill.[55]

As the sun fell near the horizon, Confederate infantry fell upon Culp's Hill. While this attack progressed, two Confederate brigades formed into lines out of sight of the Federals near Gettysburg. Using the town, a small ridge, and the growing darkness as cover, they approached within a few hundred yards of the Northern lines. Suddenly, they burst upon the outmanned troops at the foot of the hill well to the right of the 26th. The defenders got off one volley before being overwhelmed.[56]

Pausing briefly to reform their lines, the Confederates surged up the hill. At the crest of the hill lay six guns of Rickett's battery along with four belonging to Wiedrich's German battery. The 6th North Carolina of Hoke's brigade, now under Isaac Avery, headed for Rickett's battery. Alongside them Harry Hay's famed "Louisiana Tigers" followed the 9th Louisiana toward Wiedrich's position. Retreating up the slope ahead of this host, the Union infantry rallied behind the batteries.[57] During those crucial moments the sounds of battle reached Colonel Krzyżanowski standing with Schurz beyond the cemetery gatehouse. With less than 400 men, members of the 58th and 119th New York regiments, he ordered the small force to fix bayonets and led them forward, accompanied by Schurz and an aide.[58] Bayonets slashed and jabbed. Musket butts became lethal clubs. By sheer physical force, the defenders gradually expelled the Tigers from the emplacements.[59]

Throughout the attack the Sigel Regiment held its position, looking nervously over its collective shoulder as the sounds of battle moved perilously up the other side of the hill, reached the crest, and then receded back down the slope. To their front they detected movement as John B. Gordon's Confederate brigade began to form in support of the rebel attack, but with the repulse of Avery and Hays no attempt was made on the lines held by the 26th.

Back in town Michael Jacobs, professor of mathematics at Gettysburg College, wrote in his diary: "The rebels returned to our street at ten p.m., and prepared their supper; and soon we began to hope that all was not lost. Some of them expressed their most earnest indignation at the foreigners—the Dutchmen—for having shot down so many of their men. This led us to believe that the Eleventh Corps, of whom many were foreign Germans, and whom, on the previous evening, they tauntingly told us they met at Chancellorsville—had done their duty and had nobly redeemed their character."[60]

The early morning hours of July 3 offered little opportunity for rest. Frequent flurries of musket fire from pickets dueling with Confederate snipers kept men in a state of semi-consciousness most of the night. Early that afternoon some 150 guns opened fire upon Cemetery Ridge. Confederate gunners directed their fire to the left of the Sigel Regiment's position. To keep their minds off the bombardment, the troops cleaned their guns, polished their buttons, and sewed their tattered clothing. No one doubted that General Lee would soon launch yet another attack upon their position. When it finally came, everyone was relieved to see the assault directed at the center of the Northern portion, considerably to the left of the line held by the Sigel Regiment.

With the repulse of Pickett's Charge, Southern sharpshooters renewed their activities with a vengeance throughout the evening. Nevertheless, by morning a strange silence hung over the battlefield. At daybreak a patrol probed into Gettysburg only to find the Confederates withdrawn. About 8:00 a.m. Krzyżanowski led the 119th New York and 26th Wisconsin across the wide, flat plains toward Seminary Ridge. He approached the rise with caution, trying to determine whether General Lee's forces might still be lurking about. Moving forward with his men spread out in skirmish order, the colonel ascended the low, sloping ridge to find the enemy gone. He made prisoners of forty-seven stragglers, then reported the welcome news to headquarters. The Battle of Gettysburg was over.[61]

The Pursuit

After some delay, the Army of the Potomac began its pursuit of Lee's retreating army on the morning of July 5. Col. Jacobs returned from leave on the afternoon of July 4, in time to lead the Sigel Regiment off toward Emmitsburg early on the evening of the 5th. Struggling over roads turned "horribly muddy" by the rain and the thousands of feet that preceded them, they halted at midnight to camp about "five or six miles from Cemetery Hill." On the following day they moved south to Emmitsburg, camping near the spot they occupied the night before the battle began. That evening news arrived of the fall of Vicksburg, but many were reluctant to believe it, as Winkler explained, "lest we will be disappointed again."[62]

At 4:00 a.m. on the 7th the column moved out of Emmitsburg, crossed the Catoctin Mountains, and marched to Middletown some thirty miles away. On the road all day struggling up and down the mountains, they did not halt until after 9:00 p.m. amid "a furious rain that drenched us to the skin." Winkler felt lucky to find a loyal Union family who treated the men very well. That night he "Had a nice, clean, white bed to sleep in" which he considered a great "luxury."[63]

On the 8th they marched to Boonsboro where the rebels attacked Gen. Judson Kilpatrick's cavalry. Rushing forward, Winkler hoped they would "have another battle this side of the river" where "we can concentrate a large force and, if their retreat is cut off, we can give the rebels a blow which will go far to end the war." When they arrived at the scene of the action west of town, however, the rebels had already retreated and the Badgers settled into camp for the night.[64]

Relieved by a division of the Fifth Corps on July 9, the Eleventh Corps concentrated in an area at the foot of South Mountain. The sound of artillery fire could be heard in the distance throughout the day and into the next morning, but nothing further developed. On the 10th they marched to within about three miles of Hagerstown, expecting a fight at any time, but again nothing developed and there appeared to be some confusion about the whereabouts and intentions of Lee's army. "We have no knowledge of the movement of the enemy at our headquarters," Winker reported, "but from the quiet that prevails infer his retreat across the Potomac."[65]

Marching with the remainder of the Eleventh Corps, the Sigel Regiment passed through Hagerstown on July 11 to the cadence of enthusiastic "hurrahs" from the local emergency militia. Citizens lined the streets, showering the men with an ovation of cheers that heartened them beyond words. Continuing on, the Northern army finally caught up with the Confederates the next day between Funkstown and Hagerstown, following the retreating Southern columns to Williamsport where the pursuit was finally given up on the 14th.[66]

Winkler expressed concern that the public, its expectations heightened by sensational news stories of the Northern victory, would be disappointed by Lee's escape, but he was content to see an end to the campaign. He thought an attack by the greatly weakened Northern regiments on the "strong defensive position of the enemy" would have been problematical. The army "needs more men and re-organization before it will be reliably effective."[67] Few outside the army agreed with him. Both the public and the president were disappointed the Southern army escaped back to Virginia. Regardless, coupled with the fall of Vicksburg, the repulse of Lee's invasion turned the tide of Southern victories into the beginning of Northern ascendancy. Later generations of historians would generally refer to Gettysburg as the "high tide" of the Confederacy.

Carl Kindt, Company A, a laborer from Franklin.

The Result

The Battle of Gettysburg marked a milestone in the history of the Army of the Potomac. For the first time the Federal army in the East won an unmistakable victory in a major battle with the Army of Northern Virginia. In the encounter, the Sigel Regiment once again behaved well. Placed in an open field with no cover, assailed from front and flank by both infantry and artillery, the regiment held its ground stubbornly until ordered to retire. It fell back in orderly fashion to the almshouse line until once again flanked and ordered to retire. Becoming separated during this retreat, the two major sections of the regiment rallied on the outskirts of Gettysburg where they served as part of the rear-guard for the retreating Eleventh Corps. Coming off the field with its honor intact, the regiment rallied again at the foot of Cemetery Hill where it assumed a position it held for the balance of the battle, dueling constantly with Confederate sharpshooters for the next two days. Of the contest on July 1, Confederate corps commander Richard Ewell proclaimed his assault on the Eleventh Corps line that included the 26th Wisconsin an "obstinate contest."[68] Their sacrifice helped save the crucial Cemetery Hill position as a rallying point for the Army of the Potomac.

The price was high. While their casualties at Chancellorsville were heavy, those at Gettysburg were worse. According to Fox's *Regimental Losses*, of all the regiments that fought at Gettysburg the 26th ranked 15th in aggregate loss with its killed numbering more than 12%. Of the 458 officers and men reported as present for duty on the monthly muster of June 30, 61 were killed or died of wounds, at least 150 wounded, and 41 captured or missing, a casualty rate of more than 55%. When deductions are made for the pickets under Lt. Traeumer, stretcher bearers, and others not on the battle line, the loss probably approaches two-thirds of those actually engaged. Every member of the color guard was either killed or wounded, and only four of the officers who were present on the field of battle escaped unhurt.[69]

Our regiment was almost completely annihilated," Wickesberg told his parents.[70] In Company G, Karl Karsten lamented his unit's loss in a letter to a friend. "We have only fought two battles but we have suffered terribly in both of them so that our beautiful regiment has been decimated greatly."[71] Losses were so severe that when the pursuit of Lee ended and time permitted, the regiment was consolidated into five companies. Only later that fall, with the return of the sick and wounded and the addition of some of those who returned from detached duty, did it resume its normal organization.[72]

In the aftermath of the battle the newspapers praised the army, its commander, and, uncharacteristically, some reports included kind words for the Eleventh Corps. On July 4 the *New York Times*, previously a bastion of anti-German criticism, reported the Eleventh Corps redeemed the disgrace of Chancellorsville.[73] But the good-will engendered by the triumph did not long survive the echo of the guns. Subsequent stories in many newspapers completely neglected the crucial part played by the Eleventh Corps at Gettysburg. Before long many Northern newspapers began criticizing the corps, and particularly its German element, for "running away" on the first day of the battle. Disheartened and bewildered, the men felt betrayed, their enormous sacrifices forgotten. While few enlisted men deserted, many vowed never to re-enlist once their terms of service expired. Among the officers, some sought transfers to other theaters of operation where their contributions might better be appreciated. Others resigned. In the Sigel Regiment, Major Henry Baetz submitted a detailed letter of resignation criticizing the absence of any official denunciation of the fictitious "news" stories. In his case, the anger and disgust that drove his pen must have been extreme for he had no immediate need to resign other than as a protest. He would have received a discharge anyway due to the wounds he suffered at Gettysburg.[74]

Chapter 8

"SAD AND POIGNANT MEMORIES"

Recovery and Transfer

s the armies began their withdrawal from Gettysburg, they left in their wake the disrupted lives of many thousands both in and out of uniform. For the captives, the Confederate retreat brought grueling marches with little prospect of anything other than dehumanizing rebel prisons. For the wounded, the battle for survival frequently meant amputation, pain, lonely confinement far from family and friends, and often death. For those at home, the news of the battle brought the conflicting emotions of joy over the victory and anxiety over the fate of loved ones. For the Sigel Regiment, the withdrawal brought continued hard marching and sacrifice.

The Captives

At dawn on the morning of July 2, Joseph Arnold, a sergeant in Company E, shared some of his remaining hardtack with Capt. Domschcke and Lt. Wallber. To accompany it, he made the last of his coffee, sharing that with the two officers also. Soon after they finished, the Confederates separated the prisoners, placing officers in one area and enlisted men in another. The separation complete, the rebels offered to parole each group and send the men to Carlisle for exchange. Since government policy prohibited accepting this type of agreement, Domschcke and Wallber declined. Among the enlisted men there was uncertainty about what should be done. Arnold asked permission to discuss the proposal with his officers and the rebels agreed. Arnold sought out Domschcke, who advised him the "government would not recognize such parole." If the enlisted men accepted it, they "must assume responsibility for the consequences." Domschcke then said: "We officers are going to Richmond. I advise you men to do likewise." Arnold returned to the enlisted men, who all agreed to reject the offer of parole.[1]

The Southerners marched the captives about one and one-half miles behind the front lines and gave them the first rations they received since their capture. Domschcke found them "homeopathic in quantity" consisting of a small piece of "raw meat with a handful of wheat flour and a few grains of salt." Although grateful for the meager food, Domschcke believed "Malice accompanied this gift of rations, for we had almost nothing in which to cook or bake it." According to Wallber, the two officers "stood there asking ourselves, what shall we do with this manifestation of rebel generosity?" They finally decided to tie the flour in a rag for later use. Domschcke wrapped the precious powder, but while marching tragedy struck. He explained: "I lost my grip on the bundle. The flour spilled on the wet grass. The two of us, famished, looked with pain at what we had lost." Wallber also remembered the incident: "Two more sorrowful people could not be imagined as we looked down upon our loss, for we were very, very hungry. But we still had our meat, and this we cooked in a small tin cup which I had saved. This was the only food for the day. Our next flour ration, however, was guarded more carefully." They also "learned to bake," Domschcke explained, "though we owned neither pot not pan nor oven. I rolled dough on an oilcloth and shaped little loaves. Wallber meanwhile kindled a fire and hunted up small stones and ringed the fire with them. Stones hot, we put the loaves on them and with sticks tilted the stones to the fire and left them until one side of the loaves baked. We turned the loaves to repeat the process. Only with disgust could I nibble such bread now; but we wolfed it then and craved more."[2]

From the field where they were kept, Domschcke and Wallber "heard the fire of musketry and the roaring of cannon" as the Confederates attacked first the Round Tops and then Culp's Hill and Cemetery Hill, "but were unable to find out who had been victorious. The prisoners coming in did not know. In the evening, the rebel bands played lively airs and we judged from this, that the enemy had the best of the encounter. We laid down to rest with sad misgivings."[3]

The morning of July 3 found them "lying on the ground near General Pickett's headquarters." There they saw the Confederate general emerge from his tent, in Wallber's words, "his long locks reaching to his shoulders, artistically arranged, his high riding boots brilliantly polished. [H]is external appearance without a fault, he mounted his horse. In looking at his cheeks and nose, we divined that their color was not caused by drinking sodawater only. With a haughty air, imbued with his own importance he galloped to the front." Domschcke described Pickett as "The archetype of a Virginia slave baron [who] strutted briskly, proud in bearing, head lifted in arrogance. On horseback he looked like the ruler of a continent. Obviously he took pains with appearance—riding boots aglitter, near-shoulder-length hair tonsorially styled—but the color of his nose and upper cheeks betrayed that he pandered the inner man. Pleasures of the bottle left indelible tracks."[4]

As the day wore on a "dismal silence" blanketed the battlefield. It was, Domschcke thought, "That eerie silence" which "usually precedes the battle's catastrophes." He was right. "[I]n the afternoon, hell broke loose. The thunder of cannon shook the earth. We surmised that this clash would decide the contest." Wallber was equally struck by the moment: "Our hearts were beating fast, our anxiety was at fever heat, for it was clear to us that this day was significant. When night approached, cannon and musketry firing ceased. What was the result? The musicians remained silent. Could we base any hopes on this? No news came to us. In utter despair, tired and hungry, we spent the night lying on the green sward."[5]

The prisoners awoke to the sun on Independence Day. "But what a 4th was this!" Wallber thought. "At home it was a day of jubilation, while here we did not know whether the enemy had not succeeded in shaking the foundation of our republic. We were huddled together on a field, surrounded by a fence, on the outside of which sentinels were posted,—weatherbeaten fellows, clad in torn gray garments, who eyed us malignantly. The weather had turned gloomy and we sat around with heavy hearts, wondering what news we would likely hear, when one of our officers, disregarding all possible consequences, gave vent to his feelings and in honour of the day began a patriotic song. We others took courage and all joined in the chorus. The sentinels pricked up their ears, looked at us, but said nothing. This seemed encouraging, for we reasoned that they would hardly permit us to indulge in this harmless pleasure had they been victorious. Their severity was too well known to us, why then in this case were they so lenient? Why could we sing *John Brown*, and *Rally Round the Flag*? This leniency must have its reason. Could it mean that they were beaten on July 3rd?" Soon afterward "a curious commotion was visible around us. Troops commenced to maneuver, orderlies galloped to and fro, and the immense wagon train began to move." Wallber and Domschcke knew for the first time the rebels were "skedaddling."[6]

"Our hearts rejoiced when we realized that the Rebels had lost and were fleeing," Domschcke recalled. But joy was tempered by the reality of their own plight. "At the same time, however, we knew our fate. We would be carried along with the retreating army, away from the land of freedom, to the Hell of treason and barbarism—to Richmond, where the arch-Rebel Jefferson Davis reigned. Never had joy and grief so crowded at once into our souls: joy at the victory of our army, grief at our own lot."[7]

The prisoners marched south with the rebel army. A "terrible rainstorm" broke out at about noon, but spirits rose as the men anticipated being freed by advancing Union troops. "We waited anxiously for the release, but alas, day after day vanished, when we realized that our hope was in vain. Our fears for a long imprisonment were to become true."[8]

On the 5th the column wound through Fairfield. "Women of all ages stood in the doorways," Domschcke recalled, "saw our many blue uniforms, and wept, believing all to be lost. We shouted reassurance: 'The Rebel army is retreating, we'll soon be back!' A beautiful young woman sobbed bitterly and begged God to protect us."[9]

The following morning the rebels, finding themselves greatly burdened by the host of slow-moving prisoners, once again offered the Northerners parole. Once again the Federals refused. "How could we agree to something so desired by the enemy?" Domschcke asked. After the refusal, the column moved on, conditions becoming worse. "We began a torturous and exhausting march," Domschscke remembered. "What a horrid night! Our concourse moved at a crawl, having to halt nearly every five minutes. Given neither rest nor enough to eat, and therefore tired and weak, we lay down at once on the muddy road wherever we paused, so as to get the most of each moment of every respite."[10]

Hunger became overpowering. "In the absence of rations we picked a few ears of wheat, which we found in a field adjoining our camp, to appease in a measure our hunger."[11]

Guarded by the survivors of Pickett's ill-fated charge, they had another opportunity to view the general after the decimation of his division. They found him a changed person. Wallber noted "a dark shadow hovered over his red physiognomy." To Domschcke, "a pall seemed to cloak" the Southern general.[12]

At last, after four days of increasing misery, the column reached Virginia. As Domschcke crossed the river into the Old Dominion State, "Gloomy prospects joined sad and poignant memories; recent days had been painful. We looked back across the Potomac that separated us again from the land of the free, our eyes caressed longingly the Maryland mountains where our army must be." Wallber also looked "yearningly" on "the picturesque land we were to leave behind and a feeling of loneliness overcame us." On July 18 they arrived in Richmond as captives rather than victors.[13]

The Wounded

On the sanguinary field north of Gettysburg the evening of July 1 found the ground littered with dead and wounded. Confederates found Morris Wingler with his brain membrane exposed and carried him to a field hospital in grave condition. Corp. Henry Klinker, his ankle shattered, lay on the field in agony, in and out of consciousness. Nearby, Ludwig Kuhn struggled against the pain of the musket ball in his chest. Corp. Carl Krueger suffered through three days on the open field, his wound undressed, without food and water. Eventually Confederates carried them all as prisoners to field hospitals. 1st Sergt. Peter Guttmann, his skull fractured by a pistol ball that fortunately did not penetrate his cranium, also lay on the field for three days until finally taken to a farmhouse. When the Confederates withdrew from the town on July 4 they and many of their friends were freed from rebel captivity. Wingler lay in the field hospital before being sent to the South Street Hospital in Philadelphia where surgeons finally extracted the ball from his skull. Kuhn, suffering from haemoptysis, was treated in the field hospital with cold water dressings, linseed poultices, and cerate dressings. Transferred to Saterlee Hospital in Philadelphia on July 9, he recovered there until transferred to the Veteran Reserve Corps in December. Bothered by constant pain, he found it hard to sleep or lie flat resulting in a disability discharge on July 9, 1864. Krueger spent five months recovering in a hospital before rejoining the regiment in December. Guttmann stayed in the farmhouse for three weeks recuperating from his injury.[14]

In the little church in Gettysburg that served as a hospital, Dr. Huebschmann ministered to friend and foe alike during the balance of the battle. When the Confederates retreated, they allowed him to remain to tend the wounded who were, with few exceptions, also allowed to remain. Huebschmann cut a ball from near Lt. Grode's spine and the officer, though "still in a feeble condition," was able to rejoin the regiment in September. His leg smashed, Lt. Col. Boebel did not receive medical attention until July 4 when Union troops recaptured him from the retreating Confederates. After enduring a painful amputation in the field hospital at Gettysburg, he was transferred to Letterman hospital to recuperate. His wound effectively ending his military career, he went home to Milwaukee in August. William Ehrmann, wounded in the leg, struggled to the field hospital where he recuperated for 24 days before being sent to Harrisburg. Lucky that the ball did not damage the bone, he nevertheless did not rejoin the regiment until eight months later at Chattanooga. Others were not as fortunate. Pvt. Mathias Schwister of Company E died in Gettysburg on July 5; Peter Kruescher of Company C lasted until July 8; Joseph Balmes of Company C died on July 10; and Christian Stier of Company F succumbed on July 14. Others lingered longer, but death arrived nonetheless: Sergt. August Braatz of Company B lasted until August 1. Carl Behling of Company E stayed in the Eleventh Corps hospital until July 10. Transferred to Jarvis Hospital in Baltimore, he suffered from "profuse, exhausting hemorrhage." The condition reappeared on July 23 for two hours. On August 6 he ate "a hearty dinner" when suddenly a "profuse hemorrhage occurred" and he died in ten minutes. Franz Benda of Company F had the ball extracted from his hip in the Eleventh Corps hospital. Transferred to Camp Letterman on August 6, the attending surgeon noted that he suffered from "a compound fracture of the femur." Six days later he developed diarrhea and "hectic fever." Treated with "exhibition of tonics, stimulants, and anodynes," he died of "exhaustion" on August 20.[15]

Others, less seriously wounded, left Gettysburg for a variety of hospitals in Washington, Baltimore, Philadelphia, and elsewhere. Lackner was taken to the field hospital where he shared a tent with Sergt. Major Metzel until July 7, much of it during a drizzling rain. On the 7th, 2nd Lt. William Steinmeyer of Company B, 1st Lt. Sigmund Juenger of Company A, Corp. Philip Grosch, also of Company A, and Lackner "procured a wagon, rode to Littleton & then per Cattle cars to Baltimore." The foursome left Baltimore on the 9th for Philadelphia, and from there journeyed to Milwaukee, arriving on July 11. Lackner "immediately left to visit my parents." He remained home recuperating until August 22 when he left via the Great Lakes route to rejoin his regiment. He found it at Catlett's Station on August 28.[16]

Sgt. Metzel was removed to a hospital in Washington, D. C., where he died on July 20. Others succumbed to wounds or infection throughout the coming months: Anton Texton on July 22, William Lauer on July 25, William Feldmann on August 2, Carl Behling on August 8, William Hartmann on August 16, John Wildhagen and Joseph Zbitowsky on September 3.[17]

Charles Hafemann and Karl Wickesberg were sent to the U. S. General Hospital in West Philadelphia where their wounds steadily improved. In a little more than a week Wickesberg felt well enough to visit Philadelphia, but he chafed at the daily confinement. "[W]e are treated like prisoners and not wounded people," he complained in a letter to his parents. "I wish to God the war would be over soon, because I would like to come home now, and live with you."[18]

The Folks at Home

As the Fourth of July approached in this, the third year of the war, Milwaukeeans determined to celebrate the patriotic anniversary "with an eclat exceeding all previously known in the annals of the city." Officials appointed a committee to plan the activities. Throughout the city, individuals and organizations clamored to participate as a means, perhaps, of showing their support for the nation and their troops in the field. Historian Frank A. Flower described the fateful occasion:

The day was ushered in, as usual, with the ringing of bells and firing of cannon, an immense procession formed, consisting of committees, city officers, military led by General Pope, returning soldiers and citizens on foot, civic societies, and a long train of gaily decked vehicles of every description. It was formed and marched under Dr. E. B. Walcott, Chief Marshal, supported by several aids. As it marched, the citizens sang with voices that drowned the martial music, the new war-songs of the people, the 'Battle Cry of Freedom,' 'John Brown's Body,' and others. But, as it marched, a great shadow of anxiety pervaded it, which neither songs nor shouts could hide. A terrible battle, on the issues of which might hang the life of the Republic, had been fought at Gettysburg, of which only a few imperfect telegraphic reports of the first two days struggle had been received, sufficient to show that it was the bloodiest and most desperate of the war, but not assuring a victory to the Federal troops. So, with hearts heavy with foreboding, the great assembly gathered on the bluffs of Lake Michigan, at the head of Division street, to wait for further tidings of the battle, and listen to the patriotic speeches of the day. Governor Salomon spoke first, in his usual strong and loyal style. He was followed by Hon. James R. Doolittle. He had finished his exordium, was fairly on in his speech, and had just alluded to the uncertainties hanging over the field of Gettysburg, exhorting his audience to prepare with patriotic hearts for the worst, when a messenger, hot and breathless with running and with joy, handed him a dispatch. During its perusal the silence of death fell on the vast audience. When he read it aloud—'The Battle of Gettysburg, after three days of hard fighting, has resulted, yesterday, in a complete victory to the Federal army, and the total route [*sic*] of the Confederate's—shouts of triumph went up, loud and prolonged, 'The Battle Cry of Freedom,' was sung, and then 'John F. Potter' swelled the general din of joy, with a salute of thirty-four guns, under the vigorous manipulation of Geo. Godfrey. The cloud was dissipated, and the day was bright as the sun that shone above. Following Senator Doolittle, the speaking was continued by General Pope, Levi Hubbell, G. G. Bellows and Governor Yates, of Illinois. A balloon ascension in the afternoon, and a grand illumination and fire-works in the evening, closed the most exciting and most joyous 'Fourth' ever celebrated in Milwaukee.[19]

Despite the holiday celebration and the joy of the victory in far-away Pennsylvania, anxiety grew as thoughts of loved ones became fears for their safety. After so many battles, there were no illusions the victory had come without cost. People frequented the telegraph office and scanned the daily newspapers for some word of casualties. As usual, this most important of information came painfully slow. On July 13 the *Milwaukee Sentinel* reported: "We learn through Mr. Coleman, of the *Atlas*, that Mr. Domschcke, formerly associated with him in the publication of that paper, and who was a Lieutenant in the 26th Regiment, was taken prisoner during the recent battles in Pennsylvania."[20] Almost daily, individually and in groups, the fate of loved ones became known and the joy of victory was too often replaced by the grim reality of capture, injury, or death.

On the 31st the *Sentinel* published a story from W. Y. Selleck, secretary of the Soldier's Aid Society, who was in Washington, D. C., after having visited the Army of the Potomac. "I visited the 2d, 3d, 6th, and 7th regiments, and also met some of the officers of the 26th Regiment. I left the army on Saturday last at 2 o'clock p.m. crossing at Berlin into Virginia. The regiments from Wisconsin are in good condition, what there is left of them. The 2d had 54 muskets in the field, the 6th about 130, the 7th a little over 200, the 5th about 400, the 3d about 300, and the 26th less than 300."[21] This could only have been chilling news to families still awaiting word of loved ones. In anticipation, the various aid societies redoubled their work and the *Turnverein* decided to use the proceeds from its annual Thomas Paine dinner to support the widows and orphans of its soldiers.[22]

On July 28 President Lincoln moved to replace the losses of the summer campaigns calling for another 500,000 men. In Milwaukee, the call met with mixed reaction, some citizens being resigned to see the war through to its conclusion, while others felt the seemingly endless slaughter must end. "The office of the examining physicians of the Enrollment Board was crowded with persons seeking exemption for physical disabilities," Flower wrote. "Never before had the city shown such a display of disease. The whole city was undergoing a general diagnosis. One half seemed suddenly stricken with disease, and the other disclosed the existence of chronic ailments hitherto suffered in secret. A maimed hand or foot came to be deemed a great boon, and hernia, sufficient to gain exemption, was deemed a blessing. Happy indeed was he who lacked a toe or wore a truss. The large drafts from the able-bodied population already made, had left comparatively few of that class for enrollment, while the class exempt for disability had remained undiminished. Nearly half of those who applied for examination previous to the draft were not entered on the enrollment list."[23]

As November approached and the day for the next draft drew near, anxiety rose among those of military age. "This year," Flower wrote, "immediately after the draft, commenced the grand exodus of cowards into Canada, and to other countries outside the United States. Milwaukee's first installment was in the 1,047 who failed to report. Something akin to infamy ought to attach to those who returned to enjoy the blessings of a reunited and happy country, which they were too cowardly to help to preserve. There are gradations in the depths of cowardice; if it be deemed disgrace to flee from the face of the enemy, to what lower depths does he sink who, ignoring the call to duty, flees from the chance of facing danger. This role of poltroons is preserved in the archives of the country they dishonored. Let these pages record the names and deeds of nobler men."[24]

The Survivors

By the end of the Gettysburg Campaign Krzyżanowski's brigade was in bad shape. In the Sigel Regiment, the privations of military life and the trauma of two major battles were too much for some. Although spared most of the horrors of combat, Damkoehler grew increasingly homesick, lamenting his absence as word reached him of his wife's illness. "How many times I have cursed the moment in which I determined even to risk my life to help our government. If I had remained at home I could have helped you in your sickness, and could have looked after the children so they wouldn't become wild. And I am so far distant from you all, I can hardly write words with certainty that you will receive them and must realize that you are suffering and in need of help which I cannot give."[25] Overcome by their experiences, four privates and a sergeant deserted between July and September. Yet, while many grumbled and longed for the day they could go home, Damkoehler and the rest continued to do their duty whenever called.[26]

The regiment—which performed so well at Chancellorsville during Jackson's devastating attack, and north of Gettysburg in another untenable situation—was now but a mere shell of its former self. So few men answered the morning muster that Colonel Jacobs temporarily consolidated the regiment into five companies. Throughout the Eleventh Corps many regimental strengths shrank to less than 200 men. Those who remained were without adequate shoes, clothing, and equipment. On September 9, Capt. H. N. Stinson inspected the regiment's weapons while it was encamped at Catlett's Station, Virginia. The rifles were .58 calibre English-made Enfields marked "Tower 1862" that had been issued at Milwaukee before the regiment left for the front. "The arms appear to be kept clean and in good order by the men," Stinson reported, but they were nevertheless in need of replacement. He explained:

> The defect alleged against the arms are 1st that a great many of the guns have locks so defective that they will not explode a cap, when an attempt is made to fire the gun, at the first trial, and that it is often necessary to snap a rifle a number of times before it will go off. This defect is so general as to be *very serious*, and increases gradually. 2nd that many of the arms do not shoot straight and that they are an inferior weapon. 221 rifles are serviceable and 8 unserviceable. Except that no armourer has been employed, it would appear that efforts have been made to keep the arms in repair. No surplus arms on hand. Parts of unserviceable arms cannot be used to repair a sufficient number to effectively arm the command. No arms have been condemned in order to be turned in. None have burst. Regular property returns have been made for the last quarter. I certify that I have carefully inspected the arms of the 26th Wisconsin Vols., and find them as above stated, and respectfully recommend that they be exchanged for the Springfield Rifled Musket.[27]

To strengthen the depleted corps, the Washington War Department once again reshuffled its regiments. At the end of July, new troops arrived to fill some of the gaps left by the devastating spring and summer campaigns. Krzyżanowski's brigade received a pair of veteran New York regiments, the 68th and 141st. The 82nd Ohio left the brigade and was reassigned elsewhere.[28] In another change, Capt. Winkler was finally relieved of staff duty at his request and returned to the Sigel Regiment on July 18. With the absence of Lt. Col. Boebel and Major Baetz because of wounds sustained at Gettysburg, as ranking captain Winkler found himself second in command behind Col. Jacobs.[29]

After resting for a few days following Lee's escape, the regiment crossed the Potomac at Berlin, Maryland, marching eighteen miles into Virginia on July 19 amid very hot weather described by one soldier as "intensely sultry." At first they met with enthusiastic welcomes. In one "little village," the "female portion of the inhabitants displayed themselves conspicuously in Sunday attire, remembered a Wisconsiner, waving welcome to our forces with handkerchiefs and national flags." Later, as they marched slowly through the lush undulating Loudon Valley, the reception changed. "The sentiment displayed along our yesterday's march was not very friendly," Winkler wrote. "Ladies curled their lips in proud disdain as we passed, and in some places went so far as to lock up their wells to prevent our soldiers getting water."[30]

Camping on the 25th near the intersection of the Warrenton Branch and the Orange and Alexandria Railroad at Warrenton Junction, they engaged in picket and patrol duty until September 16. The July weather was "intensely hot" with water "very scarce and very bad. A glass of fresh water is a luxury wholly out of question." The pickets, whom Winkler supervised, were stationed beyond Weaverville, between Warrenton Junction and Catlett's Station. There the captain enjoyed the luxury of a real bed in Mrs. Weaver's home, as well as "a good supper of bread and milk."[31]

At Warrenton Junction the regiment received pay for two months. Charles Graefe had his picture taken to send home. "We have it quite good here," he told his family, "and are of good spirit and have plenty to eat, fresh bread every day. We want to buy for our head general [Krzyżanowski] a new sword as he did so much for us and as he was so brave in the battle of Gettysburg and near Chancellorsville and because he helped us so much to get out of this terrible fighting and raining of munition."[32]

Sergeant Wickesberg, recently recovered from his Gettysburg wounds, rejoined the regiment at Warrenton Junction. "I feel much better now than in the hospital, because now I am with my *kameraden* again," he exclaimed. Although the regiment received pay twice,

Wickesberg did not get anything, probably because he was listed as being in the hospital on the previous muster rolls. He had not been paid in a full six months.[33]

The weather continued oppressive into August. "All is very quiet and monotonous," Winkler reported. "Holidays, Sundays, work days, all are alike, but it takes constant and careful attention to know what day of the week and month it is." One of the few activities other than picket and patrol occurred on September 2 when the brigade formed for review by Gen. Howard. As the 26th marched by the general, Winkler heard him proclaim it a "Bully regiment!"[34]

Speculation, always a favorite pastime, spawned new rumors. Some believed the corps would be broken up, some that it would be transferred to New Orleans, to Texas, or elsewhere. When the First Division received orders to proceed to Alexandria during the first week of August, the prevalent rumors correctly divined its ultimate destination as Charleston, South Carolina. Its removal from the corps spread new rumors about the fate of the remaining troops, but it would be another month before any further move occurred.[35]

While the army sparred with Lee's forces at a respectable distance, its critical supply lines along the Orange and Alexandria Railroad came under repeated attacks. Clearly Meade could not ignore these threats to his vital supply lines. The War Department decided to assign the Eleventh Corps to protect them, spreading it out in a large fan-shaped arc with its headquarters at Catlett's Station. As part of this redeployment, Krzyżanowski's brigade left Warrenton Junction for Rappahannock Station on September 16.[36] The Sigel Regiment marched at 1:00 p.m., not arriving at its destination, some fourteen miles away, until 10:00 p.m. There the men "bivouacked for the night and took position on a hill by the railroad bridge on the south side of the river," a "very important place that requires careful guarding."[37]

The next day they began making themselves at home. "We collected a lot of boards and were building huts and made it real comfortable for ourselves," Damkoehler explained.[38] "[W]e have to guard the railroad," Karsten wrote to a friend, "where we have to keep an attentive eye, guerrillas are not quite stupid. We are located on a hill which is surrounded by rifle pits and trenches; and which was earlier a graveyard and is full of graves."[39] To Winkler, the position "resembles that of our army at Gettysburg, only on a smaller scale."[40]

With their camps now somewhat more permanent, the men could use off-duty hours to write home, visit friends, engage in regimental contests, or join an occasional hunting party. German musicians found themselves much in demand throughout the army. But all was not peaceful. Diseases flourished throughout August and September. A severe epidemic of typhoid fever swept through the camps disabling scores of men. Ernst Damkoehler reported suffering from fever and diarrhea. Although he went to see the doctor, it "didn't help and soon [he] developed headaches on [his] left side and eye." He felt "very tired." His weight plunged from 150 pounds to 126.[41] Although Damkoehler began to recover and soon pronounced himself "pretty well," disease took the lives of several including Hermann Pagenkopf of Company B, Joseph Stauber of Company E, Anton Pfeiffer of Company I, and Robert Salter of Company G. Another fatality was Private Alois Koetzdinger of Company F who accidentally drowned in the Rappahannock River on September 18. Toward the end of August, Krzyżanowski contracted bronchitis and received twenty days sick leave to recuperate. On September 6 he boarded a train for Washington, leaving Col. Jacobs in command of the brigade. The change left Winkler temporarily in command of the Sigel Regiment.[42]

Meanwhile, a thousand miles away, events began to unfold that would have a profound affect on the Eleventh Corps. For weeks Northern and Southern armies vied for position in an intricate series of maneuvers near Chattanooga, Tennessee. The campaign culminated on September 19-20 when General Braxton Bragg's Confederates defeated the Union forces in a bloody battle along Chickamauga Creek in Northwest Georgia. General William S. Rosecrans led his vanquished army back to Chattanooga where he determined to hold the city. While Bragg settled down to conduct a siege, Rosecrans telegraphed urgent appeals for help to the War Department in Washington.[43]

Responding to Rosecran's appeals, Secretary of War Stanton, with the President's approval, ordered General Meade to immediately dispatch two corps to join the forces gathering for the relief of Chattanooga. Meade chose the Eleventh and Twelfth Corps, while the War Department assigned Joseph Hooker to lead them west.[44] Marching orders arrived at the Eleventh Corps headquarters suddenly on September 24. The men received orders to prepare to leave immediately. Winkler, away on court martial duty, returned to the regiment at 4:00 p.m. to find everything in readiness, the men waiting to be loaded onto railroad cars for the move. They waited until "a little before midnight" when "the order came that we must start at once and march as far as Manassas Junction."[45]

Colonel Jacobs led the brigade north from Rappahannock Station, marching all night until he reached Catlett's Station. After a three-hour rest, the march continued until the tired command arrived at Manassas Junction about 5:00 p.m. the next day. Within four hours the men "were packed into the dirty baggage cars and started" for the trip to Alexandria, across the river from Washington. Krzyżanowski rejoined his brigade as it paused to cook five days rations while changing trains in Alexandria. Shortly, a long line of boxcars belonging to the Baltimore and Ohio Railroad appeared. The men clamored aboard, forty to sixty bodies shoving into each of the cramped cars. The pungent smell of manure greeted them, but speed was of the essence. No time could be wasted in cleaning out the wastes of the freight car's recent occupants. According to Winkler, "The cars were so crowded, it was almost impossible to live in them."[46]

On the morning of September 26 the leading elements of the movement passed through Martinsburg, reaching Cumberland, Maryland, by mid-afternoon. Karsten noted the Sigel Regiment reached Harpers Ferry, which it found "almost all burnt down," at 2:00 p.m., pushing on to Martinsburg at 6:00 p.m. where they received coffee and bread.[47] "We passed some fine scenery yesterday between Washington and here," Winkler wrote as the train paused at a town along the Baltimore & Ohio Railroad in western Virginia. "We were at Harper's Ferry at about sunset." Still uncertain of their destination, the captain believed the prevailing rumor they were destined to reinforce Rosecrans in Chattanooga. It was obviously an emergency move, "and that, to my judgment, can be nothing but Rosecrans need of reinforcements."[48]

At 8:00 a.m. on the 27th the train brought the Sigel Regiment to New Creek. At Benwood, on the Ohio River, the trains halted to deposit their load of human cargo at 4:00 a.m. on the 28th. Grateful for the opportunity to get some fresh air, the men crossed the river on a pontoon bridge to Bellaire on the Ohio side of the river. Once again racing across the countryside, the air within the cars became hot and foul smelling.

There was no opportunity to obtain food, water, or fresh air. Men found it impossible even to tend to the natural necessities of life. "I could write pages if I wanted to give you a good description of our oppressions on the train where we were packed together like herrings," Damkoehler wrote. It was "a terrible fatigue for animals and humans."[49]

Sickened by the crowded conditions in the acrid cars, some soldiers chose to climb outside in search of relief. Perched precariously atop the boxcars, they enjoyed the fresh air and open scenery of southern Ohio, but the urge to avoid the stifling atmosphere below placed the men in grave jeopardy when the speeding trains passed under low bridges or entered darkened tunnels.[50]

By afternoon they passed through Zanesville, arriving in Columbus that evening. Enthusiastic crowds greeted the troops with welcoming cheers as their trains sped out of Ohio, into Indiana. Wherever a momentary halt occurred the citizens offered refreshments to the huddled mass of humanity within the boxcars. Travel through the North proved quite different than marching along hostile Virginia roads, but was tiring nonetheless. "This mode of traveling is so fatiguing," Winkler complained. "We have seen little of papers for some days, and the account of the Battle of Chattanooga was very meager. It seems unquestionable that Rosecrans suffered very severely and was pretty badly defeated, but he seems to hold and maintain a strong position."[51]

From Indianapolis, which they passed at 10:00 a.m. on September 29, the tracks turned south to Jeffersonville, a town on the Ohio River. Ferries carried men and equipment to Louisville on the morning of September 30, where Winkler and some of the officers enjoyed the opportunity for a hearty breakfast at the Louisville Hotel before again boarding trains for Nashville. "It is tiresome and wearisome on the cars," Winkler complained, "I feel the fatigue, but we have to take them again." Lackner characterized it only as "a hard ride in Cattle cars."[52]

The bulk of the Eleventh and Twelfth Corps reached the Tennessee city by October 1.[53] Krzyżanowski's brigade arrived at Bridgeport, Alabama, on October 2, 1863, only eight days after leaving Rappahannock Station. Within eleven and one-half days, two entire army corps numbering 17,500 men rested on the banks of the Tennessee River. In that short space of time ten batteries of artillery with forty-five guns, 717 wagons and ambulances, over 4,400 horses and mules, and all of the two corp's baggage traveled over some 1,192 miles of track. It was at that time the largest, most successful railroad movement in the entire history of warfare. Of more immediate interest to Col. Jacobs and his men, it brought them to an entirely new theater of operations away from the prejudice and misfortunes of the Army of the Potomac.[54]

Chapter 9

"A COMFORTLESS LIFE"
Alabama and Tennessee

hen Capt. Winkler stepped off the cramped train in Bridgeport, Alabama, at 3:00 a.m. on October 7 he entered a desolate, foreboding world. His gaze fell upon "a very wild country" with "nothing but wooded mountains" as far as the eye could see. The town of Bridgeport contained "not a house," but consisted only of "a platform twenty yards long" running along the "single railroad track."[1] But Karl Wickesberg was pleased because the weather was so mild. "It is still pretty warm here. In Virginia they started having hoarfrost already. But here we do not have to worry about that yet."[2]

Since early July the tri-state area surrounding Chattanooga sweltered under a scorching sun that hardened the ground until it cracked. Not a single drop of rain fell in three months. Nature chose to remedy this oversight with a vengeance shortly after the Eleventh Corps arrived in Bridgeport. Overnight a torrential downpour turned parched, blistered earth into deep, clinging mud that entombed everything with wheels. Roads became impassable. Supplies grew scarce. When men opened barrels of crackers they were greeted by hundreds of glutted worms. Improperly packaged salt-pork rotted into contaminated refuse. For several days, until the deluge abated, the men subsisted on half-rations.[3] Soon Wickesberg's early enthusiasm for Bridgeport waned. "We had pretty bad times here already. The whole army was on half rations. And then the things we got were rotten yet. The crackers, for instance, had worms in them. And we did not have anything else except that lousy stuff and a little coffee with it, and a little bacon. But anyone who had only a penny left bought himself some bread for it because there are bakeries here. We sometimes had pretty bad food already, but it never was as bad as now."[4] Damkoehler's impressions were similar: "Here we have the same rations which are crackers, sugar and coffee and one half pound of meat. No rice or beans. Our troops are half-starved and work day and night digging trenches....It is worse for the riding horses. We have no corn for them. They are eating in the fields now while I am writing."[5] Winkler, too, found the plight of the animals especially severe. The "mules and horses look wretched and are almost wholly without forage."[6]

Sutlers scalped food and other supplies at outrageous prices in blatant profiteering. With the rail lines behind them temporarily cut, news also became a scarce commodity. "There is no mail communication," Winkler wrote, "no communication at all."[7] Many soldiers followed Karl Wickesberg's lead by writing home for "pectoral tea," leather boots, foodstuffs, and new clothing, but the letters could not begin their journeys until the rail lines were restored.[8]

While they waited for the supply line to reopen, and for the rain to subside enough for Hooker's command to take to the roads, new changes occurred in the command structure. Within the regiment, Major Baetz, suffering from the effects of his Gettysburg wound and still smarting from the anathemas heaped upon the Germans in the Eleventh Corps, resigned. Capt. Winkler accepted promotion to major in his stead. In the three months between September 1 and November 30 several other changes occurred: Charles Schmidt replaced Winkler as captain of Company B, with Joseph Maschauer replacing Schmidt as first lieutenant of Company H; Lt. George P. Traeumer replaced Philip Schlosser who resigned as adjutant; Conrad Grode rose to first lieutenant in Company A; Robert Mueller replaced John P. Seemann as captain of Company C; and Christian Phillip replaced Otto Troemel whose Gettysburg wounds required him to resign as first lieutenant in Company F.[9]

Other changes took place in the brigade when Carl Schurz reorganized his division into three brigades, replacing the previous two brigade structure. As a result, Krzyżanowski's brigade lost the veteran 75th Pennsylvania and 68th New York. Four regiments remained: the 26th Wisconsin, Captain Michael Esembaux's 58th New York, Lt.

Colonel John T. Lockman's 119th New York, and Lt. Colonel William T. Logie's 141st New York.[10]

While the troops waited to move toward the besieged federal forces in Chattanooga, Krzyżanowski's brigade, under the temporary command of Colonel Jacobs, conducted picket and fatigue duties and sent out daily reconnaissance patrols to ascertain the strength and position of the enemy—glamorless, tiring tasks, but necessary for the success of the coming campaign. In one of the larger actions, a rebel force estimated at 1,000 men threatened a tunnel at Cowan, Tennessee, on the Elk River, driving in the pickets, cutting telegraph wires, and obstructing the railroad tracks. To meet this challenge, Gen. Hooker ordered the Eleventh Corps to dispatch a like force "under your most resolute officers" to guard the important tunnel and rail lines in that area.[11] Since transport was limited, Assistant Adjutant General Theodore Meysenburg cautioned that "Special pains must be taken to transport as many men as possible on the limited number of cars."[12]

Under Jacobs' command, the better part of the brigade, reinforced by a regiment from the 1st Brigade, prepared to move. Winkler, in command of the Sigel Regiment while Jacobs commanded the brigade, found it "rather hard" to rouse the exhausted men, "but in a few moments they were out." The men marched down to the platform where the entire force crowded into two small trains for the thirty-mile journey.[13] By 11:00 p.m. on Saturday, October 9, the trains were underway. Moving at a very slow rate, they arrived at Stevenson, only ten miles from their starting point, at 4:00 a.m. After "a long stop," they moved on into the rising sun, finally arriving at their destination well after daylight. There they found the rebels—probably a small raiding party rather than the large host reported by the skittish tunnel guards—nowhere to be found. Winkler detailed Adjutant Traeumer and fifty men to remove the obstacles from the tracks and air shafts, mostly rocks and logs thrown there in haste by the raiders the previous evening. Meanwhile, he went to the top of the hill to survey the surrounding countryside while the other regiments searched and secured the area, then everyone boarded the trains for the trip back to camp. Karsten recorded their arrival in camp as 3:00 a.m.[14]

Winkler found the whole affair an unnecessary annoyance resulting from the failure of the tunnel guards and their supports to do their duty properly. Because of their "unsoldierly" conduct and "panic-stricken flight," the force had to be sent from Bridgeport on what was essentially, by then, a wild goose chase.[15] The same sense of frustration can be felt in Sergt. Wickesberg's description of the incident: "Everything was so secret and quiet that we did not know what it meant. We had to get ready, and off we went to the railroad. We were packed into the railroad cars like sardines. Into oxcars and horsecars, nobody cared where. Then we left. After about a 35 mile ride, we had reached our destination. And we were supposed to take a few hundred Rebels prisoner, where there were no Rebels."[16]

Another such expedition began on Friday, October 23. The previous night, orders arrived for the Sigel Regiment to be ready to march at 6:00 a.m. "with one day's rations, from which we inferred that we would be back at night." Under the command of Lt. Col. Charles Asmussen, Chief of Staff of the Eleventh Corps, the 26th, in company with the 143rd New York from the 1st Brigade, 3rd Division, marched off along the Branch Railroad via Shellmound to Gordon's coal mines. The purpose of the expedition was to rescue a locomotive and freight cars, a mission Gen. Howard felt some anxiety over because "they are so near the rebels that it is rather risky staying out so far."[17]

"It was raining cats and dogs," Karsten wrote in his diary. "We had to help rebuild the railroad bridge which was burned by the rebels. Also, we had to get a locomotive and several cars from the coal mine where the rebels tried to burn them. I saw the famous Nickajack Cave as well as the salt mines."[18] Rather than a one-day task, the force did not return until about 9:00 p.m. on the evening of the 24th, their one-day's rations long since consumed. "It rained nearly all the time," Winkler reported, "and we had rather a rough time of it and were so glad to get home."[19]

Back in Bridgeport, the regiment continued picket and fatigue duties, drilled daily, and complained all the while about the "dismal" weather with its incessant rain and mud. A reconnaissance made by three companies to the south of the Tennessee River under Capt. Fuchs captured two rebel scouts, but otherwise there was only routine camp life. Trains arrived only infrequently, thus news and provisions were sparce and could not be counted upon from day to day. Even the prospect of change was welcomed, but often proved disappointing. "As we retired at half past eight o'clock last night," Winkler wrote on October 16, "the sky was brilliant with its thousands of stars. It was a cheering sight for us, somewhat as the rainbow must have been to Noah, for even if it did not tell us that the days of deluge were past forever, it did seem to promise that to-day's sun should rise unobscured; but in this land of treason, signs are false, the first peer through the opening of my tent this morning showed lowering skies."[20]

By mid-October the weather also began to turn cold, alternating between warm days and cold nights as the onset of winter neared. Winkler found "such a scarcity of blankets" that he slept "in full-dress uniform, lacking only boots and spurs," but nevertheless had "to tremble with cold all night."[21] The troops suffered proportionally more, especially those exposed on the picket lines or in the rifle pits during the long, damp, cold nights. But as the days passed, plans began to unfold for the final push to relieve the besieged Union forces in Chattanooga.

Wauhatchie

To coordinate the relief of Chattanooga, in mid-October the government appointed Gen. Ulysses S. Grant to command of the new Military Division of the Mississippi. Grant arrived in Chattanooga on October 23 to assume personal command of the Union efforts. At the time, Bragg's Confederate army occupied the heights to the east and south of the city, with its cavalry operating north of the city. This left only a long, circuitous wagon route of some sixty miles as the lifeline connecting the city to federal supply bases. With the onset of the rainy days of October, this route became problematical at best. A shorter route via Kelley's and Brown's ferries existed, but Confederate forces in Lookout Valley and on Raccoon Mountain made this route inaccessible. Grant assigned Hooker's force the important task of opening this vital supply line into the city.[22]

To accomplish this mission, Hooker needed to secure possession of a rail and water route into the city. With this objective in mind his infantrymen crossed the Tennessee River on the night of October 26, the Eleventh Corps in the advance, to begin the campaign. Orders arrived in the Sigel Regiment on the previous evening directing it to be ready to march at 9:00 a.m. On the road at the appointed time, the men crossed the Tennessee River, moving northeasterly along the railroad

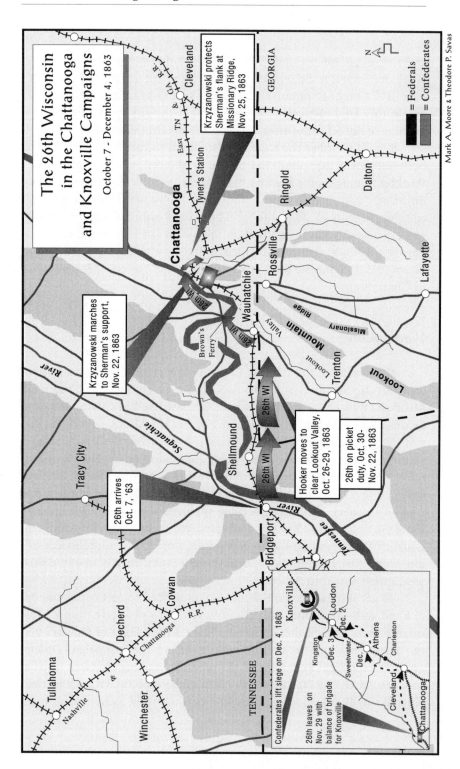

The 26th Wisconsin in the Chattanooga and Knoxville Campaigns
October 7 - December 4, 1863

Krzyzanowski protects Sherman's flank at Missionary Ridge, Nov. 25, 1863

Krzyzanowski marches to Sherman's support, Nov. 22, 1863

Hooker moves to clear Lookout Valley, Oct. 26-29, 1863

26th on picket duty, Oct. 30- Nov. 22, 1863

26th arrives Oct. 7, '63

Confederates lift siege on Dec. 4, 1863

26th leaves on Nov. 29 with balance of brigade for Knoxville

= Federals
= Confederates

Mark A. Moore & Theodore P. Savas

following the base of Raccoon Mountain in the direction of the besieged city. The road, which Karsten described as "mountainous and bad," was in "very bad" condition, the marching through constant "mire" being "very disagreeable." At Lookout Creek Confederate pickets burned a wooden railroad bridge, but skirmishers quickly put the rebels to flight and the column continued on, crossing the narrow stream with relative ease. Cautiously, they advanced into Lookout Valley.[23]

Posted high above the narrow, rocky roads, on the steep, craggy slopes of Lookout Mountain, Confederate artillery lobbed shells upon the blue-clad infantry below. The column advanced with prudent caution, flankers in place to guard against any ambush. As they trudged along, the report of hostile muskets burst upon the skirmishers from a woods bordering the dirt road. Col. Krzyżanowski rushed reinforcements forward, outflanking the woods and turning it into a trap for its occupants. With the proficiency of veterans who gained their experience in a year of hard campaigning in Virginia, the men methodically cleared the hostile area at a cost of one man dead and one wounded. The rebel loss in this small affair was four killed and at least eight wounded.[24]

By 3:00 p.m. the Sigel Regiment reached Brown's Ferry on the Tennessee River, the perilous transit into Lookout Valley accomplished. Apparently pleased with the successful march, General Hooker ordered a halt for the evening before all his forces arrived. "We got into camp at night in quite a pleasant valley," Winkler reported, "pitched our tents and went to sleep at an early hour."[25]

Although most of the units lay around Brown's Ferry, General John W. Geary's division halted at Wauhatchie about three to four miles away. Observing this division of forces, Confederate General Bragg determined to destroy Geary's isolated force by means of a daring night assault by Longstreet's Corps. Longstreet ordered General Micah Jenkins' division to attack Geary, taking care also to dispatch General Evander Law to prevent Hooker from sending relief to the isolated Union division. Law placed his blocking force on a small hillock overlooking the Brown's Ferry-Wauhatchie Road.[26]

While Longstreet maneuvered his forces for the attack, Hooker, repeating his earlier errors at Chancellorsville, congratulated himself upon the success of his movement. In the twilight hours of October 28 he remained inactive, allowing his troops to cook supper, relax, and retire for the evening. As darkness enveloped Lookout Valley, firing occasionally broke out along the picket lines. Once again, as he had done nearly six months before, Hooker took little notice of it.[27]

Back near Wauhatchie, where Geary's division of the Twelfth Corps encamped for the evening, Ernst Damkoehler moved slowly forward with the Eleventh Corps supply trains. The hour was already late and there remained four miles of unsafe roads between them and their own corps, so the quartermaster halted the supply train to spend the night with Geary's troops. Damkoehler and his comrades "started a fire and covered ourselves with our saddle blankets and after we got a cup of coffee from some soldiers, we believed ourselves very comfortable." They were not. About 11:00 p.m. sudden firing broke out along Geary's lines. Startled by the unexpected commotion, Damkoehler "got up and saddled the horses," but still "did not believe they would attack."[28]

No sooner had Damkoehler returned to his campfire than Longstreet's veterans of the Army of Northern Virginia surged out of the darkness, thousands of piercing rebel yells shattering the nighttime calm. "We lay down again by the fire, and all of a sudden our pickets were driven back and the Rebels followed twice as fast. Not even 200 steps away from us we heard their yelling as they made the charge and at the same time fired several volleys into us. We were directly by a Battery and the wagon train of the 12th Corps for which the Rebels had especially meant it. We also received the whole hail of musketry and I can't understand that not one of us or the horses were wounded. It took a short time to jump up and put the bridles on the horses and we (as non-combatants) took the safest way out and rode back to the train."[29]

While Damkoehler escaped the rebel onslaught, his comrades in the Sigel Regiment, some four miles away, were only just becoming aware of the nearby danger. About 11:00 p.m. the familiar sound of guns echoed down the valley from Wauhatchie. Roused by this unexpected alarm, officers and men rose at once. A quick series of orders brought the men into line, ready to respond when needed. As Colonel Jacobs formed his ranks, Hooker instructed Schurz to move his division to Geary's aid. Krzyżanowski's brigade fell in line behind Hector Tyndale's brigade, which led a hasty rush into the darkness. Colonel Friedrich Hecker's brigade followed Krzyżanowski, with Orland Smith's brigade from Steinwehr's division bringing up the rear.[30]

The Sigel Regiment marched back along the narrow road it advanced upon that afternoon. Though illuminated by a bright moon, the shadows of surrounding hills and woods produced an eerily ominous scene. Suddenly a volley of musketry blazed out of the darkness to strike down several unsuspecting men in Tyndale's lead brigade. Schurz ordered Tyndale to advance on the unseen enemy, sending an aide to instruct Krzyżanowski to halt and await the outcome of the fight. It was a sound move. For all Schurz knew the murky shadows ahead might conceal an entire army.[31]

As soon as he received Schurz's order, Krzyżanowski stopped his advance, moved his brigade off the roadway to make room for the others, and formed his regiments in an open field facing the firing. Drawn up in reserve in double lines, the Sigel Regiment stood prepared to either receive an assault or move forward as the situation might dictate. While they deployed, Colonel Hecker, receiving no order to halt, continued along the road until he passed Krzyżanowski's stationary brigade. At that point Hecker met General Howard's aide, who ordered him to halt in reserve near Krzyżanowski's brigade.[32]

By the time Orland Smith's command arrived, Tyndale's troops had successfully uncovered the rebel positions. Side by side, Smith and Tyndale advanced up the small hillock against Law's Confederates. In minutes the Southerners began retreating. As they did, Hooker arrived upon the field in front of Krzyżanowski's brigade. Standing beside each other, the general and the Polish colonel peered into the night to catch a glimpse of the distant muzzle flashes.[33] Finally, an order from Schurz obliged Krzyżanowski to move part of his brigade forward to close a gap between the brigades of Tyndale and Smith. The order specifically directed the colonel to lead his men in person because the position was one of great importance. In less than ten minutes Krzyżanowski led the 26th Wisconsin and another regiment into the breach, holding his ground until the conflict ended. His remaining two regiments, much depleted in strength after posting the division's pickets and detailing men to escort prisoners back to Chattanooga, constituted barely more than color guards.[34]

When order finally replaced confusion, Hecker's brigade, reinforced by Krzyżanowski's 141st New York, received belated orders to advance to Geary's aid. Krzyżanowski spent a sleepless night holding the position assigned to him. At 6:00 a.m. he received orders to advance to Wauhatchie. Although the infantry firing had long since ceased, the column was subjected to shellfire from the rebel batteries

Anton Ewens, Company A. A Cooper from Milwaukee, wounded in Lookout Valley

on Lookout Mountain. One missile exploded amid the 26th Wisconsin, severely wounding Corp. Albin Knolle and Pvt. Anton Ewens in Company E, but the column pushed on, covering the distance to Geary's position in about an hour. The troops arrived at Geary's head-quarters at 7:15 a.m. and went into place on his far right where they extended the defensive line to include a vital railroad junction. "We stayed there on the right through rain and mud," Winkler wrote, "without tents, and very short of provisions, until very late" on the night of October 31, "without sleeping at all, watching the guns on the mountains right opposite, expecting every moment that they would open upon us." According to Gen. Geary's report, the men carried out their task of constructing breastworks and traverses with a great deal of skill and cheerfulness.[35]

The Battle of Wauhatchie was a disorganized affair that spawned differing accounts among the various after-action reports. Neither Confederate nor Union losses approached the terrible tolls exacted by Chancellorsville or Gettysburg, yet the result was impressive. The gateway to Chattanooga stood open and the Union army in that besieged city received a new lease on life.

Relieving Chattanooga

Once the vital supply line to Chattanooga was open it had to be protected. For the first three weeks in November the task of protecting this "Cracker Line" went to Hooker's force. It was a glamorless assignment, but one essential to the success of the Chattanooga campaign. Confederate artillery on the summit of Lookout Mountain, 1,464 feet above the valley below, dominated the landscape for miles around. Every day Southern gunners hurled shells into the Union lines. Though they did little actual damage, the shells did create some tense moments. The constant booming of rebel guns became so much a part of the soldier's daily lives they fashioned a game out of it. Eager eyes scanned Lookout Mountain for the puff of smoke that invariably identified the firing of a cannon. When one occurred the soldiers quickly placed bets on where the deadly projectile would hit. Yet, the seemingly random firing was not without effect. As the Sigel Regiment hugged the ground in its exposed rifle pits, shells from Lookout Mountain wounded two men. On another occasion, a rebel shell landed between Winkler's tent and the cook's tent, burrowing several feet into the ground without exploding.[36]

Daily life was difficult, rain continued to fall at frequent intervals and rations were slow to arrive, often necessitating a reduction to three-quarter rations for days at a time. Winkler complained "We have lived such a comfortless life ever since we left Bridgeport; we have not been in camp since; we have been always moving about, digging rifle pits in every position we occupied, and been constantly on the watch for an attack from the enemy. We have nothing with us but shelter tents and often we were not allowed to put them up, and crackers and coffee with bacon and occasionally a little fresh beef is all we have to subsist on."[37] As the month progressed, rations became scarce. For a week, chilling rains fell almost daily. Intensified by the cool, damp climate, sickness spread through the ranks.[38]

Expecting at any moment to be moved about, as had become the practice in the valley, the men foresook the usual practice of making their camp more comfortable. When the weather turned cold they paid the price for this decision. "It is very cold," Winkler wrote, "and my fingers are too numb for writing." Since they thought their stay would be only temporary, they "had not deemed it worth while to go to such extravagance as to build fire-places. As I went shivering to bed last night, I made up my mind that I would have a fire-place if it were only for one day's use."[39]

While the regiment lay in Lookout Valley, a command change took place. At the time of the reorganization of Schurz's division, Col. Jacobs had temporary command of Krzyżanowski's brigade. Thus, when a new third brigade was created for the division its command went to Col. Friedrich Hecker of the 82nd Illinois. Since Hecker was his junior, Jacobs felt offended, believing he should have been named commander of the new brigade. In response to Jacobs' protest, Gen. Howard, commanding the Eleventh Corps, assured the angered colonel there was no evaluation of his capabilities in comparison to those of Hecker's, and no slight was intended. "You were commanding a brigade," Howard explained, and "I was told were likely to continue so. Col. Hecker is an energetic man as well as yourself. I thought of combining those three Regts. for their good but with no thought of disparagement of you or your Regt. I did not think that you ranked him till my attention was called to it Friday. Col. Hecker is not 'preferred' to you in any sense i.e. I mean by me that I know of."[40]

Shortly after this incident, Jacobs received a letter from his brother-in-law containing the disturbing news that the colonel's wife was seriously ill and urging him to come home at once. Whether the disagreement about command of the new brigade had anything to do with Jacobs' decision to leave at this juncture, or whether it was solely because of the distressing news about his wife's condition, cannot be determined. Regardless, the colonel obtained an appointment as recruiting officer and left for Milwaukee on November 8. Command of the regiment again devolved on Winkler.[41]

Throughout most of November the regiment manned its rifle pits in the valley, cold, hungry, and tired of the monotony. When not on the firing line, the companies dug more rifle pits, built breastworks, constructed corduroy roads, and performed other laborious tasks. The heavy fog frequently seen in the valley that time of year came as a welcome relief from the daily shelling. "This is a pleasant morning," Winkler wrote on November 18, "not a breeze stirring; a heavy fog that enshrouded everything a short time ago is lifting and the sun is coming forth. Old Lookout is blind today, cannot see through the fog and has not fired a shot."[42]

Occasionally, when a train or a supply wagon would stop on its way into the besieged city, the regiment would enjoy a holiday from the hardtack and coffee that became commonplace. To further relieve the monotonous diet, the regiment went on a foraging expedition toward Trenton, leaving at 7:00 a.m. on November 11 and not returning until 3:00 a.m. on the 12th. Karsten reported marching forty miles during which he "arrested" one goose. On other occasions individual enterprise yielded rewards. One day Henry Peiper acquired a small amount of flour and other delicacies he prepared for Winkler's mess. By "taxing his culinary talents to the utmost, we had biscuits to take the place of hard tack at breakfast this morning. The judgment of the mess was that they were excellent; yes, tough biscuits, without butter, and coffee without milk, constitute an excellent breakfast. Today too, for the first time, except once at Bridgeport, since we came to this department we have had potatoes for dinner. Ah, you don't know what a luxury a potato is."[43]

Life in Lookout Valley ended abruptly on November 22 with orders to move to the support of Gen. William T. Sherman's proposed assault on the Confederate lines east of Chattanooga. Marching with three days rations and without knapsacks, the regiment, only 270 strong, crossed the Tennessee River on pontoon bridges at Brown's Ferry, moved north to Chattanooga, passed the city, recrossed the Tennessee River to the east, and moved to the far left of the Union line. There the Sigel Regiment fell into line on the right of Orland Smith's brigade, connecting with the 136th New York of that command, and immediately dug a line of rifle pits. Krzyżanowski's brigade formed in time to act as reserve for Sherman's assault on Orchard Knob. Following this successful attack, the 26th Wisconsin fought a sharp skirmish at Citico Creek that enabled the brigade to move into position to cover the otherwise exposed flank of the Northern army. The entire movement and the ensuing skirmish were accomplished without loss.[44]

For the next two days the regiment exchanged picket fire with the Confederates, capturing several deserters and some 80 to 100 prisoners.[45] While they provided cover for Sherman's troops before Chattanooga, behind them in Lookout Valley the rest of Hooker's command contended with the Confederates on Lookout Mountain. With the rest of the army looking on in disbelief, Hooker's troops moved out to the assault, battling their way up the formidable mountain nearly everyone presumed impregnable. On they went, climbing, clawing, and battling to the top, evicting the rebel defenders and seizing the dominant heights commanding the city and the valley through which flowed its lifeline of supplies. It was a pivotal event in the campaign, and Damkoehler, who had a close view of the assault from the Eleventh Corps supply train in the valley, could not wait to write home about the event. "Must tell you the good news," he wrote to Mathilde. "Lookout Mountain is ours. We are in the midst of the battle. The capture of Lookout was a sensational sight. Our boys started at the right time and drove the Rebels like wild rabbits out of their holes. The 'Hurrah' calls of our boys lasted to late in the evening when the hill was in our permanent positive possession."[46]

On the other side of Chattanooga, the men in the Sigel Regiment could hear the sounds of battle echoing up to them from the valley behind. The noise "lasted long after dark," and it was not until late at night that word arrived of their comrade's success. When it did, the men were beside themselves with joy, cheering and huzzahing well into the night. To Sgt. Wickesberg, "It seemed that the hurrah-calling did not want to end."[47]

Yet not all the Confederates were ready to give up. Forty thousand defiant men rallied to the "Stars and Bars" atop Missionary Ridge. On November 25 General Ulysses S. Grant, Federal commander-in-chief in the west, ordered an assault on the Confederate rifle pits at the base of Missionary Ridge. As the assault waves moved forward, the Sigel Regiment pushed back Southern skirmishers near Chickamauga Creek on the Union left, thus preventing the attackers from being caught in a deadly enfilading fire. In Company F, a ball passed through Frank Fisher's hat, but there were no casualties. Grant's men easily overpowered the rifle pits. Then, without orders, surged up the steep slope. With Northern generals looking on in utter disbelief the Southern troops on Missionary Ridge broke, fleeing from the scene in abject rout. Cheering Union infantry followed the retreating Confederates.[48]

That evening everyone sensed victory, though the extent was not immediately clear. Nevertheless, everyone knew the day had gone well for the Union and Winkler found everyone "jubilant." At 4:00 a.m. orders arrived to break camp and march at once. "[W]e started in the dark," Winkler recalled, "and it was very foggy." The regiment moved back toward Chattanooga, then crossed the Chickamauga River at its mouth. As it crossed, a staff officer arrived from Eleventh Corps headquarters with the welcome news they were "in pursuit of the fleeing foe." When the good news circulated, "there was rejoicing, every heart was glad. I never knew the column to march so rapidly," Winkler marveled. "We halted for a time; some one suggested this was Thanksgiving Day in Wisconsin; I thought of the holiday at home; remarks were passed, how the people were spending it in a social circle; yes, they were spending it festively, but this army was enjoying it and there was not a man who would have exchanged his proud place for a seat at the festive board."[49]

As the pursuit progressed, tons of abandoned supplies and equipment fell to the victorious troops. Confederate General Bragg had "destroyed everything," Wickesberg wrote. "He had burned everything at the railroad stations. They left their ammunition and everything and ran away as fast as they could." During the pursuit "60 to 70 prisoners fell into our hands."[50] Only danger from another quarter slowed the Union columns. Formal pursuit had to be called off on November 28. Instead of continuing after Bragg, Grant was obliged to answer the plea of Union forces under General Ambrose Burnside besieged in Knoxville by Longstreet's corps.[51]

Knoxville

Failing to prevent the opening of the "Cracker Line" to supply federal troops in Chattanooga, Gen. Bragg ordered Longstreet's infantry and Wheeler's cavalry northward to assist Gen. Samuel Jones' troops operating against Burnside in northeastern Tennessee. Bragg hoped the threat to Burnside would ease pressure on his own forces and help him reestablish a seige of Chattanooga or force Grant to abandon the city. The move succeeded in forcing Burnside inside the defensive works around Knoxville, to the great consternation of the authorities in Washington, but Grant correctly chose to ignore the threat and concentrate on defeating Bragg's army. This accomplished, under growing pressure to assist Burnside and prevent the fall of Knoxville, Grant dispatched a force under Gen. William T. Sherman to Burnside's aid.[52]

The most important factor in the relief of Knoxville was time. Burnside's army lay on the verge of starvation. A delay, even of a day or two, could spell doom for his troops. The Sigel Regiment marched lightly, forsaking tents and supply wagons for the sake of speed. Packed with ammunition, the men were able to squeeze little food into their blanket rolls or knapsacks. Marching at 6:00 a.m. on Sunday, November 29, they moved steadily through damp, cool air, following the East Tennessee and Georgia Railroad through Cleveland on the same day and Charleston on the 30th. There a detachment helped repair the railroad bridge over the Hiwassee River before the regiment crossed early on December 1. Halting to receive its share of some captured rebel flour and salt, the regiment reached Riceville without incident at noon on December 1 and pushed on through to Athens that evening.[53] "We marched through good Country & neat villages," Capt. Lackner recalled.[54] Although Winkler found "the days very pleasant," the nights were "very cold" and the marches "strenuous."[55]

More hard marching on the following day brought them through Sweetwater to Philadelphia on the evening of the 2nd. Rations soon gave out, forcing the men to forage for food as they plodded along in the wake of retreating rebels sent to disrupt their march.[56] "[W]e had to survive through food that farmers gave us or that which we took from the enemy," Sgt. Wickesberg reported.[57] Major Winkler pronounced the land "a fine agricultural country, but it is very much exhausted. It was with difficulty that we could get a cow and ox and [a] few sheep or

hogs from a farmer as we passed along, but we had to take them to subsist our column."[58] Still they pushed on, brushing aside the
Confederate rear guard whenever it appeared.

On December 3 Krzyżanowski's brigade led the advance upon
Loudon, Tennessee, a major Confederate supply base. Winkler deployed
the regiment in battle array, skirmishers out front, and pushed forward.
The brigade swept into the outskirts of the city so quickly the rebels
were forced to destroy or abandon huge quantities of stores they could
not remove. Sgt. Wickesberg reported the troops "were so close behind
[the Confederates] that they let 2 locomotives and 42 railroad cars run
into a river from a high bridge. And a hospital with 300 sick and wounded men fell into our hands." Large quantities of supplies fell to the
brigade's advance, temporarily easing the men's plight.[59]

After resting and recuperating all day Friday, a halt that allowed
the rest of the column to catch up and the bridge over the river to be
rebuilt, the advance toward Davis' Ferry resumed at 1:00 a.m. Saturday
morning. Continuing on in the face of sporadic sniping, the regiment
made remarkable speed over the muddy roadways. Major Winkler was
well-pleased with the men's performance under the trying conditions.
"[T]he regiment never marched better, with fewer stragglers; we have
been in positions that tried them too."[60]

By December 5 the Federal advance reached Little River, fifteen
miles from Knoxville. Orders arrived to resume the march to Knoxville
at 6:30 a.m. the following day, but their rapid movement had already
foiled Longstreet's plans for starving Burnside into submission.
Convinced he could not maintain his siege against the Northern reinforcements, Longstreet quietly withdrew back into Virginia. The
Confederate siege of Knoxville failed because of the rapid marching
and willing sacrifices of thousands of Union infantrymen. Not the
least of these were the officers and men of the Sigel Regiment.[61]

The end of the siege, however, brought little rest for the rescuers.
Krzyżanowski's brigade halted for one day, then, on December 7, began
the arduous march back toward Chattanooga without ever having seen
the city it helped save. With food supplies now exhausted, the nearby
farms fell prey to Northern foragers struggling to survive off the countryside, but the supplies they brought in proved "scanty and of inferior
quality." By the 10th they reached the "pretty village" of Athens, but
their plight continued. Frequent rains covered the cold, rocky roads

with a slippery mud. One man in four lacked shoes, while blankets were a luxury. Threadbare clothing proved inadequate against the icy December rains. Brutally cold winds brought sleet that produced a muddy bog by day, a frozen vice at night. Perpetually damp clothing froze to men's bodies as they slept. Equipment parked overnight had to be pried free in the morning before it could be moved. Even the supply of coffee gave out, forcing the men to roast corn or wheat kernels as a substitute. It was, Col. Krzyżanowski wrote with dramatic understatement, a "terrible ordeal."[62]

Lashed by freezing winds, pummeled by thunderstorms and sleet, threatened by lightning, many of the weary men developed colds, bronchitis, or pneumonia. We "lived entirely on the Country," Capt. Lackner wrote in his diary, and endured "the most severe marches."[63] While the officers generally managed to save some food and coffee, and thereby fared better, the men were almost totally destitute. Sunday, December 13, found the column "still wandering about without communication" as it passed through Charleston, Tennessee. "Our march is very slow," Winkler lamented. "Flour and meat is all the ration we get; wheat has been distributed to supply the place of coffee, but we have a little coffee and sugar left in our mess. We have also ample opportunity to get our flour baked into bread and sometimes to buy a pound of butter, so that we fare pretty well, but for the men it is hard. They are deficient in everything, food, blankets, and the shoes are giving out as well as salt; it is really hard on them, and therefore highly desirable that we get back to our lines of communication soon."[64]

On they marched through Calhoun, a "poor, miserable little place" on the Hiwassee River, a branch of the Tennessee. In the distance to the east, the high ranges of the Smoky Mountains were clearly visible. Despite the conditions, the scenery made a very positive impression on Winkler. "This East Tennessee is a magnificent country, the finest I have seen in the south." The weather broke somewhat on the 14th, the afternoon becoming "perfectly comfortable in the open air and in the sun."[65]

The march began again at 7:30 a.m. on the 15th, the 26th Wisconsin in the lead as the column marched through Cleveland half an hour after noon. While passing through town General Schurz rode up with good news. As Winkler explained it, he "told us...we were going back to our old camps, there to rest and receive the necessary outfit before we can enter upon another campaign. The intelligence was hailed with joy by everybody. There in that camp, the boys have their huts already built, their knapsacks and all superfluous property was left there, many of their companions who were sick when we left are still there, and of course they would rather return to those quarters—a sort of home to them—than put up new ones. I too am glad of it."[66]

Tired, sore, cold, wet, hungry, and sick, the columns of scarecrows staggered on as best they could. On the 16th Wickesberg reported they "had to march until 12 O'Clock midnight. And it was raining all the time. We had to wade up to our knees in mud. During the whole time we got our food from the enemy and the farmers."[67] Winkler "sat up all night, a drenching rain and mud knee deep preventing every thought of sleep."[68] He felt "the hardships of the campaign had been extraordinary. The men were mostly without blankets, shoes were badly worn out and on the way back quite a number were absolutely barefooted."[69] When they finally arrived back at their camps near Chattanooga on December 17, after another full day of marching, Ernst Damkoehler, who spent the campaign in camp with the corps wagon train, was shocked by the "ragged" appearance they made after their "terrible" ordeal.[70] No doubt the vision of his regiment marching in exhausted, sick, and emaciated from the rigors of the Knoxville campaign was fresh in his mind when, two weeks later, he explained to his wife that as a member of the quartermaster department, "Even though we are not so much exposed to fatigue as the soldiers in the Regiment, due to our business we are exposed to wind and weather, [but] our fate is gold towards the one of the soldiers."[71]

Thankful to be back in camp once again, the suffering men found no supplies awaiting them. No one expected them back so soon. Rather than sustenance, the men found words of censure from General Howard who chastised them for their foraging expeditions. Little else could have been expected given the privations of the campaign. Fortunately, the commanding general displayed a better understanding of the circumstances surrounding the march. In a letter to Howard, General Sherman enthusiastically praised the conduct of the Eleventh Corps during the successful campaign that saved Knoxville, and more importantly Burnside's army, from a defeat that would have dimmed the luster and importance of the victories around Chattanooga.[72]

Winter Quarters

Settling thankfully into winter quarters in Lookout Valley, the exhausted men set about making their camp more hospitable. Winkler's tent was "being fixed again with an oaken floor in it and a huge fire-place."[73] With some time to relax, and writing materials at last available, many of the men wrote extensively to family and friends to catch up on news they missed while in the field. Sgt. Wickesberg wrote to tell his parents he was "still happy and healthy."[74] Capt. Lackner penned an entry in his diary. Others assured their families of their continued good health, sought news of family and friends, or asked those at home to send postage stamps, clothing, foodstuffs, thread, or other items they needed but could not obtain.

Over the next week the regiment went on fatigue duty, building corduroy roads in and about the camps. On Christmas Eve "they brought home all the tools they had with them" and spent Christmas morning "improving their quarters, little log huts with a good chimney to heat them, and a tent to shelter them from the outside."[75] Unlike their first Christmas away from Wisconsin, few seem to have taken note of the day or described any particular celebrations to the folks back home. It seems to have passed as a welcome holiday of rest rather than anything approaching the festive occasion twelve months earlier. The arrival of the new year met a similar reception. After several days of rain and heavy winds, New Year's Day dawned a frigid nine degrees. Winkler received his officers, then set out to pay his respects to Col. Krzyżanowski and Gen. Schurz. He considered it "not much different than other days here."[76]

Yet, while most considered themselves lucky to be back in camp without having to fight a major battle, the toll of the recent campaigns was only just becoming evident. Exposed to the elements during the march up Lookout Valley and the grueling, bitter campaign to Knoxville, men fell ill at an alarming rate. Sniffles turned to colds, colds to bronchitis, bronchitis to pneumonia, with startling rapidity in an age without antibiotics. August Jaeger died in Lookout Valley on November 5. August Schwenecke passed away in Bridgeport, Alabama, on December 2. On December 10, death claimed John Ollig who had been left behind in the hospital when the regiment marched off to

Knoxville. Gotthardt Franke and Nicholas Roeder both died in a Chattanooga hospital three days after Christmas. Julius Krueger succumbed in the same city on New Year's Eve. And still death was not appeased. January claimed the lives of Christian Entz, Heinrich Lingsch, and William Lindloge. Corp. Ehlert Tiedemann and Corp. Samuel Johnston succumbed in February.[77] Officially they were all listed as having "died of disease," yet they were victims of the war as surely as if they had been torn asunder by canister. The cost of war was high.

At home in Wisconsin, as the year ended family and friends worried about their men in the service, hoping the holidays and the coming year would smile kindly on them. Col. Jacobs submitted his formal resignation on January 11, a move the *Milwaukee Sentinel* explained was due to "private affairs which fully justify him in doing so. In Howard's whole corps there is not a truer or a braver officer than Col. Jacobs."[78] Lt. Col. Boebel, his amputated leg still healing, could not take the field and would eventually submit his resignation as well. Thus, Winkler's temporary command of the regiment became permanent.[79]

The regiment stayed in Lookout Valley until January 25 when it broke camp and moved to Whiteside, Tennessee, thirteen miles from Chattanooga on the Nashville and Chattanooga railroad. Officers and men alike were disappointed to leave their now comfortable camp behind. When they arrived at their new location, they were relieved to find a pleasant campsite with fireplaces already in place for them to occupy once the units they were relieving left. One night in their tents and the next they were busily making the new campsite home. Damkoehler found it "a very nice place here, right on the Tennessee":

> We have here the Post Commissary and besides our Brigade we have perhaps 800 citizens to take care of (these are old men and women with families). All the families which are real destitute receive half rations of bacon, flour and bread. The rest of them can buy as soon as they get the order from the Provision Marshall. I feel so sorry for the poor women, of whom so many were forced to become bad. Others err through frivolity (in all it is a detestable picture how the people are humiliated).
>
> Almost every day our young people pay visits to the farms in the environs and for what reason no one can guess easily. The poverty among the people is too great. Most of the people are from the Southern Army and due to their worthless money they can do almost nothing for their families. Their farms are destroyed, fences burned down, chickens, cows and pigs were stolen by the

soldiers and only the pitiful picture of half-starved women and children was left behind. It will take a long time for the country to recover after the war is over."[80]

At their new location the men served as pickets, performed guard duty, and occasionally labored on the railroad and growing fortifications. In their spare time the officers visited Lookout Mountain where Winkler had his photograph taken sitting on the famous rock overhang.[81] In the ranks, the men made the best of camp life to relax and write home. Karl Wickesberg assured his parents of his good health and commented frequently on the unexpected moderate weather. "Up to now," he wrote on January 17, "we have only had one quarter inch of snow. But it cannot hold itself here. Sometimes it is a little cold. But up to now the frost did not penetrate 2 inches into the mud, yet. The weather here is about like April or May up there." He closed, as many did, with earnest wishes for the conclusion of the long war. "Dear Mother, I hope, God willing, the war will be over soon. Please pray for me as long as it lasts, and trust in God. He will bring everything to a good end."[82]

A week later, after receiving a letter asking whether he could get a furlough to help his father build a cabin, Wickesberg explained, "it is too cold up there." Also, "There are too many copperheads up there with you, that could tempt one too easily." Then, perhaps thinking of the broken love affair that prompted his original enlistment into the army, he noted that at home a "girl could turn one's head." Besides, before he could come home "the Star Spangled Banner has to wave through all the states of the rebellion, and Jeff Davis and his pals be exterminated."[83] Then, in another letter, he proudly requested that his family send to him "5 yards of blue ribbon, one half inch wide" so he could fashion stripes for his uniform to reflect his recent promotion to sergeant.[84]

Along with the new year, Ernst Damkoehler received the troubling news that his wife was ill again, and she and his children were in need of warm clothing for the winter. "You can imagine what impression it left on me, that deficiency in clothing and other needs is the cause of your sickness." he wrote her. "It was still my desire to surprise you this winter, but was really cured with receipt of your last lines. It would be an unexcusable sin to spend money on me to enjoy a reunion if my whole earnings are not enough to clothe you and give you the most needed necessities. Would it not be a sin to spend money for trips when the family did not have a bit of meat in the house for the last six weeks?" He promised to send her $46 as soon as they were paid.[85]

Damkoehler became increasingly concerned with newspaper reports of a particularly brutal winter in Wisconsin claiming the lives of many who could not survive the exceptional cold. "It was a great consolation for me when I received your lines and found out that you lived through all the terrible cold without any happenings," he wrote with much relief. "As the reports in the newspapers from everywhere brought to light all the casualties which the cold claimed I was overtaken with an awful fear. I thought, perhaps you were not supplied with wood and that you could not get any help in this terrible cold and other thoughts went through my mind. I was freed from all these worries and fears through your writing."[86]

When Mathilde asked about his plans to reenlist, he assured her he would not do so. "[W]ould I have anticipated that it would have lasted so long, I would never have enlisted," he confessed. Yet that did not mean he sought to escape his oath. When Wisconsin appeared ready to resort to the draft to fill its quota of men, Damkoehler explained his position in detail:

> Some one who laughed in his fist and called us nuts will make a grimace when he has to leave as a drafted man. It serves them right. The war was started and it takes soldiers to finish it. Now I can answer your question right away concerning my color. I am for war as long as a Rebel stands in the picture. If the South wants to make peace, well and good, and it should accept the offered terms. To make peace now after our conquered advantages would be treason to our country. Every good Democrat is for war and I did not expect that you wanted to put me in the category of the Copperheads. Almost every soldier, who found out the burden and fatigue of the war, wants to come home honorably and not insulted. There are just these miserable cowards who prolong the war and who are in the way of the Government. . .because they know beforehand that our Government can't step back. Most of the old Regiments enlisted once more and if the Government brings 300,000 men more in the field this winter to start a strong campaign this Spring, we hope to make an end of the Rebels during the course of next summer."[87]

Homesick and tired of the war though they may have been, most of the soldiers in the 26th Wisconsin Infantry held views similar to Damkoehler's.

By February the weather in Tennessee turned bitterly cold, precluding any further campaigning until spring. "I would have answered some time ago," Damkoehler informed his wife on February 21, "if it were not for the unbearable cold which we had here for a length of time, that held me back. As we came here from Lookout Valley it was the nicest summer weather. We did not equip our tents for cold weather and for some time it was so cold that one could not get warm near the fire."[88] Rumors, of course, abounded. Both Damkoehler and Wickesberg reported the prevailing opinion that the Eleventh and Twelfth Corps would be sent to rejoin the Army of the Potomac. Such speculation increased with the return of good weather. "The weather is excellent," Damkoehler observed in early March, "[T]he roads are in the best shape and I believe that one is only waiting for the arrival of many old Regiments to start again the 'beating-up'. . . .Our troops are in good spirit and sure of victory."[89]

Though many spoke of furloughs, few enlisted men obtained them. Sergeant Karl Karsten was among the lucky few who were able to get away, traveling to West Bend on recruiting duty.[90] Another who left, "for the good of the regiment" as he explained, was Major Winkler, who applied for permission on February 3 to return to Milwaukee to fill the regiment's depleted ranks with new recruits. Colonel John T. Lockman of the 119th New York, temporarily in command of the brigade, endorsed Winkler's request. "The 26. Regt. Wis. Vols. have shown themselves a brave & efficient Regt," explained Lockman. "Its ranks have been thinned on the well contested fields of Chancellorsville and Gettysburg. I know no other Officer in the regt. who is so well adapted to recruiting the Regt. as Major Winkler. He possesses talent, influence & energy & his presence at Milwaukee will ensure success."[91]

With him went Sgt. Charles Weinreich, Co. B; 1st Sgt. Julius Mueller, Co. C; Corp. Bartholomew Peisen, Co. D; Sgt. Charles Herrmann, Co. E; 1st Sgt. William H. Hemschemeyer, Co. F; Sgt. Philip Walldorf, Co. I, and Sgt. Henry Nolt, Co. K. Their efforts ultimately were successful in bolstering the regiment's depleted ranks with several dozen new recruits.[92]

One person Major Winkler successfully recruited did not return with him when he journeyed south again in April: Frances M. Wightman signed on as Mrs. Frederick C. Winkler on March 2, 1864.

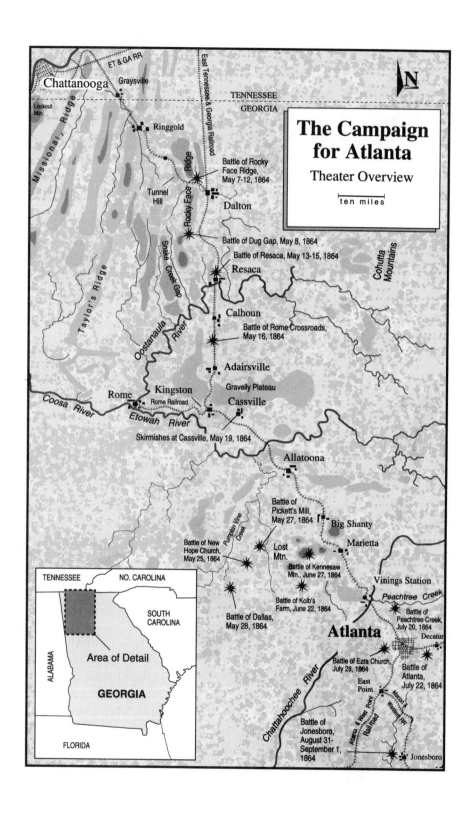

The Campaign for Atlanta

Theeater Overview

ten miles

ET & GA RR

Chattanooga   Graysville

East Tennessee & Georgia Railroad

Lookout
Mtn.

Missionary Ridge

TENNESSEE
GEORGIA

Ringgold

Battle of Rocky
Face Ridge,
May 7-12, 1864

Tunnel
Hill

Rocky Face Ridge

Dalton

Cohutta Mountains

Battle of Dug Gap, May 8, 1864

Snake Creek Gap

Battle of Resaca, May 13-15, 1864

Resaca

Taylor's Ridge

Oostanaula River

Calhoun

Battle of Rome Crossroads,
May 16, 1864

Adairsville

Coosa River

Rome   Kingston   Gravelly Plateau

Rome Railroad   Cassville

Etowah River

Skirmishes at Cassville, May 19, 1864

Allatoona

Battle of
Pickett's Mill,
May 27, 1864   Big Shanty

Pumpkin Vine Creek

Battle of New
Hope Church,
May 25, 1864   Lost
Mtn.   Marietta

Battle of Kennesaw
Mtn., June 27, 1864   Vinings Station

Peachtree Creek

Battle of Kolb's
Farm, June 22, 1864   Battle of
Peachtree Creek,
July 20, 1864

Battle of Dallas,
May 28, 1864   **Atlanta**   Decatur

Battle of Ezra Church,
July 28, 1864   Battle of
Atlanta,
July 22, 1864

East
Point

Chattahoochee River

Atlanta & West Point Railroad

Macon & Western RR

Battle of
Jonesboro,
August 31-
September 1,
1864   Jonesboro

TENNESSEE   NO. CAROLINA

SOUTH
CAROLINA

Area of Detail

ALABAMA

GEORGIA

FLORIDA

"WE HAVE TO DEAL WITH THE REBELS"
The Atlanta Campaign

While commander of the Federal armies in the west, Ulysses S. Grant advocated the consolidation of the understrength Eleventh and Twelfth Corps. Under Grant's plan, Generals Hooker and Slocum would be shelved leaving Oliver Otis Howard to command the new organization. Following Grant's appointment as General-in-Chief of the Armies of the United States on March 12, 1864, his replacement in the West, William Tecumseh Sherman, effected the consolidation. On April 4, Special Field Orders No. 105 created the new Twentieth Army Corps from the survivors of so many fields of conflict.[1] For various political and personal reasons, command of the Twentieth Corps, which retained the five-pointed star of the former Twelfth Corps as its badge, went to Joseph Hooker.[2]

As part of the reorganization that occasioned formation of the Twentieth Corps, Krzyżanowski's brigade was broken up, its regiments reassigned to bolster other understrength units. For the Badgers, the change brought assignment to the Third Brigade, Third Division, Twentieth Corps, commanded by Colonel James Wood, Jr., of the 136th New York. Formerly Orland Smith's brigade of the Eleventh Corps, it now included the 55th Ohio, 75th Ohio, 33rd Massachusetts, 136th New York, and 26th Wisconsin.[3] Major Winkler made no qualitative judgment on the reorganization, commenting only that he had known Col. Wood "a long time and have always been on friendly terms with him."[4] Sgt. Wickesberg welcomed the change. "[W]e have profited by it," he commented. "In any case, by the end of the week, we have to deal with the Rebels."[5]

One who was not happy with the changes was Ernst Damkoehler. Although "alive and in good health," the private explained to his wife Mathilde that the consolidation of the two corps meant he would have to return for duty with the regiment. "The news I have to write to you today is not very good....With the dissolving of our Brigade the Commissary Department is also out of existence, and in a few hours we also have to report to our Regiment. I was supposed to go this morning to the Regiment but through the influence of Captain Schmidt, I have to stay till the new Regiment arrives and transfer the goods to them....I think it will be hard for me in the Regiment, when in the last year I did not march 10 miles and I am not used to marching and carrying a big load on my back." With thoughts of both the hardships ahead and his family at home, he closed the letter with "A thousand kisses for you and the children."[6]

On April 22 orders arrived for the 26th Wisconsin to join its new brigade in Lookout Valley. At 6:00 a.m. the following morning, the regiment marched out of camp as the band of the 82nd Illinois played patriotic tunes. By 4:00 p.m. on a warm, sunny afternoon the men were in Lookout Valley where they pitched their tents about one mile from Brown's Ferry.[7]

The new brigade held a drill on the afternoon of April 25, but the Sigel Regiment, having only recently arrived, was excused to allow the men time to construct their camp. "To-morrow I shall commence drilling the regiment vigorously," Winkler wrote, "we must keep at it now, so as to be in good trim by the time we start on active operations, which cannot be far hence." On the 28th the regiment participated in a full division drill with both infantry and artillery firing off blank cartridges. The 29th saw a resumption of brigade drill, followed by another division outing on the 30th. "These are things we never practiced in our old brigade and division," Winkler confessed, "we are, therefore, much behind and have to work and study to keep up."[8]

As April gave way to May, Wickesberg found "The weather is nice and warm, and the trees are clad in their full green dresses."[9] With most of the sick and wounded from the previous fall's campaigns now returned, and several dozen new recruits swelling the ranks, the Sigel Regiment boasted 417 muskets. One of the new recruits was Charles Buerstatte. Born in Elberfeld, Prussia, Buerstatte arrived in the United States with his parents in 1850, settling in Manitowoc County.

Educated in the public schools, he volunteered for three years service on February 12, 1864, not yet eighteen years of age. He arrived in camp to join the Sigel Regiment in Lookout Valley on April 23, drawing his first rifled musket four days later.[10]

Buzzard Roost Gap

Following the failure of his army at Chattanooga, Bragg moved the rebel force twenty-five miles southeast to Dalton, Georgia, where he intrenched with the intention of shielding the state from invasion. In December President Davis, under increasing public pressure to relieve Bragg, appointed Joseph E. Johnston to replace the hapless commander of the Army of Tennessee. Richmond also arranged for reinforcements to bolster Johnston's forces to 60,000 infantry and 2,000 cavalry.[11]

William T. Sherman, commander of the Union armies concentrated about Chattanooga, received orders from U. S. Grant to "move against Johnston's army, to break it up, and to get into the interior of the enemy's country as far as you can, inflicting all the damage you can against their war resources."[12] Because Atlanta was an important Confederate manufacturing, transportation, and supply center, Sherman determined to move upon the city, bringing Johnston's army to a stand if possible, to deny the city and its economic support to the Confederacy. Poised to move south with Sherman were the Army of the Cumberland under Gen. George H. Thomas, the Army of the Tennessee under Gen. James B. McPherson, and the Army of the Ohio under Gen. John M. Schofield. Thomas's command included Oliver O. Howard's Fourth Corps, John M. Palmer's Fourteenth Corps, Joseph Hooker's Twentieth Corps, and Washington L. Elliott's cavalry corps. McPherson's force consisted of John A. Logan's Fifteenth Corps, Grenville M. Dodge's Sixteenth Corps, and Francis P. Blair's Seventeenth Corps. Schofield's command included his Twenty-Third Corps and Gen. George Stoneman's cavalry division. Altogether, Sherman's force numbered about 98,500 men.[13]

Striking its tents at an early hour on May 2, the 26th Wisconsin moved out of its encampment at 6:00 a.m., filing southeast over the old Chickamauga battlefield. As the men marched they passed "skeletons of horses, and every tree bears the mark of the battle, many strong trunks were broken down by artillery fire, many graves too attest the deadliness of the conflict."[14] After a trek of more than fifteen miles they arrived at Gordon's Mill, Georgia, about 3:00 p.m. By 6:00 p.m. they had erected their camp, only to receive marching orders for early the next morning.[15]

On the morning of May 3 new ammunition was distributed and the march continued. Up at 4:00 a.m. the following day, the men were on the road by 6:00, marching at a steady pace all day without a rest until they arrived at Edward's Saw and Flour Mill at Taylor's Mountain, some sixteen miles from their previous camp. In Company F, Pvt. Buerstatte embarked upon his first campaign finding the "Weather is beautiful and the air warm."[16] Having subsisted on little but crackers, coffee, and salt pork since returning to the regiment, Winkler was delighted when one of the men brought into camp "a quarter of veal" which he quickly prepared and shared with the thankful major. "[W]here he got it," the major confessed, "I have not deemed it my duty to inquire."[17]

On the 5th they paused to pitch their shelter tents at Pleasant Grove. Winkler, Buerstatte, and others took advantage of the brief opportunity to write home. Surrounded by "tall white oaks and pines," their camp rested about three miles south of Ringgold with a long, steep hill known as Taylor's Ridge separating the Sigel Regiment from the rebel positions in the direction of Dalton. Winkler hoped for a battle soon, for to move forward depleted the Northern ranks as the need to protect lengthening supply lines increased. At the same time, the retreating Confederates stood to gain in strength by concentrating their forces. He felt, however, the indications pointed to "a long march."[18]

The march continued on the 6th in a "southwesterly direction" about seven miles through hilly country to Leet's Farm. Buerstatte noted the absence of men along the route of march. "We see few men but often women and children," he observed.[19] Winkler described the new campsite: "There are a number of large farms and plantations here, also a mill and a tannery, all deserted except the mill, which seems to be feebly worked. The whole country wears a desolate aspect."[20]

The regiment crossed Taylor's Ridge "over a very rugged road" in "very hot" weather on the 7th, passing through Gordon's Springs and moving into position on a small ridge of hills in Dogwood Valley about three miles southwest of Buzzard Roost Gap. To the east, Johnston's

Buzzard Roost Gap. Photo by George Barnard

Confederate army occupied a strong north-south line along Rocky Face Ridge slightly to the west of Dalton, Georgia. Once in position, the whole regiment went on picket duty, not being relieved until noon the following day. No sooner had they rejoined the brigade on May 8 then they received orders to send out skirmishers toward the half-mile gap in the mountains occupied by the railroad line running to Dalton. The gap, a naturally strong position, was fortified and held in strength by rebel troops. Winkler pronounced it "a very wild country, nothing but mountains and gaps, and I believe the enemy's position is very strong and of such a nature that superior forces cannot be easily made to tell."[21]

Companies A and I of the Sigel Regiment went forward as skirmishers to develop the Confederate position. Since the creek to their front was very deep, they crossed gingerly on a felled tree, spread out in skirmish order, and moved carefully up the ridge leading to Rocky Face Mountain. They had gone only a few rods when Confederate skirmishers opened fire. A sharp skirmish developed about 3:00 p.m., but the rebels showed no disposition to press the issue. The skirmishing continued all afternoon with the 26th losing 1st Lt. Sigmund Juenger of Company A and 1st Sergt. Friedrich W. Stollberg, Company I, wounded. According to Major Winkler's official report, the afternoon was a success. "We had felt his position, discovered the nature, extent, and character of his works, and the object of the reconnaissance seemed to be accomplished."[22]

The following day, May 9, Company F was assigned as skirmishers, crossing the creek in front of Buzzard Roost. So close were they to the enemy lines that Karsten, newly appointed second lieutenant in the company, could "hear every command" their officers used. About noon, Company C relieved the Lake Shore Rifles, the latter having lost one man wounded during the morning's skirmishing. In the evening, the regiment returned to the division encampment in Dogwood Valley and went into camp. While near Buzzard Roost Gap the regiment received news that Grant had defeated Lee in the Wilderness. The announcement, Winkler noted, "causes universal rejoicing" among the officers and men. "The soldiers hope to see the war come to an end this year," Buerstatte wrote. "So do the enemy prisoners, some of whom look quite bewildered."[23]

Since Johnston's position appeared too strong to assail directly, Sherman maneuvered to force the Confederates out of their works.

Sending McPherson's force to the west and south to turn Johnston's southern flank, Sherman ordered Thomas's force to attack Johnston's lines in sufficient strength to hold him in place to cover McPherson's move. At the same time, Schofield's small Army of the Ohio was to demonstrate southward, threatening Johnston's northern flank to prevent the Confederates from shifting troops southward.[24]

On May 11 the 26th marched south at daylight toward Snake Creek Gap on the road to Dalton. As they marched, Gen. Hooker rode by the trudging infantry, "[W]e greeted him with hurrahs," Karsten wrote.[25] They halted at noon and went to work making improvements on the road leading through the gap so it could accommodate both wagons and infantry at the same time. Johnston withdrew southward on the night of May 12, retreating to Resaca where he established new fortifications to obstruct Sherman's advance.[26] The Sigel Regiment followed.

Resaca

Johnston placed his army in defensive positions north and west of Resaca, their line resembling an inverted capital letter L with its flanks resting along the banks of the Connasauga and Oostanaula Rivers. At 8:00 a.m. on the 13th, the Twentieth Corps moved to support McPherson's advance on the western portion of the Confederate line. McPherson soon ran into a strong rebel position along Camp Creek, supported by earthworks along a ridge west of Resaca.[27]

The 26th Wisconsin moved into position in front of the Confederate intrenchments, about 370 strong, on May 13. As soon as fighting broke out, the regiment went into line of battle. Soon orders arrived for it to form into column as a reserve to support McPherson's troops holding the front line. Throughout the late morning and early afternoon the men were under arms, relaxing as best they could, but always anticipating the call to action at any moment. Later in the afternoon, when a breakthrough threatened, the regiment deployed again in line of battle and marched into a dense wood where they halted and formed "in rear of a line of another Corps in whose front there was quite an active skirmish fire."[28] There they stood, ready to advance, until the sun began to set.

After dark the regiment went to "relieve the front line...taking position in line of battle on the brow of a high hill heavily timbered, confronting the position of the enemy on another hill across a flat open valley cut by a creek."[29] There they remained throughout the night and the morning of the 14th while McPherson's corps attacked with mixed results. As the day wore on, Buerstatte found time between alarms to consign an entry to his diary. "Since yesterday and today a lively skirmish has been occurring in front of us. We were lying here in battleline. The enemy is resisting heavily and we will soon get into the fire because our advance troops are already in it....We hear loud gunfire to the left and in front of us and it seems the enemy is being driven back."[30]

The regiment remained in this position until nearly midnight on the 14th. Company B held the skirmish line, maintaining a sporadic but dangerous fire throughout the day that cost the life of Albert Jahns and wounded Philip Liebenstein, William Jaeger, Frederick Siebold, and John N. Perschbacher. Behind the skirmish line, Confederate minie balls whistled randomly among the men in the skirmish reserve, Company K, and in the regiment's main battle line. One spent ball struck Frank Kuechenmeister of Company K a glancing blow in the left foot just below the ankle creating a severe bruise. Despite the pain, he stayed with his company and around midnight a regiment of the Fourteenth Corp relieved them. Several others had bullet holes through their clothing. The men marched about a half mile to the rear where they rested briefly until daylight. In the immediate presence of the enemy, they slept but little that night, their thoughts no doubt focused on the work of the coming day.[31]

At daylight on Pentecost Day, May 15, Winkler led the 26th at the head of Wood's brigade to the extreme southern flank of the Northern army where Sherman determined to turn the Confederate left. There, the brigade deployed about noon to lead an assault on the Confederate lines. The Sigel Regiment formed in the woods with its left resting on the Resaca Road where it connected with the 33rd Massachusetts. Beyond the 33rd in line were the 136th New York, 55th Ohio, and 73rd Ohio. Soon after the regiment formed, Col. Wood arrived to order it's alignment adjusted for the assault. "I was then ordered to swing my right forward so as to occupy an oblique position to the road," Winkler reported, and "to face a hill on the left of the road which I was told at the same time I was to occupy when the Brig. moved forward."

Without hesitation, the major issued the proper orders, moving the men swiftly into the desired formation. From their new position the men could see out across the valley and up a long slope dotted with enemy rifle pits to a row of foreboding breastworks. They all knew what the next few moments would bring. Some checked their gun locks or ammunition, others fingered their bayonets. No doubt they all felt the growing anxiety as they awaited the command to advance which, for some, would surely bring crippling wounds or death. Who would the angel of death tap this bright May day?[32]

When the order to advance finally came, Winkler sent his skirmishers forward, followed by the rest of the regiment. Up the hill they ran, struggling to keep their balance against the incline. In Company K, Franz Kuechenmeister hobbled up the slope, his wounded ankle paining him at every step. The men moved forward at the double-quick, the skirmishers quickly driving their rebel counterparts from their rifle pits. From the top of the hill, a volley exploded forth as the *freiwilligen* moved steadily up the long slope. Luckily, most of the Confederates aimed high, their shots whistling over the heads of the advancing men but causing few casualties. In a few seconds the Sigel Regiment was in among the breastworks, scattering the rebel defenders. As Winkler stood atop the hill, the 33rd Massachusetts arrived beside the 26th and lay down to present a smaller target to Confederate sharpshooters. Winkler "ordered my men to do the same with gun in hand & skirmishers out."[33]

Looking to his rear for support, the major "saw skirmishers of the 1st Brig. coming out of the woods on the right of the road advancing toward my line from the rear. Immediately behind them a line of battle appeared, crossed the road obliquely & marched up the hill behind my line, while at the same time another line of battle broke forth from the woods on the right of the road into the open field in front & then pushed obliquely to the left across the road & came directly in front of my line. Col. Wood just passing by in rear of my regiment I called his attention to them."[34]

Beyond the line taken by this initial assault lay the main Confederate's defense line. Well-placed on a parallel ridge, the rebel works were separated from the new position of the Sigel Regiment by "a narrow valley, covered with a dense growth of young pines." It was a formidable position, placed on a steep incline with all the approaches

The Battleground at Resaca. Photo by George N. Barnard.

easily covered by rifle fire and supported by a four-gun battery.[35] As Winkler watched, the battle line advancing from his rear "passed right over my men & pushed forward into the thicket in my front where it was at once concealed from my sight."[36]

The Federal assault drove in the Confederate skirmishers, pressing toward the main Confederate line. But the rebel fire was heavy and dense timber along the slope broke the alignment of the attacking force. "A heavy musketry fire immediately opened in my front," Winkler remembered, and "a large number of troops came rushing back in disorder through my line & lay down behind it."[37] The movement caused considerable confusion in the Union line. According to Col. Wood, the brigade commander, the 1st Brigade "ran over and through" the 26th "creating so much confusion as to render the regiment almost unserviceable, as well as causing great hindrance to the regiment next to it. Major Winkler, with commendable skill and ability, with no little difficulty extricated his men from the confused mass into which they had become and brought them again reformed into line."[38]

Although the main rebel lines were gained in places, including a penetration by the Sigel Regiment, the first assault failed. His own men realigned, as Winkler watched, officers ran about rallying the other troops, most of whom reformed, moved once again in front of the 26th, and there "lay down flat in front of it." Looking to his left, Winkler saw the 33rd Massachusetts begin to move forward. Sensing a general advance, he brought the 26th to its feet and ordered it forward. The major described it thusly: "I called out to the troops in front of me to be still & let me pass over but to no avail. As my line came on they jumped up & mixed in with it. The woods were so dense that I could see but a very small portion of my line & nothing of the regiment on my left. I had no orders but concluded to push on. The confusion rising from the large number of troops of different organizations scattered through that thicket became greater & greater in the advance. We met but little opposition from the enemy till we got within very short distance of his rifle pits on top of the hill. We pushed forward to right under those pits & a number of my men & also men of other regiments got into them, but with that promiscuous crowd which had now usurped the places of lines of battle it was impossible to lend them the necessary support, & they had to hasten out again." Near the rebel lines the regiment was exposed to a severe fire of canister and musketry. In the Wenze Guard, one of the lead missles found Ernst Damkoehler, knocking him to the ground with a painful wound. The deadly fire forced the regiment to the ground to avoid destruction. Any movement drew instant fire. Winkler "then endeavored to reform in line on the slope of the hill but receiving quite a heavy fire from our own men in the rear was obliged to fall back to the foot of the hill."[39] Buerstatte, in his first major action, commented that "Our regiment moved ahead in good formation, but the other regiments broke up and we had to retreat."[40] Damkoehler, unable to escape, was captured by the advancing Confederates. By the next day he was on his way to Andersonville prison.

At the bottom of the hill Winkler formed a thin line from a scattering of troops he was able to rally. "I took it forward & participated in a number of charges that were attempted upon the enemys position partly by our & partly by the 2nd Division all of which however resulted only in an increase of confusion." When it became obvious that no further advantage could be gained, Winkler sent Capt. Fuchs back to the hill originally taken to round up any of the 26th who might be there and to obtain further orders from Col. Wood. When no orders arrived after a few minutes, the major led his small command back to Wood's position where he found Fuchs and the rest of the regiment. There he also found Col. Wood who told him to remain in position until further orders.[41]

Soon, a Confederate counterattack pressed across the valley and up the hill Winkler held, but aimed to the left of his position. Thinking to be of assistance, he ordered the Sigel Regiment to the left, "but found the hill so thickly covered with troops that I could only find a place in the fourth line." The rebel assault repelled, the Sigel Regiment held its ground until dusk when the brigade was relieved and went into camp for the night.[42]

As the regiment fought, holding Johnston's army in place, Sherman's wide flanking movement crossed the Connesauga River at Lay's Ferry, threatening Confederate supply and communication lines with Atlanta. Johnston withdrew that night, moving his forces southward once again. About 10:00 a.m. on the 16th the Sigel Regiment joined the pursuit, moving across the Connesauga River on a log bridge and on to Field's Mill on the Coosawattee River. Crossing in a ferry, it halted for the night on the far bank.[43] "The enemy was beaten this morning," Buerstatte wrote. "We have the last stragglers of the Rebs behind us. We captured more material and ammunition. The guns they left behind are all destroyed. The road is scattered full of dead horses, pieces of clothing, weapons, cartridge containers, etc. These are the tracks of an army in flight."[44] "Our success in last Sunday's fight was neither brilliant nor all that it might have been," Winkler concluded, "but was sufficient to induce the enemy to leave his fortifications and retreat in haste." Leading his men south, the major was surprised by the lack of care the Confederates gave their own wounded: "The way the rebels left many of their own wounded in the field, wholly destitute and uncared for, is shocking."[45]

Though victorious, the regiment paid dearly for its success. "This was a horrible fight," Buerstatte wrote. "Dead and wounded lay everywhere."[46] The dead included 1st Lt. Christian Phillip of Company F, Julius Suettinger in Company C, Michael Wagner of Company F, and, in Company H, the carpenter from Herman, Wisconsin, Sergt. Karl Wickesberg. Shot through the breast in the Union advance, Wickesberg was carried to the nearby field hospital where he spent the night in considerable agony before succumbing early the following morning. Capt. Karl Schmidt sent Wickesberg's death certificate to his uncle in Wisconsin, along with an accounting of $154.94 due the deceased sergeant for back pay and clothing, and a request for payment of $6 a comrade had lend to the deceased for the purchase of a watch.[47]

While losses were not as high as at Chancellorsville or Gettysburg, they were every bit as bitter to their comrades and to family and friends at home. "We were considerably disappointed," Buerstatte commented. Total losses for the two days were seven killed and 43 wounded.[48]

Cassville

As Confederate forces retired grudgingly southward toward Atlanta, Northern troops followed warily seeking an opportunity to flank the rebels and cut them off from the Georgia crossroads that was Sherman's ultimate goal. Johnston moved south to Calhoun, then on to Adairsville without finding a suitable place to impede Sherman's rapid advance. The Sigel Regiment followed in the rebel's wake, march-

Sgt. Karl Wickesberg, a carpenter from Herman. Killed in action at Resaca.

Courtesy of Alfred Wickesburg

ing southeasterly through Calhoun in hot, humid weather. Crossing the Connesauga River on a rough log bridge, they marched on until nightfall when they were ferried across the Coosawattee River at Field's Mill above the junction of the former stream. All along the way, Karsten reported, "we saw lots of munitions which the rebels could not take with them and could not destroy."[49]

After a few brief hours of sleep, the officers woke the men early, but orders to move did not arrive until noon. At 1:00 p.m. on May 17 they were on the march again, moving southwesterly over roads described as "very rough" making the marching "slow."[50] "We are finding while marching," Buerstatte commented, "many dead and wounded left behind by the enemy." On they plodded hour after hour, making only average time because of congestion and the poor conditions of the narrow, winding southern roads. Evening found them two miles west of Calhoun where they stopped for the night. "In the evening we got to the enemy area and built breastworks overnight," Buerstatte wrote. "Enemy cavalry is in front of us. We are extremely exhausted from the long march."[51] Winkler also considered the march, through "a very fine country, of large—once wealthy—plantations," difficult, commenting that everyone felt "very much undone."[52]

On the 18th Johnston halted north of Cassville, intent upon striking Schofield's small force before it could be supported by the rest of Sherman's troops. Poor coordination and faulty intelligence, however, prevented the attack and Johnston fell back that evening to a new position south of Cassville. The Sigel regiment moved out at 5:00 a.m., marching south under a hot sun until it encountered Johnston's skirmishers, backed by a section of artillery, in mid-afternoon. Winkler ordered the regiment into line of battle to support skirmishers from

Jacob Mahloch, Company H, a farmer from Rhine. Wounded at Resaca.

Courtesy of Russell Scott

another regiment of the brigade, advancing slowly but not becoming directly involved. That night the men "slept on our arms."[53]

Early the following morning the Confederates fell back further to Allatoona Pass. Winkler led his men "due south" on a reconnaissance, skirmishing intermittently until he came in sight of "a large body of rebels" around noon. Since the brigade was alone in the advance, it retired to a small hill where a battery unlimbered and opened fire. The Sigel Regiment deployed near a farm house, constructing a makeshift breastwork out of material from nearby slave shacks to receive the anticipated Confederate attack, but the rebels declined the invitation.[54]

After it became apparent the Confederates did not mean to attack, the brigade, now reinforced, continued its advance about 2:30 p.m. with the Sigel Regiment in the lead, Companies A and G deployed as skirmishers. Having gone only about a half mile, the skirmishers became embroiled in a "brisk" exchange, driving the rebels back into the hills surrounding Cassville. Despite the sustained firing, the 26th suffered no losses.[55] "All the rebels wish," Winkler believed, "is to get away; they do not fight with spirit; they give up to every attack, and many are glad to come in and surrender at every opportunity."[56]

During the late afternoon the army concentrated near Cassville, a village Winkler found "pretty" with "several churches but deserted and desolate."[57] In the early evening the brigade again advanced in battle order against the town, being opposed by rebel skirmishers and artillery fire well into the night. When the firing finally died down, the Sigel Regiment was sent about a mile to the rear to rest after the successful day's fight.[58]

The short nights, long marches and frequent skirmishes greatly debilitated the men. Muscles grew sore, bodies weary, and minds constantly on edge from the strain of sustained contact with the enemy. But the marches and fighting accomplished a purpose. With every move the Confederates fell relentlessly back toward Atlanta, the constant pressure making it impossible for them to dig in for a stand.

From Dallas to New Hope Church

While the army concentrated, the 26th enjoyed two days of welcome rest. Fresh meat, dried apples, and cornmeal arrived to the delight of officers and men alike. In the oppressive heat everyone sought shade, but drills continued and a dress parade was staged for a group of general officers.[59] "The heat is terrible," Buerstatte wrote, "and we are all almost 'finished.'"[60]

Despite the rest, picket duty and skirmishing continued. Winkler was visiting the skirmish line on May 24 when a rebel minie ball struck a sergeant standing only a few feet from the major. "He was but a few steps from me when he was shot," Winkler wrote, "and fell right down with a loud and most painful moan."[61]

"One does not realize it," Buerstatte mused, "but today is Sunday."[62] Winkler, too, felt it was "a much pleasanter Sunday morning than it was a week ago, not in point of weather alone, but it is more Sunday like. No booming of cannon, no rattling of musketry, no ordering voices harsh with excitement, no shrieks of wounded, no groans of dying, no confusion of battle disturbs the holy quiet of the Sabbath Day. A week ago the riot of human weakness, folly and passion seemed to contend with the goodness of God and for a time almost to gain mastery over it; Nature was calm and placid, the happy birds sung merrily in green boughs, the air was balmy and soft, all beckoned the beneficence of the Ruler above, but man converted this scene of peaceful calm to a pandemonium of terror and destruction until Night kindly threw its mantle over the scene and screened the combatants from each other's view. Brave men may, but I believe there are very few, if any, who take delight in battle, and very few who in the heat of an engagement will not welcome the coming night as that of a friend who will stop the fierce wrangle and bring relief to the struggling men. There is something so providentially kind in it to those who have survived the dangers of the day, in the fall of night upon the battle field. It brings relief to the anxious heart and inspires it with gratitude to God for the favors shown during those hours of danger."[63]

The peacefulness of the Sabbath was but temporary. After resting his army, Sherman again sent McPherson in a wide flanking move aimed at Dallas, Georgia, a crossroads west of Marietta astride one of the main roads into Atlanta. In preparation, Winkler received orders to have the regiment ready to march at 4:00 a.m. on May 23. As he explained them, the orders called for "light fighting order with twenty day's rations and haversacks and wagons, so as to be independent of the railroad. The rations are reduced and the deficiency is to be supplied by foraging."[64] Buerstatte felt lucky when, as the time for the movement drew near, Lackner's Company F was temporarily detached and "assigned to train guard duty."[65] While Company F marched off to take its turn shepherding the trains, Winkler led the rest of the regiment southward once again, crossing the Etowah River on a pontoon bridge in the afternoon and pressing on the following day to Burnt Hickory.[66] Along the way, Karsten came upon several chickens which he and his comrades "transported into the other world."[67]

The Twentieth Corps arrived at Dallas on May 25. The Sigel Regiment marched shortly after 8:00 a.m., crossing Pumpkin Vine Creek and continuing on over "very rough country, hills and woods" to New Hope Church. As the troops moved forward, the lead regiment of John Geary's 2nd Division met Confederate resistance and a sharp fight developed. The balance of the corps was up, in position, and ready to advance by early afternoon. A heavy skirmish line drove the enemy back steadily until the rebels reached a fortified ridge where they determined to make a stand. Col. Wood aligned his brigade with the 55th Ohio and 136th New York in the front line, the 73rd Ohio and 33rd Massachusetts in the second line, and the 26th Wisconsin in the third. Moving forward about 4:00 p.m. with its right along the road, the brigade arrived at a ravine "commanded by an opposite hill, which the rebels held in force with infantry and artillery.[68]

Wood ordered his men forward against the strongly held position and a "bloody fight" ensued. According to Winkler, "The rebel's fire was very rapid and, owing to their advantageous position, far more effective than ours." On the left, a Confederate force enfiladed the brigade caus- ing casualties in the lead regiments. Wood ordered the 73rd Ohio to change front and drive the rebels back, but the regiment met fierce resistance that arrested its advance short of the objective. The 33rd Massachusetts changed front to support the 73rd, coming into line on the extreme left of the brigade to extend the flank of the 73rd. But the Confederate position, covered by well-placed rifle pits, was too strong. Despite the added weight of volleys from the 33rd, the two regiments could advance no further. Hugging the ground and the little cover avail- able, they fought it out with the rebels despite mounting casualties.[69]

Riddled by well-aimed Confederate fire, the 73rd suffered so severely Wood ordered the Sigel Regiment forward to replace it.[70] "We attacked quite fiercely," Winkler reported, "and fought a sharp battle which lasted until night, when we held all the ground we had gained."[71] The Badgers kept up a heavy musketry, inflicting and suffer- ing casualties in a lengthy exchange of fire that cost the regiment dear- ly. In Company B, Ferdinand Huebner was shot through the left arm, Adam Truss in his right hand, Charles Jaeger in the left leg, August Ninon in the thigh, Bernard Kuckhan in the side, and John Weiffenback in the left shoulder. Weiffenback succumbed to his wound in a Chattanooga hospital on June 3.[72]

In Company C, Edward Langer was killed, John Christen wounded in the right leg, John Lauer hit above the eye, and Thurlius Shaefer shot in the right leg. Lauer later died in a Chattanooga hospital. Shaefer, his leg amputated, also succumbed in the same Tennessee city.[73]

Company E was particularly hard hit. Sergt. Philip Zipp was wounded, Corp. Magnus Schneider wounded, Corp. Henry Diener wounded, Corp. François Knein shot in the right foot, Pvt. Friedrich Zirbel hit in arm, George Kraus shot in the head, Paul Glatzel wound- ed in the leg, Friedrich Lankow shot in the leg, Charles Stier hit in the leg, Franz Oehlke shot in the arm, Samuel Proechel wounded in the left shoulder, and Heinrich Wagner shot through the shoulder. George Krause died in the hospital on May 28; Henry Diener lasted until

October 1. Magnus Schneider and François Knein hobbled back along the narrow roadway toward the field hospital, but took a wrong turn at a fork in the road and fell into rebel hands. Their mistake proved fatal. They were taken to Andersonville prison where Schneider died on September 24 and Knein on October 8.[74]

In the intense fire and smoke shrouding the battlefield, Capt. John Fuchs and Adjutant George P. Traeumer were conspicuous in their efforts to keep the men in "a firm, steady, unwavering line," firing at any targets that presented themselves. "Our fire had been so hot," Winkler observed, "that the rebels had been obliged to slacken theirs very much, and when we ceased firing, they showed no disposition to renew it."[75]

In Company G, Robert Templeton and Emerson Smith were killed. The wounded included Cyrus W. Shafer, Charles Hafemann, William Sery and George Dellenback. Frederick Dristler was captured. Company H lost Pvt. Heinrich Behler wounded. Company I had Rudolph Laisse wounded and Chauncy Lacy and John Swoboda missing. In Company K, Jacob Klink and Friedrich Roell were killed; and Sergt. Henry Nolt wounded in the hand. Lacy and Swoboda were later found wounded, but recovered. Dellenbach died of his wounds at Kingston, Georgia, on July 2. Distler was taken to Andersonville prison where he died on August 14. Charles Hafemann lay on the field for hours, unable to regain the Union lines. While he awaited his fate, maggots crawled about his wound feasting on the fresh blood and flesh. Eventually retrieved when the Confederates retired, he was treated at the field hospital before being sent north to a hospital in Jeffersonville, Indiana, then to Madison General Hospital in Wisconsin where he spent the rest of the war recuperating.[76]

Eventually, a heavy evening thunderstorm and the darkness of an overcast night ended the grueling fight. "When it was dark," Winkler wrote, "we ceased firing, fixed bayonets, closed up the intervals the casualties of the contest had caused, and were ready for further action, offensive or defensive."[77] Winkler placed pickets out front and sent Sergt. Fritz Laich of Company K on a reconnaissance, but the sergeant apparently scouted too far in the intense darkness and was captured. He was taken by the rebels to Andersonville prison where he died of disease on September 30, 1864.[78]

That evening the men "had to sit and be rained upon without shelter and without a fire." After midnight they were relieved and marched a short distance to the rear where the men spent most of the night constructing protective intrenchments. "[H]ungry, wet, without a blanket," Winkler recalled, "we did not have a very pleasant night of it." Finally, at daylight, they received coffee, meat, crackers, and blankets, and were able to stand down for a brief rest.[79]

With the day's fight at an end, the regiment moved to a less exposed position where the tired men enjoyed a well-earned rest. In all, the "contest" cost the Badgers one officer and six men killed, 31 wounded, and two missing.[80] In a war where so many fell, Winkler took the time to comment on the deaths of Templeton and Smith: "They were both excellent men, cool and brave. Truer and braver hearts have never fallen in battle."[81]

Golgotha Church to Noses' Creek

Following the action at New Hope Church, Sherman moved eastward in an attempt to force Johnston out of his strong position. Heavy rains delayed further action, as did Sherman's desire to build up his store of supplies in the event his lengthening supply lines should be cut by roving Confederate cavalry. In the meantime, Johnston gradually drew his lines back to a position anchored on Kennesaw Mountain north of Marietta, then turning southward several miles west of and paralleling the railroad line to Atlanta.[82]

The Sigel Regiment stayed in reserve on May 26, resting and replenishing its ammunition. On the 27th Lackner's command returned about midnight from guarding the trains, camping in a "thickly wooded" area near Burnt Hickory. Buerstatte and his comrades enjoyed little rest as the "Rebs greeted us with cannonfire this morning." After breakfast the regiment moved forward to relieve a unit of the 1st Brigade, taking its turn behind the front-line breastworks.[83] During the succeeding days the regiment's skirmishers were continually engaged. "There is constant watching, constant skirmishing between the lines," Winkler informed those at home, "which sometimes changes into a severe fight; neither party seems inclined to attack the other. What the result of this will be, I don't know; it would seem that a hard battle will have to be fought, but our doings is a riddle to me. The monotony of sitting here day after day, night after night, on the same spot, and now and then going to look over the breast works when picket firing becomes active to see what it means, is rather dull and does not afford a very good subject for writing."[84] Though "dull" and "monotonous" to some, the skirmishing meant more to others. In Company E it cost the life of Reinhold Krause.

On the evening of May 29 the rebels launched a brief attack, but it was easily repulsed without serious loss while the 26th was in reserve. The regiment filed into the breastworks again on May 30, but was relieved that night without further incident and spent the 31st once again in reserve.[85] Winkler found the waiting "tedious, hard," with "nothing to do, nothing to read, no news, no information of anything. As you may suppose, our camps are rife with thousands of rumors."[86] They did not have long to wait for rumors to be replaced with orders. During the night instructions arrived for a move and the following morning the entire division set out on a march to the left.[87]

The next morning, June 1, found the regiment camped near New Hope Church. The men were up before dawn, cooking coffee and preparing to march once again. Winkler believed his men were "all in excellent spirits and in good condition and ready for any duty."[88] But the march over hills and through ravines soon turned difficult as "torrents of rain" came and went on June 2. "We are all wet through and through," Buerstatte reported, "and there is an awful lot of mud! mud!"[89] The rains continued off and on for the next three days, dampening the mens clothing and spirits alike. Skirmishing continued intermittently. On the evening of June 2 the regiment had quite a scare when a random rebel shell suddenly landed amid its campsite grazing one man. The next day found it occupying a position before the rebel entrenchments on Pine Knob.[90]

During the march the roads became so muddy it was difficult for the supply wagons to move forward, relegating the troops to hard tack and coffee for several days. On the 4th a small ration of bacon made breakfast a treat. That night the regiment camped near a deserted farm with a large apple orchard about nine miles from Marietta. Winkler reported the men "feasted on beef and apple sauce for desert."[91]

At daylight on June 5 the Twentieth Corps marched southward once again, seeking the next Confederate defensive line north of Atlanta, thought to be on the south side of the Chattahoochee River. Although rations once again became scarce, the weather finally cleared, sparing the marching men from the constant dampness of the previous days. On the 6th Karsten went with Company G and part of Company H to act as flankers, digging rifle pits to protect the left of the army from surprise attack. The following day Buerstatte noted in his diary he was "learning what the word 'hunger' means." That day the regiment "encamped on a hill" where the men "had to build breastworks deep into last night." Once the construction was completed, however, it enjoyed several days of rest.[92]

On June 15 the corps advanced once again, fighting its way forward some two miles, but the Sigel Regiment was lucky enough to be held in reserve during the action. Under intense pressure, the rebels abandoned their works between Pine Knob and Lost Mountain, retiring to "a very strong position well intrenched near Golgotha Church. About 2:00 p.m. Winkler led his men forward, meeting the rebels around 6:00 p.m. near Big Shanty. For half an hour the regiment was "subjected to the sharpest artillery fire that [Winkler] experienced since Gettysburg. The noise of whizzing and exploding shells, especially in the woods, is terrific, but compared to infantry its destructiveness is slight." Buerstatte, experiencing a major bombardment for the first time, painted a somewhat more desperate picture: "We laid for 2 hours through cannon and rifle fire on the ground and dared not get up." Two men were wounded.[93]

The regiment lay on its arms until the danger passed, then set about building protective breastworks well into the night. Throughout the next day picket firing alternately raged and subsided, while the artillery lobbed shells over the woods into enemies unseen on each side. At sunset the rebels "opened a brisk discharge of shells" on a battery the Sigel Regiment was supporting, the shells bursting around the regiment "with most uncomfortable vividness." Several exploded directly overhead, yet the men miraculously escaped injury.[94]

The following morning, June 17, skirmishers from the 26th Wisconsin met the rear guard of Gen. Patrick Cleburne's veteran Confederate division near Muddy Creek. A brisk skirmish that Karsten described as "quite lively" developed with the Confederates hard-pressed to hold their positions. As pressure increased on the Southern lines, a sudden, unexpected rush by the Germans surprised the rebels and drove them from the field. In the pursuit, Jacob Baldes of Company B captured a prized Confederate battle flag as a trophy.[95]

The rebels retired to Noses' [or Noyes'] Creek where they again intrenched. On the 19th the Confederates abandoned these lines and retired southward again. The Sigel Regiment followed, advancing "once more with difficulty," crossing "several creeks very much swollen in consequence of the late heavy rains," and running into rebel skirmishers again shortly after noon. "We advanced 2 miles," Buerstatte wrote. The rain "was perfectly furious" during the day as the advance was preceded by active skirmishing. With resistance stiffening, the 26th was ordered into line on the right of the brigade and sent forward into a wooded area. Pushing through, the men came upon "an open field commanded by a wooded hill held by rebel skirmishers."

While the main body of the regiment halted, the skirmishers moved forward to engage the enemy. In the sharp fighting that followed, the 26th lost only one man killed and four wounded, with one of the captains receiving a bullet through his haversack.[96] Among the wounded were 1st Sergt. Jakob Blum of Company I, Frederick William Matuschka of Company I, William Richter of Company I, and Conrad Knöpp of Company K. Lt. Karsten escaped with "a glancing shot on the foot" and was back with the regiment the next day. The dead man was Heinrich Gessner of Company B. But the advance was successful, the rebels being forced to abandon their works. "The Rebs left their defenses," Buerstatte noted. They were "strong defenses, which were built a long time ago."[97]

The regiment did not arrive in camp near Culp's House and Kennesaw Mountain until about 11:00 p.m. Despite the success of the day, Winkler was not pleased. Several mistakes in command occurred on the skirmish line and the major's inquiries turned up unsettling information. "One of my line officers misbehaved himself again," he wrote. "I found that night that he had been under the influence of liquor. I am determined to stop everything of that kind and have put him in arrest and preferred charges, and shall try to get him punished exemplarily; there is certainly nothing more revolting than an officer getting drunk when charged with the responsibilities as commanding men under fire. Still you see drunken officers in every battle; they shall not, however, be seen in my regiment."[98] Winkler does not state who the offending officer was, but it was probably 1st Lt. Leopold Melchior who was placed under arrest that month and dismissed from the service under a General Field Order dated September 8, 1864.[99]

Kennesaw Mountain

On June 20 the regiment stayed in place until 5:00 p.m. when it was ordered to advance in a heavy rain storm to the support of the 1st Division. The troops formed outside the breastworks, waiting fruitlessly in line under a constant rain until dark when they returned to their original position. The downpour continued through the night. The rain had a very detrimental effect on both men and equipment. By the end of the campaign, every drum in the regiment was useless, the drumheads having been ruined. Winkler proposed taking up a collection when the regiment was paid to buy new ones. "Since the first of June," he wrote, "we have had just three days it did not rain; every brook is a river and the roads are terrible. If we did not have the railroad we would have to go back or starve." That night Winkler and his staff officers did not starve. During the day Commissary Sergeant Samuel Meyer located a sutler and bought a can of strawberries, a can of tomatoes, a "little box of sardines," and some flour. The resulting dinner of pancakes and the other delicacies "made a very agreeable change for dinner."[100]

The morning of June 22nd dawned sunny and warm. "It is a bright, pleasant morning," Winkler felt, "justifying the hope that it will not rain to-day."[101] Before the morning could be fully enjoyed, orders arrived to make ready to advance. Moved quickly to the front at Kolb's Farm, across a broad field from the rebel lines entrenched in a woods, the Sigel Regiment made ready to attack. Guns loaded and capped, bayonets fixed, the men waited for the signal to advance. It came about noon. Up and over their own works the men jumped, moving quickly to the attack. Shouting lustily as they ran across the wide field swept by a "destructive" Confederate fire, the men pushed on into the woods on the opposite side, carrying the first line of rebel defenses. In the forefront was Charles Stamm of Company C who felt "somewhat ambitious to give the rebels as good as they sent and suddenly found himself alone, far in advance of the Union lines. Bullets were flying and he concluded to join his comrades, which he did on the double quick."[102]

The regiment halted about 300 yards from the main Confederate line. There they hastily erected breastworks to protect their prize from any Southern counterattack. In this greatly exposed position, commanded by the main rebel battle line, the 26th held all afternoon under a deliberate fire delivered from well-covered Confederate positions. "The bullets flew around and over us thick and fast," Winkler wrote. One "tore a large piece of the brim" of his hat, passing "within half an inch" of his head. All about him men hugged the ground, trying to protect themselves as best they could while keeping up a fire against their tormenters. A minie ball shot a hole through the skirt of Capt. Lackner's coat, while another dented his scabbard without injuring the brave officer. Another ball glanced off a tree, striking Winkler in the knee, but its force was spent and it did no serious damage. The major tried to pick it up as a souvenir, but it was so hot he could not keep it in his hand.[103]

Unlike most fights where there was a brief few minutes of intense activity and anxiety, following the initial charge the afternoon unfolded slowly, the pressure building in intensity as minute after minute, hour after hour, balls zipped and whined about the prone men, striking with sickening thuds anyone rising above the sparce cover. Adolph Kuhlig was struck almost simultaneously in the foot and by another missle that inflicted "a severe wound in the head." In Company F, a minie ball found Frank Fisher, tearing through "a small portfolio he carried," ripping through some papers, an oil blanket and some clothing with such force it shattered a wooden pipe and sliced into his side, the force knocking him unconscious. In Company I, John Koepnick was killed, while the lengthening toll of wounded included John Groff, William Klatt, Rudolf Kreofsky, Joseph Mickolosky, Friedrich Mueller, Anton Neumeister, Ernst Schreiber, John Style, John Swoboda, and George Boyer.[104]

Despite the severity of the enemy fire on its exposed position, the 26th Wisconsin held until nightfall when it was relieved by other troops. "Today was again another bloody day near Marietta," Buerstatte wrote in his diary.[105] The cost for the day was "very heavy," with nine men killed and thirty wounded.[106] After so much death on so many fields, the losses this day made a particularly curious impression on their commander. "It is with a heavy heart that I contemplate the loss," he wrote the next morning. "The loss of so many of my good boys yesterday affected me very much more than at any other time; it was, I believe, because I saw everything so plainly and talked to many of the

Anton Neumeister, Company I, a blacksmith from Mequon.
Wounded at Kennesaw Mountain.

Courtesy of the U.S. Army Military History Institute

wounded myself. The engagement was slow and lasted so long; one had an opportunity to see all so plainly, and then, while both at Resaca and near Dalton the great majority of the wounds were light, most of them yesterday were severe, many of them fearful. Now the intelligence that the result of the fighting yesterday has been largely in our favor, has reconciled us somewhat to our individual loss."[107]

After a brief rest, the regiment moved forward again to a position of great importance guarding the road from Powder Springs to Marietta. Its first task was fatiguing construction work, building "breastworks in view of the enemy who provided us with cannonball music." After finishing the entrenchments, the Wisconsinites settled into a duel with Confederate sharpshooters, backed by occasional artillery fire, that lasted until July 3.[108] The weather was exceptionally hot, water very scarce, and there was nothing to cover the men from the direct sun except small trees taken from nearby woods and fashioned into makeshift arbors. Winkler found the position "like so many we have had during this campaign, very close to the enemy's pickets, and as the pickets keep firing constantly, a great many bullets are thrown into the line." Winkler had the men construct extra breastworks for protection, including a four foot high earth and log entrenchment to protect the regimental headquarters from the "intrusion of stray bullets." Two men were wounded along the front lines, a ball passed through Capt. Steinmeyer's tent just above where he was reclining, only narrowly missing him, and another sliced through Karsten's tent about eighteen inches from the ground the lieutenant and his tentmates were resting upon. Winkler pronounced it "a disagreeable mode of fighting," unlike the large-scale battles of Virginia, and very taxing on the nerves. When the troops should have been at rest between battles, "there is constant firing all around, and you are never out of danger and can hardly move about without indiscreet exposure."[109] Total losses during this period were 11 killed and mortally wounded and 36 wounded.[110]

On the morning of July 2 the Sigel Regiment joined the 73rd Ohio in a reconnaissance toward the right to locate and connect with the Twenty-third Corps, a mission it accomplished without loss while capturing a large number of rebel deserters and stragglers. The lack of serious resistance, coupled with the number of prisoners, convinced Winkler the "Johnnies" were "demoralized."[111] Appearances, however, could be deceiving. Even as he pondered the rebel's seeming demise, Confederate Gen. Johnston was planning his next move.

Peach Tree Creek

Following the failure of a general assault on the Confederate lines on June 27, an attack the 26th fortunately missed, Sherman returned to his flanking strategy, sending McPherson off on another turning movement. By July 3 the Confederates once again abandoned their lines, retreating southward to a strong position along the Chattahoochee River only a few miles from Atlanta. The Sigel Regiment followed at 6:00 a.m., marching all day under a "broiling sun" until the rebels took up a new line behind Nickajack Creek. All along the march beaten rebels surrendered until by nightfall the division had taken, according to Karsten, some 500 captives. The following day, a year after the end of the Battle of Gettysburg, Buerstatte and Company F stood picket duty, returning about noon. Karsten accompanied part of the regiment and the 73rd Ohio on a reconnaissance. During the afternoon a "terrible cannonade" commenced in front and to the left, but without effect. That evening they marched an additional three miles, stopping to construct yet another set of breastworks before retiring for a brief sleep.[112]

Rising early on the 5th, news soon arrived that the rebels had once again abandoned their lines to retreat farther south. Throughout the day the regiment marched through "the greatest heat in which many of our men collapsed from exhaustion." Pushing ahead hard on the heels of the retreating rebels, by nightfall they were in position on a hill about two miles from the Chattahoochee River. After throwing up the usual breastworks, they were allowed to rest for a few days in relative calm.[113] The weather cleared and became "beautiful," while the halt allowed the men time to rest and recuperate to some extent from the rigors of the previous weeks.[114] While there, a communication from Governor John T. Lewis arrived making official Winkler's promotion to lieutenant colonel to replace Hans Boebel who lost a leg at Gettysburg. Capt. Lackner received a promotion to succeed Winkler as major. Another arrival from Milwaukee was Quartermaster Sergeant George Jones who returned with two new flags Winkler described as "a United States banner with our last year's battles inscribed in gilt and the name of the regiment, and a blue state flag with the coat of arms of the state in the center on one side and an eagle on the other, with the name of the regiment gilded on a red circular strip underneath."[115] The old national flag, the frayed and battered veteran of so many fields, was returned to Wisconsin for safekeeping.

While in camp, an unofficial truce also prevailed along the river separating the two forces. "Our pickets are on the northern bank and have agreed with the rebel pickets on the other side not to shoot. There they were this morning, within talking distance of each other, not the least bitter feeling disturbing the friendly intercourse. The rebels were freely walking about on the south bank, washing their clothes and spreading them in the sun to dry, while our men were doing the same

1864 Issue National Flag, 26th Wisconsin Volunteer Infantry, first carried at Peach Tree Creek and in all subsequent battles.

Courtesy of the Wisconsin Veterans Museum

on this side; some of our men had even been across and traded off coffee and sugar for tobacco."116

The regiment stood for a general inspection on the 16th, but little else disturbed the tranquility until the following day. Then, orders arrived to clean up the camp and prepare to march. Later that day they crossed the Chattahoochee on pontoons, marching to within seven miles of Atlanta on the 18th. There they halted and remained in place throughout July 19th.117

Once again on the march early on Wednesday morning, July 20, the regiment moved forward from Buck Head at a steady pace, crossing Peach Tree Creek "shortly before noon." In the afternoon they halted to rest at the foot of a hill separating them from the front lines. In Company C, Charles Stamm recalled that "we came to an old dead corn field and had stacked our arms with a view of getting some supper. The Kenosha members of the regiment had made it a custom to stick together and when we stacked arms [George C.] Limpert went out and got some wood to make a fire. Charley Vollmer scouted out to get some water for the coffee and I was out gathering blackberries."[118] Throughout the large field, the other companies settled in for what they thought would be a peaceful evening bivouac. Beyond the hills to their front, the Confederates had other ideas.

Frustrated with the continual retreat of Johnston's army, President Davis replaced him with aggressive Gen. John Bell Hood on July 17. By July 20, John Newton's 2nd Division, Fourth Corps, was across Peach Tree Creek supported by the balance of the corps and by elements of the Twentieth Corps. Sensing an opportunity to crush the Northern army while its various units were separated by the creek, Hood ordered a major assault by the corps of Alexander P. Stewart and William J. Hardee.[119]

Beginning around 3:00 p.m, the Southern assault rolled forward, driving into Newton's Division and threatening to overrun it. As part

Oil painting depicting the 26th Wisconsin, in center, marching into action at Peach Tree Creek, Georgia. The artist was Carl Dilg, a painter from Milwaukee who served in Company B and was wounded at Chancellorsville.

Courtesy of Thomas A. Kuhn

of the assault, George Maney's Division of Hardee's Corps smashed into a gap that developed between Newton's and Geary's divisions, threatening to break through the line and inflict a smashing defeat on the Union host. As the sounds of battle suddenly descended upon the Sigel Regiment's campsite men rushed to arms while Winkler ordered them into line. Stamm had gathered about a quart of berries when the sounds of firing reached him. Quickly he ran back to retrieve his musket. Although no orders arrived, when Colonel Harrison began moving his 1st Brigade forward to the right of the 26th, Winkler ordered his men forward, up the hill in their front and down the reverse slope. The rest of Wood's Brigade followed as soon as its regiments were ready, the 20th Connecticut falling in on the left of the Sigel Regiment, with the 73rd Ohio behind the Badgers and the 55th Ohio behind the 20th Connecticut. Most of the 136th New York was detached on picket and acting as skirmishers.[120]

Reaching the bottom of the slope on the reverse side of the first hill, they moved through a "fringe of trees and bushes" lining the ravine. When the regiment emerged from the shrubs, Confederate troops swarmed over the next hill, opening fire on the Badgers below. The grey infantry was W. S. Featherston's Mississippi brigade of A. P. Stewart's Corps, intent on penetrating the weak spot in the federal line.[121]

In Company C, Stamm's musket misfired. As he threw it down, a bullet cut down Capt. Robert Mueller so Stamm picked up his sword. Soon another soldier fell and the private took his musket to resume firing.[122] To Buerstatte, the "the gunfire exceeded anything I had ever heard before. We loaded and fired as fast as possible."[123] But as they fought, troops on their left fell back before Stewart's attack and Confederate infantry concealed in a dense woods only sixty yards away poured a deadly enfilading fire into the regiment. Assailed by heavy fire from front and flank, Winkler ordered the men to lie down and hold their ground. There, amid a withering crossfire, exposed as well to a "scorching" hot sun that made each effort a progressively more difficult task, the regiment fought to hold its ground and prevent a rebel breakthrough. "For a time the conflict was desperate," Winkler wrote. "I took every man who could be spared on the right to re-enforce the left."[124]

In front of them, the 33rd Mississippi Infantry, some 400 strong, swept down the opposite ridge intent upon destroying Winklers's small

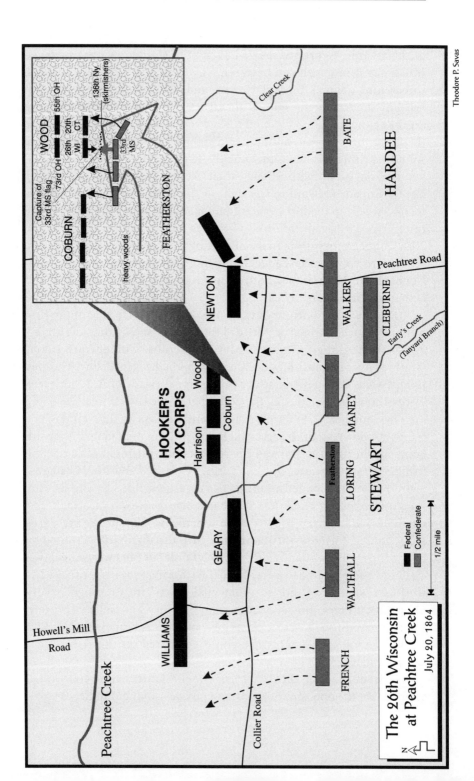

Theodore P. Savas

Clear Creek

HARDEE

BATE

Peachtree Road

WALKER

CLEBURNE

Early's Creek

(Tanyard Branch)

NEWTON

MANEY

STEWART

Wood

LORING

Featherston

HOOKER'S
XX CORPS

Harrison   Coburn

GEARY

WALTHALL

Howell's Mill

Road

WILLIAMS

FRENCH

Collier Road

Peachtree Creek

Federal
Confederate

1/2 mile

**The 26th Wisconsin
at Peachtree Creek**

July 20, 1864

N

Inset map:

WOOD

55th OH

136th Ny.
(skirmishers)

26th 20th
WI. CT.

73rd OH

33rd
MS

Capture of
33rd MS flag

COBURN

heavy woods

FEATHERSTON

band, now less than 260 muskets. On they came, closer and closer, until they were only ten paces away. At that moment Winkler shouted an order, the regiment sprang up with the alacrity and precision of the veterans they were, and loosed a deadly volley that staggered the Mississippians. Watching from behind the lines, Col. Wood was impressed with the courage and precision of his Wisconsin regiment. "Cooly and deliberately," he wrote in his official report, "the men poured into their [the Confederate] line a well-directed, withering, and destructive fire, which covered the ground with dead and wounded."[125]

Stunned by the sudden death about them, the Confederates recoiled as Winkler ordered his men to charge. The Badger's charge prompted the rest of Wood's Brigade to advance on their left, protecting them somewhat from the vicious enfillading fire. In the forefront of the Badger's attack, urging his men on, Capt. John Seemann fell. On they

Flag of the 33rd Mississippi Infantry captured by the 26th Wisconsin at Peach Tree Creek. Note the many bullet holes and tears that testify to the intensity of the fight.

Courtesy of the Old Capitol Museum of Mississippi History.

Capt. William Steinmeyer, Company E, a gunsmith from Milwaukee. Wounded at Peach Tree Creek.

Frank A. Kuechenmeister, Company K, a mechanic from Milwaukee. Wounded at Peach Tree Creek.

Courtesy of Erv Seeger

Ferdinand Scholz, Company A, a cigar-maker from Milwaukee. Wounded at Peach Tree Creek.

Stephan Fiess, Company A, a carpenter from Milwaukee. Killed in action at Peach Tree Creek.

went, up the hill, scattering the Mississippians before them. Led by Capt. Fuchs, Company C surged forward, its leader seizing the coveted Confederate regimental flag. Others captured six officers swords and some forty prisoners. Still they moved on until they reached the crest of the hill where they established a defensive line along a fence.[126]

They were barely in position when another danger arose. From the dense woods to the left, "a heavy volley" tore into the ranks of the Sigel Regiment. In Company A, a musket ball entered Julius Semich's right eye, destroying it and passing through the bone to lodge at the second molar on the left side of his head. Another ball struck Franz Kuechenmeister in Company K, smashing his hand so badly the lower portion of his right arm would have to be amputated. The regiment "replied with vigor" for about fifteen minutes until the 20th Connecticut arrived on its left flank and Confederate fire slackened. Their ammunition exhausted, the men scavenged for what they could find in the cartridge boxes of the dead and wounded rebels. Then a force of Southerners came rushing at them in a counterattack aimed at retaking the hill, but, with the help of a four-gun battery that unlimbered on the hill behind them, the 26th repelled the new assault before it could get very close.[127]

With the rebel counterattack defeated, a lull ensued. Looking about him, Winkler noted that "The intense heat of the sun, added to the heat of the contest, had utterly exhausted the men, and when the excitement was over quite a number fell into a swoon." To Col. Wood, they appeared "nearly exhausted by the extreme heat of the day and the severe fighting." He ordered the 73rd Ohio forward to relieve them, noting in his report that "On being relieved the regiment fell back about fifty yards to the rear, where it took position in line of battle, ready to spring to their guns in case of necessity."[128]

Turning to retire to the second line, the weary men had a full view of the dead and dying littering the slope behind them. Making his way to the field hospital, Kuechenmeister picked up a souvenir he later took home to Wisconsin, a cedar canteen inscribed "W. E. Ratcliffe, 33d Mississippi Infantry." Among the fallen littering the slope were Confederate Colonel Jabez L. Drake and most of the officers of the 33rd Mississippi, nearly 50 Confederate soldiers, and too many of their own friends and comrades.[129] "This was a sight which I had never seen before and hope never to see again," wrote Buerstatte. "The entire field was scattered with dead, wounded and dying. The wounded moaned so much that I could hardly watch."[130]

Capt. John P. Seemann, Company I, a commissioner from Milwaukee. Killed in action at Peach
Tree Creek.

Courtesy of the U.S. Army Military History Institute

John Held, Company D, a cooper from
Racine. Killed in action at Peach Tree
Creek

John Fuhrmann, Company E, a farmer
from Princeton. Injured while building
breastworks at Peach Tree Creek.

Courtesy of Eliot Held   *Courtesy of Steven Miske.*

Moving back down the hill, "the men were so exhausted they could hardly move; some had to be carried back though not wounded." Their "guns were so hot from rapid firing that the men could not touch the barrels." The oppressive heat, the unshielded sun, the constant fear and exhilaration of the sharp action, the exhausting charge up the hill, and the dogged defense left many completely exhausted, while others were pushed to the edge of their mental endurance. To Winkler, Adjutant George Traeumer "seemed to be in hysterics, and for a time I almost feared that he was dying." Others were in similar condition, and Winker felt so tired he "had not strength to speak above a whisper."[131]

The extraordinary fight lasted only about 45 minutes, but it cost the regiment dearly. Among the nine dead were Captains John P. Seemann of Company I and Robert Mueller of Company C. Others included Sergeants Stephen Feiss and Bernhard Ott, Corporals John Held and Franz Reuter, and Privates William Arnn, Xavier Braun, Gerhard Niephaus, William Sasse, and Jacob Weber. The 36 wounded included Captain William Steinmeyer of Company E and Lieutenant Nicholas Wollmer of Company G. The latter lingered on in pain until August 21 when he died. Julius Semich, his eye destroyed and a ball lodged in his head, was carried to the field hospital and then sent north. Miraculously, he survived to join the Veteran Reserve Corps before being discharged for disability and pensioned. But the losses were not without purpose. The stand of the 26th Wisconsin's *freiwilligen* in the ravine blunted the Confederate assault, and its charge up the hill, followed by the rest of Wood's Brigade, took the Confederate line in flank and rear, relieving the pressure on Newton's Division and allowing that unit to hold its shaky position.[132] So effective was the fire of the Sigel Regiment and the other units of Wood's brigade that every Confederate regimental commander save one was killed or wounded and Featherston's brigade reported that the "severe fire" cut down 616 of its 1,230 effectives, a loss of 50% of its strength.[133]

Winkler was elated with the performance of his men: "At last I have some good news. We fought the hardest battle and won the greatest victory yesterday of all the campaign, and my regiment covered itself with glory. We were attacked by superior numbers, the forces on our left failed us; we were outflanked, but we whipped the enemy, turned, and pursued him to the position we coveted, got it and held it."[134]

Nor was Winkler the only one impressed. In the 33rd Massachusetts, Col. Adin Underwood credited the Sigel Regiment with "pluckily" holding fast in the face of a "heavy fire" from front and flank, pouring in "a heavy fire which scattered the enemy's front," and leading the counterattack that "relieved the pressure on Newton's division."[135] In his report on the battle the brigade commander, Colonel Wood, singled out the Badgers for special praise:

> To us it was a brilliant feat of arms. We encountered the enemy in superior numbers in the open field. We met his offensive attack with an offensive return; his charge with a countercharge. The victory was complete and decisive....Where all behaved well, it may be regarded as invidious to call attention to individuals, yet it seems to me that I cannot discharge my whole duty in this report without pointing out for especial commendation the conduct of the 26th Wisconsin Volunteer Infantry, and its brave and able commander. The position of this regiment in the line was such that the brunt of the attack on this brigade fell upon it. The brave, skillful and determinate manner in which it met this attack, rolled back the onset, pressed forward in a counter charge and drove back the enemy, could not be excelled by the troops in this or any other army, and is worthy of the highest commendation and praise. It is to be hoped that such conduct will be held up as an example for others, and will meet the appropriate reward.[136]

Occasional gunshots rang out during the night as edgy pickets fired at whatever shadows presented themselves. Removed from the front line, the men in the Sigel Regiment replenished their ammunition, helped carry the wounded from behind the lines, then settled down to a long, uneasy night with little chance for rest. Three stretchers kept at work all night retrieving the wounded, the men taking turns on this difficult humanitarian duty.[137] Charles Stamm estimated Union troops buried "over 137" rebel soldiers and claimed he fired 113 shots during the fight.[138] The next day Buerstatte captured the mood in his diary: "This morning our regiment, after a sleepless night, had to bury the dead Rebs which laid before our regiment. They were all from the 33rd Mississippi Regiment. Our regiment lost 9 dead and 36 wounded. We buried over 50 Rebs, among them Colonel Drake and most of the officers of the 33rd Miss. Regiment. Now we had to clean our guns."[139]

Throughout the day on July 21 the regiment remained on alert about a half mile from the Confederate front line fortifications as enemy sharpshooters sent an occasional shot into its position. That night the rebels silently abandoned their works, continuing their retreat southward toward the fortifications surrounding Atlanta.[140]

In the aftermath of the fight, his friends carried Lt. Wollmer, a very popular officer, to the field hospital where he lingered on in pain until succumbing to his wounds on August 21. His remains were sent home to Manitowoc where his funeral attracted "an immense concourse of people" including Major Henry Baetz and Wollmer's friends from the *Manitowoc Freier Sängerbund*. In honor of their deceased friend, the officers of the regiment contributed $123 which Major Lackner transmitted to Wollmer's widow and three children with "our sincere condolence" for the loss of her husband, their "brother officer" who "has ever been a true friend, and a brave and respected comrade." In response, Mrs. Wollmer accepted the gift:

> with warm and hearty thanks, for the reason that it comes from my husbands comrades, who served with him for two years, who fought by his side in so many battles for our dear and bleeding country; for the reason that it comes from brave men who amid the roar of the cannon, in the throng of the battle and the groans of the wounded and dying, have yet preserved a feeling heart for a poor widow and orphans, whom they are not acquainted with, but know that they exist, and that Lt. Wollmer was their supporter and protector. Gentlemen, receive my warm thanks, and may the God of Battles preserve you, and permit you, happier than my poor husband was to come home again to your dear wives and children; permit you to be received with that love you deserve, and may you enjoy for long, long time, the blessings of liberty and peace of our beloved country, which when it calls out her heroes among the first will be the officers of the 26th Regiment.[141]

Siege of Atlanta

After suffering heavy casualties at Peach Tree Creek, Hood retired back into the fortifications around Atlanta. On the 22nd, in a probe of McPherson's exposed flank, that general was killed and replaced as commander of the Army of the Tennessee by Oliver O. Howard. Hooker, offended because he ranked Howard and coveted the position, angrily resigned command of the Twentieth Corps. Sherman replaced him with Henry Slocum, former commander of the Twelfth Corps.[142]

The same day McPherson met his fate, the Sigel Regiment marched in pursuit of the retreating rebels. "The boys are in good spirits," Winkler wrote, "they are ready for the most desperate deeds."[143] On they marched into the dwindling daylight. "Toward evening," Buerstatte wrote, "the Rebs greeted us with cannonfire." Four guns were brought forward and placed along the regiment's position to reply to the rebel fire, quickly silencing the offending guns. When the day's march concluded the men set to work constructing the usual breastworks only two and one-half miles from Atlanta. From their position, Buerstatte marveled that "One can see the towers of Atlanta," while Winkler felt "very confident now that Atlanta will soon be ours."[144] Within a few hours, however, a Confederate sharpshooter found Sergt. Franz Warver, a shoemaker from Racine. His arm amputated, he was taken to Nashville where he lost his battle for life on October 14.

Saturday, July 23, found them on the march again, moving off to the right where they were ordered to support Dilger's Ohio battery in the opening stages of the bombardment of Atlanta. Buerstatte noted with concern that "Heavy defenses rise before us."[145] On the 27th, two men were slightly wounded by a shell. Four days later the men were suddenly ordered to arms, placed in line and hurriedly marched off to support the right wing. After marching only a short way, they alternately halted and moved, making little progress but all the while standing exposed to the horrible sunlight. "The heat was intense," Winkler reported, "over a dozen men were attacked by sunstroke." About noon, during a brief halt, Winkler unpacked a small package of tartaric acid he received from home and mixed it with water to make a crude lemonade he found "good and refreshing." Gaining the right flank, exhausted by the fatiguing march, the men went to work to construct breastworks before being allowed any rest. Placed on the right flank in a refused position, the brigade formed the extreme right of the entire army. "We have built miles of breastworks," Winkler commented, "but have never yet fought in any of them."[146]

On August 3 orders arrived for the Sigel Regiment to move into the front lines besieging the rebel city. Thus began more than three weeks of brutal trench warfare during which the men were "constantly engaged in siege and fatigue duty," taking part in "several reconnaissances and many skirmishes, losing three men killed and four wounded." Though changing its position several times, the regiment was constantly under fire from sharpshooters and artillery ranging from 20-pound Parrott guns to huge 64-pounders.[147]

The days wore on, one like another, causing men to lose track of time. "One almost doesn't realize it [is Sunday] because the bombardment continues without letup," Buerstatte wrote. "We received a little whiskey today. The Rebs bothered us very much. They lobbed 64-pounders at us."[148] Aside from the rebels, the static life in the trenches was made more uncomfortable by the constant heat and bothersome insects. "I have not seen an honest blade of grass in Georgia," Winkler wrote, "our horses look poor; the heat and flies are hard on them, and feed so poor and scanty....There are thousands of little flies which are the greatest annoyance. They are everywhere, swarming in clouds in the air, settling like locusts on our sugar, mixing like spice with our apple sauce, and floating like ducks in our coffee and tea."[149] The intense heat, constant digging to extend and strengthen the lines, the annoying flies, and the deadly sharpshooters made each day a lengthy misery. "Not until night can we get the benefit of night's sweet restorer," commented Winkler.[150]

Annoyances aside, life in the trenches was quite dangerous. Tragedy could strike without warning. "This constant firing, when not really fighting, is the greatest annoyance of this campaign, and the losses it involves are so painful." On August 8 Reinhold Nemitz was "dangerously wounded" while standing only about ten paces from Winkler's tent. "This poor boy this morning seemed to feel it so deeply; he sobbed amid his groans and faltered forth, 'Oh, I have gone through so many battles, and now I must be wounded here in camp.' He gave directions to write to his father and said he could not live. In a pitched battle, we have so much to occupy us, but here in camp it is horrible to see our men wounded."[151] Nemitz died that same day. During the reconnaissances and skirmishes attending the seige operations the regiment lost two men killed and two wounded. It nearly suffered another when a ball tore through the boot on Frank Fisher's left foot. Carried in an ambulance to a field hospital after being wounded at Kennesaw Mountain, the surgeons cut a ball "as flat as a 25-cent piece" out of him before he regained consciousness. Taken to a hospital in Chattanooga, it took Fisher seven weeks to recuperate enough to rejoin the regiment outside Atlanta. Only just returned, he escaped personal injury in this close call.[152]

Amid the constant annoyances and danger in the trenches, documents arrived from the governor's office appointing Winkler colonel of the regiment and Lackner lieutenant colonel. Ironically, because of the losses in the regiment its aggregate number fell to less than the number required for the appointment of a colonel. Winkler and Lackner, after all they and their men had accomplished in the march to Atlanta, could not be mustered in their new ranks.[153]

On the evening of August 25 orders arrived for the regiment to retire to the rear. Quietly, so as not to arouse a Confederate reaction, the men withdrew from the trenches and formed into line of march. Moving westward to Turner's Ferry on the Chattahoochee River, they crossed on a pontoon bridge and began building the ever-present breastworks to guard the river crossing.[154] "This army is great on digging," Winkler wrote. "Our main work nowadays is done with pick and spade. Every position that is taken is very strongly fortified, and as long as we remain in a place the boys seem to make it their pastime to keep constantly adding to the strength of their works. They learned from the rebels."[155]

Occasional cavalry raids and a Confederate reconnaissance in force on the 28th kept the men ever vigilant, but the new camp was much more appealing than life in the trenches. "We have a very nice place here now," Winkler wrote, "a shady grove—and it would not be bad if we were to stay for a time." With the move the weather also turned more amenable. "We are enjoying pleasant weather now with our easy times; the nights are very cool, everything is wet in the morning."[156]

While in the new camp, life returned to some semblance of routine order. Newspapers and mail arrived more frequently, and Winkler's thoughts turned to politics. Though favoring the Republicans, he was not particularly inclined to Lincoln's renomination. "I confess that I am not a very great, enthusiastic admirer of his, and I think the country might afford us an abler and a stronger Chief Magistrate, but it is hard to say who that man is, or at least who the proper man in the present crisis would be."[157] With the nomination of McClellan by the Democrats meeting in Chicago, Winkler pronounced himself "glad" as "he is certainly the most respectable and patriotic" of the Democratic candidates. "[W]hatever may be said of his political opinions, his antecedents and avowed principles admit of no doubt as to his loyalty to the United States and his hostility to the Rebellion."[158] Winkler believed that Lincoln would be re-elected if the military prospects brightened, but felt confident with McClellan should the election go the other way. "[I]f McClellan should be chosen, unless he repudiates every act and word of his past life, his course cannot be essentially different. It is quite remarkable how diametrically opposed McClellan's course has been to that advocated by the present peace faction of the Democratic party."[159]

On September 1 a minister from Ohio, a former resident of Madison, Wisconsin, visited the 73rd Ohio and came over to the Badger's camp, accompanied by the 73rd's band, to visit. Rev. Britton made a pleasant speech, the band played lively aires, and for one evening the war seemed far away.[160]

The regiment held its position at Turner's Ferry for a week before moving forward again. But this time the march to the front was one of victory. Two officers and seventy men were detached as a reconnaissance party that entered the city of Atlanta and found it abandoned by the rebel army.[161] Karsten noted the houses throughout town were destroyed or damaged. An entry in Buerstatte's diary dated September 2 describes it thusly: "This morning we left our quarters at the river at 5:00 o'clock and filed through wood and field, over hill and dale toward Atlanta. We came to the city at 10:00 o'clock. The city immediately surrendered. We drove 30 Reb cavalry before us through the city. Several stores were broken into and tobacco was taken from them. Many Germans live here."[162] Winkler was more succinct: "I have good news—Atlanta is ours."[163]

With the fall of Atlanta, the campaign effectively came to an end. The result was aptly described by Lt. Col. Winkler: "Hood has fought four battles, one north, one east, and one west, and finally one south of the city, and raided our railroad. He gained the satisfactory result of holding the city long enough to see a great portion of it devastated and then left it, his army broken, reduced and demoralized, and valuable stores of munitions of war left a prey to the flames."[164] At a time when Grant's offensive in Virginia had ground to a halt with tremendous casualties causing war-weariness to grip the North on the eve of the important 1864 presidential election, the fall of Atlanta gave renewed hope to Northerners and did more than anything else to insure the reelection of Abraham Lincoln.

Chapter 11

MARCHING THROUGH GEORGIA

March to the Sea

O n a warm, clear September evening Lt. Col. Winkler and Major Lackner "took a moonlight ride" around the city of Atlanta, stopping for a while at Gen. Thomas' headquarters "where the excellent band of the 33rd Massachusetts discoursed some of its exquisite music." The two officers found Atlanta a "fine city; there must have been a great deal of wealth in it. There are many large mansions and it looks much like a western city." Daily its citizens fled to the Southern lines, taking what little they could carry with them. The few Union sympathizers likewise began leaving "for a grand migration northward," making the city nearly deserted save for the roaming soldiery.[1]

In the camps outside the formerly rebel city the soldiers gained renewed hope the war would soon be over. On September 8th Gen. Sherman's General Order was read to the troops, congratulating them on their great victory and thanking them for their sacrifices. Before the end of September news arrived of "the splendid victory won by General Sheridan in the Shenandoah Valley" and everyone was once again "jubilant."[2] Although Confederate cavalry continued to harass Union supply lines and attack isolated posts, it was clear to everyone that the fall of Atlanta marked a turning point on the road to ultimate victory. Yet, another battle lay just around the corner.

As the army sat outside Atlanta recuperating from the campaign and planning its next moves, the battlefield moved north to Wisconsin where the fall elections loomed crucial. All that had been achieved in the recent months of suffering could be undone by a victory of the

Northern peace faction. On both the federal and state levels the political contests raged unabated that fall, the soldiers taking a lively interest in the campaigns. While opinions on the presidential race were mixed, the soldiers were overwhelmingly in favor of prosecuting the war to a successful conclusion, most supporting the candidacy of Abraham Lincoln as a means of securing that end. In the Sigel Regiment the men looked with interest on the race for mayor of Milwaukee where the incumbent, Abner Kirby, was said to be sympathetic to Copperhead views.[3]

As the campaign developed, politicians actively courted the soldier vote. "We are overwhelmed with a flood of political prints and pamphlets," Winkler wrote. "I don't know how my regiment will vote; it used to be strongly democratic, still I think the officers are, save one or two, for Lincoln. I never talk to them on political subjects. I am going to vote the Republican ticket straight through, but beyond that will not meddle with politics." To Winkler, at least, the choice was clear. An anti-war victory at the polls would be disastrous to the Union cause. No admirer of Lincoln, he felt the Illinoisan "personally no abler or stronger than McClellan, but the influences which surround him, both of political and military men, are such as to support and strengthen him. I have little doubt that Lincoln will be elected, but the greater his majority, the more emphatic will be the blow to the enemies of the country."[4]

When the election finally arrived, the Sigel Regiment, drawn from largely Democratic areas of Wisconsin and returning an overwhelming Democratic vote in elections the previous year, cast 112 votes for Lincoln and 88 for McClellan. In other Badger regiments the vote was not as close. Altogether, Wisconsin soldiers in the army returned a decisive majority vote for Lincoln, giving him 11,372 votes while casting only 2,428 for other candidates. Without these votes, Lincoln would have lost the state. Similarly, the "soldier vote" proved pivotal in electing Republicans to several local, state, and congressional offices, including General Halbert E. Paine as Republican congressman from Milwaukee.[5] In the end, the results so painfully won on the battlefield were sustained at the ballot box.

While the election campaign unfolded, the Sigel Regiment recuperated from its summer ordeal. Concerts, reviews, and other diversions occurred with regularity, but news was infrequent due to rebel raids on the railroad lines. "We get no mail," Winkler complained in early October, "no trains have gone north from Chattanooga for some time. We get no information as to the actual state of things and have to be contented as best we can."[6] Some of the news that did get through was unsettling. Families at home often wrote of illness, anxiety, and economic hardship. Two years after the regiment mustered in, many families found their state funds suddenly cut off. Concern increased to the point where 1st Lt. Joseph Maschauer wrote directly to Wisconsin Governor Lucius Fairchild:

> Sir,
>   Many of my men complain that their families do not get the state pay which they heretofore received and I thought it proper to send you a list of the strength of my company as it was on the 1st of May 1864. We have not been paid of[f] since Dec. 31st 1863 and some of my men's families are therefore suffering. In hope that you will be kind enough to correct errors. I remain,
>
> Very Respectfully,
> Your Obedt servant

During the day the men drilled and performed fatigue duties, constructing and improving fortifications and laying corduroy roads. All things considered, however, the time spent outside Atlanta after its fall was a very welcome relief. On October 5, after most had given up hope of ever being paid again, the paymaster at last arrived in camp. Some received as much as eight or nine months pay, enough to make spirits soar. To Winkler it was "more money than they know what to do with."[7] The ill and the lightly wounded returned for duty, food improved, the oppressive humidity gave way to milder weather, and morale continued high as word of Union successes in other theaters speard throughout the camps.

The life of relative ease came to an end on October 7 when Winkler received orders to move the regiment north to reinforce the 1st Brigade guarding the railroad bridge over the Chattahoochee River. The regiment marched off to its new assignment the next morning, reporting to Col. Franklin C. Smith that same day. They found their new camp devoid of even rudimentary necessities, let alone amenities, and "very cold." The first night there they "were fairly driven into bed last night by the cheerless cold." The next night was no better. "To-night we sleep in our uniforms," Winkler wrote, "otherwise there is no standing it."[8]

As the days passed, Winkler returned briefly to Atlanta for courts martial duty, leaving the regiment in the hands of Major Lackner. On the 19th the men prepared three days rations, then Lackner led them off on a reconnaissance and foraging expedition into the countryside toward Roswell, Georgia. On the 20th they came within a mile of that town, camping there overnight. The next morning, loading their forage wagons with corn, they left at noon for Marietta, covering sixteen miles in six hours. The expedition returned to camp on the 21st without loss.[9]

While rebel raiders continued to stage hit-and-run attacks on isolated posts and pickets, the regiment got along quite well once it put its camp in order. Farmers from the surrounding countryside "bring butter, eggs, chickens, etc. to our picket line and are there met by our men, who trade coffee and sugar for them. Our foragers have brought in a few things, geese, ducks, apples, etc."[10] Occasional foraging expeditions broke the routine, but otherwise all remained quiet as October turned to November.

On the first day of the new month orders arrived for the Sigel Regiment to "prepare at once for an active campaign with very limited transportation."[11] Speculation ran wild about the meaning of the orders, most feeling the army would be off in pursuit of Hood's Confederate army then in northern Alabama. Other speculation was that Gen. Sherman would leave a force to protect Atlanta and northern Georgia, while driving with his main army toward either Mobile or Savannah. Winkler approved. "The rebel army in its present demoralized state ought to be followed up," he wrote. "I am ready for my part. If I could start out with four hundred muskets, as I did four months ago, it would be more gratifying. Three officers and thirty-two men killed, four officers and one hundred and fifty three men wounded, are the casualties of the regiment in the last campaign; besides there is a large number of men sick in many of the large hospitals. That terrible army disease, scurvy, has made inroads upon us." To compensate for the losses he received a single recruit. "[T]hink of it," he mused sarcastically, "one recruit." In any event, given the lateness of the season Winkler did not think it would be "a very long campaign or a bloody one."[12] Although one recruit arrived, Lt. Karsten left for home on furlough on October 25, having submitted his resignation.

While the regiment made ready to move, little information arrived from the outside world. Artillery and musketry fire echoed through their position from Atlanta on November 9 as some Georgia militia and cavalry clashed briefly with the federal garrison, but otherwise the days were uneventful. "We have had a good long rest and must not complain," Winkler counseled.[13]

Finally, at 4:00 p.m. on November 13, orders arrived to destroy their camp, the railroad, the bridge, and be ready to march the next morning. "We all went out at once," Winkler remembered, "and worked long after dark; the whole railroad is in ruins. That large bridge we have been so anxious to guard all this time, is no more."[14] When they returned to camp late that night the men received a ration of whiskey for their efforts. Up early the next morning, they finished packing before putting the torch to their campsite, destroying anything that might be of any service to the Confederates after they left. At 10:00 a.m. Winkler led the regiment off along the road to Atlanta, a new campaign of uncertainty before them.[15]

To the Sea

After being forced out of Atlanta, Gen. John Bell Hood moved the Confederate Army of Tennessee north to attack Sherman's supply and communication lines in the hope this would force him to abandon Atlanta. Failing this, and convinced he could neither retake Atlanta nor successfully oppose Sherman's force in the open countryside, Hood moved his army into northern Alabama where he made ready to invade Tennessee, a strategy he hoped would force Sherman to abandon Georgia and allow the Confederates to recruit and reprovision in the Volunteer State. Faced with Hood's movement north, Sherman decided to concentrate the Fourth and Twenty-third Corps and scattered Union forces in Tennessee and Kentucky to oppose the Confederate invasion under the command of Gen. George H. Thomas. Meanwhile, Sherman determined to lead the rest of his forces southeastward through the Georgia heartland, destroying railroads, factories, government stores, and other resources supporting the Southern war effort in a bold drive to the Atlantic seacoast. Such a move, he reasoned, would have three desirable effects: it would destroy much of the economic infrastructure of the Southern war effort, it would strike a blow at Southern morale, and it would place Sherman in position to move north through the

Carolinas to cooperate with Grant's forces in capturing Richmond and destroying Lee's Army of Northern Virginia.[16]

Under Sherman's plan the men would advance in two giant wings. The right wing, consisting of the Army of the Tennessee under Gen. Oliver O. Howard, included the Fifteenth and Seventeenth Corps. The left wing, styled the Army of Georgia and led by Gen. Henry Slocum, included the Fourteenth and Twentieth Corps. The cavalry, Gen. Judson Kilpatrick's 3rd Division, was to protect the flanks and rear of Sherman's forces, while also scouting ahead and foraging for supplies. Altogether, Sherman's force contained 55,000 infantry, 5,000 cavalry, 2,000 artillerymen, and 64 guns. To oppose him the Confederacy could muster only 3,000 Georgia militia and state troops under Gen. Gustavus W. Smith and Gen. Joseph Wheeler's cavalry force of about 10,000 troopers.[17]

On November 15, as Winkler led his small command back to the rendezvous near Atlanta, Sherman burned the remaining stores and military equipment in the city, loaded twenty day's rations into the limited wagon train that would be his supply base on the march, and issued orders for the advance of his army. Led temporarily by Gen. Alpheus S. Williams, the Twentieth Corps included the divisions of Nathaniel J. Jackson, John W. Geary, and William T. Ward. The Sigel Regiment was attached to the 3rd Brigade of Ward's 3rd Division. In addition to the Badgers, the brigade included its comrades of the recent campaign, the 20th Connecticut, 33rd Massachusetts, 55th Ohio, 73rd Ohio, and 136th New York. As the corps moved out on its eastward journey, the 26th found itself assigned to the rear of the column, behind the corps supply train. Always an odious position, the marching was slow and haphazard because of the frequent stops and starts of the wagons ahead. Winkler found it "very tedious marching," taking all night to cover the sixteen miles to Stone Mountain. After only a brief rest and time to have breakfast, the column resumed its march through "the desolate village of Decatur."[18] On they trudged through the morning, afternoon, and well into the evening, crossing the Yellow River at Rock Bridge on the evening of the 16th before finally falling out for a few brief hours of sleep.[19]

Marching along the railroad line to Augusta, the regiment spent considerable time tearing up the rails, burning the ties, and destroying anything the Confederates might use to aid their war effort. On the

17th they passed through Sheffield where they "commenced foraging with good success."[20] They reached Social Circle about 10:00 a.m. on the 18th, some fifty-one miles from Atlanta, still tearing up and destroying the railroad as they went. At Madison on the morning of November 19 they destroyed another 250 to 300 yards of track before turning southward, away from the railroad, moving along the Oconee River toward the Georgia capitol at Milledgeville.[21]

"The country is full of large plantations," Winkler noted, and "some of the villages are very beautiful. Madison has magnificent mansions and gardens, roses and other flowers are in full bloom everywhere."[22] Amid the picturesque setting, destruction continued wherever potential military supplies or equipment could be found. Nor was destruction the only punishment visited upon the countryside. "We began to live from that which we found on the plantations," Buerstatte confided to his diary on the evening of the 19th, "such as potatoes, pigs, chickens, sheep and cornmeal." The 20th brought three days of rain and mud to further complicate the marching, but the column pushed on regardless of the weather.[23]

On November 22 they plodded into Milledgeville still under rainy skies, an army at once of destruction and liberation. Winkler found the "white people of Georgia are cold and for the most part intensely Secesh, and remain true to the most terrible resolutions that they will never give up, but the negroes...are the most devoted friends of the Yankee soldiers. Their demonstrations are literally frantic. They dance and shout and clap their hands when they see our column approach. Whatever a soldier may ask for, they hasten to do for him. Whatever their masters have, he will get. It is claimed the negroes are so well contented with their slavery; if it ever was so, that day has ceased to be. Hundreds of men go with us, and thousands would if they could take their families along."[24]

After spending a day in the Georgia capital, the column moved off again, struggling through flooded swamps and swollen creeks to Sandersville. The weather cleared on the 23rd, but strong winds continued to buffet the men as they pushed along trying to maintain their pace. Buerstatte noted the men "crowded ourselves quite close together" in the narrow roadway.[25] On November 26 the advance brushed away Wheeler's Confederate cavalry after "a light skirmish" and the column wound its way into Sandersville. Despite the weather and the

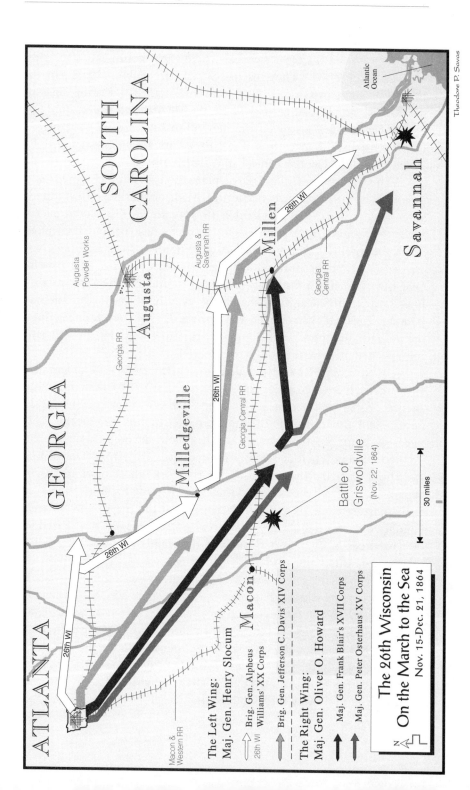

Theodore P. Savas

ATLANTIC
OCEAN

SOUTH
CAROLINA

GEORGIA

Augusta Powder Works

Augusta

Augusta & Savannah RR

Millen

26th WI

Georgia RR

Georgia Central RR

Milledgeville

26th WI

Georgia Central RR

Savannah

Macon

Battle of
Griswoldville
(Nov. 22, 1864)

26th WI

Macon & Western RR

30 miles

The Left Wing:
Maj. Gen. Henry Slocum

⇨ Brig. Gen. Alpheus
26th WI Williams' XX Corps

⇨ Brig. Gen. Jefferson C. Davis' XIV Corps

The Right Wing:
Maj. Gen. Oliver O. Howard

⬆ Maj. Gen. Frank Blair's XVII Corps

⬆ Maj. Gen. Peter Osterhaus' XV Corps

**The 26th Wisconsin
On the March to the Sea**
Nov. 15-Dec. 21, 1864

N

lack of rest, Winkler found the men "all in very good condition." By now he "supposed Savannah to be our objective point; we are about half way now. I hope the remainder of our journey will be as successful."[26]

The regiment stood for inspection on the morning of November 27, moving out again about 10:00 a.m. While Kilpatrick's cavalry dueled almost daily with Wheeler's Confederate horsemen, infantry skirmishes were few as the lines of march pressed on through Davisboro to the Ogeechee River with the 26th still acting as rear guard. Approaching Louisville, "a great deal of bridging and 'corduroying' was necessary" to negotiate "innumerable rivers, creeks and swamps."[27] Passing through Louisville on the 29th, they bivouacked southeast of town that evening and spent the next day engaged in what Buerstatte termed "a well-deserved rest."[28]

"Our duty has been very easy lately," Winkler opined, but he was appalled by the depredations daily inflicted upon the Southern inhabitants. "Some of the most outrageous depredations and excesses are daily committed by our soldiers here," he lamented. "Citizens are robbed daily of everything. It is really heart-rending to enter some of these houses and see how like demons our soldiers have behaved." Winkler sent guards to several nearby homes to protect them from marauding soldiers.[29] Yet, the Sigel Regiment was not reluctant to secure its needs from the countryside. In his official report on the campaign, Col. Winkler admitted that "two men and a pack-mule from each company, sent out daily, brought in sufficient to subsist the command wholly."[30]

December 1 found the regiment on the road again. Though daily skirmishes occurred at the head of the column and along its flanks, the rear guard remained untested. The roads turned bad, swollen swamps and creeks caused delays necessitating construction of corduroy roads and bridges, but while the march was frequently slowed it could not be stopped. Mile after mile the armies drew nearer their goal. By December 3 they were near Springfield on the west bank of Jack's Branch. "We are in a poor country now," Winkler informed those at home, "pine forests and swamps, and here and there a small plantation. So far we have been able to forage all the sweet potatoes and fresh meat we wanted. Sweet potatoes have been the great staple of the Army of Georgia."[31]

"Today is Sunday but we had to march anyhow," Buerstatte wrote on December 4. "The entire area around Andersonville is swampy and roads are bad."[32] Regardless, the relentless march continued. On the 6th they reached Springfield. The next day Buerstatte described marching "among ruins and mud" about twenty-five miles from Savannah, while on the 9th artillery firing echoed back from the front and left flank as Wheeler made a final attempt to interfere with Sherman's progress toward his destination. Moving along the Charleston and Savannah Railroad, December 10 found the Sigel Regiment within four and one-half miles of its coastal objective.[33] "Before us and near us we hear cannonfire near the 14th Corps and 17 A.C.," Buerstatte wrote. "The 14th is to our left and 17 A.C. is to our right and in front of us." At noon the firing grew loud and word came for the brigade to form into line of battle with the 26th on the extreme left, but nothing further developed and they soon stood down.[34]

With the army at the very gates of Savannah, siege operations commenced immediately with the 26th held in reserve. "The bombing continues without stopping near us," Buerstatte wrote on December 11. "Our rations are now short and one discovers what hunger feels like."[35] After two days of bombardment, a division of the Fifteenth Corps stormed Fort McAllister, opening communication and supply lines to Adm. Dahlgren's fleet and the Union base at Port Royal.[36]

After the fall of Fort McAllister, Winkler rode down to the river to see the area. He found "immense rice plantations" and "a large number of mills....The rebel troops were very kind to leave the immense stores of rice undisturbed; it is the only thing we have, except captured beef, to feed our army."[37] But the time for sightseeing was limited, as the siege moved closer to a conclusion the Sigel Regiment moved closer to the front, assigned to the first assault wave in the upcoming attack on the Confederate works protecting the city. Moved to a position on the right of the brigade between the Charleston and Savannah and the Central Railroads, the regiment found itself opposite a rebel fort mounting heavy guns that showered their earthworks with spherical case shot "loaded with balls two inches in diameter."[38]

Protected by strong earthworks, the men kept well hidden from the rebel artillery and sharpshooters. Meanwhile, preparations for the assault continued. Experienced eyes examined every foot of terrain, concluding the task would not be easy. "For several hundred yards we would have to go through a deep swamp," Winkler explained, "where all the trees, brush, briers, and vines had to be cut down; serious apprehensions were, therefore, entertained that, although successful, the losses would be great."[39] By now the veterans of so many fields knew full well what the proposed assault would mean. No one looked forward to the death and destruction certain to accompany such a desperate attack. Thus, when orders arrived on the morning of December 21 for Winkler to get his regiment in line and be prepared to "move upon the enemy at once," he feared the worse. Great relief swept through the regiment, and "much rejoicing," when news arrived that the rebels had fled across the Savannah River during the night, abandoning the city to the Yankees.[40]

As soon as the Confederate retreat became known, Sherman's army moved in to occupy the seacoast city. On the morning of the 21st orders arrived for the Sigel Regiment to advance. "The Rebs have left," Buerstatte announced, "and we had to pack in 5 minutes and march toward Savannah, where we set up quarters 1 mile west of the city. We now have as much rice as we want. The Rebs have fled to South Carolina. We captured much rice, cannons and munitions which the enemy left behind. We also captured many prisoners."[41] The historic march to the sea was over, the Confederacy sliced into parts, and its ability to continue the war seriously damaged. Winkler pronounced it "the most successful campaign known in military history."[42]

With the fall of Savannah, Sherman set about consolidating his position and preparing his next move. On Christmas Eve men in the Sigel Regiment cleaned their quarters. Buerstatte reported that "Each person planted a Christmas tree in front of his tent" to create a festive atmosphere. Christmas morning the regiment stood for inspection, then "received a 1/2 unit [of] crackers, rice and meat."[43] Despite the meager fare, there was much to be thankful for on this, their third Christmas away from home. The capture of Atlanta, the reelection of Lincoln, the successful march through Georgia, and the surrender of Savannah were crippling blows to the Confederacy. Yet, other good news also brightened the day and the prospects for the future. In the fall Union forces swept the Shenandoah Valley clear of Confederates, destroying Jubal Early's rebel army. Grant had Lee bottled up in Petersburg, and as they approached Savannah came the welcome news that Hood had been roughly handled at Franklin, Tennessee. Now came the news that Hood had "met with a crushing defeat" at Nashville, virtually destroying his army. Things could hardly look brighter for the Union cause. "The rebels are crippled everywhere," Winkler wrote with obvious joy, sensing that the coming year might finally be the last in what appeared only weeks ago to be a seemingly interminable war.[44]

Chapter 12

THROUGH THE HEART OF SECESSION

The Carolinas Campaign

*W*ith the fall of Savannah, Gen. Grant determined to employ Sherman's troops in conjunction with the Army of the Potomac and Gen. Benjamin Butler's Army of the James to overwhelm and destroy the Army of Northern Virginia. To implement this, Sherman was to feint toward Charleston and Augusta, then push his 60,000 troops northward through the Carolinas to a rendezvous with Grant's forces besieging Richmond and Petersburg. To oppose the advance the Confederates rushed troops into South Carolina from scattered points, but by the beginning of February could muster only 22,500 men under Gen. Pierre G. T. Beauregard. When Robert E. Lee was finally installed as general-in-chief of all Confederate armies, he brought Gen. Joseph E. Johnston in to command the defense of the Carolinas with Beauregard remaining as his second-in-command.[1]

Before Sherman's move could begin, provision had to be made to supply his forces as they moved northward. To this end, Grant ordered the capture of Ft. Fisher and Wilmington, North Carolina. With these in hand, Northern forces could push forward from Wilmington and New Bern to Goldsboro, providing Sherman with considerably shorter and more reliable supply lines as he advanced. After an unsuccessful attempt in December, Ft. Fisher fell on January 15, 1865. Wilmington passed into federal hands on February 22. By mid-March, Union forces were in Goldsboro, completing preparations for Sherman's resupply.[2]

While these preparations were underway, Sherman concentrated his forces, planned feints toward Charleston and Augusta to confuse the Confederates as to his intentions, and established a bridgehead on the north side of the Savannah River. To carry out these plans, Howard's Fifteenth and Seventeenth Corps went by ship to the head of Port Royal Sound. In Slocum's army, the Fourteenth Corps moved thirty miles upriver before crossing, while the Twentieth Corps received the assignment of crossing the river at Savannah.[3]

Into the "Hot-bed of Secession"

The day after Christmas Winkler received orders to move the Sigel Regiment across to the north side of the Savannah River the following day.[4] "[T]hat will take us into South Carolina," he thought, "that hot-bed of secession. If the people of that state had been listeners to the conversations of officers and soldiers here lately, they would know their doom is no enviable one. It seems to be a favorite contemplation with all, how they will plunder upon getting into South Carolina....Soldiers like sweet potatoes and young pork, varied with poultry, much better than lean beef and hard tack. It is cheaper also for the United States. Then there are some railroads there too, that ought to be fixed."[5]

On the 27th, marching orders were postponed, giving the men an opportunity to enjoy beautiful, summer-like weather. Daily drills resumed, but this did not seem to bother anyone as the food, the rest, and the continuing good news kept morale high. On December 30 Gen. Sherman reviewed the entire Twentieth Corps, the men making a fine impression.[6]

Early on New Year's Eve morning the regiment filed out of its camp in the rain, marched about two miles to the South Branch, and crossed the stream to Hutchinson's Island. The weather turned cold and unpleasant as the men sat on the island waiting to cross to the South Carolina shore. On the far bank, Southern cavalry roamed about sniping at any federals within range. Winkler loaded his sharpshooters into boats, but they could find no suitable landing place along the marshy northern riverbank. As the rain fell and the temperature dipped, the men sat all day in the mud waiting to cross. Engineers moved forward, but the wind rose, becoming "so furious" it "agitated the water so much" it foiled every attempt to bridge the waterway with pontoons.[7] When night finally fell, the thoroughly wet, cold men retraced their steps back to camp where they "received sugar and full cracker rations."[8]

Pleasant weather returned on New Year's Day, along with orders to remain ready to march at a moment's notice. The regiment left camp at 7:00 a.m. on January 2, marching to the city docks where the men filed aboard the steamer *Planter* at noon.[9] Sgt. Major George Jones recalled taking a "pleasant boat ride around the point of Green Island," landing about an hour later at Cheve's Landing on the shores of "the birthplace of Secession."[10] While the ship returned to the south shore to bring over the rest of the brigade, the men cooked "a dinner of rice and coffee." By 3:00 p.m. the balance of the brigade crossed and the entire force marched off "along the banks of an artificial canal" used to irrigate the surrounding rice fields.[11]

Covering some four miles, as darkness fell the men came to a pine forest where they stacked arms and made themselves "happy over the cup of rice and coffee."[12] Even in the twilight the scenery made an impression on the men. "Near our camp are two fine houses which have lately been deserted by the chivalrous owners. The natural growth of the trees here are chiefly red pine, interposed with here and there a live oak, palmetto or cedar—but the hand of art has embroidered many more beautiful shrubs among which the Magnolia ranks as king. It is indeed a combination of branches with it's dark green leaves so thick it is velvety in such profusion as to almost hide from the misgiving grew the larger blossoms of dark red that rival the rose in display of—and all thru the winter."[13]

Early the next morning Winkler sent out a reconnaissance party of fifty men to scout the area ahead. Little more than a mile from camp they ran into rebel cavalry pickets sparking a lively exchange of fire. The *freiwilligen* pushed forward, driving the enemy back another mile before the Confederates rallied on their reserves and resistance stiffened. Back in camp, Winkler gathered together twenty men as soon as the first firing echoed through camp, leading them forward to investigate the unexpected fight.[14]

Winkler arrived to find the rebels barricaded in entrenchments on either side of the road, their positions covered on each flank by "impassable swamps." Flanking parties failed to find a way through the

marshes, and a personal inspection by Winkler proved similarly unpro-
ductive.[15] Not to be denied, Winkler led a small band out on a wide
flanking movement, "over a rice field dike" and through a swampy
canebrake finally reaching a road leading to the Confederate rear, only
to be seen by rebel pickets who raised the alarm. "The 'Johnnie's soon
'smella mice' and 'skedaddled'," Sgt. Major Jones commented.
Winkler's men pursued briefly, but "as it was getting late" they
returned to camp with "nobody hurt."[16]

On the 4th the regiment "packed up" and marched a mile or two
northeast, camping "in a large open field on Hardees Plantation" in
Beaufort, South Carolina. Buerstatte described the campground as "low
and swampy." The following morning Winkler led 150 men on a reconnaissance "some four or five miles" beyond the scene of the earlier skirmish without finding any sign of Confederate activity. "We searched,"
Buerstatte wrote in his diary, "but found no enemy."[17]

With rain falling almost daily, and preparations to complete
before Sherman could move north in force, many believed they would
remain in the area for some time. "Orders were given the boys today to
build comfortable quarters as we should probably remain here several
weeks," Jones reported, adding that "I do not place much confidence in
the latter part at best."[18]

Rain returned on the 6th, followed by falling temperatures and
wind on the 7th. The clear, cold morning with the "stiff northwest
breeze" reminded Jones of his "cold Northern home." Winkler "shivered" thorough the night, confessing his "teeth have chattered a good
deal this last week." Buerstatte complained of the rain, adding concern
over "bad rations and bad water."[19] Regardless of whether they
believed they would stay, Winkler send out a wagon to secure bricks
for a fireplace, while Jones, Buerstatte, and the rest began constructing
more comfortable dwellings. With typical soldierly pessimism, Jones
reported on the 9th: "Finished and moved into my house today and
consequently am now ready for marching orders."[20]

Heavy thunder showers drenched the camp on the 10th, but subsided the following day. The weather remained cloudy until the sun
returned on the 12th. To pass the time, Jones read *The Grinnell Arche
Expedition* and played chess with Winkler, managing to finish "second
best" in all but one of the games. Mail arrived on the 13th, prompting
Jones to confide to his diary: "What a relief to hear once more that

those who are near and dear to me are still well and happy." Company drills began on the 14th, a "beautiful" day according to Buerstatte, after a long absence during the campaign through Georgia.[21]

About this time, Rev. John Kilian arrived from Greenfield to assume the vacant post of chaplain. An Evangelical Lutheran who "speaks but very little English," Kilian held services on Sunday, January 15, the first time Sgt. Jones could remember "service has been held in the 26th since being in the field." Winkler considered him "a very plain, unsophisticated little man from North Greenfield, knowing little of the world beyond the limit of his flock, but he is energetic and devoted to his cause and to his duty."[22] Regardless, apparently the new chaplain's first sermon on future destiny and reconciliation was impressive for both Jones and Buerstatte commented on it in their diaries. Jones labeled it "an interesting sermon," while both noted that it was drawn from 2nd Corinthians, Chapter 5, verses 19-21: "God was reconciling the world to himself in Christ, not counting their trespasses against them and entrusting to us the message of reconciliation. So we are ambassadors for Christ, as if God were appealing through us. We implore you on behalf of Christ, be reconciled to God. For our sake he made him to be sin who did not know sin, so that we might become the righteousness of God in him."[23]

Though relatively easy duty, and close to the city, food was surprisingly limited. "Prices are exorbitant here," Winkler complained, "it is very expensive to live. Provisions are still coming in scantily. If it were not for the abundance of rice, our men would actually suffer want. Our animals live on rice in the sheaf exclusively; forage, they have none at all."[24] Buerstatte, too, felt the effects of the limited diet and was disappointed when a new supply of flour that arrived proved to be spoiled. "We received 'hundred-year old' flour which was alive with worms," he commented wryly.[25]

On the 16th, command of the brigade passed to Col. William Cogswell. Winkler described him as a "very attentive" officer who "strictly forbids all wanton destruction of private property. I think he is by far the best officer we have had at the head of this brigade."[26] That day and the next the Sigel Regiment remained ready to march, but without orders to move. The men took advantage of the rest to write home, play chess, read, and otherwise pass their off-duty hours. On the 17th the division marched to Hardeeville, but the 26th and the 136th New York remained behind to wait for the division supply wagons. Jones "Had a good meal of raw oysters today, the first in a long long time."[27]

The regiment marched at 8:00 a.m. on the 18th, moving over muddy roads at an average pace. The men passed two or three "deserted homes" and "a few small clearings but for most of the way the road led through a heavy pine forest." The column reached Hardeeville, "a small country village of about a dozen wood houses, everywhere surrounded by a pine forest" and located on the Charleston and Savannah Railroad, about 1:00 p.m., camping "on the left of the Brigade." The men covered "about ten miles."[28] For the next several days the skies once again opened, deluging the surrounding countryside. Jones found the weather "very disagreeable," so he tried to remain inside as much as possible, spending some of his time beating Captain Steinmeyer at chess.[29]

But the rain was a serious matter. "The Savannah River is swollen," Winkler reported, "the dikes along the rice fields are said only just to loom out of the water. Our corduroy went off with the tide and the roads are unfathomable. It is manifest that this weather will seriously interfere with the projective campaign. The swamps about here are about enough in dry weather, but in such times as these there is no way of moving."[30] Jones also deduced the effects of the rain on Sherman's plans. "The roads in this flat country are already almost impassible, and the present campaign is at a 'standstill.'" To make their stay more comfortable, "The 'Yank's have torn the depot down to build themselves houses."[31]

The weather continued bad for the next week. "Though there were a few stars visible on retiring last night," Jones wrote, "yet the first sound that greeted my ears on awaking this morning was the dismal 'patter of the rain' on the roof. Rained all day. The roads now are a perfect sea of water."[32] The difficult conditions notwithstanding, Company F went on a foraging expedition that morning, finding no trace of the enemy and bringing back "corn, sweet potatoes and pork" despite the "bad roads." A dress review enlivened the 24th, but the temperature turned cold enough by the 25th that Buerstatte reported water froze into ice a half-inch thick overnight.[33]

Despite the weather, Major Lackner led a reconnaissance party of 115 men "mounted on pack mules" out of camp at 8:30 a.m. on the 24th. Moving off along the Augusta Road in the direction of Robertsville, about two miles beyond Purysburg the column found the road obstructed by felled trees about "every fifteen to twenty feet." "The road is bad," Lackner reported, "some portions of it we found under water and others miry." About a mile beyond Enni's Crossroads

Brig. Gen. William Cogswell commanding the Third Brigade, Third Division, Twentieth Corps, including the 26th Wisconsin.

Courtesy of the U.S.Army Military History Institute.

Lackner ran into a picket of twenty-five men from Wheeler's rebel cavalry. Skirmish firing broke out as both forces deployed. Lackner dismounted twenty-five of his men and sent them off through the swamps to the right to circle around the flank of the Southern force and cut off the road to their rear. Before the maneuver could be completed, the enemy fled. Lackner pursued about three miles, "occasionally exchanging shots," until he finally halted when informed that some 300 to 500 of Wheeler's men were at Robertsville, with others in surrounding towns.[34]

Lackner retired to Enni's Crossroads, leaving forty men to guard the road. He and his patrol spent a horrible night out in the cold, wet countryside before advancing the next day along the Sister's Ferry Road to Grahamville, finding no further evidence of the enemy. "This road is unobstructed, dry, and in good condition," he reported. At

Grahamville he met a force of Gen. Foster's Union cavalry, remaining there until midnight when he led the column back to camp via the Charleston and Purysburg Road. He brought with him for the officer's mess "a duck, a goose and some sweet potatoes." The successful reconnaissance, including the skirmish on the 24th, was accomplished without loss.[35]

Thursday, January 26, dawned "a fine clear day," pleasant enough to hold another dress parade in the evening. "If this fine weather continues," Jones predicted, "we will probably march in a few days." Orders arrived two days later.[36] It was "a clear cold day." The night before water "was frozen in all the little ponds...as thick as a silver dollar." As Jones sat in his shelter wondering what the pending movement would bring, his mind turned to those no longer there. With feeling and foreboding, he committed his thoughts on the eve of a new campaign to his diary: "The loss of so many companions and friends within the last year, makes those that are left, doubly dear to me."[37]

On to Columbia

Reveille sounded the beginning of the campaign at 4:30 a.m. on January 29. Coffee, breakfast, and packing created a bustle of activity, but the regiment completed its tasks in time to be in line of march at the appointed hour of 7:00 a.m., ready to move out along the Robertsville Road. Jones, promoted to adjutant only ten days previously, thought they "Traveled very fast & without any interruptions," passing mostly through "a wilderness of pine." He remembered passing only a single house all day, covering twenty miles over the poor roads without the customary stop for dinner. Just before dark they halted "in a large corn field" where the men quickly set up their bivouac under orders to be ready to march again at 7:00 a.m., most no doubt as "tired & weary" as the new adjutant.[38]

The next morning, "Just as the sun was peeping above the horizon our bugler sounded the 'forward' and we were again on the move." They passed through a country "mostly under cultivation," but found "the inhabitants have all fled leaving their houses and in many cases their furniture to the mercy of the 'Yanks.'" Jones found the "air was cool and bracing and we marched without a moments halt until we

The Carolinas Campaign

Monroe's Crossroads: March 10, 1865
Averasboro: March 16, 1865
Bentonville: March 19-21, 1865

NORTH CAROLINA
Greensboro
Salisbury
Raleigh
Stewart
Smithfield
Hampton
Hardee
Bragg
Charlotte
Monroe's Crossroads
Averasboro
SHERMAN
Cox
Cheraw
Cheraw
Bentonville
Fayetteville
Goldsboro
New Bern
COLUMBIA
26Th WI
TERRY
Wilmington
(Fort Fisher falls on January 15, 1865)
SOUTH CAROLINA
Augusta
SHERMAN
26Th WI
GEORGIA
Charleston
ATLANTIC OCEAN
Savannah

After Savannah, Georgia, fell in December 1864, Gens. William T. Sherman and Ulysses S. Grant conferred on what the Union armies should do to bring to the war to a close. Grant wanted to transport Sherman's men to Virginia for a decisive campaign against Robert E. Lee's Army of Northern Virginia, which for months had been stuck in trenches defending Richmond and Petersburg. Sherman, however, wanted instead to march north to Virginia via the Carolinas. In addition to wreaking havoc and disorganizing the Southern defenders, Sherman's drive northward would further depress morale across the Confederacy and hasten its collapse.

As Sherman's armies marched into South Carolina, the important coastal fortification guarding Wilmington, Fort Fisher, fell to a massive amphibious assault on January 15, 1865, sealing off the last major route of supply for Lee's army. Columbia, the state's capital, witnessed Sherman's army on February 17, and there seemed little the under strength Confederates could do to stop Sherman. In accordance with Lee's wishes, Joseph E. Johnston was appointed to command on February 22, although he did not think he could do much to stop the enemy. Johnston, however, turned in perhaps his best performance of the war, waging a series of actions designed to delay and destroy portions of Sherman's army. The finale came on March 19 at Bentonville, where the Southerners crushed the head of one Federal column before the reality of numbers played itself out.

The 26th Wisconsin, marching with William Cogswell's brigade (Third Division, XX Corps), played a significant role in the fighting at Averasboro on March 16. Although the brigade was seriously engaged at Bentonville on the 19th, the 26th was in the second line and saw but light action.

Joe Johnston retreated from the Bentonville battlefield on March 21-22, and surrendered his army at Durham on April 26, 1865.

Theodore P. Savas

reached" Robertsville, "some seven miles from our starting point," around noon. They camped about three miles to the northeast of the village at the Maner plantation.[39]

On the morning of the 31st the Sigel Regiment marched through Robertsville, a town Jones described as "a little larger than Hardeesville, with a fine church and splendid shade trees. The 'Chivalry' have nearly all left. The chief productions of the surrounding country for the past year appears to have been corn and cotton." Once clear of the village they pushed on to "a large cornfield about three miles from Sisters Ferry."[40]

For the next week the regiment march unopposed through the heart of secession, living off "cornmeal, pork and sweet potatoes."[41] "We...have been marching and working every day," Winkler wrote, "yet we are very well off, marching through the enemy's country in pleasant weather, living on the best of fare, and tearing up the most vital railroads in the south far and wide, without the slightest opposition."[42] From Robertsville they marched through Lawtonville on the morning of February 3, camping on the evening of the 4th at Allendale. There the regiment's forage party came in with "an abundance of supplies."[43]

On the morning of February 6 the column crossed the Big Salkehatchie River at Buford's Bridge, pushing on to the Little Salkehatchie which it crossed at Dowling's Mills on the 7th. They marched "without interruption" throughout the day, finally arriving at the Augusta and Charleston Railroad one or two miles east of Graham's Station, fifty-six miles from their starting point, that evening. Moving west along the route of the railroad, they spent the next three days destroying all the railroad property in their path. A train fell victim to their advance on February 8, another at Blackville on the following day, and a third on the 10th when they marched through Williston.[44] Winkler reported the men "worked vigorously at the destruction of the railroad till night." The two divisions employed in the movement west from Graham's Station on the South Carolina Railroad "destroyed every bit of the road, taken up and heated, bent and twisted every rail, and burned every tie to a mile west of" White Pond, at the Thirty-third Mile Post some "twenty miles from Graham."[45]

Not all of the depredations fell on railroad property and military stores. Adin Underwood of the 33rd Massachusetts remembered finding thousands of bags of peanuts. The men confiscated these, roasting the goobers over their campfires well into the evening. One day, while Underwood sat in the parlor of a South Carolina house, "A couple of Germans from the Twenty-Sixth Wis. regiment loafed into the room. Upon spying a piano one seated himself before it and began to play opera, ballads, marches and, at last, jigs and 'hoe-downs,' upon which Dutchy number two mounted the instrument and began 'shaking her down' on the top. At the final wind-up, where the dance ends with a bang, he brought his foot down, and with it the butt of his rifle, driving it clear through the piano. We then dragged it into the road, where we took the large bass wires for bails to our coffee kettles, using the rosewood case to cook the coffee with."[46]

Aside from the tremendous damage done to the Confederate economic infrastructure supporting the war effort, Sherman's movement forced the outnumbered Confederates to retire north and west. In their wake, Howard pushed his forces through Orangeburg and on toward Columbia, while Slocum circled through Windsor and on to Lexington. On February 11 the Sigel Regiment "waded the Big Salkehatchie River in water over our knees" and turned toward Columbia. The following day the men "crossed the South Edisto River," at Guignard's Bridge, then moved over the North Edisto at Jone's Bridge, arriving within four miles of Columbia on the 16th.[47]

From Columbia the column turned northwestward as Sherman pursued the Confederates concentrating near Cheraw. Although the movement was slowed by the muddy roads, the men plodded on, crossing the Saluda River on a pontoon bridge at Mount Zion Church, about ten miles away, on the 18th. Turning northeast, they crossed the Broad River on the 20th, then pushed on through Winnsboro to Rocky Mount on the Catawba River on the 21st, crossing once again on pontoons on the evening of the 22nd. "[W]e have plenty to eat and are filling our wagons besides," Winkler exulted, "and no enemy has the temerity to show his face."[48]

At the Catawba, one of the regiment's foragers reported being told by "a white woman and a negro" named Moses that two Union officers who had escaped from a rebel prison were living "on an island in the river." The regiment was ordered across the river at midnight, but Winkler obtained permission to leave thirty men behind to try and effect a rescue the next morning. He selected Companies B and K, leaving them under the command of Capt. William H. Hemschemeyer of Company I. The captain led his men off the next morning, returning a short time later having rescued Lt. William Smith of the 14th New York Cavalry and Lt. Spaulding of the 2nd U. S. Cavalry.[49]

Crossing the Wateree River on pontoons on the 23rd, the column pushed on through Russell's Cross Roads to Hanging Rock on the 26th, crossed Little Lynch's Creek and Black Creek, finally arriving at Chesterfield Court House about 4:00 p.m. on March 3.[50] By this time the campaign had already lasted longer than the march through Georgia to the sea. Winkler's horse was "wholly giving out," and the men were no doubt tired, but victory was a strong antidote for their weariness. Pressing on to Westfield Creek, the column "took a by-road to Grady's farm" where it camped for the night.[51] Sherman finally reached Cheraw the following day, only to find that Gen. William Hardee's Confederates had once again retired before the Northern advance, this time retreating all the way into North Carolina.[52]

By Sunday, March 5, the Sigel Regiment lay "quietly" in its camp west of the Great Pedee River near the boundary line between the two Carolinas. For most it was a day of rest, but Winkler spent time preparing for the next move. "The country around here is poor and it may be hard to subsist the army," Winkler explained, "but I have almost a wagon-load of salted hams and shoulders and had a corn mill running part of yesterday. My foragers have taken possession of another mill about seven miles away."[53] One of those foragers was Charles Buerstatte who reported moving across the border into North Carolina where "I put on my first pair of civilian pants and wore a stove-pipe hat."[54] The war, once so cruel and horrible, had for some become a pleasant escapade, the days of privation seemingly a distant memory.

Throughout the campaign, according to Winkler's official report, "foragers provided us with an abundance of supplies." In the month between February 4 and March 4, for example, Winkler estimated his foragers brought in 800 pounds of wheat flour, 4,000 pounds of corn meal, 550 bushels of sweet potatoes, 13,000 pounds of meat, 900 pounds of lard, 150 pounds of dried fruit, and 1,200 bushels of corn for animal fodder. They also destroyed about 300 bales of cotton. As successful as they were, however, the foragers were not immune from danger. While out on a foraging expedition between Cheraw and Seedsville on March 5, Capt. August Bartsch and ten men were "engaged in grinding corn at a mill" when they were approached by a cavalry force dressed in Union blue. Too late they discovered the Southern subterfuge and all were taken prisoner, condemned to spend the balance of the war in rebel prisons. The unfortunate captives included Corp. Wilhelm Marx, Co. D; George Dascher, Co. K; Frederick Pieper, Co. H; Sergt. Ludwig Hill, Co. H; Eugene Hook, Co. G; Carl Boettscher, Co. C; Christian Caflisch, Co. K; Jacob Gall, Co. I; Corp. Wilhelm Muehlheisen, Co. D. and Frederick Engelking of Co. H. [55]

Despite the losses, spirits remained high. "We hear reports of successes gained by General Grant before Petersburg," Winkler wrote, "but Charleston is ours and Wilmington too. It would seem, with such forces closing around him, that Lee must feel that his last hour has come. It is said that there are thirty thousand rebels on the other side of the river. They may give us a little trouble in crossing, but cross we will, and they will have to retire, they dare not fight us. A prisoner has afforded the boys a great deal of amusement by telling us that these forces were intended to cut off and capture General Howard's command." Everywhere the news was good, the Confederates were on the run and no serious resistance was anticipated. Several miles to the north, where the Confederate forces were concentrating as quickly as possible, Joseph Johnston had other ideas.[56]

Averasboro

Hampered by lack of railroad equipment, poor roads, and other obstacles, Johnston nevertheless determined to concentrate all available forces at Fayetteville, North Carolina, in the hope of arresting Sherman's progress. When Bragg was unable to slow the Union advance at Kinston on March 7-10, Johnston's plans were once again thwarted. Establishing his headquarters at Raleigh, the Confederate commander feared the loss of that city would disrupt supplies to Lee's army in Virginia. Thus, he determined to attack Sherman before the two wings of the Union army could be united.[57]

The Sigel Regiment left its camp on March 6, marched through

Cheraw that evening, and crossed the Great Pedee River on pontoons about 3:00 a.m. Advancing into the Tarheel State, the column marched over "bad roads," forded several streams including the Lumber River and Rockfish Creek, arriving at the Cape Fear River near Fayetteville on March 11.[58]

On Sunday, March 12, the men rested and attended "church services" before crossing the river on the 13th. Winkler found Fayetteville "a fine place, as large as Savannah. The arsenal was broken down, as it was apprehended that burning it might endanger adjacent buildings." Unlike their neighbors to the south, "Orders have said that the people of North Carolina are not to be treated like enemies; nothing but necessary stores are to be taken, and no ruthless burning, etc. will be tolerated. I fear it will not be found easy to enforce this order."[59]

On the 14th Major Lackner led four companies of the Sigel Regiment on an expedition to hold the crossing at Goose Creek while the rest of the regiment moved forward with the brigade in a reconnaissance-in-force toward the Black or South River. As the force approached the river it encountered a small force of rebel cavalry. Col. Cogswell deployed five companies of the 55th Ohio and, after a "hot fire for twenty minutes," drove the enemy across the river. The mission completed, the force retraced its steps back to camp. The 26th Wisconsin marched twenty-two miles meeting no serious resistance and suffering no casualties.[60]

The lack of resistance convinced many the Confederates would no longer fight. "I see the northern papers predict a great battle," Winkler wrote, "I doubt it. Our numbers will be so imposing that prudence will advise the Confederates to retreat."[61] Ahead of them, however, Johnston at last moved his army forward, sending Hardee's corps off toward Averasboro to intercept the advance of the Twentieth Corps. Sherman advanced from Fayetteville on the 15th, his army moving in three columns with Slocum on the left or northern flank aiming for Smithfield, then turning east toward Bentonville. The Fifteenth Corps formed the middle column, and Howard's force the right or southern wing.[62]

The Sigel Regiment marched out of Fayetteville along the Raleigh Plank Road at 6:30 a.m. on the morning of March 15, not halting until 5:00 p.m. The following day the march resumed at the same hour, covering about five miles over "difficult and muddy roads" and crossing

A view from the John Smith house looking north. The 26th Wisconsin advanced just to the east of this photograph. Photo by Mark A Moore.

Taylor's Hole Creek. A mile beyond the creek Slocum's column ran into Hardee's men dug in on a ridge between the river and a swampy area near Averasboro. Two divisions formed for the attack, including Ward's Division containing the Sigel Regiment which deployed with three regiments in the first line and three in the second. By the time Ward arrived on the field a brigade of Gen. Kilpatrick's cavalry and Hawley's Brigade of the 1st Division were already "hotly engaged."[63]

Winkler formed his men into line of battle two ranks deep, pushed his skirmishers forward, and "a very hot skirmish ensued." After halting for a few minutes, the brigade received orders to move to the relief of the 2nd Brigade, 1st Division, which had been skirmishing for some time. To fill the space assigned them, all six regiments had to be moved forward into the first line with the 33rd Massachusetts advanced as skirmishers. The brigade advanced about 250 yards to the vicinity of the Smith house where a lively skirmish developed. After about an hour, the Federals advanced further, taking possession of "a slight line of

Martin Hahn, Company C, a wagon-maker from Milwaukee. Wounded at Bentonville, his foot was amputated.

breastworks."[64]

With Confederate resistance stiffening, reinforcements moved forward to support the skirmish line, which gradually fought its way forward over a period of several hours until it seized a "stronger line of works" some distance from the first. The skirmishers continued on, pressing the rebels back another mile through swampy ground until the Southerners retired within their main defensive works leaving their dead and wounded in Union hands. Winkler led the Sigel Regiment forward, realigning its ranks under the cover of a hill beyond the swamp, some seventy-five yards from the skirmish line and another fifty from the rebel works. In what Winkler described as "sharp skirmishing" that "lasted until night," the federals pushed Hardee's men steadily back from one position to another, driving them back about two and one-half miles, taking "two lines of light breastworks," and capturing "three pieces of artillery and two hundred prisoners." The battle lasted until night, the rebels putting up an "obstinate" defense in "a strong line of breastworks, extending from the Cape Fear River on his right to the Black River on his left."[65]

Unable to hold his lines, Hardee retreated toward Smithfield during the night. Though ending favorably for the Union, the rambling fight cost the regiment two officers and five men killed. Among the dead were Capt. Charles Schmidt of Company B, 1st Lt. Friedrich R. Klein of Company C, Corp. Jacob Gilgen of Company A, Corp. Herman Lindemuth of Company E, Pvt. Charles Busse of Company B, Pvt. Johann Gruhlke of Company E, and Pvt. Gottlieb Strutz of Company H. Ten others were wounded. Of the latter, John Schmidt of Co. F and Charles Oestreich of Co. E would later succumb to their injuries.[66] The unopposed romp through South Carolina was over; war was still a serious, deadly affair.

Bentonville

On March 17 Slocum advanced toward Bentonville while Johnston planned another delaying action. Concentrating 21,000 troops around Smithfield, the Confederates determined to attack Slocum before Sherman could bring Howard to his aid. The Sigel Regiment followed the rebel retreat along the Smithfield Road "until noon," then headed back toward the battlefield. On the 18th they moved out again, turning east and wading the Black River in water Buerstatte described as "over our hips." Stuck at the rear of the column behind a wagon train they were to guard, Winkler found the roads "very bad." It took them "all that day, and until almost five the next morning" to move only twelve miles.[67]

After only three hours of rest they were on the road again, covering eleven miles on a "fair road" when the sound of artillery broke the

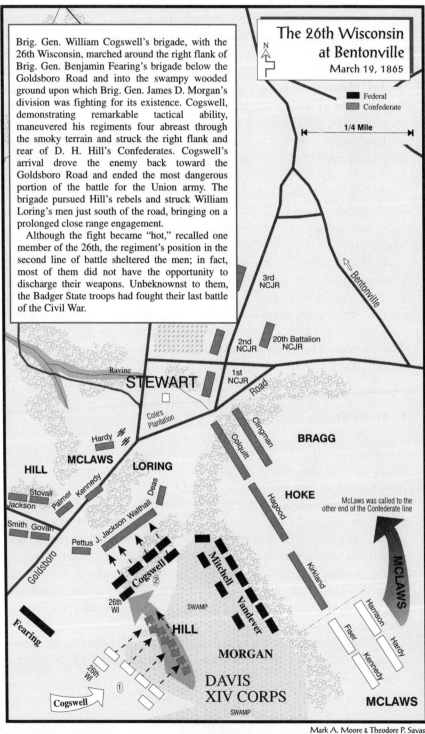

The 26th Wisconsin at Bentonville
March 19, 1865

Brig. Gen. William Cogswell's brigade, with the 26th Wisconsin, marched around the right flank of Brig. Gen. Benjamin Fearing's brigade below the Goldsboro Road and into the swampy wooded ground upon which Brig. Gen. James D. Morgan's division was fighting for its existence. Cogswell, demonstrating remarkable tactical ability, maneuvered his regiments four abreast through the smoky terrain and struck the right flank and rear of D. H. Hill's Confederates. Cogswell's arrival drove the enemy back toward the Goldsboro Road and ended the most dangerous portion of the battle for the Union army. The brigade pursued Hill's rebels and struck William Loring's men just south of the road, bringing on a prolonged close range engagement.

Although the fight became "hot," recalled one member of the 26th, the regiment's position in the second line of battle sheltered the men; in fact, most of them did not have the opportunity to discharge their weapons. Unbeknownst to them, the Badger State troops had fought their last battle of the Civil War.

Federal
Confederate

1/4 Mile

Mark A. Moore & Theodore P. Savas

calm. What they heard was an attack by Johnston on Slocum's advanced elements. At 11:00 a.m. the order came to leave the wagon trains and move forward at once. Rushing another four miles at the double-quick, they arrived about 1:00 p.m. near Bentonville to find a full-scale battle underway with Slocum marshalling his troops to withstand repeated Confederate assaults. Wading a stream in "water over our knees," the Sigel Regiment moved into an open field where its brigade formed behind the batteries deployed in rear of the 1st Division. While the columns maneuvered into lines of battle, "down in the woods beyond" the men could hear "musketry fire going on." Two divisions of the Fourteenth Corps had run headlong into strong Confederate resistance and found themselves outflanked and sorely pressed.[68]

About 3:00 p.m., as the brigade passed the Harper house, Lt. Col. Charles Asmussen arrived with orders to move to the right of the road and hurry forward to support the Fourteenth Corps which was being hard pressed by Johnston's vigorous assault. Asmussen had been sent by Gen. Alpheus S. Williams, commanding the Twentieth Corps, to find the first brigade he could and rush it forward to plug a critical gap between the 1st and 2nd Divisions of the Fourteenth Corps. Winkler ordered the regiment to prepare to move, then marched forward with the brigade into "a swampy wood" where orders arrived "to advance." Two brigades of the Fourteenth Corps had become "disconnected," Winkler explained, "and our brigade was sent down to set things right" and close the gap that had developed. In fact, the federal line had been broken and the Fourteenth Corps was in imminent danger of being driven from the field. Four brigades of Lee's Corps of the Army of Tennessee under Maj. Gen. Daniel Harvey Hill were advancing through a gaping hole in the Northern line, opposed only by the 17th New York and 10th Michigan.[69]

Moving forward, Cogswell's brigade formed to the right of the Goldsborough Road, with the 20th Connecticut on the left near the road, the 26th Wisconsin in support in the second line. The brigade pushed into the gap between Gen. James D. Morgan's 2nd Division and Gen. William P. Carlin's 1st Division of the Fourteenth Corps. It could not have arrived at a more advantageous time and position. Smashing into the right flank and rear of Hill's force, shattering his attack, the federals drove through a woods, across a swamp, and into an open pine woods, cutting off a portion of the Confederate troops and taking scores of prisoners and the colors of the 26th Tennessee Infantry.[70] According to Buerstatte, the fight became "hot," but the Badgers, placed in the second line, had no opportunity to fire. Instead, they had to endure the frustrating experience of remaining in position while stray minie balls and occasional artillery shells landed about them. The fight continued on until nightfall "when the enemy withdrew, leaving his dead and many of his wounded on the field.[71] One of the latter proved to be a lieutenant from the 33rd Mississippi Infantry, the same unit the Sigel Regiment had mauled at Peach Tree Creek.[72]

In the end, Johnston's attempt to defeat Slocum failed and the Confederates once again abandoned the field during the night. According to Nathaniel Hughes, one recent historian of the Battle of Bentonville, "Some consider Cogswell's role the most important of all" in restoring the Union lines and bringing about the victory. "Cogswell's timely and powerful attack," Hughes concluded, "after 'coming on the field with tired troops,' had saved Morgan, restored the Union line, and broken the Confederate attack. The initiative passed. It was a remarkable, if not decisive performance."[73]

Losses in the Sigel Regiment were one killed and five wounded. The wounded included Henry Erdmann, Martin Hahn, Carl Koerner, Charles Buerstatte, and Charles Thieme. The dead man was Pvt. Mathias Reisenbegler, a butcher from Two Rivers. No one knew it then but he had the dubious distinction of being the last soldier from the 26th to be killed in action during the war.[74]

The Army was Electrified

Following the action at Bentonville, Johnston retired toward Smithfield. On the 22nd, Sherman advanced toward Goldsboro, arriving there the same day. When all his forces were consolidated, the Northern general mustered about 80,000 troops. Johnston, collecting all his available forces around Smithfield, could muster little more than 18,000 effectives.[75]

The Sigel Regiment spent March 20 building fortifications near Bentonville. On the 21st the Wisconsin regiment and the 33rd Massachusetts conducted a reconnaissance about one mile from the camp, drawing a few shots from rebel sharpshooters, but finding little.

The men spent the rest of the day building fortifications before marching for Goldsboro on the 22nd. The regiment crossed a pontoon bridge over the Neuse River on the 23rd, camping at the intersection of the Wilmington and Weldon with the North Carolina Railroad, within five miles of its destination, that evening. On the 24th the men 'marched in parade through Goldsboro," moving about three miles north of town where the men erected their camp under instructions to stay for the next few days. Spirits were high. The rebels were retreating on every hand, the weather continued mild and enjoyable, and their arrival at the federal supply depot brought the prospect of new uniforms and a well-deserved rest. Yet, reminders of war continued. While out foraging, Franklin Terry of Company C was captured near Goldsboro, North Carolina, on March 24.[76]

"We finished our campaign at ten this morning," Winkler wrote home on March 24. "It has been a long and toilsome one, but it is accomplished." Though success was at hand, any thoughts of joy were greatly tempered. "Our rejoicing over the successes of the campaign," Winkler wrote to the Governor on March 25, "is allayed with sorrow for our losses." Winkler's hope for an end to active campaigning was, however, premature. His army rested, its supplies replenished, Sherman moved again on April 1. Assigned to guarding the wagon train, the 26th Wisconsin marched to Kingston on the Neuse River, some twenty-seven miles to the southeast, where it arrived about noon the next day. After spending the 3rd "quartered in a wagonshop," the regiment retraced its steps back to Goldsboro. Leaving Kingston at 6:00 a.m. on April 4, the men marched without rest until 3:00 p.m., covering some twenty miles. On the road again early on the 5th, they arrived at their old campsite about 10:00 a.m.[77]

While events unfolded, the Badgers spent the next four days in camp, staging a review for Gen. Howard on the 6th and undergoing inspection by Gen. Cogswell on the 7th. While there, "the army was electrified" by "news of the capture of Richmond." Marching orders arrived on Sunday, April 9. That night the men attended church services, unaware that Robert E. Lee had surrendered the Army of Northern Virginia that very day.[78]

April 10 dawned dismal and wet. At 5:30 a.m. the regiment broke camp, marching toward Raleigh in the rain. The march continued on into the 11th, the pace rapid and seemingly purposeful. Despite the rain, the weather was "very warm," the woods about them "quite green" in the bloom of spring. "We marched hard," Buerstatte reported, "and many collapsed from exhaustion." They passed through "the small town of Smithfield" on the morning of the 12th where the delirious news reached them of Lee's surrender. The men were celebrating the good news when, according to Charles Stamm, "an Orderly rode up to the speaker with a dispatch announcing the assassination of Lincoln." Everyone's demeanor instantly changed, thoughts of celebration suddenly far from their minds.[79]

Crossing the Neuse River on pontoons, the regiment camped at Swift Creek at 3:30 p.m. An hour later orders arrived for them to rush to support Gen. Kilpatrick's cavalry, but they were soon countermanded. Unbeknown to the men, as they marched the seventeen miles to Raleigh on the 13th, Joseph Johnston requested a cease fire. The war that was so destructive, so deadly, with so many sacrifices, was drawing to a close with such relative quiet as to be anticlimactic. As if to mock the war itself, the regiment camped that evening near the North Carolina insane asylum.[80]

Sherman reviewed the Twentieth Corps on April 21. The Sigel Regiment marched again on the 24th, with orders to move to the front. After marching all day along the Aven's Ferry road to Jones's Cross Roads on the 25th, the men rested for two days while Johnston and Sherman agreed upon the final terms for the surrender off the Confederate army. The capitulation became official on April 26, but news apparently did not arrive in the Sigel Regiment for another two days. The day after the surrender Buerstatte commented only that "We lay still," while his entry for the 28th says simply "We marched again to Raleigh." There, on April 29, as they camped outside the city, news of the capitulation apparently arrived. Perhaps unwilling to believe it could be true after so many false camp rumors, Buerstatte commented only that "General Johnston probably has surrendered his army."[81]

Chapter 13

"THE BOYS ARE ALL JUBILANT"
Journey Home

*I*n the west the last spasms of the war sputtered on throughout the summer, but for all practical purposes except the lives of those involved, the Civil War ended with the surrender of the troops under Robert E. Lee and Joseph E. Johnston. For men ravaged by the privation and suffering of endless months of warfare, the intense emotional experiences of combat, and the often gruesome deaths of friends and comrades, the end must have been one of inestimable relief. It was over; they were going home.

On to Richmond

"On to Richmond!" For years the press echoed this sentiment as one Union commander after another tried in vain to subdue the Southern capital. Now the Sigel Regiment was to march on that famous city again, but this time as peaceful visitors. The march began at 7:30 a.m. on the last day of April. Surrender or not, life in the army continued as usual. Buerstatte's diary for April 30 reads simply: "We marched north with 20 cartridges per man."[1]

By the next morning they were crossing the Neuse River at Manteo's Mills, heading north to the Tarr River which they crossed that evening. The morning of the 3rd found them marching through Williamsboro, continuing on to the Roanoke River which they crossed on pontoons that afternoon, once again entering Virginia nineteen eventful months after they headed west to Tennessee.[2]

"The days are very warm," Buerstatte wrote on the 4th. "We have yet to go 76 miles to Richmond."[3] On across the Meherrin River, they camped briefly before resuming the trek at 5:00 a.m. on the 5th. Moving steadily at a regular pace, they covered eighteen miles through countryside covered with red and white oak, broken only once by a "field of wheat just heading out." At noon they crossed the Nottoway River, stopping for an hour on the northern shore to have dinner. When they resumed the march, they covered only a mile before halting for the night because, according to Jones, the "extreme heat made the horses give out on the road."[4]

A brief overnight rain Jones found "just enough" to "lay the dust and for a couple of hours it was cool and pleasant." They reached the Southside Railroad at Blacks and Whites Station where they recognized the St. Andrew's Cross on the caps of their former comrades in the Sixth Corps, Army of the Potomac. Leaving another fourteen miles behind them, they "camped a little after noon in a pleasant pine grove," intent upon avoiding the sweltering afternoon heat.[5] On the 7th they marched at 4:30 a.m., crossed the Appomattox River on a pontoon bridge "about two miles below Bivel's Bridge," and went into camp "near Clover Hill a little after noon having made about 18 miles." [6]

On the road again at 5:00 a.m. on the 8th they wound through "the little village of Clover Hill," a station on the Richmond and Petersburg Railroad which George Jones supposed "to have been chiefly important for it's coal mines." After covering seventeen miles, they camped "in a pine woods" near Manchester about seven miles from Richmond. "This may be the end of our on to Richmond movement," Jones quipped, "having made 170 miles in 4 years."[7]

After two days of rest, the regiment marched again at 11:00 a.m. on May 11, covering the final few miles into the former capital of the Confederacy. "We marched on parade through the city of Manchester," Buerstatte wrote. "A brigade of the 3rd Division of the 24th Army Corps was lined up on the main street and it greeted us with thundering hurrays and drums."[8] Adj. Jones, too, was impressed with the soldierly salute offered by their comrades. As he described it, "Gen'l. Devlin's division of the 24th Corps was paraded on the principal street in Manchester reaching nearly the whole length of the town and received us with 'present arms,' bands playing, and their hearty cheers." [9]

Feeling proud and joyous, the men crossed the James River into the capital city. The column wound past Libby Prison, where Captain Bernhard Domschcke and Adjutant Albert Wallber were imprisoned after Gettysburg, and Castle Thunder before turning down the city's main street. Passing the Capitol and City Hall, Jones was much taken by the "equestrian bronze statue of Washington in the Capitol Square," which he pronounced "the finest one [he] ever saw."[10] Despite the wartime destruction, Buerstatte found it "a large, beautiful city."[11] Their curiosity satisfied, the column marched about three miles beyond the city where it camped for the night at the small hamlet of Nish.

Old Familiar Country

Beginning early each morning to avoid the increasing heat of the afternoons, the regiment made "slow progress" on the 12th because of the "heavy rain" the previous night, but still made it across the Chickahominy and Stoney Rivers.[12] The next day it reached the Fredericksburg Railroad at Ashland, which Jones found to be a "pretty little town of about a dozen houses," before crossing the South Anna River "on an old trestle bridge and the New Found River on a bridge of rails."[13] The Little River and the Richmond and Gordonsville Railroad yielded to their advance on the 14th as they crossed the Virginia Central Railroad and "caught a glimpse of the Smoky summits of the Blue Ridge" before sunset.[14]

May 15 found them entering what Winkler called "the old familiar country."[15] Crossing the Mattapony and Po Rivers, they marched through Spottsylvania Court House, according to Jones "a little town of some dozen houses now full of air holes and ventilation caused by Yankee Artillery about a year ago."[16] They marched along Lee's old earthworks for about two miles. "[I]t really looked wild," Buerstatte felt. "The trees lay around in all directions, there were the breastworks, and hands, feet and heads stuck out of the graves. The area was scattered for miles with canisters, knapsacks and various articles of war."[17] Ironically, that night they camped on the old Chancellorsville battlefield, coming full circle since their baptism of fire two years previously. They found "Two old destroyed brick buildings still stand there as a mute reminder that a farm was there."[18]

Adjutant Jones could not resist the temptation to investigate further. When the column marched the next morning he directed his horse toward the Hawkins Farm and the other familiar landmarks. "Took a ride over the ill-fated field when we were so badly defeated 2 years ago," he wrote. "Every spot seemed as natural and familiar to me as the dear yard at home. Distinguished the graves of 1 or two 26th boys, but by far the greater part are buried here or there over the field without a board to mark their resting place. I overtook the column at U. S. Ford, crossed the river on a pontoon. Marched by the way of Hartwood Church to within about 9 miles of Catletts Station, having made 22 miles."[19]

Leaving the Rappahannock and its bloody memories behind, the men crossed the Cedar River, marching on past Weaverville and Catlett's Station to camp at Brentsville eighteen miles away.[20] All along the way new grass covered the scarred and burned sections destroyed during the years of warfare. "The sod," Jones thought, "is very fertile and splendid" so that in future years "this section will again blossom" now that it is "under the system of free labor."[21]

Reville sounded at 2:30 a.m. on May 18, with the column on the road by 4:30. Buerstatte found the day "very warm," while Jones pronounced it "very warm indeed and the marching very severe on the boys."[22] But on they trudged for nineteen miles, not stopping until they passed through Fairfax Station, within fourteen miles of Alexandria, camping in the fields beyond around 4:00 p.m. With no particular reason for the tiring march, Buerstatte complained they "had to march very hard with little to eat. Half the company collapsed from exhaustion."[23]

Heavy overnight rain, along with a cool, cloudy day, eased the march on the 19th as the regiment covered the remaining miles, camping a short distance outside Alexandria, across the Potomac River from Washington.[24] At last they could enjoy several days of rest. That afternoon Major Lackner and Adjutant Jones rode into town, the latter finding it "changed but very little since I was here 18 months ago."[25] The following day Governor Lewis made "a flying visit" to speak to the regiment, but everyone's thoughts were far from Virginia or whatever words the governor chose to impart. "The boys are all jubilant over the prospect of soon getting home," Jones reported.[26] Before they could leave, another duty remained.

As part of the ceremonies attending the muster-out of the volunteer armies, there was a "Grand Review" of the troops planned for May 23-24. On the first day the Army of the Potomac marched through Washington to be reviewed by the President, leading political figures, and prominent military officers. The next day was the turn of the western armies, the Army of the Tennessee and the Army of Georgia. An estimated 150,000 men passed in review during the two days.[27]

Impatiently, the men waited for the review. Two days of rain made the waiting more difficult, confining them to their tents when not on duty. The weather cleared on the 23rd, dawn bringing with it a "beautiful bright cool day." Jones occupied his time reading newspapers to catch up on recent events and the planned festivities, while lamenting being unable to see the first day of the Grand Review. "Should have been much pleased to have witnessed the review of the Glorious Old Army of the Potomac today, but must be content seeing Sherman's army reviewed tomorrow."[28]

Rested and revitalized, the men rose early Wednesday morning, ready to march at 5:00 a.m. Their knapsacks and equipment were loaded into wagons to follow as they would not be returning to the state where so many of their friends lay forever.[29] At the appointed hour, Winkler led his men across Long Bridge over the Potomac River into Washington to participate in the Grand Review as part of the 3rd Brigade, 3rd Division, Twentieth Corps, Army of Georgia. While crossing the bridge, the men were hailed by Friedrich W. Kutler, a former "Twenty-sixer" from Company D who was wounded at Chancellorsville and assigned to guard duty with Company I, 24th Veteran Reserve Corps. Hailing old friends as the regiment passed, Kutler watched them move on to the Review. As Buerstatte described it: "We marched past Alexandria, across the Potomac River, past the Capital, and up Pennsylvania Avenue through Washington....We were reviewed by Lieutenant General U.S. Grant, Major General W.T. Sherman, and other Generals."[30]

Buerstatte found Washington "a large, beautiful city," while Jones marveled that "nearly every house displayed the glorious old Stars and Stripes. The people manifested in every way their appreciation of the Army." But the adjutant was less impressed with the marching itself: "The review was the grandest one I ever witnessed in point of numbers, both of spectators and troops, but I have seen much better marching, than was executed by the mass today. This probably [due] to their being in columns closed in mass which is a poor formation to exhibit good marching."[31]

The review completed, the regiment continued on north of the city where it camped "in a dense forest" of pines near Ft. Lincoln. Adjutant Jones expressed the feelings of everyone as they pitched their tents yet again: "[I] hope this will be the last camp of the 26th as we expect to be mustered out here."[32]

With everyone anxious to get home, time seemed to pass very slowly in the new camp. Surprisingly, considering their proximity to Washington and the huge federal supply bases in the area, a food shortage developed during the next week. Rations that arrived were contaminated and it had been so long since they were paid few had resources to buy anything at the sutler's inflated prices. "[W]e can't buy our rations," Buerstatte complained, "we must go hungry and our money is short."[33] Part of the problem was administrative. The blank muster rolls required before the men could be paid off and sent home had not yet arrived.[34]

Most of the officers visited town, but the enlisted men generally stayed in camp biding their time as best they could. Adj. Jones made the most of his time, visiting the Patent Office, the Capitol, and the Smithsonian Institution. "I never spent a day more beneficially," he declared. "The architecture, sculpture and painting exhibits in the Capitol is truly magnificent. The painting which most struck my fancy was the battle of Chasultyseck [Chapultepec], and the sculpture of the dying Tecumseh could not be excelled in expression even by life itself."[35]

The blank muster forms arrived on May 28, which meant considerable work for Adjutant Jones who was responsible for making sure all the paperwork was completed properly. "Work is now crowding fast," he reported, "as the sooner we get our necessary papers completed the sooner we will go home."[36] The first few days of June were busy ones for the adjutant and the other officers and sergeants charged with completing the muster rolls, regimental accounts, and other paperwork that had to be finished before the regiment could be discharged. For the others, cards, chess, reading, and visits to nearby regiments helped pass the time.

A visit from Wisconsin's former governor Alexander Randall briefly interrupted the monotony on Sunday, June 4. On a "calm quiet Sabbath" afternoon, the Sigel Regiment and the other four Wisconsin regiments in the Army of Georgia marched out to greet Randall, now Assistant Postmaster General of the United States. After a march of three miles, the regiments formed in line while the ex-governor, accompanied by Gen. Slocum, inspected their ranks. This formality completed, the regiments "closed up in long columns by division," forming a large square, to hear Wisconsin's Gen. Harrison Hobart formally introduce Randall. Randall delivered what Winkler described as a "patriotic" speech, following which the assembled soldiers gave "three cheers" and "went home."[37] Jones was somewhat less than impressed by the occasion and Randall's remarks: "[T]he ex-Gov. made rather a vague speech, not very interesting to the boys, we returned home concluding that considering the heat and clouds of dust which we had to endure, that we had paid rather dear for the whistle."[38]

The company officers completed their muster rolls by June 6, leading Jones to believe "there is a prospect of our getting home next week."[39] But more frustration awaited. With the paperwork complete, Winkler and Jones visited the mustering officer, Capt. Beecher, only to find "he will not get to them for a week, so it is quite uncertain when we will get off."[40]

While they waited, Gen. Slocum hosted a supper for corps, division, brigade, and regimental commanders. Winkler attended, finding the evening "passed off very pleasantly; the toasts and speeches were very good."[41] For Buerstatte, however, another engagement arrived. He and the others who mustered in during 1864 found they were not yet eligible for discharge. Instead, on June 9 he penned the following entry in his diary: "We 64'ers left the 26th Regiment and were reassigned to the 3rd Wisconsin Regiment."[42] While his comrades awaited their homeward journey, Buerstatte's service would continue amid strangers in another regiment.

Adjutant Jones' diary entry for June 8 summarized the general feeling in the regiment: "Too warm to work, so I idled away my time as best I could. Time seems to go very slowly now that I can almost count the days I am yet to remain in the service."[43] While many grew impatient, Winkler was realistic. "It is no small job to make out all the papers and comply with all the red tape necessary to get a regiment out of the service, I assure you, but think it will be a week before we start" for home.[44]

Home to Wisconsin

The regiment's time finally came on June 13. In the morning the men officially mustered out of federal service, boarding a train that afternoon for the long trip to Wisconsin. Chugging and jolting off through Baltimore, they turned west, unaware that yet another trial awaited them before they would see their loved ones. Suddenly, as they jostled along with thoughts of home flooding their minds, their train rushed headlong into a passenger train on the Baltimore & Ohio line. Cars flew from the tracks, people and equipment tumbled about, and screams mixed with the sounds of wrenching iron and splintering wood. John Adam Schneider of Company D, riding on a platform between two cars to get some fresh air, was thrown between two cars as debris came to rest all about him. Miraculously, rescuers pulled him from the wreckage unhurt. Nine people were killed in the crash and about thirty injured, but in the Sigel Regiment only Company A's Adolf Kuhlig was "slightly injured."[45]

Despite the accident and his narrow escape, the entire trip impressed Schneider as "a perfect ovation" from every city and town the troops passed through. From Pittsburgh the train turned northwest to Cleveland and Detroit before arriving at Grand Haven, Michigan, where the men boarded a steamer for the trip across Lake Michigan to Milwaukee.[46]

While the men waited about Washington, committees of their fellow-citizens prepared to celebrate their arrival. The Chamber of Commerce appointed a Committee of Reception to make arrangements for honoring the arrival of all the city's various regiments and batteries, while in the German community Philip Schlosser, the Sigel Regiment's former adjutant, coordinated activities for a Committee of Festivities to mark the arrival of *"unser deutsches regiment."*[47] Their only concern was when the troops would arrive. To solve the problem, the organizers announced that "The exact time and hour of the arrival of the Regiment not being known yet, the citizens will be notified of its arrival by signal gun-shots."[48]

When the ship hove into sight on the horizon, three guns fired to alert the citizenry of its approach. As the boat entered the harbor, thirteen guns roared a salute while church bells rang to summon the populace to "give a cordial welcome to the returning heroes." Citizens flocked to the docks, the boat easing its way to shore about noon amid growing festivities. The *Turnverein*, the *Leiderkranz*, and the other German societies formed in the streets, while cannons fired, bands played, and joyous greetings filled the air.[49]

Once ashore, the men were surrounded by family, friends, and well-wishers eager to greet the returning veterans. Most of the soldiers had not seen their families and friends in more than two and one-half years. Accompanied by a military escort from Camp Reno, the soldiers were ushered to the Fair Building on Main Street where Gen. Halbert E. Paine arranged for refreshments and "the first welcome" was "tendered to them by their friends and the public."[50]

The initial welcome complete, the triumphant march continued through streets lined solidly with rows of spectators. Led by Christian Bach's Band playing lively, patriotic music, under the direction of Drum Major John Spoerl, the procession's divisions represented a cross-section of Milwaukee's community, with its German population especially evident. Following the band in the first division came the Marshal of the Day, Gen. Philip Best, and his assistants on horseback, then the Milwaukee *Turnverein*, the *Schuetzen Verein*, the *Liederkranz*, and representatives of other societies. The mayor and city officials led the second division, followed by civil and military officers and the orators of the day in carriages, two companies of the U. S. Veteran Reserve Corps, and a second band. The Citizen's Committee of Reception led the final division, followed by former members of the regiment, the 26th Wisconsin Volunteer Infantry led by Col. Winkler, a section of artillery, and finally the relatives of the soldiers and citizens of Milwaukee.[51] Some may have felt the eerie similarity of the procession to that of the October day, now so long ago, when 988 young and hearty men marched purposefully through these very streets on their way to end the rebellion. They returned now, only 270 in number, thin, rugged, weathered veterans of so many fields where innocence and idealism were numbered among the casualties.

Through the city's streets the procession marched, winding its festive way to the Turner Hall on Fourth Street "where the different companies were seated at tables spread with a splendid banquet, and attended by the lady friends of the soldiers. The hall and tables were beautifully decorated with evergreen wreaths and festoons, flags and flowers, and the galleries were crowded with ladies. Across the street in front of the hall was a splendid triumphal arch, surmounted with flags and trimmed with evergreens, and a bevy of Halo girls dressed in white stood on a raised platform, on either side, waving their handkerchiefs in welcome."[52]

Following a sumptuous banquet, ex-Governor Edward Salomon "welcomed the officers and men in an eloquent speech in German, which was frequently and vociferously applauded."[53] Moritz Schoeffler and Bernhard Domschcke contributed emotional remarks to an occasion deeply felt by all. "Our German citizens determined," the *Milwaukee Sentinel* explained, "on the arrival of the Twenty-sixth Regiment, to give it such a welcome as should testify their high appreciation of its gallant services in the cause of civil liberty."[54] All concerned considered the day an eminent success.

The ceremonies concluded, the men spent the next few days renewing old acquaintances while occupying what, to veterans of so many campsites through various states and all manner of weather, must have seemed like luxurious accommodations at Camp Washburn. The end finally came on June 29 when the soldiers were paid off and the regiment disbanded, each of the comrades in arms now a private citizen, free to resume life as a civilian.[55]

These survivors from Company A chose to remember their wartime comrades by preparing this commemorative collage when they mustered out of service. Left to right, top row, August Schmidt, Christian Buerkey, Otto Gross, Raimund Kiefer; 2nd row, George Kissinger, Charles Musewald, George Andrecht, Gotthold Jaenig, William Bogk; 3rd row, Louis Hüsselmann, Adolf Kuhlig, Joseph Scholz, Frank M. Fiess, August Nitschke, Joseph Berlage; middle row, Joseph Wolf, William Hausberg, August Bielefeld, Capt. John William Fuchs, Eduard Seeliger, William Koch, Ulrich Leuenberger,; 5th row, Anton Czoernig, William Nero, Philip Kissinger, Richard Stoltz, Michael Moldenhauer, Philip Bauer; 6th row, Fritz Lüscher, William Mätzold, Charles Prien, Anton Nolde, August Beitz; bottom row, William Lück, Heinrich Roth, Christian Dauffenbach, John Schauss.

Courtesy of the Milwaukee County Historical Society.

Chapter 14

"FAME'S ETERNAL CAMPING GROUND"

Aftermath

The muffled drum's sad roll has beat
  The soldier's last tattoo;
No more on life's parade shall meet
  The brave and daring few.
On fame's eternal camping ground
  Their silent tents are spread,
And Glory guards with solemn round
  The bivouac of the dead.

"The Bivouac of the Dead"
by Theodore O'Hara

*F*or most of the "Boys in Blue" who marched and fought with *"unser deutsches regiment,"* the Civil War was the single most important event in their lives, an event that shaped and molded their futures as it had their years in uniform. Of those who survived the experience, most went home to resume their lives as best they could. Some went on to prominence, some did not, but every one was a different person for the experience they shared during those unforgettable thirty-three months.

Col. William H. Jacobs returned to banking, serving as president of the Second Ward Bank and becoming a principal backer of the Wisconsin Central Railroad, which later became the Soo Line. He also pursued political office, becoming county Clerk of the Courts and later serving as State Senator for 1875 and 1876. An owner of large landholdings in northern Wisconsin and Michigan, he was instrumental in organizing the Industrial Exposition, active in supporting musical organizations, and was always "actively identified with the interests of the city." In recommending him to a position as U.S. Consul to the German states, Halbert E. Paine, a member of the U.S. House of Representatives, characterized his standing as "so high that I have never heard any complaint, charge, or suspicion against him in any capacity. He is a gentleman of unusual talent." Twenty years after leading the Sigel Regiment off to war, he died September 11, 1882, at the age of fifty-one. On his death, the *Wisconsin Magazine of History* noted that "He was very popular and greatly lamented."[1]

Lt. Col. Frederick C. Winkler received brevet promotions to the ranks of colonel and brigadier general in recognition of his services in the field. Following the war he resumed the practice of law in partnership with A. R. R. Butler. In 1873 he became a partner in the firm of Jenkins, Elliott & Winkler, later becoming senior partner in the respected firm of Winkler, Flanders, Smith, Bottom & Vilas. During the course of his career he served as president of the Milwaukee County Bar Association and Wisconsin State Bar Association, and vice president of the American Bar Association. A zealous Republican, he became a member of that party's State Central Committee in 1869, served as a delegate to the Republican National Conventions in 1880 and 1894, was a member of the Wisconsin State Assembly in 1872, championed civil service reform, and served as a member of the Milwaukee City Board of School Commissioners in 1878-1880. An activist in veterans affairs, he was a member of the Grand Army of the Republic and gained election as Commander of the Wisconsin Commandery of the Loyal Legion of the United States. A member of the Menomonee Valley Improvement Commission and vice president of the Milwaukee Art Association, he served as Trustee of the Northwestern Mutual Life Insurance Company for thirty-two years. He and his wartime bride had nine children. He died in Los Angeles at the age of eighty-three while visiting one of his daughters on March 22, 1921. President Theodore Roosevelt called him "a man whom I have always considered a model for me and my sons to follow as an American citizen of the highest and best type."[2]

Lt. Col. Hans Boebel, his right leg amputated because of the wound he received while commanding the regiment at Gettysburg, was elected Milwaukee city treasurer and later appointed Deputy Revenue Collector. An active member of the Milwaukee *Turnverein*, in 1881 he was elected treasurer of the Gymnastic Seminary [Normal School] of the North American Union of Gymnastic Societies, established to train gymnastic teachers. "In all his private relations," a biographical sketch noted, "he has sustained the same modest, loyal and manly course which made him prominent in his army relations."[3]

Major Henry Baetz, forced to resign because of the effects of his Gettysburg wound, was elected as a Republican to the office of Treasurer of Manitowoc County in 1866 and 1868. In 1869 voters elected him State Treasurer, a position he was re-elected to in 1871. In 1876 he moved to Milwaukee where he began a career in journalism and gained election as Librarian of the Public Library, resigning that post in 1880 to accept the position of Secretary of the State Board of Immigration. In 1883 he was hired by Philip Best as general purchasing agent for what became the Pabst Brewing Company. He was also part owner and operator of the Pabst Mine near Ironwood, Michigan. A member of the Wisconsin Academy of Sciences, Arts and Letters, the Wisconsin Archeological Society, the Milwaukee Musical Society, and the Old Settler's Club, he served as president of the Deutscher Club and the *Deutsche Gesellschaft von Milwaukee*. He retired in 1904, passing away in Milwaukee on January 2, 1910.[4]

Major Franz Lackner's services were honored with a brevet promotion to the rank of lieutenant colonel. After returning to Wisconsin he ran the Terrace Gardens at West Highland Avenue and North Ninth Street for a while before moving to Chicago where he worked for fifty-six years as a prominent corporate attorney. He was elected president of the Chicago Bar Association, was an active member of the Civic Committee that removed a group of corrupt city politicians from office, served on the Committee on Relief following the famous Chicago Fire, and was appointed by the governor of Illinois a member of the committee to draft a new Chicago city charter. A member of the Union League Club, the University Club, and charter member of the *Turnverein*, he was elected national president of the latter organization. Upon his retirement at the age of seventy-five, he moved to South Pasadena, California, where he passed away at the age of eighty-eight on December 20, 1928. His biographical entry described him as "An able lawyer of high principles, a patriot who promptly placed his life at the service of his country, an upright, courageous gentleman, he will long be remembered for the prominent part which he played in this country's history and for the fine and inspiring life that he led."[5]

Capt. Bernhard Domschcke, captured at Gettysburg, spent the rest of the war as a Confederate prisoner in Richmond, Danville, Macon, Charleston, Columbia, and elsewhere, suffering exceptional privation. Following the war he resumed his journalistic career in October, 1866, as editor-in-chief of the *Daily Herold,* and was later elected national president of the *Turnverein.* He also wrote an excellent personal account of his experiences as a prisoner of war which he published in 1865 as *Zwanzig Monate in Kriegsgefangenschaft: Erinnerungen.* Translated into English and published 122 years later, it remains one of the best primary sources available on life in the Confederate prisons. Never recovering from the damage done to his health by his wartime incarceration, he suffered serious health problems, dying prematurely at the age of forty-three on May 5, 1869.[6] His passing was a cause for universal mourning. Thousands of people moved through the Turner Hall "to take a farewell glance at the features of the lamented dead. The casket was placed in the middle of the hall, and was draped with the Stars and Stripes, and covered with a beautiful wreath and bouquets of flowers." An enormous funeral cortege, reminiscent of the procession at the reception of the Sigel Regiment in Milwaukee in 1865, accompanied the body through the streets of the city to its final resting place in Forest Home. "The rites over," the *Milwaukee Sentinel* reported, "the large assembly dispersed, with the consciousness that they had paid the last tokens of respect to one who ably defended the right; one whose name will be borne in grateful remembrance by every patriot and lover of freedom throughout the land."[7]

Adjutant Albert Wallber marched south from Gettysburg with his captors, eventually being confined in Richmond's notorious Libby Prison. There, he joined a group plotting an escape. Using a table knife, chisel, and spittoon, the men took turns digging through a masonry wall into a storage basement, then into the street nearby. On February 9, 1864, 109 Union prisoners dressed in civilian clothing escaped through the makeshift tunnel. Many were recaptured within hours, but Wallber pressed on, tracked by bloodhounds and mounted patrols. Crossing streams and wading swamps in freezing weather, thorns and brambles tearing at his clothing, without food, his only aid came from slaves who pointed the way to safety and shared their meager rations with him. His feet badly frozen, his body emaciated, and suffering from exposure, he finally reached the Union lines after five grueling days, one of 57 who eventually made it to safety. Following the war he wrote a memoir of his experiences in prison and the successful escape, co-authored with Bernhard Domschcke a description of life in Confederate prisons titled *"Erinnerungen: 20 Monate in Gefangenschaft,"* participated actively in veterans affairs, and spoke before many patriotic gatherings. Rising to become vice president of the Weisel & Vilter Manufacturing Company in Wisconsin, he was an active member of the Milwaukee *Turnverein*, the *Deutsche Gesellschaft*, Robert Chivas Post No. 2, G.A.R., and the German English Academy which he served as president. He died in Milwaukee on December 17, 1911.[8]

Lt. Karl Doerflinger, his ankle shattered by a minie ball at Chancellorsville, lay unattended for days. Because of the delay in securing proper medical attention, his leg had to be amputated at the thigh. While he lay wounded, a letter from Col. Jacobs to the *Daily Herold* informed Milwaukeeans that "The palm of the day was due to the young hero, Doerflinger, who 'stormed' ahead of the regiment and each time was hailed by it with fiery enthusiasm."[9] Surviving the battle and the horrors of amputation, Doerflinger returned home a hero but suffered pain for the rest of his life. He submitted to five operations to try and rectify the damage done by the poor amputation, but none were successful. As late as 1908 he had two additional inches amputated in an attempt to relieve the increasing pain.[10]

Despite the loss of his leg and the recurring pain it caused, Doerflinger became a teacher at Peter Engelmann's famous German-English Academy. In 1869 he left for Europe where he studied the German kindergarten system, joining the Milwaukee Kindergarten Society shortly after his return. Due largely to his efforts, Milwaukee became the first city in the United States to mandate a kindergarten. He was also a member of the Board of Regents of the state normal schools for three years and developed a proposal for establishing a Department of Education in the university system. Over the years Doerflinger became a recognized national leader in educational reform,

advocating the inclusion of kindergartens and manual training in public school systems. As president of the Doerflinger Book and
Publishing Company he became publisher of the progressive journal
New Education, as well as *Education-Journal,* the organ of the
National German American Teacher's Association, the children's
monthly *Onkel Karl,* and several other books and education journals.
A member of the Wisconsin Natural History Society for more than
forty years, he served as secretary for a dozen years, is credited with
discovering the Wisconsin Meteorite, and was instrumental in establishing the first public museum in Milwaukee, serving as its initial
head. A leading advocate of forest conservation and scientific reforesta-
tion, he lectured on scientific farming and crop rotation, and visited
Mexico "to study the cultivation of coffee, cocoa, rubber, vanilla and
other products."[11]

In 1889-1893 "he traveled in Europe for the recovery of his health,
and for study and observation." Upon his return, he invested in the
Doerflinger Artificial Limb Company, becoming its president. He was
a member of the Milwaukee Musical Society, the Liberal League, the
Fortnightly Club, E. B. Walcott Post of the G.A.R., the Deutscher Club,
and others. Active, as well, in the Milwaukee *Turnverein,* he rose to
president in 1881 and was instrumental in Milwaukee's first place fin-
ishes in the national *Turnfests* in 1873, 1875, and 1879, and in the
international festival at Frankfort-am-Main in 1880. In 1870, while visiting Europe, "he took off [his] artificial leg and took part in all save the
running events in a gymnastic festival sponsored by the Gymnastic
Union of the Upper Rhine," finishing in eleventh place. He died
November 9, 1911.[12]

Surgeon Franz Huebschmann served at the U.S. General Hospital
in Milwaukee for several months before becoming Milwaukee city
physician. In 1866 his neighbors elected him city alderman from the
Second Ward. Appointed county physician in 1868, he became a member of the Board of Health in 1869 and was elected vice president of the
Milwaukee Medical Society the following year. A member of the City
Charter Convention in 1867, he also served as Democratic state senator in 1871 and 1872. According to one author, he "possessed a warm
heart, an active mental organization, affable and courteous habits and
pleasing address, and made a multitude of warm friends." He died in
Milwaukee on March 21, 1880.[13]

Charles Buerstatte returned home a twice-wounded veteran of nearly a dozen engagements at the age of eighteen. He enrolled in Baldwin (Ohio) University where he obtained an education as a pharmacist. He married in 1871, fathering ten children. After working for two years as a drug clerk, he opened Manitowoc Drugs on South 8th Street in 1872, operating it for forty years before turning it over to his sons. The business finally closed in 1967.[14]

The twelve *freiwilligen* who were the first to follow West Bend editor Jacob Mann into Company G fared poorly. Fully one-half died in service, three were either discharged or transferred because of disabilities they incurred, two were wounded, and only one escaped unscathed. Jacob Dexheimer and Killian Schnepf were killed at Chancellorsville; Charles Hafemann was wounded at Gettysburg and New Hope Church, spending the rest of the war in the hospital; John Horn was discharged for disability; Julius Jewlson was killed at Gettysburg; Conrad Mack died of disease in Virginia; John Remmel served most of the war before being transferred to the Veteran Reserve Corps due to disability; John Schultz was wounded at Gettysburg; Peter Stoffel died of wounds he received at Resaca; Robert H. Templeton was killed at Dallas; and Jacob Wagner was discharged for disability. Only Jacob Heip, who became a lieutenant in Company K but resigned before seeing action, returned home unscathed.[15]

None of the four volunteers that came south to Milwaukee from Sturgeon Bay to join Company I escaped uninjured. Georg Boyer was wounded at Kennesaw Mountain, Phillip Feldman died of wounds received at Gettysburg, and George Heilmann was transferred to the Veteran Reserve Corps due to disability. Ernst Damkoehler, wounded and captured at Resaca, was sent to Andersonville prison where he succumbed quickly to his wounds and the lack of adequate medical treatment on June 26, 1864, without ever seeing his infant son, his other seven children, or his beloved Mathilde again. He is buried in Grave 2522 near Americus, Georgia.[16]

In Company C the close band of friends and relatives from Greenfield also left behind them many ruined hopes and dreams. Leopold Drewes was injured in an accident and hospitalized when the regiment mustered out. Julius Stirn and Nicholas Friedrich were transferred to the Veteran Reserve Corps due to service-incurred disability. After surviving the Confederate prison at Belle Isle, Asmus Holz was exchanged and returned to the regiment. Captured again during the Atlanta campaign, he died of disease at Andersonville, August 20, 1864. Louis Manz's wound resulted in permanent stiffening of his hand, making him unfit to resume his trades as coppersmith and saw mill operator. He settled in Hale's Corners after the war where he became a letter carrier and served over fifty years before retiring in 1915. He died at the Soldier's Home, the oldest living letter carrier in the United States.[17] Adam Wuest recovered from his wound and followed the regiment through Georgia and the Carolinas to the end of the war. He settled in Milwaukee for some time, but never married his wartime sweetheart Christina Schmidt. Later he moved to Franksville, Racine County, where he opened a tavern. Like many, his wartime experience was the great event in his life. Eventually he moved to Richmond, Virginia, to be nearer the scenes of his service. His brother-in-law, Adam Muenzenberger, the devout cobbler who agonized through the deaths of two sons and longed for a return to his beloved Barbara, died of disease in a Richmond prison on December 3, 1863.[18]

"Meine Lieben Kameraden!"

One feeling many of the veterans shared was their desire to maintain the friendships they made in the service. On the Fourth of July, 1867, the citizens of Milwaukee gathered for their traditional observance of the national holiday. It was a cool, clear day, a day the *Milwaukee Sentinel* described as "all that could be asked by any one except the vendors of lemonade and other liquids for assuaging thirst."[19] Five thousand people attended the celebration in the German community, with Bach's Band leading a procession of all the civic, social, and cultural societies from Turner Hall to Williamsburg where the festivities took place. There, Bach's Band played, the male chorus of the *Musik Verein* sang, a *Puppintheater* [Puppet Theater] entertained the "younger patriots," and everyone found good company. A highlight of the afternoon was "an eloquent oration on national affairs by Captain Bernhard Domschcke," followed that evening by dancing and fireworks.[20]

Members of the Sigel Regiment participated in the Fourth of July celebrations as individuals, or members of organizations like the

Turnverein, the *Musik Verein,* the *Liederkranz,* or the various G.A.R. posts. Before long, the veterans felt the need to maintain the friendships developed during the wartime years, preserve the memory of their deeds, and honor their deceased comrades-in-arms in more formal fashion. The day before the Fourth of July celebration in 1870, the regiment held a reunion. According to the *Sentinel,* "The numerous friends of the Twenty-sixth were notified, on Saturday, of their assemblage yesterday, by the receipt of a silk magenta badge, announcing the fact. They assembled for roll-call on Market Square soon after noon yesterday, and proceeded to the Milwaukee Garden, where an address was delivered, speeches made, and a good dinner enjoyed. This regiment did good service in the war, and the reunion was a pleasant occasion. Over two hundred of the old veterans, of German nativity, were together, and a large number of friends besides. The day and evening were given to the exchange of reminiscences of the times that tried men's souls."[21] Later that same year a "Soldiers Reunion" took place in Milwaukee on September 28, prompting members of the 26th Wisconsin to plan a second reunion to coincide with the fall celebration.[22]

Each year the local reunions continued. On January 10, 1875, about forty veterans met at Baeder's on Fourth Street to organize and "complete arrangements for a reunion," but this time they also sought to mold a permanent regimental association. As officers, they elected Col. William Jacobs as president, Adjutant Philip Schlosser as vice president, and Quartermaster Adolf Hensel as secretary. They also empowered the president "to appoint a committee to draft a constitution and by-laws with a view to permanent organization, and to appoint a committee on finance."[23] The following month a well-attended meeting received the report of the Committee on Constitution and By-Laws which recommended the creation of a fund to support destitute veterans, collection of an annual membership fee of one dollar from "all who are able to pay it," and the appointment of a three-man executive committee to determine whether applicants for aid were "really deserving of support." Winkler argued convincingly that the provisions for the destitute should wait because the veterans were not all residents of Milwaukee and "all had not yet signed the roll." He suggested that special collections be taken up for the needy, while membership dues be reserved for the expenses of the association. After some discussion, the assembled veterans voted to form a permanent organization "to bring them into closer relations with each other, and to encourage annual reunions." Annual dues of one dollar would be collected, but "this fee is not obligatory to the exclusion of worthy comrades who are in destitute circumstances." The association was to be administered by a president, vice president, secretary, treasurer, and an executive committee of three members "of which the officers shall be ex-officio members." Winkler was nominated to fill the vacant treasurer's position, but declined due to the press of his professional duties. In his place the men elected Capt. William Steinmeyer. As an executive committee, they chose Winkler, W. Joseph Schultz, and Charles Trapschuh. After considering the anniversary of the Battle of Chancellorsville, the meeting determined to hold the next reunion instead on Sunday, July 4, the anniversary of the Battle of Gettysburg, and assigned the task of planning the event to the executive committee.[24]

At a meeting held in a hall owned by William A. Koch, himself a veteran of the regiment, on May 31, the veterans named Joseph Maschauer, Charles Trapschuh, and Joseph A. Berlage a committee on finance, while Adj. Schlosser and Trapschuh were assigned "to confer with the owners of parks with a view of ascertaining accommodations and terms."[25] The veterans met again a week later on June 6 to complete arrangements. The Committee on Finance reported a "considerable sum had been subscribed, and the prospects were favorable to the collection of an amount that would cover the expense that the gathering would entail." Schlosser and Trapschuh reported the "terms of Mr. Dreher, of the Milwaukee Garden, were the most liberal," whereupon "his place was named as the one at which the reunion is to take place." Invitations were sent to all the Milwaukee area veterans, and to Major Lackner in Chicago and Capt. Hubert Dilger, a battery captain who served much of the war in close concert with the 26th, also in Chicago.[26]

On the appointed day, the veterans and their guests met at the West Side Turner Hall at 1:00 p.m., from whence, escorted by the Juneau Guard and led by the stirring music of a band, they marched to the Milwaukee Garden. Accompanied by representatives of the 5th, 6th, 9th, 11th, and 24th Wisconsin regiments, the veterans of the 26th included men from "Racine, Menomonee Falls, Fond du Lac, and other cities and towns in the interior." According to the *Sentinel*, "There were about eighty of the plucky regiment that had battled for their country on many a field during the war for the Union, and the day was

delightfully spent in recounting incidents and experiences of soldier-
life during the great rebellion." Later, at the afternoon banquet,
Winkler, Jacobs, Boebel, Lackner, Dr. Vette, Dr. Huebschmann and
others "addressed their old comrades in brief and pithy speeches, and,
in the evening, all joined in a grand ball in honor of the event. The
reunion was so successful in its arrangements that there is a decided
sentiment in favor of annual meetings here on the Fourth of July."[27]

Reunions of the veterans residing in the Wisconsin area continued to be held annually, the fifteenth anniversary of their departure
for the war also being duly noted in ceremonies at Koch's Hall in
October 1877. Similarly, the twentieth anniversary of their departure
was occasion for special celebrations in 1882. At 2:00 p.m. on
September 3:

> the battle-scarred heroes assembled at the headquarters on Fourth
> street, just north of State, 200 strong, and headed by Zeitz's
> Military Band, marched to Milwaukee Garden, where a reunion
> was indulged in, the battles of the war fought over again in
> imagery, and a jolly good time indulged in. The war-worn colors of
> the regiment that had been so heroically defended on many a well-
> fought field were displayed in the line, but they had been so rent
> with war's rough usage that it was necessary that they should be
> covered with gauze to present even a semblance of their originali-
> ty. The afternoon was spent pleasantly at the garden in social con-
> verse, enlivened by patriotic airs from the band. The scenes of the
> camp-fire, the march and the battle were brought vividly to mind
> by the presence of so many comrades of the campaign. The enthu-
> siasm knew no bounds as the stirring notes of "Rally Round the
> Flag, Boys," "John Brown's Body Lies Mouldering in the Grave,"
> "Dixie," "The Star Spangled Banner," and other well-remembered
> airs were played, and many a gray-haired veteran, forgetful of all
> else, sang himself hoarse over the chorus, and danced with the
> zest of a youth in his teens. At 6 o'clock the soldiers sat down to a
> pork-and-beans supper, in the dining-room, and in the evening the
> dancers took possession of the large pavilion, but this proving
> inadequate, the dining-room was also utilized, and at both places
> the votaries of Terpsichore indulged the favorite pastime until an
> early hour this morning.[28]

Among those present, the *Sentinel* commented that "Uncle Sam's civil service was represented by six letter-carriers, viz.: Charles Thieme, Henry Urich, William Weidner, Henry Larch, Louis Manz and Antoine Ewens, who followed the fortunes of the regiment through the war." A favorite of the reunions in the mid-1880s was Hector, the twice-wounded gray horse ridden by Adj. Philip Schlosser through almost two years of war.[29]

The regiment's silver anniversary in 1887 was cause for special celebration and remembrance. Aside from the usual Fourth of July ceremonies, a reunion of the surviving comrades-in-arms took place on August 27-28. A committee consisting of Philip J. Schlosser, Ferdinand Scholz, Philip G. Hunkel, Henry Van Ewyk, Henry Klinker, Charles Trapschuh, William Steinmeyer, and Hans Boebel, and about thirty of the veterans residing in Milwaukee met at Robert Chivas Post, G.A.R., to plan the two-day event and issue invitations to all of their comrades who could be located.[30]

The festivities began with a reception and informal campfire at Robert Chivas Hall on Saturday evening, August 27. The *Sentinel* reported "The hall had been especially decorated for the occasion and about the walls were shields bearing the names of the engagements in which the regiment participated. The windows were profusely decorated with foliage, while the national colors were tastily hung about the room."[31]

The following day the veterans marched from the hall to Market Square where they halted briefly at the spot where they held their last formal review before leaving for the war twenty-five years before. "The sun was shining and the ground was hard and dry," the *Milwaukee Sentinel* reported, "when the tramp of the old soldier boys re-echoed along Third street at 1 P. M. in the air of a war-time melody. About 150 veterans made up the procession, which was just a block long, and perhaps fifty of these were from out of town. The total number of survivors is said to be 320."[32] The correspondent thought "They were a vigorous fine-looking body of men. Here and there was one who had left a leg or an arm on a Southern field, while others bore the evidence of their gallant service in scars that were not exposed."[33]

From Market Square the procession moved on to Schuetzen Park which was decorated in the national colors for the occasion with the names of the regiment's battles posted on the trees. At 4:00 p.m. the veterans assembled to have their picture taken from the grand stand, after which Mayor Emil Wallber rose to address them, telling them how proud he was of "the most German regiment of the most German city of America."[34] Following the mayor's speech, shouts rang out for Gen. Winkler, and "that gentleman limped to the platform and was received with cheers." The cheers turned to deafening shouts and applause as he greeted the assembled veterans as *"Meine Lieben Kameradden!"* [My Dear Comrades]. But the wildest ovation was reserved for Col. Boebel who "came forward with the assistance of his wooden leg, and made a one-minute speech that took the old veterans by

Johann Bentz, Company C, a farmer from Kenosha. Photo taken at the 1888 reunion

Courtesy of Russell Scott

Christian R. Caflisch, Company K, a farmer from Honey Creek who was captured while foraging on March 5, 1865. Photo taken in later years.

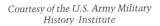

Courtesy of the U.S. Army Military History Institute

Philip Mathes, Company H, a farmer from Rhine who was wounded at Gettysburg. Photo taken at a post-war reunion.

Courtesy of Russell Scott

storm." Thoughtfully, he intoned: *"Jungens, wenn ich die alten Gesichter so wiedersehe, dann rappelts hier, (placing his hand over his heart.) Last uns immer unsere Schulldigkeit wie damals thun und all Schlechtigkeiten zum Teufel jugen"* [Boys, when I see all the old faces, then my heart pounds. Let's do our duty now, as we did then, and leave everything bad to the devil.]. The speeches over, the picnic and entertainment lasted well into the night.[35]

The celebration in 1888 was also particularly special, for in that year twenty-six veterans of the Sigel Regiment journeyed to Gettysburg to participate in the dedication of a monument to memorialize their contributions on that bloody field. On this occasion, arrangements were made by a committee consisting of Frederick E. Winkler, Albert Wallber, William Sternmeyer and Philip Schlosser. Rendezvousing at the Second Ward Bank, the old veterans formed behind the American Cadet Band to march through the city's streets to the railroad station. Their old regimental colors crowned with a wreath of laurels, they marched through Market Square, dipping their colors as they passed over the ground where they held their last parade before leaving for Virginia twenty-six years before. They left Milwaukee in a group at 10:00 a.m., June 28, traveling by rail to Chicago as they had done that fateful fall in 1862.[36]

Enroute, the veterans of the 26th were joined by Gen. Lucius Fairchild and about twenty-five veterans from other Wisconsin cities. As the official head of Wisconsin's delegation, the general was charged with accepting the Wisconsin monuments on Wisconsin Day at the battlefield.[37] "It is a sacred mission which takes surviving soldiers of the Civil War from Wisconsin to Gettysburg," the *Milwaukee Sentinel* declared. "That turning point of fortune to the Union forces was a field fruitful of graves for Wisconsin men and grief for Wisconsin. That delegation of gray and grizzled veterans, conspicuous for the number of empty sleeves and honorable scars which it carries goes to dedicate seven modest monuments to the memory of nearly half a thousand men from the Badger state who unsuccessfully attempted to run the awful gauntlet which death maintained for two days."[38]

The year 1889 brought to Milwaukee a national encampment of the Grand Army of the Republic with more than 100,000 veterans and guests in attendance. Over 300 veterans from the Sigel Regiment met during the week at Philip Schlosser's Hall on the corner of Third Street

Survivors of the 26th Wisconsin at the dedication of their monument at Gettysburg, July 1, 1888. Left to Right: Ferdinand Huebner, Ferdinand Krueger, Henry Van Eweyk, Julius Meiswinkel, Charles J. Meyers, Frederick Siebold, Sigmund Juenger, William Franke, Julius Ernst Lasche, Philip Jacob Schlosser, Nicolaus Friedrich, Frank A. Kuechenmeister, John Charles Trapschuh, Adolph Kuhlig, Charles B. Thieme, William Joseph Scholz, Paul Van de Plasche, Louis Huesselmann, George Dittmar, Ferdinand Scholz, Friedrich Janzen, Daniel Steuerwald, John F. Luscher, Frank M. Fiess, Sebastian Guckenberger. *Courtesy of the Milwaukee County Historical Society.*

and Reservoir Avenue, before marching to Schuetzen Park for a grand picnic on August 26.[39] Another noteworthy meeting occurred in 1894 when Gen. Oliver O. Howard spoke at the Congregational Church on Grand Avenue. According to Doerflinger, he "Spoke with the highest appreciation of the courage and other good qualities of the German soldiers of the Eleventh Corps that were formerly under his command."[40]

The local reunions continued each year, the number of veterans slowly diminishing as the years passed. In 1902, committee members Karl Doerflinger, Philip J. Schlosser and Albert Wallber invited the survivors to Schützen Park for the annual commemoration. By 1913, only a few remained. But in that year, the last grand reunion was held in conjunction with the fiftieth anniversary of the Battle of Gettysburg. To celebrate the anniversary of the battle that, more than any other, came to represent the war in microcosm, veterans from North and South met on the field where the fortunes of the nation hung in the balance a half century before. Records of the Wisconsin commission charged with responsibility of making arrangements for the encampment at Gettysburg indicate the following veterans of the Sigel Regiment planned to visit the scene of their wartime sacrifices: William Sery, Company G; Nicholas Kolngen, Company C; Charles Baje, Company C; August Nitschke, Company A; William H. Rintelmann, Company A; Charles Gottschalk, Company B; Herman Schultz, Company B; Peter Hoffmann, Company C; August Luedtke, Company E; Mathew Dambach, Company B; Franz Friedrich, Company I; Frank Rezac, Company I; William Lueck, Company A; Peter Wirshem, Company C; Jacob Mahloch, Company H; Henry Waack, Company F; Edward Carl, Company K; Phipp Zipp, Company E; Frederick C. Winkler, Colonel; Henry Fink, Company B; Theodore Koerner, Company K; Charles J. Trapschuh, Company A; Carl F. O. Kindt, Company C; Henry W. Rintelmann, Company A; Ferdinand Scholz, Company A; John Hammen, Company K; Paul Von der Plasche, Company B; Ernst Schreiber, Company I; Jacob Schneeberger, Company D; Peter Lorsch, Company D; John Wemmert, Company D; Ferdinand Haese, Company F; John Steffen, Company H; Martin Kohn, Company H; William Schumacher, Company B; George W. Jones, Company G; Gottlieb Metzner, Company G; George Dascher, Company K; Albert Kittel, Company K; and Peter Schneller, Company K.[41]

The Honors of War

Organized at Milwaukee from men of that city and the surrounding counties, the 26th Wisconsin Volunteer Infantry was formed under the spirit of the German republican movement of 1848. Sent to join the Army of the Potomac in Virginia in October, 1862, the regiment endured hard marches, debilitating weather, disease, and boredom before its baptism of fire the following spring. When it finally "saw the elephant" at Chancellorsville it behaved with great gallantry and determination despite being placed in an untenable position. Its heroic stand contributed significantly to the escape of the Eleventh Corps baggage train, artillery, and troops who would have been cut off if the Badgers had not held as long as they did. Moving north to Gettysburg, the regiment again behaved well in defeat on July 1, acting as rear guard on the retreat through town. Their conduct as sharpshooters and skirmishers during the balance of that battle elicited praise from those who witnessed their courage.

Transferred to Tennessee, the Sigel Regiment served with honor during the campaigns to relieve the sieges of Chattanooga and Knoxville before joining Sherman's march on Atlanta. In that decisive campaign they shouldered much of the burden of marching, fatigue, and combat, being almost always in the presence of the enemy during the four months from the beginning of May, 1864, to the fall of Atlanta. Their battle honors read like a history of that grueling march: Buzzard Roost Gap, Resaca, Cassville, Dallas, New Hope Church, Golgotha Church, Nose's Creek, Kennesaw Mountain, Kolb's Farm, Peach Tree Creek, Atlanta. In each of these actions they served well, playing crucial roles at Resaca and Peach Tree Creek while gaining special praise from their brigade commander.

After the fall of Atlanta, the regiment joined Sherman's march to the sea, participating in the siege of Savannah and the battles of Averasboro and Bentonville. Once again, the men served with distinction, earning the respect of those around them. Their brigade commander during this time, Brig. Gen. William Cogswell, later stated in an official report to the Secretary of War that the 26th Wisconsin was "one of the finest military organizations in the service."[42]

Its success came at a very high price. The 26th Wiscsonsin Volunteer Infantry enrolled 1,002 men on its original muster rolls.

During its term of service it received 87 additions: 84 recruits in 1864, two recruits in 1865, and one substitute. Thus, its total aggregate strength was 1,089. Of this number, death claimed 254. The regiment also lost 125 through transfer and 232 by discharge. Of those transferred, aside from the recruits whose terms of service did not end with the Sigel Regiment, most went to the Veteran Reserve Corps or the Invalid Corps as a result of wounds or other service-related disabilities. Similarly, aside from some early resignations by officers during the first several months in the field, most discharges resulted from battle wounds and disabilities. In the end, 447 mustered out with the regiment, or separately in the various hospitals where its casualties slowly recovered. Including those who were killed in action, died of wounds, or died of disease, the chance that a Wisconsin soldier would die in the Civil War was one in seven. In the Sigel Regiment it was one in four. In all, at least 34 officers and 583 enlisted men became casualties during the war, a total of 55.7% of those enrolled.[43] When approximately 109 officers and men who resigned were discharged, deserted, or transferred to other units before the regiment's first combat in May, 1863, are deducted about 62.9% of those who served until at least May, 1863, become casualties, only a few short of two-thirds of the regiment.

The most comprehensive study of casualties in the Union army is *Regimental Losses in the American Civil War 1861-1865* by William F. Fox. According to Fox, the Sigel Regiment sustained the fifth highest number of casualties of any Northern regiment engaged at Chancellorsville and the fifteenth highest at Gettysburg. With 191 killed in action or died of wounds, the regiment placed fourth among all Wisconsin regiments in the total number of killed.[44] But, because the aggregate strength of regiments varied considerably, Fox believed the most appropriate way to evaluate losses was on a percentage basis. "[T]he proper way to judge the relative losses of regiments during their term of service is to accompany the statement of the losses with the figures of the total enrollment," he explained, "and compare the percentages as well as the losses. The regiments in the following list can fairly claim the honor of having encountered the hardest fighting in the war. They may not have done the most effective fighting, nor the best fighting; but they evidently stood where the danger was thickest, and were the ones that faced the hottest musketry. They were all well-known, reliable commands, and served with unblemished records."

Applying this criteria, the Sigel Regiment's 17.2% killed in action placed it second among Wisconsin regiments and a remarkable fifth among the multitude of regiments from all the states wearing the blue.[45] Commenting specifically on the 26th Wisconsin, Fox characterized it as "A German regiment whose gallantry and soldierly bearing reflected credit upon its nationality."[46] Writing about Gettysburg for the Military Order of the Loyal Legion in 1896, Edwin E. Bryant stated: "In the roll of honor of Wisconsin's regiments, none are more deserving, none have a more glorious record than this regiment."[47] Fox agreed, placing the regiment at the pinnacle of his list of the most gallant regiments in the volunteer service.[48]

Despite its honorable service and sacrifice in some of the most important campaigns and engagements of the war, the 26th Wisconsin has been largely ignored by historians in its home state. One example of this is the work of Richard N. Current, a prominent state and national historian who wrote the most comprehensive history of Wisconsin. In it he lists all of the Wisconsin regiments that fought at Gettysburg and explains their contributions; all, that is, except the Sigel Regiment. Although he lists the 26th as present, he otherwise ignores it. Worse still is Robert W. Wells's popular "official" history *Wisconsin in the Civil War,* which is sold at the State Historical Society in Madison and at other state-supported outlets. Although covering the contributions of other Wisconsin units, Wells virtually ignores the Sigel Regiment. In discussing Gettysburg he says only that "The 26th Wisconsin, with just one previous battle under its belt, got into little of the fighting as a unit. It did, however, furnish numerous men for picket duty—a task that involved skirmishing in advanced positions. It lost 41 men killed, 137 wounded, 26 prisoners and six missing." If this is "little of the fighting," one wonders what would constitute significant action. Apparently it never occurred to Wells that regiments do not usually lose 210 casualties "skirmishing" on "picket duty."[49] Yet another example of this neglect can be seen in the Wisconsin Military Museum where, as of this writing, aside from a German-language recruiting poster there is virtually no mention of the Sigel Regiment or its sacrifices in the otherwise admirable displays.

The men who marched with the Sigel Regiment were farmers and cobblers, singers and gymnasts, Catholics and freethinkers. Some enlisted to preserve the Union, some to eliminate slavery, some because of the excitement of the day, some for the bounties, and some for personal reasons. They had as many human foibles and failings as anyone: they jockeyed for promotion, complained of the hunger and the weather, blamed the generals and politicians for hardships and failures, and thought longingly of home. But when it came to fighting, the men acquitted themselves exceptionally well. There were many regiments, both North and South, that fought with courage and determination in defense of their principles during the war. Few fought harder, sacrificed more, or contributed as much as the *freiwilligen* of the 26th Wisconsin Volunteer Infantry—"*unser deutsches regiment.*"

Veterans of the 26th Wisconsin gatheered for their 50th anniversary commemoration at Whitefish Bay on August 21, 1912.

Courtesy of Fred Turk and the Milwaukee County Historical Society

Appendix A

OFFICERS AND STAFF, OCTOBER 6, 1862

Wilhelm H. Jacobs, Colonel
Charles Lehmann, Lieutenant Colonel
Philip Horwitz, Major
Philip J. Schlosser, Adjutant
Frederick W. Hundhausen, Quartermaster
Dr. Franz Huebshmann, Surgeon
Dr. Theodore Fricke, First Asstnt. Surgeon
Dr. Simon von der Vart, Second Asstnt. Surgeon

William Vette, Chaplain
Hermann Fuerstenberg, Sergeant Major
Adolph Hensel, Quartermaster Sergeant
Oswald Schhubert, Commissary Sergeant
William Hoffman, Hospital Steward
Gottfried Luther, Principal Musician

Company A, Flying Rangers
  William George, Captain
  Christian Sarnow, First Lieutenant
  August F. Mueller, Second Lieutenant
Company B, German Americans
  Frederick C. Winkler, Captain
  William E. Huttman, First Lieutenant
  Karl H. Doerflinger, Second Lieutenant
Company C, Milwaukee Guards
  John P. Seeman, Captain
  John W. Fuchs, First Lieutenant
  Bernhard Domschcke Second Lieutenant
Company D, Salomon Rifles
  August Ligowsky, Captain
  August Schueler, First Lieutenant
  Charles Ottilie, Second Lieutenant
Company E, Fond du Lac Turners
  Anton Kittlar, Captain
  Charles W. Neukirch, First Lieutenant
  John F. Hagen, Second Lieutenant

Company F, Lake Shore Rifles
  Henry Baetz, Captain
  Charles Pizzala, First Lieutenant
  Albert Wallber, Second Lieutenant
Company G, Washington County Rifles
  Jacob E. Mann, Captain
  William Smith, First Lieutenant
  Julius Meiswinkel, Second Lieutnt.
Company H, Second Ward Guard
  Hans Boebel, Captain
  Joseph Wedig, First Lieutenant
  Charles Vocke, Second Lieutenant
Company I, Wenze Guard
  Franz Landa, Captain
  Henry J. Berninger, First Lieutenant
  John Orth, Second Lieutenant
Company K, Sigel Guard
  Louis Pelosi, Captain
  Jacob Heipp, First Lieutenant
  Edward Carl, Second Lieutenant

Appendix B

DEMOGRAPHICS

The regimental descriptive books and papers contain known occupations for 1,063 of the men in the Sigel Regiment. These are as follows:

Occupation	Number	Occupation	Number
Architect	1	Druggist	1
Artist	1	Dyer	2
Baker	6	Editor	4
Banker	2	Engineer [b]	3
Barber	3	Farmer	409
Barkeeper	2	Farmhand	1
Blacksmith	32	Fisherman	4
Bookbinder	5	Gardner	8
Bookkeeper	2	Gilder	1
Bootmaker	1	Grinder	1
Brewer	8	Gunsmith	1
Broommaker	4	Harnessmaker	3
Butcher	25	Hostler	1
Cabinetmaker	6	Hotelkeeper	1
Carpenter [a]	74	Hunter	1
Carver	1	Ironworker	1
Chemist	1	Joiner	3
Cigarmaker	6	Laborer [c]	113
Clergyman	1	Lawyer	3
Clerk	22	Liveryman	1
Commissioner	1	Locksmith	2
Confectioner	1	Machinist	2
Cooper	37	Manufacturer	1
Coppersmith	1	Mason	10
Drayman	1	Mechanic	8
Driver	1	Merchant	18

Occupation	Number	Occupation	Number
Merchant	18	Tailor	21
Miller	10	Tanner	1
Molder	1	Teacher [f]	5
Moulder	2	Teamster	11
Musician	4	Tinsmith	7
Painter	8	Tobacconist	1
Papermaker	1	Tradesman	3
Patternmaker	1	Trunkmaker	1
Peddler	1	Turner	2
Physician [d]	8	Typefounder	1
Pianomaker	1	Varnisher	1
Pilecutter	1	Vinegarmaker	1
Potter	4	Wagoner	1
Porter	6	Wagonmaker	15
Printer	6	Watchmaker	2
Register of Deeds	1	Weaver [g]	5
Ropemaker	2	Wheelwright	2
Saddler	11	Well Digger	1
Sailor	3		
Saloonkeeper	3		
Servant	1		
Shoemaker	51		
Smith	1		
Soldier	4		
Stonecutter [e]	2		

[a] Includes two ship carpenters.
[b] Includes one topographical engineer.
[c] Includes one listed as workman.
[d] Includes three surgeons.
[e] Includes one stonemason.
[f] Includes one music teacher.
[g] Includes one carpetweaver.

ENROLLMENT & PRESENT FOR DUTY

The following is a table describing the strength of the regiment according to the monthly muster rolls on file in the National Archives, Washington, D.C. The data given is as of the end of the month indicated. Those present but not available for duty included the sick, men on extra duty, or those under arrest. The absent included some who were sick, wounded, on detached duty, on leave, or absent without leave. The column "% Present For Duty" indicates the percentage of the Total who were available for duty. The "% Total Mustered" indicates the percentage present for duty compared with the original 988 mustered in Milwaukee at the beginning of October, 1862.

Month	Present			Present For Duty			Absent			Total	% Present For Duty	% Total Mustered
	Off.	Men	Total	Off.	Men	Total	Off.	Men	Total			
1862												
Oct.	38	922	960	38	823	861	-	21	21	988	87.1	87.1
Nov.	31	833	867	27	780	807	4	58	62	976	82.7	81.7
Dec.	30	812	842	28	695	723	7	120	127	969	74.6	73.2
1863												
Jan.	31	718	749	26	646	672	6	200	206	955	70.4	68.0
Feb.	27	769	796	24	634	658	6	130	136	932	70.6	66.6
Mar.	33	760	793	31	611	642	4	118	222	911	70.5	65.0
Apr.	33	709	742	33	652	685	4	147	151	893	76.7	69.3
May	21	550	571	17	467	484	11	234	245	816	59.3	49.0
June	22	534	556	20	438	458	11	233	244	796	57.5	46.4
July	13	322	335	9	273	282	20	342	362	697	40.5	28.5
Aug.	16	332	348	10	265	275	15	319	334	682	40.3	27.8
Sept.	19	349	368	11	247	258	10	294	304	672	38.4	26.1
Oct.	18	331	349	11	288	299	9	316	325	674	44.4	30.3
Nov.	17	346	363	14	296	310	6	307	313	676	45.9	31.4
Dec.	19	355	374	15	293	308	6	285	291	665	46.3	31.2

Month	Present			Present For Duty			Absent			Total	% Present	% Total
	Off.	Men	Total	Off.	Men	Total	Off.	Men	Total		For Duty	Mustered
1864												
Jan.	15	380	395	13	318	331	10	237	247	642	51.6	33.5
Feb.	13	408	421	12	329	341	9	227	236	657	51.9	34.5
Mar.	16	417	433	15	350	365	8	213	221	654	55.8	36.9
Apr.	17	483	500	15	390	405	4	176	280	680	59.6	41.0
May	13	367	380	11	318	329	7	274	281	666	49.4	33.3
June	19	323	342	16	293	309	6	296	302	643	48.1	31.3
July	17	277	294	14	252	266	6	317	323	617	43.1	26.9
Aug.	17	256	273	14	213	227	4	309	313	586	38.7	23.0
Sept.	13	285	298	12	238	250	4	270	274	572	43.7	25.3
Oct.	13	280	293	13	244	257	4	269	273	566	45.4	26.0
Nov.	14	283	297	14	253	267	4	262	266	563	47.4	27.0
Dec.	15	276	291	15	248	263	3	259	262	553	47.6	26.6
1865												
Jan.	15	287	302	14	252	266	3	251	254	550	48.4	26.9
Feb.	15	266	281	14	234	248	3	265	268	549	45.2	25.1
Mar.	15	234	249	15	206	221	1	268	269	518	42.7	22.4
Apr.	17	262	279	17	236	253	5	231	236	515	49.1	25.6
May	18	288	306	18	258	276	2	201	203	509	54.2	27.9

Appendix D

ENGAGEMENTS

Chancellorsville, Virginia, May 1-5, 1863.
Gettysburg, Pennsylvania, July 1-4, 1863.
Funkstown, Maryland, July 12-13, 1863.
Wauhatchie, Tennessee, October 28-29, 1863.
Citico Creek, Tennessee, November, 1863
Missionary Ridge, Tennessee, November 23-25, 1863.
Buzzard Roost Gap, Georgia, May 8-9, 1864.
Rocky Face Ridge, Georgia, May 8-11, 1864.
Resaca, Georgia, May 13-16, 1864.
Cassville, Georgia, May 19, 1864.
Burnt Hickory, Georgia, May 23, 1864.
Dallas, Georgia, May 25, 1864.
New Hope Church, Georgia, May 25-June 1, 1864.
Pine Mountain, Georgia, June 11-14, 1864.
Golgotha Church, Georgia, June 15-16, 1864.
Lost Mountain, Georgia, June 15-17, 1864.
Muddy Creek, Georgia, June 17, 1864.
Noses' Creek [or Noyes' Creek], Georgia, June 19, 1864.
Kennesaw Mountain, Georgia, June 19-July 2, 1864.
Kolbs' Farm, Georgia, June 22, 1864.
Peach Tree Creek, Georgia, July 19-21, 1864.
Atlanta, Siege of, Georgia, July 22-September 2, 1864.
Savannah, Siege of, Georgia, Dec. 10-21, 1864.
Lawtonville, South Carolina, February 2, 1865.
Goldsboro Road, North Carolina, March 14, 1865.
Averasboro, North Carolina, March 15-16, 1865.
Bentonville, North Carolina, March 19-20, 1865.
Mill Creek, North Carolina, March 22, 1865.

Appendix E

FATALITIES

During its service, the 26th Wisconsin Volunteer infantry enrolled 1,089 men. It was officially credited with 188 killed in action or died of wounds, the fifth highest percentage of any Northern regiment. In addition to this, I have added to the list Ernst Damkoehler who died in a Confederate prison from the effects of wounds received in action, and Jacob Klein and Charles Woetzel, MIA at Chancellorsville and believed KIA. At least one source indicates Bruno Benim and William Lindloge died of wounds received in action, but I have been unable to confirm these with any additional sources and thus have not included them. Its "official losses" were as follows:

Unit	KIA & DOW			DOD, Prison, etc.		Total			%
	Off.	Men	Total	Off.	Men	Total	Enroll	Dead	Dead
Staff	-	2	2	-	-	0	12	2	16.7
Co.A	1	10	11	-	7	7	101	18	17.8
Co.B	1	21	22	-	8	8	103	30	29.1
Co.C	2	17	19	-	5	5	103	24	23.3
Co.D	-	18	18	-	3	3	105	21	20.0
Co.E	1	19	20	-	13	13	114	33	28.9
Co.F	2	17	19	-	11	11	116	30	25.9
Co.G	2	24	26	-	10	10	112	36	32.1
Co.H	-	19	19	-	6	6	101	25	24.8
Co.I	2	15	17	-	8	8	112	25	22.3
Co.K	1	14	15	-	6	6	110	21	19.1
Total	12	176	188	-	77	77	1,089	265	24.3

But the numbers do not tell the whole story. For each number there was a man, a living human being with family, friends, and acquaintances who mourned his loss. The names of the 191 who were killed in action or died of wounds are as follows:

Name	Rank	Company	Battle
Arm, William	Private	F	Peach Tree Creek
Backhaus, William	Corporal	B	Gettysburg
Balmes, Jacob	Private	C	Gettysburg
Behnke, Henry	Private	I	Chancellorsville
Beling, Carl	Private	E	Gettysburg
Benda, Franz	Private	F	Gettysburg
Berlandi, Philip	Corporal	C	Gettysburg
Braatz, August	Sergeant	B	Gettysburg
Braun, Xaver	Private	E	Peach Tree Creek
Braunschweig, Frederick	Private	B	Gettysburg
Bruckert, Charles	1st Sergeant	I	Gettysburg
Burg, Lorenz	Private	E	Chancellorsville
Busse, Charles	Private	B	Averasboro
Carstangen, Hugo	Sergeant Major	Staff	Chancellorsville
Casper, Carl	Private	B	Chancellorsville
Chalaupka, George	Corporal	D	Gettysburg
Conrad, August	Private	H	Resaca
Daily, Richard	Private	G	Chancellorsville
Dallmann, John	Private	C	Gettysburg
Damkoehler, Ernst	Private	I	Resaca
Dellenbach, George	Private	G	Burnt Hickory
Detsch, Michael	Private	H	Kennesaw Mountain
Dexheimer, Jacob	Private	G	Chancellorsville
Diefenthaler, Philip	Corporal	H	Gettysburg
Distelhorst, Henry	Private	B	Chancellorsville
Dronkers, Dingenis	Private	D	Gettysburg
Dross, Louis	Private	D	Chancellorsville
Eberhard, Jacob	Private	B	Gettysburg
Ehlert, Frederick	Sergeant	B	Gettysburg
Feiss, Stephen	Sergeant	A	Peach Tree Creek
Feistel, Edward	Private	B	Gettysburg
Feldmann, Philip	Private	I	Gettysburg
Ferge, Gottlieb	Corporal	I	Gettysburg
Fleck, August	Corporal	K	Chancellorsville
Fritz, Ferdinand	Private	G	Gettysburg
Fuchs, Moritz	Corporal	E	Chancellorsville
Gathmann, Andreas	Private	A	Peach Tree Creek

Name	Rank	Company	Battle
Gessner, Henry	Private	B	Kennesaw Mountain
Geumann, Christian	Private	A	Gettysburg
Gilgen, Jacob	Corporal	A	Averasboro
Giljohann, Frederick	Private	I	Atlanta
Gottfried, Wenzel	Private	H	Chancellorsville
Gross, Joseph	Corporal	D	Chancellorsville
Gruhlke, Johann	Private	E	Averasboro
Guenther, Henry	Corporal	G	Chancellorsville
Hacker, Henry	Private	F	Resaca
Hartmann, Jacob	Private	H	Chancellorsville
Hartmann, William	Private	B	Gettysburg
Held, John	Corporal	D	Peach Tree Creek
Hermann, Hermann	Private	C	Chancellorsville
Herrmann, John	Private	K	Gettysburg
Hess, William	Sergeant	F	Gettysburg
Hilger, Henry	Private	B	Chancellorsville
Indermauer, Jacob	Private	K	Chancellorsville
Jahns, Albert	Private	B	Resaca
Jewlson, Julius	Private	G	Gettysburg
Klein, Friedrich Rudolph	1st Lieutenant	C	Averasboro
Klein, Jacob*	Private	E	Chancellorsville
Klink, Jacob	Private	K	Burnt Hickory
Koch, Joseph	Private	C	Gettysburg
Koehler, George	Corporal	G	Gettysburg
Koenig, Theodor	Private	A	Resaca
Köpnick, John	Private	I	Kennesaw Mountain
Koerner, Carl	Private	D	Bentonville
Kraus, Geroge	Private	E	Burnt Hickory
Krause, Reinhold	Private	E	Burnt Hickory
Krauss, John	Corporal	A	Gettysburg
Kreuscher, Peter	Private	C	Gettysburg
Krueger, Christian	Sergeant	C	Kennesaw Mountain
Krueger, Gottlieb	Private	F	Kennesaw Mountain
Kruse, Diedrich	Private	I	Gettysburg
Kuehn, August	Private	E	Resaca
Kuhlke, August	Private	B	Chancellorsville
Kuhlmann, Charles	Private	B	Kennesaw Mountain
Kuhn, George	Private	H	Kennesaw Mountain
Kuhn, Peter	Private	G	Gettysburg
Langer, Edward	Private	C	Dallas
Lankow, Frederick	Private	E	Burnt Hickory

Name	Rank	Company	Battle
Lasstofka, Wenzel	Private	I	Chancellorsville
Lau, Johan	Private	I	Chancellorsville
Lauer, John	Private	C	Burnt Hickory
Lauer, William	Private	B	Chancellorsville
Lauermann, Jacob	Private	G	Chancellorsville
Leken, Henry	Private	C	Gettysburg
Lindemuth, Hermann	Corporal	E	Averasboro
Mathes, Philip	Corporal	H	Gettysburg
Mayer, John G.	Private	H	Gettysburg
Meier, Heinrich	Private	E	Gettysburg
Mengeld, Martin	Private	K	Chancellorsville
Metzl, Alexander	Sergeant Major	Staff	Gettysburg
Michel, Jacob	Sergeant	C	Kennesaw Mountain
Milke, William	Private	D	Peach Tree Creek
Möhr, Henry	Corporal	H	Gettysburg
Muelhaupt, August	Corporal	C	Chancellorsville
Mueller, Robert	Captain	C	Peach Tree Creek
Müller, Valentine	Private	H	Peach Tree Creek
Nell, Philip	Corporal	H	Resaca
Nemitz, Reinhold	Private	A	Atlanta
Nero, Frederick	Private	I	Chancellorsville
Neukirch, Charles W.	Captain	E	Chancellorsville
Neumann, Joseph	Private	C	Gettysburg
Neusser, Paulus	Corporal	I	Gettysburg
Niephaus, Gerhard	Private	F	Peach Tree Creek
Oehlke, Franz	Private	E	Dallas
Oestreich, Charles	Corporal	F	Averasboro
Ott, Bernhard	Sergeant	K	Peach Tree Creek
Paul, John	Private	A	Kennesaw Mountain
Pfau, Andreas	Private	D	Gettysburg
Phillip, Christian	1st lieutenant	F	Resaca
Pickeruhn, August	Private	F	Chancellorsvile
Pizzala, Charles	Captain	G	Chancellorsville
Rausch, Michael	Private	K	Chancellorsville
Regenbrecht, George	Corporal	I	Gettysburg
Reisenbegler, Mathias	Private	F	Bentonville
Reuter, Franz	Corporal	H	Peach Tree Creek
Rinke, Anton	Private	C	Resaca
Ritger, John	Corporal	G	Gettysburg
Roehr, Hermann	Private	F	Chancellorsville
Röhrig, Friedrich	Private	K	Gettysburg

Name	Rank	Company	Battle
Röll, Friedrich	Private	K	Burnt Hickory
Romag, Henry	Private	E	Kennesaw Mountain
Rook, Peter	2nd Lieutenant	F	Gettysburg
Rost, August	Private	A	Chancellorsville
Rothacker, David	Private	K	Gettysburg
Rusco, George W.	Corporal	G	Chancellorsville
Sasse, William	Private	B	Peach Tree Creek
Schaeffer, Thurlius	Corporal	C	Burnt Hickory
Schara, Franz	Private	F	Gettysburg
Schlenstedt, Hermann	Private	E	Gettysburg
Schmidt, Charles	Captain	B	Averasboro
Schmidt, Christian	Sergeant	F	Chancellorsville
Schmidt, John	Private	F	Averasboro
Schmidt, Johan	Private	G	Chancellorsville
Schmidt, Leopold	Private	F	Gettysburg
Schneider, Nicholas	Private	E	Kennesaw Mountain
Schnepf, Killien	Private	G	Chancellorsville
Schueler, August	Captain	K	Chancellorsville
Schwartz, Heinrich	Private	D	Chancellorsviile
Schwister, Mathias	Private	E	Gettysburg
Seemann, John P.	Captain	I	Peach Tree Creek
Sihlsdorf, Frederick	Private	G	Gettysburg
Smith, Emerson	Private	G	Burnt Hickory
Smith, William	Captain	I	Gettysburg
Sohns, Charles	Private	D	Kennesaw Mountain
Sonnenschein, Frederick	Private	K	Chancellorsville
Spranger, Frederick	Private	H	Resaca
Stamm, Leonhard	Private	A	Gettysburg
Steinhof, Frederick	Private	K	Chancellorsville
Steinmetz, Joseph	Private	G	Chancellorsville
Stier, Christian	Private	F	Gettysburg
Stoeffel, Peter	Private	G	Resaca
Stollberg, Frederick	Private	I	Gettysburg
Stellenwerk, Joseph	Private	I	Chancellorsville
Stoppels, François	Private	D	Gettysburg
Strutz, Gottlieb	Private	H	Averasboro
Style, John	Private	I	Kennesaw Mountain
Suttinger, Julius	Private	C	Resaca
Templeton, Robert H.	Corporal	G	Burn Hickory
Textor, Anton	Private	H	Gettysburg
Thiele, Frederick	Private	D	Chancellorsville

Name	Rank	Company	Battle
Thuerwaechter, Michael	Corporal	E	Chancellorsville
Tolzmann, August	Private	B	Chancellorsville
Vetter, John C.	Private	G	Chancellorsville
Vondrom, Charles	Private	B	Chancellorsville
Voss, Frederick	Private	F	Chancellorsville
Wachter, George	Sergeant	I	Chancellorsville
Waetzel, Charles	Private	E	Chancellorsville
Wagner, Michael	Private	F	Resaca
Walldorff, Philip	Sergeant	I	Resaca
Warver, Franz J.	Sergeant	D	Atlanta
Weber, Jacob	Private	D	Peach Tree Creek
Weifenbach, John	Private	B	Burnt Hickory
Weinand, John	Corporal	G	Chancellorsville
Wendorff, Frederick	Private	B	Kennesaw Mountain
Westhoff, August	Private	D	Kennesaw Mountain
Wickesberg, Charles	Sergeant	H	Resaca
Wildhagen, Johan	Private	D	Gettysburg
Winkelmann, Christian	Corporal	E	Chancellorsville
Winter, Frederick	Private	F	Peach Tree Creek
Woerner, Frederick	Private	H	Chancellorsville
Woetzel, Charles**	Private	E	Chancellorsville
Wolf, Albert	Private	G	Resaca
Wollmer, Nicholas	1st Lieutenant	G	Peach Tree Creek
Woller, Ferdinand	Private	E	Atlanta
Young, Martin	1st Lieutenant	A	Gettysburg
Young, Nicholas	Private	G	Gettysburg
Zbitowsky, Joseph	Private	D	Gettysburg
Zilhsdorf, Franz	Private	G	Chancellorsville
Zöger, Mathias	Private	G	Chancellorsville
Zuehlsdorff, Frederick	Private	B	Gettysburg
Zünke, John A.	Private	H	Chancellorsville

* Jacob Klein was originally listed as MIA, but the muster out papers indicate he was probably "killed on the skirmish line" There is no record of his capture or return after the war, so I have included him here.

** Charles Woetzel was originally listed as MIA at Chancellorsville, but was "presumed" killed when no record of him surfaced after the war.

The following were taken prisoner during various battles and died in Confederate prisons. Thirteen died of disease or unknown causes. One is known to have died of wounds and is thus listed and counted in the section above.

Name	Rank	Company	Place
Bahn, Ernst	Private	B	Richmond, Va.
Damkoehler, Ernst *	Private	I	Andersonville, Ga.
Distler, Frederick	Private	G	Andersonville, Va.
Duehring, Ferdinand	Private	B	Richmond, Va.
Eichmeier, Adolph	Private	E	Richmond, Va.
Held, Carl	Private	H	Andersonville, Ga.
Holz, Asmus	Private	C	Andersonville, Ga.
Jenkins, Michael	Private	I	Belle Isle, Va.
Jenny, John	Private	E	Richmond, Va.
Knien, François	Corporal	E	Andersonville, Ga.
Laich, Fritz	Sergeant	K	Andersonville, Ga.
Muenzenberger, Adam	Private	C	Richmond, Va.
Schneider, Magnus	Corporal	E	Andersonville, Ga.
Stoltze, George	Private	C	Richmond, Va.

* Also listed as DOW above.

The following died of disease contracted during their service with the 26th Wisconsin Infantry.

Name	Rank	Company
Balke, Frederick	Private	K
Braun, Ferdinand	Private	I
Cassel, Alfred	Corporal	G
Crowley, John	1st Sergeant	G
Diener, Henry	Corporal	E
Entz, Christian	Private	B
Franke, Gotthard	Private	K
Gathmann, Andreas	Private	A
Hammang, Paul	Private	E
Hauptmann, Jacob	Private	A
Heidenreich, Josef	Private	F
Hoffranz, Peter	Private	D
Jaeger, August	Private	B
Jaeger, Heinrich	Private	A
Johnston, Samuel	Corporal	G

Name	Rank	Company
Kaufmann, Conrad	Private	F
Kowar, Joseph	Private	I
Kruger, Julius	Private	F
Krull, Fritz	Private	E
Lang, Lorenz	Private	I
Lindloge, William	Private	F
Lingsch, Heinrich **	Private	B
Lippmann, Henry	Sergeant	F
Mack, Conrad	Private	G
Marquardt, Charles	Private	I
Müller, John	Private	K
Müller, William	Private	A
Nachtsheim, Johan	Private	K
Oehlke, Franz	Private	E
Ollig, John	Private	A
Ostertag, John	Private	E
Pagenkopf, Hermann	Private	B
Parbs, Charles	Private	E
Pfeiffer, Anton	Private	I
Pleuss, Dietrich	Private	F
Raatz, Hermann	Private	F
Roeder, Nikolaus	Private	F
Salter, Robert	Private	G
Schaefer, George	Private	H
Schnorrenberg, Peter	Private	G
Schwenicke, August	Private	H
Seidemann, Friedrich	Private	D
Sommer, Gotthard	Private	H
Spangenberg, Wilhelm	Private	A
Stamp, Philip	Private	H
Stange, William	Private	E
Stauber, Joseph	Private	E
Strupp, Jacob	Private	G
Stubanus, Andreas	Private	G
Temke, Fritz	Private	E
Tiedemann, Ehlert	Private	F

** One source lists him as DOW June 28, '64.

The following two died from miscellaneous causes not reported above.

Name	Rank	Company	Cause
Koetzdinger, Alois	Private	F	Drowned
Thiele, Henry	Private	B	Suicide

Appendix F

ROSTER

The following list is based on that found in *Roster of Wisconsin Volunteers, War of the Rebellion, 1861-1865,* with additions and changes reflecting information found in the regimental descriptive book, regimental muster rolls, regimental morning reports, miscellaneous regimental papers and reports in the National Archives, annual reports of the Adjutant General of Wisconsin, contemporary newspapers, G.A.R. papers, and in the various other sources noted in the bibliography of this book. In instances where there is contradictory evidence, I have followed the final list of casualties submitted to the Wisconsin Adjutant Generals' Office unless there are at least two other original sources citing contrary information. Similarly, given the various spellings of some names, I have followed the spelling of the *Germania* anniversary article unless compelling evidence suggested an error there. Where alternate names were frequently given, they appear in parentheses. The names in brackets are original names before they were anglicized.

Key to Abbreviations

CIA	=	Captured in Action
Disch.	=	Discharged
DOW	=	Died of Wounds
DOD	=	Died of Disease
ENL	=	Enlisted
KIA	=	Killed in Action
MO	=	Mustered Out
RES	=	Resigned
Trans.	=	Transferred
VRC	=	Veteran Reserve Corps

FIELD & STAFF

Colonel

William H. Jacobs [Wilhelm Heinrich Jacobs]; banker, Milwaukee; ENL Aug. 16, '62; slightly WIA Chancellorsville, May 2, '63; RES Jan. 11, '64; president of Fifth Ward branch of the Second Ward Savings Bank; a principal backer of the Wisconsin Central Railroad, which later became the Soo Line; president of the Milwaukee *Musikverein*; treasurer of Brewers' Protective Insurance Co.; instrumental in organizing the Industrial Exposition; director of Bank of Commerce; elected county Clerk of the Courts; served in the state Senate as Democrat in 1875 and 1876; sang as tenor in operas; founding member and first president of Twenty-Sixth Regiment Association formed in 1874; elected to state senate in 1875 and 1876. At his death on September 11, 1882, the *Wisconsin Magazine of History* noted that "He was very popular and greatly lamented."

Lieutenant Colonels

Charles Lehmann; soldier, Milwaukee; ENL Aug. 16, '62; RES Jan. 16, '63.

Hans Boebel [Böbel]; printer, Milwaukee; appointed Jan. 18, '63 from Capt. Co. H; WIA Gettysburg, July 1, '63, lower half of right femur amputated; disch. due to disability because of wounds, May 28, '64; after war served as clerk in office of City Treasurer; twice elected Milwaukee City Treasurer beginning 1871 and in 1874 appointed to federal position as Deputy Revenue Collector; officer in Milwaukee *Turnverein* and noted dramatic actor in its stage productions; in 1881 he was elected treasurer of the Gymnastic Seminary [Normal School] of the North American Union of Gymnastic Societies; prominent freethinker and Republican; member of Robert Chivas Post No. 2, G.A.R.; member of Twenty-Sixth Regiment Association.

Frederick C. Winkler; lawyer, Milwaukee; appointed June 27, judge advocate general of XI Corps from fall 1862 through July 1863; appointed major Nov. 17, '63; recruiting duty Jan. 1-Feb. 27, '64; appointed colonel Aug. 17, '64, but not mustered; MO June 13, '65; brevet promotions to the ranks of colonel and brigadier general in recognition of his services in the field; resumed law practice after war; president of Milwaukee Public Museum; president of the Milwaukee County Bar Association and Wisconsin State Bar Association; vice president of American Bar Association; member of Wisconsin State Assembly in 1872; commander of Wisconsin Commandry of the Loyal Legion of the United States; trustee of Northwestern Mutual Life Insurance Co. for 32 years; member of Republican Partys' State Central Committee in 1869; served as a delegate to the Republican National Conventions in 1880 and 1894; member of the Wisconsin State Assembly in 1872; member of the Milwaukee City Board of School Commissioners in 1878-1880; member of the

Menomonee Valley Improvement Commission; vice president of the Milwaukee Art Association; member of E.B. Walcott Post No. 1, G.A.R.; elected Commander of the Wisconsin Commandry of the Loyal Legion of the United States; founding member and member of first executive committee of Twenty-Sixth Regiment Association; attended fiftieth anniversary at Gettysburg in 1913; died in Los Angeles March 22, 1921. President Theodore Roosevelt called him "a man whom I have always considered a model for me and my sons to follow as an American citizen of the highest and best type."

Majors

Phillip Horwitz; merchant, Milwaukee, ENL Aug. 16, '62; RES Feb. 5, '63; traveling agent for Schoeffers' Tyrolean Vocalists after war; member of Robert Chivas Post No. 2, G.A.R.; died in Milwaukee November 8, 1886.

Henry Baetz [Heinrich Bätz]; register of deeds, Manitowoc; appointed Mar. 15, '63 from Capt. Co. F; severely WIA in right leg at Gettysburg, July 1, '63; RES Oct. 8, '63; held many local and civic offices including president of village of Manitowoc; elected as a Republican to the office of Treasurer of Manitowoc County in 1866 and 1868; elected state treasurer in 1869 and 1871 serving four years; moved to Milwaukee in 1875 and began a career in journalism; elected first Milwaukee city librarian 1878-80; first salaried secretary to State Board of Immigration, 1880-83; employed by Pabst Brewing Co. in 1883 and served for 21 years until retirement in 1904; part owner and operator of the Pabst Mine near Ironwood, Michigan; member of the Wisconsin Academy of Sciences, Arts and Letters, the Wisconsin Archaeological Society, the Milwaukee Musical Society, and the Old Settlers' Club; served as president of the Deutscher Club and the *Deutsche Gesellschaft von Milwaukee*. Died in Milwaukee Jan. 2, 1910.

Francis [Franz] Lackner; lawyer, Milwaukee; appointed June 27, '64 from Capt. Co. F; acting Inspector General of 3rd Div, 11 Corps Jan. 11 '64 until consolidation of XI and XII Corps; appointed lieutenant colonel, Oct. 19, '64, but not mustered; brevet lieutenant colonel U.S. Vols., Mar. 13, '65; MO June 13, '65; ran the Terrace Gardens in Milwaukee after war; moved to Chicago as corporate attorney; member of Chicago Bar Association and American Bar Association; president of Chicago Law institute; president of the Chicago Bar Association; member of Chicago Union League, University Club, and *Turnverein*; president of national *Turnverein*; member of Civic Committee for political reform; member of Committee on Relief after Chicago Fire of 1871; member of committee to draft new city charter; retired in 1916 and moved to California; died in South Pasadena on December 20, 1928.

Adjutants

Phillip Jacob Schlosser; merchant, Milwaukee; ENL Aug. 20, '62; RES Sept. 12, '63; officer of Sixth Ward Branch of the Second Ward Bank in Milwaukee after war; officer in Knights of Pythias; member of Robert Chivas Post No. 2, G.A.R.; founding member and first vice president and later treasurer of Twenty-Sixth Regiment Association formed in 1874; died Feb. 2, 1906.

George P. Traeumer; engineer, Milwaukee; appointed Sept. 16, '63 from 2nd Lieut. Co. I; disch. Jan. 14, '65, for disability; operated construction company; served several terms as member of Board of Public Works and eight years as county clerk; active as trustee of Milwaukee *Turnverein;* led popular German band; commanded state troops during labor riots in Milwaukee in 1886 and fired on strikers killing two and wounding fourteen; member of Robert Chivas Post No. 2, G.A.R.; member of Robert Chivas Post No. 2, G.A.R.; member of Twenty-Sixth Regiment Association.

George William Jones; farmer, Jackson; appointed Jan. 19, '65 from Sergt. Major; MO June 13, '65; farmer in West Bend after war; president of the Washington County Agricultural Society; chairman of the Washington County Greenback Committee; member and captain of the G.A.R. in Washington County; member of Twenty-Sixth Regiment Association; attended fiftieth anniversary at Gettysburg in 1913.

Quartermasters

Frederick W. Hundhausen; physician, Milwaukee; ENL Aug. 22, '62; 2nd Brigade Quartermaster Jan. '64 until consolidation of XI and XII Corps; disch. July 30, '64, disability; opened saloon on corner of Mason and Broadway; served as school commissioner and city treasurer; founding member of Twenty-Sixth Regiment Association; died in hospital at the National Soldiers' Home in Milwaukee July 14, 1878.

Adolph Hensel; clerk, Milwaukee; appointed Feb. 11, '65 from 1st Lieut. Co. B; MO June 13, '65; founding member and first secretary of Twenty-Sixth Regiment Association formed in 1874.

Surgeons

Francis Huebschmann [Franz Hübschmann]; physician, Milwaukee; ENL as Surgeon Aug. 14, '62; in charge of division hospital at Chancellorsville; assigned to duty at corps hospital Jan. 10, '64; RES Sept. 23, '64; served at the U.S. General Hospital in Milwaukee for several months before becoming Milwaukee city physician; elected city alderman from the Second Ward in 1866; appointed county physician in 1868; member of the City Charter Convention in 1867; became a member of the Board of Health in 1869; elected vice president of the Milwaukee Medical

Society in 1870; served as Democratic state senator in 1871 and 1872; founding member of Twenty-Sixth Regiment Association; died in Milwaukee March 21, 1880.

Simon Von der Vaart; physician, Milwaukee; ENL as 1st Asst. Surgeon, Aug. 30, '62; appointed Surgeon Oct. 19, '64; MO June 13, '65

Theodore Fricke; physician, Watertown; ENL as 2nd Assistant Surgeon Sept. 8, '62; RES Mar. 7, '63.

Charles Georgii; Milwaukee; appointed 2nd Assistant Surgeon Apr. 17, '63; RES July 26, '63.

Chaplains

William Vette; editor, Milwaukee; quartermaster dept. Oct. '62; appointed chaplain Nov. 6, '62 from Co. D; resigned Apr. 2, '64; founding member of Twenty-Sixth Regiment Association.

John Kilian; clergyman, Greenfield; ENL Nov. 5, '64; MO June 13, '65.

Sergeant Majors

Hermann Fuerstenberg [Fürstenberg]; farmer, Milwaukee; appointed Sept. 17, '62 from Co. D; promoted 2nd Lieut. Co. D, Nov. 6, '62.

Peter Fernekes; tinsmith, Milwaukee; appointed Nov. 6, '62 from 1st Sergt. Co. C; promoted 2nd Lieut. Co. I, Dec. 22, '62.

Adolph Cordier; merchant, Milwaukee; appointed Dec. 22, '62 from Sergt. Co. K; promoted 2nd Lieut. Co. F, Mar. 15, '63.

Hugo Carstanjen; chemist, Milwaukee; appointed Mar. 15, '63 from Sergt. Co. D; KIA May 2, '63, Chancellorsville, Va.

Alexander Metzel [Metzl]; banker, Milwaukee; appointed May 3, '63 from Sergt. Co. B; WIA Gettysburg July 1, '63; DOW due to pyemia at Washington, D.C., July 20, '63.

Nicolaus Wollmer; farmer, Greenfield; appointed July 20, '63 from Co. D; promoted 1st Lieut. Co. G, Apr. 13, '64.

Friedrich Rudolph Klein; artist, Milwaukee; appointed Apr. '64 from Sergt., Co. K; promoted 1st Lieut. Co C., Oct. 19, '64.

George William Jones; farmer, Jackson; appointed Nov. 1, '64 from Q.M. Sergt.; promoted Adjutant, Jan. 19, '65.

Henry Sontag; clerk, Milwaukee; appointed Mar. 28, '65 from Corp. Co. B; MO June 13, '65; member of Twenty-Sixth Regiment Association.

Quartermaster Sergeants

Adolph Hensel; clerk, Milwaukee; appointed Sept. 17, '62 from Co. C; promoted 1st Lieut. Co. B, June 4, '63.

George William Jones; farmer, Jackson; appointed July 1, '63 from Corp. Co. G; promoted Sergt. Major, Nov. 1, '64.

Frederick Reuss; clerk, Milwaukee; appointed Nov. 1, '64 from Sergt. Co. B; MO June 13, '65; member of Wolcott Post No. 1, G.A.R.

Commissary Sergeants

Oswald Schubert; merchant, Milwaukee; appointed Sept. 1, '62 from Corp. Co. I; reduced to ranks and trans. to Co I, Dec. 10, '62.

Samuel Meyer; tradesman, Racine; appointed Dec. 10, '62 from Co. D; MO June 13, '65.

Hospital Stewards

William Hoffmann; barber, Milwaukee; Aug. 12,'62; disch. Mar. 8, '63, disability.

August Krueger; Milwaukee; Oct. 20, '63; MO June 13, '65; lived in Sheboygan after war; member of Twenty-Sixth Regiment Association.

Principal Musician

Gottfried G. Luther; mechanic, Milwaukee; ENL Aug. 20, '62; trans. to Co. C, Feb. 11, '63.

COMPANY A, FLYING RANGERS

Captains

William Georg; confectioner, Milwaukee; rank from Sept. 3, '62; RES Mar. 10, '63; elected Milwaukee city councilman from 9th Ward; founding member of Twenty-Sixth Regiment Association; died in November, 1878.

John William Fuchs; soldier, Milwaukee, veterinary surgeon; rank from Nov. 15, '63 from 1st Lieut. Co. C; WIA Gettysburg, July 1, '63; captured colors of 33rd Mississippi Infantry at Peach Tree Creek, Ga., July 20, '64; appointed Major, Oct. 19, '64, but not mustered; brevet Major, U.S. Vols., Mar. 13, '65; MO May 15, '65.

First Lieutenants

Christian Sarnow; carpenter, Milwaukee; rank from Sept. 3, '62; RES Nov. 19, '62 due to illness; elected alderman in 1874 and 1875; member of state assembly in 1877 and 1879.

August F. Mueller; clerk, Milwaukee; rank from Dec. 15, '62; 2nd Lieut., Sept 3, '62; RES Feb. 6, '63; member of Wolcott Post No. 1, G.A.R.

Martin Young; merchant, Milwaukee; rank from Mar. 15, '63; enlisted Aug. 15, '62; Sergt.; 2nd Lieut., Feb. 1, '63; KIA July 1, '63, Gettysburg, Pa.; buried in Gettysburg National Cemetery, Wisconsin Plot, grave D-1.

Conrad Grode; carpenter, Milwaukee; rank from Nov. 17, '63; enlisted Aug. 18, '62; Corp., Sergt.; 2nd Lieut., Mar. 15, '63; WIA Gettysburg July 1, '63; RES Jan. 13, '64; after war was contractor and builder, but injuries forced him to abandon that business and he opened a book store; suffered from rheumatism; member E.B. Walcott Post No. 1, G.A.R.

Sigmund Juenger; carpenter, Milwaukee; rank from Mar. 1, '64; enlisted Aug. 19, '62; Sergt., 1st Sergt.; 2nd Lieut. Co. G, June 1, '63, but not mustered; detached to brigade quartermaster dept.; WIA Gettysburg July 1, '63; WIA Buzzard Roost, May 8, '64; disch. due to wounds July 30, '64.

Frank Fiess; carpenter, Milwaukee; rank from Apr. 6, '65; enlisted Aug. 15, '62; Corp., Sergt., 1st Sergt.; MO June 13, '65; member of Robert Chivas Post No. 2, G.A.R.; founding member of Twenty-Sixth Regiment Association.

Second Lieutenants

August F. Mueller; rank from Sept. 3, '62; promoted 1st Lt. Dec. 15, '62.

Martin Young; Milwaukee; enlisted Aug. 15, '62; Sergt.; 2nd Lieut., Feb. 1, '63; promoted 1st Lieut Mar. 15, '63.

Conrad Grode; Milwaukee; enlisted Aug. 18, '62; Corp., Sergt.; 2nd Lieut., Mar. 15, '63; promoted 1st Lieut. Nov. 17, '63.

Enlisted Men

Andrecht, George; ropemaker, Milwaukee; Aug. 16, '62; Corp.; CIA Chancellorsville; rejoined regt. Jan. '64; MO June 13, '65.

Bauer, Philip; shoemaker, Milwaukee; ENL Aug. 21, '62; MO June 13, '65; member of Twenty-Sixth Regiment Association.

Beitz, August; banker, Milwaukee; ENL Aug. 21, '62; division bakery; WIA and CIA Chancellorsville; exchanged and rejoined regt. Oct. 3, '63; MO June 13, '65; member of the Twenty-Sixth Regiment Association.

Berlage, Joseph A.; carpenter, Milwaukee; ENL Aug. 15, '62; Corp.; WIA Gettysburg; rejoined regt. Dec. 20, '63; reduced to ranks Mar. 16, '65; MO June 13, '65; founding member of Twenty-Sixth Regiment Association and member of first finance committee.

Bielefeld, August; farmer, Cedarburg; ENL Aug. 21, '62; Corp., Sergt.; MO June 13, '65.

Bissing, Franz; butcher, Milwaukee; ENL Aug. 21, '62; hospital cook; sent to hospital Jan. '63; disch. Mar. 11, '63, disability.

Bogk, William; carpenter, Milwaukee; ENL Aug. 21, '62; detailed as hospital cook; MO June 13, '65; member of Robert Chivas Post No. 2, G.A.R.; founding member of Twenty-Sixth Regiment Association.

Bruce, William; merchant, Milwaukee; ENL Aug. 20, '62; disch. at Milwaukee Sept. 20, '62, disability.

Buerkey, Christian; shoemaker, Milwaukee; ENL Aug. 20, '62; MO June 13, '65; member of Robert Chivas Post No. 2, G.A.R.

Czoernig, Anton; laborer, Milwaukee; ENL Aug. 15, '62; MO June 13, '65; member of Robert Chivas Post No. 2, G.A.R.

Dauffenbach, Christian; potter, Reeseville; ENL Aug. 21, '62; Corp.; MO June 13, '65; member of Robert Chivas Post No. 2, G.A.R.

Dittmar, Georg; wheelwright, Milwaukee; Aug. 15, '62; WIA Chancellorsville, May 2, '63; trans. to VRC, June 22, '64.

Engel, George; clerk, Milwaukee; ENL Aug. 15, '62; brigade teamster; detached as nurse at field hospital; discharge May 20, '65, disability.

Eyssenhardt, Adelbert; farmer, Milwaukee; ENL Aug. 15, '62; Corp., Sergt.; WIA Gettysburg; trans. to VRC, Apr. 6, '64.

Fiess, Stephan; carpenter, Milwaukee; ENL Aug. 15, '62; Corp. and Sergt.; KIA, July 20, '64, Peach Tree Creek, Ga.

Gathmann, Andreas; farmer, Oak Creek; ENL Aug. 16, '62; company cook; DOD in field hospital near Atlanta, Ga., July 27, '64.

George, Adolph; carpenter, Milwaukee; ENL Aug. 15, '62; disch. at Gainesville, Va., Nov. 23, '62, disability.

Geumann, Christian; blacksmith, Milwaukee; ENL Aug. 15, '62; KIA July 1, '63, Gettysburg, Pa.

Gilgen, Jacob; shoemaker, Milwaukee; ENL Aug. 15, '62; Corp.; KIA Mar. 16, '65, Averasboro, N.C.

Graetz, Bernhardt; brewer, Milwaukee; ENL Aug. 15, '62; company cook; disch. at Stafford Court House, Va., Feb. 26 '63, disability.

Grosch, Philip; potter, Milwaukee; ENL Aug. 15, '62; Corp.; sent to hospital from Stafford Court House, Va., Jan. 20, '63; disch. at Madison, Wisc., July 24, '63, disability (rheumatism).

Gross, Otto; carpenter, Milwaukee; ENL Aug. 21, '62; MO June 13, '65.

Grunder, Jacob; carpenter, Oak Creek; ENL Aug. 19, '62; WIA in head at Chancellorsville; trans. to VRC at Washington, D.C., June 9, '64; MO Aug. 19, '65; member of Robert Chivas Post No. 2, G.A.R.

Hauptmann, Jacob; laborer, Milwaukee; ENL Aug. 15, '62; DOD (typhoid fever) in regimental hospital at Stafford Court House, Va., Jan. 17, '63.

Hausburg, William; farmer, Mequon; ENL Aug. 21, '62; WIA June, '64; MO June 13, '65; moved to Chicago after the war; attended regimental reunions.

Hensel, William; wagonmaker, Milwaukee; ENL Aug 15, '62; regimental teamster; sent to hospital Jan. 20, '63; disch. at Madison, Wisc., July 20, '63, disability.

Huesselmann Louis; butcher, Milwaukee; ENL Aug. 20, '62; regimental butcher; MO June 13, '65; member of Robert Chivas Post No. 2, G.A.R.; founding member of Twenty-Sixth Regiment Association.

Jaeger, Heinrich; farmer, Milwaukee; ENL Aug. 14, '62; company cook; DOD of typhoid fever at regimental hospital, Centreville, Va., Nov. 30, '62.

Jaenig, Gotthold; tailor, Mequon; ENL Aug. 21, '62; WIA and CIA Chancellorsville; rejoined regt. Oct. 3, '63; MO June 13, '65.

Joergi, Ulrich; potter, Milwaukee; Aug. 15, '62; sent to hospital Oct. '62; disch. Feb. 2, '63, disability.

Kaempfer, Anton; saloonkeeper, Milwaukee; ENL Aug. 15, '62; brigade ambulance teamster; sent to hospital Dec. 17, '62; disch. Feb. 14, '63, disability.

Kiefer, Raymond; farmer, Milwaukee; ENL Aug. 21, '62; company cook; severely WIA and CIA Chancellorsville; exchanged and rejoined regt. Oct. 3, '63; MO June 13, '65.

Kissinger, George; shoemaker, Milwaukee; ENL Aug. 18, '62; WIA Gettysburg; rejoined regt. Jan. 3, '64; MO June 13, '65.

Kissinger, Philip; clerk, Milwaukee; ENL Aug. 18, '62; Corp.; WIA Gettysburg; MO June 13, '65; member of Robert Chivas Post No. 2, G.A.R.; member of Twenty-Sixth Regiment Association.

Klett, Richard; soldier, Mequon; ENL Aug. 21, '62; sent to hospital May 20, '64; trans. to VRC, Mar. 15, '65; MO at Milwaukee Aug. 19, '65; member of Robert Chivas Post No. 2, G.A.R.

Klinke, Julius; weaver, Milwaukee; ENL Aug. 21, '62; trans. from Co. D Oct. 4, '62; detailed to Gen. Sigel and returned to regt. Nov. 30, '62; deserted from Washington hospital, June 20, '63 (final report of casualties says Aug. 5, '63; muster out roll says deserted at Frederick, Md., when sent from hospital back to regt.).

Koch, William; carpenter and cabinet maker, Milwaukee; ENL Aug. 15, '62; MO June 13, '65; resumed carpentry after war; in 1874 opened saloon and restaurant in Milwaukee; active Republican; founding member of Twenty-Sixth Regiment Association; member of Robert Chivas Post No. 2, G.A.R; died in Milwaukee May 24, 1901.

Koenig, Theodor; music teacher, Milwaukee; ENL Aug. 15, '62; CIA Chancellorsville; exchanged and rejoined regt. Oct. 3, '63; severely WIA in side May 15, '64, Resaca, Ga.; DOW at General Hospital, Nashville, Tenn., July 3, '64 (final report of casualties says July 5, '64 at Louisville, Ky.).

Kraus, John; laborer, Milwaukee; ENL Aug. 20, '62; Corp.; KIA July 1, '63, Gettysburg, Pa.; buried in Gettysburg National Cemetery, Wisconsin Plot, grave C-16.

Krompass, Peter; wheelwright, Milwaukee; ENL Aug. 15, '62; sent sick to hospital Mar. '63; trans. to VRC, Nov. 15, '63; MO June 26, '65.

Kuhlig, Adolph; tailor, Milwaukee; ENL Aug. 20, '62; Corp.; provost guard; slightly WIA at Gettysburg, July 1, '63; WIA in foot and head at Kennesaw Mt., June 22, '64; MO June 13, '65; member of Robert Chivas Post No. 2, G.A.R.; member of Twenty-Sixth Regiment Association; attended dedication of regimental monument at Gettysburg in 1888; suffered from war wounds; moved to Southern Illinois for several years for health, then became clerk in Milwaukee in 1880; employed in Milwaukee city water department from 1884 to death on October 19, 1889.

Kuntz, Adam; mason, Milwaukee; ENL Aug. 15, '62; Corp.; disch. Mar. 7, '63, disability.

Labonde, Peter; farmer, Milwaukee; ENL June 27, '62 from Co. D; WIA Chancellorsville; absent wounded at MO of Regt.

Leuenberger, Ulrich; painter, Milwaukee; ENL Aug. 15, '62; MO June 13, '65.

Lueck [Lück], William; Lebanon; ENL Aug. 14, '62; company cook; MO June 13, '65; attended fiftieth anniversary at Gettysburg in 1913.

Luscher, Friedrich; farmer, Milwaukee; ENL Aug. 20, '62; regimental teamster; MO June 13, '65.

Luscher, John; engineer, Milwaukee; Aug. 15, '62; Sergt.; disch. Jan. 17, '63, disability.

Maetzold [Mätzold], William; shoemaker, Cedarburg; ENL Aug. 21, '62; CIA Chancellorsville; exchanged and rejoined regt. Oct. 3, '63; MO June 13, '65.

Moegling, Christoph; miller, Milwaukee; ENL Aug. 21, '62; hospital nurse; CIA Gettysburg; rejoined regt. May 22, '65; MO June 13, '65.

Moldenhauer, Michael; Cedarburg; ENL Aug. 21, '62; detached as bugler to 3rd Division, June 10, '64 to July 12, '64; WIA Averasboro, March 16, '65; disch. at Madison, Wisc., May 27, '65.

Mueller, John B.; carpenter, Grafton; ENL Aug. 19, '62; company cook; sent to hospital Mar. '63; trans. to VRC, Mar. 16, '64.

Mueller, Georg Frederick; shoemaker, Milwaukee; ENL Aug. 19, '62; regimental teamster; detached to provost guard, 3rd Brigade, 3rd Div.; WIA Averasboro; absent wounded at MO of regt.

Mueller, William; cooper, Cedarburg; ENL Aug. 20, '62; DOD (typhoid fever) in General Hospital at Windmill Point, Va., Feb. 2, '63.

Mueller, William [Wilhelm]; shoemaker, Milwaukee; ENL Aug. 15, '62; sent to hospital Sept. 25, '63 at Rappahannock Station, Va.; disch. Feb. 22, '65, disability.

Musewald, Carl; cooper, Milwaukee; ENL Aug. 19, '62; Corp.; MO June 13, '65.

Nemitz, Reinhold; farmer, Milwaukee; ENL Aug. 20, '62; KIA on skirmish line near Atlanta, Ga., Aug. 8, '64.

Nero, William; shoemaker, Mequon; ENL Aug. 20, '62; detached as brigade pioneer; MO June 13, '65; member of Robert Chivas Post No. 2, G.A.R.

Nitschke, August; varnisher, Milwaukee; ENL Aug. 15, '62; Corp., Sergt., 1st. Sergt.: WIA in head May 15, '64, Resaca; absent sick at MO of regt.; lived in

Appleton after war; member of Twenty-Sixth Regiment Association; attended fiftieth anniversary at Gettysburg in 1913.

Nolde, Anton; farmer, Mequon; ENL Aug. 21, '62; brigade pioneer; CIA Gettysburg; exchanged and rejoined regt. Nov. 17, '63; MO June 13, '65.

Ollig, John; cooper, Milwaukee; ENL Aug. 16, '62; DOD Dec. 10, '63, General Hospital, Lookout Valley, Tenn.

Opitz, Hermann; farmer, Mequon; ENL Aug. 21, '62; company cook; WIA in left foot May 15, '64, Resaca; disch. at Madison, Wisc., Feb. 7, '65, disability.

Otto, Caspar; saddler, Milwaukee; ENL Aug. 15, '62; sent to hospital Oct. '62; disch. Dec. 22, '62, disability.

Paul, John; shoemaker, Mequon; ENL Aug. 21, '62; WIA June 22, '64, Kennesaw Mountain; DOW in general field hospital, June 24, '64.

Perlewitz, Hermann; painter, Milwaukee; ENL Aug. 15, '62; Sergt.; left sick at Centreville, Va., Dec. 10, '62; disch. Mar. 19, '63, disability.

Pfeifer, Peter; laborer, Milwaukee; ENL Aug. 21, '62; drummer; WIA Chancellorsville, May 2, '63; WIA Averasboro; trans. to VRC; MO May 18, '65.

Prien, Charles A.; painter, Milwaukee; ENL Aug. 20, '62; Corp.; MO June 13, '65.

Reifenstuhl, Friedrich; tailor, Milwaukee; ENL Aug. 15, '62; disch. at Stafford Court House, Va., Mar. 27, '63, disability.

Rintelmann, Henry W.; farmer, Cedarburg; ENL Aug. 19, '62; Corp., Sergt.; CIA Gettysburg July 1, '63 and held at Belle Island in Richmond, Va., then Andersonville, Savannah, Millers, Blackshire, Thomasville, and finally back to Andersonville, Ga.; paroled "in a most horrible condition" May or June '65; disch. at Milwaukee, June 29, '65; confined in hospital at Milwaukee after release; paroled June '65; absent sick at MO of regt.; member of Robert Chivas Post No. 2, G.A.R.; attended fiftieth anniversary at Gettysburg in 1913.

Rintelmann, William H.; farmer, Cedarburg; ENL Aug. 18, '62; CIA Gettysburg July 1, '63; exchanged May, '65; absent sick at MO of regt.; disch. at Milwaukee May 20, '65; attended fiftieth anniversary at Gettysburg in 1913.

Ritschie, John; tobacconist, Milwaukee; ENL Aug. 15, '62; 1st Sergt.; left sick at Fairfax, Va., Nov. 1, '62; muster roll says "has since been reported as deserted and as now being in Canada"; deserted ca. Jan. 1, '63.

Rost, August; barber, Fond du Lac; ENL Aug. 21, '62; KIA May 2, '63, Chancellorsville, Va.

Roth, Heinrich; carpenter, Cedarburg; ENL Aug. 21, '62; Sergt.; regimental bugler Mar. 15, '63; reduced to ranks July 21, '64; brigade bugler Feb. 4, '65; MO June 13, '65; returned to Cedarburg after war; member of Twenty-Sixth Regiment Association.

Schauss, John; bookbinder, Milwaukee; ENL Aug. 15, '62; CIA Gettysburg; exchanged and rejoined regt. Nov. 17, '63; MO June 13, '65.

Schieffeneder, Anton; mechanic, Milwaukee; ENL Aug. 15, '62; Musician; CIA Gettysburg July 1, '63; paroled between Dec. '64 and Feb. '65; exchanged Mar. '65; absent sick at MO of regt.; disch. at Milwaukee June 29, '65.

Schmidt, August; farmer, Milwaukee; ENL Aug, 15, '62; company cook; CIA Chancellorsville; paroled and rejoined regt. Oct. 3, '63; MO June 13, '65.

Schmidt, Christian F.; mechanic, Milwaukee; ENL Aug. 15, '62; sent to hospital Dec. 10, '62; discharged Feb. 25, '63 due to disability; member of Robert Chivas Post No. 2, G.A.R.

Schoepperle, Michel; miller, Mequon; no further record, probably not mustered.

Scholz, Ferdinand; cigarmaker, Milwaukee; ENL Aug. 15, '62; provost guard; WIA Kennesaw Mountain, July 1, '64; WIA Peach Tree Creek and taken to hospital at Nashville; absent wounded at MO of regt.; member of Robert Chivas Post No. 2, G.A.R.; founding member of Twenty-Sixth Regiment Association; attended fiftieth anniversary at Gettysburg in 1913.

Scholz, Joseph William; butcher, Milwaukee; Aug. 15, '62; Corp., Sergt.; CIA Gettysburg; MO June 13, '65; founding member and member of first executive committee of Twenty-Sixth Regiment Association.

Seeliger, Eduard; coppersmith, Milwaukee; ENL Aug. 16, '62; Corp., Sergt.; WIA Gettysburg; MO June 13, '65.

Semisch, Julius; carpenter, Mequon; ENL Aug. 21, '62; provost guard; WIA Peach Tree Creek, July 20, '64, by ball entering the right orbit and destroying right eye before lodging in left side of head at 2nd upper molar; trans. to VRC, Mar. 13, '65; MO Sept. 8, '65.

Sentz, Hermann; Wauwatosa; ENL Aug. 18, '62; WIA Gettysburg; trans. to VRC, Feb. 10, '64; disch. June 28, '65, disability.

Spangenberg, Wilhelm; butcher, Milwaukee; ENL Aug. 18, '62; ambulance teamster; DOD of typhoid fever in regimental hospital at Stafford Court House, Va., Dec. 31, '62.

Stamm, Leonard; painter, Milwaukee; ENL Aug. 15, '62; KIA July 2, '63, Gettysburg, Pa.

Steinacker, Ferdinand; cooper, Milwaukee; ENL Aug. 19, '62; sent to hospital Apr. '63; disch. at Washington, D.C., July 30, '63, disability.

Stoltz, Richard; gilder, Milwaukee; ENL Aug. 15, '62; Corp.; provost guard; MO June 13, '65.

Streiff, Jacob; shoemaker, Milwaukee; ENL Aug. 15, '62; quartermaster dept.; sent to hospital Nov. '62; disch. Mar. 19, '63, disability.

Thieme, Charles Bernhard; wagonmaker, Milwaukee; ENL Aug. 15, '62; WIA by gunshot in right arm at Gettysburg July 1, '63; rejoined regt. Nov. 22, '63; WIA Bentonville, N.C., Mar. 19, '65; disch. June 28, '65, disability; Regimental Descriptive Book says "good soldier"; muster roll says "fought well, like a good soldier"; member of regimental veterans association; postal letter carrier after war; member of Robert Chivas Post No. 2, G.A.R.

Trapschuh, John (also given as Charles John); carpenter, Milwaukee; ENL Aug. 20, '62; CIA Gettysburg; paroled and rejoined regt. Nov. 17, '63; MO June 13, '65; member of Robert Chivas Post No. 2, G.A.R.; founding member and member of first executive committee and first committee on finance of Twenty-Sixth Regiment

Association; attended fiftieth anniversary at Gettysburg in 1913.

Treudel, Sebastian; carpenter, Milwaukee; ENL Aug. 15, '62; sent to hospital Apr. '63; disch. Aug. 8, '63, disability.

Van Eweyk, Henry; painter, Farmers; ENL Aug. 21, '62; Corp.; monthly reports note he deserted with John Ritchie and was "said to be in Canada"; returned from desertion and rejoined regt. at Stafford Court House, Va., Apr. 5 '63; WIA Peach Tree Creek, July 20, '64; promoted Capt. Co. D, 45th Wis. Inf., Feb 27, '65; founding member of Twenty-Sixth Regiment Association.

Vetter, Gustav; miller, Milwaukee; ENL Aug. 20, '62; trans. due to disease to VRC, Mar. 1, '64; member of Robert Chivas Post No. 2, G.A.R.; founding member of Twenty-Sixth Regiment Association.

Werner, William; laborer, Milwaukee; ENL Aug. 15, '62; Corp.; sent to hospital Apr. '63; disch. Apr. 10. '63, disability.

Wohlfahrt, Rudolph; tailor, Milwaukee; ENL Aug. 15, '62; sent to hospital Oct. '62; disch. at General Hospital, Philadelphia, June 14, '63, disability; founding member of Twenty-Sixth Regiment Association.

Wolff, Joseph; vinegar maker, Milwaukee; ENL Aug. 15, '62.; detached to brigade commissary dept. Oct. 9, '63; rejoined regt. Feb. 14, '64; MO June 13, '65.

COMPANY B, GERMAN AMERICANS

Captains

Frederick C. Winkler; lawyer, Milwaukee; rank from Sept. 3, '62; Judge Advocate 11th Army Corps., from Nov. 15, '62; trans. to Gen. Schurzs' staff, Apr. 9, '63 until July '63; promoted Major, Nov. 17, '63.

Charles Schmidt; cooper, Milwaukee; appointed Nov. 24, '63 from 1st Lieut., Co. H; KIA Mar. 16, '65, Averasboro, N.C.

Peter Guttmann; soldier, Milwaukee; appointed Apr. 6, '65 from 1st Lieut. Co. D; MO June 13, '65.

First Lieutenants

William E. Huttmann; Milwaukee; rank from Sept. 3, '62; RES Dec. 9, '62.

Francis Lackner; lawyer, Milwaukee; appointed Dec. 20, '62 from 2nd Lieut., Sept 3, '62; promoted Capt. Co. F, Mar. 15, '63.

Adolph Hensel; clerk, Milwaukee; appointed June 4, '63 from Q.M. Sergt.; promoted Q.M., Feb. 11, '65.

Second Lieutenants

Charles H. Doerflinger [Karl Dörflinger]; architect, Milwaukee; rank from Dec. 20, '62; enlisted Aug. 15, '62; 1st Sergt.; promoted 1st Lieut., Co. K, Mar. 15, '63.

William Steinmeyer; gunsmith, Milwaukee; appointed Mar. 15, '63; enlisted Aug. 15, '62; Sergt., 1st Sergt.; slightly WIA Gettysburg; promoted 1st Lieut., Co. E, Nov. 17, '63.

Enlisted Men

Backhaus, Wilhelm H.; gardener, Milwaukee; ENL Aug. 15, '62; Corp.; KIA July 1, '63. Gettysburg, Pa.

Bahn, Ernst; farmer, Milwaukee; ENL Aug. 21, '62; WIA and CIA Gettysburg; DOD in Confederate prison at Richmond, Va., Feb. 8, '64.

Baldes, Jacob; carpenter, Milwaukee; ENL Aug. 15, '62; Corp.; captured Confederate flag during skirmish at Muddy Creek, Ga., June 17, '64; MO June 13, '65; member of Twenty-Sixth Regiment Association; died in July 1880.

Bergmann, August; farmer, Lebanon; ENL Aug. 21, '62; MO June 13, '65.

Braasch, William; farmer, Ixonia; ENL Aug. 21, '62; WIA Gettysburg; trans. to VRC, Mar. 13, '64.

Braatz, August; farmer, Ixonia; ENL Aug. 21, '62; Sergt.; WIA by gunshot in head at Gettysburg, July 1, '63; DOW in hospital at Baltimore, Md, Aug. 9, '63.

Braunschweig, Frederick; farmer, Lebanon; ENL Aug. 21, '62; KIA July 1, '63, Gettysburg, Pa.

Braunschweig, William; farmer, Lebanon; ENL Aug. 21, '62; Corp., Sergt.; WIA July 20, '64; absent wounded in hospital at Madison, Wisc., at MO of regt.; disch. May 22, '65 at Madison, Wisc.; lived in Watertown after war; member of Twenty-Sixth Regiment Association.

Busse, Charles; Milwaukee; ENL Jan. 20, '64; KIA Mar. 16, '65, Averasboro, N.C.

Casper, Anton; farmer, Milwaukee; ENL Aug. 15, '62; MO June 13, '65.

Casper, Carl; farmer, Lebanon; ENL Aug. 20, '62; KIA May 2, '63, Chancellorsville, Va.

Dambach, Mathias {or Matthew}; laborer, Polk; Aug. 16, '62; WIA Gettysburg; CIA near Atlanta, Ga., Nov. 11, '64; MO June 29, '65; attended fiftieth anniversary at Gettysburg in 1913.

Daniel, Ferdinand (or Frederick); gardener, Milwaukee; Aug. 15, '62; company cook; absent sick in hospital at Jeffersonville, Ind., since July 15, '64; MO at Milwaukee June 17, '65.

Diemer, Nicholas; farmer, Dubuque, IA; ENL Aug. 21, '62; trans. to VRC, Apr. 28, '64; MO at New York City Sept. 11, '65.

Diestelhorst, Henry; saddler, Milwaukee; ENL Aug. 15, '62; KIA May 2, '63,

Chancellorsville, Va.

Dilg, Carl; painter, Milwaukee; ENL Aug. 15, '62; WIA Chancellorsville May 2, '63; detached to topographical corps; deserted from Emory Hospital Convalescent Camp, June 18, '63; returned to regiment; MO June 13, '65; after the war he painted a large canvas of the Twenty-Sixth Wisconsin going into action at Peach Tree Creek.

Duehring, Ferdinand; farmer, Lebanon; ENL Aug. 21, '62; CIA Gettysburg; DOD in Confederate prison at Richmond, Va., Mar. 11, '64.

Duehring, William; farmer, Lebanon; ENL Aug. 21, '62; WIA Gettysburg; MO June 13, '65.

Eberhard, Jacob; tradesman, Milwaukee; ENL Aug. 15, '62; KIA July 1, '63, Gettysburg, Pa.

Ehlert, Frederick; machinist, Milwaukee; ENL Aug. 13, '62; Corp., Sergt.; KIA July 1, '63, Gettysburg, Pa.

Entz, Christian; shoemaker, Milwaukee; ENL Aug. 18, '62; DOD at Chattanooga, Tenn., Jan. 8, '64.

Eppler, Edward; farmer, Ixonia; ENL Aug. 21, '62; trans. to VRC, Oct. 3, '63.

Erdmann, Johann; broommaker, Wauwatosa; ENL Aug. 20, '62; regimental and brigade teamster; MO June 13, '65; lived in Cedarburg after war; member of Twenty-Sixth Regiment Association.

Ewald, William; teamster, Newton; ENL Aug. 15, '62; WIA Chancellorsville; WIA Peach Tree Creek, July 20, '64; DOW Aug. 1, '64, Chattanooga, Tenn.

Fahrner, Simon; dyer, Milwaukee; ENL Aug. 15, '62; disch. at Stafford Court House, Va., Mar. 21, '63, disability.

Feistel, Eduard; farmer, Franklin; ENL Aug. 21, '62; KIA July 1, '63, Gettysburg, Pa.

Fink, Henry; clerk, Milwaukee; ENL Aug. 15, '62; WIA by musket ball in right forearm at Chancellorsville and arm rendered useless; gangrene set in and bones removed May 16, '63; sent to hospital in Falmouth, then Judiciary Square Hospital in Washington, D.C., then to Madison, Wisc.; trans. to VRC Mar. '64; disch. due to wounds May 10, '64; became travelling salesman; opened own business in 1867 dealing in wool, hides, and furs; sold business in 1878 and went into real estate; member of Wilkin Manufacturing Co.; member of Milwaukee County Board of Supervisors, 1870-1874; an "enthusiastic and zealous Republican"; appointed collector of internal revenue for First District of Wisconsin in 1889 and U. S. Marshal from 1877 to 1885; elected member of state assembly in 1876 and 1877; member Milwaukee *Turnverein*; member of E.B. Walcott Post No. 1, G.A.R.; founding member of Twenty-Sixth Regiment Association; attended fiftieth anniversary at Gettysburg in 1913; died Jan. 13, 1925.

Fischer, Carl; laborer, Polk; ENL Aug. 21, '62; detached as pioneer; disch. at Jeffersonville, Ind., Feb. 25, '65, disability.

Friedrich, Carl A.; blacksmith, Milwaukee; ENL Aug. 21, '62; disch. at Columbia Hospital, Washington, D.C., Feb. 25, '64, disability.

Froehlich, Julius; clerk, Milwaukee; ENL Aug. 19, '62; Corp.; disch. in hospital at Washington, D.C., Dec. 20, '62, disability.

Gessner, Heinrich; mason, Milwaukee; ENL Aug. 15, '62; KIA June 19, '64, Kennesaw Mountain, Ga.

Gnewach, Wilhelm; farmer, Lebanon; ENL Aug. 21, '62; ambulance corps; MO June 13, '65.

Gottschalk, Charles; teamster, Wauwatosa; ENL Aug. 20, '62; regimental and brigade teamster; detached to surgeons department temporarily in July '63; MO June 13, '65; lived in Mequon after war; member of Twenty-Sixth Regiment Association; attended fiftieth anniversary at Gettysburg in 1913.

Groth, Heinrich; farmer, Lebanon; ENL Aug. 21, '62; disch. at Milwaukee Oct. 6, '62, disability.

Grundke, John; carpenter, Wauwatosa; ENL Aug. 13, '62; Corp., Sergt.; WIA by gunshot in leg Chancellorsville; disch. Apr. 22, '64, disability; member of Robert Chivas Post No. 2, G.A.R.

Haag, John; farmer, Polk; ENL Aug. 20, '62; disch. at Baltimore, Md., Feb. 17, '63, disability.

Hartmann, William; farmer, Ixonia; Aug. 20, '62; WIA by shot in lower leg at Gettysburg; DOW in hospital at Philadelphia Aug. 16, '63.

Heide, Louis C.; lawyer, Milwaukee; ENL Aug. 15, '62; brigade quartermaster dept.; disch. at Philadelphia, Pa., Dec. 25, '62, disability.

Hilger, Henry; saddler, Wauwatosa; ENL Aug. 21,'62; musician; WIA in shoulder and back at Chancellorsville; DOW Aug. 16, '63 (one source says deserted from hospital at Philadelphia, Pa., Dec. 5, '63).

Huebner, August; blacksmith, Ixonia; ENL Aug. 21, '62; WIA Chancellorsville; sent to hospital Oct. 15, '63; absent at MO of regt.

Huebner, Ferdinand; farmer, Ixonia; ENL Aug. 21, '62; member of color guard; WIA in left arm May 25, '64; absent wounded in Nashville, Tenn., at MO of regt.

Hunkel, Philip; bookkeeper, Chicago, IL; ENL Aug. 13, '62; WIA Gettysburg; disch. Dec. 22, '63, disability; member of Robert Chivas Post No. 2, G.A.R.; member of Twenty-Sixth Regiment Association.

Jaeger, August; farmer, Lebanon; ENL Aug. 21, '62; DOD in XI Corps Hospital in Lookout Valley, Tenn., Nov. 5, '63.

Jaeger, Carl; farmer, Ixonia; ENL Aug. 21, '62; clerk; WIA in left leg June 25, '64; disch. at Jefferson Barracks, Mo., Oct. 22, '64, disability.

Jaeger, Hermann; farmer, Lebanon; ENL Aug. 21, '62; absent sick in hospital at Lookout Mountain, Tenn., at MO of regt.

Jaeger, William; farmer, Milwaukee; ENL Aug. 21, '62; WIA and left leg fractured May 14, '64 at Resaca; disch. at Philadelphia, Pa., Jan. 11, '65, disability.

Jahns, Albert; clerk, Milwaukee; ENL Aug. 13, '62; WIA Gettysburg; KIA May 14, '64, Resaca, Ga.

Juderjahn, Wilhelm; Milwaukee; ENL Aug. 15, '62; company cook; CIA Chancellorsville; MO June 13, '65; member of Robert Chivas Post No. 2, G.A.R.

Kelz, George; blacksmith, Milwaukee; ENL Aug. 21, '62; disch. Oct. 6, '62, disability.

Koch, Henry; shoemaker, Milwaukee; ENL Aug. 14, '62; Corp.; absent sick in hospital since Oct. 25, '63; MO at Milwaukee Aug 10, '65.

Kucknan, Bernard; farmer, Portland; ENL Aug. 21, '62; WIA Gettysburg; WIA in side May 25, '64; absent wounded in hospital at Louisville, Ky., at MO of regt.

Kuhlmann, Charles; bookkeeper, Milwaukee; ENL Aug. 20, '62; WIA Gettysburg; WIA near Marietta, Ga., June 22, '64; DOW at Nashville, Tenn., July 19, '64.

Kulke, August; farmer, Lebanon; ENL Aug., 21, '62; severely WIA Chancellorsvillè; DOW in hospital at Brooks Station, Va., May 20, '63.

Latzke, John A.; farmer, Ixonia; ENL Aug. 21, '62; MO June 13, '65.

Lauer, William; clerk, Milwaukee; ENL Aug. 21, '62; severely WIA in knee at Chancellorsville; DOW at Washington, D.C. June 25, '63.

Laufer, Carl; cooper, Milwaukee; ENL Aug. 13, '62; Corp.; WIA May 15, '64 at Resaca; sent to hospital at Nashville, Tenn., MO at Nashville May, 30, '65.

Liebenstein, Philip; farmer, Greenfield; ENL Feb. 23, '64; WIA in left arm May 14, '64 at Resaca; trans. to VRC, Apr. 1, '65; disch. May 26, '65, disability.

Liebenstein, William; farmer, Greenfield; ENL Feb. 29, '64; trans. to Co. B, 3rd Wis. Inf., June 9, '65; MO July 18, '65; elected to local offices and state assembly in 1893.

Lingsch, Heinrich; mason, Milwaukee; ENL Aug. 15, '62; company cook; DOD at Murfreesboro, Tenn., Jan. 20, '64.

Maasch, Theodor; farmer, Ixonia; ENL Aug. 21, '62; slightly WIA in finger May 15, '64 at Resaca; MO June 13, '65.

Meiswinkel, Julius; clerk, Milwaukee; ENL Aug. 16, '62; 1st Sergt.; promoted 2nd Lieut. Co G, Sept. 18, '62.

Metzel, Alexander; banker, Milwaukee; ENL Aug. 19, '62; Corp., Sergt.; promoted Sergt. Major, May 3, '63.

Meyer, Bernhard; miller, Milwaukee; ENL Aug. 15, '62; Sergt., 1st Sergt.; WIA in breast at Chancellorsville; trans. to VRC, Mar. 1, '64; MO at Washington, D.C., June 24, '65.

Miller, Friedrich; farmer, Polk; ENL Aug. 16, '62; MO June 13, '65.

Moldenhauer, August; farmer, Lebanon; ENL Aug. 21, '62; WIA Chancellorsville, disch. Oct. 5, '63, disability.

Mueller, Julius; farmer, Lebanon; ENL Aug. 20, '62; WIA Gettysburg; trans. to VRC, Apr. 28, '64; member of Robert Chivas Post No. 2, G.A.R.; founding member of Twenty-Sixth Regiment Association.

Ninon, August; Ixonia; ENL Aug. 21, '62; WIA in thigh May 25, '64; MO June 13, '65.

Pagenkopf, Herman; farmer, Ixonia; ENL Aug. 20, '62; CIA Gettysburg; exchanged and DOD (chronic diarrhoea) at Annapolis, Md., Dec. 7, '63.

Penner, William; clerk, Milwaukee; ENL Aug. 13, '62; Corp., Sergt.; MO June 13, '65.

Perschbacher, John A.; farmer, Kewaskum; Feb. 22, '64 from Co. F; slightly

WIA in left foot at Resaca; trans. to Co. B, 3rd Wis. Inf., June 9, '65.

Petsch, Ferdinand; farmer, Lebanon; ENL Aug. 21, '62; MO June 13, '65.

Prengel, Theodor; clerk, Milwaukee; ENL Aug. 15, '62; Corp.; color bearer; WIA Gettysburg and CIA in hospital but left behind when rebels retreated July 4, '63; MO June 13, '65; opened own dry goods store after war and later worked 40 years for government; member of Robert Chivas Post No. 2, G.A.R.; founding member of Twenty-Sixth Regiment Association.

Raabe, Gottlieb; farmer, Lebanon; ENL Aug. 21, '62; WIA Gettysburg; MO June 13, '65.

Raasch, August; farmer, Ixonia; ENL Aug. 21, '62; WIA Gettysburg; absent in hospital at Madison, Wisc., at MO of regt.

Rauth, Henry; printer, Milwaukee; ENL Aug. 21, '62; Sergt.; promoted 2nd Lieut. Co. C, Mar. 15, '63.

Reuss, Frederick; clerk, Milwaukee; ENL Aug. 15, '62; Sergt.; brigade commissary clerk; promoted Q.M. Sergt., Nov. 1, '64.

Sasse, Wilhelm; farmer, Milwaukee; ENL Aug. 21, '62; KIA July 20, '64, Peach Tree Creek, Ga.

Schape, August; tinsmith, Milwaukee; ENL Aug. 18, '62; slightly WIA Chancellorsville; MO June 13, '65.

Schick, Frederick; butcher, Milwaukee; ENL Aug. 18, '62; ambulance corp; clerk to judge advocate; trans. to VRC, Mar. 14, '64; MO June 27, '65.

Schlueter, Henry; farmer, Franklin; ENL Aug. 21, '62; disch. Oct. 6, '62, disability.

Schulz [or Schultz], Hermann; farmer, Milwaukee; ENL Aug. 19, '62; WIA Gettysburg; sent to Ft. Schuyler Hospital in New York City; disch. 1864; attended fiftieth anniversary at Gettysburg in 1913.

Schulze, Gotthard; ropemaker, Milwaukee; ENL Aug. 21, '62; disch. Dec. 20, '62, disability.

Schumacher, Wilhelm; farmer, Ixonia; ENL Aug. 21, '62; MO June 13, '65; attended fiftieth anniversary at Gettysburg in 1913.

Siebold, Frederick; machinist, Milwaukee; ENL Aug. 21, '62; Corp.; WIA Chancellorsville; WIA slightly in left arm at Resaca; promoted 2nd Lieut. Co. F, 45th Wis. Inf., Dec. 6, '64; moved to St. Paul, Minn., after war; attended regimental reunions.

Sonntag, Henry; clerk, Milwaukee; ENL Aug. 13, '62; Corp.; promoted Sergt. Major, Mar. 28, '65.

Staib, Charles; clerk, Milwaukee; ENL Aug. 15, '62; Corp.; clerk at division headquarters; MO June 13, '65.

Tesch, Theodor; carpenter, Lebanon; ENL Aug. 20, '62; Corp.; MO June 13, '65.

Thiele, Henry; merchant, Milwaukee; ENL Aug. 21, '62; committed suicide at Stafford Court House, Va., Feb. 28, '63.

Truss, Adam; broommaker, Milwaukee; ENL Aug. 21, '62; WIA in right hand May (or June ?) 25, '64; MO June 13, '65; engineer at county jail after war; member of Robert Chivas Post No. 2, G.A.R.

Tulzmann, August; teamster, Milwaukee; ENL Aug. 21, '62; KIA May 2, '63, Chancellorsville, Va.

Upmann, Frederick G.; shoemaker, Milwaukee; ENL Aug 14, '62; Corp., Sergt.; MO June 13, '65; member of Robert Chivas Post No. 2, G.A.R.; founding member of Twenty-Sixth Regiment Association.

Von der Plasche, Paul; farmer, Polk; ENL Aug. 21, '62; hospital nurse; orderly at division headquarters; MO June 13, '65; lived in Brookfield after war; member of Twenty-Sixth Regiment Association; attended fiftieth anniversary at Gettysburg in 1913.

Vondran, Charles; farmer, Farmington; ENL Aug. 21, '62; severely WIA in breast at Chancellorsville; DOW in hospital at Brooks Station, Va., May 25, '63.

Weiffenbach, John; farmer, Polk; ENL Aug. 19, '62; WIA Gettysburg; WIA in left shoulder May 25, '64; DOW June 3, '64 Chattanooga, Tenn.

Weinreich, Charles; teamster, Milwaukee; ENL Aug. 15, '62; Corp., Sergt.; member of color guard; recruiting duty Jan. 1-Feb. 27, '64; WIA in foot at Resaca; WIA July 20, '64; absent wounded in hospital at Keokuk, Iowa, at MO of regt.; lived in Platteville after war; member of Twenty-Sixth Regiment Association.

Wendorff, August; gardener, Milwaukee; ENL Aug. 18, '62; WIA July 20, '64; disch. at Madison, Wisc., Jan 10, '65, disability.

Wendorff, Friedrich; farmer, Lebanon; ENL Aug. 21, '62; WIA Gettysburg; WIA June 22, '64 and upper one-third of left arm amputated; DOW (enteric fever) at Nashville, Tenn., July 19, '64.

Wendorff, Johann; farmer, Ixonia; ENL Aug. 21, '62; company cook; MO June 13, '65.

Will, Frederick; farmer, Ixonia; ENL Aug. 21, '62; Corp. Sergt., 1st Sergt.; MO June 13, '65.

Wrede, Louis; Wauwatosa; ENL Aug. 15, '62; musician; MO June 13, '65.

Zuehlsdorff, Friedrich; merchant, Milwaukee; ENL Aug. 15, '62; KIA July 1, '63, Gettysburg, Pa.

COMPANY C, MILWAUKEE GUARDS

Captains

John P. Seemann; commissioner, Milwaukee; rank from Sept. 3, '62; WIA Chancellorsville; detached to Provost Marshal 3rd Div. 11th Army Corps, from Nov. 6, '62 until July 4, '63; dismissed from service for absence without leave Sept. 23, '63; from Oct. 21, '63 until Dec. 30, '63, reinstated and recommissioned as Capt. Co. I.

Robert Mueller; farmer, Milwaukee; appointed Nov. 17, '63; ENL Aug. 18, '62; Sergt., 1st Sergt.; 2nd Lieut., Nov 14, '62; 1st Lieut., Mar. 15, '63; WIA in arm at

Chancellorsville; rejoined regt. Aug. 7, '63; KIA July 20, '64, Peach Tree Creek, Ga.

Henry Rauth; printer, Milwaukee; appointed Oct. 19, '64 from Sergt. Co. B; 2nd Lieut., Mar. 15, '63; WIA and CIA Chancellorsville; exchanged June 6, '63 and rejoined regt. June 11, '63; 1st Lieut., Nov. 17, '63; MO June 13, '65; moved to St. Louis after war.

First Lieutenants

John William Fuchs; soldier, Milwaukee; appointed Sept. 3, '62 from Sergt. Co. C, 5th Wis. Inf.; promoted Capt. Co. A. Mar. 15, '63.

Friedrich R. Klein; artist, Milwaukee; appointed Oct. 19, '64 from Sergt. Major; KIA Mar. 16, '65, Averasboro, N.C.

Julius Mueller; distiller, Milwaukee; appointed Apr. 6, '65; ENL Aug. 16, '62; Sergt., 1st Sergt.; recruiting duty Jan. 1-Feb. 27, '64; MO June 13, '65.

Second Lieutenant

Bernhard Domschcke; editor, Milwaukee; rank from Sept. 3, '62; promoted 1st Lieut. Co. G, Nov. 14, '62.

Enlisted Men

Arft, John; ship carpenter, Milwaukee; ENL Aug. 20, '62; WIA Gettysburg; trans. to VRC, Nov. 15, '63; MO Aug. 24, '65, term expired.

Awe, Fritz; farmer, Spring Prairie; ENL Aug. 20, '62; left sick Feb. 11, '63; trans. to VRC, Sept. 30, '62; MO June 26, '65.

Baje, Charles; blacksmith, Milwaukee; ENL Aug. 21, '62; WIA Chancellorsville May 2, '63; WIA Gettysburg and sent to Harvey General Hospital in Madison, Wisc.; disch. Nov. 28, '64, disability; attended fiftieth anniversary at Gettysburg in 1913.

Balmes, Joseph; wagonmaker, Milwaukee; ENL Aug. 20, '62; WIA Gettysburg with gunshot compound fracture of right hip; DOW in field hospital at Gettysburg July 10, '63; buried in Wisconsin Section at Gettysburg National Cemetery, grave B-19.

Benecke, Henry; locksmith, Franklin; ENL Aug. 15, '62; disch. by medical director of XI Corps Dec. 26, '62, disability.

Bentz, John; farmer, Kenosha; ENL Aug. 18, '62; company cook; MO June 13, '65; returned to Kenosha after war; member of Twenty-Sixth Regiment Association; died in 1899.

Berens, Vincenz; carpenter, Granville; ENL Aug. 20, '62; company cook; MO June 13, '65.

Beres, Christian; farmer, Greenfield; ENL Aug. 21, '62; Corp.; MO June 13, '65; founding member of Twenty-Sixth Regiment Association.

Beres, John; farmer, Greenfield; ENL Aug. 21, '62; WIA Chancellorsville; trans. to VRC Sept. 30, '63; MO June 26, '65.

Berger, Fredrich; laborer, Milwaukee; ENL Aug. 16, '62; company cook; CIA Gettysburg; paroled Mar. or Apr. '64; rejoined July 10, '64; MO June 13, '65.

Berlandi, Philip; carpenter, Milwaukee; ENL Aug. 21, '62; Corp; KIA July 1, '63, Gettysburg, Pa.

Bigalke, Hermann; clerk, Milwaukee; ENL Aug. 16, '62; WIA Chancellorsville; rejoined regt. July 21, '64; WIA Averasboro Mar. 16, '65; MO May 19, '65.

Boettscher, Carl; wagonmaker, Milwaukee; ENL Aug. 15, '62; WIA at Dallas, Ga., June 22, '64; rejoined regt. Nov. 11, '64; CIA at Thompsons' Cr. near Cheraw, S.C., Mar. 5, '65; exchanged Apr. 4, '65; MO June 13, '65.

Botzet, Peter; laborer, Wauwatosa; ENL Aug. 20, '62; left sick June 11, '63; trans. to VRC, Dec. 12, '63; MO June 28, '65.

Brandenburger, Philip; farmer, Granville; ENL Aug. 21, '62; officers' cook; detached to provost guard of XI Corps Nov. 1, '62; rejoined July 20, '63; absent sick since Oct. 26, '63; in Harvey General Hospital at Madison, Wisc., at MO of regt.

Christen, John M.; tanner, Milwaukee; ENL Aug. 12, '62; detached to provost guard of XI Corps; rejoined Aug. 6, '63; WIA in right leg and CIA when he took the wrong road to the hospital at Dallas, Ga., May 25, '64; held prisoner in Confederate prison at Andersonville, Ga.; survived but absent prisoner at MO of regt.

Dallmann, Johann; farmer, Kenosha; ENL Aug. 18, '62; KIA July 1, '63, Gettysburg, Pa.

Depke, Frederick (or Ferdinand); fisherman, Milwaukee; ENL Aug. 21, '62; absent sick Feb. 4 to July 27, '63; detached to brigade provost guard May 23, '64 to June 1, '65; MO June 13, '65.

Drewes, Leopold; carpenter, Greenfield; ENL Aug. 15, '62; Corp.; injured by accident, Oct. 5, '64 when leg fractured by falling tree in camp; absent sick at MO of regt.

Ehlert, Theodor; laborer, Milwaukee; ENL Aug. 18, '62; teamster; MO June 13, '65; member of Robert Chivas Post No. 2, G.A.R.

Erdmann, Henry; butcher, Milwaukee; ENL Aug. 21, '62; Corp., Sergt.; color sergt.; WIA Bentonville, N.C., Mar. 19, '65; MO May 29, '65.

Fernekes, Peter; tinsmith, Milwaukee; ENL Aug. 21, '62; 1st Sergt.; promoted Sergt. Major, Oct. 23, '62.

Fischer, Christian; laborer, Milwaukee; ENL Aug. 16, '62; officers' cook; left sick Apr. 14, '63; trans. to VRC, Aug. 1, '63.

Friedrich, Nicolaus; laborer, Greenfield; ENL Aug. 21, '62; left sick Dec. 10, '62; trans. to VRC, Mar. 15, '64; MO June 26, '65; member of Robert Chivas Post No. 2, G.A.R.; member of Twenty-Sixth Regiment Association.

Fritz, Michael; blacksmith, Yorkville; ENL Aug. 21, '62; CIA Chancellorsville; rejoined regt. Oct. 3, '63; absent sick since May 22, '64; MO May 22, '65.

Gebhardt, Henry; tailor, Milwaukee; ENL Aug. 13, '62; musician; left sick Sept.

5, '63; rejoined regt. and trans. to ranks at own request July 21, '64; left sick Apr. 7, '65; MO June 21, '65; founding member of Twenty-Sixth Regiment Association.

Gerber, Friedrich; shoemaker, Milwaukee; ENL Aug. 21, '62; company cook; left sick May 22, '64; rejoined regt. May 21, '65; MO June 13, '65.

Gerber, William; teamster, Milwaukee; ENL Aug. 21, '62; severely WIA Gettysburg; trans. to VRC, Mar. 15, '64.

Guckenberger, Sebastian; farmer, Oak Creek; ENL Aug. 21, '62; severely WIA in ankle at Gettysburg, July 1, '63; trans. to VRC, Nov. 1, '63; MO Aug. 16, '65; became farmer in Oak Creek after war and fathered fourteen children; member of Robert Chivas Post No. 2, G.A.R.; member of Twenty-Sixth Regiment Association.

Hahn, Martin; wagonmaker, Milwaukee; ENL Aug. 20, '62; Corp., Sergt.; WIA Bentonville, N.C., foot amputated; absent wounded at MO of regt.

Hansgen, Mathias; farmer, Paris; ENL Aug. 19, '62; disch. by medical director of XI Corps Apr. 14, '63, disability.

Henrichs, John E.; cigarmaker, Milwaukee; ENL Aug. 20, '62; monthly report states "deserted at Milwaukee about 24 Sept. '62."

Hensel, Adolph; clerk, Milwaukee; ENL Aug. 20, '62; prom. Q.M. Sergt., Sept 17, '62.

Hermann, Hermann; printer, Milwaukee; ENL Aug. 21, '62; severely WIA by three gunshots in left knee and forearm at Chancellorsville; DOW in hospital at Washington, DC., June 17, '63.

Hoffmann, Peter; farmer, Meeme; ENL Aug. 21, '62; WIA Gettysburg July 2, '63; rejoined regt. Oct. 3, '63; left sick May 2, '64; rejoined regt. Apr. 9, '65; MO June 13, '65; attended fiftieth anniversary at Gettysburg in 1913.

Holz (or sometimes Holtz), Asmus; laborer, Greenfield; ENL Aug. 18, '62; CIA Gettysburg; DOD (scorbutus) in Confederate prison Aug. 2, '64, Andersonville, Ga., and buried in grave 4570.

Hunzicker, Rudolph; cigarmaker, Milwaukee; ENL Aug. 21, '62; WIA Gettysburg July 2, '63; rejoined regt. Dec. 20, '63; MO June 13, '65.

Jarnt, Friedrich; Kenosha; ENL Aug. 21, '62; WIA June 22, '64 near Kennesaw Mtn. and sent to the United States General Army Hospital No. 19 in Nashville, Tenn.; trans. to VRC, Jan. 20, '65.

Kindt, Carl; laborer, Franklin; ENL Aug. 20, '62; left sick Dec. 10, '62; returned to regiment at an unspecified date; trans. to VRC, Jan. 1, '65; member of E.B. Walcott Post No. 1, G.A.R.; attended fiftieth anniversary at Gettysburg in 1913; died Jan. 12, 1921.

Klinker, Henry; brewer, Milwaukee; ENL Aug. 21, '62; Corp.; reduced to ranks Feb. 27, '63; WIA by minie ball in left ankle at Gettysburg and CIA but left behind after rebel retreat; leg amputated three inches below knee; disch. due to wounds Apr. 9, '64; member and trustee of Robert Chivas Post No. 2, G.A.R.; founding member of Twenty-Sixth Regiment Association.

Koch, Joseph; carpenter, Milwaukee; Aug. 18, '62; Corp.; reduced to ranks June 1, '63; KIA July 1, '63, Gettysburg, Pa.

Koepke, August; carpenter, Milwaukee; ENL Aug. 21, '62; WIA in face at

Chancellorsville; detached as pioneer June 6, '63; rejoined regt. June 20, '64; left sick Nov. 1, '64; rejoined Apr. 9, '65; MO June 13, '65; member of Robert Chivas Post No. 2, G.A.R.; member of Twenty-Sixth Regiment Association.

Kohsow, Helmuth; saddler, Milwaukee; Aug. 13, '62; Sergt; left sick Apr. 14, '63; disch. at Alexandria, Va., Oct. 9, '63, physical disability.

Kolngen, Nicolaus; carpenter, Granville; ENL Aug. 20, '62; CIA Gettysburg; rejoined regt. Dec. 19, '63; detached to train Apr. 4 to July 30, '64; MO June 13, '65; attended fiftieth anniversary at Gettysburg in 1913.

Kraemer, Johann N.; farmer, Spring Prairie; ENL Aug. 20, '62; absent sick Apr. 14 to May 30, '63; detached as pioneer June 20, '64; rejoined regt. June 1, '65; MO June 13, '65.

Krenscher, Peter; farmer, Paris; ENL Aug. 20, '62; WIA by shot in left side at Gettysburg; DOW in field hospital at Gettysburg July 8, '63; buried in Gettysburg National Cemetery, Wisconsin Plot, grave B-17.

Krueger, Christian; saddler, Kenosha; ENL Aug. 18, '62; Sergt.; CIA Chancellorsville; rejoined regt. Dec. 10, '63; WIA June 22, '64, Kennesaw Mountain, Ga.; DOW in field hospital June 24, '64.

Krueger, Ferdinand; farmer, Kenosha; ENL Aug. 21, '62; Corp.; CIA Gettysburg; rejoined regt. Sept. 6, '63; WIA Peach Tree Creek July 20, '64; ; trans. to VRC, Feb. 25, '65.

Langer, Edward; laborer, Kenosha; ENL Aug. 21, '62; KIA, May 25, '64, Dallas, Ga.

Lauer, John; clerk, Kenosha; ENL Aug. 21, '62; severely WIA Chancellorsville; WIA above the eye May 25, '64, Burnt Hickory, Ga.; DOW in field hospital at Chattanooga, Tenn., June 19, '64.

Leitzmann, Charles [Carl] cooper, Milwaukee; ENL Aug. 21, '62; Sergt.; detached to ambulance corps Nov. 1, '62; suffered from scurvy and dysentery during seige of Atlanta; rejoined regt. June 1, '65; MO June 13, '65; member of Twenty-Sixth Regiment Association; died in Milwaukee County of tuberculosis Dec. 17, 1890.

Leken, Henry; drayman, Kenosha; ENL Aug. 16, '62; KIA July 1, '63, Gettysburg, Pa.

Limpert, George C.; farmer, Kenosha; ENL Feb. 2, '64; Corp.; trans. to Co. C, 3rd Wis. Inf., June 10, '65; returned to Kenosha after war; member of Twenty-Sixth Regiment Association.

Luther, Gottfried G.; mechanic, Milwaukee; ENL Aug. 20, '62; Principal Musician; reduced to ranks Feb. 11, '63; slightly WIA Chancellorsville; rejoined regt. July 20, '63; left sick Oct. 26, '63; rejoined regt. Feb. 14, '64; left sick May 23, '64; rejoined regt. May 21, '65; MO June 13, '65.

Manz, Lewis; cooper, Greenfield; ENL Aug. 21, '62; WIA in hand and CIA Chancellorsville; held prisoner in Richmond and after exchange rejoined regiment in Tennessee Nov. 18, '63; trans. to VRC, Mar. 1, '64; disch. Sept. 22, '64, due to wounds; wound resulted in permanent stiffening of his hand, making him unfit to resume his trades as coppersmith and saw mill operator; after war returned to Hales' Corner and became postal letter carrier for over fifty years; retired in 1915; member of Robert Chivas Post No. 2, G.A.R.; member of Twenty-Sixth Regiment Association; died at Soldiers' Home as oldest letter carrier in U.S.

Mathias, Gottlieb; cooper, Milwaukee; ENL Aug. 21, '62; detached to ambulance corp Oct. 20, '63; rejoined regt. June 1, '65; MO June 13, '65; member of Knights of Pythias; founding member of Twenty-Sixth Regiment Association; died in March, 1876.

Mathias, Jack; laborer, Belgium; ENL Aug. 21, '62; left sick Dec. 10, '62; rejoined regt. June 10, '63; WIA Gettysburg; trans. to VRC, Nov. 1, '63; MO Aug. 5, '65.

Mayer, Leopold; carpenter, Milwaukee; ENL Aug. 15, '62; Corp.; company cook; absent sick June 20 to July 30, '63; MO June 13, '65.

Michel, Jacob; cooper, Greenfield; ENL Aug. 21, '62; Corp., Sergt.; WIA and CIA Chancellorsville; rejoined regt. Oct. 3, '63; WIA June 22, '64, Kennesaw Mountain, Ga.; DOW at Chattanooga, Tenn., July 12, '64.

Muelhaupt, August; carpenter, Milwaukee; ENL Aug. 18, '62; Corp., WIA in arm and leg at Chancellorsville; DOW in Stanton Hospital at Washington, D.C., Jan. 1, '64.

Mueller, Charles; farmer, Milwaukee; ENL Aug. 20, '62; brigade teamster; left sick Apr. 14, '63; WIA Chancellorsville; trans. to VRC, Sept. 1, '63; disch. June 10, '65, disability.

Muenzenberger, Adam; shoemaker, Greenfield; ENL Aug. 16, '62; Corp., Sergt.; CIA Gettysburg; DOD in Confederate prison Dec. 3, '63, Richmond, Va.

Neumann, Joseph; grinder, Milwaukee; ENL Aug. 15, '62; KIA July 1, '63, Gettysburg, Pa.

Paulus, Nicolaus; laborer, Paris; Aug. 21, '62; WIA Gettysburg; rejoined regt. some time before mid-Oct., '63; MO June 13, '65; lived in Kenosha after war; member of Twenty-Sixth Regiment Association.

Petermann, Ferdinand; laborer, Franklin; ENL Aug. 21, '62; left sick Feb. 11, '63; trans. to VRC, Sept. 30, '65; MO July 6, '65.

Radatz, Friedrich; laborer, Kenosha; ENL Aug. 15, '62; left sick Aug. 26, '64; rejoined regt. Apr. 9, '65; MO June 13, '65; returned to Kenosha after war; member of Twenty-Sixth Regiment Association.

Riegger, Benedict; laborer, Franklin; ENL Aug. 15, '62; WIA Gettysburg; WIA June 22, '64 near Kennesaw Mtn. and sent to General Hospital No. 1, Chattanooga, Tenn.; absent wounded at MO of regt.

Rinke, Anton; farmer, Mt. Pleasant; ENL Aug. 17, '62; WIA and right arm fractured May 15, '64, Resaca, Ga.; DOW in field hospital June 2, '64.

Rook, Peter; painter, Kenosha; ENL Aug. 14, '62; Sergt., 1st Sergt.; acting 2nd Lieut. Co. F, June 1, '63, but not mustered; KIA July 1, '63, Gettysburg, Pa.

Schaefer, Gustav; Milwaukee; ENL Aug. 21, '62; musician; muster out papers say "Accompanied the regiment in all campaigns."; MO June 13, '65.

Schaeffer, Thurlius; butcher, Milwaukee; ENL Aug. 20, '62; WIA Gettysburg; WIA May 25, '64, at Dallas, Ga.; right leg amputated and DOW at Chattanooga, Tenn., June 20, '64.

Scherer, Carl; saddler, Milwaukee; ENL Aug. 20, '63; severely WIA Gettysburg; disch. at West Philadelphia, Pa., Oct. 5, '63, disability.

Schmarbeck, Friedrich; farmer, Kenosha; ENL Aug. 14, '62; left sick Nov. 5, '64; rejoined regt. May 21, '65; MO June 13, '65.

Schoenleber, Julius; shoemaker, Milwaukee; ENL Aug. 18, '62; officers' cook; CIA Gettysburg; exchanged and trans. to VRC, Jan. 15, '64; MO July 3, '65; member of Robert Chivas Post No. 2, G.A.R.

Schroeder, August; harnessmaker, Kenosha; ENL Aug. 14, '62; Corp., Sergt.; WIA June 22, '64, Kennesaw, Mountain, Ga., and sent to hospital; MO June 28, '65.

Schuele, John George; molder, Milwaukee; ENL Aug. 20, '62; Corp.; WIA slightly in head May 15, '64, near Resaca and in hospital at Louisville, Ky.; rejoined regt. Aug. 23, '64; MO June 13, '65; member of Rank and File Post No. 240, G.A.R.; member of Twenty-Sixth Regiment Association.

Segrist, Henry; shoemaker, Clifton; ENL Feb. 24, '64; slightly WIA Resaca May 15, '64, and sent to hospital in Louisville, Ky.; trans. to Co. C, 3rd Wis. Inf., June 10, '65; MO May 30, '65.

Sprengling, Andreas; laborer, Milwaukee; ENL Aug. 13, '62; WIA in both thighs at Chancellorsville; trans. to VRC, Aug. 10, '63; pensioned as invalid.

Stamm, Charles Frederick; blacksmith, Pleasant Prairie; Feb. 2, '64; trans. to Co. C, 3rd Wis. Inf., June 10, '65; MO July 15, '65; elected mayor of Kenosha in 1887.

Steinly, Deany [also C. D. Steinle]; butcher, Milwaukee; ENL Aug. 21, '62; Corp.; severely WIA by gunshot in hip at Chancellorsville; disch. Apr. 11, '64, disability; member of Robert Chivas Post No. 2, G.A.R.; founding member of Twenty-Sixth Regiment Association.

Stirn, Julius; laborer, Greenfield; ENL Aug. 21, '62; ammunition wagon teamster; WIA in foot at Chancellorsville; in Aug. '64 still in hospital at Philadelphia; trans. to VRC, Dec. 30, '64.

Stoltze, George; tinsmith, Milwaukee; ENL Aug. 20, '62; CIA Gettysburg; DOD in Confederate prison Feb. 5, '64, Richmond, Va.

Suettinger, Julius; mechanic, Milwaukee; ENL Aug. 14, '62; CIA Chancellorsville; rejoined regt. Oct. 3, '63; KIA May 15, '64, Resaca, Ga.

Tarry, Franklin; farmer, Paris; ENL Aug. 21, '62; detached as brigade teamster Mar. 14, '63; CIA Mar. 26, '65, Goldsboro, N.C., while on foraging expedition; absent prisoner of war at MO of regt.

Thurm, Heinrich; farmer, Kenosha; ENL Aug. 21, '62; disch. at Alexandria, Va., Aug. 12, '63, physical disability.

Trümper, August; laborer, Milwaukee; ENL Aug. 13, '62; Corp., 1st Sergt.; WIA Peach Tree Creek July, '64; MO, June 13, '65.

Urich, Heinrich; laborer, Milwaukee; ENL Aug. 14, '62; Corp.; slightly WIA Chancellorsville; rejoined July 5, '63; reduced to ranks by own request July 10, '63; WIA Resaca, May 15, '64; and lost fore finger on left hand; absent wounded at MO of regt.; member of Robert Chivas Post No. 2, G.A.R.; member of Twenty-Sixth Regiment Association; postal letter carrier after the war.

Vollmer, Charles; farmer, Pleasant Prairie; ENL Feb. 2, '64; trans. to Co. C, 3rd Wis. Inf., June 10, '65.

Wachenfeld, Heinrich; baker, Kenosha; ENL Aug. 20, '62; MO June 13, '65.

Wallich, Ferdinand; typefounder, Milwaukee; ENL Aug. 20, '62; absent sick Feb. 1 to July 28, '63; MO June 13, '65.

Weber, Mathias; blacksmith, Milwaukee; ENL Aug. 20, '62; brigade blacksmith; assigned to ammunition train Feb. 19, '63; rejoined regt. June 1, '65; MO June 13, '65.

Weber, Peter; farmer, Paris; ENL Aug. 20, '62; WIA Chancellorsville; WIA July 20, '64, Peach Tree Creek; rejoined regt. Nov. 1, '64; MO June 13, '65.

Weidner, Charles [Karl[; carpenter, Milwaukee; ENL Aug. 15, '62; detached to pioneer corps Nov. 8, '62; rejoined regt. June 20, '64; WIA June 22, '64, Kennesaw Mountain, Ga., and sent on furlough to Milwaukee; disch. at Harvey Hospital, Madison, Wisc., May 22, '65 due to disability; member of Robert Chivas Post No. 2, G.A.R.; founding member of Twenty-Sixth Regiment Association. Brother of William below and Adolf Weidner, Co.I.

Weidner, William; tinsmith, Milwaukee; ENL Aug. 14, '63; MO June 13, '65; member of Robert Chivas Post No. 2, G.A.R.; member of Twenty-Sixth Regiment Association; postal letter carrier after the war. Brother of Charles Weidner above and Adolf Weidner, Co.I. Died June 27, 1887.

Weiss, Dominique; laborer, Milwaukee; ENL Aug. 21, '62; severely WIA in shoulder, arm and foot at Chancellorsville; trans. to VRC, Apr. 1, '64; MO Sept. 8, ' 65.

Weller, Charles; laborer, Kenosha; ENL Aug. 14, '62; slightly WIA at Chancellorsville; left sick June 12, '63; rejoined regt. Jan. 7, '64; left sick May 22, '64; rejoined regt. Sept. 12, '64; left sick Nov. 5, '64; MO May 14, '65.

Winkler, Morris; farmer, Pt. Washington; ENL Aug. 21, '62; severely WIA Gettysburg by musket ball entering frontal bone of head and exposing membrane; treated in Seminary Hospital until July 8, then sent to South Street Hospital in Philadelphia where ball extracted and he remained through '64; trans. to VRC, Jan. 9, '65; MO 30, '65; suffered from dimness of vision in right eye, headaches, and dizziness; received pension for total disability.

Wirschim [or Wirshem], Peter; laborer, Kenosha; ENL Aug. 21, '62; Corp.; MO June 13, '65; attended fiftieth anniversary at Gettysburg in 1913.

Wittig, Anton; fisherman, Milwaukee; ENL Aug. 20, '62; MO June 13, '65.

Wuest, Adam; farmer, Greenfield; ENL Aug. 20, '62; WIA in left hand at Resaca May 15, '64 and sent to Cumberland Hospital, Nashville, Tenn.; middle finger amputated; rejoined regt. Sept. 27, '64; MO June 13, '65; settled in Milwaukee after war; later moved to Franksville, Racine County, where he opened a tavern; eventually moved to Richmond, Virginia.

Zimmermann, Louis; farmer, Milwaukee; ENL Aug. 15, '62; Corp.; WIA June 22, '64, Kennesaw Mountain, Ga.; rejoined regt. Apr. 23, '65; MO June 13, '65.

Zimmermann, Philip; laborer, Milwaukee; ENL Feb. 8, '64; trans. to Co. C, 3rd Wis. Inf., June 10, '65.

COMPANY D, SALOMON RIFLES

Captains

August Ligousky; topographical engineer, Madison; rank from Sept. 3. '62; Topographical Engineer of 3rd Div., XI Corp., from Nov. 25, '62, until June, '64; disch. July 19, '64.

Joseph Maschauer; farmer, Milwaukee; appointed Oct. 19, '64 from 1st Lieut. Co. H; later commanded Company I beginning about Apr. 20, '65; MO June 13, '65; founding member of Twenty-Sixth Regiment Association and member of first committee on finance.

First Lieutenants

August Schueler; engineer, Milwaukee; appointed Sept. 3, '62; to Capt. Co. K. Mar. 15, '63.

Edward Carl; Sauk City; appointed Mar. 15, '63, 2nd Lieut. Co, K; promoted Capt. Co. K, June 1, '63.

August Bartsch; blacksmith, Madison; appointed June 1, '63; ENL Aug. 11, '62; 1st Sergt; 2nd Lieut., Mar. 15, '63; WIA Gettysburg July 1, '63; promoted Capt. Co. G, Apr. 13, '64.

Leopold Melchior; brewer, Milwaukee; appointed Apr. 13, '64; ENL June 4, '62; Sergt., 1st Sergt; 2nd Lieut., June 1, '63; severely WIA Gettysburg; listed as "present in arrest" in June '64; report dated Aug, 31, '64 notes "1st. Lt. Leop. Melchior in arrest or confinement"; dismissed from service Sept. 8, '64.

Peter Guttmann; soldier, Milwaukee; appointed Oct. 19, '64; ENL Aug. 19, '62; Corp., Sergt., 1st Sergt; WIA Gettysburg; promoted Capt. Co. B, Apr. 6, '65.

Henrich Elsner; harnessmaker, Milwaukee; appointed Apr. 6, '65; ENL July 18, '62; Corp., Sergt., 1st Sergt.; WIA Chancellorsville; commanded company beginning Apr. 20, '65; MO June 13, '65.

Second Lieutenants

Charles Ottilie; physician, West Bend; rank from Sept. 10, '62; trans. to 1st Asst. Surgeon, 9th Wis Inf., Oct. 5, '62 and later became surgeon of that regt.

Hermann Fürstenberg; farmer, Milwaukee; appointed Nov. 6, '62; ENL July 6, '62; promoted Sergt. Major, Sept. 17, '62; promoted 1st Lieut. Co. G, Feb. 1, '63.

Enlisted Men

Ahlers, Diedrich; sailor, Milwaukee; ENL Aug. 21, '62; company cook; pioneer; WIA in leg at Chancellorsville; detached to provost guard at Philadelphia, Pa., and on detached service at MO of regt.

Arnold, Isaac; miller, Milwaukee; ENL July 31, '62; trans. to 19th Wis. Inf., Sept. 20, '62.

Baer, Friedrich; farmer, Madison; ENL June 30, '62; company cook; WIA in face at Gettysburg; rejoined regt. Aug. 31, '63; MO June 13, '65.

Bockmann, Otto; farmer, Racine; ENL Aug. 18, '62; Corp., Sergt., 1st Sergt.; muster out papers say "He has never been absent from his company since enlisted."; MO June 13, '65; founding member of Twenty-Sixth Regiment Association.

Boch (or Boclo), Hugo; druggist, Cedarburg; ENL Aug. 21, '62; medical dept.; disch. Feb. 1, '63, disability.

Boehmer, William; moulder, Milwaukee; ENL Mar. 28, '64; WIA June 22, '64; trans. to Co. D, 3rd Wis. Inf., June 10, '65.

Bolte, August; carpenter, Milwaukee; ENL Aug. 15, '62; WIA in right foot and CIA Gettysburg; paroled Mar. or Apr. '64; rejoined regt. June 15, '64; MO June 13, '65; member of Robert Chivas Post No. 2, G.A.R.

Carstanjen, Hugo; chemist, Milwaukee; ENL July 27, '62; Sergt.; absent sick Jan. 22 to Feb. 2, '63; promoted Sergt. Major, Mar. 15, '63; KIA Chancellorsville, May 2, '63.

Chalaupka, George; carpenter, Racine; ENL Aug. 21, '62; Corp.; KIA July 1, '63, Gettysburg, Pa.

Daehme (or Daehmer), Christian; farmer, Milwaukee; ENL Aug. 12, '62; disch. Sept. 20, '62.

Deis, Balthasar; shoemaker, Racine; ENL Dec. 23, '63; absent sick Oct. 9, '64; trans. to Co. D, 3rd Wis. Inf., June 10, '65.

Dronkers, Dingenius; farmer, Franklin; ENL June 11, '62; KIA July 1, '63, Gettysburg, Pa.

Dross, Louis; blacksmith, Racine; ENL Aug. 21, '62; KIA May 2, '63, Chancellorsville, Va.

Farber, Peter; farmer, Franklin; ENL Aug. 2, '62; absent sick Dec. 4, '62; trans. to VRC, Nov. 15, '63; lived in Waukesha after war; member of Twenty-Sixth Regiment Association.

Francksen, William; farmer, Milwaukee; June 5, '62; Corp., Sergt.; WIA Gettysburg; absent wounded at MO of regt.

Fuehling, Adam; wagonmaker, Ottowa; ENL Aug. 19, '62; WIA and CIA Chancellorsville; deserted May 17, '63.

Gerhaeuser, John L.; laborer, Racine; ENL Aug. 19, '62; WIA Gettysburg and right arm amputated; disch. with pension due to wounds July 27, '64.

Gleichmann, Georg; carpenter, Ottowa; ENL Aug. 19, 62; absent sick Sept. 21, '63 to Jan. 18, '64; MO June 13, '65.

Gregg, Martin; farmer, Madison; ENL June 27, '62; trans. to 19th Wis. Inf., Sept.

20, '62.

Gross, Joseph; saddler, Milwaukee; ENL July 25, '62; Corp.; KIA May 2, '63, Chancellorsville, Va.

Hardrath, Friedrich; farmer, Racine; ENL Aug. 20, '62; disch. Sept. 21' 62.

Heck, Peter; farmer, Racine; ENL Aug. 21, '62; company cook; muster out papers say "He has been present since the organization of the company."; MO June 13, '65.

Held, John; cooper, Racine; ENL Aug. 19, 62; Corp.; absent sick Oct. 28, '63 to June 5, '64; KIA July 20, '64, Peach Tree Creek, Ga.

Hess, Lewis; farmer, Caledonia; ENL Aug. 20, '62; WIA Gettysburg, July 1, '63; trans. to VRC, Nov. 13, '63; MO July 29, '65.

Hilger, Joseph; miller, Racine; ENL Aug. 20, '62; WIA in leg at Gettysburg; rejoined regt. Sept. 2, '64; MO June 13, '65.

Hoffarth, Peter; laborer, Milwaukee; ENL Aug. 12, '62; deserted at Milwaukee Oct. 5, '62; arrested in Chicago Nov. 11, '64 and joined regt. Apr. 9, '65; trans. to Co. D, 3rd Wis. Inf., June 10, '65.

Hoffranz, Peter; farmer, Ozaukee; ENL Aug. 21, '62; DOD in field hospital at Stafford Court House, Va., Feb. 1, '63.

Horter, Conrad; shoemaker, Racine; ENL Dec. 7, '63; trans. to Co. D, 3rd Wis. Inf., June 10, '65.

Huntz, Michael; laborer, Racine; ENL Aug. 20, '62; Corp., Sergt.; WIA Peach Tree Creek July 20, '64; rejoined regt. Apr. 19, '65; never absent until wounded; MO June 13, '65; returned to Racine after war; member of Twenty-Sixth Regiment Association.

Jentz, Friedrich; farmer, Milwaukee; Aug. 21, '62; musician (drummer); muster out papers say "He has never been absent from his company since its organization."; MO June 13, '65; owned barber shop after war; member of Robert Chivas Post No. 2, G.A.R.

Jonson, Friedrich; laborer, Milwaukee; ENL June 4, '62; Sergt.; severely WIA in head at Gettysburg; rejoined regt. Aug. 31, '63; trans. to 16th Illinois Infantry, Oct. 8, '63; member of Twenty-Sixth Regiment Association.

Kehrein, Eduard; laborer, Milwaukee; ENL Aug. 19, '62; company cook; WIA in leg at Gettysburg; rejoined regt. Nov. 30, '63; WIA in finger on left hand at Resaca, May 15, '64; rejoined regt. Aug. 20, '64; MO June 13, '65.

Klein, Heinrich; merchant, Milwaukee; ENL Aug. 20, '62; company cook; muster out papers say "He has never been absent from the company since its organization."; MO June 13, '65.

Klein, Jacob; farmer, Milwaukee; ENL Aug. 12, '62; deserted at Milwaukee Oct. 5, '62 and "said to be in Minnesota."

Kleinschmidt, John; carpenter, Racine; ENL Dec. 7, '63; WIA June '64; trans. to Co. D, 3rd Wis. inf., June 10, '65.

Klinke, Julius; weaver, Milwaukee; ENL Aug. 21, '62; Sergt.; reduced to ranks and trans. to Co. A, Sept. 22, '62.

Koerner, Carl; farmer, Mt. Pleasant; ENL Feb. 29, '64; WIA Bentonville, Mar. 19, '65; DOW Apr. 24 or 27, '65.

Kohn, Ludwig; brewer, Racine; ENL Aug. 18, '62; severely WIA by conoidal musket ball entering right scapula and lodging in thoracic cavity at Gettysburg; removed to Satterlee Hospital in Philadelphia July 9, '63; trans. to VRC, Mar. 15, '64; discharged June 9, '64; suffered from pain making it hard to sleep and could not lie flat; returned to Racine after war; member of Twenty-Sixth Regiment Association.

Korte, Heinrich; farmer, Madison; ENL Aug. 12, '62; severely WIA in breast and finger shot off at Gettysburg; trans. to VRC, Mar. 15, '65.

Kraemer, William; farmer, Watertown; ENL Aug. 14, '62; WIA Peach Tree Creek July 20, '64; rejoined regt. May 19, '65; MO June 13, '65.

Kretschmar, Friedrich; tailor, Milwaukee; ENL July 1, '62; muster out papers say "He has never been absent from the company since its organization."; MO June 13, '65.

Kropf, Franz; farmer, Madison; ENL Aug. 13, '62; CIA Chancellorsville; rejoined regt. Oct. 17, '63; absent sick since Apr. 5, '65; MO June 30, '65.

Krueger, Charles [Karl]; farmer, Milwaukee; ENL Aug. 21, '62; WIA Gettysburg; absent sick July 20, '64 to Feb. 12, '65; MO June 13, '65; founding member of Twenty-Sixth Regiment Association.

Kuder, Theodore; teacher, Milwaukee; Aug. 7, '62; detached to topographical corps; provost marshals' clerk; Corp.; muster out papers say "never absent"; MO June 13, '65.

Kutler, Friedrich; baker, Racine; Aug. 18, '62; WIA in right hip by minie ball and CIA at Chancellorsville; paroled fifteen days later and sent to hospital at Stafford Court House, Va., then to Harvey Hospital in Washington, D.C., then to Convalescent Camp in Alexandria, Va.; trans. to VRC, Mar. 10, '64; guarded rebel prisoners and participated in repulse of Jubal Earlys' raid in 1864 where he suffered from sunstroke; was on guard duty at Long Bridge in the District of Columbia when the 26th Wisconsin marched by enroute to the Grand Review in May, 1865; MO June 29, '65; settled as a baker in Appleton, Wisc. in 1869., member of G.A.R. Post 133.

Kwabil, Frank J.; manufacturer, Racine; ENL Aug. 19, '62 WIA Chancellorsville May 2, '63; trans. to VRC, Mar. 31, '64, MO June 26, '65.

Labonde, Peter; farmer, Milwaukee; ENL June 27, '62; trans. to Co. A, Dec. 2, '62.

Lacker, Lorenz; merchant, Milwaukee; ENL Aug. 7, '62; teamster; detached to topographical corps; absent sick beginning July 6, '64; MO Aug. 29, '65.

Lorsch, Peter; teamster, Racine; Aug. 19, '62; brigade quartermaster dept; severely WIA by three gunshots at Chancellorsville; absent wounded at MO of regt.; member of Robert Chivas Post No. 2, G.A.R.; attended fiftieth anniversary at Gettysburg in 1913

Marx, Wilhelm; farmer, Milwaukee; ENL June 16, '62; Corp.; CIA Thompsons' Cr. near Sneedsville, N.C., Mar. 5, '65; paroled Apr. '65; MO May 24, '65.

Menger, Georg; shoemaker, Racine; ENL Aug. 18, '62; CIA Gettysburg; absent prisoner at MO of regt.

Meyer, Samuel; tradesman, Racine; ENL Aug. 18, '62; quartermaster department Oct. '62; promoted Commissary Sergt., Dec.10, '62.

Meyers, John; pilecutter Milwaukee; ENL Aug. 15, '62; company cook; WIA June 22, '64, Dallas, Ga.; disch. due to wounds May 27, '65; founding member of Twenty-Sixth Regiment Association.

Milke, Wilhelm; farmer, Saukville; ENL Aug. 21, '62; member of color guard; WIA July 20, '64, Peach Tree Creek; DOW at 3rd Div. hospital, Nashville, Tenn., Aug. 7, '64.

Monreau, Joseph; butcher, Watertown; ENL Aug. 21, '62; musician; absent Apr. 27 to May 17, '65; MO June 13, '65.

Moulton, Harvey; farmer, Madison; ENL July 2, '62; trans. to 19th Wis. Inf., Sept. 20, '62.

Mower, John; farmer, Wauwatosa; ENL June 12, '62; Corp.; severely WIA by three gunshots at Chancellorsville; trans. to VRC, Nov. 13, '63; disch. at Philadelphia, Pa., June 15, '65, disability.

Muecklich, Otto ; cabinetmaker, Burlington; ENL Aug. 20, '62; company cook; MO June 13, '65. Muster out papers say "He has been present since the organization of the company."

Mueller, John W.; cooper, Milwaukee; ENL Aug. 19, '62; disch. Sept. 22, '62.

Muehlheisen, Wilhelm; bookbinder, Racine; ENL Aug. 20, '62; Corp.; WIA June 15, '64, New Hope Church, Ga.; rejoined regt. July 25, '64; CIA Thompsons' Cr. near Sneedsville, N.C., Mar. 5, '65; paroled Apr. '65; absent at MO of regt.

Nieland, Joseph; farmer, Watertown; ENL June 8, '62; absent sick Feb. 11 to Aug. 12, '64; sent sick Oct. 12, '64 to General Hospital at Prairie du Chein, Wisc., and there MO June 30, '65.

Nittel, William; bookbinder, Madison; ENL Aug. 15, '62; deserted at Milwaukee Oct. 5, '62; rejoined regt. at Catletts' Station, Va., July 31, '63; Corp.; WIA Averasboro, N.C.; MO June 13, '65.

Oertel, Georg; weaver, Milwaukee; ENL June 18, '62; Corp.; hospital nurse; disch. June 16, '63, disability.

Peisen, Bartholomew; shoemaker, Racine; ENL Aug. 21, '62; Corp.; recruiting duty Jan. 1-Feb. 27, '64; WIA Peach Tree Creek July 20, '64; third finger of left hand amputated; disch. at Chattanooga, Tenn., May 22, '65; returned to Racine after war; member of Twenty-Sixth Regiment Association; later moved to Cedar Falls, Iowa in fall of 1865 and to Eldora, Iowa, in 1868; died Feb. 2, 1915.

Pfau, Andreas; laborer, Racine; ENL Aug. 18, '62; KIA July 1, '63 Gettysburg, Pa.

Rasmussen, Niels; farmer, Mt. Pleasant; Aug. 18, '62; WIA Chancellorsville; trans. to VRC, Nov. 13, '63; MO July 19, '65.

Rasmussen, Peter; farmer, Mt. Pleasant; ENL Aug. 18, '62; absent sick beginning Dec. 4, '62; absent sick at MO of regt.

Reith, Joseph; shoemaker, Mt. Pleasant, ENL Jan. 25, '64; brigade forager; trans. to Co. D, 3rd Wis, Inf., June 10, '65.

Rippchen, Heinrich; cooper, New Berlin; ENL Mar. 31, '64; trans. to Co. D, 3rd Wis, Inf., June 10, '65.

Rosenthal, Henry; harnessmaker, Racine; ENL Aug. 20, '62; WIA Gettysburg; rejoined regt. Dec. 25, '63; absent sick since Mar. 5, '65; absent sick at MO of regt.

Schaefer, August; shoemaker, Milwaukee; ENL Aug. 15, '62; Sergt.; absent sick Dec. 4, '62; reduced to ranks Mar. 15, '63; trans. to VRC, Sept 1, '63; member of Robert Chivas Post No. 2, G.A.R.; member of Twenty-Sixth Regiment Association.

Schaefer, John; farmer, Caledonia; ENL Aug. 21, '62; Corp.; WIA June 22, '64, Kennesaw Mountain, Ga.; MO June 13, '65.

Scherer, Joseph B.; farmer, Madison; ENL June 27, '62; trans. to 19th Wis. Inf., Sept. 20, '62.

Schelp, Heinrich; farmer, Racine; ENL Aug. 20, '62; CIA Gettysburg and imprisoned at Belle Isle, Richmond, Va.; paroled Mar. or Apr. '64; rejoined regt. July 1, '64; MO June 13, '65.

Schlie, Carl; shoemaker, Milwaukee; ENL Aug. 21, 62; Corp. Sergt.; absent sick June 15 to Sept. 7, '64; MO June 13, '65; founding member of Twenty-Sixth Regiment Association.

Schneeberger, Jacob; baker, Racine; ENL Aug. 18, '62; pioneer; WIA June 22, '64, Kennesaw Mountain, Ga.; rejoined regt. Apr. 20, '65; MO June 13, '65; returned to Racine after war; founding member of Twenty-Sixth Regiment Association; attended fiftieth anniversary at Gettysburg in 1913.

Schneider, Adam [or John Adam]; moulder, Racine; ENL Aug. 21, '62; Corp.; muster out papers say "He has been with his company since its organization."; MO June 13, '65; suffered from rheumatism after war; worked as skilled moulder for J. I Case T. M. Co.; elected sheriff in 1886 with support of labor and Democratic Party; member G.A.R. Post No. 17; member of Masonic Order.

Schwartz, Heinrich; carpenter, Milwaukee; ENL Aug. 15, '62; WIA May 2, '63, Chancellorsville, Va.; DOW May 9, '63.

Seidemann, Friedrich; farmer, Milwaukee; ENL Aug. 21, '62; absent sick beginning Oct. 17, '63; DOD Oct. 4, '63, Nashville, Tenn.

Slemmer, Georg; butcher, Milwaukee; ENL Aug. 3, '62; deserted at Milwaukee Oct. 5, '62 and "said to be in Minnesota."

Smertczek (or Smerchak) [Smrcek], Frank; farmer, Caledonia; ENL Aug. 18, '62; Corp.; WIA in right leg May 15, '64, Resaca; disch. March 27, '65, disability.

Smertczek (or Smerchak) [Smrcek], Joseph; farmer, Caledonia; ENL Aug. 18, '62; absent sick beginning July 20, '64; MO June 30, '65.

Sohns, Charles; farmer, Milwaukee; ENL Aug. 31, '62; WIA Kennesaw Mountain, Ga., June 22, '64; DOW June 25, '64.

Spaar, Andreas; shoemaker, Mt. Pleasant; ENL Jan. 25, '64; absent sick beginning Oct. 7, '64; trans. to Co. D, 3rd Wis. Inf. June 10, '65.

Stopples, François; farmer, Franklin; ENL June 23, '62; hospital nurse; KIA July 1, '63, Gettysburg, Pa.

Struss, August; cooper, Milwaukee; ENL Aug. 15, '62; disch. at Philadelphia, Pa., Dec. 2, '63, disability; member of Robert Chivas Post No. 2, G.A.R.

Thiele, Friedrich; laborer, Caledonia; ENL Aug. 20, '62; WIA May 2, '63, Chancellorsville, Va.; DOW May 9, '63.

Tondorf, Nicolaus; cooper, Racine; ENL Aug. 18, '62; absent sick Feb. 11 to

Dec. 18, '63; MO June 13, '65.

Van Hag, Wilhelm; laborer, Racine; ENL Aug. 21, '62; brigade forager; absent sick May 27 to Sept. 7, '64; MO June 13, '65.

Vette, William; editor, Milwaukee; ENL Aug. 14, '62; promoted Chaplain, Nov. 6, '62.

Wade (or Wait), William; farmer, Milwaukee; ENL June 11, '62; trans. to 19th Wis. Inf., Sept. 20, '62.

Waldschmidt, Heinrich; blacksmith, Milwaukee; ENL Aug. 15, '62; disch. Oct. 5, '62.

Warver, Franz Joseph; shoemaker, Racine; ENL Aug. 16, '62; Corp., Sergt.; WIA July 23, '64, Atlanta; left arm amputated; DOW at Nashville, Tenn., Oct. 14, '64.

Weber, Jacob; carpenter, Milwaukee; ENL June 26, '62; KIA July 20, '64, Peach Tree Creek, Ga.

Wemmert, John; farmer, Caledonia; ENL Aug. 21, '62; hospital nurse; MO June 13, '65; muster out papers say: "He was present with the company since its organization."; attended fiftieth anniversary at Gettysburg in 1913.

Wergin, Bernhard; blacksmith, Milwaukee; ENL June 4, '62; WIA Gettysburg; trans. to VRC, Feb. 10, '64.

Westhoff, August; watchmaker, Milwaukee; ENL Aug. 15, '62; WIA in arm at Gettysburg; rejoined regt. Aug. 31, '63; KIA June 22, '64, near Kennesaw, Mountain, Ga.

Wildhagen, John; cabinetmaker, Madison; ENL June 7, '62; temporary ambulance guard; WIA and CIA at Gettysburg July 1, '63; DOW in parole camp at Annapolis, Md., Sept. 3, '63.

Wiskow, Charles; shoemaker, Milwaukee; ENL Aug. 15, '62; company cook; detached to topographical dept., 3rd division, XI Corps; MO June 13, '65. Muster out papers say: "He has been present with the company since its organization."

Wollmer, Nicholas; farmer, Greenfield; ENL Aug. 20, '62; adjutants' clerk; promoted Sergt. Major, July 20, '63.

Zbitowsky, Joseph; farmer, Caledonia; ENL Aug. 21, '62; WIA in leg at Gettysburg July 1, '63; DOW (tetanus) in hospital in New York Harbor Sept. 3, '63.

COMPANY E, FOND DU LAC TURNERS

Captains

Anton Kettler (or Kittlar); gardener, Fond du Lac; rank from Sept. 3, '62; resigned Mar. 8, '63; returned to Fond du Lac, and later settled in Byron.

Charles W. Neukirch; accountant, Fond du Lac; appointed Mar. 15, '63; 1st Lieut., Sept. 3, '62; WIA May 2, '63, Chancellorsville, Va.; DOW in Seminary Hospital, Georgetown, D.C, May 12, '63.

Peter Fernekes; tinsmith, Milwaukee; appointed June 1, '63 from 2nd lieut., Co. I; 1st Lieut., Mar. 15, '63; resigned Apr. 19, '64.

William Steinmeyer; gunsmith, Milwaukee; appointed May 3, '64 from 2nd Lieut., Co. B; 1st Lieut. Nov. 17, '63; WIA in right shoulder July 20, '64, Peach Tree Creek; MO June 13, '65; became retail grocer in Milwaukee; owner of William Steinmeyer Co. which closed in 1949; founding member and first treasurer of Twenty-Sixth Regiment Association; member of the Military Order of the Loyal Legion of the United States; commander of Robert Chivas Post No. 2, G.A.R., in 1885 and 1886; died in Milwaukee May 10, 1892.

First Lieutenants

Henry Greve, Manitowoc, appointed June 1, '63 from 2nd Lt., Co. K; resigned Sept. 8, '63.

Casper Buechner, mechanic, Fond du Lac; appointed May 3, '64; ENL Aug. 15, '62; Sergt., 1st Sergt.; WIA Gettysburg; rejoined regt. Dec. 12, '63; promoted Capt. Co. K Feb. 11, '65.

Joesph Arnold; butcher, Fond du Lac; appointed Feb. 11, '65; ENL Aug 15, '62; Sergt., 1st Sergt.; CIA Gettysburg; paroled and exchanged Mar. 7, '64; MO June 13, '65.

Second Lieutenants

John F. Hagen; carpenter, Fond du Lac; rank from Sept. 3, '62; resigned Feb. 12, '63.Anton Vogt; tailor, Fond du Lac; appointed Mar. 15, '63; ENL Aug. 15, '62; 1st Sergt; resigned Aug. 5, '63; returned to Fond du Lac and became proprietor of beer hall.

Enlisted Men

Altmann, Alois; butcher, Fond du Lac; ENL Aug. 19, '62; CIA Gettysburg; paroled Mar. '65; rejoined regt. Apr. 22, '65; left sick Apr. 23, '65; MO May 24, '65.

Arndt, Karl; blacksmith, Fond du Lac; ENL Aug. 15, '62; WIA Gettysburg; trans. to VRC, Mar. 2, '64; MO June 26, '65.

Behling, Carl; laborer, Franklin; ENL Aug. 18, '62; WIA by gunshot through upper lobe of left lung July 1, '63, Gettysburg; treated in XI Corps hospital until July 10 when transferred to Jarvis Hospital in Baltimore; suffered profuse hemorrhaging and DOW Aug. 8, '63.

Behling, Friedrich; laborer, Franklin; ENL Aug. 18, '62; left sick Oct. 26, '63; rejoined regt. May 22, '63; MO June 13, '65.

Beumel, Carl; brewer, Fond du Lac; ENL Aug. 21, '62; company cook; WIA Chancellorsville; listed as deserted before going into battle July 1, '63; pardoned by

War Dept. Special Order No. 315, Sept. 22, '64; returned and rejoined regt. Dec. 22, '63; listed as "at present under arrest or confinement at Div. [headquarters] 11 Corps" in Lookout Valley, Tenn.; returned from confinement Oct. 16, '64; MO June 13, '65.

Boege, Rudolph; barber, Fond du Lac; ENL Aug. 15, '62; musician; detailed briefly as nurse, Oct. 28, '64; disch. at Bridgeport, Ala., May 2, '64, disability.

Braun, John; laborer, Fond du Lac; ENL Aug. 15, '62; Corp., Sergt.; WIA Chancellorsville May 2, '63; WIA and CIA Gettysburg; paroled and exchanged Mar. 7, '64; MO June 13, '65.

Braun, Xaver; laborer, Fond du Lac; ENL Aug. 15, '62; musician; WIA in hand at Gettysburg; rejoined regt. Nov. '63; KIA July 20, '64, Peach Tree Creek, Ga.

Burg, Lorenz; farmer, Fond du Lac; ENL Aug. 13, '62; KIA May 2, '63 Chancellorsville, Va.

Burggraff, William; cooper, Fond du Lac; ENL Feb. 22, '64; WIA May 8, '64; rejoined regt. Apr. 9, '65; trans. to Co. E, 3rd Wis. Inf. June 10, '65.

Czarnecki, Walenti; farmer, Fond du Lac; ENL Aug. 18, '62; generally listed as deserted before going into battle July 1, '63, but final report on casualties says "supposed killed or deserted."

Deifel, William; mason, Milwaukee; ENL Aug. 20, '62; detached briefly to Pioneer Corps June 1-4, '63; detached to Co. I, 1st Bn., Invalid Corps at Albany Barracks, Albany, N.Y., Aug. 26, '63; trans. to VRC, Sept. 25, '63; company Morning Reports indicate trans. to Invalid Corps Oct. 17, '63; MO June 20, '65.

Diener, Henry; mechanic, Fond du Lac; ENL Aug. 15, '62; Corp.; WIA May 25, '64; DOD (chronic diarrhoea) at Mound City, Ill., Oct. 1, '64.

Dreblob, Eduard; farmer, Madison; ENL Feb. 4, '64; company cook; WIA Peach Tree Creek; trans. to Co. E, 3rd Wis. Inf., June 10, '65.

Eichmeier, Adolph; miller, Fond du Lac; ENL Aug. 15, '62; Corp.; CIA Gettysburg; DOD in Confederate prison at Richmond, Va., Dec. 9, '63.

Ewens, Anton C.; cooper, Milwaukee; ENL Aug. 16, '62; WIA in upper right thigh and CIA at Chancellorsville; paroled May 15, '63 and sent to Douglas Hospital in Washington, DC; rejoined regt. in mid-Sept. '63; WIA in left foot by shell near Lookout Mountain, Oct. 28, 1863; operation to remove portion of bone in foot due to gangrene, Nov. 16, 1863; disch. at Madison, Wisc., due to wounds Oct. 28, '64; member Twenty-Sixth Regiment Association; postal letter carrier after war; became mail carrier, superintendent of the Twelfth Street branch office, and later a real estate dealer in Milwaukee; member of Wolcott Post No. 1, G.A.R.; died May 17, 1916.

Fischer, William; blacksmith, Fond du Lac; ENL Aug. 15, '62; slightly WIA at Chancellorsville; trans. to VRC, Jan. 8, '64.

Flamig, Henry; farmer, Fond du Lac; ENL Aug. 15, '62; WIA in hip at Chancellorsville; trans. to VRC, Oct. 12, '63.

Fuchs, Moritz; merchant, Fond du Lac; ENL Aug. 15, '62; Corp.; KIA May 2, '63, Chancellorsville, Va.

Fuhrmann, John; farmer, Princeton; ENL Jan. 4, '64; injured while building breastworks at Peach Tree Creek, Ga.; trans. to Co. E, 3rd Wis. Inf., June 10, '65; MO

July 18, '65; after war moved to Westfield, Wisc.; married and had ten children; died April 4, 1919.

Gaubatz, Reinhardt; wagonmaker, Fond du Lac; ENL Aug. 20, '62; teamster with ammunition wagon and later quartermaster; detached to Gen. Schurzs' headquarters April 16, '63 to Apr. 19, '64; WIA Resaca May 15, '64; disch. at Madison, Wisc., due to wounds Oct. 28, '64.

Gelhar, Gottfried; farmer, Princeton; ENL Jan. 27, '64; trans. to Co. E., 3rd Wis. Inf., June 10, '65.

Glatzel, P. Paul; laborer, Fond du Lac; ENL Aug. 15, '62; WIA in leg May 25, '64; disch. at Camp Randall, Wisc., due to wounds Sept. 22, '65.

Gross, Johann Ludwig; farmer, Milwaukee; ENL Aug. 15, '62; pioneer; WIA Gettysburg; rejoined regt. Feb. '64; MO June 13, '65; lived in New Berlin after war; member of Twenty-Sixth Regiment Association.

Gross, Friedrich Wilhelm; farmer, Milwaukee; ENL Jan. 15, '64; WIA June 22, '64; rejoined regt. Sept. 17, '64; MO June 13, '65.

Gruhlke, Johann; farmer, Princeton; ENL Jan. 18, '64; KIA Mar. 16, '65, Averasboro, N.C.

Haertley, Mathias; wagonmaker, Fond du Lac; ENL Aug. 15, '62; WIA Gettysburg; corps escort; absent sick May 10, '64; rejoined regt. Feb. 10, '65; MO June 13, '65; lived in Mayville after war; member of Twenty-Sixth Regiment Association.

Hagemann, Christian; shoemaker, Fond du Lac; ENL Aug. 19, '62; Corp. Sergt; MO June 13, '65.

Hammang, Paul; farmer, Fond du Lac; ENL Aug. 15, '62; DOD at Stafford Court House, Va., Jan. 28, '63.

Hansen, Friedrich; farmer, Eden; ENL Aug. 21, '62; WIA Chancellorsville; rejoined regt. Dec. '63; absent sick since Apr. 12, '65; MO July 13, '65.

Herrmann, Charles; cabinetmaker, Waupun; ENL Aug. 15, '62; Corp., Sergt.; recruiting duty Jan. 1-Feb. 27, '64; WIA June 15, '64; disch. at Madison, Wisc., due to wounds Feb. 3, '65.

Herzog, Heinrich; laborer, Fond du Lac; ENL Aug. 20, '62; disch. at Milwaukee Dec. 6, '62, disability.

Hilgert, Jacob; shoemaker, Fond du Lac; ENL Aug. 15, '62; disch. at Stafford Court House, Va., Mar. 29, '63, disability.

Hubatzschek, Robert; cigarmaker, Fond du Lac; ENL Aug. 15, '62; company clerk; left sick Sept. 24, '63; trans. to VRC, Jan. 15, '64; returned to Fond du Lac after war; member of Twenty-Sixth Regiment Association.

Jahnke, Friedrich W.; farmer, Milwaukee; ENL Aug. 18, '62; MO June 13, '65; lived in Appleton after war; member of Twenty-Sixth Regiment Association.

Jenner, Nicholas; tailor, Fond du Lac; ENL Aug. 18, '62; Corp., Sergt.; WIA Gettysburg; WIA slightly in left leg at Resaca (company Morning Report says May 18, '64); MO June 13, '65.

Jenny, John; teamster, Kenosha; ENL Aug. 19, '62; teamster; CIA Gettysburg; DOD in Confederate prison at Richmond, Va., Jan. 28, '64.

Kefer, Ferdinand; butcher, Fond du Lac; ENL Aug. 15, '62; Corp.; WIA Chancellorsville; rejoined regt. Nov. '63; absent sick since July 4, '64 at MO of regt.

Kiefer, Nicholas; farmer, Fond du Lac; ENL Aug. 15, '62; CIA Chancellorsville, May 2, '63; disch. July 18, '64.

Klein, Jacob; farmer, Friendship; ENL Aug. 21, '62; MIA May 2, '63 Chancellorsville and presumed dead. Muster out papers say "Probably killed on the skirmish line."

Knein, François; wagonmaker, Empire; ENL Aug. 20, '62; Corp.; color bearer; WIA and CIA at Dallas, Ga., May 25, '64 (company Morning Report says May 28); DOD (diarrhea) in Confederate at Andersonville, Ga., prison Oct. 8, '64 and buried in grave 10536.

Knolle, Albin; wagonmaker, Fond du Lac; ENL Aug. 15, '62; Corp; WIA by shell near Lookout Mountain, Oct. 28, '63; (one source says Nov. 5, '63) trans. to VRC, Jan. 10, '65; returned to Fond du Lac after war; member of Twenty-Sixth Regiment Association.

Kraus, George; wagonmaker, Fond du Lac; ENL Aug. 15, '62; WIA Chancellorsville and placed in Invalid Detachment, Lincoln Hospital, Washington, D.C.; WIA in head at Burnt Hickory near Dallas, Ga., May 25, '64; DOW in hospital on May 26, '64 (company Morning Report says WIA May 27 and DOW May 29).

Krause, Reinhold; laborer, Fond du Lac, ENL Aug. 15, '62; KIA while on skirmish line May 27 or 29, '64 at Burnt Hickory near Dallas, Ga.

Krause, William A. E.; farmer, Byron; ENL Aug. 18, '62; left sick June 18, '64; rejoined regt. May 20, '65; MO June 13, '65.

Krueger, August; laborer, Fond du Lac; ENL Aug. 20, '62; deserted on march from Dumfries to Stafford Court House, Va., Dec. 15, '62.

Krueger, Carl; tradesman, Milwaukee; ENL Aug. 19, ' 62; Corp., Sergt.; color corp. at Chancellorsville; WIA in leg early on July 1, '63 at Gettysburg and left on field three days before wound attended; returned to regt. Nov. '63; reduced to ranks by order of Lt. Col. Winkler, Oct. 15, '64; MO June 13, '65.

Krull, Fritz; laborer, Wauwatosa; ENL Aug. 15, '62; taken sick and missing on march from Berea Church to Stafford Court House, Va., Feb. 5, '63 and presumed to have DOD.

Kuehn, August; Madison; ENL Feb. 4, '64; WIA in right arm and left hand May 15, '64, Resaca, Ga.; DOW in hospital at Resaca, Ga., June 19, '64.

Kunert, Carl; laborer, Princeton; ENL Jan. 23, '64; trans. to Co. E, 3rd Wis. Inf., June 10, '65.

Lange, Wilhelm; laborer, Princeton; ENL Jan. 13, '64; WIA July 5, '64; trans. to Co. E, 3rd Wis. Inf., June 10, '65.

Lankow, Friederich; tailor, Fond du Lac; ENL Aug. 15, '62; WIA and CIA at Chancellorsville; WIA in leg May 25, '64; DOW at Chattanooga, Tenn., June 4, '64 (final report of casualties says DOW June 7, '64).

Lechelt, Johann; farmer, Princeton; ENL Jan. 27, '64; trans. to Co. E, 3rd Wis. Inf., June 10, '65.

Leisgang, George; farmer, Granville; ENL Aug. 21, '62; provost guard; detached as hospital nurse, Apr. 25, '64; Corp.; MO June 13, '65; returned to Granville after war; member of Twenty-Sixth Regiment Association.

Lindemuth, Herman; wagonmaker, Fond du Lac; Aug. 19, '62; Corp.; WIA Mar. 16, '65, Averasboro, N.C.; DOW in field hospital Mar. 17, '65.

Luedtke, August; farmer, Fond du Lac; ENL Aug. 21, '62; company cook; WIA Chancellorsville; MO June 13, '65; attended fiftieth anniversary at Gettysburg in 1913.

Meier, Heinrich; laborer, Fond du Lac; ENL Aug. 20, '62; KIA July 1, '63, Gettysburg, Pa.

Meyers, Charles J.; merchant, Fond du Lac; ENL Aug. 15, '62; Sergt.; regimental adjutants' clerk; detached to special duty at brigade headquarters, June 12 to July 27 '63; MO June 13, '65; member of Robert Chivas Post No. 2, G.A.R.; founding member of Twenty-Sixth Regiment Association.

Oehlke, Franz; farmer, Madison; ENL Feb. 4, '64; WIA in arm and CIA at Dallas, Ga., May 25, '64; DOW in Confederate prison at Andersonville, Ga., Oct. 27, '64 and buried in grave 11545.

Ostertag, John; blacksmith, Fond du Lac; ENL Aug. 21, '62; slightly WIA Chancellorsville; sent to hospital Apr. 20, '64 and DOD at Chattanooga, Tenn., May 2, '64.

Pommerich, John; laborer, Fond du Lac; ENL Aug. 15, '62; WIA Gettysburg July 1, '63; rejoined regt. Nov. 2, '64; brigade forager under Gen. Sherman; MO June 13, '65.

Proechel, Samuel; blacksmith, Princeton; ENL Jan. 27, '64; WIA in left shoulder May 25, '64; rejoined regt. Sept. '64; trans. to Co. E, 3rd Wis. Inf., June 10, '65.

Reichardt, John; tailor, Fond du Lac; ENL Aug. 15, '62; Sergt.; disch. at Washington, D.C., Mar. 25, '63, disability.

Reinecke, Friedrich; butcher, Milwaukee; ENL Aug. 14, '62; left sick May 1, '64; trans. to VRC, Dec. 31, '64; MO June 29, '65.

Rietz, Ernst Leo; farmer, New Holstein; ENL Aug. 20, '62; Corp.; company cook; CIA Chancellorsville, May 2, '63; MO June 13, '65.

Romag, Heinrich; farmer, Fond du Lac; ENL Aug. 15, '62; company cook; cook to regimental medical dept., Aug. 19 to Aug. 24, '63; KIA June 22, '64 at Kennesaw Mountain, Ga.

Rosenthal, William; farmer, Fond du Lac; ENL Aug. 15, '62; WIA in abdomen at Chancellorsville; WIA June 22, '64; disch. at Madison, Wisc., due to wounds May 13, '65.

Rossmann, Hans; laborer, Fond du Lac; ENL Aug. 18, '62; disch. at Stafford Court House, Va., Mar. 24, '63, general disability and old age.

Ruebsaamen, Carl; farmer, Fond du Lac; ENL Aug. 21, '62; WIA Gettysburg July 1, '63; trans. to VRC, Jan. 13, '64; MO June 29, '65.

Rumpel, Christian; farmer, Waupun; ENL Aug. 15, '62; provost guard; CIA Gettysburg; paroled and exchanged Mar. 7, '64, then absent sick; trans. to VRC, Apr. 13, '65; MO Sept. 16, '65.

Ruppelt, Oswald; farmer, Princeton; ENL Jan. 14, '64; trans. to Co. E, 3rd Wis. Inf., June 10, '65.

Saack, Friedrich Wilhelm; carpenter, Marshfield; ENL Feb. 27, '64; provost guard; left sick Feb. 26, '65; trans. to Co E, 3rd Wis. Inf., June 10, '65.

Schaefer, Charles; farmer, Empire; ENL Aug. 21, '62; company cook; WIA in right hand May 15, '64 at Resaca; rejoined regt. Apr. 23, '65; MO June 13, '65.

Schlensted, Hermann; cooper, Wauwatosa; ENL Aug. 13, '62; company cook; KIA July 1, '63, Gettysburg, Pa.

Schmidt, Carl; laborer, Fond du Lac; ENL Aug. 20, '62; Corp.; MO June 13, '65.

Schmidt, William; farmer, Fond du Lac; ENL Aug. 15, '62; company cook; teamster; MO June 13, '65.

Schmitz, Joseph; farmer, Fond du Lac; ENL Aug. 21, '62; disch. at Washington, D.C., Mar. 11, '63, disability.

Schneider, Magnus; farmer, Fond du Lac; ENL Aug. 15, '62; Corp.; WIA and CIA at Dallas, Ga., May 25, '64 (company Morning Report says May 28); DOD (scorbutus) in Confederate prison at Andersonville, Ga., Sept. 24' 64 and buried in grave 9693.

Schneider, Nicholas; farmer, Taychedah; ENL Aug. 15, '62; KIA June 22, '64 at Kennesaw Mtn. near Marietta, Ga.

Schnur, John; farmer, Fond du Lac; ENL Aug. 15, '62; deserted on the march from Dumfries to Stafford Court House, Va., about Dec. 15, '62.

Schueler, Fritz; farmer, Fond du Lac; ENL Aug. 21, '62; deserted from hospital in Chicago May 20, '63.

Schneller, John; farmer, Fond du Lac; ENL Aug. 15, '62; WIA Gettysburg; rejoined regt. Nov. '63; detached to corps headquarters Apr. 4, '64; MO June 13, '65.

Schwister, Mathias; farmer, Granville; ENL Aug. 21, '62; WIA by gunshot at Gettysburg July 1, '63; DOW in Corps Hospital July 5, '63; buried in Gettysburg National Cemetery, Wisconsin Plot, grave B-20.

Soll, Friedrich; cabinetmaker, Fond du Lac; ENL Aug. 15, '62; left sick July 1, '63; served as volunteer nurse in XI Corps Hospital at Gettysburg beginning July 4, '63; trans. to VRC, Jan. 15, '64; MO June 30, '65.

Sporer, John; tailor, Fond du Lac; ENL Aug. 15, '62; left sick Apr. 20, '64; rejoined regt. Apr. 19, '65; left sick May 11, '65; MO Aug. 14, '65.

Stange, William; tailor, Fond du Lac; ENL Aug. 15, '62; WIA in head at Chancellorsville; DOD (typhoid fever) Aug. 4, '63, Convalescent Camp, Va.

Stark, John; farmer, Menomonee; ENL Aug. 18, '62; WIA July 16, '64 (final report says July 19); trans. to VRC, Dec. 28, '64; MO July 5, '65 at Indianapolis, Ind..

Stauber, Joseph; carpenter, Fond du Lac; ENL Aug. 18, '62; detached to Pioneer Corps and returned on Aug. 1, '63; left sick Sept. 26, '63; DOD (chronic diarrhoea) Oct. 15, '63, in hospital in Alexandria, Va.

Stengel, August; farmer, Fond du Lac; ENL Aug. 21, '62; WIA Chancellorsville, May 2, '63; trans. to VRC, Oct. 12, '63; MO June 29, '65.

Stier, Charles; saddler, Fond du Lac; ENL Aug. 21, '62; Sergt; WIA in leg at Gettysburg; rejoined regt. Dec. '63; detached as brigade saddler, Nov. 11, '63 to Apr. 22, '64; detached to brigade headquarters, Apr. 29, '64; WIA in leg May 25, '64;

rejoined Apr. 1, '65; MO June 13, '65.

Strub, John; laborer, Fond du Lac; ENL Aug. 20, '64; MO June 13, '65.

Tempke, Fritz; laborer, Fond du Lac; ENL Aug. 19, '62; DOD (typhoid fever) at Nashville, Tenn., July 6, '64.

Thuerwaechter, Michael; tailor, Fond du Lac; ENL Aug. 15, '62; Corp.; KIA May 2, '63, Chancellorsville, Va.

Uerling, Franz; farmer, Lamartine; ENL Aug. 21, '62; sent sick to Douglas Hospital in Washington, then to a hospital in Chicago; deserted from hospital in Chicago May 20, '63.

Urban, John; carpenter, Princeton; Jan. 27, '64; WIA Peach Tree Creek; trans. to Co. E, 3rd Wis. Inf., June 10, '65.

Wagner, Heinrich; farmer, Granville; Aug. 18, '62; Corp.; slightly WIA Chancellorsville; rejoined regt. Feb. '64; WIA through shoulder May 25, '64; MO June 13, '65.

Walz, Michael; farmer, Granville; ENL Aug. 21, '62; provost guard; WIA Chancellorsville, May 2, '63, then in Invalid Detachment, Douglas Hospital, Washington, D.C.; detached to brigade headquarters, Mar. 20 to Apr. 28, '64; detached to Pioneer Corps Apr. 29, '64; MO June 13, '65.

Waskowitz, John; carpenter, Fond du Lac; ENL Aug. 15, '62; WIA Chancellorsville; trans. to VRC, Sept. 13, '63; MO June 29' 65.

Weiss, Christian; laborer, Milwaukee; ENL Aug. 14, '62; WIA Gettysburg July 1, '63; trans. to VRC, May 30, '64; MO July 3, '65.

Wildfang, Ernst; farmer, Fond du Lac; ENL Aug. 21, '62; company cook; detailed as nurse in 3rd Div., XX Corps hospital Apr. 9, '65 and later sick; MO May 24, '65.

Winkelmann, Christian; farmer, Fond du Lac; ENL Aug. 15, '63; Corp.; KIA May 2, '63, Chancellorsville, Va.

Witzel, Friedrich; farmer, Empire; ENL Aug. 21, '62; WIA Aug. 24, '64; WIA Mar. 16, '65; absent wounded at MO of regt.; lived in Manitowoc after war; member of Twenty-Sixth Regiment Association.

Woetzel, Charles; baker, Fond du Lac; ENL Aug. 15, '62; baker; MIA May 2, '63 Chancellorsville and presumed KIA.

Woller, Ferdinand; farmer, Fond du Lac; ENL Aug. 21, '62; detached to XI Corps Provost Guard April 11 to May 20, '63; WIA Gettysburg; rejoined regt. Aug. '63; WIA Aug. 14, '64; DOW at Nashville, Tenn., Aug. 16, '64 (final report on casualties says in field hospital).

Zapfe, August; laborer, Fond du Lac; ENL Aug. 15, '62; WIA twice in breast at Gettysburg; trans. to VRC Dec., 12, '63; MO July 10, '65.

Zech, Joseph Anton; carpenter, Fond du Lac; ENL Aug. 18, '62; disch. at Washington, D.C., June 3, '63, disability.

Zeihger, David; farmer, Milwaukee; ENL Mar. 18, '64; left sick July 3, '64; rejoined regt. Apr. 9, '65; trans. to Co. E, 3rd Wis. Inf., June 10, '65; member of Robert Chivas Post No. 2, G.A.R.

Zeihger, Gottlob; cooper, Milwaukee; ENL Aug. 18, '62; WIA and CIA

Gettysburg; WIA June 19, '64 (company Morning Report says July 16, '64); absent wounded at MO of regt.

Zipp, Philip; mechanic, Fond du Lac; ENL Aug. 15, '62; Sergt.; WIA May 25, '64; disch. due to wounds Oct. 20,' 64 at Madison, Wisc.; attended fiftieth anniversary at Gettysburg in 1913.

Zirbel, Friedrich; farmer, Janesville; ENL Aug. 21, '62; WIA in arm May 25, '64; MO May 26, '65.

COMPANY F, LAKE SHORE RIFLES

Captains

Henry Baetz; register of deeds, Manitowoc; rank from Sept. 9, '62; promoted Major, Mar. 15, '63.

Francis Lackner; lawyer, Milwaukee; appointed Mar. 15, '63, from 1st Lieut. Co. B; served as staff officer on Gen. Schurzs' staff; WIA at Gettysburg July 1, '63; promoted Major, June 27, '64.

Andrew J. Fullerton; farmer, West Bend; appointed Oct. 19, '64; from 1st Sergt., Co. G; 1st Lieut., June 8, '64; MO June 13, '65; lived in Young Hickory after war; member of Twenty-Sixth Regiment Association.

First Lieutenants

Charles Pizzala; soldier, Manitowoc; rank from Sept. 9, '62; promoted Capt. Co. G, Dec. 20, '62.

Bernhard Domschcke; editor, Milwaukee; appointed Nov. 14, '62 from Co. G; promoted Capt. Co H, Mar. 15, '63.

Otto Troemel; printer, Manitowoc; appointed Mar. 15, '63; ENL Aug. 21, '62; 1st Sergt.; 2nd Lieut., Feb. 1, '63; WIA Gettysburg; disch. Oct. 30, '63, disability.

Christian Phillip; farmer, Sauk City; appointed Oct. 30, '63 from 2nd. Lieut., Co. K; KIA May 15, '64, Resaca, Ga.

Second Lieutenants

Albert Wallber; clerk, Milwaukee; rank from Aug. 20, '62; promoted 1st Lieut. Co. I, Feb. 1, '63.

Adolph Cordier; merchant, Milwaukee; appointed Mar. 15, '63 from Sergt. Major; WIA in leg at Chancellorsville, 1st Lieut. Co. G, June 1, '63, but not mustered; disch. due to wounds Jan. 22, '64.

Karl Karsten; farmer, West Bend; appointed Apr. 13, '64; from 1st Sergt. Co. G; 1st Lieut., Oct. 19, '64, but not mustered; disch. Jan. 13, '65.

Enlisted Men

Arm (sometimes Aarm), William; farmer, Greenfield; ENL Feb. 23, '64; KIA July 20, '64, Peach Tree Creek, Ga.

Arndt, Gottfried; farmer, Centreville; ENL Aug. 21, '62; WIA Chancellorsville; disch. Feb. 5, '64, disability.

Benda, Franz; farmer, Manitowoc; ENL Aug. 21, '62; WIA in left hip and compound fracture of pelvis and femur at Gettysburg and treated in XI Corps hospital where the ball was extracted; transferred to Letterman Hospital at Gettysburg, Pa., Aug. 6 and DOW there Aug. 20, '63; buried in Gettysburg National Cemetery, Wisconsin Plot, grave C-19.

Boeling, Charles; broommaker, Milwaukee; ENL Aug. 16, '62; trans. to Co. K, Oct. 3, '62.

Boenig, Friedrich; farmer, Kossuth; ENL Aug. 21, '62; left sick Dec. 10, '63; trans. to VRC, July 1, '63.

Boettcher, Gottfried; laborer, Two Rivers; ENL Feb. 29, '64; trans. to Co. F, 3rd Wis. Inf., June 10, '65.

Bornemann, Conrad; tailor, Columbus; ENL Aug. 21, '62; Corp., Sergt.; WIA Gettysburg; rejoined regt. Dec. 19, '63; trans. to Invalid Corps, Mar. 1, '64; MO June 27, '65.

Braeutigam, Adam; tailor, Manitowoc; ENL Aug. 19, '62; Corp.; left sick Sept. 10, '62; trans. to Invalid Corps, Mar. 15, '64; MO July 29, '65.

Braunreiter, Joseph; farmer, Manitowoc; ENL Aug. 21, '62; WIA Chancellorsville; rejoined regt. Apr. 23, '64; left sick May 11, '64 to Oct. 17, '64; MO June 13, '65.

Buerstatte (also given as Buerstaedter), Charles; wagonmaker, Two Rivers; ENL Feb. 18, '64; slightly WIA at Resaca, May 15, 1864; slightly WIA in March, 1865, probably at Bentonville, N.C.; trans. to Co. F, 3rd Wis. Inf., June 10, '65; enrolled in Baldwin (Ohio) University and became a pharmacist; married in 1871, fathering ten children; worked two years as a drug clerk, then opened Manitowoc Drugs on South 8th Street in 1872, operating it for forty years before turning it over to his sons. The business finally closed in 1967.

Burkhardt, Christoph; farmer, Manitowoc; ENL Aug. 21, '62; WIA in arm and side at Chancellorsville; trans. to Invalid Corps, Mar. 1, '64; MO Aug. 21, '65.

Burkhardt, Felix; laborer, Two Rivers; ENL Feb. 20, '64; company cook; trans. to Co. F, 3rd Wis. Inf., June 10, '65.

Czamburek, Mathias; farmer, Manitowoc; ENL Aug. 21, '62; left sick Nov. 3, '64; absent sick at MO of regt.

Cziskowsky, Anton; laborer, Manitowoc; Dec. 26, '63; Corp.; trans. to Co. F, 3rd Wis. Inf., June 10, '65.

Dargel, Eduard; farmer, Schleswig; ENL Aug. 21, '62; slightly WIA Gettysburg;

deserted at Lookout Mountain, Tenn., Nov. 22, '63.

Dieterich, Carl; gunsmith, Two Rivers; ENL Aug. 21, '62; Corp.; regimental teamster; CIA Gettysburg; exchanged Aug. 20, '63; left sick Oct. 8, '63; rejoined regt. Nov. 17, '63; left sick Oct. 8, '64; MO June 13, '65.

Dieterich, Heinrich; mason, Gibson; Aug. 21, '62; CIA Gettysburg; rejoined regt. Nov. 17, '63; left sick Oct. 8, '64 to May 21, '65; MO June 13, '65.

Dimler, Edward; surgeon, Eaton; ENL Aug. 21,' 62; detached as nurse in regimental hospital Oct. 18, '62; MO June 13, '65

Doerfer, Peter; laborer, Milwaukee; ENL Feb. 18, '64; trans. to Co. F, 3rd Wis. Inf., June 10, '65.

Donath, August; farmer, Schleswig; ENL Aug. 21, '62; WIA Chancellorsville; trans. to Invalid Corps, Jan. 15, '64; MO July 3, '65.

Edler, Johann; laborer, Milwaukee; ENL Aug. 20, '62; disch. Oct. 3, '62.

Ehrdenreich, John D.; laborer, Manitowoc; ENL Dec. 27, '63; left sick Oct. 8, '64; rejoined regt. June 3, '65; trans. to Co. F, 3rd Wis. Inf., June 10, '65.

Erickson, Knud; farmer, Manitowoc; ENL Jan. 4, '64; provost guard; trans. to Co. F, 3rd Wis. Inf., June 10, '65.

Fischer, Frank [Frantisek Fiser]; shoemaker, Manitowoc; ENL Aug. 20, '62; Corp.; WIA June 22, '64, Kennesaw Mountain, Ga; MO June 13, '65; after war engaged in agricultural produce and implements in Manitowoc; moved to Milwaukee in 1888 to become foreman of George C. Cribb Manufacturing Co. agricultural machinery company; member of G.A.R. Post 18.

Greve, Henry; carpenter, Manitowoc; ENL Aug. 21, '62; Sergt., 1st Sergt.; promoted 2nd Lieut. Co. K, Mar. 15, '63.

Hacker, Henry; shoemaker, Two Rivers; ENL Aug. 21, '62; WIA Gettysburg; WIA Resaca; KIA May 25, '64, Burnt Hickory, Ga.

Haese, Ferdinand; farmer, Rockland; ENL Aug. 21, '62; Corp.; sent sick to div. hospital, Goldsboro, N.C., Mar. 8, '65; MO June 30, '65 while in Swift Hospital at Prairie du Chien, Wisc.; lived in Manitowoc after war; member of Twenty-Sixth Regiment Association; attended fiftieth anniversary at Gettysburg in 1913.

Heidenreich, Joseph; farmer, Newton; ENL Aug. 21, '62; DOD of typhoid fever in hospital at Stafford Court House, Va., Feb. 6, '63.

Hein, Jacob; laborer, Two Rivers; ENL Aug. 21 '62; Corp., Sergt.; left sick at Bridgeport, Ala., Oct. 26, '63; rejoined regt. June 6, '64; MO June 13, '65.

Hemschemeyer, William H.; saloonkeeper, Manitowoc; ENL Aug. 21, '62; Sergt., 1st Sergt.; recruiting duty Jan. 1-Feb. 27, '64; promoted 1st Lieut. Co. I, Apr. 13, '64.

Henkel, Gottlieb; butcher, Milwaukee; Aug. 21, '62; detached as pioneer May 18, '64; from Co. K; MO June 13, '65.

Hess, William; joiner, Two Rivers; ENL Aug. 21, '62; Sergt.; WIA July 1, '63, Gettysburg, Pa.; DOW July 3, '63.

Hoefer, Peter; farmer, Milwaukee; Mar. 26, '64; left sick Dec. 31, '64; rejoined regt. Apr. 23, '65; trans. to Co. F, 3rd Wis. Inf., June 10, '65.

Hoefling, William; merchant, Two Rivers; ENL Aug. 21, '62; WIA

Chancellorsville; rejoined regt. May 21, '65; MO June 13, '65.

Holzschuh, Anton; farmer, Centreville; ENL Aug. 20, '62; musician; CIA Gettysburg; rejoined regt. Nov. 16, '63; left sick Apr. 7, '65; MO May 19, '65; returned to Centreville after war; member of Twenty-Sixth Regiment Association.

Jaenig, Ernst; farmer, Centreville; ENL Aug. 21, '62; left sick Apr. 25, '63 to May 20, '63 and Oct. 21, '63 to Sept. 30, '64; pontoon driver in Army of the Cumberland; MO June 13, '65.

Jaura (sometimes Jura), Wenzel; farmer, Manitowoc; ENL Aug. 21, '62; WIA Chancellorsville; rejoined regt. May 20, '63; WIA and CIA Gettysburg; trans. to Invalid Corps, May 6, '64.

Joachimsthal, Joseph; farmer, Manitowoc; ENL Aug. 21, '62; WIA in leg at Chancellorsville; trans. to Invalid Corps, Jan. 1, '65.

Kaufmann, Conrad; laborer, Two Rivers; ENL Feb. 29, '64; DOD (dysentery) at Chattanooga, Tenn., Aug. 15, '64.

Kempf, John; farmer, Centreville; ENL Aug. 21, '62; severely WIA in both legs and face at Gettysburg; disch. Dec. 31, '63, disability.

Kihm, John; farmer, Eaton; ENL Aug. 21, '62; Corp.; WIA May 15, '64, Resaca and spent rest of war in hospital; MO June 9, '65; returned to Eaton after war; member of Twenty-Sixth Regiment Association.

Kletzin, Abraham; farmer, Schleswig; ENL Aug. 21, '62; company cook; detached as ambulance teamster Nov. 6, '62; rejoined regt. Apr. 1, '63; brigade teamster; WIA Gettysburg; MO June 13, '65.

Koenig, Joseph; farmer, Schleswig; ENL Aug. 21, '62; CIA Gettysburg; rejoined regt. Oct. 3, '63; left sick Apr. 20, '64; absent sick at MO of regt.

Koenke, August; farmer, Schleswig; ENL Aug. 21, '62; WIA in nose and ear at Chancellorsville; disch. Aug. 18, '63, disability.

Koetzdinger, Alois; farmer, Manitowoc; ENL Aug. 15, '62; drowned Sept. 17,'63, Rappahannock River, Va.

Krajnik, Joseph; farmer, Manitowoc; ENL Aug. 21, '62; left sick Sept. 24, '63; disch. May 25, '64, disability. Muster out records say "never was in battle."

Krueger, Ferdinand J. G. [brother of Gottlieb and cousin of Julius]; farmer, Newton; ENL Aug. 21, '62; Corp., Sergt., 1st Sergt., MO June 13, '65; farmer in Manitowoc after war; moved to Milwaukee in 1887; member of Robert Chivas Post No. 2, G.A.R.

Krueger, Gottlieb Michael [brother of Ferdinand and cousin of Julius]; farmer, Newton; ENL Aug. 21, '62; WIA Gettysburg; rejoined regt. Feb. 12, '64; KIA June 22, '64 at Kennesaw Mountain, Ga.

Krueger, Julius [cousin of Ferdinand and Gottlieb]; farmer, Liberty; ENL Aug. 21, '62; DOD in hospital at Chattanooga, Tenn., Dec. 30, '63.

Kuhn, Martin; laborer, Two Rivers; ENL Aug. 21, '62; left sick Dec. 10, '62; deserted Apr. 30, '63 from hospital (adjutant generals' records indicate deserted Aug. 27, '63).

Kuhnel, Anton; brewer, Two Rivers; ENL Aug. 21, '62; Sergt.; CIA Gettysburg; absent at MO of regt.

Kunkel, John; farmer, Two Rivers; ENL Aug. 21, '62; WIA Gettysburg; trans. to VRC, May 31, '64; MO July 24, '65.

Kunz, Albert; ship carpenter, Manitowoc; Aug. 15, '62; WIA and CIA at Gettysburg; absent in hospital at MO of regt.

Lebal, John; farmer, Cooperstown; ENL Aug. 21, '62; WIA Gettysburg; trans. to Invalid Corps, Jan. 15, '64; MO July 13, '65.

Leubner, Paul; tinsmith, Manitowoc; ENL Aug. 21, '62; detached as ambulance teamster Nov. 2, '62; rejoined regt. June 1, '65; MO June 13, '65.

Lindloge, William; farmer, Liberty; ENL Aug. 21, '62; left sick Oct. 11, '64; DOD Jan. 28, '65, Madison, Wis. (adjutant generals' list says DOW June 28, '64).

Lippmann, Henry; farmer, Liberty; ENL Aug. 21, '62; Corp., Sergt.; left sick Dec. 10, '62 to Jan 30, '63; WIA Peach Tree Creek July, '64; DOD (dysentery) at Chattahoochie, Ga., Oct. 23, '64.

Lorenz, Charles; farmer, Centreville; ENL Aug. 20, '62; left sick Dec. 17, '63 to July 10, '64; MO June 13, '65.

Ludwig, Albert; farmer, Chilton; ENL Feb. 26, '64; brigade cattle guard; trans. to Co. F, 3rd Wis. Inf., June 10, '65.

Mantowsky, Bartholomaeus; laborer, Maple Grove; ENL Aug. 20, '62; detached as brigade teamster Nov. 24, '62; rejoined regt. Apr. 20, '64; left sick Apr. 24, '65; ; MO June 10, '65.

Mathias, Friedrich; laborer, Milwaukee; ENL Feb. 11, '64; trans. to Co. F, 3rd Wis. Inf., June 10, '65.

Meier, Carl; farmer, Mishicot; ENL Aug. 21, '62; WIA May 15, '64, Resaca, Ga.; rejoined regt. May 21, '65; MO June 13, '65; lived in Two Rivers after war; member of Twenty-Sixth Regiment Association.

Mendlick, Henry; laborer, Manitowoc; ENL Aug. 21, '62; WIA Chancellorsville May 2, '63; disch. May 9, '63, disability.

Muench, Franz; clerk, Manitowoc; ENL Aug. 21, '62; Corp.; CIA and probably WIA at Chancellorsville; disch. Sept. 2; '63, disability.

Neitzel, John; blacksmith, Manitowoc; ENL Aug. 21, '62; left sick Feb. 28, '64 to July 10, '64; left sick Sept. 9, '64; MO May 3, '65.

Neumann, Philip; shoemaker, Manitowoc; ENL Aug. !8, '62; Corp.; CIA Gettysburg; paroled Mar. 7, '64; WIA Peach Tree Creek; MO June 13, '65.

Niemann, Friedrich; Two Rivers; ENL Feb. 14, '64; trans. to Co. F, 3rd Wis. Inf., June 10, '65.

Niephaus, Gerhard; farmer, Manitowoc; Aug. 15, '62; severely WIA Gettysburg; rejoined regt. Dec. 29, '63; KIA July 20, '64, Peach Tree Creek, Ga.

Oestreich, Carl; laborer, Manitowoc; Aug. 21, '62; Corp.; KIA Mar. 16, '65, Averasboro, N.C.

Olm, August; laborer, Schleswig; ENL Aug. 21, '62; Sergt.; sent to hospital Nov. 11, '64; rejoined regt. Jan. 12, '65 at Savannah, Ga.; severely WIA Averasboro and sent to hospital in Goldsboro, N.C.; MO July 5, '65; lived in Centreville, Sheboygan Co., after war; member of Twenty-Sixth Regiment Association.

Ott, Bernhard; mason, Prairie du Sac; ENL Aug. 14, '62; trans. to Co. K, Oct. 3, '62.

Parbs, Charles; farmer, Greenfield; ENL Feb. 22, '64; DOD of dysentery in field hospital near Atlanta, Ga., Sept. 13, '64 (final report of casualties says Aug. 15, '64).

Perschbacher, John N.; farmer, Kewaskum; ENL Feb. 22, '64; trans. to Co. B, Sept. 1, '64.

Pickeruhn, August; farmer, Schleswig; ENL Aug. 21, '62; KIA May 2, '63, Chancellorsville, Va.

Pleuss, Dietrich; farmer, Newton; ENL Feb. 29, '64; left sick May 24, '64; DOD Dec. 31, '64, Evansville, Ind.

Puls, August; farmer, Manitowoc; ENL Aug. 21, '62; WIA Gettysburg; detached to ambulance corps Nov. 20, '63; rejoined regt. Apr. 20, '64; MO June 13, '65.

Puls, Friedrich; farmer, Kossuth; ENL Aug. 19, '62; WIA in knee at Chancellorsville; rejoined regt. May 1, '64; MO June 13, '65.

Raatz, Hermann; farmer, Two Rivers; ENL Aug. 21, '62; admitted to 3rd Div. hospital at Alexandria, Va., January 22, '63 and DOD (typhoid fever) Jan. 31, '63 (tubercules also found in lungs).

Reisenbegler, Mathias; butcher, Two Rivers; ENL Feb. 22, '64; KIA Mar. 19, '65, Bentonville, N.C.

Roeder, Nikolaus; farmer, Manitowoc; ENL Aug. 15, '62; DOD Dec. 28, '63, Chattanooga, Tenn.

Roehr, Hermann; farmer, Schleswig; ENL Aug. 21, '62; KIA May 2, '63, Chancellorsville, Va.

Rost, Friedrich August; farmer, Schleswig; ENL Aug. 21, '62; company cook; muster out papers say "never left the Regt."; MO June 13, '65; member of Robert Chivas Post No. 2, G.A.R.; founding member of Twenty-Sixth Regiment Association.

Rothacker, David; laborer, Sauk City; ENL Aug. 15, '62; trans. to Co. K, Oct. 3, '62.

Rusch (or sometimes Rush), Louis; farmer, Rockland; ENL Aug. 20, '62; company cook; WIA Peach Tree Creek; MO May 29, '65; lived in Manitowoc after war; member of Twenty-Sixth Regiment Association.

Schara, Franz; farmer, Manitowoc; ENL Aug. 21, '62; WIA in hand July 1, '63, Gettysburg, Pa.; DOW July 3, '63.

Schimeck, Franz; mason, Manitowoc; ENL Aug. 21, '62; CIA Gettysburg; paroled Feb. '64; rejoined regt. July 1, '64; MO June 13, '65.

Schmidt, Leopold; farmer, Kossuth; ENL Aug. 21, '62; KIA July 1, '63, Gettysburg, Pa.

Schmidt, Christian; laborer, Two Rivers; ENL Aug. 21, '62; Corp., Sergt.; KIA May 2, '63, Chancellorsville, Va.

Schmidt, Friedrich; farmer, Maple Grove; ENL Aug. 15, '62; left sick Oct. 27, '63 to Jan. 5, '64 and May 10, '64 to May 21, '65; MO June 13, '65.

Schmidt, Jacob; laborer, Lake; ENL Feb. 27, '64; WIA Peach Tree Creek; in hospital when trans. to Co., F, 3rd Wis. Inf., June 10, '65.

Schmidt, John; Manitowoc; ENL Dec. 28, '63; WIA July, '64; KIA Mar. 16, '65, Averasboro, N.C.

Schneider, Michael; farmer, Newton; ENL Aug. 21, '62; WIA Gettysburg and middle third of right femur amputated; second amputation Aug. 13, '63; disch. due to wounds Jan. 29, '64.

Scholz, Joseph; farmer, Chilton; ENL Feb. 26, '64; trans. to Invalid Corps, Dec. 28, '64; MO July 13, 65.

Schubert, Oswald; merchant, Milwaukee; ENL Aug. 18, '62 from Co. I; Sergt, 1st Sergt.; promoted 1st Lieut. Co. I, Nov. 15, '64.

Schultz, Joachim; farmer, Liberty; ENL Aug. 21, '62; CIA Chancellorsville; rejoined regt. Oct. 3, '63; WIA Peach Tree Creek; rejoined regt. Apr. 1, '65; MO June 13, '65; lived in Manitowoc after war; member of Twenty-Sixth Regiment Association.

Seemann, John; farmer, Manitowoc; ENL Dec. 30, '63; left sick May 17, '64; rejoined regt. Oct. 27, '64; trans. to Co. F, 3rd Wis. Inf., June 10, '65.

Simonek, Jan; (Simonek) laborer, Manitowoc; ENL Aug. 21, '62; severely WIA in left arm at Gettysburg; treated in hospital in Newark, NJ; trans. to VRC, Nov. 20, '63; MO July 6, '65 at Trenton Barracks, Trenton, NJ; resided in Green Bay after war; moved to Medford, WI, in 1882 where he ran a feed buisness until he died Mar. 25, 1914.

Škala, John Friedrich; farmer, Mishicot; ENL Aug. 18, '62; trans. to Invalid Corps, Oct. 3, '63; MO July 3, '65.

Skarda, Jacob; farmer, Manitowoc; ENL Jan. 4, '64; detached as pioneer Apr. 9, '65; trans. to Co. F, 3rd Wis. Inf., June 10, '65.

Spinker, Henry; carpenter, Manitowoc; ENL Dec. 31, '63; trans. to Co. F, 3rd Wis. Inf., June 10, '65.

Stiede, Charles; blacksmith, Two Rivers; ENL Feb. 12, '64; left sick May 15, '64; in hospital when trans. to Co. F, 3rd Wis. Inf., June 10, '65.

Stier, Christian; farmer, Newton; ENL Aug. 21, '62; WIA in small of back at Gettysburg, July 1, '63; DOW July 14, '63; buried in Gettysburg National Cemetery, Wisconsin Plot, grave A-17.

Stuempges, Julius; farmer, Newton; ENL Aug. 21, '62; Corp.; MO June 13, '65.

Swegkar, Waclaw [Vaclav Svejkar]; farmer, Manitowoc; ENL Aug. 21, '62; WIA June 22, '64, Kennesaw Mountain; absent in hospital at MO of regt.

Taube (or sometimes Tanbe), Daniel; farmer, Newton; ENL Aug. 31, '62; WIA in leg at Chancellorsville; rejoined regt. Jan. 10, '64; sent to hospital sick June 6, '64; disch. Sept. 17, '64, disability.

Tiedemann, Ehlert; farmer, Schleswig; ENL Aug. 21, '62; Corp.; member of color guard; left sick Feb. 9, '64; DOD Feb. 17, '64, Nashville, Tenn.

Todl, Adolf; printer, Manitowoc; ENL Aug. 20, '62; Corp., Sergt.; WIA in leg at Gettysburg; deserted from hospital at Ft. Schuyler, N.Y., Aug. 27, '63.

Utke, Wilhelm; farmer, Liberty; ENL Aug. 21, '62; WIA Chancellorsville; absent sick until Apr. 7, '65; MO June 13, '65.

Vogt, John; farmer, Centreville; ENL Aug. 21, '62; Corp., Sergt.; MIA Chancellorsville (probably CIA); WIA July 20, '64, Peach Tree Creek; rejoined regt. Apr. 7, '65 at Goldsboro, N.C.; MO June 13, '65.

Voigt, Wilhelm; farmer, Mishicot; ENL Aug. 21, '62; WIA Chancellorsville; discharge June 9, '64, disability.

Voss, Friedrich; farmer, Schleswig; ENL Aug. 21, '62; KIA May 2, '63, Chancellorsville, Va.

Waanish, Watigas (or Mathias); farmer, Manitowoc; ENL Aug. 21, '62; sick Oct. 27, '63 to Jan. 6, '64; MO June 13, '65.

Waack, Henry; farmer, Newton; ENL Aug. 21, '62; musician; note in muster out papers says "never left the regiment"; MO June 13, '65; attended fiftieth anniversary at Gettysburg in 1913.

Wagner, Michel; blacksmith, Two Creeks; ENL Aug. 21, '62; detached to brigade blacksmith May 24, '63; rejoined regt. Apr. 20, '64; ; KIA May 15, '64, Resaca, Ga.

Winter, Christian; laborer, Milwaukee; ENL Aug. 13, '62 from Co. K; WIA Chancellorsville May 2, '63 and sent to McDougall General Hospital May 3, '63; sent sick to hospital Apr. 4, '65; MO Aug. 7, '65.

Winter, Friedrich W.; laborer, Kewaskum; ENL Feb. 22, '64; WIA Peach Tree Creek, Ga.; DOW at Cumberland Hospital, Nashville, Tenn., Aug. 16, '64.

Zurmuehlen, Friedrich; farmer, Two Rivers; ENL Aug. 21, '62; hospital nurse; CIA Chancellorsville; rejoined regt. Oct. 3, '63; MO June 13, '65.

COMPANY G, WASHINGTON COUNTY RIFLES

Captains

Jacob E. Mann; editor, West Bend; rank from Sept. 10, '62; resigned Dec. 8, '62.

Charles Pizzala; soldier, Manitowoc; appointed Dec. 20, '62 from 1st Lieut. Co. F; KIA May 2, '63, Chancellorsville, Va.

Hermann Fuerstenberg [Fürstenberg] laborer, Milwaukee; appointed June 1, '63 from 2nd Lieut. Co D; 1st Lieut., Feb. 1, '63; WIA Gettysburg; resigned Feb. 8, '64.

August Bartsch; blacksmith, Madison; appointed Apr. 13, '64 from 1st Lieut. Co. D; CIA near Sneedsville, N.C., Mar. 5, '65; MO May 15, '65; died in Denver, Colorado, Aug. 17, 1876.

First Lieutenants

William Smith; Milwaukee; Sept. 10, '62; promoted Capt. Co. I, Dec. 15, '62.

Bernhard Domschcke; Milwaukee; appointed Nov. 14, '62 from 2nd Lieut., Co. C; trans. to Co. F.

Nicholas Wollmer; farmer, Greenfield; appointed Apr. 13, '64 from Sergt. Major; WIA July 20, '64, Peach Tree Creek, Ga.; DOW Aug. 21, 64.

Lambert Weiss; farmer, Addison; appointed Apr. 6, '65; ENL Aug. 20, '62; Corp., Sergt., 1st Sergt.; MO June 13, '65.

Second Lieutenants

Julius Meiswinkel; clerk, Milwaukee; rank from Sept. 18, '62 from 1st Sergt. Co. B; resigned Feb. 6, '63; member of Robert Chivas Post No. 2, G.A.R.; member of Twenty-Sixth Regiment Association.

John Orth; clerk, Milwaukee; appointed Feb. 1, '63; from Co. I; wounded by accident while on picket line, Nov,'62; resigned June 23, '63.

Enlisted Men

Abbott, Edward; miller, Jackson; ENL Aug. 21, '62; disch. Oct. 4, '62, disability.

Abbott, Martin; farmer, Jackson; ENL Aug. 21, '62; WIA in finger and CIA Chancellorsville; hospital nurse May 15, '63 to Nov. 14, '64; rejoined regt. Nov. 14, '64; MO June 13, '65.

Allen, Henry; farmer, Trenton; ENL Aug. 12, '62; Corp., 1st Sergt.; CIA Chancellorsville; rejoined regt. Oct. 3, '63; MO June 13, '65.

Andreas, Carl; farmer, Milwaukee; ENL Aug. 20, '62; MO June 13, '65.

Bantin, Henry; laborer, West Bend; ENL Aug. 18, '62; disch. at Philadelphia, PA, June 8, '63, disability due to chronic diarrhoea.

Blenker, Henry; farmer, Addison; ENL Aug. 21, '62; Sergt; WIA in breast and hip at Chancellorsville; trans. to VRC, Jan. 15, '65; MO Sept. 16, '65.

Carey, John; farmer, Trenton; ENL Aug. 15, '62; Corp; left sick May 2, '64; rejoined regt. Apr. 10, '65; MO June 13, '65.

Cassel, Alfred H.; farmer, Jackson; ENL Aug. 21, '62; Corp.; DOD (typhoid bronchitis; one source says smallpox) in hospital at Stafford Court house, Va., Mar. 25, '63; buried in Fredericksburg Cemetery, Division C, Section B, grave 373.

Crowley, John; farmer, Jackson; ENL Aug. 21, '62; 1st Sergt.; DOD (consumption or typhoid fever) in hospital at Stafford Court House, Va., Jan. 5, '63.

Daily, Richard; laborer, Trenton; ENL Aug. 15, '62; WIA in hips and DOW in field hospital May 2, '63, Chancellorsville, Va.

Daul, Bernhard; farmer, Addison; ENL Aug. 21, '62; WIA Gettysburg; rejoined regt. Aug. 26, '63; MO June 13, '65.

Dellenbach, George; farmer, Addison; ENL Aug. 20, '62; slightly WIA Gettysburg; rejoined regt. Aug. 26, '63; WIA May 25, '64; DOW July 2, '64, Kingston, Ga.

Dellenbach, Peter; farmer, Addison; ENL Aug. 20, '62; WIA in back at Chancellorsville; rejoined regt. Oct. 18, '63; absent sick July 23, '64 to Oct. 10, '64; absent sick Apr. 10, '65 to June 5, '65; MO June 13, '65; spent postwar years on family farm.

Dexheimer, Jacob; carpenter, Menomonee Falls; ENL Aug. 13, '62; KIA May 2, '63, Chancellorsville, Va.

Dimler, Louis; surgeon, Sheboygan; ENL Aug. 11, '64 as voluntary substitute; trans. to Co. G, 3rd Wis. Inf., June 10, '65.

Distler, Frederick; farmer, Trenton; ENL Aug. 21, '62; WIA Chancellorsville; CIA May 25, '64 at Dallas, Ga.; DOD (diarrhea) in Confederate prison at Andersonville, Ga., Aug. 16, '64 and buried in grave 5830.

Dowland, Frederick J.; teacher, Trenton; ENL Aug. 21, '62; WIA at Chancellorsville; CIA May 25, '64; trans. to VRC, Feb. 13, '65; MO Aug. 3, '65.

Eichhorst, Friedrich; laborer, Jackson; ENL Aug. 12, '62; absent sick May 10, '63 to Jan. 8, '64; absent sick July 17, '64 through MO of regt.

Emmett, George H.; farmer, Jackson; ENL Aug. 12, '62; Corp.; WIA in right leg Chancellorsville; trans. to VRC, Sept. 17, '64; MO July 8, '65.

Firks, William; farmer, Herman; ENL Sept. 24, '62; nurse at General Hospital in Chattanooga, Tenn., Nov. 20, '63 to Jan. 10, '64; WIA June 13, '64, Dallas, GA; absent wounded in hospital at Milwaukee at MO of regt.

Fitting, John; farmer, Addison; ENL Aug. 21, '62; WIA Gettysburg and sent to hospital in Philadelphia, PA; absent wounded at MO of regt.

Frensz, Charles; farmer, West Bend; ENL Aug. 21, '62; slightly WIA Chancellorsville; severely WIA Gettysburg; disch. due to wounds Dec. 4, '63.

Frensz, Christian; farmer, West Bend; ENL Aug. 21, '62; Corp., Sergt.; WIA Gettysburg; rejoined regt. Jan. 8, '64; MO June 13, 65.

Fritz, Ferdinand; farmer, Addison; ENL Aug. 21, '62; KIA July 1, '63, Gettysburg, Pa.

Fullerton, Andrew J.; farmer, Jackson; ENL Aug. 21, '62; 1st Sergt.; slightly WIA Chancellorsville; promoted 1st Lieut. Co. F, June 8, '64.

Groshans (or Grosshaus), Louis; farmer, Addison; ENL Aug. 21, '62; WIA Dec. 10, '62; trans. to VRC, July 1, '63; MO Aug. 21, '65.

Guenther, Henry; blacksmith, Addison; ENL Aug. 20, '62; Corp.; KIA May 2, '63, Chancellorsville, Va.

Guenther, John H.; farmer, Addison; ENL Aug. 21, '62; Corp.; WIA in fleshy part of leg and CIA at Chancellorsville; rejoined regt. Aug. 9, '63; MO June 13, '65.

Hafemann, Charles; blacksmith, West Bend; ENL Aug. 12, '62; WIA Gettysburg, July 1, '63 and taken to General Hospital in Philadelphia, Pa.; WIA in left leg above knee May 25, '64 and sent to General Hospital in Jeffersonville, Ind., then to General Hospital in Madison, Wisc.; MO May 18, '65; received disability pension; moved to farm near Wayside, Wisc.

Heinz, Jacob; farmer, Addison; ENL Aug. 18, '62; severely WIA Gettysburg; trans. to VRC, Mar. 31, '65.

Hook, Eugene; farmer, Addison; ENL Aug. 20, '62; WIA Gettysburg; CIA Thompsons' Cr. near Cheraw, S.C., Mar. 5, '65; paroled Apr. 2, '65; MO June 13, '65; lived in Mayville after war; member of Twenty-Sixth Regiment Association.

Horn, John; laborer, West Bend; Aug. 12, '62; Sergt., 1st Sergt.; disch. at Washington, D.C., Apr. 10, '63, disability.

Hughes, William; farmer, Trenton; ENL Aug. 21, '62; severely WIA Gettysburg; rejoined regt. Sept. 16, '63; WIA Peach Tree Creek and sent to hospital in Keokuk, Iowa; absent wounded at MO of regt.

Jewlson, Julius; farmer, Trenton; ENL Aug. 12, '62; KIA July 1, '63, Gettysburg, Pa.

Johnson, Samuel; farmer, West Bend; ENL Aug. 12, '62; Corp.; hospital nurse; DOD at Murfreesboro, Tenn., Mar. 5, '64 (final report of casualties says Feb. 22, '64).

Jones, George William; farmer, Jackson; ENL Aug. 21, '62; Corp.; judge advocates' clerk; promoted Q.M. Sergt., July 1, '63.

Karsten, Karl; farmer, West Bend; ENL Aug. 13, '62; Corp., Sergt., 1st Sergt.; promoted 2nd Lieut. Co. F, Apr. 13, '64.

Keller, John; laborer, Milwaukee; ENL Aug. 21, '62; disch. at Washington, D.C., Mar. 3, '63, disability.

Knobel, Jacob; Addison; ENL Aug. 18, '62; WIA in shoulder and knee Chancellorsville; trans. to VRC, Nov. 15, '64.

Koehler, George; carpenter, Barton; ENL Aug. 21, '62; Corp.; KIA July 1, '63, Gettysburg, Pa.

Kuhl, Peter; laborer, Addison; ENL Aug. 20, '62; left regt. sick Aug. 24, '64 in hospital in Washington, D.C.; MO June 9, '65.

Kuhn, Peter; carpenter, Wayne; ENL Aug. 21, '62; WIA with compound fracture of lower right leg July 1, '63, Gettysburg, Pa.; DOW July 9 in XI Corps hospital (final report of casualties says DOW at Gettysburg July 15, '63); buried in Gettysburg National Cemetery, Wisconsin Plot, grave B-18.

Lauermann, Jacob; farmer, Jackson; ENL Aug. 21, '62; KIA May 2, '63, Chancellorsville, Va.

Mack, Konrad; farmer, West Bend; ENL Aug. 12, '62; DOD (typhoid fever) at Stafford Court House, Va., Dec. 23, '62; buried in Fredericksburg Cemetery, Row B, Section B, grave 26.

Maier (or Mayer), John; farmer, Trenton; ENL Aug. 21, '62; severely WIA Chancellorsville; rejoined regt. May 24, '65; MO June 13, '65.

Metzner, Gottlieb; blacksmith, West Bend; ENL Aug. 21, '62; severely WIA Gettysburg and sent to hospital in Ft. Schuyler, NY, then to Chattanooga, Tenn.; rejoined regt. May 28, '65; MO June 13, '65; attended fiftieth anniversary at Gettysburg in 1913.

Mueller, Henry A.; blacksmith, Addison; ENL Aug. 20, '62; Corp.; WIA in right cheek at Chancellorsville; treated in field hospital at Aquia Creek; WIA in left cheek and shoulder at Gettysburg, CIA and treated by Confederate surgeon; treated in hospital in West Philadelphia; trans. to Camp Randall Hospital in WI, Aug. 25, '63; trans. to Invalid Corps, Dec. 28, '63; trans. to VRC Mar. 15, '65; MO Sept. 8, '65; married in St. Lawrence, Washington County, after war; moved briefly to Missouri, then to Milwaukee where he opened a store specializing in religious and school items; member of Rank and File Post No. 240, G.A.R.; died in Milwaukee, May 29, 1915.

Perthold, Louis; farmer, Farmington; ENL Aug. 21, '62; disch. at Washington, D.C., Apr. 30, '63, disability.

Phillipsen, Peter; butcher, Milwaukee; ENL Aug. 15, '62; brigade teamster, 2nd brigade, 3rd div., XI Corps; rejoined regt. Apr. 28, '64; WIA Peach Tree Creek and 3 1/2 inches of upper left arm removed; sent to hospital in Milwaukee; disch. May 27, '65, disability.

Remmel, Johann; farmer, West Bend; ENL Aug. 12, '62; Sergt.; trans. to VRC, Jan. 10, '65; MO June 30, '65.

Reidl, Wenzl; cooper, Trenton; ENL Aug. 21, '62; left regt. sick Apr. 26, '63 to general Hospital, Philadelphia, PA; rejoined regt. July 21, '64; MO June 13, '65.

Rilling, John; farmer, West Bend; ENL Aug. 18, '62; disch. at Columbian College Hospital, Washington, D.C., Feb. 13, '63, disability.

Ripplinger, Peter; farmer, Addison; ENL Aug. 18, '62; slightly WIA Chancellorsville; trans. to VRC, Sept. 12, '64; MO July 5, '65.

Ritger, John; farmer, Addison; ENL Aug. 21, '62; Corp.; severely WIA and DOW while acting as color bearer July 1, '63, Gettysburg, Pa.

Rusco, George W.; joiner, West Bend; ENL Aug. 12, '62; Corp.; KIA May 2, '63, Chancellorsville, Va.

Rusho, Anthony; farmer, Trenton; ENL Aug. 21, '62; Corp.; disch. at Philadelphia, Pa, May 28, '63, disability.

Saaler, John; shoemaker, Menomonee; ENL Aug. 19, '62; disch. Mar. 3, '63, disability.

Salter, Robert [brother of William]; farmer, Jackson; ENL Aug. 15, '62; WIA Gettysburg; left regt. sick July 24, '63; DOD (typhoid fever) Aug. 23, '63, Harewood Hospital, Washington, D.C.

Salter, William [brother of Robert]; farmer, Jackson; ENL Aug. 21, '62; Sergt.; WIA and CIA Chancellorsville; paroled and exchanged; deserted at Indianapolis, Ind., Sept. 30, '63; fled to Canada and married; returned to U.S. under general amnesty and resided in Chilton, Wisc.

Schaefer, Friedrich; farmer, Wayne; ENL Aug. 21, '62; WIA Chancellorsville; trans. to VRC, Nov. 1, '63; MO July 13, '65.

Schmidt, John; farmer, Jackson; ENL Aug. 15, '62; KIA May 2, '63, Chancellorsville, Va.

Schnepf, Killian; farmer, West Bend; ENL Aug. 13, '62; KIA May 2, '63, Chancellorsville, Va.

Schnorrenberg, Peter; farmer, Addison; ENL Aug. 21, '62; DOD (consumption) in hospital at Stafford Court House, Va., Feb. 2, '63.

Schuh, Charles; teamster, West Bend; ENL Aug. 13, '62; Corp.; member of color guard; MO June 13, '65.

Schuh, George; carpenter, Addison; ENL Aug. 21, '62; severely WIA Gettysburg and sent to hospital at Ft. Schuyler, NY; trans. to VRC, Feb. 15, '64.

Schuh, Joseph; farmer, Addison; ENL Aug. 21, '62; Corp.; member of color guard; MO June 13, '65.

Schultz, John; farmer, Addison; ENL Aug. 12, '62; Corp.; Sergt.; severely WIA Gettysburg; rejoined regt. May 2, '64; MO June 13, '65.

Sery (or Serie), Wilhelm; laborer, Milwaukee; ENL Aug. 15, '62; pioneer; slightly WIA May 25, '64, Dallas, Ga.; rejoined regt. Apr. 10, '65; MO June 13, '65; attended fiftieth anniversary at Gettysburg in 1913.

Shafer, Cyrus W.; farmer, Trenton; ENL Aug. 15, '62; corps escort; WIA Chancellorsville; slightly WIA May 25, '64, Dallas, Ga.; rejoined regt. Feb. 3, '65; detached as orderly to XX Corps HQ, Feb. 14 to June 10, '65; MO June 13, '65.

Shattuck, James H.; Jackson; ENL Aug. 12, '62; disch. Apr. 9, '63, disability.

Sihlsdorf, Frederick; farmer, Addison; ENL Aug. 21, '62; KIA July 1, '63, Gettysburg, Pa.; buried in Gettysburg National Cemetery, Wisconsin Section, grave 8.

Simon, William; hotelkeeper, Barton; ENL Aug. 15, '62; disch. Jan. 5, '63, disability.

Smith, Emerson L.; farmer, West Bend; ENL Aug. 12, '62; CIA Chancellorsville; exchanged and rejoined regt. Oct. 2, '63; KIA May 25, '64 at Burnt Hickory near Dallas, Ga.

Stecher, Peter; laborer, Milwaukee; ENL Aug. 15, '62; drummer; MO June 13, '65.

Steinmetz, Joseph; farmer, Trenton; ENL Aug. 18, '62; teamster; KIA May 2, '63, Chancellorsville, Va.

Steuerwald, Daniel; farmer, West Bend; ENL Aug. 21, '62; detached as regimental teamster Dec. 9, '62; corps escort; MO June 13, '65; elected to local offices and state assembly in 1887.

Steuerwald, Frederick; farmer, Trenton; ENL Aug. 20, '62; detached as regimental teamster Dec. 9, '62; corps escort; MO June 13, '65.

Stoeffel, Peter; farmer, West Bend; ENL Aug. 12, '62; company cook; WIA in foot May 15, '64, Resaca, Ga.; DOW at Chattanooga, Tenn., June 19, '64.

Stollberg, Gustav; shoemaker, Milwaukee; ENL Aug. 21, '62; musician; MO June 13, '65.

Story, Albert; farmer, Trenton; ENL Aug. 18, '62; WIA and CIA Gettysburg; prisoner in Richmond and paroled Aug. 1, '63 to U. S. General Hospital at Annapolis, Md. and remained there until muster out; MO June 29, '65.

Strupp, Jacob; farmer, Addison; ENL Aug. 21, '62; left regt. sick Feb. 6, '63; rejoined regt. July 24, '63; left regt. sick Mar. 15, '64; DOD at Madison (or Jeffersonville), Ind., Apr. 4, '64 (final list of casualties says at Chattanooga, Tenn.).

Strupp, Mathias; laborer, Addison; ENL Aug. 21, '62; WIA Chancellorsville; rejoined regt. July 5, '63; Corp.; MO June 13, '65.

Stubanus, Andreas; farmer, Greenfield; Aug. 20, '62; WIA Chancellorsville; WIA Gettysburg; rejoined regt. Apr. 5, '64; left regt. sick July 4, '64; DOD at Jeffersonville, Ind., Aug. 28, '64.

Templeton, Robert H.; farmer, Trenton; ENL Aug. 12, '62; Corp; KIA May 25, '64 at Burnt Hickory near Dallas, Ga.

Treutel, Henry; blacksmith, Addison; ENL Aug. 21, '62; Corp.; trans. to VRC, July 10, '64; MO July 5, '65.

Ullweling, Peter; farmer, Addison; ENL Aug. 21, '62; WIA Chancellorsville; disch. Nov. 18, '64, disability.

Vetter, Johann C.; laborer, Brookfield; ENL Aug. 16, '62; WIA May 2, '63, Chancellorsville; leg amputated and DOW at Brooks Station, Va., May 8, '63.

Wagner, Jacob; blacksmith, West Bend; ENL Aug. 12, '62; Corp.; disch. at Philadelphia, Pa, Feb. 14, '63, disability due to rheumatism.

Walter, John; farmer, Wayne; Aug. 21, '62; Corp.; WIA Gettysburg and sent to hospital in Philadelphia; MO papers say "received notice that he was in confinement at Louisville, Ky. for desertion."; absent at MO of regt.

Walter, Peter; farmer, Wayne; Aug. 21, '62; company clerk; severely WIA Gettysburg; trans. to VRC, Jan. 10, '65.

Wehe, William; farmer, Addison; ENL Aug. 18, '62; Corp.; company cook; absent sick Dec. 10, '62 to Apr. 20, '63; MO June 13, '65.

Weinand, Jacob; blacksmith, Trenton; ENL Aug. 15, '62; Corp.; KIA May 2, '63, Chancellorsville, Va.

Wiedemann, Joachim; shoemaker, Wayne; ENL Aug. 21, '62; WIA Gettysburg and sent to hospital in Philadelphia; absent wounded at MO of regt.

Wolf, Albert; farmer, Herman; ENL Sept. 24, '62; WIA in foot and forearm May 15, '64, Resaca, Ga.; DOW June 19, '64, Chattanooga, Tenn. (final list of casualties says at Kennesaw Mtn. June 27, '64).

Wolter, Frederick; farmer, West Bend; ENL Aug. 21, '62; comp. cook; MO June 13, '65.

Young, Michael; farmer, Trenton; ENL Aug. 15, '62; disch. May 15, '63, disability.

Young, Nicholaus; farmer, Trenton; ENL Aug. 15, '62; WIA with compound fracture of right thigh at Gettysburg July 1, '63; DOW at Letterman Hospital, Gettysburg, Pa., August 8, '63 (final report of casualties says DOW July 15, '63).

Zihlsdorf, Franz; farmer, Addison; ENL Aug. 21, '62; KIA May 2, '63, Chancellorsville, Va.

Zoeger [Zöger], Mathias; farmer, West Bend; Aug. 18, '62; WIA in knee May 2, '63, Chancellorsville; leg amputated and DOW at Washington, DC., June 24, '63.

COMPANY H, SECOND WARD GUARD

Captains

Hans Boebel; printer, Milwaukee; rank from Sept. 3, '63; promoted Lieut. Col., Jan. 18, '63.

Bernhard Domschcke (also spelled Domschke); editor, Milwaukee; appointed Mar. 15, '63 from 1st Lieut. Co. F; CIA Gettysburg; spent the rest of the war as a

Confederate prisoner in Richmond, Danville, Macon, Charleston, Columbia, and elsewhere; resigned Apr. 24, '65; edited *Daily Herold* after war; wrote an excellent personal account of his experiences as a prisoner of war which he published in 1865 as *Zwanzig Monate in Kriegsgefangenschaft: Erinnerungen*; national president of *Milwaukee Turnverein*, 1866-67; chair of 7th Ward Republican Club; member of State Board of Immigration; died at age 43 due to effects of Confederate prisons on May 5, 1869.

First Lieutenants

Joseph Wedig; lawyer, Sheboygan; rank from Sept. 3, '62; resigned Feb 26, '62.

Charles Vocke; draftsman, Madison; appointed Mar. 15, '63; 2nd Lieut., Sept. 3, '62; resigned May 13, '63.

Carl Schmidt; professor, Milwaukee; appointed June 1, '63; ENL Aug. 14, '62; 1st Sergt; 2nd Lieut. Mar. 15, '63; promoted Capt. Co. B, Nov. 24, '63.

Joseph Maschauer; farmer, Milwaukee; appointed Nov. 24, '63; ENL Aug. 21, '62; Sergt., 1st Sergt; 2nd Lieut., June 1, '63; severely WIA Gettysburg; promoted Capt. Co. D, Oct. 19, '64.

Second Lieutenants

Charles Vocke, draftsman, Madison; appointed Sept. 3, '62; promoted 1st. Lt.

Enlisted Men

Anhalt, William; farmer, Rhine; ENL Aug. 20, '62; company cook; WIA and CIA Chancellorsville; rejoined regt. Oct. 3, '63; MO June 13, '65; lived in Sheboygan after war; member of Twenty-Sixth Regiment Association.

Ballhorn, John (or Jacob); carpenter, Sheboygan; ENL Aug. 15, '62; Corp.; MO June 30, '65; lived in Sheboygan after war; member of Twenty-Sixth Regiment Association.

Barbiere, Guiseppe; musician, Milwaukee; ENL Aug. 20, '62; WIA and CIA Chancellorsville; deserted from parole camp at Alexandria, Va., June, '63.

Beck, Ludwig; farmer, Rhine; ENL Aug. 20, '62; WIA in leg at Gettysburg; trans. to VRC, Feb. 15, '64.

Behrend, Friedrich; carpenter, Milwaukee; ENL Aug. 21, '62; disch. Jan. 5, '63, disability.

Behrends, Bernard; tailor, Milwaukee; ENL Aug. 14, '62; Corp.; disch. Apr. 7, '63, disability.

Benim, Bruno; farmer, Milwaukee; ENL Aug. 20, '62; disch. July 15, '63, disability (one source says DOW received at Gettysburg).

Boehler [Böhler], Henry; tailor, Milwaukee; ENL Aug. 15, '62; WIA Gettysburg; rejoined regt. Nov. '63; WIA May 25, '64; MO June 13, '65; member of Robert Chivas Post No. 2, G.A.R.

Bommerl, Anton; blacksmith, Milwaukee; ENL Aug. 18, '62; disch. Mar. 21, '63, disability.

Buettner, Josep; farmer, Russel; ENL Aug. 21, '62; Corp.; MO June 13, '65; lived in Sheboygan after war; member of Twenty-Sixth Regiment Association.

Conrad, August; farmer, Sheboygan; ENL Aug. 15, '62; WIA May 25, '64, Resaca; DOW at Louisville, Ky., Aug. 25, '64.

Daub, John; carpenter, Milwaukee; ENL Aug. 19, '62; deserted Sept. 25, '62 (one source says Sept. 6) at Milwaukee.

Detsch, Michael; farmer, Sheboygan; ENL Aug. 24, '62; WIA June 22, '64; DOW at Chattanooga, Tenn., July 13, '64.

Diefenthaeler, Philip; farmer, Rhine; ENL Aug. 21, '62; KIA July 1, '63, Gettysburg, Pa.

Ehrmann, William; farmer, Milwaukee; ENL Aug. 20, '62; Sergt., 1st Sergt.; WIA in leg at Gettysburg, July 1, '63; MO June 13, '65; suffered from effects of wound after war; member Robert Chivas Post, G.A.R.

Engelking, Frederick; carpenter, Rhine; ENL Aug. 21, '62; Corp., Sergt.; CIA Thompsons' Cr. near Cheraw, S.C., Mar. 5, '65; paroled Apr., '65; MO June 13, '65; lived in Sheboygan after war; member of Twenty-Sixth Regiment Association.

Flentze, Theodor; shoemaker, Rhine; ENL Aug. 21, '62; disch. Mar. 11, '63, disability.

Frick, John; farmer, Rhine; ENL Aug. 21, '62; detached to brigade headquarters Dec. 17, '64; MO June 13, '65.

Goelz, Adam; carpenter, Milwaukee; ENL Aug. 21, '62; WIA Gettysburg; rejoined regt. Nov. '63; absent sick at MO of regt.

Goetzmann, Gustav; barkeeper, Milwaukee; ENL Aug. 16, '62; Corp., Sergt.; trans. to VRC, Dec. 2, '63; MO July 1, '65; member of Robert Chivas Post No. 2, G.A.R.; founding member of Twenty-Sixth Regiment Association.

Gottfried, Wenzel; carpenter, Milwaukee; ENL Aug. 18, '62; KIA May 2, '63, Chancellorsville, Va.

Graefe, Charles [Karl] A.; carpenter, Sheboygan; ENL Aug. 16, '62; WIA in right arm May 15, '64, Resaca; trans. to VRC Mar. 13, '65; MO Aug. 19, '65; right arm permanently incapacitated; died in Sheboygan, April 10, 1928.

Grasse, Charles; cooper, Sheboygan; ENL Aug. 15, '62; Corp.; slightly WIA Chancellorsville; trans. to VRC, Nov. 15, '63; MO Aug. 4, '65.

Gropp, Henry; miller, Sheboygan; ENL Aug. 18, '62; Corp.; MO May 30, '65.

Harsch, Christian; butcher, Prairie du Chien; ENL Aug. 15, '62; Sergt.; WIA Chancellorsville; trans. to VRC, Nov. 6, '63.

Hartmann, Jacob; farmer, Rhine; ENL Aug. 21, '62; KIA May 2, '63, Chancellorsville, Va.

Hartmann, Philip; farmer, Rhine; ENL Aug. 21, '62; MO June 13, '65. MO papers say he "was never absent from his command."

Hein, Anton; shoemaker; Russel; ENL Aug. 21, '62; deserted Oct. 10, '62 at Baltimore, MD.

Held, Carl; laborer, Milwaukee; Aug. 15, '62; CIA Gettysburg; DOD (dysentery) in Confederate prison at Andersonville, Ga., Apr. 1, '64 and buried in grave 303.

Hill, Ludwig; blacksmith, Milwaukee; ENL Aug. 15, '62; Sergt.; CIA Thompsons' Cr. near Cheraw, S.C., Mar. 5, '65; paroled Apr. '65; absent sick at MO of regt.

Hoberg, Christopher; cooper, Norway Prarie; Feb. 12, '64; WIA May 15, '64, Resaca; rejoined regt. Sept. '64; detached to brigade headquarters; trans. to Co. H, 3rd Wis. Inf., June 10, '65.

Imig, Frederick; printer, Sheboygan; ENL Aug. 15, 62; WIA and CIA Chancellorsville; paroled and returned to regt. ca. Oct. 3, '63; trans. to VRC, Apr. 22, '64.

Jintra, H. Wenzel; workman, Milwaukee; ENL Aug. 16, '62; MO June 13, '65; enlisted in 45th New York Vols.

Kapinos, Wenzel; laborer, Milwaukee; ENL Aug. 16, '62; WIA Chancellorsville; WIA May 15, '64, Resaca; rejoined regt. Apr. '65; MO June 13, '65.

Kirschner, Ferdinand; farmer, Paycheedah; ENL Aug. 19, '62; teamster and later ambulance guard; MO June 13, '65.

Kohn, Martin; carpenter, Moselle; ENL Aug. 20, '62; Corp.; WIA May 10, '64, Resaca; disch. for disability; attended fiftieth anniversary at Gettysburg in 1913.

Krebs, Otto; harnessmaker, Sheboygan; ENL Aug. 20, '62; Corp.; CIA Gettysburg; MO June 13, '65.

Krueger, Carl; laborer, Waukesha; ENL Aug. 15, '62; hospital nurse; MO June 13, '65; member of Robert Chivas Post No. 2, G.A.R.

Kuhn, George; farmer, Rhine; ENL Aug. 21, '62; company cook; KIA, June 22, '64 at Kennesaw Mtn. near Marietta, Ga.

Kuhn, Philip; saloonkeeper, Milwaukee; ENL Aug. 14, '62; Corp., Sergt.; WIA in left elbow Gettysburg; sent to hospital in Chester, PA; rejoined at Chattanooga in Jan. or Feb. '64; absent sick (probably since Nov. '64) in Jeffersonville, IN, at MO of regt.; disch. at hospital in Milwaukee, May 26, '65; moved to Chicago after war; member of George H. Thomas Post No. 5, G.A.R; died in Chicago, Sept. 30, 1895.

Lauermann, Joseph; shoemaker, Milwaukee; ENL Aug. 15, '62; sick in hospital Dec. 2, '64 to Mar. 28, '65; MO June 19, '65.

Levit, Jacob; merchant, Milwaukee; ENL Aug. 15, '62; absent sick since Nov. 18, '64 at MO of regt.

Mahloch, Jacob; farmer, Rhine; ENL Aug. 20, '62; WIA by bullet through left calf at Resaca, Ga, May 15, '64; taken to General Hospital in Murfreesboro, Tenn.; rejoined regt. Oct. 1, '64; MO June 13, '65; returned to Sheboygan after war and became farmer near Schleswig, later moving to Keil in Manitowoc Co.; member of Post 190, G.A.R. and Post 99, American Legion; attended fiftieth anniversary of regiment in Milwaukee; attended fiftieth anniversary at Gettysburg in 1913; died June

29, 1930, as last surviving Civil War veteran in Keil, Wisc. Buried in Sts. Peter and Paul Catholic Cemetery, Keil, Wisc.

Mathes, Philip; farmer, Rhine; ENL Aug. 20, '62; WIA in foot at Gettysburg; rejoined regt. Nov. '63; WIA May 15, '64, Resaca; disch. due to wounds at U.S. General Hospital, Prairie du Chien, Wisc., June 30, '65; farmer in Rockville, Wisc., after war; member of G.A.R. post in Keil, Wisc.

Mattes [or Mathes], Philip; farmer, Rhine [some sources say Sheboygan]; ENL Aug. 20, '62; Corp.; KIA July 1, '63, Gettysburg, Pa.

Mauer, Peter; farmer, Rhine; ENL Aug. 20, '62; Corp.; WIA Peach Tree Creek; absent sick at MO of regt.

Mayer (or Meyer), John George; shoemaker, Milwaukee; ENL Aug. 15, '62; KIA July 1, '63, Gettysburg, Pa.

Meiners, Heinrich; laborer, Milwaukee; ENL Aug. 15, '62; Corp.; WIA Gettysburg; disch. due to wounds Dec. 25, '63.

Möhr, Henry; cooper, Milwaukee; ENL Aug. 21, '62; Corp.; KIA July 1, '63, Gettysburg, Pa.

Müller, Valentine; farmer, Rhine; ENL Aug. 20, '62; WIA July, '64; DOW at Kingston, Ga., Aug. 17, '64.

Nell, Philip; carpenter, Rhine; ENL Aug. 21, '62; member of color guard; WIA May 15, '64, Resaca; DOW at Louisville, Ky., July 25, '64.

Nytes, Jacob; carpenter, Sheboygan; ENL Aug. 21, '62; Sergt., 1st Sergt.; slightly WIA Chancellorsville; WIA May 15, '64, Resaca; disch. at Madison, Wisc., to be mustered as 2nd Lieut., Co. I, 45th Wis. Inf., Sept. 24, '64.

Oberbeck, Ludwig; laborer, Sheboygan; ENL Aug. 15, '62; company cook; MO June 13, '65.

Pieper, Carl; farmer, Moselle; ENL Aug. 21, '62; MO June 13, '65.

Pieper, Friedrich; carpenter, Sheboygan; ENL Aug. 15, '62; CIA Thompsons' Cr. near Cheraw, S. C., Mar. 5, '65; paroled Apr. '65; absent in Parole Camp at MO of regt.; lived in Sheboygan after war; member of Twenty-Sixth Regiment Association.

Pieper, Henry; blacksmith, Sheboygan; ENL Aug. 21, '62; regimental carpenter; MO June 13, '65.

Polaschack (or Pollaschek), Adolf; laborer, Milwaukee; ENL Aug. 13, '62; disch. Apr. 15, '63, disability.

Rausche, Frederick; tailor, Sheboygan; ENL Aug. 19, '62; Corp.; Sergt.; WIA Gettysburg; trans. to VRC; disch. due to wounds Sept. 21, '64.

Redetski, Samuel; farmer, Russel; ENL Aug. 21, '62; trans. to VRC, Oct. 1, '64; disch. Oct. 24, '64, disability.

Reichenberg, Richard; butcher, Milwaukee; ENL Aug. 14, '62; brigade butcher and later ambulance driver in Aug. '63; listed in most sources as deserted Sept. 25, '63, from Annapolis, MD, but monthly report states deserted from furlough July 4, '63.

Remeck (or Reineck), Henry; farmer, Rhine; ENL Aug. 22, '62; Corp.; slightly WIA Chancellorsville; rejoined regt. July 10, '63; MO June 13, '65.

Reuter, Franz; ironworker, Milwaukee; ENL Aug. 15, '62; Corp.; KIA July 20, '64, Peach Tree Creek, Ga.

Roessler, Carl; musician, Milwaukee; ENL Aug. 15, '62; musician; MO June 13, '65.

Roll (sometimes listed as Boll), Erasmus; farmer; Russel; ENL Aug. 21, '62; WIA Chancellorsville; trans. to VRC, Sept. 7, '63.

Rosenbauer, John; farmer, Rhine; ENL Aug. 21, '62; company cook; WIA by musket ball in arm and CIA at Chancellorsville; rejoined regt. Apr. 8, '64; WIA May 15, '64, Resaca; MO June 13, '65.

Roth, John C. [also known as F. Conrad Roth]; cigarmaker, Milwaukee; ENL Aug. 14, '62; teamster for 2nd brigade, 3rd division, XI Corps; WIA in shoulder and right breast at Chancellorsville; trans. to VRC, Oct. 3, '63; lived in Madison after war; member of Twenty-Sixth Regiment Association.

Schaefer, Carl; farmer, Herman; ENL Aug. 19, '62; disch. Apr. 6, '63, disability.

Schaefer, George; shoemaker, Milwaukee; ENL Aug. 19, '62; DOD at Berea Church, Va., Feb. 2, '63.

Schmahl, George; farmer, Rhine; ENL Aug. 21, '62; WIA Averasboro; disch. due to wounds at General Hospital, Davids' Island, NY, Oct. 21, '65.

Schmidt, Friedrich; carpenter, Mosel; ENL Aug. 21, '62; disch. Oct. 5, '62, disability.

Schmitz, John; carpenter, Sheboygan; ENL Aug. 15, '62; company cook; MO June 13, '65.

Schrage, Friedrich; teamster, Sheboygan; ENL Aug. 21, '62; disch. due to disability at Brooks Station, Va., July 16, '63; lived in Menasha after war; member of Twenty-Sixth Regiment Association.

Schwenicke (sometimes given as Schroennicke) August; farmer, Rhine; ENL Aug. 21, '62; DOD Dec. 2, '63, Bridgeport, Tenn.

Siebelist, Rudolph; carpenter, Milwaukee; ENL Aug. 14, '62; Corp., Sergt.; WIA May 15, '64, Resaca; rejoined regt. July '64; WIA Peach Tree Creek; absent wounded at MO of regt.; member of Robert Chivas Post No. 2, G.A.R.

Smitka, Franz; butcher, Milwaukee; ENL Aug. 13, '62; Sergt.; disch. Mar. 21, '63, disability.

Sommer, Gotthard (or Gottlieb); farmer, Moselle; ENL Aug. 21, '62; DOD (typhoid fever) Nov. 17, '62, Fairfax Court House, Va.

Spranger, Friedrich; farmer, Rhine; ENL Aug. 21, '62; WIA at Resaca, Ga., May 15, '64; DOW in field hospital May 16, '64.

Stamp, Philip; farmer, Rhine; ENL Aug. 21, '62; DOD at Washington, D.C., Oct. 26, '62.

Steffen, John; cooper, Sheboygan; ENL Aug. 21, '62; pioneer; WIA and CIA Gettysburg; rejoined regt. Nov. 17, '63; MO June 13, '65; attended fiftieth anniversary at Gettysburg in 1913.

Steffen, Joseph; cooper, Sheboygan; ENL Aug. 15, '62; WIA Gettysburg; rejoined regt. Apr. 30, '64; MO June 13, '65.

Steinbach, Jacob; carpenter, Sheboygan; ENL Aug. 15, 62; WIA in leg at Gettysburg; rejoined regt. Mar. '64; MO June 13, '65.

Steinhaus, Friedrich; farmer, Mosel; ENL Aug. 21, '62; WIA Gettysburg, leg amputated; absent wounded at MO of regt.

Streiber, Adam; farmer, Rhine; ENL Aug. 21, '62; disch. for disability.

Strutz, Gottleib; farmer, Rhine; ENL Aug. 21, '62; KIA Mar. 16, '65, Averasboro, N.C.

Textor, Anton; laborer, Milwaukee; ENL Aug. 16, '62; WIA in shoulder at Gettysburg July 1, '63; DOW in Jarvis Hospital at Baltimore, Md., July 22, '63.

Thiele, Friedrich; farmer, Rhine; ENL Aug. 20, '62; WIA Gettysburg; rejoined regt. Jan. 3, '64; MO June 13, '65; died in 1877.

Trester, Hubert; merchant, Sheboygan; Aug. 20, '62; regimental muster roll states deserted from Falmouth, Va., Dec. '63 and fled to Canada; monthly report states "Left regt. on Furlough expiring May 23. Declared before leaving he should not return to regt. His wife keeps store at Sheboygan, Wisc."; arrested at Detroit, Mich., Mar. 13, '65; MO roll says "deserted while on furlough June 8, 1863." MO June 13, '65.

Voigt, Robert; saddler, Sheboygan; ENL Jan. 22, '64; WIA May 15, '64, Resaca; rejoined regt. Apr. '65; trans. to Co. H, 3rd Wis. Inf., June 10, '65.

Wagner, Michael; farmer, Moselle; ENL Aug. 21, '62; WIA Chancellorsville; trans. to VRC, Sept. 12, '63; MO June 28, '65.

Wapler, Albert; Milwaukee; ENL Aug. 14, '62; musician (drummer); company cook; trans. to VRC Sept. 12, '63; member of Robert Chivas Post No. 2, G.A.R.; founding member of Twenty-Sixth Regiment Association.

Welsh, Henry; farmer, Moselle; ENL Aug. 18, '62; WIA Chancellorsville; disch. Oct. 14, '63, disability.

Wickesberg, Karl; carpenter, Herman; ENL Aug. 15, '62; Sergt.; WIA in wrist at Gettysburg July 1, '63; DOW May 15, '64, Resaca, Ga., of wounds received the same day; buried in grave 570, Section K, national cemetery, Chattanooga, Tenn.

Woerner, Friedrich; farmer, Rhine; ENL Aug. 21, '62; KIA May 2, '63, Chancellorsville, Va.

Zeiger, Franz; farmer, Rhine; Aug. 20, '62; WIA Gettysburg; WIA Peach Tree Creek; absent wounded at MO of regt.

Zimmermann, Philip J.; carpenter, Rhine; ENL Aug. 20, '62; WIA and CIA Chancellorsville; rejoined regt. Oct. '63; MO June 13, '65.

Zimmermann, Wilhelm; farmer, Wauwatosa; ENL Aug. 15, '62; disch. Jan. 22, '63, disability.

Zinke, Adam; cooper, Milwaukee; ENL Aug. 18, '62; WIA and CIA at Chancellorsville; trans. to VRC, Aug. 19, '63; MO June 28, '65.

Zinke [or Zünke], John Adam; carpenter, Milwaukee; ENL Aug. 18, '62; KIA May 2, '63, Chancellorsville, Va.

COMPANY I, WENZE GUARD

Captains

Franz Landa; Milwaukce; rank from Sept. 3, '62; resigned Nov. 19, '62; died in Milwaukee, April, 1872.

William Smith; Milwaukee; appointed Dec. 15, '62 from 1st Lieut. Co. G; KIA July 1, '63, Gettysburg, Pa..

John P. Seemann; commissioner, Milwaukee; appointed Dec. 30, '63 from Co. C; KIA July 20, '64, Peach Tree Creek, Ga.

William H. Hemschemeyer; saloonkeeper, Manitowoc; appointed Oct. 19, '64 from 1st Sergt. Co. F; 1st Lieut., Apr. 13, '64; MO June 13, '65; lived in Manitowoc after war; elected to local offices and state assembly in 1879 and 1880; member of Twenty-Sixth Regiment Association.

First Lieutenants

Henry J. Berninger; teacher, Milwaukee; rank from Sept. 17, '62; trans. to Co. K.

Albert Wallber; clerk, Milwaukee; appointed Feb. 1, '63; from 2nd Lieut. Co. F; brigade ordnance officer Feb. 1, '63; Adjutant, May 10, '63, but not mustered; CIA Gettysburg; escaped from Libby Prison Feb. 9, '64; resigned Apr. 3, '64; co-authored with Bernhard Domschcke a description of life in Confederate prisons titled "Erinnerungen: 20 Monate in Gefangenschaft"; became vice president of Weisel & Vilter Manufacturing Company in Milwaukee; secretary of Milwaukee Brewers' Association; president of the German-English Academy in Milwaukee; member of *Milwaukee Turnverein*; prominent local dramatic actor; member of *Deutsche Gesselschaft*; member of Wolcott Post No. 1, G.A.R.; member of Robert Chivas Post No. 2, G.A.R.; member of Military Order of the Loyal Legion of the United States; died in Milwaukee Dec. 17, 1911.

Oswald Schubert; merchant, Milwaukee; appointed Nov. 15, '64; ENL Aug. 18, '62; Corp.; quartermaster dept.; promoted Commissary Sergt. and detached to commissary dept. Sept. 1, '62; rejoined Co. Dec. 10, '62; trans. to Co. F, May 2, '64; from 1st Sergt. Co. F; MO June 13, '65.

Second Lieutenants

John Orth; Milwaukee; rank from Sept. 10, '62; wounded by accident at Thoroughfare Gap, Oct. 5, '62; trans. to Co. G.

Peter Fernekes; tinsmith, Milwaukee; appointed Dec. 22, '62 from Sergt., Major; promoted 1st Lieut. Co. E, Mar. 15, '63.

George P. Traeumer [Träumer]; engineer, Milwaukee; appointed Mar. 15, '63; ENL Aug. 20, '62; 1st Sergt.; promoted Adjutant, Sept. 16, '63.

Enlisted Men

Baatz, Julius; farmer, Milwaukee; ENL Jan. 4, '64; trans. to Co. I, 3rd Wis. Inf., June 10, '65.

Baatz, William; farmer, Mequon; ENL Aug. 18, '62; WIA and CIA Chancellorsville; rejoined Oct. 4, '63; MO June 13, '65.

Baerecke, Maximilian; miller, Milwaukee; ENL Aug. 15, '62; Sergt.; reduced to private July 1, '63; detailed as brigade pioneer May 22, '64; rejoined regt. June 1, '65; MO June 13, '65; member of Robert Chivas Post No. 2, G.A.R.

Balluff, Carl; brewer, Milwaukee; ENL Aug. 18, '62; musician; severely WIA Gettysburg; trans. to Invalid Corps, Jan. 15, '64; lived in La Crosse after war; member of Twenty-Sixth Regiment Association.

Bauer, Carl August C.; mason, Milwaukee; ENL Jan. 20, '64; trans. to Co. I, 3rd Wis. Inf., June 10, '65.

Beckmann, Charles; farmer, Mequon; ENL Aug. 19, '62; Corp.; severely WIA Chancellorsville; rejoined regt. Jan. 23, '64; MO June 13, '65.

Behnke, Heinrich; cooper, Milwaukee; ENL Aug. 20, '62; WIA May 2, '63, Chancellorsville; DOW at XI Corps hospital, Brooks Station, Va., June 10, '63.

Blum, Jacob; shoemaker, Milwaukee; ENL Aug. 20, '62; Corp., Sergt.; WIA June 19, '64 near Kennesaw Mountain, Ga., and sent to hospital in Nashville, Tenn.; trans. to VRC, Jan. 10, '65; MO July 15, '65.

Borkenhagen, Gustav; cooper, Milwaukee; Jan. 20, '64; trans. to Co. I, 3rd Wis. Inf., June 10, '65.

Boyer, George; farmer, Brown; ENL Aug. 19, '62; detailed to ambulance corps Oct. 10, '62; rejoined regt. Apr. 20, '64; WIA Kennesaw Mountain June 22, '64 and sent to hospital in Louisville, Ky.; absent sick at MO of regt.

Braun, Ferdinand; blacksmith, Milwaukee; ENL Aug. 21, '62; medical dept. (hospital nurse); DOD (typhoid fever) at Stafford Court House, Va., Feb. 19, '63.

Braun, Gustav; wagonmaker, Milwaukee; ENL Aug. 21, '62; colonels' servant; severely WIA Chancellorsville; trans. to Invalid Corps, Sept. 1, '63.

Bruckert, Charles; dyer, Milwaukee; ENL Aug. 14, '62; Sergt., 1st Sergt.; acting 2nd Lieut., June 1, '63, confirmed but not mustered; WIA with compound fracture of lower right leg at Gettysburg, Pa, July 1, '63; leg amputated; DOW July 16, '63 and buried in Gettysburg National Cemetery, Wisconsin Plot, grave A-16.

Brueggemann, Otto; hunter, Milwaukee; ENL Aug. 21, '62; absent sick Dec. 5, '62; disch. in convalescent camp near Stafford Court House, Va., Mar. 30, '63, disability.

Bulda, Joseph; farmer, Caledonia; ENL Aug. 14, '62; company cook; WIA July 7, '64; absent sick Nov. 1, '64 in U.S. General Hospital at Prairie du Chien, Wisc.; MO June 30, '65.

Crusius, Christian; farmer, Milwaukee; ENL Aug. 21, '62; Sergt.; WIA and CIA Chancellorsville; rejoined regt. Oct. 4, '63; WIA Peach Tree Creek July 20, '64 and sent to hospital in Nashville, Tenn.; rejoined regt. Apr. 25, '65; 1st Lieut. Co. H, June 2, '65, but not mustered; MO June 13, '65.

Dallmann, Carl; butcher, Milwaukee; Aug. 14, '62; WIA while on picket Mar. 15, '63; trans. to VRC, Jan. 15, '64; MO June 28, '65.

Damkoehler, Ernst; farmer, Brown; ENL Aug. 19, '62; ambulance teamster; detached to brigade commissary dept. Oct. '62 until consolidation of XI and XII Corps; rejoined regt. Apr. 24, '64; WIA and CIA May 15, '64; DOW in Confederate prison at Andersonville, Ga., June 26, '64 and buried in Wisconsin section of National Cemetery near Americus, Ga., grave 2522.

Duesing (or Diesing), Johann; teamster, Milwaukee; ENL Aug. 21, '62; Corp., Sergt.; MO June 13, '65.

Dworschack, Peter; brewer, Wauwatosa; ENL Aug. 18, '62; WIA and CIA Chancellorsville; held in Richmond prison; rejoined regt. Oct. 4, '63; WIA Mar. 16, '65 and sent to Ft. Schuyler Hospital in New York City; MO May 30, '65.

Feldmann, Philip; farmer, Milwaukee; ENL Aug. 19, '62; WIA July 1, '63, Gettysburg, Pa.; DOW in XI Corps hospital Aug. 2, '63.

Felsecker, Franz J.; teacher, Milwaukee; ENL Aug. 21, '62; medical dept.; disch. in camp at Stafford Court House, Va., Jan. 19, '63, medical disability.

Ferge, C. Gottlieb; cigarmaker, Milwaukee; ENL Aug. 18, '62; Corp.; KIA July 1, '63, Gettysburg, Pa.

Fischer, Charles; printer, Milwaukee; Aug. 15, '62; Corp.; WIA Chancellorsville; disch. at Stafford Court House, Va., Mar. 30, '63, medical disability.

Fischer, Henry Albert; farmer, Sauk City; ENL Aug. 20, '62; WIA Chancellorsville; trans. to VRC, Mar. 1, '64; MO June 30, '65.

Friedrich, Franz; shoemaker, Racine; ENL Aug. 18, '62; Corp., Sergt; MO June 13, '65; attended fiftieth anniversary at Gettysburg in 1913.

Gall, Jacob; cooper, Milwaukee; ENL Mar. 25, '64; CIA Mar. 5, '65; paroled Apr. '65 and sent to hospital in Madison, Wisc.; trans. to Co. I, 3rd Wis. Inf., June 10, '65.

Gasper, Wilhelm; hosteler, Milwaukee; ENL Aug. 19, '62; colonels' servant; teamster; deserted June 6, '63 and listed as "gone to Washington by steamer"; returned; MO June 13, '65. Note on muster out papers says: "Was with the Regt. from the beginning but was in no fight."

Giljohann, Friedrich; patternmaker, Milwaukee; ENL Aug. 15, '62; musician; DOW in div. field hospital near Atlanta, Ga., of wounds received same day, Aug. 13, '64.

Graefe (or sometimes Graf), Friedrich; butcher, Milwaukee; ENL Aug. 12, '62; company cook; disch. at Stafford Court House, Va., Apr. 16, '63, medical disability.

Groff, John; farmer, Town 12; ENL Aug. 13, '62; WIA in ribs at Chancellorsville; rejoined regt. Apr. 27, '64; WIA June 22, '64 and furloughed to Milwaukee; rejoined regt. Apr. 25, '65; MO June 13, '65.

Hartung, Edward; gardener, Milwaukee; ENL Aug. 21, '62; company cook; disch. in camp at Stafford Court house, Va., Jan. 19, '63, medical disability.

Heilig, Ferdinand; shoemaker, Milwaukee; Aug. 19, '62; company cook; CIA Gettysburg and held prisoner in Richmond, Va.; dropped from rolls by misunderstanding Aug. 31, '64; placed back on rolls Apr. 30, '65; absent at MO of regt.

Heilmann, Adam; farmer, Sturgeon Bay, ENL Aug. 19, '62; absent sick Apr. 25, '63; trans. to Invalid Corps Sept. 1, '63.

Heilmann, George; Brown; ENL Aug. 19, '62; trans. to VRC, Oct. 14, '63; MO June 28, '65.

Heitefuss (or sometimes Heidefuss), Fritz; turner, Milwaukee; ENL Aug. 12, '62; Sergt.; MO June 13, '65.

Hirsch, Friedrich; cooper, Milwaukee; ENL Aug. 13, '62; detailed company cook May 25, '64; MO June 13, '65.

Hoene, Julius William Franz; turner, Milwaukee; ENL Aug. 19, '62; teamster; hospital cook and nurse; deserted near Brooks Station, Va., June 5, '63.

Hoenig, George; cooper, Milwaukee; ENL Mar. 25, '64; trans. to Co. I, 3rd Wis. Inf., June 10, '65.

Jacoby (or sometimes Jacobi), Charles; miller, Milwaukee; ENL Aug. 12, '62; WIA Chancellorsville; deserted and dropped form rolls Aug. 31, '64.

Jenkins, Michael; farmer, Milwaukee; ENL Aug. 20, '62; CIA Gettysburg; DOD in Confederate prison at Belle Isle, Richmond, Va., Oct. 8, '63.

Johnson, Edmond; farmer, Greenfield; ENL Aug. 20, '62; CIA Gettysburg July 1, '63; returned to regt. Nov. 18, '63; WIA May 15, '64, Resaca; rejoined regt. July 13, '64; WIA by shell near Atlanta, Ga., July 27, '64 and sent to U.S. General Hospital at Milwaukee; MO June 16, '65. Morning report notes "Good Soldier."

Justin, Louis; pianomaker, Milwaukee; ENL Aug. 21, '62; WIA Gettysburg; disch. at Harvey General Hospital, Madison, Wisc.; Jan. 20, '64.

Kamschulte, Clemens; carpenter, Milwaukee; ENL Aug. 21, '62; WIA and CIA Chancellorsville; exchanged Sept. 25, '63; dishonorably disch. Oct. 1, '63 (Adjutant Generals' report lists him as deserting and dropped from rolls Oct. 31, '64).

Kaul, Jacob; farmer, Milwaukee; ENL Aug. 15, '62; detached as teamster with ambulance corps Dec. 1, '62; absent sick May 14, '64; rejoined regt. May 24, '65; MO June 13, '65; after war retired to live on earnings from real estate holdings and also engaged in furniture business; active Republican; died in 1873.

Klatt, Wilhelm; musician, Milwaukee; ENL Aug. 18, '62; WIA June 22, '64 and sent to hospital at Mound City, Ill., then to U.S. Hospital at Prairie du Chien, Wisc.; absent wounded at MO of regt.

Koege, John; merchant, Milwaukee; Aug. 15, '62; Corp.; WIA Chancellorsville; reduced to ranks Jan. 1, '64; deserted and dropped from rolls Apr. 30, '64.

Koepnick [Köpnick], John; tailor, Milwaukee; ENL Aug. 14, '62; KIA, June 22, '64 at Kennesaw Mtn. near Marietta, Ga.

Kolberg, Johann; sailor, Milwaukee; ENL Aug. 21, '62; regimental quartermaster dept.; absent sick Feb. 15, '63; disch. at U.S. General Hospital, Cleveland, OH, Mar. 9, '64, disability.

Kowar, Joseph; farmhand, Caledonia; ENL Aug. 19, '62; DOD (heart disease) at Milwaukee Sept. 19, '62.

Kraft, Gottlieb; smith, Milwaukee; ENL Aug. 21, '62; disch. at Stafford Court House, Va., Mar. 30, '63, medical disability.

Krecklow, William; farmer, Milwaukee; ENL Jan. 20, '64; absent sick May 7 to June 1, '64; WIA June 22, '64; rejoined regt. Aug. 30, '64; trans. to Co. I, 3rd Wis. Inf., June 10, '65.

Krell (or Krill), Jacob; farmer, Rochester; Aug. 19, '62; absent sick Apr. 21, '63; trans. to Invalid Corps, July 1, '63.

Kreofsky, Rudolph; fisherman, Milwaukee; ENL Aug. 14, '62; company cook; WIA June 22, '64, Kennesaw Mountain and taken to hospital in St. Louis, Mo.; rejoined regt. Apr. 16, '65; MO June 13, '65.

Kruse, Diedrich; farmer, Mequon; ENL Aug. 20, '62; KIA July 1, '63, Gettysburg, Pa.

Kundecker (or sometimes Kundiger), Friedrich; sailor, Milwaukee; ENL Aug. 12, '62; disch. at Stafford Court House, Va., Mar. 30, '63, medical disability.

Lacy (or sometimes Lechky), Chancey; Waterford; ENL Aug. 18, '62; WIA in both legs at Chancellorsville; rejoined regt. Jan. 3, '64; WIA May 25, '64 and sent to hospital in Jeffersonville, Ind.; trans. to VRC, Dec. 4, '64.

Laisse, Rudolph; blacksmith, Milwaukee; ENL Aug. 15, '62; WIA May 25, '64; absent sick Nov. 1, '64 in U.S. General Hospital, Madison, Wisc.; MO June 30, '65.

Lang, Lorenz; liveryman, Milwaukee; ENL Aug. 15, '62; absent sick from Nov. 1, '64; DOD Nov. 10, '64, U.S. General Hospital, Nashville, Tenn.

Lastofka (or Latofska), Wenzel; laborer, Milwaukee; ENL Aug. 14, '62; WIA by musket ball in axilla and right humerus near neck at Chancellorsville; right arm amputated May 15 and DOW July 10, '63.

Lau, Johann; farmer, Mequon; ENL Aug. 19, '62; KIA May 2, '63, Chancellorsville, Va.

Lehmann, Wilhelm; shoemaker, Milwaukee; ENL Aug. 18, '62; WIA Chancellorsville; trans. to VRC, Sept. 22, '64; MO July 14, '65.

Lew (or Leu), Henry; fisherman, Milwaukee; ENL Aug. 15, '62; pioneer; WIA Gettysburg; disch. at Saterlee Hospital, Philadelphia, PA, May 24, '65.

Luedolph (or sometimes Lydolf), Heinrich; shoemaker, Mequon; ENL Aug. 21, '62; musician; nurse in field hospital; absent sick Jan. 16, '63 to Apr. 26, '64; absent sick beginning Nov. 1, '64 and absent sick in U.S. General Hospital, Prairie du Chien, Wisc., at MO of regt.

Marquardt, Charles; cooper, Milwaukee; ENL Jan. 20, '64; absent sick beginning June 21, '64; DOD at U.S. General Hospital, Chattanooga, Tenn., June 27, '64.

Matuschka, Frederick William; cooper, Milwaukee; ENL Mar. 25, '64; WIA June 19, '64 and sent to hospital in Nashville, Ind.; rejoined regt. Nov. 3, '64; trans. to Co. I, 3rd Wis. Inf., June 10, '65.

Mechtel, Leonard; papermaker, Milwaukee; ENL Aug. 18, '62; Corp.; absent sick Apr. 25 to June 3, '63; MO June 13, '65.

Mikulesky (or sometimes Michalosky), Joseph; farmer, Caledonia; ENL Aug. 21, '62; WIA Kennesaw Mountain June 22, '64 and sent to U.S. General Hospital, Knoxville, Tenn.; absent wounded at MO of regt.

Mueller, Friedrich; laborer, Milwaukee; ENL Aug. 21, '62; WIA June 22, '64 and sent to hospital in Jeffersonville, Ind.; trans. to VRC, Jan. 10, '65; MO July 14, '65.

Mueller, Wilhelm Max; laborer, Milwaukee; ENL Aug. 18, '62; Corp.; disch. in camp near Stafford Court House, Va., Jan. 19, '63, medical disability.

Muhlack, Friedrich; laborer, Milwaukee; ENL Aug. 21, '62; absent sick Nov. 1, '64 to Jan. 5, '65; MO June 13, '65.

Nero, Friedrich; joiner, Mequon; ENL Aug. 18, '62; WIA Chancellorsville; right arm amputated May 6 and DOW at King Street Hospital, Alexandria, Va., June 14, '63.

Neumann, Johann Friedrich; laborer, Milwaukee; ENL Aug. 14, '62; Corp.; WIA Aug. 15, '64; rejoined regt. Sept. 28, '64; MO June 13, '65.

Neumeister, Anton; blacksmith, Mequon; ENL Aug. 18, '62; WIA Gettysburg; WIA Kennesaw Mountain June 22, '64; absent wounded in Harvey General Hospital, Madison, Wisc., at MO of regt.

Neumeister, Julius; farmer, Mequon; Aug. 19, '62; WIA Gettysburg; rejoined regt. July 21, '64; absent sick Jan. 2, '65 to May 20, '65; MO June 13, '65.

Paider, Joseph [Josef Paidr]; potter, Milwaukee; ENL Aug. 19, '62; Corp.; MO June 13, '65; moved to Kewaskum after war; member of Twenty-Sixth Regiment Association.

Pazdernick, Wenzel; cooper, Milwaukee; ENL Aug. 20, '62; absent sick Mar. 30, '63; trans. to VRC, Nov. 15, '63; founding member of Twenty-Sixth Regiment Association.

Pfeiffer, Anton; gardener, Green Bay; ENL Aug. 21, '62; absent sick July 10, '63; DOD of dyspepsia in 3rd Division hospital at Alexandria, Va., Oct. 10, '63.

Regenbrecht, George; farmer, Greenfield; ENL Aug. 15, '62; Corp.; KIA July 1, '63, Gettysburg, Pa.

Rezac, Frank [Frantisek Rezac]; farmer, Rochester; ENL Aug. 19, '62; WIA Gettysburg; trans. to VRC, Mar. 15, '64; MO June 26, '65; attended fiftieth anniversary at Gettysburg in 1913.

Richter, William; driver, Milwaukee; ENL Aug. 21, '62; CIA Gettysburg and held prisoner in Richmond, Va.; WIA June 22, '64; rejoined regt. Apr. 20, '65 at Raleigh, NC; absent at MO of regt.

Ruehl (or Reihl), Jeremais; mason, Milwaukee; ENL Aug. 21, '62; company cook; MO June 13, '65.

Rosewal, Josef; farmer, Caledonia; ENL Aug. 21, '62; CIA Gettysburg and held prisoner in Richmond, Va.; rejoined regt. Nov. 18, '63; absent sick Apr. 27, '64; trans. to VRC, Jan. 10, '65; MO July 5, '65.

Scherz, Georg; gardener, Milwaukee; ENL Aug. 14, '62; Corp.; furlough granted Apr. 23, '63; trans. to Invalid Corps, Sept. 1, '63; MO June 26, '65.

Schreiber, Ernst; cooper, Milwaukee; ENL Aug. 13, '62; CIA Gettysburg; WIA Kennesaw Mountain June 22, '64 and sent to hospital in Nashville, Tenn.; MO June 13, '65; attended fiftieth anniversary at Gettysburg in 1913.

Schwaibald, Jacob; carpenter, Milwaukee; ENL Aug. 16, '62; absent sick Dec. 15, '62; disch. in convalescent camp at Alexandria, Va., Jan. 15, '63, disability; member of Robert Chivas Post No. 2, G.A.R.; founding member of Twenty-Sixth Regiment Association.

Schwetz, Johann; shoemaker, Caledonia; Aug. 21, '62; absent sick June 16, '63; rejoined regt. Apr. 21, '64; absent sick Nov. 1, '64 to Apr. 7, '65; MO June 13, '65.

Smertcheck [Smrcek], Vincens; farmer, Caledonia; ENL Aug. 21, '62; absent sick Oct. 6, '62; deserted and dropped from rolls Apr. 30, '64 (another source says he died Jan. 14, '63 at Columbia Hospital, Washington, D.C.).

Smith, John B.; carpenter, Milwaukee; ENL Aug. 18, '62; WIA and CIA Chancellorsville and held prisoner in Richmond, Va.; trans. to Invalid Corps, Jan. 15, '64; MO July 13, '65.

Stauff, Jacob; peddler, Milwaukee; ENL Aug. 12, '62; Corp.; WIA Gettysburg; absent sick Nov. 20, '63 to Dec. 12, '63; color corp. and color bearer, May 26, '64; MO June 13, '65; member of Robert Chivas Post No. 2, G.A.R.; founding member of Twenty-Sixth Regiment Association.

Stegemann, Joachim; farmer, Mequon; ENL Aug. 19, '62; absent sick Apr. 3, '63' trans. to Invalid Corps Aug. 1, '63; MO June 23, '65; returned to farming in Mequon after war; died in 1873.

Stellenwerk, W. Joseph; brewer, Milwaukee; ENL Aug. 18, '62; KIA May 2, '63, Chancellorsville, Va.

Stilb, John N.; shoemaker, Kenosha; ENL Aug. 12, '62; WIA Gettysburg July 1, '63; disch. at U.S. General Hospital, Camp Chase, OH, Jan. 2, '64; returned to Kenosha after war; member of Robert Chivas Post No. 2, G.A.R.; member of Twenty-Sixth Regiment Association.

Stollberg, Carl; farmer, Milwaukee; ENL Aug. 19, '62; Corp.; disch. at Stafford Court House, Va., Mar. 30, '63, medical disability; member of Robert Chivas Post No. 2, G.A.R.; founding member of Twenty-Sixth Regiment Association.

Stollberg, Friedrich; welldigger, Milwaukee; ENL Aug. 19, '62; KIA July 1, '63, Gettysburg, Pa.

Stollberg, Friedrich William; farmer, Milwaukee; ENL Aug. 19, '62; Corp., Sergt., 1st Sergt.; WIA May 8, '64 at Buzzard Roost and sent to U.S. General Hospital in Jeffersonville, Ind.; trans. to VRC, Oct. 20, '64; MO July 14, '65; member of Robert Chivas Post No. 2, G.A.R.; founding member of Twenty-Sixth Regiment Association.

Stuetze, Gustav Adolph; teamster, Milwaukee; ENL Aug. 16, '62; wagonmaster; absent sick Sept. 12, '63 to Apr. 24, '64; failed to report on expiration of furlough Feb. 23, '64; returned to regt. and absent sick Apr. 24, '64 to Apr. 10, '65; MO June 13, '65.

Style, John; butcher, Milwaukee; ENL Aug. 12, '62; WIA Gettysburg; rejoined regt. Apr. 29, '64; KIA June 22, '64, at Kennesaw Mtn. near Marietta, Ga.

Swoboda, John; farmer, Manitowoc Rapids; ENL Aug. 19, '62; WIA and CIA Gettysburg and held prisoner in Richmond, Va.; rejoined regt. Nov. 25, '63; WIA June 22, '64 and sent to hospital in Jeffersonville, Ind.; rejoined regt. Apr. 7, '65; MO June 13, '65.

Wachter, Georg A.; carver, Milwaukee; ENL Aug. 18, '62; Sergt.; KIA May 2, '63, Chancellorsville, Va.

Walldorf, Philip; barkeeper, Milwaukee; ENL Aug. 15, '62; company cook; detailed as officers' servant Nov. '62; Corp., Sergt.; WIA Chancellorsville; recruiting duty Jan. 1-Feb. 27, '64; WIA May 15, '64 at Resaca, Ga.; DOW in division field hospital May 18, '64.

Walz, Georg; farmer, Milwaukee; Aug. 20, '62; absent sick Apr. 9 to May 21, '65; MO June 13, '65; lived in Granville after war; member of Twenty-Sixth Regiment Association.

Weidner, Adolph; cabinetmaker, Milwaukee; ENL Aug. 13, '62; WIA Gettysburg July 1, '63; rejoined regt. July 21, '64; MO June 13, '65; founding member of Twenty-Sixth Regiment Association; member of Wolcott Post No. 1, G.A.R. Brother of Charles and William Weidner, Co. C.

Winkelmann, John; cooper, Milwaukee; ENL Jan. 20, '64; trans. to Co. I, 3rd Wis. Inf., June 10, '65; member of Wolcott Post No. 1, G.A.R.

Wolfgram, Friedrich; farmer, Milwaukee; ENL Aug. 21, '62; WIA Gettysburg July 1, '63; absent sick at Harvey General Hospital, Madison, Wisc.; trans. to VRC; MO Aug. 19, '65; founding member of Twenty-Sixth Regiment Association.

Womastick, Franz; laborer, Milwaukee; ENL Aug. 14, '62; absent sick July 16, '64 at U.S. General hospital, Madison, Wisc.; MO May 26, '65. Note in muster out papers says "No History. Coward."

Zion, William; laborer, Greenfield; ENL Mar. 26, '64; detached to corps escort Feb. 24, '65; trans. to Co. I, 3rd Wis. Inf., June 10, '65.

COMPANY K, SIGEL GUARD

Captains

Louis Pelosi; Milwaukee; rank from Sept. 3, '62; resigned Mar. 12, '63.

August Schueler; engineer, Milwaukee; appointed Mar. 15, '63 from 1st Lieut, Co. D; WIA May 2, '63, Chancellorsville, Va.; leg amputated and DOW; buried in Fredericksburg Cemetery, Row B, Section C, grave 556.

Edward Carl; Sauk City; appointed June 1, '63; 2nd Lieut., Sept 3, '62; promoted 1st Lieut. Co. D, Mar. 15, '63; from 1st Lieut. Co. D; resigned Sept 26, '64; attended fiftieth anniversary at Gettysburg in 1913.

Caspar Buechner; mechanic, Fond du Lac; appointed Feb. 11, '65 from 1st Lieut. Co. E; MO June 13, '65; returned to Fond du Lac after war; member of Twenty-Sixth Regiment Association.

First Lieutenants

Jacob Heip; West Bend; appointed Sept. 10, '62; resigned Nov. 19, '62.

Henry Berninger; Milwaukee; appointed Sept 17, '62 from Co. I, resigned Feb. 26, '63.

Charles H. Doerflinger [Karl Dörflinger]; architect, Milwaukee; appointed Mar. 15, '63 from 2nd Lieut. Co. B; WIA in left ankle at Chancellorsville; lower 1/3 of left femur amputated June 27, '63 but poorly done and end of bone not covered with flesh, thus very sensitive and painful; reamputation June 27, '63; disch. due to wounds Feb. 25, '64; became a teacher at Peter Engelmanns' famous German-English Academy; member of Milwaukee Kindergarten Society; became nationally known author, editor, educator, and businessman; member of the Board of Regents of the state normal schools; president of Doerflinger Artifical Limb Company; president of the Doerflinger Book and Publishing Company; publisher of the progressive journal *New Education*, as well as *Education-Journal*, the organ of the National German American Teachers' Association, the childrens' monthly *Onkel Karl*, and several other books and education journals; member of the Wisconsin Natural History Society; active member of Milwaukee *Turnverein*, the Milwaukee Musical Society, the Liberal League, the Fortnightly Club, E. B. Walcott Post of the G.A.R., the Deutscher Club, and others; elected president of Milwaukee *Turnverein* in 1881; founding member of Twenty-Sixth Regiment Association; visited Chancellorsville battlefield in 1887 and collected relics on the Hawkins Farm; see last chapter for his varied professional activities; died Nov. 9, 1911.

Friedrich Th. Koerner; merchant, Milwaukee; Mar. 18, '64; ENL Aug. 15, '62; 1st Sergt.; WIA in leg at Chancellorsville; WIA with flesh wound in both legs May 25, '64 at New Hope Church, Ga.; Capt., Oct. 19, '64, but not mustered; disch. due to wounds Oct. 26, '64.

Second Lieutenants

Henry Greve; carpenter, Manitowoc; appointed Mar. 15, '63 from 1st. Sergt. Co. F; severely WIA by two gunshots in leg at Chancellorsville; promoted 1st Lieut. Co. E, June 1, '63.

Christian Philip; Sauk City; appointed June 1, '63; ENL Aug. 15, '62; Corp., Sergt.; promoted 1st Lieut. Co. F, Oct. 30, '63.

Enlisted Men

Balke, Friedrich; farmer, Honey Creek; ENL Jan. 16, '64; absent sick May 26 to July 10, '64; sent to div. hospital Aug. 22, '64; DOD at Atlanta, Ga., Sept. 30, '64.

Bartsch, Anton; laborer, Prairie du Sac; ENL Aug. 12, '62; sent to hospital Dec. 8, '62; returned to regt. Apr. 11, '63; CIA Chancellorsville; sent to parole camp at Annapolis, MD; trans. to VRC, Sept. 17, '64; MO July 14, '65.

Baumgarten, Henry; stonecutter, Milwaukee; ENL Aug. 21, '62; CIA Chancellorsville; returned to regt. Nov. 12, '63; MO June 13, '65.

Becker, Robert; musician, Germantown; ENL Aug. 15, '62; Corp.; CIA

Chancellorsville; returned to regt. Oct. 2, '63; absent sick Aug. 2, '64 to Sept. 17, '64; MO June 13, '65.

Becker, Rudolph; farmer, Germantown; ENL Aug. 15, '62; drummer to Aug. 10, '64; detached as brigade orderly Aug. 10, '64 until MO June 13, '65.

Best, Anton; farmer, Milwaukee; ENL Feb. 1, '64; trans. to Co. K, 3rd Wis. Inf., June 10, '65.

Betz, Michel; laborer, Franklin; ENL Aug. 18, '62; member of color guard; absent sick Mar. 10, '64 to Oct. 14, '64; MO June 13, '65.

Boeling, Charles; broommaker, Milwaukee; ENL Aug. 16, '62 from Co. F; sent to hospital Feb. 8, '64; trans. to VRC, Jan. 10, '65; MO at Indianapolis, Ind., July 22, '65; member of Robert Chivas Post No. 2, G.A.R.

Bremser, Heinrich; trunkmaker, Milwaukee; ENL Aug. 13, '62; WIA Chancellorsville, arm; disch. Aug. 1, '63, disability; member of Twenty-Sixth Regiment Association.

Burkhardt, Peter; tinsmith, Milwaukee; ENL Aug. 17, '62; WIA Chancellorsville; trans. to VRC, Nov. 15, '63.

Caflisch, Christian R.; farmer, Honey Creek; ENL Dec. 31, '63; CIA while foraging for regt. near Chesterfield Court House, near Cheraw, SC, Mar. 5, ' 65; paroled Apr. '65; trans. to Co. K, 3rd Wis. Inf., June 10, '65; disch. June 20, '65 at Madison, Wisc..

Cleaver, John L.; clerk, Milwaukee; ENL Aug. 21, '62; disch. at Centreville, Va., Dec. 11, '62, medical disability.

Cordier, Adolph; merchant, Milwaukee; ENL Aug. 16, '62; Sergt., promoted Sergt. Major, Dec. 22, '62.

Crandall, Jerome; farmer, Milwaukee; ENL Feb. 3, '64; WIA May 15, '64 at Resaca; trans. to VRC, Jan. 10, '65; MO Aug. 30, '65.

Dascher, George; farmer, Sauk City; Aug. 12, '62; absent sick June 12, '63 to June 30, '63; CIA at Chesterfield Court House while foraging for regt. near Cheraw, SC., Mar. 5, '65; paroled Apr. '65; absent sick at MO of regt.; discharged June 20, '65 at Milwaukee; attended fiftieth anniversary at Gettysburg in 1913

Diehl, Christian; farmer, Troy; ENL Aug. 13, '62; Corp.; WIA in face at Chancellorsville; trans. to VRC, Nov. 15, '63.

Dietz, Christian H.; carpetweaver, Milwaukee; ENL Aug. 14, '62; company cook; WIA Chancellorsville; absent sick July 1, '63 to Oct. 18, '63; detached to extra duty Feb. '64 until MO June 13, '65.

Fleck, August; shoemaker, Milwaukee; Aug. 15, '62; Corp.; KIA May 2, '63, Chancellorsville, Va.

Franke, Gotthard; farmer, Franklin; ENL Aug. 21, '62; sent to XI Corps hospital Nov. 22, '63; DOD in XI Corps hospital at Chattanooga, Tenn., Dec. 28, '63.

Franke, William; locksmith, Milwaukee; ENL Aug. 14, '62; WIA and CIA Chancellorsville; returned to regt. Nov. 12, '63; WIA May 15, '64 at Resaca; returned to regt. Apr. 20, '65; MO June 13, '65; member of Robert Chivas Post No. 2, G.A.R.

Fuchs, Theobald; farmer, Sauk City; ENL Aug. 14, '62; absent sick Oct. '62 to Dec. '62; Corp.; absent sick Aug. 28, '64 to Sept. 15, '64; MO June 13, '65.

Gäss (or Goetz), John; farmer, Oak Creek; ENL Aug. 13, '62; detached as div. teamster Nov. '62; WIA in shoulder and leg at Gettysburg; disch. Apr. 27, '64, disability.

Gasser, Jacob; farmer, Sauk City; ENL Aug. 15, '62; deserted before going into battle July 1, '63; MO June 20, '65.

Grochowsky, Charles; shoemaker, Milwaukee; ENL Aug. 21, '62; Corp., Sergt.; member of color guard; WIA Gettysburg July 1, '63; returned to regt. Dec. 18, '63; MO June 13, '65.

Hager, Gustav; farmer, Honey Creek; ENL Jan. 2, '64; trans. to Co. K, 3rd Wis. Inf., June 10, '65.

Hammen, John; bootmaker, Milwaukee; ENL Aug. 6, '62; WIA Chancellorsville; returned from hospital ca. Oct. 3, '63; trans. to VRC, July 12, '64; MO June 31, '65; member of Robert Chivas Post No. 2, G.A.R.; founding member of Twenty-Sixth Regiment Association; attended fiftieth anniversary at Gettysburg in 1913.

Hartmann, Conrad; laborer, Sauk City; ENL Aug. 13, '62; WIA Kennesaw Mountain, July '64, while in breastworks; WIA Peach Tree Creek; MO June 13, '65; wounded arm remained lame for rest of life.

Hauser, Jacob; farmer, Sauk City; ENL Aug. 11, '62; deserted in Milwaukee Oct. 6, '62 (monthly report says Oct. 5).

Heck, Sebastian; farmer, Milwaukee; ENL Aug. 20, '62; detached to ambulance guard Dec. 10, '62 until MO June 13, '65.

Heim, John; laborer, Milwaukee; ENL Aug. 18, '62; detached as div. teamster Jan. '63; returned to regt. May 1, '64; detached as brigade teamster Sept. '64 until MO June 13, '65.

Heldstab, Christian; farmer, Sauk City; Aug. 13, '62; WIA Chancellorsville; returned to regt. June '63; absent sick May 28, '64 to June 3, '65; MO June 13, '65.

Henkel, Gottleib; butcher, Milwaukee; ENL Aug. 21, '62; trans. to Co. F, Oct. 3, '62.

Herrmann, John; porter, Milwaukee; ENL Aug. 14, '62; WIA in arm at Chancellorsville; KIA July 1, '63, Gettysburg, Pa.

Hertner, Anton; farmer, Sauk City; ENL Aug. 15, '62; deserted on march between Emmitsburg and Middletown, Md., July 8, '63.

Hetzel, David; butcher, Germantown; ENL Aug. 20, '62; slightly WIA at Chancellorsville; sent to hospital May 2, '64; trans. to VRC, July 20, '64; retransferred Mar. 18, '65; rejoined regt. Apr. 27, '65; M.O. June 13, '65.

Hoffmann, William; surgeon, Milwaukee; ENL Aug. 13, '62; disch. at Stafford Court House, Va., Mar., '63, medical disability.

Hornburg, Julius; bookbinder, Milwaukee; ENL Aug. 17, '62; Corp.; sent to hospital Sept. 26, '63; returned to regt. Jan. '64; trans. to VRC, Mar. 1, '64; MO June 28, '65.

Indermauer, Jacob; farmer, Sauk City; ENL Aug. 13, '62; officers' servant; KIA May 2, '63, Chancellorsville, Va.

Jochem, Peter; shoemaker, Washington Co.; ENL Aug. 15, '62; MO June 13, '65.

Kipp, William H.; farmer, Sauk City; ENL Aug. 17, '62; detached duty as brigade teamster Jan. '63 to Aug. '63; sent to hospital Sept. 28, '63; returned to regt. Sept. 2, '64; MO June 13, '65.

Kittel, Albert; farmer, Milwaukee; ENL Aug. 21, '62; officers' cook; teamsters' cook Feb. '63 to Nov. 15, '64; MO June 13, '65; member of Wolcott Post No. 1, G.A.R.; member of Robert Chivas Post No. 2, G.A.R.; attended fiftieth anniversary at Gettysburg in 1913.

Klein, Friedrich Rudolph; artist, Milwaukee; ENL Aug. 5, '62; Color Corporal, Sergt.; absent sick Apr. '63 to Jan. '64; reduced from Sergt. to ranks, July '63; promoted Sergt. Major, Mar., '64.

Klink, Jacob; cooper, Milwaukee; ENL Aug. 19, '62; absent sick June 12 to June 30, '63; KIA May 23, '64 at Burnt Hickory near Dallas, Ga.

Knechtel, Theodor; farmer, Milwaukee; ENL Aug. 12, '62; company cook; sent to hospital Apr. '63; trans. to VRC, Nov. 15, '63; MO July 13, '65.

Knoepp, Conrad; farmer, Sauk City; ENL Aug. 18, '62; WIA in thigh and CIA Chancellorsville; returned to regt. Oct. 2, '63; WIA June '64; MO June 13, '65.

Koerner, Hugo; carpenter, Milwaukee; ENL Aug. 15, '62; Corp; severely WIA Chancellorsville; disch. July 15, '63, disability.

Koerner, Theodore; carpenter, Milwaukee; ENL Aug. 14, '62; drummer; MO June 13, '65; attended fiftieth anniversary at Gettysburg in 1913.

Krantz, Christoph; porter, Milwaukee; ENL Aug. 20, '62; company cook; MO June 13, '65.

Kremer, William; blacksmith, Milwaukee; ENL Aug. 18, '62; sent to hospital Jan. 28, '63; returned to regt. July 31, '63; WIA May 15, '64, Resaca; MO May 31, '65.

Kuechenmeister, Franz; mechanic, Milwaukee; Aug. 14, '62; Corp.; WIA in left foot at Resaca, Ga., May 14, '64; WIA in right arm at Peach Tree Creek, Ga, July 20, '64; MO June 13, '65; after war returned to trade as model maker, then obtained job as adjuster and repairer with sewing machine company; letter carrier in Milwaukee beginning in 1884.

Laich, Fritz; clerk, Milwaukee; ENL Aug. 18, '62; detailed on extra duty June 28 to July 5, '63; Sergt.; CIA Burnt Hickory, Ga., May 23, '64; DOD (Scorbutus) in Confederate prison at Andersonville, Ga., Sept. 16, '64 and buried in grave 8944.

Lasche, Julius Ernst; clerk, Milwaukee; ENL Aug. 5, '62; sent to hospital Jan. 27, '63; trans. to VRC, Nov. 1, '63; MO Aug. 16, '65; founding member of Twenty-Sixth Regiment Association.

Lehmann, Henry; farmer, Milwaukee; ENL Feb. 6, '64; cattle guard; trans. to Co. K, 3rd Wis. Inf., June 10, '65.

Lorch, Heinrich; saddler, Milwaukee; ENL Aug. 12, '62; Corp., Sergt.; WIA Peach Tree Creek; amputated shaft of right humerous July 22, '64; absent wounded at MO of regt.; member of Twenty-Sixth Regiment Association; postal letter carrier after war.

Mann, Friedrich; merchant, Milwaukee; ENL Aug. 15, '62; Sergt.; detached to topographical corps; sent to hospital Jan. 27, '63; WIA Chancellorsville; disch. Sept. 6, '63, disability.

Matzke, Christian; laborer, Milwaukee; ENL Aug. 12, '62; WIA Chancellorsville; trans. to VRC, Nov. 15, '63; MO Sept. 22, '65.

Mengelt (or Mengold), Martin; farmer, Sauk City; ENL Aug. 15, '62; KIA May 2, '63, Chancellorsville.

Morsbach, Albert; farmer, Sauk City; ENL Aug. 13, '62; WIA Chancellorsville and absent sick until MO June 13, '65.

Mueller, Friedrich; weaver, Milwaukee; ENL Aug. 19, '62; WIA Chancellorsville; returned to regt. July 19, '63; MO June 13, '65.

Mueller, John; stonemason, Honey Creek; ENL Aug. 14, '62; DOD (heart disease) Apr. 15, '63, Stafford Court House, Va.

Munder (or Munter), Wilhelm; laborer, Milwaukee; ENL Aug. 15, '62; sent to hospital Apr. '63; trans. to VRC, Sept 1, '63; MO June 26, '65.

Mundloch, Hubert; gardener, Milwaukee; ENL Aug. 14, '62; WIA Chancellorsville; WIA Gettysburg and absent until MO May 25, '65.

Nachtsheim, Johann; cooper, Greenfield; ENL Aug. 15, '62; CIA Gettysburg July 1, '63; DOD Dec. 5, '64, in parole camp at Alexandria, Va. (Adjutant Generals' Report says he DOD in rebel prison, but he probably died in a parole camp shortly after release).

Neusser, Paulus; bookbinder, Rock County; ENL Aug. 15, '62; Corp.; KIA July 1, '63, Gettysburg, Pa.

Nolt, Henry; farmer, Sauk County; ENL Aug. 15, '62; Sergt., 1st Sergt.; WIA Chancellorsville; recruiting duty Jan. 1-Feb. 27, '64; WIA in hand May 25, '64 but remained with regt.; MO June 13, '65.

Orth, Carl; farmer, Milwaukee; ENL Aug. 21, '62; sent to hospital June 12, '63; returned Dec. 20, '63; WIA Peach Tree Creek July 20, '64; absent until MO June 12, '65.

Ott, Bernhardt; mason, Prairie du Sac; ENL Aug. 14, '62 from Co. F; CIA Chancellorsville; returned to regt. Sept. '63; WIA July 20, '64, Peach Tree Creek, Ga.; DOW July 21, '64.

Pidgeon, Richard; painter, Milwaukee; ENL Aug. 21, '62; disch. at Stafford Court House, Va., Mar. 29, '63, medical disability.

Pfeifer, Thaddeus; farmer, Sauk City; ENL Aug. 21, '62; company cook; sent to hospital Nov. 18, '62; trans. to VRC, Nov. 15, '63.

Pfeil, Gottlob; shoemaker, Sauk City; ENL Aug. 15, '62; detached to ambulance guard Dec. 10, '62; returned to regt. May 27, '63; absent sick since Aug. 9, '64; MO June 2, '65.

Phillipp, Christian; farmer, Prairie du Sac; promoted Sergt. to 1st Lt., Co. F, Oct. 30, '63; see entry under Co. F.

Philipp, Lucius (or Luziers); laborer, Sauk City; ENL Aug. 15, '62; WIA Chancellorsville; trans. to VRC, Jan. 10, '64; MO July 21, '65.

Preiss, Friedrich; tailor, Milwaukee; ENL Aug. 12, '62; Sergt.; disch. Sept. 19, '63, disability.

Rau, Ludwig; farmer, Honey Creek; ENL Jan. 11, '64; sick leave beginning Aug. 4, '64; trans. to Co. K, 3rd Wis. Inf., June 10, '65.

Rau, Peter; farmer, Honey Creek; ENL Jan. 11, '64; sent sick to hospital May 2, '64; returned to regt. Apr. 9, '65; trans. to Co. K, 3rd Wis. Inf., June 10, '65.

Rausche, Michel; farmer, Sauk City; ENL Aug. 15, '62; KIA May 2, '63, Chancellorsville, Va.

Redel, Frederick; farmer, Milwaukee; ENL Feb. 4, '64; trans. to Co. K, 3rd Wis. Inf., June 10, '65.

Remmele, Friedrich; farmer, Honey Creek; ENL Jan. 18, '64; WIA Peach Tree Creek July 20, '64; returned to regt. Apr. 9, '65; trans. to Co. K, 3rd Wis. Inf., June 10, '65.

Roehrig [Röhrig], Friedrich; laborer, Wauwatosa; ENL Aug. 21 '62; KIA July 1, '63, Gettysburg, Pa.

Roell [Röll], Friedrich; tailor, Milwaukee; ENL Aug. 15, 62; WIA and CIA Chancellorsville; DOW at McClellan Hospital, Philadelphia, May 25, '63.

Rothacker, David; laborer, Sauk City; ENL Aug. 15, '62 from Co. F; detaches to div. as teamster Dec. '63; returned to regt. Apr. '63; KIA July 1, '63, Gettysburg, Pa.

Sasse, Friedrich; farmer, Milwaukee; ENL Aug. 14, '62; WIA in leg at Gettysburg; trans. to VRC, Jan. 15, '64; MO July 13, '65.

Schallschlaeger, John; porter, Greenfield; ENL Aug. 19, '62; sent to hospital Dec. 8, '62; trans. to VRC, Nov. 15, '63; member of Robert Chivas Post No. 2, G.A.R.

Schlosser, Ludwig; wagonmaker, Sauk City; ENL Aug. 21, '62; WIA in foot at Chancellorsville; returned to regt. May 7, '64; sent to hospital Aug. 2, '64; trans. to VRC, Jan.10, '65; MO July 5, '65.

Schmidt, Friedrich; carpenter, Milwaukee; ENL Aug. 13, '62; ambulance corps; detached to pioneer corps Dec. 10, '62; rejoined regt. May 7, '64; sent to hospital May 12, '64; absent thereafter and MO May 31, '65.

Schneller, Peter; farmer, Troy; ENL Aug. 12, '62; Corp.; WIA Gettysburg; returned to regt. Dec. 17, '63; absent sick since Aug. 2, '64; MO May 26, '65; attended fiftieth anniversary at Gettysburg in 1913.

Schnitzler, William; merchant, Milwaukee; ENL Aug. 19, '62; ambulance corps; detached to pioneer corps Dec. 10, '62 through MO June 13, '65.

Schoenfeld, Edward; watchmaker, Pt. Washington; ENL Aug. 12, '62; disch. at Stafford Court House, Va., Mar. 21, '63, medical disability.

Schroeder, Hubert; cabinetmaker, Milwaukee; ENL Aug. 18, '62; Corp.; WIA Gettysburg; returned to regt. Oct. '63; absent sick since May 26, '64 at MO of regt.

Seitz, John; carpenter, Milwaukee; ENL Aug. 20, '62; WIA Chancellorsville; trans. to VRC, Mar. 31, '64.

Seitz, Joseph; painter, Milwaukee; ENL Aug. 21, '62; WIA Chancellorsville; MO June 13, '65.

Siebenaler, Michel; laborer, West Bend; ENL Aug. 20, '62; MO June 13, '65.

Sonnenschein, Friedrich; porter, Milwaukee; ENL Aug. 21, '62; hospital nurse; severely WIA Chancellorsville; DOW May 25, '63, Philadelphia, Pa.

Stanger, John; porter, Milwaukee; ENL Aug. 18, '62; WIA Chancellorsville; returned to regt. July 21, '64; MO June 13, '65.

Steinhof, Friedrich; farmer, Milwaukee; ENL Aug. 20, '62; WIA Chancellorsville; DOW at Harewood Hospital, Washington, D.C., May 17, '63.

Stievens, John; farmer, Franklin; ENL Aug. 18, '62; WIA in hand at Chancellorsville; absent at MO of regt.

Taege Fritz; butcher, Milwaukee; ENL Aug. 14, '62; company cook; absent sick at MO of regt.

Theurich, Julius; tailor, Milwaukee; ENL Aug. 13, '62; Corp.; WIA and CIA Chancellorsville; returned to regt. Oct. 2, '63; sent to hospital Oct. 26, '63; trans. to VRC, Jan. 10, '65.

Thies, Henry; tinsmith, Milwaukee; ENL Aug. 18, '62; Corp.; WIA badly in foot at Chancellorsville; listed as deserted from furlough July 4, '63; returned to duty; trans. to VRC, Jan. 10, '65.

Van Wald, Leonhard; farmer, Prairie du Sac; ENL Aug. 13, '62; sent to hospital Dec. 8, '62; returned to regt. Jan. '63; WIA Gettysburg; trans. to VRC, Jan. 15, '64; MO July 13, '65.

Wagner, Heinrich; farmer, Wauwatosa; ENL Aug. 20,'62; detached as brigade teamster Oct. 11, 62; sent to hospital some time in '63; returned from hospital ca. Oct. 3, '63; brigade teamster until MO June 13, '65.

Walser, Hubert; farmer, Troy; ENL Aug. 13, '62; WIA May 15, '64, Resaca; returned to regt. May 4, '65; MO June 13, '65.

Wenig, Oswald; wagoner, Troy; ENL Aug. 20, '62; deserted on march between Emmitsburg and Middletown, Md., July 8, '63.

Wichner, August; laborer, Milwaukee; ENL Aug. 21, '62; detached to div. teamster Mar. 4, '63, from there detached to brigade ambulance corps, June 12, '63 and there until MO June 13, '65.

Wimmer, Joseph; farmer, Honey Creek; ENL Jan. 7, '64; WIA May 15, '64 at Resaca; returned to regt. Apr. 26, '65; trans. to Co. K, 3rd Wis. Inf., June 10, '65.

Winter, Bernhardt; carpenter, Milwaukee; ENL Aug. 20, '62; sent to hospital Apr. 1, '63; trans. to VRC, Sept. 7, '63.

Winter, Christian; laborer, Milwaukee; ENL Aug. 13, '62; trans. to Co. F., Oct. 3, '62.

Wintermantle, Christian; farmer, Franklin; ENL Aug. 20, '62; Corp.; cattle guards; absent sick Jan. '63 to Mar. '63; MO June 13, '65.

Witwen, John Peter; farmer, Troy; ENL Aug. 15, '62; Corp.; absent sick Dec. 12, '62 to Aug. 9, '63; extra duty Oct. 13, '63 to Sept. 25, '64; company cook; MO June 13, '65.

Wunderlich, Leopold; servant, Milwaukee; ENL Aug. 15, '62; Corp.; sent to hospital Jan. '63; disch. at hospital in Madison, Wisc., July 15, '63, disability.

Zeiger, Joseph; carpenter, Milwaukee; ENL Aug. 13, '62; Corp., Sergt.; CIA Chancellorsville; returned to duty Oct. 2, '63; MO June 13, '65.

RECRUITS NOT ON COMPANY ROLLS

Cahill, John; Jamesville; ENL Feb. 8, '65; deserted Feb. 17, '65 from Camp Randall; arrested Madison Mar. 25, '65; deserted Apr. 24, '65 while passing through a crowd of people at the depot in Chicago; monthly report states "This man deserted immediately on arriving at Camp, undoubtedly enlisted for the purpose of deserting."

Clark, William; Milwaukee; ENL Apr. 5, '64.

Dunn, John; Milwaukee; ENL Apr. 5, '64.

Kealey, John; Milwaukee; ENL Apr. 5, '64.

Notes

Chapter 1: Unser Deutsches Regiment

1. Lankevich, 5-9.

2. Zink, 25; Zeitlin, 4; Current, 44.

3. Zeitlin, 8.

4. Bruce, 174; Zeitlin, 8; "The German in Wisconsin," mss, 10.

5. Lankevich, 12, 14; Zeitlin, 10; "The German Element in Milwaukee," MSS in the State Historical Society, Madison, 7, 12-13.

6. Bruncken, 226-227; Current, 135; Schurz quoted in "Germans in Wisconsin," 9.

7. Bruncken, 226-227; Current, 135.

8. Current, 123-124, 129; "German Element," 6, 10, 13; Lankevich, 18, 20-21.

9. "German Element," 12.

10. "German Element," 8, 10.

11. Zeitlin, 14; Mueller, 2; *Turnverein Milwaukee* (Milwaukee: Milwaukee Turnverein, 1896); Koss, "Geschichte der Gründung,'" in his *Milwaukee*; Current, 143-144; Bruncken, 225, 235; Lankevich, 17; Overmoehle, 215.

12. *Turnverein Milwaukee*; Mueller, 2; Metzner, 15; Zucker, *Forty-Eighters*, p. 280; Kaufmann, 484; Hense-Jensen; *Milwaukee Turners 140th Anniversary*, 4; Chivas Post, 544.

13. Current, 123-124.

14. Lacher, 19.

15. Koss, 151; Osten, 1.

16. Knoche, 114-115, including quotation about Huebschmann on 114; Flower, 1011; Osten, 1.

17. Bruncken, 228; Knoche, 116-117; quote from Koss, 153.

18. Knoche, 118; Koss, 231; Flower, 1012.

19. Current, 197, quotation from 200.

20. Flower, 224; Current, 202, 203; Bruncken, 232.

21. Bernhard Domschcke, biographical papers, MS in Wisconsin Historical Society; Schlichter, 324-25, 328; Flower, 636; Zucker, *Forty-Eighters*, 287-288.

22. Current, 222.

23. Overmoehle, 179; *Atlas*, April 18, 1857.

24. Current, 232, quotation from 223.

25. *Milwaukee Sentinel*, August 28, 1856

26. Current, 223

27. Knoche, 121; Flower, 1012; quotation from Current, 264.

28. Current, 264.

29. Bruce, 175; Gregory, "Elections," 61; Current, 237, quotation from 263.

30. Current, 268; Meyer, 26; *Seebote,* November 6, 1858.

31. Current, 282, 284; Bruce, 175; Gregory, "Elections," 61.

32. Gregory, "Elections," 61.

33. Bruce, 587.

34. Bruce, 587; Flower, 693; Meyer, 28; *Banner und Volksfreund,* April 16, 1861.

35. Zeitlin, 28-29; Mueller; Current, 307; Metzner, 21.

36. Flower, 721; *Milwaukee Sentinel,* August 19, 1862, 1.

37. *Milwaukee Sentinel,* August 13, 1862, 1.

38. Flower, 1100; Zucker, " Forty-Eighters," 307.

39. *Milwaukee Sentinel,* August 14, 1862, 1.

40. *Milwaukee Sentinel,* November 5, 1861, 1, February 6, 1862, 1, and July 29, 1862.

41. *Milwaukee Sentinel,* September 25, 1861, 2, and November 9, 1886.

42. *Milwaukee Sentinel,* August 13, 1862, 1, March 23, 1921, 1, and March 24, 1921, 14; *Men of Progress,* 194.

43. Lackner diary, September 7, 1862.

44. *Memoirs of Milwaukee County,* 49; quotation from *Men of Progress,* 419-420.

45. Flower, 638.

46. *Milwaukee Sentinel,* August 14, 1862, 1.

47. *Milwaukee Sentinel,* August 13, 1862, 1, and August 15, 1862, 1.

48 Koss, *Milwaukee Sentinel,* August 19, 1862; Lacher, 50.

49. Flower, 636; *Milwaukee Sentinel,* August 21, 1862, 1, and quotation from August 22, 1862, 1.

50. *Milwaukee Sentinel,* September 29, 1862, 1.

51. West Bend *Post,* August 9, 1862.

52. West Bend *Post,* August 16, 1862; Karsten diary, August 13, 1862.

53. West Bend *Post,* August 30, 1862; Manitowoc *Pilot,* August 15, 1862, 3.

54. West Bend *Post,* September 13, 1862; Karsten diary, September 3, 1862.

55. Falge, Vol. I; Flower, 997; *Memoirs of Milwaukee County,* p. 778-780.

56. Baensch, 87-90; Lacher, 50; Manitowoc *Pilot,* August 15, 1863, 3.

57. Manitowoc *Tribune,* September 10, 1862, 2.

58. Charles W. Neukirch to Col., August 26, 1862, in 26th Wisconsin file, Civil War Papers, Series XII, Wisconsin Veterans Museum.

59. Lamers, "Humble." 68.

60. Muenzenberger Letters, introduction by William M. Lamers, 4-5; *Milwaukee Sentinel,* August 19, 1862.

61. Damkoehler letters.

62. Damkoehler to Mathilde, September 1, 1862.

63. Damkoehler to Mathilde, September 1, 1862.

64. *Milwaukee Sentinel*, August 26, 1862, 1.

65. *Milwaukee Sentinel*, September 1, 1862, 1.

66. *Adjutant General*, 402.

67. Lackner diary, September 7, 1862.

68. Milwaukee *Pionier*, September 17, 1862. The quotations in question were attributed by the newspaper only to "E.R." A search of the regimental muster rolls indicates only one person with those initials, Ernst Rietz. Hence, I have used his name in place of the initials.

69. Francis Lackner diary September 7, 1862.

70. *Milwaukee Sentinel*, September 18, 1862, 1; *Adjutant General*, 402; Regimental Papers, Box 2, National Archives; Love, 395.

71. Regimental Papers, Box 2, National Archives.

72. Lackner diary, September 7, 1862; Karsten diary, September 17, 1862.

73. Damkoehler to Mathilde, September 1, 1862.

74. *Milwaukee Sentinel*, September 23, 1862, 1 and quote from August 29, 1862, 1.

75. *Milwaukee Sentinel*, September 10, 1862.

76. *Milwaukee Sentinel*, September 10, 1862.

77. *Milwaukee Sentinel*, September 10, 1862.

78. *Milwaukee Sentinel*, September 9, 1862.

79. Regimental Papers, Box 2, National Archives.

80. Flower, 720.

81. Doerflinger, "Familiar History," n.p.

82. Undated news clipping, *State Journal*, State Historical Society of Wisconsin.

83. Muenzenberger to wife, September 30, 1862.

84. *Milwaukee Sentinel*, October 4, 1862, 1 and October 6, 1862, 1; quote from *Daily Milwaukee News*, October 5, 1862, 1; Flower, 720.

85. *Milwaukee Sentinel*, October 4, 1862, 1.

86. *Milwaukee Sentinel*, October 4, 1862, 1 .

87. *Milwaukee Sentinel*, October 4, 1862, 1 .

88. *Milwaukee Sentinel*, October 4, 1862, 1 .

89. Muenzenberger to wife, September 30, 1862.

90. Lackner diary, October 17, 1862.

91. E. R. to *Pionier*, Milwaukee *Pionier*, September 17, 1862.

92. *Milwaukee Sentinel*, October 7, 1862, 1.

93. *Daily Milwaukee News*, October 7, 1862, 1.

94. *Milwaukee Sentinel*, October 7, 1862, 1; quotation from Winkler, *Letters*, 1.

95. Lackner diary, October 17, 1862.

96. Doerflinger, 5.

97. Winkler, *Letters*, 1.

98. *Milwaukee Sentinel*, October 7, 1862, 1.

99. *Milwaukee Sentinel*, October 7, 1862, 1.

Chapter 2: Soldiering

1. Crusius to *Pionier*, October 12, 1862 (hereafter cited as Crusius). The letters to the *Pionier* were signed only "C.C." In them, their author is angry that Lt. Berninger has been transferred from his company, refers to Lt. Orth as being of "our company," and also mentions Lt. Fernekes. All of these officers were in Company I. The only soldier in that company with the initials "C.C.," and in fact the only one with a last name beginning with "C.," is Christian Crusius; thus I have used his name throughout as the author of the letters.
2. Lackner diary, October 17, 1862.
3. Winkler, *Letters*, 1.
4. Lackner diary, October 17, 1862.
5. *Milwaukee Sentinel*, October 8, 1862, 1.
6. *Milwaukee Sentinel*, October 8, 1862, 1. The West Bend *Post*, October 11, 1862, says they arrived at 7:00 p.m. and left a little after 10:00 p.m.
7. *Milwaukee Sentinel*, October 9, 1862, 2; Karsten diary, October 7 and 8, 1862.
8. *Milwaukee Sentinel*, October 9, 1862, 2.
9. Winkler, *Letters*, 1.
10. Crusius, October 12, 1862.
11. Muenzenberger to wife, October 14, 1862.
12. Doerflinger, 5.
13. Crusius, October 12, 1862; Winkler, *Letters*, 1-3; quotation from Lackner diary, October 17, 1862.
14. Winkler, *Letters*, 3; Frederick C. Winkler to Gen. August Gaylord, August 25, 1864.
15. Karsten diary, October 13, 1862.
16. Crusius, October 12, 1862.
17. Lackner diary, October 17, 1862.
18. Muenzenberger to wife, ca. October 11. 1862.
19. Doerflinger, 5; Karsten diary, October 12, 1862.
20. Doerflinger, 5.
21. Zucker, *passim*; Wittke, 229; Pula, "Sigel Regiment," 32.
22. Pula, "Sigel Reigment," 32; Pula, *For Liberty and Justice*, passim.
23. Crusius, October 12, 1862; Karsten diary, October 14, 1862.
24. Lackner diary, October 17, 1862.
25. Winkler, *Letters*, 4-5.
26. Lackner, October 17, 1862.
27. Damkoehler to Mathilde, October 19, 1862.
28. Muenzenberger to wife, October 14, 1862.
29. Lackner, October 19, 1862.
30. Winkler, Letters, 2, 3.
31. Lackner diary, October 17, 1862; *Pionier*, November 1, 1862.
32. Muenzenberger to wife, October 14, 1862.
33. Muenzenberger to wife, October 30, 1862.
34. Lackner diary, October 19, 1862.
35. Winkler, *Letters*, 4.
36. Damkoehler, October 19, 1862.
37. Damkoehler to Mathilde, October 19, 1862.
38. Wickesberg, 2.
39. Wickesberg, October 16, 1862.

40. Muenzenberger to wife, October 30, 1862.
41. Lackner diary, October 28, 1862.
42. Lackner diary, October 30, 1862.
43. Winkler, *Letters*, 7.
44. Winkler, *Letters*, 6.
45. Muenzenberger to wife, October 30, 1862.
46. Winkler, *Letters*, 6.
47. Damkoeher to Mathilde, October 19, 1862.
48. Muenzenberger to wife, October 14, 1862.
49. Damkoehler to Mathilde, October 19, 1862.
50. Lackner diary, October 17, 1862.
51. Damkoehler to Mathilde, October 19, 1862.
52. Muenzenberger to wife, October 14, 1862.
53. Damkoehler to Mathilde, October 19, 1862.
54. Winkler, *Letters*, 8.
55. Winkler, *Letters*, 8 (including quotations); Lackner diary, October 21, 1862.
56. Lackner diary, October 21, 1862.
57. Lackner diary, October 21, 1862.
58. Winkler, *Letters*, 8.
59. Winkler, *Letters*, 8.
60. Lackner diary, October 21, 1862.
61. Muenzenberger to wife, October 30, 1862.
62. Muenzenberger to wife, November 25, 1862.
63. Lackner diary, October 21, 1862.
64. Damkoehler to Mathilde, October 19, 1862.
65. Crusius, November 1, 1862.
66. Karsten diary, October 22, 23, 24, 1862.
67. Huebschmann to wife, November 11, 1862, Huebschmann Papers, Folder 1.
68. Damkoehler to Mathilde, October 19, 1862.
69. Winkler, *Letters*, 9.
70. Crusius, November 1, 1862; Winkler, *Letters*, 9; Karsten diary, October 31, 1862.
71. Crusius, November 1, 1862.

Chapter 3: On the March

1. Crusius, November 1, 1862.
2. Winkler, *Letters*, 10-11.
3. Lackner diary, November 29, 1862.
4. Winkler, *Letters*, 12.
5. Winkler, *Letters*, 13; Karsten diary, November 2, 1862.
6. Lackner diary, November 29, 1862; Karsten diary, November 2, 1862.
7. Winkler, *Letters*, 12.
8. Lackner diary, November 29, 1862.
9. Winkler, *Letters*, 12-13.
10. Lackner diary, November 29, 1862.

11. Lackner diary, November 29, 1862.

12. Crusius, November 23, 1862.

13. Lackner diary, November 29, 1862.

14. Lackner diary, November 29, 1862.

15. Muenzenberger to wife, November 29, 1862.

16. Lackner diary, November 29, 1862.

17. Muenzenberger to wife, November 12, 1862.

18. Crusius, November 23, 1862.

19. Karsten diary, November 4, 1862.

20. Wickesberg to parents, November 4, 1862.

21. Winkler, *Letters*, 14.

22. Lackner diary, November 29, 1862.

23. Lackner diary, November 29, 1862.

24. Crusius, November 1, 1862.

25. Muenzenberger to wife, November 29, 1862.

26. *Milwaukee Sentinel*, November 9, 1862, 1.

27. *Milwaukee Sentinel*, November 9, 1862, 1.

28. Gregory, "Presidential Elections," 60-64.

29. Lackner diary, November 29, 1862.

30. Crusius, November 23, 1862.

31. Damkoehler to Mathilde, November 10, 1862.

32. Winkler, *Letters*, 14.

33. Lackner diary, November 29, 1862.

34. Damkoehler to Mathilde, November 10, 1862.

35. Winkler, *Letters*, 15.

36. Damkoehler to Mathilde, November 11, 1862.

37. Lackner diary, December 1, 1862 and quotation from November 29, 1862.
38. Lackner diary, December 1, 1862.
39. Winkler, *Letters*, 18.
40. Winkler, *Letters*, 18-19.
41. Winkler, *Letters*, 16.
42. Quote from Winkler, *Letters*, 15-16; Damkoehler to Mathilde, November 11, 1862.

43. Crusius, November 23, 1862.
44. Damkoehler to Mathilde, November 11, 1862.
45. Damkoehler to Mathilde, November 10, 1862.
46. Damkoehler to Mathilde, November 11, 1862.
47. Muenzenberger to wife, November 12, 1862.
48. Muenzenberger to wife, November 16, 1862.
49. Lackner diary, December 1, 1862.
50. Lackner diary, December 1, 1862.
51. Muenzenberger to wife, November 19, 1862.
52. Damkoehler to wife, December 22, 1862.
53. *Milwaukee Sentinel*, November 26, 1862, 2.

54. *Milwaukee Sentinel,* December 4, 1862, 1.

55. Muenzenberger to wife, December 9, 1862.

56. Muenzenberger to wife, November 27, 1862.

57. Doerflinger, 1.

58. Muenzenberger to wife, December 7, 1862.

59. Muenzenberger to wife, November 27, 1862.

60. Muenzenberger to wife, December 7, 1862.

61. Barbara Muenzenberger to Adam, December 8, 1862.

62. Muenzenberger to wife, November 19, 1862.

63. Lackner diary, December 1, 1862.

64. Winker, *Letters,* 22.

65. West Bend *Post,* February 28, 1863.

66. Muenzenberger to wife from Centreville, but undated.

67. Lackner diary, December 9, 1862.

68. Lackner diary, December 1, 1862.

69. Lackner diary, December 5, 1862.

70. Muenzenberger to wife, December 7, 1862.

71. Muenzenberger to wife from Centreville, but undated; quotations from Sentinel, April 11, 1863, 1, 5.

72. Muenzenberger to wife, November 19, 1862.

73. Lackner diary, December 1, 1862.

74. Lackner diary, December 1, 1862.

75. Quiner, 139-146; quotation from Korn, "Civil War Drafts in Milwaukee," 7; Meyer, 33.

76. Quiner, 146-147; Korn, "Drafts in Milwaukee," 7-12; *Milwaukee Sentinel,* November 10 and 11, 1862.

77. Muenzenberger to wife from Centreville, not dated.

78. Winkler, *Letters,* 20.

79. Muenzenberger to wife from Centreville, undated; Karsten diary, December 2, 1862.

80. Muenzenberger to wife from Centreville, undated.

81. Lackner diary, December 9, 1862.

82. *History of Milwaukee,* 799; Lackner diary, December 9, 1862; Muenzenberger to wife, December 9, 1862 and December 16, 1862.

83. Lackner diary, December 26, 1862.

84. Quotations from Crusius, December 18, 1862; Muenzenberger to wife, December 16, 1862.

85. Crusius, December 18, 1862.

86. Lackner diary, December 26, 1862; Muenzenberger to wife, December 16, 1862.

87. Lackner diary, December 26, 1862.

88. Muenzenberger to wife, December 16, 1862.

89. Lackner diary, December 26, 1862; Karsten diary, December 11, 1862.

90. Muenzenberger to wife, December 16, 1862.

91. Lackner diary, December 26, 1862.

92 Lackner diary, December 26, 1862.

93. Muenzenberger to wife, December 16, 1862; Crusius, December 18, 1862;

Karsten diary, October 13, 1862.

94. Lackner diary, December 26, 1862.

95. Damkoehler to Mathilde, December 22, 1862.

96. Damkoehler to Mathilde, December 22, 1862.

97. Lackner diary, December 26, 1862.

98. Muenzenberger to wife, December 16, 1862; Lackner diary, December 26, 1862.

99. Winkler to Gaylord, August 25, 1864.

100. Lackner diary, December 26, 1862.

101. Muenzenberger to wife, December 16, 1862.

102. Crusius, December 18, 1862.

103. Muenzenberger to wife, December 16, 1862.

104. Lackner diary, December 26, 1862.

105. Muenzenberger to wife, December 16, 1862.

106. Wickesberg to parents, December 25, 1862.

107. Lackner diary, December 26, 1862.

108. Muenzenberger to wife, December 17, 1862.

109. Lackner diary, December 26, 1862.

110. Crusius, December 18, 1862; Muenzenberger to wife, December 17, 1862.

111. Crusius, December 18, 1862.

112. Muenzenberger to wife, December 17, 1862.

113. Muenzenberger to wife, December 17, 1862; Lackner diary, December 26, 1862.

114. Lackner diary, December 26, 1862.

115. Muenzenberger to wife, December 28, 1862.

116. *Roster of Wisconsin Volunteers, passim.*

117. Muenzenberger to wife, December 21, 1862.

118. Muenzenberger to wife, December 17, 1862.

119. Damkoehler to Mathilde, December 22, 1862.

120. Wickesberg to parents, December 25, 1862.

121. Muenzenberger to wife, December 21, 1862.

122. Lackner diary, December 26, 1862; Karsten diary, December 25, 1862.

123. Winkler, Letters, 25; Muenzenberger to wife, January 1, 1863; Crusius, January 29, 1863; quote from Lackner diary, January 1, 1863.

124. Muenzenberger to wife, January 1, 1863.

125. Lackner diary, January 1, 1863.

126. Quotes from Muenzenberger to wife, January 1, 1863; also Crusius, January 29, 1863.

127. Quotes form Lackner diary, January 1, 1863; also Wickesberg to parents, January 1, 1863.

128. Muenzenberger to wife, January 1, 1863.

129. Lackner diary, January 1, 1863.

130. Wickesberg to parents, January 1, 1863.
131. Lackner diary, January 1, 1863.
132. Winkler, *Letters*, 24.
133. Muenzenberger to wife, January 1, 1863.
134. Wickesberg to parents, January 1, 1863.

Chapter 4: Marking Time

1. "Geschichte der Gründung"; Flower, 742; quote from *Milwaukee Sentinel*, November 11, 1862, 1.
2. *Milwaukee Sentinel*, January 8, 1863, 1.
3. *Milwaukee Sentinel*, January 27, 1863, 1.
4. Damkoehler to Mathilde, January 17, 1863.
5. Karsten diary, January 5, 1863.
6. Crusius, January 29, 1863.
7. Lackner diary, January 5, 1863.
8. Lackner diary, January 11, 1863.
9. Muenzenberger to wife, January 6, 1863.
10. Muenzenberger to wife, January 6, 1863.
11. Damkoehler to Mathilde, January 17, 1863.
12. Wickesberg to parents, January 18, 1863.
13. Muenzenberger to wife, January 6, 1863.
14. Muenzenberger to wife, January 9, 1863.
15. Lackner diary, February 5, 1863.
16. Muenzenberger to wife, January 30, 1863.
17. Damkoehler to Mathilde, February 2, 1863.
18. Muenzenberger to wife, January 6, 1863.
19. Wickesberg to parents, January 18, 1863.
20. Winkler, *Letters*, 29.
21. Muenzenberger to wife, January 6, 1863.
22. Muenzenberger to wife, January 9, 1863.
23. Doerflinger, 6.
24. Wickesberg to parents, January 18, 1863.
25. Muenzenberger to wife, March 12, 1862.
26. Muenzenberger to wife, January 6, 1863.
27. Muenzenberger to wife, February 16, 1863.
28. Muenzenberger to wife, February 16, 1863.
29. Winkler, *Letters*, 36.
30. Lackner diary, January 16, 1863.
31. Crusius, January 29, 1863.
32. Crusius, January 29, 1863.
33. Love, 397; quote from Winkler, *Letters*, 30.
34. Regimental Papers, Box 2, National Archives.
35. Doerflinger, 6.
36. Crusius, January 29, 1863.
37. Lackner diary, February 5, 1863.
38. Muenzenberger to wife, February 20, 1863.

39. Muenzenberger to wife, February 20, 1863.
40. Lackner diary, February 5, 1863.
41. Damkoehler, February 2, 1863.
42. Doerflinger, 6.
43. Crusius, January 29, 1863.
44. Lackner diary, February 5, 1863.
45. Love, 397.
46. Lackner diary, February 12, 1863.
47. Damkoehler to Mathilde, February 23, 1863.
48. Crusius, February 16, 1863.
49. Damkoehler to Mathilde, February 23, 1863.
50. Muenzenberger to wife, January 29, 1863.
51. West Bend *Post*, March 7, 1863.
52. Lackner diary, February 15, 1863.
53. Damkohler to Mathilde, February 23, 1863.
54. Doerflinger, 5.
55. Crusius, March 15, 1863.
56. Muenzenberger to wife, February 25, 1863.
57. Muenzenberger to wife, February 7, 1863; Lackner diary, February 15, 1863.
58. Muenzenberger to wife, January 30, 1863 and February 20, 1863.
59. Muenzenberger to wife, February 27, 1863.
60. Muenzenberger to wife, February 27, 1863.
61. Muenzenberger to wife, January 30, March 23, and April 12, 1863.
62. *Milwaukee Sentinel*, April 11, 1863.
63. *Wisconsin Roster*, II, 312, 313, 316, 324, 329, 336; Winkler, *Letters*, 28; Lackner diary, February 27, 1863.
64. Lackner diary, February 27, 1863.
65. *Roster of Wisconsin Volunteers*, 312; quotation from Winkler, *Letters*, 38.
66. Crusius, February 17, 1863.
67. West Bend *Post*, March 7, 1863.
68. Damkoehler to Mathilde, February 23, 1863.
69. Muenzenberger to wife, January 31, 1863.
70. Muenzenberger to wife, February 7, 1863.
71. Muenzenberger to wife, February 16, 1863; quotation from February 25, 1863.
72. Muenzenberger to wife, February 27, 1863.
73. Lackner diary, February 28, 1863; *Milwaukee Sentinel*, March 8, 1863, 1.
74. Winkler, *Letters*, 31.
75. Doerflinger, 7.
76. Damkoehler to Mathilde, February 2, 1863.
77. Crusius, February 16, 1863.
78. Winkler, *Letters*, 35.
79. Wickesberg to parents, March 7, 1863.
80. Muenzenberger to wife, March 15, 1863.
81. Muenzenberger to wife, March 12, 1863.
82. Lackner diary, March 15, 1863; *Roster of Wisconsin Volunteers*; Wickesberg to parents, March 7, 1863.
83. Crusius, March 15, 1863.
84. Muenzenberger to wife, March 12, 1863.
85. *Milwaukee Sentinel*, April 7, 1863, 2.
86. *Milwaukee Sentinel*, March 12, 1863.
87. Winkler, *Letters*, 40.
88. Doerflinger, 7.

89. Pula, *For Liberty and Justice*, 73-74.
90. Damkoehler to Mathilde, April 12, 1863.
91. Muenzenberger to wife, April 2, 1863.
92. Muenzenberger to wife, March 7, 1863.
93. Lackner diary, February 15, 1863.
94. Muenzenberger to wife, March 7, 1863.
95. Muenzenberger to wife, March 12, 1863.
96. Anonymous letter to *Milwaukee Sentinel*, April 7, 1863.
97. Muenzenberger to wife, April 12, 1863.
98. Damkoehler to Mathilde, February 23, 1863.
99. *Milwaukee Sentinel*, March 18, 1863, 1.
100. *Milwaukee Sentinel*, April 11, 1863, 2.
101. Anonymous letter to *Milwaukee Sentinel*, April 7, 1863.
102. Winkler, *Letters*, 38.
103. *Milwaukee Sentinel*, April 7, 1863.
104. Muenzenberger to wife, April 2, 1863.
105. Muenzenberger to wife, April 6, 1863.
106. Damkoehler to Mathilde, April 12, 1863.
107. Muenzenberger to wife, April 6, 1863.
108. Damkoehler to Mathilde, April 12, 1863.
109. Winkler, *Letters*, 43.
110. Karsten diary, April 10, 1863.
111. Muenzenberger to wife, April 12, 1863.
112. Brooks, 45, 56.
113. Love, 397.
114. Lackner diary, April 19, 1863.
115. Damkoehler to Mathilde, April 14, 1863.
116. Muenzenberger to wife, April 14, 1863.
117. Muenzenberger to wife, April 17. 1863.
118. Muenzenberger to wife, April 17, 1863.
119. Muenzenberger to wife, April 20, 1863.
120. Muenzenberger to wife, April 20, 1863.
121. Damkoehler to Mathilde, April 12, 1863.
122. Lackner diary, April 9 and April 19, 1863; quotes from Winkler, *Letters*, 45.

Chapter 5: Chancellorsville

1. Lackner diary, May 7, 1863.
2. Winkler, *Letters*, 46.
3. Muenzenberger to wife, May 7, 1863.
4. Lackner diary, May 7, 1863; Doerflinger, 7.
5. Lackner diary, May 7, 1863.
6. Lackner diary, May 7, 1863; quotation from Winkler, *Letters*, 46.
7. Lackner diary, May 7, 1863.
8. Winkler, *Letters*, 46-47; Doreflinger, 7.
9. Lackner diary, May 7, 1863.
10. Lackner diary, May 7, 1863; quotation from Lackner diary, May 7, 1863.
11. Lackner diary, May 7, 1863.
12. Lackner diary, May 7, 1863.

13. Doerflinger, 7.

14. Lackner diary, May 7, 1863; see also Muenzenberger to wife, May 7, 1863.

15. Winkler, *Letters*, 49.

16. General Order No. 47 quoted from Bigelow, 223.

17. Lackner diary, May 7, 1863.

18. Winkler, *Letters*, 45.

19. Schurz, Chancellorsville Report, 650; Muenzenberger, letter to wife, May 7, 1863.

20. Steele, 335-336; Schurz, Chancellorsville Report, 650; quotation from Bigelow, 258.

21. Dodge, *Addresses*, 96; Howard, *Autobiography*, 361.

22. Winkler, *Letters*, 50.

23. Muenzenberger to wife, May 7, 1863.

24. Carpenter, 50; Bigelow, 278; Hamlin, 55; Catton, *Glory Road*, 182; Hassler, 142.

25. Carpenter, 51-52; Couch, 163; Hamlin, 75-76; Bigelow, 285; Hassler, 143.

26. Carpenter, 50; Bigelow, 278; Hamlin, 55; Catton, *Glory Road*, 182.

27. Bigelow, 285; Quiner, 748.

28. Steele, 340; Howard, *Autobiography*, 371; Raphelson, 167-168; Fitzhugh Lee, 238; Love, 399; Doerflinger, 3.

29. Bigelow, 133, 290; Catton, *Glory Road*, 182; Hamlin, 55-57, 65; Alexander, 333.

30. Love, 399; Lackner diary, May 7, 1863; Doerflinger, 2.

31. Wickesberg to parents, May 21, 1863.

32. Winkler report, August 25, 1864.

33. Doerflinger, 2.

34. Doerflinger, 2.

35. Doerflinger to mother, May 15, 1863.

36. Doerflinger, 3.

37. Muenzenberger to wife, May 19, 1863.

38. Muenzenberger to wife, May 19, 1863.

39. Doerflinger, 3; *Daily Milwaukee News*, May 17, 1863, 1.

40. Wickesberg to family, May 21, 1863.

41. *Roster of Wisconsin Volunteers*, passim.

42. Regimental Descriptive Book, 26th Wisconsin Infantry; Doerflinger, 8; Muenzenberger, letter to wife, May 7, 1863; Andrew Sprengling Papers, Milwaukee County Historical Society; *Roster of Wisconsin Volunteers*, 318-321.

43. Doerflinger, 8.

44. Krzyżanowski, Chancellorsville Report, 667; Doerflinger, 8; Muenzenberger, letter to wife, May 7, 1863.

45. Krzyżanowski, Chancellorsville Report, 667.

46. Quiner, 749; *Roster of Wisconsin Volunteers*, 334-336; *Medical and Surgical History*, Surgical, II, 639.

47. Quiner, 749; *Roster of Wisconsin Volunteers*, 329-331.

48. *Medical and Surgical History*, Surgical, II, 639; Regimental Descriiptive Book, 26th Wisconsin Infantry; Doerflinger, 8; Lackner diary, May 7, 1863.

49. Krzyżanowski, Chancellorsville Report, 666-667; Schurz, Chancellorsville Report, 667; *Milwaukee Sentinel*, May 23, 1863; Quiner, 749.

50. Doerflinger, 3, 8; Krzyżanowski, Chancellorsville Report, 667; "Personal War Sketches," E. B. Walcott Post No. 1, 294.

51. Doerflinger, 3.

52. "Das 26. Wisconsin Regiment," *Herold*, May 23, 1863.

53. Lackner diary, May 7, 1863; *Medical and Surgical History,* Surgical, II, 957.

54. Doerflinger, 9.

55. Doerflinger, "General Schurz bei Chancellorsville,"176.

56. Lackner diary, May 7, 1863; Underwood, 53.

57. Doerflinger to mother, May 15, 1863.

58. Doerflinger, 3.

59. Doerflinger to mother, May 15, 1863.

60. Doerflinger, 1, 9.

61. Krzyżanowski, Chancellorsville Report, 667; *O.R.,* I, XXV, I, 547, 657-658).

62. Lackner diary, May 7, 1863; *O.R.,* I, XXV, I, 547, 657-658; *Annual Report of the Adjutant General of the State of Wisconsin,* 403.

63. Lackner diary, May 7, 1863; Muenzenberger to wife, May 7, 1863.

64. Muenzenberger to wife, May 7, 1863.

65. Lackner diary, May 7, 1863.

66. Winkler, *Letters,* 50.

67. Lackner diary, May 7, 1863; *O.R.,* I, XXV, I, 547, 657-658.

68. Muenzenberger to wife, May 7, 1863.

69. Muenzenberger, letter to wife, May 7, 1863; Schurz, Chancellorsville Report, 657; Schurz, *Reminiscences,* II, 431-432; William Houghton, letter to father, May 8, 1863.

70. Muenzenberger to wife, May 7, 1863.

71. Lackner diary, May 7, 1863.

72. Muenzenberger to wife, May 7, 1863.

73. Winkler, *Letters,* 51.

74. Lackner diary, May 7, 1863.

75. Muenzenberger to wife, May 11, 1863.

76. Muenzenberger to wife, May 7, 1863.

77. Muenzenberger to wife, May 7, 1863.

78. Fox, *Regimental Losses,* 34, 436; Regimental Descriptive Books, 26th Wisconsin Infantry.

79. "Personal War Sketches," E. B. Walcott Post No. 1, G.A.R., 294.

80. Underwood, 47.

81. *O.R.,* I, XXV, I, 267.

82. *O.R.,* I, XXV, I, 655.

83. Fox, 399.

84. Doerflinger, 3.

85. Doerflinger, 3, 9.

86. *Herald,* May 23, 1863.

87. Letter, Dennis R Moore to author, February 7, 1995.

88. Milwaukee *Sentinel,* May , 1863.

89. *The New York Times,* May 5, 1863, 1, 8; *Morning Telegraph* (Harrisburg, PA), May, 1863; *Pittsburgh Post,* May 6 and May 8, 1863; *Indianapolis Daily Journal,* May 1863; *Frank Leslies' Illustrated Newspaper,* May 23, 1863, 130.

90. Schurz, *Reminiscences,* II, 423 (contains letter from Schimmelfennig); Schurz, Chancellorsville Report, 658; *The New York Times,* May 28, 1863.

91. "Das 11. Armce-Corps in der letzten Schlacht bei Chancellorsville," *Herold,* May 23, 1863.

92. *Milwaukee Sentinel,* May 23, 1863, 1.

93. Muenzenberger, letter to wife, May 19, 1863.

94. Damkoehler to Mathilde, May 1, 1863.

95. Winkler, *Letters,* 51-52.

96. Doerflinger, 9.

97. Wickesberg, letter to family, May 21, 1863.

Chapter 6: North to Pennsylvania

1. Winkler, *Letters*, 55.
2. Muenzenberger to wife, May 19, 1863.
3. Damkoehler to Mathilde, May 28, 1863.
4. Lackner diary, May 23, 1863; Love, 402; Muenzenberger to wife, June 7, 1863.
5. Lackner diary, Stafford C.H., May 7, 1863.
6. Damkoehler to Mathilde, May 28, 1863.
7. Muenzenberger to wife, May 23, 1863.
8. Winkler, *Letters*, 58.
9. Damkoehler to wife, May 28, 1863.
10. Winkler, *Letters*, 54.
11. Winkler, *Letters*, 58.
12. Lackner diary, May 7, 1863.
13. Muenzenberger to wife, May 23, 1863.
14. *Medical and Surgical History*, Surgical, II, 630, 957; F. Phister letter "To Whom it May Concern," November 17, 1898, Charles E. Estabrook Correspondence, State Historical Society (Wisconsin); Karl Doerflinger, Misc. Papers and Letters, Charles E. Estabrook Correspondence.
15. K.R., "Das 26. Wisconsin Regiment," *Herold*, May 23, 1863; *Milwaukee Daily News*, May 17, 1864, 1.
16. Muenzenberger to wife, May 19, 1863, quote from May 31, 1863; *O.R.*, I, XXV, I, 660.
17. Winkler, *Letters*, 52.
18. Muenzenberger to wife, May 23, 1863.
19. Lackner diary, May 23, 1863.; quote from Domschcke, *Twenty Months*, 26.
20. Winkler, Letters, 52.
21. Dyer, 320; *Annual Report of the Adjutant General of Ohio*, 1863. 342; *Union Army*, II, 408.
22. *Roster of Wisconsin Volunteers*, 312-339.
23. Winkler, *Letters*, 60, 64.
24. Muenzenberger to wife, June 7, 1863.
25. Winkler, *Letters*, 60.
26. Damkoehler to Mathilde, May 28, 1863.
27. Winkler, *Letters*, 60.
28. Winkler, *Letters*, 61.
29. Muenzenberger to wife, May 31, 1863.
30. Esposito, 93.
31. Winkler, *Letters*, 62.
32. Love, 402; *Annual Report of the Adjutant General of the State of Wisconsin*, 403; Muenzenberger to wife, June 22, 1863.
33. Muenzenberger to wife, June 22, 1863.
34. Emil Koenig, Report of the 58th New York at Gettysburg, *O. R.*, I, XXVII, I, 739; Howard, *Autobiography*, 386, 390; Muenzenberger to wife, June 22, 1863; Lackner diary, December 22, 1863.
35. Love, 402; *Annual Report of the Adjutant General of the State of Wisconsin*, 403; Muenzenberger to wife, June 22, 1863; quote from Winkler, *Letters*,

62-63; Karsten diary, June 14, 1863.

36. Muenzenberger to wife, June 22, 1863.

37. Love, 402.

38. Domschcke, *Twenty Months*, 26; Damkoelher to Mathilde, June 22, 1863; Karsten diary, June 17, 1863; Muenzenberger to wife, June 22, 1863.

39. Koenig, Gettysburg Report, p. 739; Muenzenberger to wife, June 22, 1863; Love, 402.

40. Winkler, *Letters*, 63.

41. Damkoehler to Mathilde, June 22, 1863; Wallber, "From Gettysburg to Libby Prison," 191; Winkler, *Letters*, 63; Muenzenberger to wife, June 23, 1863.

42. Damkoehler to Mathilde, June 22, 1863.

43. Muenzenberger to wife, June 22, 1863.

44. Muenzenberger to wife, June 22, 1863.

45. Muenzenberger to wife, June 24, 1863.

46. Love, 402; quotes from Domschcke, *Twenty Months*, 26-27.

47. Winkler, *Letters*, 64.

48. Wallber, "From Gettysburg to Libby Prison," 191.

49. Howard, *Autobiography*, 386; Wickesberg, letter to family, July 6, 1863.

50. Winkler, *Letters*, 65.

51. Hassler, 156, 159, 160, 163; Comte de Paris, III, 914; Schurz, *Reminiscences*, III, 4.

52. Karsten diary, June 28, 1863; Winkler, *Letters*, 66.

53. *O.R.* I, XXVII, I, 140; I, XXVII, III, 255-288, 260, 336.

54. Muenzenberger to wife, June 30, 1863.

55. Winkler, *Letters*, 66, 67.

56. Domschcke, *Twenty Months*, 27; letter from Winkler to Gen. August Gaylord, August 25, 1864; Regimental Muster Roll, Box 1, National Archives.

57. Winkler, *Letters*, 67-68.

58. Muenzenberger to wife, June 30, 1863.

59. Winkler, *Letters*, 68.

Chapter 7: Gettysburg

1. Domschcke, *Twenty Months*, 27.

2. Koenig, Gettysburg Report, 739-740; Howard, *Autobiography*, 408.

3. Love, 417.

4. Arnold to Mother, undated, Oshkosh Historical Society.

5. Fox, *New York at Gettysburg* 15; Schlicher, 452; Schurz, *Reminiscences*, III, 4; Carl Schurz, Report on the Battle of Gettysburg, *O. R.*, I, XXVII, I, p. 727; Dodge, "Left Wounded," 318.

6. Wallber, "From Gettysburg to Libby Prison," 191-192.

7. Schlicher, 452; Dodge, "Left Wounded," 318; Schurz, Gettysburg report, 727; Domschcke, *Twenty Months*, quotatiuon from 27.

8. Love, 417.

9. Dodge, "Left Wounded," 318; Wickesberg, letter to family, July 6, 1863.

10. Domschcke, *Twenty Months*, 27; Karsten diary, July 1, 1863.

11. Arnold to Mother, undated, Oshkosh Historical Society.

12. *Pennsylvania at Gettysburg* 438; Schurz, Reminiscences, III, 7; Schurz, Gettysburg Report, 727.

13. Wickesberg to parents, July 6, 1863.

14. Doubleday, 138; Comte de Paris, 559, 570; Frederick C. Winkler, "Winkler's Reminiscences of Frank Haskell," unpublished manuscript in the University of Wisconsin-Milwaukee Library, n.d., 4-5, 7.

15. Schlicher, 452.

16. 26th Wisconsin Infantry, regimental morning reports and muster rolls, Boxes 1 and 2, National Archives; Arnold to Mother, undated, Oshkosh Historical Society.

17. Winkler, *Letters*, 68.

18. Benjamin A. Willis, Report of the 119th New York at Gettysburg, *O. R.*, I, XXVII, I, 742; Dodge, "Left Wounded," 317, 319; Fox, New *York*, 15.

19. Damkoehler to Mathilde, August 4, 1863; *Roster of Wisconsin Volunteers*, 312-313.

20. Love, 417; *Annual Report of the Adjutant General of the State of Wisconsin*, 403.

21. *Pennsylvania at Gettysburg*, I, 438; Karsten diary, July 1, 1863; Downey,. 48; Vanderslice, 66.

22. Wallber, "From Gettysburg to Libby Prison," 191.

23. Hubert Dilger, Report on Gettysburg, *O. R.*, I, XXVII, I,. 754; Thomas W. Osborn, Report on the Eleventh Corps Artillery at Gettysburg, *O. R.*, I, XXVII, I, 745; Schurz, *Reminiscences*, 8; III, Bates, *Martial Deeds*, 225.

24.Gordon, 151; Early, 267-268.

25. Gordon, 151; Early, 267-268.

26. Charles K. Fox, *Gettysburg* 16; Downey, 49-50.

27. *Annual Report of the Adjutant General of the State of Wisconsin*, 403; Winkler to Gaylord, August 25, 1864.

28. Winkler to Gen. August Gaylord, August 25, 1864.

29. Schurz, *Reminiscences*, III, *passim; Medical and Surgical History*, Surgical, III, 82, 293, 314; Scott,. 267-268; Kaufmann, 480; Regimental Descriptive Book, 26th Wisconsin Infantry.

30. *Roster of Wisconsin Volunteers*, 312-313.

31. *Soldiers' and Citizens' Album*, 822-823.

32. *Roster of Wisconsin Volunteers*, 316-318; Quiner, 751; West Bend *Post*, August 1, 1863.

33. *Roster of Wisconsin Volunteers*, 316-318; Quiner, 751; Winkler to Col. F. Firmin, May 1, 1864.

34. *Roster of Wisconsin Volunteer*, 318-321; *Medical History*, 178; Paul Miller to Frank Turk, February 1996; *Medical History*, 479-80; Donnabelle Gerhardt to author, July 16, 1996; Emma Van Waring Craig to Dear Laura, July 24, 1949; August Bartsch to unknown, October 15, 1864.

35. Wickesberg to parents, July 6, 1863.

36. *Roster of Wisconsin Volunteers*, 329-331; Quiner, 751; *Soldiers' and Citizens' Album*, 280.

37. Krzyżanowski, *Wspomnienia*, 79.

38. Pula, *For Liberty and Justice*, 100-102.

39. Nichols, *Medical and Surgical History*, Surgical, I, 493 and III, 82.

40. Howard, *Autobiography*, 417; W. Fox, *Gettysburg*, 22; Charles H. Howard, "The First Day at Gettysburg," 258; Schurz, *Reminiscences*, III,. 10-11; Oliver O. Howard, Gettysburg report, 703-704; Winkler to Gen. August Gaylord, August 25, 1864.

41. Arnold to mother, undated, historical Files, Oshkosh Public Museum, Oshkosh, Wisconsin.

42. Wickesberg to parents, July 6, 1863; Lackner diary, December 22, 1863; Wallber, "From Gettysburg to Libby Prison," 192; Winkler to Gaylord, August 25, 1864; *Annual Report of the Adjutant General of the State of Wisconsin*, 403; Love, 417.

43. Winkler, *Letters*, 69-70; Winkler to Gaylord, August 25, 1864.

44. Winkler, *Letters*, 70-71.

45. Winkler, *Letters*, 71.

46. Lackner diary, December 22, 1863; Wickesberg to parents, July 6, 1863; Winkler to Gaylord, August 25, 1864.

47. Zucker, *Forty-Eighters*,. 54, 111; Lonn, 327; Kaufmann, 514; Osten, 1.

48. Longstreet, 356; Simonhoff, 77; W. Fox, *New York*, 25; Butts, 78, 80; Phisterer, *New York*, 3405, 3409; Schlicher, 435; William H. Jacobs, Report of the 26th Wisconsin at Gettysburg, *O. R.*, I, XXVII, 746; Schurz, *Reminiscences*, III, 35-36; Gordon, *Reminiscences*, 151; Muenzenberger to wife, August 30, 1863; Wickesberg, letter to family, July 9, 1863.

49. Lackner diary, December 22, 1863.

50. Milwaukee Features File, Microfilm #450, Milwaukee County Historical Society; Osten, 1.

51. Wallber, "From Gettysburg to Libby Prison," 192-193.

52. Domschcke, *Twenty Months*, 28.

53. *Annual Report of the Adjutant General of the State of Wisconsin*, 403; *Milwaukee Sentinel*, January 11, 1875, 8; Love, 417; Koenig, Gettysburg report, 740; Schurz, *Reminiscences*, III, 20; Winkler to Gaylord, August 25, 1864; Karsten diary, July 1, 1863.

54. Simonhoff, 77-78; Butts, 83.

55. Downey, 87, 97-99; Schurz, *Reminiscences*, III, 22; Simonhoff, 78; Koenig, Gettysburg report, 741; *Medical and Surgical History*, Surgical, III, 302; Regimental Descriptive Book, 58th New York Infantry.

56. Beecham, 198; Alexander, 411 Hunt, 312.

57. Moore, 120; Howard, Gettysburg report, 706; Young, 432; Vanderslice, 93; Kaufmann, 563.

58. Schurz, *Reminiscences*, III, 24-25; Howard, *Autobiography*, 429; Schurz, Gettysburg report, 731.

59. Regimental Descriptive Book, 58th New York Infantry; Schurz, *Reminiscences*, 24-25.

60. Earl Schenck Miers and Richard A. Brown, . 183.

61. *Annual Report of the Adjutant General of the State of Wisconsin*, 404; Karsten diary, July 4, 1863; Miers and Brown, 183.

62. Winkler, *Letters*, 73; Winkler to Gaylord, August 25, 1864.

63. Winkler, *Letters*, 72; Karsten diary, July 7, 1863.

64. *Annual Report of the Adjutant General of the State of Wisconsin*, 403; Winkler, *Letters*, 73-74.

65. Winkler, *Letters*, 74-75; Karsten diary, July 9, 1863, says they were relieved by the Sixth Corps.

66. *Annual Report of the Adjutant General of the State of Wisconsin*, 403.

67. Winkler, *Letters*, 75.

68. Ewell as quoted in Young, *Gettysburg*.

69. *Annual Report of the Adjutant General of the State of Wisconsin*, 403.

70. Wickesberg to parents, July 6, 1863.

71. Karsten to Dear Friend Carl, September 21, 1863.

72. *History of Milwaukee*, 800; Fox, *Regimental Losses*, 34, 439; *The Annual Report of the Adjutant General of the State of Wisconsin* lists the regiment's loss as 41 killed, 137 wounded, 26 captured, 6 missing—a total of 210 casualties.

73. *The New York Times,* July 4, 1863, 1; Schurz, *Reminiscences,* III, 53; Krzyżanowski, *Wspomnienia,* 78.

74. Schurz, *Reminiscences,* III, 53.

Chapter 8: Recovery and Transfer

1. Joseph Arnold, "Belle Island," pubished in Domschcke, *Twenty Months,* 135; Domschcke, *Twenty Months,* 29; Wallber, "From Gettysburg to Libby Prison," 193. Wallber's account closely parallels Domschcke's, including enough exact wording to suggest Wallber drew heavily on Domschcke's account in writing his own.

2. Domschcke, *Twenty Months,* 29; Wallber, "From Gettysburg to Libby Prison," 193.

3. Wallber, "From Gettysburg to Libby Prison," 194; Domschcke, *Twenty Months,* 29. The quotes are from Wallber, but they paraphrase Domschcke's earlier work.

4. Wallber, "From Gettysburg to Libby Prison," 194; Domschcke, *Twenty Months,* 29.

5. Domschcke, *Twenty Months,* 29; Wallber, "From Gettysburg to Libby Prison," 194.

6. Wallber, "From Gettysburg to Libby Prison," 194, italics added.

7. Domschcke, *Twenty Months,* 31.

8. Wallber, "From Gettysburg to Libby Prison," 195.

9. Domschcke, *Twenty Months,* 32.

10. Wallber, "From Gettysburg to Libby Prison," 196; quotes from Domschcke, *Twenty Months,* 32, 33.

11. Wallber, "From Gettysburg to Libby Prison," 197.

12. Wallber, "From Gettysburg to Libby Prison," 194; Domschcke, *Twenty Months,* 30.

13. Domschcke, *Twenty Months,* 34; Wallber, "From Gettysburg to Libby Prison," 198.

14. Chivas Post, 133, 519; Paul Miller to Fred Turk, February 1996; *Medical and Surgical History,* Medical, 178, 479-480.

15. *Wisconsin Losses in the Civil War,* 134-135; *Soldiers' and Citizens' Album,* 280, 716, 823; *Medical and Surgical History,* Surgical, I, 493 and III, 82.

16. Lackner diary, December 22, 1863.

17. *Roster of Wisconsin Volunteers,* 313; *Wisconsin Losses in the Civil War,* 134-135.

18. Wickesberg to parents, July 14, 1863 and July 28, 1863, quotations from the latter.

19. Flower, 724-725.

20. *Milwaukee Sentinel,* July 13, 1863, 1.

21. *Milwaukee Sentinel,* July 31, 1863, 2.

22. "Geschichte der Gründung."

23. Flower, 730.

24. Flower, 725.

25. Damkoehler to Mathilde, August 4, 1863.

26. *Roster of Wisconsin Volunteers,* 312-339.

27. Report by Capt. H. N. Stinson, September 9, 1863, in Regimental Papers, Box 2, National Archives.

28. Winkler Papers; Quiner, p. 75; *O. R.,* I, XXVII, III, 803.

29. Winkler, Letters, 77.
30. *Annual Report of the Adjutant General of the State of Wisconsin,* 403;Winkler, *Letters,* 76, quotes from 78; Karsten diary, July 19, 1863.
31. *Annual Report of the Adjutant General of the State of Wisconsin,* 403;Winkler, *Letters,* 78-79.
32. Karl August Graefe to parents and family, Sepember 8, 1863.
33. Wickesberg to parents, September 11, 1863.
34. Winkler, *Letters,* 83.
35. Winkler, *Letters,* 80-81.
36. Winkler Papers; Howard, Gettysburg Campaign, 710; Letter, George G. Meade to Henry Halleck, July 29, 1863, *O. R.,* I, XXVII, I, 105; Howard, *Autobiography,* 448; *Annual Report of the Adjutant General of the State of Wisconsin,* 403.
37. Quote from Winkler, *Letters,* 85; Karsten diary, September 16 and 17, 1863.
38. Damkoehler to Mathilde, November 8, 1863.
39. Karsten to Dear Friend Carl, September 21, 1863; Karsten diary, September 17, 1863.
40. Winkler, *Letters,* 85-86.
41. Damkoehler to Mathilde, September 7, 1863.
42. Kryżanowski's pension form, Adjutant General's Office, War Department; Regimental Descriptive Book, 26th Wisconsin Infantry; Winkler Papers; Karsten diary, September 18, 1863.
43. Atkinson, 4; Hebert, 250.
44. Osborn, "East Tennessee," 348; Catton, *Never Call Retreat,* 255.
45. Quotes from Winkler, *Letters,* 88; Butts, 96; Remington, 113; *Union Army,* II, 93; Osborn, "East Tennessee," 349-350; Bates, *History,* II, 920; Karsten diary, September 24, 1863.
46. Butts, 96; Remington, 113; Union Army, II, 93; Osborn, "East Tennessee," 349-350; Bates, *History,* II, 920; quotes from Winkler, *Letters,* 88 and 89; Karsten diary, September 24 and 25, 1863.
47. Karsten diary, September 26, 1863.
48. Winkler, *Letters,* 88.
49. Damkoehler to Mathilde, November 8, 1863; Winkler report, August 25, 1864; Karsten diary, September 27 and 28, 1863.
50. Howard, *Autobiography,* 435; Regimental Descriptive Book, Cos. A-D, 58th New York Infantry.
51. Winkler, *Letters,* 88; Karsten diary, September 28, 1863.
52. Winkler, *Letters,* 89; Lackner diary, December 22, 1863; Karsten diary, September 29 and 30, 1863.
53. Howard, *Autobiography,* 453, 455; Turner,. 292; Remington,. 113.
54. Wladimir Krzyżanowski, Itinerary of Krzyżanowski's Brigade in the Knoxville Campaign, *O. R.,* I, XXXI, I, 111; Winkler Papers; Osborn, "East Tennessee," 350; Brooks, 64; *Evening Post* (New York), September 26, 1863; Schurz, *Reminiscences,* III, 56.

Chapter 9: Alabama and Tennessee

1. Winkler, *Letters,* 90; Karsten diary, October 3, 1863.
2. Wickesberg to parents, October 2, 1863.

3. Fullerton, *Battles and Leaders*, III, 719; Winkler Papers; Howard, *Autobiography*, 457; Butts, 96; Wickesberg, letter to family, October 17, 1863.

4. Wickesberg to parents, October 17, 1863.

5. Damkoehler to Mathilde, November 8, 1863.

6. Winkler, *Letters*, 89.

7. Winkler, *Letters*, 90.

8. Wickesberg to parents, October 17, 1863.

9. *History of Milwaukee*, 800; *Roster of Wisconsin Volunteers*.

10. Krzyżanowski, Knoxville campaign,. 111; Dyer, 456; *O. R.*, I, XXXI, I, 804.

11. *Annual Report of the Adjutant General of the State of Wisconsin*, 404; Telegraph from Hooker to Howard, October 9, 1863, in the W. H. Jacobs Papers.

12. Letter, Theodore A. Meysenburg, Assistant Adjutant General, XI Corps, to "Comdg officer 2 Brigade 3 Division," October 9, 1863, in W. H. Jacobs Papers.

13. Winkler, *Letters*, 91.

14. Winkler, *Letters*, 91; *Annual Report of the Adjutant General of the State of Wisconsin*, 404; Letter, Theodore A. Meysenburg, Assistant Adjutant General, XI Corps, to "Comdg officer 2 Brigade 3 Division," October 9, 1863, in W. H. Jacobs Papers; Winkler to Gaylord, August 25, 1864; Karsten diary, October 11, 1863.

15. Winkler, *Letters*, 91-92.

16. Wickesberg to parents, October 17, 1863.

17. *Milwaukee Sentinel*, November 12, 1863, 4; Howard to wife, October 24, 1863, O. O. Howard Papers, Bowdoin College, Brunswick, Maine.

18. Karsten diary, October 23, 1863.

19. Winkler, *Letters*, 95; Winkler to Gaylord, August 25, 1864.

20. Winkler, *Letters*, 92; Winkler to Gaylord, August 25, 1864.

21. Winkler, *Letters*, 94.

22. Boatner, 142-143.

23. Adolph von Steinwehr, Report on the Battle of Wauhatchie, *Rebellion Record*, III, 587; Joseph Hooker, Report on the Battle of Wauhatchie, *Rebellion Record*, VII, 583; Krzyżanowski, Knoxville campaign, 112; Schurz, *Reminiscences*, III, 59; Ulysses S. Grant, "Chattanooga," *Battles and Leaders*, III, 687; Butts, 98; Winkler, Letters, 95; Karsten diary, October 27, 1863.

24. Schurz, *Reminiscences*, III,. 59-60; Winkler Papers; Butts, 98.

25. Winkler, *Letters*, 96.

26. Schurz, *Reminiscences*, III, 59-60; Hooker, Wauhatchie report, 584; Grant, "Chattanooga," 687; Butts, 98; Howard, *Autobiography*, 463-464.

27. Boatner, 895-896.

28. Damkoehler to Mathilde, November 8, 1863.

29. Damkoehler to Mathilde, November 8, 1863.

30. Osborn, "East Tennessee," 359; Howard, *Autobiography*, 467; Schurz, *Reminiscences*, III, 60-65.

31. Schurz, *Reminiscences*, III, 61, 65; Winkler Papers; Osborn, "East Tennessee," 360.

32. *Ibid.*

33. Proceedings of the Court of Inquiry, 151, 165-166, 170, 183; Butts, 98-99.

34. Proceedings of the Court of Inquiry, 151, 165-166, 170, 183; Butts, 98-99; Osborn, "East Tennessee," 361; Howard, *Autobiography*, 467; Hooker, Wauhatchie report, 584; Schurz, *Reminiscences*, III, 62-64; Steinwehr, Wauhatchie report, 587; Winkler to Gaylord, August 25, 1864.

35. Schurz, Wauhatchie report,. 110-111; Proceedings of the Court of Inquiry, 160, 189-190; Howard, *Autobiography*, 470; John W. Geary, Report on Wauhatchie, *O. R.*, I, XXXI, I, 118; quote from Winkler, *Letters*, 97; Karsten diary, October 29, 1863.

36. *O. R.*, I, XXXI, III,; Lackner diary, December 22, 1863; Schurz, *Reminiscences*, III, 69, 71; Howard, *Autobiography*, 472.

37. Winkler, *Letters*, 97; Winkler to Gaylord, August 25, 1864.

38. New York State Monument on Lookout Mountain; Phisterer, New York, 2518; *O. R.*, I, XXXI, II, 17; Howard, *Autobiography*, 479; Schurz, *Reminiscences*, III, 72.

39. Winkler, *Letters*, 98.

40. Letter, O. O. Howard to "Col" [Jacobs], October 20, 1863, in W. H. Jacobs Papers.

41. *History of Milwaukee*, 800; Winkler, *Letters*, 98.

42. Winkler, *Letters*, 100.

43. Winkler, *Letters*, 100; Winkler to Gaylord, August 25, 1864; Karsten diary, November 12, 1863.

44. *O. R.*, I, XXXI, II, 373, 378, 382; Schurz, *Reminiscences*, III, 72; Winkler Papers; Winkler report, August 25, 1864; *Annual Report of the Adjutant General of the State of Wisconsin*, 404; Wickesberg to parents, December 19, 1863; Winkler to Gaylord, August 25, 1864.

45. Wickesberg to parents, December 19, 1863.

46. Damkoehler to Mathilde, November 25, 1863.

47. Wickesberg to parents, December 19, 1863.

48. Boatner, 145-147; *Union Army*, 136; Schurz, *Reminiscences*, III, 74; *Annual Report of the Adjutant General of the State of Wisconsin*, 404; *Soldiers' and Citizens' Album*, 324.

49. Winkler, *Letters*, 103, 108.

50. Wickesberg to parents, December 19, 1863.

51. Schurz, *Reminiscences*, III, 78; Oliver Otis Howard, Report on Knoxville, *O. R.*, I, XXXI, II, 350; *Annual Report of the Adjutant General of the State of Wisconsin*, 404.

52. Boatner, 143.

53. Schurz, Knoxville relief, 382-383; Schurz, *Reminiscences*, III, 78; Winkler Papers; Winkler report, August 25, 1864; Wickesberg, letter to family, December 19, 1863; Quiner,752.

54. Lackner diary, December 22, 1863.

55. Winkler, *Letters*, 103.

56. *Annual Report of the Adjutant General of the State of Wisconsin*, 404; Winkler Papers; Wicksberg to parents, December 19, 1863; Schurz, Knoxville relief, 382-383; Quiner, 752.

57. Wickesberg to parents, January 17, 1864.

58. Winkler, *Letters*, 103-104.

59. Winkler Papers; Schurz, Knoxville relief, 382-383; Quiner, 752; quote from Wickesberg to parents, January 17, 1864.

60. *Annual Report of the Adjutant General of the State of Wisconsin*, 404; Winkler, *Letters*, 104-105.

61. Winkler Papers; *Annual Report of the Adjutant General of the State of Wisconsin*, 404.

62. Quiner, 752; Winkler Papers; Schurz, *Reminiscences*, III, 80-83; Colonel Aden C. Cavins, letter to wife, December 19, 1863; *History of Milwaukee*, 800; Love, 999; Krzyżanowski, *Wspomnienia*, 80; *Annual Report of the Adjutant General of the State of Wisconsin*, 404.

63. Lackner diary, December 22, 1863.

64. Winkler, *Letters*, 105.

65. Winkler, *Letters*, 106.

66. Winkler, *Letters*, 107.

67. Wickesberg to parents, December 19, 1863.

68. Winkler, *Letters*, 107.

69. Winkler report, August 25, 1864.

70. Damkoehler to Mathilde, letter fragment, January 3, 1864.

71. Damkoehler to Mathilde, letter fragment, January 3, 1864.

72. Schurz, *Reminiscences*, III,. 82-85; Butts, 102; Oliver Otis Howard, letter to Officers of Eleventh Corps, December 8, 1863, *O. R.*, I, XXXI, III, 358.

73. *Annual Report of the Adjutant General of the State of Wisconsin*, 404; quote from Winkler, *Letters*, 109.

74. Wickesberg to parents, December 19, 1863.

75. Winnkler, *Letters*, 110.

76. Winkler, *Letters*, 111.

77. *Wisconsin Losses in the Civil War*, 135-137.

78. *Milwaukee Sentinel*, January 11, 1864, 1.

79. *History of Milwaukee*, 800.

80. Damkoehler to Mathilde, February 21, 1864.

81. Winkler, *Letters*, 114; *Annual Report of the Adjutant General of the State of Wisconsin*, 404.

82. Wickesberg to parents, January 17, 1864.

83. Wickesberg to parents, January 24, 1864. .

84. Wickesberg to family, April 10, 1864.

85. Damkoehler to Mathilde, January 3, 1864.

86. Damkoehler to Mathilde, February 21, 1864.

87. Damkoehler to Mathilde, January 3, 1864.

88. Damkoehler to Mathilde, February 21, 1864.

89. Damkoehler to Mathilde, March 7, 1864.

90. Karsten to Dear Friend Carl, March 24, 1864; Regimental morning reports and papers, National Archives.

91. Regimental Papers, Box 2, National Archives.

92. Regimental Papers, Box 2, National Archives.

Chapter 10: The Atlanta Campaign

1. Hebert, 260, 271-272; *O. R.*, I, XXXII, I, 32; Wittke, *Refugees*, 236-237.

2. Underwood, 202; Hebert, 260, 271-272; *O. R.*, I, XXXII, I, 32.

3. Dyer, 456; Sandburg, II, 257; Carl Schurz, letter to parents, April 24, 1864.

4. Winkler, *Letters*, 118.

5. Wickesberg to parents, May 1, 1864.

6. Damkoehler to Mathilde, April 17, 1864.

7. Karsten diary, April 23, 1864.

8. Winkler, *Letters*, 118.

9. Wickesberg to parents, May 1, 1864.

10. Buerstatte, 5, February 12 and April 23, 1864.

11. Boatner, 30.

12. Boatner, 30.

13. Boatner, 30; *West Point Atlas*, 146.

14. Winkler, *Letters*, 119.

15. Winkler, *Letters*, 119; Karsten diary, May 3, 1864.

16. Buerstatte, May 5, 1864; Karsten diary, May 4, 1864.

17. Winkler, *Letters*, 121.

18. Winkler, *Letters*, 120.

19. Buerstatte, May 7, 1864; Karsten diary, May 6, 1864. Leet's Farm was also called Leet's Tanyard.

20. Winkler, *Letters*, 120-121.

21. Winkler, *Letters*, 121-122; Buerstatte, May 8, 1864; *O.R.*, I, XXXVIII, II, 431, 463; Karsten diary, May 7, 1864.

22. Winkler, *Letters*, 121-122; Buerstatte, May 8, 1864; *O.R.*, I, XXXVIII, II, 431, 463; *Roster of Wisconsin Volunteers*, 313, 336; Quiner, 753; quote from *O.R.*, I, XXXVIII, II, 431.

23. Buerstatte, May 11, 1864; *O.R.*, I, XXXVIII, II, 431; Karsten diary, May 9, 1864.

24. Boatner, 705.; *West Point Atlas*, 144-145.

25. Karsten diary, May 3, 1864.

26. Winkler, *Letters*, 122; Buerstatte, May 11, 1864; Boatner, 691.

27. Boatner, 691-692.

28. Letter, Winkler to Capt. E. H. Pratt, A.A.A.G., 3rd Brigade, 3rd Division, XX Corps, May 21, 1864, in F. C. Winkler Papers, Milwaukee County Historical Society [hereafter cited as Winkler, Resaca Report]; Love, 703; Karsten diary, May 13, 1864.

29. Winkler, Resaca Report; Love, 703.

30. Buerstatte, May 14, 1864.

31. Winkler, Resaca Report; Love, 703; *Roster of Wisconsin Volunteers*, 317; Franz Kuechenmeister, Claim for Pension, October 14, 1891; Karsten diary, May 14, 1864.

32. Quotes from Winkler, Resaca Report; Underwood, 208; Buerstatte, May 15, 1864.

33. Quotes from Winkler, Resaca Report; Love, 703; *Annual Report of the Adjutant General of the State of Wisconsin*, 406; Kuechenmeister, Claim for Pension, October 14, 1891.

34. Winkler, Resaca Report.

35. Love, 704; Underwood, 208.

36. Winkler, Resaca Report; *Annual Report of the Adjutant General of the State of Wisconsin*, 406; Love, 704; *History of Milwaukee*, 800.

37. Winkler, Resaca Report.

38. *O.R.*, I, XXXVIII, II, 435; *Annual Report of the Adjutant General of the State of Wisconsin*, 406; Love, 704; *History of Milwaukee*, 800.

39. Winkler, Resaca Report; Underwood, 208-209; *O.R.*, I, XXXVIII, II, 464.

40. Buerstatte, May 15, 1864.

41. Winkler, Resaca Report.

42. Winkler, Resaca Report.

43. *Annual Report of the Adjutant General of the State of Wisconsin*, 406; *O.R.*, I, XXXVIII, II, 436, 464.

44. Buerstatte, May 16, 1864.

45. Winkler, *Letters*, 123.

46. Buerstatte, May 15, 1864.

47. *Roster of Wisconsin Volunteers*, 320, 326, 328, 333; *Milwaukee Sentinel*, May 31, 1864, 1.

48. Love, 704; *History of Milwaukee*, 800; quote from Buerstatte, May 15, 1864.

49. Winkler, *Letters*, 123; Karsten diary, May 16, 1864.

50. Love, 706; *O.R.*, I, XXXVIII, II, 464.

51. Buerstatte, May 17 and 18, 1864.

52. Winkler, *Letters*, 123.

53. *O.R.*, I, XXXVIII, II, 464; Karsten diary, May 18, 1864.

54. Boatner, 32; *West Point Atlas*, 144; quotes from *O.R.*, I, XXXVIII, II, 464; Karsten diary, May 19, 1864.

55. *Annual Report of the Adjutant General of the State of Wisconsin*, 406; Buerstatte, May 19, 1864; Winkler, Resaca Report.

56. Winkler, *Letters*, 123; Karsten diary, May 19, 1864.

57. Winkler, *Letters*, 126.

58. *O.R.*, I, XXXVIII, II, 464.

59. Winkler, *Letters*, 124.

60. Buerstatte, May 22, 1864.

61. Winkler, *Letters*, 125.

62. Buerstatte, May 22, 1864.

63. Winkler, *Letters*, 125-126.

64. Winkler, *Letters*, 124.

65. Buerstatte, May 23, 1864.

66. *Annual Report of the Adjutant General of the State of Wisconsin*, 406.

67. Karsten diary, May 23, 1864.

68. *O.R.*, I, XXXVIII, II, 464; Underwood, 215; Winkler, *Letters*, 127; *O.R.*, I, XXXVIII, II, 464.

69. Underwood, 215; Love, 710; *O.R.*, I, XXXVIII, II, 464.

70. Underwood, 215; Love, 710.

71. Winkler, *Letters*, 127.

72. *Roster of Wisconsin Volunteers*, 316-318; *Milwaukee Sentinel, June* 11, 1864, 1.

73. *Roster of Wisconsin Volunteers*, 318-320; *Milwaukee Sentinel*, June 11, 1864, 1.

74. *Roster of Wisconsin Volunteers*, 324-326; *Milwaukee Sentinel*, June 11, 1864, 1.

75. Winkler, *Letters*, 127.

76. *Roster of Wisconsin Volunteers*, 3329-339; *Milwaukee Sentinel*, June 11, 1864, 1; letter, Fred Turk to author, January 31, 1995.

77. Winkler, *Letters*, 127.

78. Underwood, 215; Love, 710; Winkler, *Letters*, 127; *Roster of Wisconsin Volunteers*, 338; *Milwaukee Sentinel*, June 11, 1864, 1.

79. Winkler, *Letters*, 127.

80. Love, 710; *Annual Report of the Adjutant General of the State of Wisconsin*, 406 (this source and Winkler's report cite casualties including five men killed, one officer and thirty-one men wounded, and two men missing); Underwood, 215; *O.R.*, I, XXXVIII, II, 465.

81. Winkler, *Letters*, 128.

82. Boatner, 32, 432; *West Point Atlas*, 146-147.

83. Buerstatte, May 27 and 28, 1864.

84. Winkler, *Letters*, 128-129.

85. Buerstatte, May 30, 1864 and May 31, 1864.

86. Winkler, *Letters*, 129.

87. Buerstatte, May 27, 1864; *Annual Report of the Adjutant General of the State of Wisconsin*, 406; *O.R.*, I, XXXVIII, II, 465; *Milwaukee Sentinel*, June 11, 1864, 1.

88. Winkler, *Letters*, 129.

89. Buerstatte, June 2, 1864.

90. Buerstatte, June 5, 1864; Winkler, *Letters*, 130; *Annual Report of the Adjutant General of the State of Wisconsin*, 406.

91. Buerstatte, June 5, 1864; Winkler, Letters, 130.

92. Winkler, *Letters*, 131; Buerstatte, June 5, 1864, June 8, 1864, and quotes

from June 7, 1864; Karsten diary, June 6, 1864.

93. Winkler, *Letters*, 133; Buerstatte, June 16, 1864; Karsten diary, June 15, 1864.

94. Buerstatte, June 17, 1864; Winkler, Letters, 133.

95. *Annual Report of the Adjutant General of the State of Wisconsin*, 406; Love, 719; *O.R.*, I, XXXVIII, II, 22, 465; Karsten diary, June 17, 1864.

96. Winkler, *Letters*, 134; *O.R.*, I, XXXVIII, II, 465.

97. Buerstatte, June 19, 1864; Karsten diary, June 19, 1864.

98. Winkler, *Letters*, 134.

99. Regimental muster rolls, report for September, 1864, National Archives.

100. Winkler, *Letters*, 135, 169.

101. Winkler, *Letters*, 135.

102. Winkler, *Letters*, 135; Buerstatte, June 22, 1864; *History of Milwaukee*, 800; *O.R.*, I, XXXVIII, II, 22, 465; quote from *Soldiers' and Citizens' Album*, 275.

103. Winkler, *Letters*, 135-137; Buerstatte, June 22, 1864; *History of Milwaukee*, 800; *O.R.*, I, XXXVIII, II, 22, 465.

104. *Soldiers' and Citizens' Album*, 324, 423; Regimental muster rolls, report for September, 1864, National Archives.

105. Love, 719; Buerstatte, June 22, 1864.

106. *O.R.*, I, XXXVIII, II, 466; Winkler to Gaylord, August 25, 1864; Love, 719, says five killed and 33 wounded.

107. Winkler, *Letters*, 135-136.

108. Love, 719; *Annual Report of the Adjutant General of the State of Wisconsin*, 406; Buerstatte, June 23, 1864.

109. Winkler, *Letters*, 137-138; ; Karsten diary, June 30, 1864.

110. Love, 719.

111. Winkler, *Letters*, 145.

112. Boatner, 453; *West Point Atlas*, 144-147; quote from Winkler, *Letters*, 145; *Annual Report of the Adjutant General of the State of Wisconsin*, 407; *O.R.*, I, XXXVIII, II, 466; Buerstatte, July 4, 1864; Karsten diary, July 3, 1864.

113. Buerstatte, July 6, 1864; *Annual Report of the Adjutant General of the State of Wisconsin*, 407; *O.R.*, I, XXXVIII, II, 466.

114. Buerstatte, July 9, 1864.

115. Winkler, *Letters*, 147, 148.

116. Winkler, *Letters*, 148-149; *Soldiers' and Citizens' Album*, 325.

117. *Annual Report of the Adjutant General of the State of Wisconsin*, 407; *History of Milwaukee*, 800; *O.R.*, I, XXXVIII, II, 466; Buerstatte, July 16, July 17, July 18, and July 19, 1864.

118. "Recall Famous Fight," *Kenosha News*, June 20, 1914; *O.R.*, I, XXXVIII, II, 466.

119. Boatner, 625-626.

120. Underwood, 226; *Kenosha News*, June 20, 1914; Boatner, 626; *O.R.*, I, XXXVIII, II, 442, 466.

121. Evans, 212; *O.R.*, I, XXXVIII, II, 442, 466.

122. Underwood, 226; Love, 728; *Kenosha News*, June 20, 1914.

123. Buerstatte, July 20, 1864.

124. Underwood, 226; Love, 728; *Annual Report of the Adjutant General of the State of Wisconsin*, 407; Winkler, *Letters*, 151; *O.R.*, I, XXXVIII, II, 442, 466-467.

125. Underwood, 226; Love, 728; *Annual Report of the Adjutant General of the State of Wisconsin*, 407; *O.R.*, I, XXXVIII, II, 442.

126. Love, 728; *History of Milwaukee*, 800; *Annual Report of the Adjutant General of the State of Wisconsin*, 407; *O.R.*, I, XXXVIII, II, 442; *Kenosha News*, June 20, 1914; Buerstatte, July 20, 1864.

127. Buerstatte, July 20, 1864; *Medical and Surgical History*, Medical, 341; Kuechenmeister, Claim for Pension, October 14, 1891.

128. Love, 728; Underwood, 226; *Annual Report of the Adjutant General of the State of Wisconsin*, 407; *O.R.*, I, XXXVIII, II, 443.

129. *Kenosha News*, June 20, 1914; *History of Milwaukee*, 800; *Annual Report of the Adjutant General of the State of Wisconsin*, 407; Evans, XI, 212.

130. Buerstatte, July 20, 1864; *Soldiers' and Citizens' Album*, 773.

131. Winkler, *Letters*, 152.

132. Love, 728; *History of Milwaukee*, 800 (the latter places the loss at 6 killed and 39 wounded); Underwood, 226.

133. Evans, XI, 212; *Medical and Surgical History*, Medical, 341.

134. Winkler, *Letters*, 149.

135. Underwood, 226.

136. *O.R.*, I, XXXVIII, II, 443.

137. Buerstatte, July 21, 1864; Winkler, *Letters*, 149.

138. *Soldiers' and Citizens' Album*, 226.

139. Buerstatte, July 21, 1864; Soldiers' and Citizens' Album, 773.

140. *Annual Report of the Adjutant General of the State of Wisconsin*, 407; *O.R.*, I, XXXVIII, II, 467.

141. Manitowoc *Pilot*, September 2, 1864, 1 and November 25, 1864, 1.

142. Boatner, 32-33.

143. Winkler, *Letters*, 150.

144. Buerstatte, July 22, 1864; Winkler, *Letters*, 150, 151.

145. Buerstatte, July 23, 1864.

146. Winkler, *Letters*, 154-155.

147. *Annual Report of the Adjutant General of the State of Wisconsin*, 407; Love, 736.

148. Buerstatte, August 21, 1864.

149. Winkler, *Letters*, 155.

150. Winkler, *Letters*, 160.

151. Winkler, *Letters*, 159.

152. *Annual Report of the Adjutant General of the State of Wisconsin*, 407, says the regiment lost 13 casualties; Love, 736; Buerstatte, August 27, 1864; *O.R.*, I, XXXVIII, II, 467, says casualties were two killed and two wounded; *Soldiers' and Citizens' Album*, 324.

153. *History of Milwaukee*, 800.

154. *Annual Report of the Adjutant General of the State of Wisconsin*, 407; Love, 736; Buerstatte, August 27, 1864.

155. Winkler, *Letters*, 158.

156. Winkler, *Letters*, 163.

157. Winkler, *Letters*, 131-132.

158. Winkler, *Letters*, 164.

159. Winkler, *Letters*, 166.

160. Winkler, *Letters*, 164.

161. *O.R.*, I, XXXVIII, II, 467.

162 .Buerstatte, September 2, 1864; Karsten diary, September 4, 1864.

163. Winkler, *Letters*, 164.

164. Winkler, *Letters*, 167.

Chapter 11: March to the Sea

1. Winkler, *Letters*, 170.
2. Winkler, *Letters*, 170; Karsten diary, September 8, 1864.
3. Bruce, 591; Klement, 42-44.
4. Winkler, *Letters*, 176.
5. Winkler, *Letters*, 179; Current, 412; Gregory, 62; Klement, 42-44.
6. Winkler, *Letters*, 171.
7. Winkler, *Letters*, 171.
8. *Annual Report of the Adjutant General of the State of Wisconsin*, 408.; Buerstatte, October 8, 1864; quotes from Winkler, *Letters*, 173; O.R., I, XXXIX, I, 679, 685, 692;
9. Winkler, *Letters*, 175; Buerstatte, October 19, 1864 and October 21, 1864; Karsten diary, October 20 and 21, 1864.
10. Winkler, *Letters*, 176; Karsten diary, October 21, 1864.
11. Winkler, *Letters*, 177.
12. Winkler, *Letters*, 168-169, 177.
13. Winkler, *Letters*, 178; Buerstatte, November 9, 1864.
14. Winkler, *Letters*, 180.
15. Buerstatte, November 14, 1864; Winkler, Letters, 180; *Annual Report of the Adjutant General of the State of Wisconsin*, 408.
16. Boatner, 509.
17. Boatner, 509.
18. Winkler, *Letters*, 180; quote from *Annual Report of the Adjutant General of the State of Wisconsin*, 408.
19. *Annual Report of the Adjutant General of the State of Wisconsin*, 408; O.R., I, XLIV. O.R. uses the name Rock Bridge, but some reports refer to it as Stone Bridge.
20. Winkler, *Letters*, 180; quote from *Annual Report of the Adjutant General of the State of Wisconsin*, 408.
21. *Annual Report of the Adjutant General of the State of Wisconsin*, 408; O.R., I, XLIV.
22. Winkler, *Letters*, 180.
23. Buerstatte, November 20, 21, 22, 1864, quote from November 19, 1864.
24. Winkler, *Letters*, 181; *Annual Report of the Adjutant General of the State of Wisconsin*, 408; O.R., I, XLIV.
25. Buerstatte, November 23, 1864; *Annual Report of the Adjutant General of the State of Wisconsin*, 408.
26. Winkler, *Letters*, 181.
27. Buerstatte, Novemnber 27, 1864; quote from *Annual Report of the Adjutant General of the State of Wisconsin*, 408; O.R., I, XLIV.
28. Buerstatte, November 29 and 30, 1864, quote from latter; O.R., I, XLIV.
29. Winkler, *Letters*, 182.
30. O.R., I, XLIV,.
31. Winkler, *Letters*, 183.
32. Buerstatte, December 4, 1864.
33. Buerstatte, December 7 and 9, 1864; O.R., I, XLIV; *Annual Report of the Adjutant General of the State of Wisconsin*, 408.
34. Buerstatte, December 10, 1864; O.R., I, XLIV.
35. *Annual Report of the Adjutant General of the State of Wisconsin*, 408; Buerstatte, December 11, 1864.

36. Boatner, 512; *Annual Report of the Adjutant General of the State of Wisconsin*, 408.

37. Winkler, *Letters*, 185.

38. Winkler, *Letters*, 185; *O.R.*, I, XLIV.

39. Winkler, *Letters*, 187.

40. Boatner, 512; *Annual Report of the Adjutant General of the State of Wisconsin*, 408; quotes from Winkler, *Letters*, 187.

41. Buerstatte, December 21, 1864.

42. Winkler, *Letters*, 185.

43. Buerstatte, December 24 and 25, 1864.

44. Winkler, *Letters*, 188.

Chapter 12: The Carolinas Campaign

1. Boatner, 123-125.

2. Boatner, 124-125.

3. Boatner, 125.

4. Buerstatte, December 26, 1864.

5. Winkler, *Letters*, 189.

6. Buerstatte, December 27 and 30, 1864.

7. Winkler, *Letters*, 190.

8. Buerstatte, December 31, 1864.

9. *Annual Report of the Adjutant General of the State of Wisconsin*, 408; Buerstatte, January 1 and 2, 1865.

10. Jones, January 2, 1865; *O.R.*, I, XLVII, I, 142.

11. Winkler, *Letters*, 191; quotes from Jones, January 2, 1865.

12. Winkler, *Letters*, 191; quotes from Jones, January 2, 1865.

13. Jones, January 3, 1865.

14. Jones, January 3, 1865; Winkler, *Letters*, 191; Buerstatte, January 3, 1865.

15. Jones, January 3, 1865; quote from Winkler, *Letters*, 191-192.

16. Jones, January 3, 1865.

17. Jones, January 4, 1865; *O.R.*, I, XLVII, I, 843; Buerstatte, January 4 and 5, 1865.

18. Jones, January 5, 1865.

19. Jones, January 6 and 7, 1865; Winkler, *Letters*, 193; Buerstatte, January 6, 1865.

20. Winkler, *Letters*, 193; Buerstatte, January 6, 1865; Jones, January 8, 1865 and quote from January 9, 1865.

21. Buerstatte, January 10 and 15, 1865; Jones, January 10, 11 12, and 14, 1865 and quote from January 13, 1865.

22. Winkler, *Letters*, 195; Jones, January 14 and 15, 1865.

23. Jones, January 15, 1865; Buerstatte, January 15, 1865; *Saint Joseph Edition of the New American Bible* (New York: Catholic Book Publishing Company, 1992), 272.

24. Winkler, *Letters*, 194.

25. Buerstatte, January 15, 1865.

26. Winkler, *Letters*, 198.

27. Buerstatte, January 17, 1865; Jones, January 16 and 17, 1865; *O.R.*, I, XLVII, I, 821.

28. Jones, January 18 and 20, 1865; *Annual Report of the Adjutant General of the State of Wisconsin*, 408.

29. Buerstatte, January 19, 20, and 21, 1865; Jones, January 19, 1865.

30. Winkler, *Letters*, 196.

31. Jones, January 20, 1865.

32. Jones, January 22, 1865.

33. Buerstatte, January 22 and 25, 1865; Jones. January 21, 1865.

34. Winkler, *Letters*, 197; Jones, January 24 and 25, 1865; *O.R.*, I, XLVII, I, 845; Ennis' Crossroads was also known as Bradham's.

35. *O.R.*, I, XLVII, I, 845; Winkler, *Letters*, 197; Jones, January 24 and 25, 1865.

36. Buerstatte, January 28, 1865; Jones, January 26 and 28, 1865.

37. Jones, January 28, 1865.

38. Quotes from Jones, January 28 and 29, 1865; Buerstatte, January 29, 1865; *Annual Report of the Adjutant General of the State of Wisconsin*, 408; *O.R.*, I, XLVII, I, 143, 821, 844.

39. Quotes from Jones, January 30, 1865; Buerstatte, January 30, 1865; *O.R.*, I, XLVII, I, 143, 844.

40. Jones, January 31, 1865.

41. Buerstatte, February 1 and 3, 1865.

42. Winkler, *Letters*, 198.

43. Buerstatte, February 8, 9, and 10, 1865; *Annual Report of the Adjutant General of the State of Wisconsin*, 408; *O.R.*, I, XLVII, I, 844.

44. Buerstatte, February 8, 9, and 10, 1865; *Annual Report of the Adjutant General of the State of Wisconsin*, 408; *O.R.*, I, XLVII, I, 143, 821, 844. Graham's Station was also referred to as Graham's Turnout, Graham's Post Office, or simply Graham.

45. Winkler, *Letters*, 198; *O.R.*, I, XLVII, I, 821, 844.

46. Underwood, 265.

47. Boatner, 125; Buerstatte, February 11, 12 and 16, 1865; *O.R.*, I, XLVII, I, 143, 844.

48. *Annual Report of the Adjutant General of the State of Wisconsin*, 408; Buerstatte, February 17, 18, 19, and 21, 1865; *O.R.*, I, XLVII, I, 143, 844; Winkler, *Letters*, 199.

49. Winkler, *Letters*, 199-200; *O.R.*, I, XLVII, I, 822.

50. *Annual Report of the Adjutant General of the State of Wisconsin*, 409; Buerstatte, February 22, 1865; *O.R.*, I, XLVII, I, 844.

51. *O.R.*, I, XLVII, I, 823.

52. Winkler, *Letters*, 200; Boatner, 126; *O.R.*, I, XLVII, I, 143.

53. Winkler, *Letters*, 200 and quote from 201; Boatner, 126.

54. Buerstatte, March 5, 1865.

55. *O.R.*, I, XLVII, I, 844, 845; Biographical File, State Historical Society of Wisconsin; Regimental Muster Rolls, National Archives.

56. Winkler, *Letters*, 201.

57. Boatner, 126.

58. *Annual Report of the Adjutant General of the State of Wisconsin*, 409; Buerstatte, March 6 and 12, 1865; *O.R.*, I, XLVII, I, 143, 844.

59. Buerstatte, March 13 and 14, 1865; Winkler, *Letters*, 202.

60. *O.R.*, I, XLVII, I, 143, 823-824.

61. Winkler, *Letters*, 202; Annual Report of the Adjutant General of the State of Wisconsin, 409.

62. Boatner, 126.

63. Boatner, 35; Love, 962; *Annual Report of the Adjutant General of the State of Wisconsin*, 409; *O.R.*, I, XLVII, I, 824.

64. Love, 962; *Annual Report of the Adjutant General of the State of Wisconsin*, 409; *O.R.*, I, XLVII, I, 824.

65. Winkler, *Letters*, 202-203; Buerstatte, March 16, 1865; *O.R.*, I, XLVII, I, 825; Love, 962; *Annual Report of the Adjutant General of the State of Wisconsin*, 409.

66. Boatner, 126; Winkler, *Letters*, 203; Love, 962; *Annual Report of the Adjutant General of the State of Wisconsin*, 409; *O.R.*, I, XLVII, I, 844.

67. Boatner, 126; Buerstatte, March 17, 1865; Winkler, *Letters*, 203; Buerstatte, March 18, 1865. The Black River was also referred to as the South River.

68. "Water" quote from Buerstatte, March 19, 1865; other quotes fom Winkler, *Letters*, 203; Love, 964; *O.R.*, I, XLVII, I, 144, 826, 834.

69. Winkler, *Letters*, 203; Bradley, 62; Hughes, 116.

70. *O.R.*, I, XLVII, I, 826, 834; Bradley, 62; Hughes, 118.

71. Love, 964; *Annual Report of the Adjutant General of the State of Wisconsin*, 409; *O.R.*, I, XLVII, I, 826, 834.

72. Winkler, *Letters*, 203-204.

73. Hughes, 116, 118-119.

74. Love, 964; *Annual Report of the Adjutant General of the State of Wisconsin*, 409; Buerstatte, March 19, 1865 (Buerstatte says two dead and five wounded); *O.R.*, I, XLVII, I, 844.

75. Boatner, 126-127.

76. Buerstatte, March 22, 23, 24 and 25,1865; *Annual Report of the Adjutant General of the State of Wisconsin*, 409; Regimental Muster Rolls, National Archives; *O.R.*, X, XLVII, I, 826.

77. Buerstatte, April 1, 2, 3, 4 and 5, 1865.

78. *Annual Report of the Adjutant General of the State of Wisconsin*, 410; Buerstatte, April 6, 7 and 9, 1865; *O.R.*, I, XLVII, I, 144.

79. Buerstatte, April 10, 11 and 12, 1865; *Annual Report of the Adjutant General of the State of Wisconsin*, 410; *Soldiers' and Citizens' Album*, 226.

80. Boatner, 127; Buerstatte, April 13, 1865; *O.R.*, I, XLVII, I, 829.

81. Buerstatte, April 1, 24, 27, 28 and 1865; *O.R.*, I, XLVII, I, 144.

Chapter 13: Journey Home

1. Buerstatte, April 30, 1865; *O.R.*, I, XLVII, I, 144.)

2. *Annual Report of the Adjutant General of the State of Wisconsin*, 410; Buerstatte, May 1, 1865 and May 3, 1865; *O.R.*, I, XLVII, I, 829.

3. Buerstatte, May 4, 1865.

4. Jones, May 5, 1865.

5. Jones, May 6, 1865; *O.R.*, I, XLVII, I, 829.

6. Jones, May 7, 1865.

7. Jones, May 8, 1865; *O.R.*, I, XLVII, I, 145.

8. Buerstatte, May 11, 1865.

9. Jones, May 11, 1865.

10. Jones, May 11, 1865.

11. Buerstatte, May 11, 1865.

12. Jones, May 12, 1865.

13. Jones, May 13, 1865.

14. Quotes from Jones, May 14, 1865; Buerstatte, May 14, 1865; *O.R.*, I, XLVII, I, 145.

15. Winkler, *Letters*, 207.

16. Jones, May 15, 1865.

17. Buerstatte, May 15, 1865.

18. Buerstatte, May 15, 1865.

19. Jones, May 16, 1865.

20. Buerstatte, May 17, 1865; Jones, May 17, 1865.

21. Jones, May 17, 1865. Brentsville was also called Bernardsville.

22. Buerstatte, May 18, 1865; Jones, May 18, 1865.

23. Buerstatte, May 18, 1865; *O.R.*, I, XLVII, I, 145.

24. Buerstatte, May 19, 1865.

25. Jones, May 19, 1865.

26. Quotes from Jones, May 20, 1865; Winkler, Letters, 208.

27. Boatner, 351; *Annual Report of the Adjutant General of the State of Wisconsin*, 410.

28. Jones, May 23, 1865.

29. Jones, May 23, 1865.

30. Buerstatte, May 24, 1865.

31. Buerstatte, May 24, 1865; Jones, May 24, 1865.

32. Jones, May 25, 1865; *O.R.*, I, XLVII, I, 145.

33. Buerstatte, May 26, 1865.

34. Jones, May 26, 1865.

35. Jones, May 30, 1865.

36. Jones, May 28 and 29, 1865.

37. Winkler, Letters, 209.

38. Jones, June 4, 1865.

39. Jones, June 6, 1865.

40. Quote from Winkler, *Letters*, 208; Jones, June 7, 1865.

41. Winkler, *Letters*, 209.

42. Buerstatte, June 9, 1865.

43. Jones, June 8, 1865.

44. Winkler, *Letters*, June 10, 1865.

45. *Annual Report of the Adjutant General of the State of Wisconsin*, 410; *Soldiers' and Citizens' Album*, 177-178, 423.

46. *Annual Report of the Adjutant General of the State of Wisconsin*, 410; *Milwaukee Sentinel*, June 17, 1865, 1; *Soldiers' and Citizens' Album*, 177-178.

47. *Milwaukee Sentinel*, June 19, 1865, 1; Winkler, Letters, 209.

48. *Milwaukee Sentinel*, June 17, 1865.

49. *Milwaukee Sentinel*, June 19, 1865, 1.

50. *Milwaukee Sentinel*, June 19, 1865, 1; quotes from undated newspaper clipping, State Historical Society of Wisconsin.

51. *Milwaukee Sentinel*, June 19, 1865, 1; undated newspaper clipping, State Historical Society of Wisconsin.

52. *Milwaukee Sentinel*, June 19, 1865, 1; undated newspaper clipping, State Historical Society of Wisconsin.

53. *Milwaukee Sentinel*, June 19, 1865, 1.

54. Undated newspaper clipping, State Historical Society of Wisconsin; quotation from *Milwaukee Sentinel*, June 19, 1865, 1.

55. *Milwaukee Sentinel*, June 19, 1865 and June 8, 1880, 4; *Annual Report of the Adjutant General of the State of Wisconsin*, 410.

Chapter 14: Aftermath

1. Flower, 1100; Zucker, 307; Lacher, 34; *Wisconsin Magazine of History*, 1882, 487; Halbert E. Paine to ??, June 26, 1868, in William H. Jacobs Papers, Milwaukee County Historical Society.

2. *Men of Progress*, 195; Winkler, *Letters*, 218; Lamers, "Hero in Blue," 27; Watrous, 18-19; King, 96; quote from "Obituary," *Wisconsin Magazine of History*, Vol. IV, 460-61; *Milwaukee Sentinel*, March 23, 1921, 1 and March 24, 1921, 14.

3. Zucker, 280; Kaufmann, 484; Flower, 999; Hense-Jensen; *Soldiers' and Citizens' Album*, 716.

4. Flower, 997; Watrous, 778-780.

5. *Encyclopedia of Biography*, 38-39; Love, 999; Osten, 16; *Encyclopedia of Biography*, 38-39.

6. Zucker, 287-288; Flower, 635-36.

7. *Milwaukee Sentinel*, May 8, 1869, 1.

8. Legler, 276; *Chivas Post*, 141; *Soldiers' and Citizens' Album*, 593.

9. *Milwaukee Daily Herold*, May 16, 1863.

10. *National New Education*, Vol. 1, No. 2, 29-30; *Men of Progress*. 420; Watrous, 50-52.

11. *National New Education*, Vol. 1, No. 2, 29-30; *Men of Progress*. 420; Watrous, 50-52.

12. Flower, 999; *Men of Progress*, 421; Watrous, 49-51.

13. Quote from Flower, 1011; Knoche, 127; Osten, 2, gives the date of death as March 22.

14. Buerstatte letters.

15. *Roster of Wisconsin Volunteers, passim.*

16. *The Soldiers' Story*, 351.

17. *Chivas Post*, 466.

18. Muenzenberger *Letters* ms., 105-106

19. *Milwaukee Sentinel*, July 6, 1867, 1.

20. *Milwaukee Sentinel*, July 6, 1867, 1.

21. *Milwaukee Sentinel*, July 4, 1870, 1.

22. *Milwaukee Sentinel*, September 19, 1870, 1.

23. *Milwaukee Sentinel*, December 28, 1874, 8, February 13, 1875, and quotes from January 11, 1875, 8.

24. *Milwaukee Sentinel*, February 15, 1875, 5.

25. *Milwaukee Sentinel*, June 1, 1875, 5.

26. *Milwaukee Sentinel*, June 7, 1875, 8.

27. *Milwaukee Sentinel*, July 1, 1875, 5.

28. *Milwaukee Sentinel*, October 8, 1877, 8 and September 4, 1882, 6.

29. *Milwaukee Sentinel*, September 4, 1882, 3.

30. *Milwaukee Sentinel*, July 4, 1887, 3.

31. *Milwaukee Sentinel*, August 21, 1887, 3, quote from August 28, 1887, 3.

32. *Milwaukee Sentinel*, July 4, 1887, 3, August 18, 1887, 3, August 21, 1887, 3, and quotes from August 29, 1887, 4.

33. *Milwaukee Sentinel*, August 28, 1887, 3.

34. *Milwaukee Sentinel*, July 4, 1887, 3, August 18, 1887, 3, August 21, 1887, 3, and quotes from August 29, 1887, 4.

35. *Milwaukee Sentinel*, August 29, 1887, 4.

36. *Milwaukee Sentinel*, June 28, 1888, 3 and June 29, 1888, 3.

37. *Milwaukee Sentinel*, June 29, 1888, 3.

38. *Milwaukee Sentinel,* July 1, 1888, 4.

39. *Milwaukee Sentinel,* August 7, 1889, 1 and August 27, 1889, 11.

40. Doerflinger, 9.

41. *Milwaukee Sentinel,* June 26, 1913.

42. *Annual Report of the Adjutant General of the State of Wisconsin,* 410.

43. Current, 352; Love, 999; Wells, 93; Meyer, 33.

44. Fox, 436, 439.

45. Fox, 8, 14.

46. Fox, 399.

47. Edwin E. Bryant, "The Battle of Gettysburg," MOLLUS-Wisconsin, II (1896), 242.

48. Fox, 399.

49. Wells, 58.

Unpublished Sources

Arnold, Joseph. 1st lieutanant, Company E, 26th Wisconsin. Letters, Oshkosh Historical Museum, Oshkosh, Wisconsin.

Barthuli, Nadine E. "Reasons and Conditions Conducive to German Immigration into Milwaukee County," thesis presented to the School of Education, University of Wisconsin-Milwaukee, 1967. Biographical File, State Historical Society of Wisconsin, Madison, Wisconsin.

Damkoehler, Ernst. Private, Company I, 26th Wisconsin. Letters in the Library of Congress. Edited by W. L. Damkoehler. Translated by Martin Boehme, Ralph Bojar, and Carl Endres.

Descriptive Book, Robert Chivas Post No. 2, Grand Army of the Republic. Milwaukee County Historical Society.

Doerflinger, Karl. "Familiar History of the Twenty-sixth Regiment Wisconsin Volunteer Infantry," March 18, 1911. State Historical Society of Wisconsin. Author was 2nd Lieutenant, Company B, 26th Wisconsin.

Estabrook, Charles A. Correspondence, State Historical Society of Wisconsin. "German Element in Milwaukee," an unpublished essay in the Milwaukee County Historical Society, Folder MMG-260.

"Germans in Wisconsin, The," an anonymous unpublished essay in the Miscellaneous MSS collection of the Milwaukee County Historical Society.

Graefe, Karl August. Private, Company H, 26th Wisconsin. Letter in State Historical Society of Wisconsin, File SC 2058.

Howard, Oliver Otis. General commanding Eleventh Corps. Papers, Bowdoin College, Brunswick, Maine.

Huebschmann, Franz. Surgeon, 26th Wisconsin. Papers, part of the Robert Wild Papers, Box 3, Milwaukee County Historical Society.

Jacobs, William H. Colonel, 26th Wisconsin. Papers, Milwaukee County Historical Society.

Jones, George W. 2nd Lieutenant and Adjutant, 26th Wisconsin. Diary, Washington County Historical Society, West Bend, Wisconsin.

Kuechenmeister, Franz. Private, Company K, 26th Wisconsin. Papers, courtesy of Erv Seeger.

Karsten, Karl M. 2nd Lieutenant, Company F, 26th Wisconsin. Diary, microfilm copy in the State Historical Society of Wisconsin, Microfilm 251.

Lackner, Francis. Major, 26th Wisconsin. Diary, Milwaukee County Historical Society.

Milwaukee Features File, Microfilm No. 450, Milwaukee County Historical Society. Cited as: Features File.

Milwaukee Turners Foundation, Inc. Miscellaneous File Folders. Milwaukee, Wisconsin.

Muenzenberger, Adam. Acting Sergeant, Company C, 26th Regiment Wisconsin Volunteers, letters, October 1862 to November, 1863. Translated by Clara M. Lamers and William M. Lamers, 1933. Courtesy of William M. Lamers.

"Personal War Sketches," E. B. Walcott Post No. 1, Grand Army of the Republic. Milwaukee County Historical Society. Cited as: Walcott Post.

"Personal War Sketches," Rank & File Post No. 240, Grand Army of the Republic. Milwaukee County Historical Society. Cited as: Rank & File Post.

"Personal War Sketches," Robert Chivas Post No. 2, Grand Army of the Republic. Milwaukee County Historical Society. Cited as: Chivas Post.

Sprengling, Andrew. Private, Company C, 26th Wisconsin. Papers, Milwaukee County Historical Society, Milwaukee, Wisconsin.

26th Wisconsin Infantry, Series XII, Civil War Papers. Wisconsin Veterans Museum, Madison, Wisconsin.

26th Wisconsin Infantry Morning Reports. National Archives, Washington, D.C.

26th Wisconsin Infantry Morning Reports, Company E, 1863-1864. Wisconsin State Historical Society.

26th Wisconsin Infantry Regimental Descriptive Books. National Archives, Washington, D.C.

26th Wisconsin Infantry Regimental Descriptive Books. State Historical Society of Wisconsin, Madison, Wisconsin.

26th Wisconsin Infantry Regimental Papers. National Archives, Washington, D.C.

26th Wisconsin Infantry Reunion Minutes, MSS 257, Urban Archives, University of Wisconsin-Milwaukee, Milwaukee, Wisconsin.

Wickesberg, Karl. Sergeant, Company H, 26th Wisconsin. Letters, courtesy of Mr. Alfred Wickesberg, Milwaukee, Wisconsin. Wild, Robert. Papers, Milwaukee County Historical Society.

Winkler, Frederick C. Lt. Col., 26th Wisconsin. Papers, Milwaukee County Historical Society, Box 1.

_____. "Winklers' Reminiscences of Frank Haskell," unpublished manuscript in the University of Wisconsin-Milwaukee Library, n.d.

Newspapers

Amerikanische Turnzeitung.
Atlas (Milwaukee).
Banner und Volksfreund (Milwaukee).
Beobachter (West Bend).
Daily Milwaukee News.
Evening Post (New York).
Frank Leslies' Illustrated Newspaper.
Germania und Abend Post(Milwaukee).

Herold (Milwaukee).
Indianapolis Daily Journal.
Kenosha News.
Manitowoc Herald.
Manitowoc Pilot.
Manitowoc Tribune.
Milwaukee Journal.
Milwaukee Sentinel.
Milwaukee Turner.
Morning Telegraph (Harrisburg, PA).
New York Times.
Pionier am Wisconsin (Sauk City, WI).
Pittsburgh Post (Pittsburgh, PA).
Täglicher Milwaukee Seebote.
Watertown Democrat (Wisconsin).

Published Sources

Aikens, Andrew J. and Lewis A. Proctor, eds. *Men of Progress. Wisconsin.* Milwaukee: The Evening Wisconsin Company, 1897.

Alexander, Edward P. *Military Memoirs of a Confederate.* Bloomington: Indiana University Press, 1962. *Annual Report of the Adjutant General of Ohio, 1863.* Columbus: The State, 1864. *Annual Report of the Adjutant General of the State of Wisconsin with Reports from the Quartermaster General and Surgeon General, for the Year Ending December 30th, 1865.* Madison: William J. Park & Co., 1866.

Arnold, Joseph. "Belle Island," in Bernhard Domschcke, *Twenty Months in Captivity, Memoirs of a Union Officer in Confederate Prison* (Associated University Presses, 1987), 135-137. The author was 1st lieutanant, Company E, 26th Wisconsin.

Atkinson, John. *The Story of Lookout Mountain and Missionary Ridge.* Detroit: Winn and Hammond, Printers, 1893.

Baensch, Emil. "The Patriotic Record of the Manitowoc Freier Saengerbund," *Wisconsin Magazine of History,* Vol. II (1918-19), 87-91.

Bates, Samuel. *Martial Deeds of Philadelphia.* Philadelphia: 1875.

Beecham, R. K. *Gettysburg: The Pivotol Battle of the Civil War.* Chicago: A. C. McClurg, 1911.

Bigelow, John. *The Campaign of Chancellorsville.* New Haven: Yale University Press, 1910.

Boatner, Mark Mayo. *The Civil War Dictionary.* New York: David McKay Co., 1961.

Bonin, John Aubrey. "Lost Victories: Johnston and Sherman at Cassville," *Blue & Gray Magazine,* XIII, No. 6 (Summer 1996), 28-37.

Bradley, Mark L. "Last Stand in the Carolinas: The Battle of Bentonville, March 19-21, 1865," *Blue & Gray Magazine,* XIII, No. 2 (December 1995), 9-22, 56-69.

Bruce, William George. *History of Milwaukee City and County.* Chicago & Milwaukee: S. J. Clarke Publishing Co., 1922.

Bruncken, Ernest. *The Germans in Wisconsin Politics.*

Bryant, Edwin E. "The Battle of Gettysburg," *MOLLUS-Wisconsin,* II (1896).

Busey, John W. *These Honored Dead: The Union Casualties at Gettysburg* (Hightstown, NJ: Longstreet House, 1988).

Butts, Joseph Tyler, ed. *A Gallant Captain of the Civil War.* New York: F. Tennyson Neely, 1902.

"C. C." Letters signed "C. C." appearing in *Pionier am Wisconsin* in 1862 and 1863. Probably from Christian Crusius, Private, Company I, 26th Wisconsin.

Carpenter, John A. "O. O. Howard: General at Chancellorsville," *Civil War History,* III, No. 1 (March 1957).

Catton, Bruce. *Glory Road.* Garden City: Doubleday & Co., 1965.

_____. *Never Call Retreat.* Garden City: Doubleday & Co., Inc., 1965.

Comte de Paris, *History of the Civil War in America.* Philadelphia: Porter and Coates, 1883, III.

Couch, Darius N. "The Chancellorsville Campaign," *Battles and Leaders,* III.

Current, Richard N. *The History of Wisconsin, Volume II, The Civil War Era, 1848-1873.* Madison: State Historical Society of Wisconsin, 1976.

"Das 11. Armee-Corps in der letzten Schlacht bei Chancellorsville," *Milwaukee Herald,* May 23, 1863.

Davis, Burke. *Shermans' March.* New York: Random House, 1980.

"Der auszug nach Camp Sigel. Vor fünfzig jahren sich die Washington Co. Rifles dem 26. regiment," *Beobachter* (West Bend), September 6, 1912.

Dictionary of Wisconsin Biography. Madison: The State Historical Society of Wisconsin, 1960.

"Die tapferen unseres "deutschen" regiments, 1862-1912; goldene jubelfeier der 26er freiwilligen von Wisconsin," *Germania,* August 21, 1912.

Dietz, J. Stanley, complr. *The Battle Flags and Wisconsin Troops in the Civil War and War with Spain.* Madison, 1943.

Dodge, Theodore A. "Left Wounded on the Field," *Putnams' Magazine,* IV (1869).

Doerflinger, Karl. "General Schurz bei Chancellorsville," *Die Glocke,* July, 1906.

Domschcke, Bernhard. *Twenty Months in Captivity, Memoirs of a Union Officer in Confederate Prison.* Associated University Presses, 1987. Edited and translated by Frederic Trautmann. Author was captain, Company H, 26th Wisconsin.

Downey, Fairfax. *The Guns at Gettysburg.* New York: David McKay Co., 1958.

Dyer, Frederick H. *A Compendium of the War of the Rebellion.* New York: Thomas Yoseloff, 1959. 3 vols.

"E. R." Letters signed "E. R." appearing in *Pionier am Wisconsin* in 1862 and 1863. Probably from Ernst Leo Rietz, Private, Company E, 26th Wisconsin.

Early, Jubal A. *Autobiographical Sketch and Narrative of the War Between the States.* Philadelphia: J. B. Lippincott, 1912. *Encyclopedia of Biography,* .

Esposito, Vincent J. *The West Point Atlas of American Wars.* New York: Frederick A. Praeger, 1959.

Estabrook. Charles E., ed. *Record and Sketches of Military Organizations.* Madison, 1914.

_____, ed. *Wisconsin Losses in the Civil War.* Madison: Democrat Printing Company, 1915.

Falge, Louis, ed., *History of Manitowoc County, Wisconsin.* Chicago: Goodspeed Historical Association, Vol. I.

Flower, Frank A. *History of Milwaukee, Wisconsin, from Pre-historic Times to the Present Date, Embracing a Summary Sketch of the Native Tribes, and an Exhaustive Record of Men and Events for the Past Century; Describing in Elaborate Detail the City as it is Now; its Commercial, Religious, Educational and Benevolent Institutions, its Government, Courts, Press and Public Affairs; its Musical, Dramatic, Literary, Scientific and Social Societies; its Patriotism During the Late War; its Development and Future Possibilities; and including Nearly Four Thousand Biographical Sketches of Pioneers and Citizens.* Chicago: The Western Historical Company, 1881.

Fox, Charles K. *Gettysburg.* New York: A. S. Barner & Co., 1969.

Fox, William F. *New York at Gettysburg.* Albany: J. B. Lyon, 1900.

_____. *Regimental Losses in the American Civil War 1861-1865.* Albany: Albany Publishing Company, 1898.

"Frederic Charles Buerstatte, a Diary of a Soldier in the Civil War," *Manitowoc County Historical Society Newsletter,* Vol. IX, No. 2 (March 1975), pp. 5-10. English translation by George Emme. Author was a private in Company F, 26th Wisconsin.

Fullerton, Joseph S. "The Army of the Cumberland at Chattanooga," *Battles and Leaders,* III.

Gordon, John B. *Reminiscences of the Civil War.* New York: Scribners' Sons, 1904.

Goss, Warren Lee. *The Soldiers' Story of His Captivity at Andersonville, Belle Isle, and Other Rebel Prisons.* Boston: I. N. Richardson & Co., 1871.

Grant, Ulysses S. "Chattanooga," *Battles and Leaders,* III.

Gregory, John G. "Early Presidential Elections in Milwaukee," *Historical Messenger of the Milwaukee County Historical Society* (December 1964), pp. 60-64.

Hamlin, Augustus C. *The Battle of Chancellorsville.* Bangor, ME: n. p., 1896.

Hecker, Friedrich. "A Vindication of the 11th Corps," *Staats Zeitung* (Illinois).

Heinrici, Max. *Das Buch der Deutschen in Amerika.* Philadelphia: Deutsch-Amerikanischer Nationalbund, 1909.

Hense-Jensen, Wilhelm. *Wisconsins Deutsch-Amerikaner bis zum Schluss des neunzehnten Jahrhunderts.* Milwaukee: Deutschen Gesellschaft, 1909, 2 vols.

Hooker, Joseph. "Report on the Battle of Wauhatchie," *Rebellion Record,* VII.

Howard, Charles H. "The First Day at Gettysburg," *MOLLUS-Illinois,* IV.

Howard, Oliver O. *Autobiography of Oliver Otis Howard.* New York: Baker & Taylor, 1907. 2 vols.

Hughes, Nathaniel C. *Bentonville: the Final battle of Sherman and Johnston.* Chapel Hill: University of North Carolina Press, 1996

Hunt, Henry J. "The Second Day at Gettysburg," *Battles and Leaders,* III.

Kaufmann, Wilhelm. *Die Deutschen in amerikanischen bürgerkriege.* Munich and Berlin: R. Oldenbourg, 1911.

King, Charles. "Frederick C. Winkler, Distinguished Soldier and Citizen," *Historical Messenger of the Milwaukee County Historical Society,* Vol. 23, No. 3 (September, 19167), 89-98.

Klement, Frank L. "The Soldier Vote in Wisconsin During the Civil War," *Wisconsin Magazine of History,* XXVIII (September 1944), pp. 37-47.

_____. "Wisconsin and the Re-Election of Lincoln in 1864: A Chapter of Civil War History," *Historical Messenger of the Milwaukee County Historical Society* (March 1966), pp. 20-42.

_____. *Wisconsin and the Civil War.* Madison: The State Historical Society of Wisconsin, 1963.

Knoche, Carl H. "Dr. Franz Huebschmanns' Political Career," *Historical Messenger of the Milwaukee County Historical Society,* Vol. 28, No. 4 (Winter 1972), pp. 114-131.

Korn, B. C. "The Civil War Drafts in Milwaukee," *Historical Messenger of the Milwaukee County Historical Society,* September 1961, pp. 7-12.

Koss, Rudolf H. "Geschichte der Gründung und Entwicklung des Turnvereins 'Milwaukee,'" in his, *Milwaukee.* Milwaukee: Schnellpressen-Druk des 'Herold,' 1871.

_____. *Milwaukee.* Milwaukee: Schnellpressen-Druk des 'Herold,' 1871. English translation by Hans Ibsen.

Krzyżanowski, Wlodzimierz. *Wspomnienia z Pobytu w Ameryce Podczas Wojny.*

Chicago: Polish Museum of America, 1963. The author was the Sigel Regiments' brigade commander while it was in the Eleventh Corps.

Lacher, J. H. A. *The German Element in Wisconsin.* Milwaukee: Steuben Society of America, 1925.

Lamers, William M. "A Humble Soldier Dies in Libby Prison," *Lore,* Vol. 11, No. 2 (Spring 1961), 68-72.

_____. "Hero in Blue," *Lore,* Vol. 10, No 1 (Winter 1959), pp. 26-28.

Lankevich, George J. *Milwaukee Chronological & Documentary History 1673-1977.* Dobbs Ferry, NY: Oceana Publications, Inc., 1977.

Legler, Henry E. *Leading Events of Wisconsin History.* Milwaukee: The Sentinel Company, 1898.

Longstreet, James. *From Manassas to Appomattox.* Bloomington: Indiana University Press, 1960.

Love, William DeLoss. *Wisconsin in the War of the Rebellion; A history of all Regiments and Batteries the State Has Sent to the Field, and Deeds of Her Citizens, Governors and Other Military Officers, and State and National Legislators to Suppress the Rebellion.* Chicago: Church and Goodman, Publishers, 1866.

McKenna, Maurice, ed. *Fond du Lac County, Wisconsin, Past and Present.* Chicago: The S. J. Clarke Publishing Company, 1912, Vol. I.

Medical and Surgical History of the War of the Rebellion. Washington: Surgeon Generals' Office, 1870-1888. 10 vols.

Metzner, Henry. *A Brief History of the American Turnerbund.* Pittsburgh: The American Turnerbund, 1924.

Meyer, Sr. Mary D., O.P., "The Germans in Wisconsin and the Civil War: Their Atitude Toward the Union, the Republicans, Slavery, and Lincoln," M.A. thesis, The Catholic Univeristy of America, 1937.

Miers, Earl Schenck and **Richard A. Brown,** *Gettysburg.* New Brunswick: Rutgers University Press, 1948.

Milwaukee Musical Society Diamond Jubilee 1850-1925. No publisher, no date.

Milwaukee Turners One Hundredth Anniversary, 1853-1953. Milwaukee: **Milwaukee Turners, 1953.** Not paginated.

Milwaukee Turners 140th Anniversary 1853-1993. Milwaukee: Milwaukee Turner Foundation, 1993.

Moore, Allison. *The Louisiana Tigers.* Baton Rouge: Ortlieb Press, 1961.

Mueller, Theodore. "The Milwaukee Turners Through the Century," in Milwaukee Turners One Hundredth Anniversary, 1853-1953. Not paginated.

90 Years of Service: The Milwaukee Turners, 1853-1943. Milwaukee: Milwaukee Turners, ca. 1943.

Oehlerts, Donald E., complr. *Guide to Wisconsin Newspapers, 1833-1957.* Madison: State Historical Society of Wisconsin, 1958.

"Oh, It Was a Glorious Sight to See," *Milwaukee Journal,* April 9, 1865.

Osborn, Hartwell. "The Eleventh Corps in East Tennessee," *MOLLUS-Illinois,* IV.

Osten, Walter. "Dr. Francis Huebschmann: The Cultured Pioneer and Framer of Our State Constitution," *The Milwaukee Turner,* IV, No. 2 (Februaqry 1943), 1-2.

Overmoehle, Sr. M. Hedwigis, "The Anti-Clerical Activities of the Forty-Eighters in Wisconsin 1848-1860," Ph.D. dissertation, St. Louis University, 1941.

Pennsylvania at Gettysburg. Harrisburg: William Stanley Ray, 1919.

Phisterer, Frederick. *New York in the War of the Rebellion, 1861-1865.* Albany: 1890. 5 vols.

Pula, James S. *For Liberty and Justice: The Life and Times of Wladimir Krzyżanowski.* Chicago: Polish American Congress Charitable Foundation, 1978.

_____. "The Sigel Regiment," *German-American Studies,* Vol. 8 (1974), 27-52.

Quiner, E. B. *The Military History of Wisconsin: A Record of the Civil and Military Patriotism of the State, in the War for the Union.* Chicago: Clarke & Co., Publishers, 1866.

Raus, Edmund J., Jr. *A Generation on the March—The Union Army at Gettysburg.* Lynchburg, VA: H. E. Howard, Inc., 1987.

Rebellion Record. New York: G. P. Putnam, n.d.

"Recall Famous Fight: Survivors of 26th Wisconsin Recall Battle of Peach Tree Creek Before Atlanta," *Kenosha News,* June 20, 1914.

Remington, Cyrus K. *A Record of Battery I, First New York Light Artillery Vols., Otherwise Known as Wiedrichs' Battery during the War of the Rebellion.* Buffalo: 1901.

Rosengarten, J. G. *The German Soldier in the Wars of the United States.* Philadelphia: Lippincott, 1886.

Roster of Wisconsin Volunteers, War of the Rebellion, 1861-1865. Madison: Democrat Printing Company, 1886.

Sandburg, Carl. *Abraham Lincoln: The War Years.* New York: Harcourt, Brace & World, Inc. 4 vols.

Schlicher, J. J. "Bernhard Domschcke. I. A Life of Hardship," *Magazine of Wisconsin History,* March, 1946, 319-332.

_____. "Bernhard Domschcke. II. The Editor and the Man," *Magazine of Wisconsin History,* June, 1946, 435-456.

Schurz, Carl. *The Reminiscences of Carl Schurz.* New York: The McClure Co., 1907-1908. 3 vols.

Simonhoff, Harry. *Jewish Participants in the Civil War.* New York: Arco Publishing Co., Inc., 1963.

Soldiers' and Citizens' *Album of Biographical Record Containing Personal Sketches of Army Men and Citizens Prominent in Loyalty to the Union.* Chicago: Grand Army Publishing Co., 1890.

Steinwehr, Adolph von. "Report on the Battle of Wauhatchie," *Rebellion Record,* III.

Steele, Matthew F. *American Campaigns.* Washington: The Telegraph Press, 1909.

Trathen, Jean Elizabeth. "The German-American of Wisconsin and the Civil War," M.A. thesis, University of Wisconsin, 1929.

Turnverein Milwaukee. Milwaukee: Milwaukee Turnvrein, 1896.

Underwood, Adin B. *The Three Years' Service of the Thirty-Third Mass. Infantry Regiment 1862-1865.* Boston: A. Williams & Co., 1881.

Van Horne, Thomas Budd. *History of the Army of the Cumberland: Its Organization, Campaigns, and Battles, Written at the Request of Major-General George H. Thomas Chiefly from His Private Military Journal and Official and Other Documents Furnished by Him.* Cincinnati: R. Clarke & Co., 1875.

Vanderslice, John M. *Gettysburg.* Philadelphia: 1897.

Wallber, Albert. "From Gettysburg to Libby Prison," in *War Papers Read Before the Commandery of the State of Wisconsin, Military Order of the Loyal Legion of the United States.* Milwaukee: Burdick & Allen, 1914, Vol. IV, 191-200. The author was 1st lieutenant, Company I, and adjutant, 26th Wisconsin.

_____. "The Escape from the Libby," in Bernhard Domschcke, *Twenty Months in Captivity, Memoirs of a Union Officer in Confederate Prison* (Associated University Presses, 1987), 125-134. *War of the Rebellion: A Compilation of the Official Records of the Union and Confederate Armies.* Washington: Government Printing Office, 1891.

Watrous, Jerome A., ed. *Memoirs of Milwaukee County.* Madison: Western Historical Association, 1909. Vol. II.

"What Claim has Mr. C. H. Doerflinger to be heard in regard to Improvements in the American Public School System which he proposes?" *National New Education,* Vol. 1, No. 2 (October 1908), pp. 29-31.

*Wild, Robert. "Chapters in the History of the Turners," *Wisconsin Magazine of History,* Vol. IX (1925-26), 123-139.

Winkler, Frederick C. *Letters of Frederick C. Winkler 1862 to 1865.* Edited and published by William K. Winkler, 1963.

Zeidler, Anita L. and **Ann H. Spransy,** compilers. *List of the Dead: List of Wisconsin Volunteers in the Union Army From Milwaukee, Who Died in the Civil War From Action, Disease and Other Causes.* Milwaukee: Milwaukee Publishers, 1962.

Zeitlin, Richard H. *Germans in Wisconsin.* Madison: The State Historical Society of Wisconsin, 1977.

Zink, Irve William, "The Influence of the Germans in Milwaukee, M. A. Thesis, Marquette University, May, 1941.

Zucker, A. E. *The Forty-Eighters; Political Regugees of the German Revolution of 1848.* New York: Columbia University Press, 1950.

INDEX

Page numbers without descriptors are general references. Names in the appendices are not indexed.

Weber, Jacob, 263
Weber, Mathias, photo of, 133
Wedig, Joseph, Lt., 94
Weidner, Adolf, photo of, 57
Weinder, Charles, photo of, 57
Weidner, William, 328
Weiffenback, John, 244
Weinreich, Charles, Sergt., 224
Wells, Robert W., 335
Wemmert, John, 332
Wendt, Brigade Commissary, 72
Werner, Friedrich, 126
Wheeler, A. O., 28
Wheeler, Joseph, Gen., 215, 276-277, 279-280, 289
White, John, 7
Wickesberg, Karl, Sergt., 99; enlists, 44; on foraging, 54; on Battle of Fredericksburg, 74; life in camp, 78-80, 194, 220, 222; complains about pay, 84; complains about doctors, 85; complains about officers, 86; promoted corp., 99; at Chancellorsville, 120, 126; threatens Gen. Howard, 142; Gettysburg Campaign, 161, 166, 171-172, 182, 189; Chattanooga Campaign, 201-202, 204, 214-215; Knoxville Campaign, 216, 219; Atlanta Campaign, 227-228, 239; photo of, 240
Wiedrich's Battery (US), 177-178
Wightman, Frances M., 225
Wildhagen, John, 189
Williams, Alpheus S., Gen., 276, 301
Wilson, H. K., 82
Wingler, Morris, 164, 187
Winkler, Frederick C., Lt. Col., 78, 94-95, 99, 107, 114-117, 149, 151, 193, 196-197, 199, 221-222, 313; enlists company, 18, 19; leaving for war 35-36; trip to Virginia, 37, 38, 39; on Schurz, 41; camp life, 42, 44, 45, 58, 73, 78, 86, 143-145, 147, 194, 220, 224; on review by Sigel, 46, 47, 49, 50; what they carry on the march, 52; thoughts on eve of first action, 52, 88, 111,

115; on marching, 53, 195; on foraging, 54, 55, 58-59, 279, 294; on press accounts, 59, 142; appointed corps judge advocate, 58, 66; on conscription, 69; on deserters and morale, 87; on Burnside, 97; on Lincoln, 108, 268-269, 272; on blacks in South, 277; at Chancellorsville, 120, 129, 135, 142; Gettysburg Campaign, 152, 154-158, 162, 171-172, 179, 180; Chattanooga Campaign, 201-205, 207, 210-211, 213-214; Knoxville Campaign, 216, 218-219; Atlanta Campaign, 227-228, 230, 232, 234-235, 237-239, 241-251, 253-254, 257, 259, 261, 263-264, 266-269; Sherman's March to the Sea, 271-277, 279, 281-282; Carolinas Campaign, 284-288, 292-296, 298-299, 301, 303; at Grand Review, 309-311; postwar activities, 318, 325-327, 329-330, 332; photo of, 18
Wirshem, Peter, 332
Wisconsin, German population of, 1-13
Wisconsin troops: Benton Hussars, 16; Von Deutsch's Dragoons, 16; 1st, 13, 18; 2nd, 191; 3rd, 191, 311; 5th, 14, 21, 191, 326; 6th, 191, 326; 7th, 191; 9th, 14, 21, 326; 11th, 326; 24th, 326; 26th, colors of, 34, 254-255; organization of, 14-29; initial officers, 337; demographics of, 29-30, 339-340; recruiting poster, 15, 22; muster in, 26-27; presentation of colors to, 30-33; leaves for war, 34-36; movement to join the Army of the Potomac, 37-41; assigned to Eleventh Corps, 40; first campaign in Virginia, 51-64; at Gainesville, Va., 53-54; at Haymarket, Va., 54; foraging, 54, 115, 293-294; election of 1862, 55-56; camp in Centreville, 64-70; Fredericksburg Campaign, 70-75; at Stafford Court